Heterogeneous Agent Systems

Heterogeneous Agent Systems

V. S. Subrahmanian, Piero Bonatti, Jürgen Dix, Thomas Eiter, Sarit Kraus, Fatma Özcan, and Robert Ross

The MIT Press
Cambridge, Massachusetts
London, England

© 2000 Massachusetts Institute of Technology

All rights reserved. No part of this book may be reproduced in any form by any electronic or mechanical means (including photocopying, recording, or information storage and retrieval) without permission in writing from the publisher.

This book was set in Times Roman by LATEX2e.

Printed and bound in the United States of America.

Library of Congress Cataloging-in-Publication Data

Heterogeneous agent systems / V. S. Subrahmanian . . . [et al.].
   p.   cm.
  Includes bibliographical references and index.
  ISBN 0-262-19436-8 (hc : alk. paper)
  1. Heterogeneous computing. 2. Intelligent agents (Computer software) I. Subrahmanian, V. S.

QA76.88.H47 2000
006.3—dc21
                                                                           99-461972

Contents

	List of Figures	ix
	List of Tables	xi
	Preface and Acknowledgments	xiii
1	**Introduction**	**1**
	1.1 A Personalized Department Store Application (STORE)	4
	1.2 The Controlled Flight into Terrain Application (CFIT)	8
	1.3 A Supply Chain Example (CHAIN)	11
	1.4 Brief Overview of Related Research on Agents	14
	1.5 Ten Desiderata for an Agent Infrastructure	21
	1.6 A Birdseye View of This Book	23
	1.7 Selected Commercial Systems	25
2	***IMPACT* Architecture**	**29**
	2.1 Overview of Architecture	29
	2.2 Agent Architecture	31
	2.3 Server Architecture	36
	2.4 Related Work	50
3	**Service Description Language**	**53**
	3.1 Agent Service Description Language	53
	3.2 Metric of Service Descriptions	57
	3.3 Matchmaking as Nearest Neighbor Computations	60
	3.4 Range Computations	66
	3.5 Simulation Evaluation	68
	3.6 Related Work	72
4	**Accessing Legacy Data and Software**	**75**
	4.1 Software Code Abstractions	75
	4.2 Code Call Conditions	80
	4.3 The Message Box Domain	91
	4.4 Integrity Constraints	93
	4.5 Some Syntactic Sugar	96
	4.6 Linking Service Descriptions and Code Calls	98
	4.7 Example Service Description Programs	99
	4.8 Related Work	105

5	**_IMPACT_ Server Implementation**	**117**
	5.1 Overview of *dbImpact* Services	119
	5.2 *TCP/IP* String Protocol for *IMPACT* servers	122
	5.3 Sample Client-Server Interactions	133

6	**Agent Programs**	**141**
	6.1 Agent Decision Architecture	141
	6.2 Action Base	143
	6.3 Action Constraints	156
	6.4 Agent Programs: Syntax	159
	6.5 Agent Programs: Semantics	171
	6.6 Relationship with Logic Programming and Nonmonotonic Logic	197
	6.7 Related Work	204

7	**Meta Agent Programs**	**209**
	7.1 Extending **CFIT** by Route and Maneuver Planning	209
	7.2 Belief Language and Data Structures	212
	7.3 Meta-Agent Programs: Semantics	226
	7.4 How to Implement Meta-Agent Programs?	242
	7.5 Related Work	249

8	**Temporal Agent Programs**	**251**
	8.1 Actions with Temporal Duration	253
	8.2 Syntax of Taps	261
	8.3 Semantics of Taps	267
	8.4 Compact Representation of Temporal Status Sets	278
	8.5 Computing Feasible Temporal Status Sets	279
	8.6 An Application of **Tap**: Strategic Negotiations	284
	8.7 An Application of **Tap**: Delivery Agents in Contract Net Environments	288
	8.8 Related Work	292

9	**Probabilistic Agent Programs**	**295**
	9.1 Probabilistic Code Calls	297
	9.2 Probabilistic Agent Programs: Syntax	303
	9.3 Probabilistic Agent Programs: Semantics	306
	9.4 Computing Probabilistic Status Sets of Positive paps	315

	9.5	Agent Programs are Probabilistic Agent Programs	320
	9.6	Extensions to Other Causes of Uncertainty	322
	9.7	Related Work	325
10	**Secure Agent Programs**	**329**
	10.1	An Abstract Logical Agent Model	332
	10.2	Abstract Secure Request Handling	338
	10.3	Safely Approximate Data Security	347
	10.4	Undecidability Results	366
	10.5	*IMPACT* Security Implementation Architecture	368
	10.6	Related Work	394
11	**Complexity Results**	**399**
	11.1	Complexity Classes	400
	11.2	Decision Making Problems	407
	11.3	Overview of Complexity Results	411
	11.4	Basic Complexity Results	417
	11.5	Effect of Integrity Constraints	440
	11.6	Related Work	459
12	**Implementing Agents**	**461**
	12.1	Weakly Regular Agents	462
	12.2	Properties of Weakly Regular Agents	477
	12.3	Regular Agent Programs	487
	12.4	Compile-Time Algorithms	493
	12.5	The Query Maintenance Package	500
	12.6	The *IMPACT* Agent Development Environment (*IADE*)	506
	12.7	Experimental Results	509
	12.8	Related Work	515
13	**An Example Application**	**517**
	13.1	The Army War Reserves (*AWR*) Logistics Problem	517
	13.2	*AWR* Agent Architecture	519
	13.3	*AWR* Agent Implementation	520
14	**Conclusions**	**529**
	14.1	Progress Towards the Ten Desiderata	529
	14.2	Agent Desiderata Provided by Other Researchers	533

Appendix

A	**Code Calls and Actions in the Examples**		**537**
	A.1	Agents in the CFIT Example	537
	A.2	Agents in the STORE Example	541
	A.3	Agents in the CHAIN Example	544
	A.4	Agents in the CFIT* Example	548
	References		**555**
	Index		**571**

List of Figures

1.1	Interactions between Agents in STORE Example	5
1.2	Interactions between Agents in CFIT Example	10
1.3	Agents in CHAIN Example	12
2.1	Overall *IMPACT* Architecture	30
2.2	Basic Architecture of *IMPACT* Agents	33
2.3	Agent/Service Registration Screen Dump	38
2.4	Example Verb Hierarchy (Missing Edge Labels are 1)	43
2.5	Example Noun-term Hierarchy	44
2.6	Hierarchy Browsing Screen Dump	47
2.7	Thesaurus Screen Dump	48
3.1	Example Type Hierarchy	54
3.2	Performance of k-nearest neighbor algorithm: Average time per query	70
3.3	Performance of k-nearest neighbor algorithm, Average time per answer	70
3.4	Performance of range query algorithm, Average time per query	70
3.5	Performance of range query algorithm, Average time per answer	71
3.6	Experimental Results of Precision of our Algorithms	72
3.7	Experimental Results of Recall of our Algorithms	73
4.1	Sample *HERMES* mediators	100
4.2	Sample query on the profiling agent's mediator (first result)	101
4.3	Sample Queries on goodSpender Predicate and profiling Agent's Mediator	102
4.4	Sample query on the autoPilot agent's mediator	103
4.5	Sample query on the supplier agent's mediator	104
4.6	*OMA* Reference Model	109
4.7	Structure of ORB	110
4.8	*CORBA* client/server interaction	113
5.1	*IMPACT* server architecture	118
6.1	Agent Decision Architecture	142
6.2	Relationship between different Status Sets (SS)	173
7.1	Agents in of CFIT* Example	210
8.1	Cycle for Agent Reasoning	252

8.2	autoPilot's "Climb" Action	253
8.3	Checkpoints of an Action	255
8.4	Temporal Status Set and State History Function (SHF) Over Time	268
9.1	Example of Random Variable in CFIT* Example	298
9.2	Example of Probabilistic code calls in CFIT* Example	298
10.1	Agent Service Evaluation Procedure	338
11.1	Decision (left) and Search (right) Problem Complexity Classes	404
12.1	Modality ordering	474
12.2	An example AND/OR tree associated with a pf-constraint	503
12.3	Main *IADE* Screen	507
12.4	*IADE* Test Dialog Screen Prior to Program Testing	508
12.5	*IADE* Test Execution Screen	509
12.6	*IADE* Unfold Information Screen	510
12.7	*IADE* Status Set Screen	511
12.8	*IADE* (In-)Finiteness Table Screen	512
12.9	*IADE* Option Selection Screen	513
12.10	Safety Experiment Graphs	513
12.11	Performance of Conflict Freedom Tests	514
12.12	Performance of Deontic Stratification	515
13.1	Architecture of the multiagent *AWR* system	519

List of Tables

2.1	Service List for the STORE example	40
2.2	Service List for the CFIT example	40
2.3	Service List for the CHAIN example	42
3.1	Example Thesaurus	63
3.2	Example Service Table	65
4.1	The **apply** Function	97
4.2	Output Type of **apply**	98
7.1	A Basic Belief Table for agent tank1	216
7.2	A Basic Belief Table for agent heli1	217
7.3	A Belief Table for agent tank1	224
7.4	A Belief Table for agent heli1	225
11.2	Complexity of Agent Programs with Negation, $\mathcal{IC} = \emptyset$	412
11.4	Complexity of Agent Programs with Negation, arbitrary $\mathcal{IC}$	413

Preface and Acknowledgments

Though agents are a rapidly growing area of research in the artificial intelligence and Java communities, most past definitions of agenthood are behavioral—agents are programs that exhibit certain hard to specify behaviors. Principled software techniques to build agents and converting existing programs (which may have been developed in PASCAL, C, LISP, etc.) and which may have used diverse data structures did not exist. In this book, we provide a theoretically clean, yet practically realizable way to build and deploy agents on top of legacy and/or specialized data structures and code bases. We believe (and hope) this book will be of interest to anyone interested in building software agents in a principled manner and deploying them on a network such as the Internet. The chapters in the book consist of three basic parts.

1. All readers should read chapters 1–4 and 6. These chapters deal with basic ideas and requirements underlying agent design, together with basic information on how agents may be programmed, how agents may declare the services they offer, and what functionalities must be supportedby an agent infrastructure supporting interoperation between different agents.

2. Readers with specific interest in implementing agents and agent systems should read chapters 5, 12,13. These chapters specify how agents and the underlying agent interoperability infrastructure interact. They also specify details about development environments and applications of agent technology.

3. Readers with interests in advanced agent reasoning should read chapters 7–11. These chapters describe extensions of the basic agent framework so that agents can reason about beliefs, about time, about uncertainty, and about security requirements. Complexity results are also described.

The work described in this book is an international effort for which funds were provided, in part, by the Army Research Laboratory under contract DAAL01-97-K0135, the National Science Foundation under grants IRI-93-57756,IIS-9820657 and IIS-9907482, the Austrian Science Fund Project N Z29-INF and a grant from Germany's DAAD.
We note that the following chapters have been derived, in part, from our published or to be published papers referenced below:

1. Chapter 4 and 6 are derived from reference *T. Eiter and V. S. Subrahmanian and G. Pick. Heterogeneous Active Agents, I: Semantics, Artifical Intelligence 108(1-2):179–255, 1999.*
2. Chapter 7 is derived in part from *J. Dix and V. S. Subrahmanian and G. Pick. Meta Agent Programs, accepted for publication in Journal of Logic Programming.*
3. Chapter 11 is derived from *T. Eiter and V. S. Subrahmanian. Heterogeneous Active Agents, II: Algorithms and Complexity, Artificial Intelligence 108(1-2):257–307, 1999.*

4. Chapter 12 is derived from *T. Eiter and V. S. Subrahmanian and T. J. Rogers. Heterogeneous Active Agents, III: Polynomially Implementable Agents, Artificial Intelligence 117(1):107–167, 2000.*

We are grateful to T. J. Rogers, Carolyn Gasarch, John Benton and Jason Ernst for extensive work on the implementation of different parts of the *IMPACT* system. In particular, T. J. was the guiding force behind the *IMPACT* system implementation.

We received extensive technical comments from researchers worldwide including Jim Hendler, Dana Nau, Luis Pereira, Bob Kowalski, Keith Clark, Terry Swift, Alex Dekhtyar, Hector Munoz, Jeff Horty, Daniel Veit, Leon Sterling, and Mirco Nanni.

We have benefited from numerous discussions on agents with folks from the U.S. Army including Jagdish Chandra, Phil Emmerman, Larry Tokarcik, Dave Hislop, Joseph Schafer, Jack Marin, Steve Choy, Swati Allen, Tim Gregory, Uma Movva and Paul Walczak. Mike Gaughan of Lockheed Sanders was a valued collaborator.

In addition, we would like to thank Bob Prior, Michael Sims, and Judy Feldmann of the MIT Press for extensive assistance.

1 Introduction

In past decades, software developers created massive, monolithic software programs that often performed a wide variety of tasks. During the past few years, however, there has been a shift from the development of massive programs containing millions of lines of code, to smaller, *modular*, pieces of code, where each module performs a well defined, focused task (or a small set of tasks), rather than thousands of different tasks, as used to be the case with old legacy systems. Software agents are the latest innovation in this trend towards splitting complex software systems into components. Roughly speaking, a software agent is a body of software that:

- provides one or more useful *services* that other agents may use under specified conditions,
- includes a *description* of the services offered by the software, which may be accessed and understood by other agents,
- includes the ability to *act autonomously* without requiring explicit direction from a human being,
- includes the ability to succinctly and declaratively describe how an agent determines *what actions to take* even though this description may be kept hidden from other agents,
- includes the ability to *interact* with other agents—including humans—either in a cooperative, or in an adversarial manner, as appropriate.

Note that not all software agents have to have the above properties—however any software agent programming paradigm must have the ability to create agents with some or all of these properties. In addition, agents will have a variety of other properties not covered in the above list, which will be spelled out in full technical detail as we go through this book.

With the proliferation of the Internet, there is now a huge body of data stored in a vast array of diverse, heterogeneous data sources, which is directly accessible to anyone with a network connection. This has led to the need for several agent based capabilities.

Data Integration Agents: Techniques to *mix and match*, *query*, *manipulate*, and *merge* such data together have gained increasing attention. Agents that can access heterogeneous data sources, and mix and match such data are increasingly important. Several agent based techniques for such data integration have been developed (Bayardo et al. 1997; Arens, Chee, Hsu, and Knoblock 1993; Brink, Marcus, and Subrahmanian 1995; Lu, Nerode, and Subrahmanian 1996; Chawathe et al. 1994).

Mobile Agents: The rapid evolution of the Java programming language (Horstmann and Cornell 1997) and the ability of Java applets to "move" across the network, executing bytecode at remote sites, has led to a new class of "mobile" agents (Rus, Gray, and Kotz 1997; Lande and Osjima 1998; Vigna 1998b; White 1997). If such agents are to autonomously form teams with other agents to cooperatively solve a problem, it is necessary that various techniques will be needed, such as techniques for describing agent services, for comprehending agent services, and for indexing and retrieving agent services, as well as techniques to facilitate interoperability between multiple agents.

Software Interoperability Agents: As the number of Java *applets* and other freely available and usable software deployed on the web increases, the ability to pipe data from one data source directly into one of these programs, and pipe the result into yet another program becomes more and more important. There is a growing body of research on agents that facilitate software interoperability (Patil, Fikes, Patel-Schneider, McKay, Finin, Gruber, and Neches 1997).

Personalized Visualization: Some years ago, the Internet was dominated by computer scientists. That situation has experienced a dramatic change and over the years, the vast majority of Internet users will view the Internet as a tool that supports their interests, which, in most cases, will not be computational. This brings with it a need for visualization and presentation of the results of a computation. As the results of a computation may depend upon the interests of a user, different visualization techniques may be needed to best present these results to the user (Candan, Prabhakaran, and Subrahmanian 1996; Ishizaki 1997).

Monitoring Interestingness: As the body of network accessible data gets ever larger, the need to identify what is of interest to users increases. Users do not want to obtain data that is "boring" or not relevant to their interests. Over the years, programs to monitor user interests have been built—for example, (Goldberg, Nichols, Oki, and Terry 1992; Foltz and Dumais 1992; Sta 1993; Sheth and Maes 1993) presents systems for monitoring newspaper articles, and several intelligent mail-handlers prioritize user's email buffers. Techniques to identify user-dependent *interesting* data are growing increasingly important.

The above list merely provides a few simple examples of so-called *agent applications*. Yet, despite the growing interest in agents, and the growing deployment of programs that are billed as being "agents" several basic scientific questions have to be adequately answered.

(Q1) *What is an agent?*
Intuitively, any definition of agenthood is a predicate, `isagent`, that takes as input a program P in any programming language. Program P is considered an agent *if, by definition,*

isagent(P) is true. Clearly, the `isagent` predicate may be defined in many different ways. For example, many of the proponents of Java believe that `isagent`(P) is true *if and only if* P is a Java program—a definition that some might consider restrictive.

(Q2) *If program P is not considered to be an agent according to some specified definition of agenthood, is there a suite of tools that can help in "agentizing" P?*

Intuitively, if a definition of agenthood is mandated by a standards body, then it is reasonable for the designer of a program P which does not comply with the definition of agenthood, to want tools that allow program P to be reconfigured as an agent. Efforts towards a definition of agenthood include ongoing agent standardization activities such as those of *FIPA* (the Foundation for Intelligent Physical Agents).

(Q3) *What kind of software infrastructure, is required for multiple agents to interact with one another once a specific definition of agenthood is chosen, and what kinds of basic services should such an infrastructure provide?*

For example, suppose agents are programs that have (among other things) an associated service description language in which each agent is required to describe its services. Then, yellow pages facilities which an agent might access are needed when the agent needs to find another agent that provides a service that it requires. Such a yellow pages service is an example of an infrastructural service.

The above questions allow a multiplicity of answers. For every possible definition of agenthood, we will require different agentization tools and infrastructural capabilities. The main aim of this book is to study what properties *any* definition of agenthood should satisfy. In the course of this, we will specifically make the following contributions.

- We will provide a concrete definition of agenthood that satisfies the requirements alluded to above, and compare this with alternative possible definitions of agenthood;
- We will provide an architecture and algorithms for agentizing programs that are deemed not to be agents according to the given definition;
- We will provide an architecture and algorithms for creating and deploying software agents that respect the above definition;
- We will provide a description of the infrastructural requirements needed to support such agents, and the algorithms that make this possible.

The rest of this chapter is organized as follows. We will first provide three motivating example applications in Sections 1.1, 1.2, and 1.3, respectively. These three examples will each illustrate different features required of agent infrastructures and different capabilities required of individual agents. Furthermore, these examples will be revisited over and over throughout this entire book to illustrate basic concepts. In short, these examples form a common thread throughout this whole book. Later, in Section 1.4, we will provide a brief overview of existing research on software agents, and specify how these different existing paradigms address one or more of the basic questions raised by these three motivating examples. Section 1.4 will also explain what the shortcomings of these existing approaches are. In Section 1.5, we describe some general desiderata that agent theories and architectures should satisfy. Finally, in Section 1.6, we will provide a quick glimpse into the organization of this book, and provide a birdseye view of how (and where) the shortcomings pointed out in Section 1.4 are addressed by the framework described in the rest of this book.

1.1 A Personalized Department Store Application (**STORE**)

Let us consider the case of a large department store that has a web-based marketing site. Today, the Internet contains a whole host of such sites, offering on-line shopping services.

Today's Department Store: In most existing web sites today, interaction is initiated by a user who contacts the department store web site, and requests information on one or more consumer products he is interested in. For example, the user may ask for information on "leather shoes." The advanced systems deployed today access an underlying database and bring back relevant information on leather shoes. Such relevant information typically includes a picture of a shoe, a price, available colors and sizes, and perhaps a button that allows the user to place an order. The electronic department store of today is characterized by two properties: first, it assumes that users will come to the department store, and second, it does nothing more than simply retrieving data from a database and displaying it to the user.

Tomorrow's (Reactive) Department Store: In contrast, the department store of tomorrow will take explicit actions so that the department store goes to the customer, announcing items deemed to be of interest to the customer, rather than waiting for the customer to come to the store. This is because the department store's ultimate goal is to maximize profit (current as well as future), and in particular, it will accomplish this through the following means: It would like to ensure that a customer who visits it is presented items that maximize its expected profit as well as the likelihood of making a sale (e.g., they may not want to lose a sale by getting too greedy.) In particular, the department store would like to ensure that the items it presents a user (whether she visited the site of her own volition, or whether the presentation is a directed mailing), are items that are likely to be of maximal interest to the user—there is no point in mailing information about $100-dollar ties to a person who has always bought clothing at lower prices.

Section 1.1   A Personalized Department Store Application (STORE)

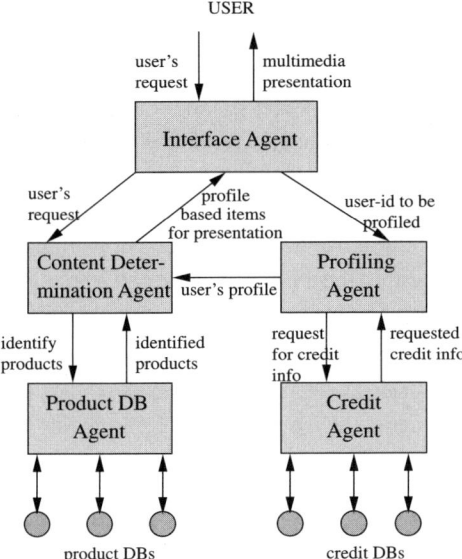

Figure 1.1
Interactions between Agents in STORE Example.

Intelligent agent technology may be used to accomplish these goals through a simple architecture, as shown in Figure 1.1. This architecture involves the following agents:

1. A Credit Database Agent: This agent does nothing more sophisticated than providing access to a credit database. In the United States, many department stores issue their own credit cards, and as a consequence, they automatically have access to (at least some) credit data for many customers. The credit database agent may in fact access a variety of databases, not just one. Open source credit data is (unfortunately) readily available to paying customers.

2. Product Database Agent: This agent provides access to one or more product databases reflecting the merchandise that the department store sells. Given a desired product description (e.g., "leather shoes"), this agent may be used to retrieve tuples associated with this product description. For example, a department store may carry 100 different types of leather shoes, and in this case, the product database may return a list of 100 records, one associated with each type of leather shoe.

3. A Profiling Agent: This agent takes as input the identity of a user (who is interacting with the Department Store Interface agent described below). It then requests the credit database agent for information on this user's credit history, and analyses the credit data.

Credit information typically contains detailed information about an individual's spending habits. The profiling agent may then classify the user as a "high" spender, an "average" spender, or a "low" spender. Of course, more detailed classifications are possible; it may classify the user as a "high" spender on clothing, but a "low" spender on appliances, indicating that the person cares more about personal appearance than on electrical appliances in his home.

As we go through this book, we will see that the Profiling agent can be made much more complex—if a user's credit history is relatively small (as would be the case with someone who pays cash for most purchases), it could well be that the Profiling agent analyzes other information (e.g., the person's home address) to determine his profile and/or it might contact other agents outside the department store that sell profiles of customers.

4. A Content Determination Agent: This agent tries to determine what to show the user. It takes as input, the user's request, and the classification of the agent as determined by the Profiling Agent. It executes a query to the product database agent, which provides it a set of tuples (e.g., the 100 different types of leather shoes). It then uses the user classification provided by the profiling agent to filter these 100 leather shoes. For example, if the user is classified as a "high spender," it may select the 10 most expensive leather shoes. In addition, the content determination agent may decide that when it presents these 10 leather shoes to the user, it will run advertisements on the bottom of the screen, showing other items that "fit" this user's high-spending profile.

5. Interface Agent: This agent takes the objects identified by the Content Determination Agent and weaves together a multimedia presentation (perhaps accompanied with music to the user's taste if it has information on music CDs previously purchased by the user!) containing these objects, together with any focused advertising information.

Thus far, we have presented how a department store might deploy a multiagent system. However, a human user may wish to have a personalized agent that finds an online store that provides a given service. For example, one of the authors was recently interested in finding wine distributors who sell *1990 Chateau Tayac* wines. An agent which found such a distributor would have been invaluable. In addition to finding a list of such distributors, the user might want to have these distributors ranked in descending order of the per bottle sales—the scenario can be made even more complex by wanting to have distributors ranked in descending order of the total (cost plus shipping) price for a dozen bottles.

Active Department Store of Tomorrow: Thus far, we have assumed that our department store agent is *reactive*. However, in reality, a department store system could be *proactive* in the following sense. As we all know, department stores regularly have sales. When a sale occurs, the department store could have a *Sale-Notification Agent* that performs the following task. For every individual I in the department store's database, the department store could:

- identify the user's profile,
- determine which items going on sale "fit" the user's profile, and
- take an appropriate action—such an action could email the user a list of items "fitting" his profile. Alternatively, the action may be to create a *personalized sale flyer* specifying for each user, a set of sale item descriptions to be physically mailed to him.

In addition, the Sale-Notification agent may *schedule future actions* based on its *uncertain beliefs about the users*. For example, statistical analysis of John Doe's shopping habits at the store may indicate the following distribution:

Day	Percentage Spent
Monday	2%
Tuesday	3%
Wednesday	3%
Thursday	2%
Friday	27%
Saturday	50%
Sunday	13%

In the above table, the tuple, ⟨Monday, 2%⟩ means that of all the money that John Doe is known to have spent at this store, 2% of the money was spent on Mondays.

The Sale-Notification agent may now reason as follows: 90% of John Doe's dollars spent at this store are spent during the Friday-Saturday-Sunday period. Therefore, I will mail John Doe promotional material on sales so as to reach him on Thursday evening.

However, there may be uncertainty in postal services. For example, the bulk mailing system provided by the US Postal Service may have statistical data showing that 13% of such mailings reach the customer within 1 day of shipping, 79% in 2 days, and the remaining 8% take over 2 days. Thus, the Sale-Notification agent may mail the sales brochures to John Doe on Tuesday.

When we examine the above department store example, we notice that:

1. The department store example may be viewed as a multiagent system where the interactions between the agents involved are clear and well defined.

2. Each agent has an associated body of data structures and algorithms that it maintains. The content of these data structures may be updated independently of the application as

a whole (e.g., user's credit data may change in the above example without affecting the Product-Database agent).

3. Each agent is capable of performing a small, but well defined set of actions/tasks.

4. The actual actions executed (from the set of actions an agent is capable of performing) may vary depending upon the circumstances involved. For example, the Credit agent may provide credit information in the above example only to the Profiling Agent, but may refuse to respond to credit requests from other agents.

5. Each agent may reason with beliefs about the behavior of other agents, and each agent not only decides what actions to perform, but also when to perform them. Uncertainty may be present in the beliefs the agent holds about other agents.

1.2 The Controlled Flight into Terrain Application (CFIT)

According to the *Washington Post (Feb. 12, 1998, page A-11)* 2,708 out of 7,496 airline fatalities during the 1987–1996 period did not happen due to pilot error (as is commonly suspected), but due to a phenomenon called *controlled flight into terrain* (CFIT). Intuitively, a CFIT error occurs when a plane is proceeding along an Auto-Pilot (not human) controlled trajectory, but literally crashes into the ground. CFIT errors occur because of malfunctioning sensors and because the autopilot program has an *incorrect belief* about the actual location of the plane. CFIT is the number one cause of airline deaths in the world. The CFIT problem is highlighted by two major plane crashes during recent years:

• The December 1995 crash of an American Airlines plane in Cali, Colombia, killing over 250 people including Paris Kanellakis, a prominent computer scientist;

• the crash of a US military plane near Dubrovnik, Yugoslavia in 1996, killing the US Commerce Secretary, Ron Brown.

We have developed a preliminary solution to the CFIT problem, and have developed a working prototype of a multi-agent solution to the CFIT problem. The solution involves the following agents:

Auto-Pilot Agent: The Auto-Pilot agent ensures that the plane stays on its allocated flight path. Most civilian flights in the world fly along certain prescribed flight corridors that are assigned to each flight by air traffic controllers. The task of the Auto-Pilot agent is to ensure that the plane stays on-course, and make appropriate adjustments (by perhaps using AI planning or 3-dimensional path planning techniques) when the physical dynamics of the plane cause it to veer off course. Techniques for agent based solutions to flight planning and air traffic control problems have been studied in the agents community by Tambe, Johnson, and Shen (1997).

Satellite Agents: We assume the existence of a set of satellite agents that will monitor the position of several planes simultaneously. Every Δt units of time, each satellite agent broadcasts a report that may be read by the location agent. Thus, if $\Delta t = 10$ and the first report is read at time 0, then this means that all the satellite agents send reports at times 0, 10, 20, ... and so on. Each satellite agent specifies where it believes the plane is at that point in time.

GPS Agent: This agent takes reports from multiple satellite agents above and merges them together. Multiplexing satellite agents together enhances reliability—if one satellite agent fails, the others will still provide a report. Merging techniques may include methods of eliminating outliers—e.g., if 9 of 10 satellite agents tell the plane it is at location A and the 10th agent tells the plane it is at location B, the last report can be eliminated. The GPS agent then feeds the GPS-based location of the plane to the Auto-Pilot agent, which consults the Terrain agent below before taking corrective action.

Terrain Agent: The Terrain agent takes a coordinate in the globe, and retrieves a terrain map for the region. In the case of our CFIT example, a special kind of terrain map is retrieved called a *Digital Terrain Elevation Data (DTED)* map. Our implementation currently includes DTED data for the whole of the continental USA, but not for the world. Given any (x, y) location which falls within this map, the elevation of that (x, y) location can then be retrieved from the DTED map by the Terrain agent. The Terrain agent provides to the Auto-Pilot agent a set of "no-go" areas. Using this set, the Auto-Pilot agent can check if its current heading will cause it to fly into a mountain (as happened with the American Airlines crash of 1996), and in such cases, it can replan to ensure that the plane avoids these no-go areas.

Figure 1.2 on the next page shows a schematic diagram of the different agents involved in this example.

The reader will readily note that there are some similarities, as well as some differences, between this CFIT example and the preceding STORE example. The example is similar to the department store example in the following ways:

- Like the STORE application, the CFIT application may be viewed as a multiagent system where the agents interact with one another in clearly defined ways.

- In both examples, each agent manages a well defined body of data structures and associated algorithms, but these data structures may be updated autonomously and vary from one agent to another.

- As in the case of the STORE example, each agent performs a set of well defined tasks.

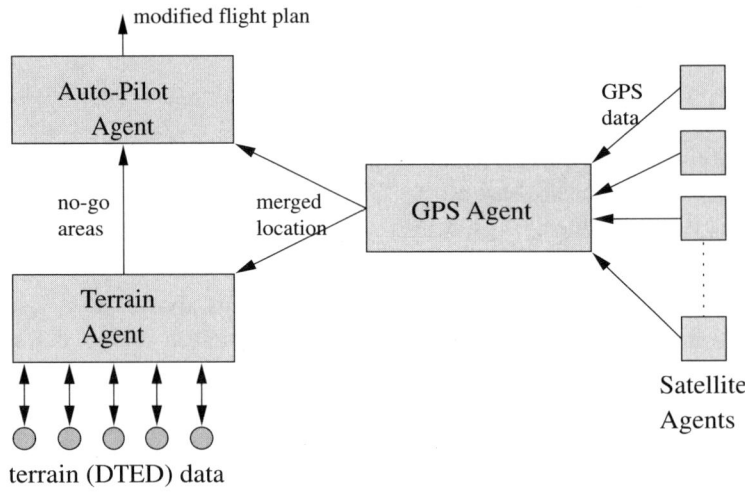

Figure 1.2
Interactions between Agents in CFIT Example.

- As in the case of the STORE example, agents may take different actions, based on the circumstances. For example, some satellite agents may send updates to one plane every 5 seconds, but only at every 50 seconds for another plane.

In addition, the following attributes (which also appear in the department store example) play an important role in the CFIT example:

Reasoning about Beliefs: The Auto-Pilot agent reasons with *Beliefs*. At any given point t in time, the Auto-Pilot agent believes that it is at a given location ℓ_t. However, its belief about its location, and the location it is really at, may be different. The task of the GPS agent in the CFIT application is to alert the Auto-Pilot agent to its incorrect beliefs, which may then be appropriately corrected by the Auto-Pilot agent.

In this example, the Auto-Pilot agent believes the correction it receives from the satellite agents. However, it is conceivable that if our plane is a military aircraft, then an enemy might attempt to masquerade as a legitimate satellite agent, and falsely inform the Auto-Pilot agent that it is at location ℓ_t^*, with the express intent of making the plane go off-course. However, agents must make decisions on how to act when requests/information are received from other agents. It is important to note that which actions an agent decides to execute depends upon background information that the agent has. Thus, if an agent suspects that a satellite agent message is not reliable, then it might choose to ignore information it receives from that agent or it may choose to seek clarification from another source. On the other hand, if it believes that the satellite agent's message is "legitimate," then it may take the information provided into consideration when making decisions. In general, agents decide how to act, based upon (i) the background knowledge that the agent has, and (ii) the beliefs that the agent currently holds.

Delayed Actions: Yet another difference with the STORE example is that the Auto-Pilot agent may choose to *delay* taking actions. In other words, the Auto-Pilot agent may know at time t that it is off-course. It could choose to create a plan at time t (creation of a plan is an explicit action) that commits the Auto-Pilot agent to take other actions at later points in time, e.g., "Execute a climb action by 50 feet per second between time $(t + 5)$ and time $(t + 10)$."

Uncertainty: If the Auto-Pilot agent receives frequent information from the Location agent, stating that it is off-course, it might suspect that some of its on-board sensors or actuators are malfunctioning. Depending upon its knowledge of these sensors and actuators, it might have different beliefs about which sensor/actuator is malfunctioning. This belief may be accompanied with a *probability* or *certainty* that the belief is in fact true. Based on these certainties, the Auto-Pilot may take one of several actions that could include returning the plane to manual control, switching off a sensor and/or switching on an alternative sensor. In general, in extended versions of our CFIT example, Auto-Pilot agents may need to reason with uncertainty when making decisions.

1.3 A Supply Chain Example (CHAIN)

Supply chain management (Bowersox, Closs, and Helferich 1986) is one of the most important activities in any major production company. Most such companies like to keep their production lines busy and on schedule. To ensure this, they must constantly monitor their inventory to ensure that components and items needed for creating their products are available in adequate numbers.

For instance, an automobile company is likely to want to guarantee that they always have an adequate number of tires and spark plugs in their local inventory. When the supply of tires or spark plugs drops to a certain predetermined level, the company in question must ensure that new supplies are promptly ordered. This may be done through the following steps.

- In most large corporations, the company has "standing" contracts with producers of different parts (also referred to as an "open" purchase order). When a shortfall occurs, the company contacts suppliers to see which of them can supply the desired quantity of the item(s) in question within the desired time frame. Based on the responses received from the suppliers, one or more purchase orders may be generated.

- The company may also have an existing purchase order with a large transportation provider, or with a group of providers. The company may then choose to determine whether the items ordered should be: (a) delivered entirely by truck, or (b) delivered by a combination of truck and airplane.

This scenario can be made significantly more sophisticated than the above description. For example, the company may request bids from multiple potential suppliers, the company may use methods to identify alternative substitute parts if the ones being ordered are not available, etc. For pedagogical purposes, we have chosen to keep the scenario relatively simple.

The above automated purchasing procedure may be facilitated by using an architecture such as that shown in Figure 1.3. In this architecture, we have an Inventory agent that

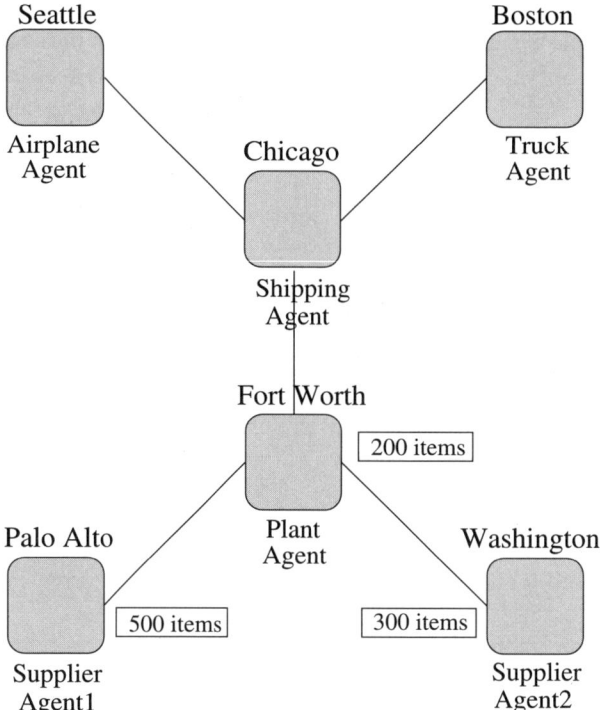

Figure 1.3
Agents in CHAIN Example.

monitors the available inventory at the company's manufacturing plant. We have shown two suppliers, each of which has an associated agent that monitors two databases:

• An ACCESS database specifying how much uncommitted stock the supplier has. For example, if the tuple ⟨widget50, 9000⟩ is in this relation, then this means that the supplier has 9000 pieces of widget50 that haven't yet been committed to a consumer.

• An ACCESS database specifying how much committed stock the supplier has. For example, if the triple ⟨widget50,1000,companyA⟩ is in the relation, this means that the supplier has 1000 pieces of widget50 that have been committed to company A.

Thus, if company-B were to request 2000 pieces of widget50, we would update the first relation, by replacing the tuple ⟨widget50, 9000⟩ by the tuple ⟨widget50, 7000⟩ and adding the tuple ⟨widget50,2000,companyB⟩ to the latter relation—assuming that company B did not already have widget50 on order.

Once the Plant agent places orders with the suppliers, it must ensure that the transportation vendors can deliver the items to the company's location. For this, it consults a *Shipping-Agent*, which in turn consults a *Truck-Agent* (that provides and manages truck schedules using routing algorithms) and an *Airplane-Agent* (that provides and manages airplane freight cargo). The truck agent may in fact control a set of other agents, one located on each truck. The truck agent we have built is constructed by building on top of ESRI's MapObject system for route mapping. These databases can be made more realistic by adding other fields—again for the sake of simplicity, we have chosen not to do so.

As in the previous two examples, the Plant agent may make decisions based on a more sophisticated reasoning process. For example:

Reasoning about Uncertainty: The Plant agent may have some historical data about the ability of the supplier agents to deliver on time. For example, it may have a table of the form:

Supplier	Item	Days Late	Percentage
supplier1	widget1	−3	5
		−1	10
		0	55
		1	20
		2	10
...	...	...	...
...	...	...	...

In this table, the first tuple says that in cases where supplier1 promised to deliver widget1, he supplied it 3 days early in 5% of the cases. The last entry above likewise says that when supplier1 promised to deliver widget1, he supplied it 2 days late in 10% of the cases. Using this table, the Plant agent may make decisions about the probability that placing an order with supplier1 will in fact result in the order being delivered within the desired deadline.

Delayed Actions: When placing an order with supplier1, the Plant agent plant may want to retain the option of cutting the contract to supplier1 if adequate progress has not been made. Thus, the Plant agent may inform supplier1 up front that 10 days after placement of the order, it will inspect the status of the supplier's performance on that order (such inspections will of course be based on reasonable and precisely stated evaluation conditions). If the performance does not meet certain conditions, it might cancel part of the contract.

Reasoning about Beliefs: As in the case of the CFIT agent, the Plant agent may make decisions based on its *beliefs* about the suppliers ability to deliver, or the transportation companies ability to ship products. For example, if the Plant agent believes that a Transportation agent is likely to have a strike, it might choose to place its transportation order with another company.

The CHAIN example, like the other examples, may be viewed as a multiagent system where the interactions between agents are clearly specified, and each agent manages a set of data structures that can be autonomously updated by the agent. Furthermore, different agents may manage different data structures.

However, a distinct difference occurs when the Plant agent realizes that neither of its Supplier agents can supply the item that is required within the given time frame. In such a case, the Plant agent may need to *dynamically find* another agent that supplies the desired item. This requires that the Plant agent has access to some kind of yellow pages facility that keeps track of the services offered by different agents. Later, in Chapters 2 and 3, we will define detailed yellow pages service mechanisms to support the need of finding agents that provide a service, when the identity of such agents is not known *a priori*.

1.4 Brief Overview of Related Research on Agents

In this section, we provide a brief overview of existing work on agents, and explain their advantages and disadvantages with respect to the three motivating examples introduced above.

Section 1.4   Brief Overview of Related Research on Agents   15

As we have already observed, the three examples above all share a common structure:

• Each agent has an associated set of data structures.

• Each agent has an associated set of low-level operations to manipulate those data structures.

• Each agent has an associated set of high-level actions that "weave" together the low level operations above that it performs.

• Each agent has a policy that it uses to determine which of its associated high level actions to execute in response to requests and/or events (e.g., receipt of data from another agent).

There are various other parameters associated with any single agent that we will discuss in greater detail in later chapters, but for now, these are the most salient features of practical implemented agents. In addition, a platform to support multi-agent interactions must provide a set of common services including, but not limited to:

1. *Registration* services, through which an agent can register the services it provides.

2. *Yellow pages* services that allow an agent to find another agent offering a service *similar to* a service sought by the agent.

3. *Thesauri* and *dictionary* services that allow agents to determine what words mean.

4. More sophisticated *ontological* services that allow an agent to determine what another agent might mean when it uses a term or expression.

5. *Security* services that allow an agent to look up the security classification of another agent (perhaps under some restricted conditions).

Different parts of various technical problems raised by the need to create multiagent systems have been addressed in many different scientific communities, ranging from the database community, the AI community, the distributed objects community, and the programming languages community, to name a few. In this section, we will briefly skim some of the major approaches to these technical problems—a detailed and much more comprehensive overview is contained in Chapter 13.

1.4.1 Heterogeneous Data/Software Integration

One of the important aspects of agent systems is the ability to uniformly access heterogeneous data sources. In particular, if agent decision making is based on the content of arbitrary data structures managed by the agent, then there must be some unified way of accessing those data structures. Many formalisms have been proposed to integrate heterogeneous data structures. These formalisms fall into three categories:

Logical Languages: One of the first logical languages to integrate heterogeneous data sources was the *SIMS* system (Arens, Chee, Hsu, and Knoblock 1993) at USC which uses a LISP-like syntax to integrate multiple databases as well. More or less at the same time as *SIMS*, a Datalog-extension to access heterogeneous data sources was proposed in the *HERMES* Heterogeneous Reasoning and Mediator System Project in June 1993 (Lu, Nerode, and Subrahmanian 1996; Subrahmanian 1994; Brink, Marcus, and Subrahmanian 1995; Marcus and Subrahmanian 1996; Adali, Candan, Papakonstantinou, and Subrahmanian 1996; Lu, Moerkotte, Schue, and Subrahmanian 1995). Shortly thereafter, the IBM-Stanford *TSIMMIS* effort (Chawathe et al. 1994) proposed logical extensions of Datalog as well. These approaches differed in their expressive power—for instance, *TSIMMIS* was largely successful on relational databases, but also accessed some non-relational data sources such as bibliographic data. *SIMS* accessed a wide variety of AI knowledge representation schemes, as well as traditional relational databases. In contrast, *HERMES* integrated arbitrary software packages such as an Army Terrain Route Planning System, Jim Hendler's UM Nonlin nonlinear planning system, a face recognition system, a video reasoning system, and various mathematical programming software packages.

SQL Extensions: SQL has long had a mechanism to make "foreign function" calls whereby an SQL query can embed a subquery to an external data source. The problem with most existing implementations of SQL is that even though they can access these external data sources, they make assumptions on the format of the outputs returned by such foreign function calls. Thus, if the foreign functions return answers that are not within certain prescribed formats, then they cannot be processed by standard SQL interpreters. Extensions of SQL to access heterogeneous relational databases such as the Object Database Connectivity (ODBC) standard (Creamer, Stegman, and Signore 1995) have received wide acceptance in industry.

OQL Extensions: Under the aegis of the US Department of Defense, a standard for data integration was proposed by a group of approximately 11 researchers selected by *DARPA* (including the first author of this book). The standard is well summarized in the report of this working group (Buneman, Ullman, Raschid, Abiteboul, Levy, Maier, Qian, Ramakrishnan, Subrahmanian, Tannen, and Zdonik 1996). The approach advocated by the *DARPA* working group was to built a *minimal core language* based on the Object Definition Language and the Object Query Language put forth earlier by the industry wide Object Data Management Group (*ODMG*) (Cattell et al. 1997). The basic idea was that the core part be a restricted version of OQL, and all extensions to the core would handle complex data types with methods.

Another important later direction on mediation includes the *InfoSleuth* effort (Bayardo et al. 1997) system, at MCC—this will be discussed in detail later in Chapter 4.

Implementations of all the three frameworks listed above were completed in the 1993–1996 time frame, and many of these are available, either free of charge or for a licensing fee (Brink, Marcus, and Subrahmanian 1995; Adali, Candan, Papakonstantinou, and Subrahmanian 1996; Lu, Nerode, and Subrahmanian 1996; Chawathe et al. 1994; Arens, Chee, Hsu, and Knoblock 1993). *Any of the frameworks listed above could constitute a valid language, by using which access is provided to arbitrary data structures.*

1.4.2 Agent Decision Making

There has been a significant amount of work on agent decision making. Rosenschein (1985) was perhaps the first to say that agents act according to states, and which actions they take are determined by rules of the form *"When P is true of the state of the environment, then the agent should take action A."* Rosenschein and Kaelbling (1995) extend this framework to provide a basis for such actions in terms of situated automata theory. For example, in the case of the department store example, the Profiling Agent may use a rule of the form *"If the credit data on person P shows that she spends over $200 per month (on the average) at our store, then classify P as a high spender."* Using this rule, the Sales agent may take another action of the form *"If the Profiling agent classifies person P as a high spender, then send P material M by email."*

Bratman, Israel, and Pollack (1988) define the *IRMA* system which uses similar ideas to generate plans. In their framework, different possible courses of actions (Plans) are generated, based on the agent's intentions. These plans are then evaluated to determine which ones are consistent and optimal with respect to achieving these intentions. This is useful when applied to agents which have intentions that might require planning (though there might be agents that do not have any intentions or plans such as a GPS receiver in the CFIT example). Certainly, the Auto-Pilot agent in the CFIT example has an *intention*—namely to stay on course, as specified by the flight plan filed by the plane, and it may need to *replan* when it is notified by the GPS agent that it has veered off course.

The *Procedural Reasoning System* (*PRS*) is one of the best known multiagent construction systems that implements BDI agents (BDI stands for *Belief, Desires, Intentionality*) (d'Inverno, Kinny, Luck, and Wooldridge 1997). This framework has led to several interesting applications including a practical, deployed application called *OASIS* for air traffic control in Sydney, Australia. The theory of *PRS* is captured through a logic based development, in Rao and Georgeff (1991).

Singh (1997) is concerned about heterogeneity in agents, and he develops a theory of agent interactions through workflow diagrams. Intuitively, in this framework, an agent is viewed as a finite state automaton. Agent states are viewed as states of the automaton, and agent actions are viewed as transitions on these states. This is certainly consistent with the three motivating examples—for instance, in the CHAIN example, when the Supplier1 agent executes an action (such as shipping supplies), this may certainly be viewed as a state transition, causing the available quantity of the supply item in question at Supplier1's location to drop.

1.4.3 Specific Interaction Mechanisms for Multiagent Systems

There has been extensive work in AI on specific protocols for multiagent interactions. Two such mechanisms are worth mentioning here:

Bidding Mechanisms: Let us return to the CHAIN example and assume that neither of the two approved suppliers (with existing contracts to funnel the purchase through) can deliver the supplies required by the Plant agent. In this case, the Plant agent needs to find another agent (one for which no contract is currently in force). The Plant agent needs to *negotiate* with the new agent, arriving at a mutually agreeable arrangement. There has been extensive work on negotiation in multiagent systems, based on the initial idea of contract nets, due to Smith and Davis (1983). In this paradigm, an agent seeking a service invites bids from other agents, and selects the bid that most closely matches its own. Schwartz and Kraus (1997) present a model of agent decision making where one agent invites bids (this is an action !) and others evaluate the bids (another action) and respond. Other forms of negotiation have also been studied and will be discussed in detail in Chapter 14.

Coalition Formation: A second kind of interaction between agents is coalition formation. Consider an expanded version of the CFIT example, in a military setting. Here, a Tank agent tank may have a mission, but as it proceeds toward execution of the mission, it encounters heavier resistance than expected. In this case, it may dynamically team with a helicopter gunship whose Auto-Pilot and control mechanisms are implemented using the CFIT example. Here, the tank is forming a *coalition dynamically* in order to accomplish a given goal. Coalition formation mechanisms where agents dynamically team up with other agents has been intensely studied by many researchers (Shehory, Sycara, and Jha 1997; Sandholm and Lesser 1995; Wooldridge and Jennings 1997). Determining which agents to team with is a sort of decision making capability.

1.4.4 Agent Programming

Shoham (1993) was perhaps the first to propose an explicit programming language for agents, based on object oriented concepts, and based on the concept of an agent state. In Shoham's approach, an agent "is an entity whose state is viewed as consisting of mental components such as beliefs, capabilities, choices, and commitments."

He proposes a language, **Agent-0**, for agent programming, that provides a mechanism to express actions, time, and obligations. **Agent-0** is a simple, yet powerful language.

Closely related to Shoham's work is that of Hindriks, de Boer, van der Hoek, and Meyer (1997) where an agent programming language based on BDI-agents is presented. They proceed upon the assumption that an agent language must have the ability to update its beliefs and its goals, and it must have a practical reasoning method (which will find a way to achieve goals). Hindriks, de Boer, van der Hoek, and Meyer (1997, p. 211) argue that *"Now, to program an agent is to specify its initial mental state, the semantics of the basic actions the agent can perform, and to write a set of practical reasoning rules."*

When compared to Singh's approach described earlier in this chapter, these approaches provide a compact way of representing a massive finite state automaton (only the initial state is explicit) and transitions are specified through actions and rules governing the actions. This is very appealing, and the semantics is very clean.

However, both approaches assume that all the reasoning done by agents is implemented in one form of logic or another, and that all agents involved manipulate logical data. While logic is a reasonable *abstraction* of data, it remains a fact of life that the vast majority of data available today is in the form of non-logical data structures that vary widely.

The second assumption made is that *all* reasoning done by agents is encoded through logical rules. While this is also reasonable as an abstraction, it is rarely true in practice. For example, consider the planning performed by the Auto-Pilot agent in the CFIT example, or the profiling performed by the Profiling agent in the department store example, or the route planning performed by the Truck agent in the in the CHAIN example. These three activities will, in all likelihood, be programmed using imperative code, and mechanisms such as those alluded to above must be able to meaningfully reason on top of such legacy code.

1.4.5 Agent Architectures

An architecture for the creation and deployment of multiagent applications must satisfy three goals:

1. First and foremost, it must provide an architecture for designing software agents.

2. It must provide the underlying software infrastructure that provides a common set of services that agents will need.

3. It must provide mechanisms for interactions between clients and the underlying agent infrastructure.

As we have already discussed the first point earlier in this section, we will confine ourselves to related work on the latter two components.

With respect to agent architectures, there have been numerous proposals in the literature, e.g., (Gasser and Ishida 1991; Glicoe, Staats, and Huhns 1995; Birmingham, Durfee, Mullen, and Wellman 1995), which have been broadly classified by Genesereth and Ketchpel (1994) into four categories:

1. In the first category, each agent has an associated "transducer" that converts all incoming messages and requests into a form that is intelligible to the agent. In the context of our CFIT example introduced this means that each agent in the example must have the ability to understand messages sent to it by other agents. However, the CFIT example shows only a small microcosm of the functioning of the Auto-Pilot agent. In reality, the Auto-Pilot needs to interact with agents associated with hundreds of sensors and actuators, and to require that the transducers anticipate what other agents will send and translate it is clearly a complex problem. In general, in an n-agent system, we may need $O(n^2)$ transducers, which is clearly not desirable.

2. The second approach is based on wrappers which *"inject code into a program to allow it to communicate"* (Genesereth and Ketchpel 1994, p. 51). This idea is based on the principle that each agent has an associated body of code that is expressed in a common language used by other agents (or is expressed in one of a very small number of such languages). This means that in the case of the CFIT example, each agent is built around a body of software code, and this software code has an associated body of program code (expressed perhaps in a different language) expressing some information about the program.

3. The third approach described in (Genesereth and Ketchpel 1994) is to completely rewrite the code implementing an agent, which is obviously a very expensive alternative.

4. Last but not least, there is the *mediation* approach proposed by Wiederhold (1993), which assumes that all agents will communicate with a mediator which in turn may send messages to other agents. The mediation approach has been extensively studied (Arens, Chee, Hsu, and Knoblock 1993; Brink, Marcus, and Subrahmanian 1995; Chawathe et al. 1994; Bayardo et al. 1997). However, it suffers from a problem. Suppose all communications in the CFIT example had to go through such a mediator. Then if the mediator malfunctions or "goes down," the system as a whole is liable to collapse, leaving the plane in a precarious position. In an agent based system, we should allow point to point communication between agents without having to go through a mediator. This increases reliability of the entire multiagent system as a whole and often avoids inefficiency by avoiding huge workloads on certain agents or servers or network nodes.

1.4.6 Match-making Services

As stated before, one of the infrastructural tasks to be provided is yellow pages services whereby agents may advertise services they offer (via the yellow pages) and the infrastructure layer allows for identifying agents A that provide a service *similar* to a service requested by agent B. For instance, in the CHAIN example, the plant agent may need to contact such a yellow pages service in order to find agents that can provide the supply item needed. The yellow pages agent must attempt to identify agents that provide either the exact supply item required, or something similar to the requested item. Kuokka and Harada (1996) present the *SHADE* and *COINS* systems for matchmaking. *SHADE* uses logical rules to support matchmaking—the logic used is a subset of *KIF* and is very expressive. In contrast, *COINS* assumes that a message is a document (represented by a weighted term vector) and retrieves the *most similar* advertised services using the *SMART* algorithm of Salton and McGill (1983). Decker, Sycara, and Williamson (1997) present matchmakers that store capability advertisements of different agents. They look for *exact* matches between requested services and retrieved services, and concentrate their efforts on architectures that support load balancing and protection of privacy of different agents.

1.5 Ten Desiderata for an Agent Infrastructure

In this book, we will describe advances in the construction of agents, as well as multiagent systems. Our intent is to provide a rich formal theory of agent construction and agent interaction that is *practically* implementable and realizable. *IMPACT* (*Interactive Maryland Platform for Agents Collaborating Together*) is a software platform for the creation and deployment of agents, and agent based systems. In this book, we will provide one set of answers to the following questions raised at the beginning of this chapter:

(Q1)   *What is an agent?*

(Q2)   *If program P is not considered to be an agent according to some specified definition of agenthood, is there a suite of tools that can help in "agentizing" P?*

(Q3)   *Once a specific definition of agenthood is chosen, what kind of software infrastructure is required to support interactions between such agents, and what core set of services must be provided by such an infrastructure?*

In particular, any solution to the above questions must (to our mind) satisfy the following important desiderata:

(D1)   Agents are for everyone: anybody who has a software program P, either custom designed to be an agent, or an existing legacy program, must be able to *agentize* their program and *plug* it into the provided solution. In particular, in the case of the CFIT example, this means that if a new Satellite agent becomes available, or a better flight planning Auto-Pilot agent is designed, plugging it in should be simple. Similarly, if a new Supplier agent is identified in the CHAIN example, we should be able to access it easily and incorporate it into the existing multiagent CHAIN example. Any theory of agents must encompass the above diversity.

(D2) No theory of agents is likely to be of much practical value if it does not recognize the fact that data is stored in a wide variety of data structures, and data is manipulated by an existing corpus of algorithms. If this is not taken into account in a theory of agents, then that theory is not likely to be particularly useful.

(D3) A theory of agents must *not* depend upon the set of actions that the agent performs. Rather, the set of actions that the agent performs must be a *parameter* that is taken into account in the semantics. Furthermore, any proposed action framework must allow actions to have effects on arbitrary agent data structures, and must be capable of being built seamlessly on top of such existing applications.

(D4) Every agent should execute actions based on some *clearly articulated* decision policy. While this policy need not be disclosed to other agents, such a specification is invaluable when the agent is later modified. We will argue that a *declarative* framework for articulating decision policies of agents is imperative.

(D5) Any agent construction framework must allow agents to perform the following types of reasoning:

• Reasoning about its beliefs about other agents.

• Reasoning about uncertainty in its beliefs about the world and about its beliefs about other agents.

• Reasoning about time.

These capabilities should be viewed as *extensions* to a core agent action language, that may be "switched" on or off, depending upon the reasoning needs of an agent. The reason for this is that different agents need to reason at different levels of sophistication. However, increasingly sophisticated reasoning comes at a computational price, viz. an increase in complexity (as we will see in the book).

Thus, it is wise to have a *base language* together with a *hierarchy* of extensions of the base language reflecting increased expressive power. Depending on which language within this hierarchy the agent wishes to use, the computational price to be paid by the agent should be clearly defined. This also requires that we have a *hierarchy* of compilers/interpreters mirroring the language hierarchy. It is in general computationally unwise to use a solver for a language "high" in the hierarchy if an agent is using a language "low" in the hierarchy (e.g., using a solver for a PSPACE-complete problem on a polynomial instance of the problem is usually not wise).

(D6) Any infrastructure to support multiagent interactions *must* provide two important types of security—security on the agent side, to ensure that an agent (if it wishes) can protect some of its information and services, and security on the infrastructural side so that one agent cannot masquerade as another, thus acquiring access to data/services that is not authorized to receive.

(D7) While the efficiency of the code underlying a software agent cannot be guaranteed (as it will vary from one application to another), guarantees are needed that provide information on the performance of an agent relative to an oracle that supports calls to underlying software code. Such guarantees must come in two forms—results on *worst case complexity* as well as accompanying *experimental results*. Both these types of results are useful, because in many cases, worst case complexity results do not take into account specific patterns of data requests that become apparent only after running experiments. Conversely, using experimental results alone is not adequate, because in many cases, we do want to know worst case running times, and experimental data may hide such information.

(D8) Efficiency of an implementation of the theory is critical in the development of a multiagent system. We must identify efficiently computable *fragments* of the general hierarchy of languages alluded to above, and our implementations must take advantage of the specific structure of such language fragments. A system built in this way must be accompanied by a suite of software tools that helps the developer build sophisticated multiagent systems.

(D9) A critical point is *reliability*—there is no point in a highly efficient implementation, if all agents deployed in the implementation come to a grinding halt when the agent "infrastructure" crashes.

(D10) The only way of testing the applicability of any theory is to build a software system based on the theory, to deploy a set of applications based on the theory, and to report on experiments based on those applications. Thus, an implementation *must be validated* by a set of deployed applications.

1.6 A Birdseye View of This Book

This book is organized as follows.

Chapter 2 introduces the reader to the overall architecture of the proposed *IMPACT* framework. It explains the issues involved in designing the architecture, what alternative architectures could have been used, and why certain design choices were made. It explains the architecture of individual agents, as well as the architecture of the agent infrastructure, and how the two "fit" together, using the STORE, CFIT, and CHAIN examples to illustrate the concepts.

Chapter 3 explains the *IMPACT* Service Description language using which an agent may specify the set of services that it offers. We describe the syntax of the language and specify the services offered by various agents in the STORE, CFIT, and CHAIN examples using this syntax. We further specify how requests for *similar* services are handled within this framework. We explain existing alternative approaches, and describe the advantages of disadvantages of these approaches when compared to ours.

Chapter 4 shows how agents may be built on top of legacy data, using a basic mechanism called a *code call condition*. We will show how such access methods may be efficiently implemented and we will describe our implementation efforts to date to do so. As in other cases, the STORE, CFIT, and CHAIN examples will be revisited here.

Chapter 5 describes the implementation of *IMPACT* Servers. These are programs that provide the "infrastructural" services needed for multiple agents to interact, including yellow pages and other services described in detail in Chapter 3. This chapter explains how to access these servers, how they were implemented, and how agents may interact to them. A theorist may wish to skip this chapter, but an individual seeking to implement an agent system may find this chapter very useful.

Chapter 6 builds on top of Chapter 4 and shows how an agent's action policies may be declaratively specified. Such declarative policies must encode what the agent is permitted to do, what it is forbidden from doing, what it is obliged to do, and what in fact, it does, given that the agent's data structures reflect a "current state" of the world. We show that the problem of determining how to "act" (which an agent must make continuously) in a given agent state may be viewed as computing certain kinds of objects called "status sets." In this chapter, we assume a frozen instant of time, and make very few assumptions about "states." These concepts are illustrated though the STORE, CFIT, and CHAIN examples.

In Chapter 7 we argue that an agent's state may (but does not have to!) contain some information about the agent's beliefs about other agents. This is particularly useful in adversarial situations where agent a might want to reason about what agent b's state before deciding what to do. The theory of Chapter 4 is extended to handle such meta-reasoning. There is also another example introduced, the RAMP example, which was particularly designed agents reasoning about beliefs.

In Chapter 8, we extend the theory of Chapter 6 in yet another direction—previously, a "frozen" instant of time was assumed. Of course, this is not valid—we all make decisions today on what we will do tomorrow, or day after, or next month. We create schedules for ourselves, and agents are no different. This chapter describes an extension of the theory of Chapter 7 to handle such temporal reasoning.

In Chapter 9, we add a further twist, increasing the complexity of both Chapter 7 and 8, by assuming that an agent may be *uncertain* both about its beliefs (about the state of the world, as well as its beliefs about other agents). The theory developed in previous chapters is extended to handle this case.

In Chapter 10, we revert to our definition of states and actions, and examine specific data structures that an agent must maintain in order to preserve security, and specific actions it can take (relative to such data structures) that allow it to preserve security. We further explore the relationship between actions taken by individual agents and the data structures/algorithms built into the common agent infrastructure, with a view to maintaining security.

In Chapter 11, we develop a body of complexity results, describing the overall complexity of the different languages developed in preceding chapters. The chapter starts out with a succinct summary and interpretation of the results—a reader interested in the "bottom line" may skip the rest of this chapter.

In Chapter 12, we identify efficiently computable fragments of agent programs, and provide polynomial algorithms to compute them. We explain what can, and what cannot, be expressed in these fragments. We then describe *IADE*—the *IMPACT* Agent Development Environment, that interested users can use to directly build agents in *IMPACT*, as well as build multi-agent systems in *IMPACT*. We will report on experiments we have conducted with *IMPACT*, and analyze the performance results we obtain.

In Chapter 13, we will describe in detail, an integrated logistics application we have built within the *IMPACT* framework for the US Army.

Finally, in Chapter 14, we will revisit the basic goals of this book—as described in Chapters 1 and 2, and explain how we have accomplished them. We identify the strengths of our work, as well as shortcomings that pave the way for future research by us, and by other researchers.

1.7 Selected Commercial Systems

There has been an increase in the number of agent applications and agent infrastructures available on the Internet. In this section, we briefly mention some of these commercial systems.

Agents Technologies Corp.'s *Copernic 98* (http://www.copernic.com/) integrates information from more than 110 information sources.

Dartmouth College's *D'Agents* project (http://www.cs.dartmouth.edu/~agent/) supports applications that require the retrieval, organization, and presentation of distributed information in arbitrary networks.

Firefly's *Catalog Navigator* (http://www.firefly.net/company/keyproducts.fly) allows users to add preference and general interest-level information to each customer's personal profile, hence providing more personalized service.

General Magic's *Odyssey* (http://www.genmagic.com/agents/) provides class libraries which enable people to easily develop their own mobile agent applications in Java. It also includes third party libraries for accessing remote *CORBA* objects or for manipulating relational databases via JDBC.

IBM's *Aglets* provide a framework for development and management of mobile agents. (http://www.trl.ibm.co.jp/aglets/). An aglet is a Java object having mobility and persistence and its own thread of execution. Aglets can move from one Internet host to another in the middle of execution, (Lande and Osjima 1998). Whenever an aglet moves, it takes along its program code and data. Aglets are hosted by an Aglet server, as Java applets are hosted by a Web browser.

Microelectronics and Computer Technology Corporation's *Distributed Communicating Agents* (DCA) for the Carnot Project (http://www.mcc.com/projects/carnot/DCA.html) enables the development and use of distributed, knowledge-based, communicating agents. Here, agents are expert systems that communicate and cooperate with human agents and with each other.

Mitsubishi Electric ITA Horizon Systems Laboratory's *Concordia* (http://www.meitca.com/HSL/Projects/Concordia/) is a full-fledged framework for development and management of network-efficient mobile agent applications for accessing information anytime, anywhere, and on any device supporting Java. A key asset is that it helps abstract away the specific computing or communication devices being used to access this data.

ObjectSpace's *Voyager* (http://www.objectspace.com/voyager/) allows Java programmers to easily construct remote objects, send them messages, and move objects between programs. It combines the power of mobile autonomous agents and remote method invocation with CORBA support and distributed services.

Oracle's *Mobile Agents* (http://www.oracle.com/products/networking/mobile_agents/html/index.html) is networking middleware designed to facilitate connectivity over low bandwidth, high latency, occasionally unreliable, connections. It may be used to help provide seamless data synchronization between mobile and corporate databases.

Softbot (software robot) programs (http://www.cs.washington.edu/research/projects/softbots/www/projects.html) are intelligent agents that use software tools and services on a person's behalf. They allow a user to communicate what they want accomplished and then dynamically determine how and where to satisfy these requests.

Stanford's *Agent Programs* (http://www-ksl.stanford.edu/knowledge-sharing/agents.html) provide several useful agent-related utilities such as a content-based router (for agent messages), a matchmaker (w.r.t. agent interests), and many more. They follow the KIF/KQML protocols (Neches, Fikes, Finin, Gruber, Patil, Senator, and Swarton 1991; Genesereth and Fikes 1992; Labrou and Finin 1997a; Finin, Fritzon, McKay, and McEntire 1994; Mayfield, Labrou, and Finin 1996; Finin et al. 1993) for knowledge sharing.

UMBC's *Agent Projects* (http://www.cs.umbc.edu/agents/projects/) include several applications such as Magenta (for the development of agent-based telecommunication applications), AARIA (for autonomous agent based factory scheduler at the Rock Island Arsenal), etc. UMBC also maintains descriptions of several projects using KQML (http://www.csee.umbc.edu/kqml/software/), a Knowledge Query and Manipulation Language for information exchange.

Some other sites of interest include the *Agent Society* (http://www.agent.org/) and a site http://csvax.cs.caltech.edu/~kiniry/projects/papers/IEEE_Agent/ agent_paper/agent_paper.html), which surveys *Java Mobile Agent Technologies*.

2 *IMPACT* Architecture

In order to describe an architecture that supports the dynamic interaction of multiple software agents, three fundamental questions need to be answered.

1. What does it mean for a program P written in some arbitrary programming language to be considered an agent (how does a suitable `isagent` predicate look)?

2. Once such a definition of the `isagent` predicate is provided, what underlying infrastructural capabilities are needed in order to allow these agents to interact meaningfully with each other?

3. How will multiple software agents communicate with one another, and how will agents and the infrastructure communicate with one another?

This chapter *sketches* out solutions to all these problems. The rest of this book will precisely describe the mathematics underlying these solutions, and go into details about algorithms for computing different problems within this architecture.

2.1 Overview of Architecture

In this section, we provide a general overview of the *IMPACT* architecture. In *IMPACT*, we have two kinds of entities:

Agents, which are software programs (legacy or new) that are augmented with several new interacting components constituting a *wrapper*. Agents may be created by either arbitrary human beings or by other software agents (under some restrictions).

IMPACT Servers, which are programs that provide a range of infrastructural services used by agents. *IMPACT* Servers are created by the authors of this book, rather than by arbitrary individuals.

Figure 2.1 on the next page provides a brief high level description of the *IMPACT* system architecture. According to this architecture, *IMPACT* agents may be scattered across the network. *IMPACT* servers may, likewise, be replicated and/or mirrored, and also located at disparate points on the network. Figure 2.1 on the following page illustrates the following:

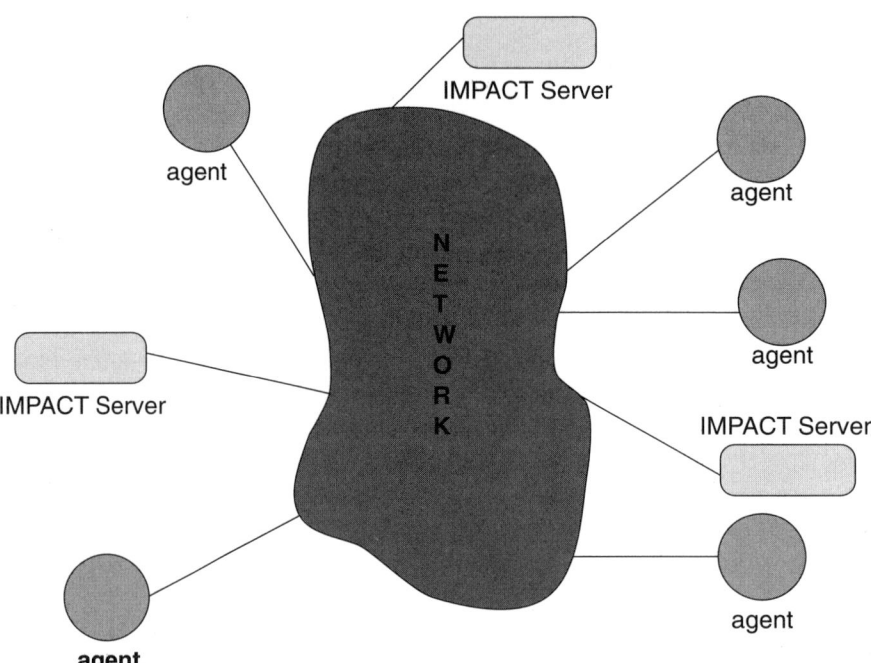

Figure 2.1
Overall *IMPACT* Architecture.

- *Agent to agent connectivity is allowed*, which facilitates interactions such as
  – Agent a requests agent b to provide a service (e.g., in the CHAIN example, the plant agent may request a supplier agent to specify by when it can provide 500 items of *widget-50*.)
  – Agent b sends agent a the answer to agent a's request.
- *Agent to server connectivity is allowed* which facilitates interactions such as
  – Agent a requests the server to identify all agents that provide a given service (e.g., in the CHAIN example, the plant agent may request the *IMPACT* server to identify all agents capable of supplying *widget-50*.
  – The server sends agent a a list of agents that the server believes are capable of providing the desired service (possibly with additional accompanying information).

- Agent a requests the server for other descriptors of a word such as car.
- The server sends to agent a a list of synonyms of the requested word.

We are now ready to describe the software-level architecture of *IMPACT* agents.

2.2 Agent Architecture

An *IMPACT* agent may be built on top of an arbitrary piece of software, defined in any programming language whatsoever. *IMPACT* agents have the following components.

Application Program Interface: Each *IMPACT* agent has an associated *application program interface* (*API*) that provides a set of functions which may be used to manipulate the data structures managed by the agent in question. The API of a system consists of a set of procedures that enable external access and utilization of the system, without requiring detailed knowledge of system internals such as the data structures and implementation methods used. Thus, a remote process can use the system via procedure invocations and gets results back in the form defined by the output of the API procedure.

For instance, in the case of the STORE example, every time the profiling agent makes a request to the credit agent, one or more functions must be executed on the data structures managed by the credit agent. The task of the API is to specify the set of such available functions, together with their signatures (input/output types).

Service Description: Each *IMPACT* agent has an associated *service description* that specifies the set of services offered by the agent. Each service has four parts:

• A *name*—for example, the gps agent in the CFIT example may provide a service called *provide: location* which specifies the location of a plane at a given instance in time.

• A *set of mandatory inputs* that must be provided in order for the function to be executable: in the STORE example, providing a potential customer's card number might be mandatory before the credit agent credit provides a credit report.

• A *set of discretionary inputs* that may (but do not have to) be provided—returning to the STORE example, providing a potential customer's name may not be mandatory.

• A *set of outputs* that will be returned by the function.

Of course, type information must be specified for all the above inputs and outputs. Chapter 3 provides a detailed description of our service description language, together with algorithms to manipulate service descriptions, and identify agents that provide a given service.

Message Manager: Each agent has an associated module that manages incoming and outgoing messages.

Actions, Constraints, and Action Policies: Each agent has a set of actions that it can physically perform. The actions performed by an agent are capable of changing the data structures managed by the agent and/or changing the message queue associated with another agent (if the action is to send a message to another agent). Each agent has an associated *action policy* that states the conditions under which the agent

- *may*,
- *may not*, or
- *must*

do some actions. The actions an agent can take, as well as its action policy, must be clearly stated in some declarative language. Furthermore, there might be constraints stating that certain ways of populating a data structure are "invalid" and that certain actions are not concurrently executable. Chapter 6 provides such a language, and describes its syntax and semantics. Chapters 8 and 9 extend this language to handle reasoning with uncertainty and time.

Metaknowledge: Some agents may hold beliefs about other agents, and use these beliefs in specifying action policies. For example, in the case of the CFIT example, the gps agent may believe that transmissions from a given satellite agent are being jammed by an enemy agent,[1] and in such a case, it may attempt to notify another agent to identify the source of the jamming signal. On the other hand, some agents may not need to reason about other agents or about the world. In the CHAIN example, the supplier agent may do nothing more sophisticated than answering a database retrieval query. Our framework for creating agents must be rich enough to support both possibilities, as well as other intermediate situations. In general, each agent may have certain *metaknowledge* structures that are used for such reasoning. Chapter 7 provides a framework for such metaknowledge structures, and how they may be manipulated.

Temporal Reasoning: In some applications, such as the CHAIN example, agents may *schedule* actions to take place in the future. For instance, the supplier agent makes a commitment to deliver certain items at certain fixed points in time in the future. This requires the ability for agents to make future commitments. Chapter 8 extends the theory of Chapter 6 to handle this situation.

Reasoning with Uncertainty: The designer of an application needs to take into account the fact that the state of an agent may be uncertain. For instance, consider the CFIT example. Here, the autoPilot agent may detect an aircraft, but does not know if the detected aircraft is a friend or a foe. Based on its sensors, it may have *uncertain beliefs* about the properties

---

[1] We understand Russia currently markets an off the shelf GPS jammer.

of the aircraft, as well as uncertainty about the *actions* that the enemy aircraft will take. Thus, the autoPilot agent needs to reason with this uncertainty in order to make a decision. Chapter 9 extends the theory of Chapter 8 to handle this case.

Security: The designer of any agent has the right to enforce any security policies that he or she deems appropriate. Some agents may have significant security components, others may have none at all. Any framework for creating agents must be rich enough to support both extremes, as well as intermediate security strategies. For instance, an agent may treat the same request from two agents differently, based on what it is willing to disclose to other agents. In the case of the CFIT example, the autoPilot agent may provide its flight path to the commander of the mission, but may not be willing to provide its flight path to other agents. In general, each agent may have certain *security* related data structures which are used for the purpose of maintaining security. Such security related data structures may well build on top of the existing meta knowledge structures that the agent has. Chapter 10 provides a framework for such security structures, and how they may be manipulated.

Figure 2.2 provides a pictorial view of how an agent is configured. The components shown in dark shade denote legacy components (which the developer of an *IMPACT* agent does not have to build), while the components shown in light shade denote components built by the person creating an *IMPACT* agent. The arrows indicate flow of data. Note that only the action policy can cause changes on the data stored in the underlying software's data structures, and such changes are brought about through appropriate function calls.

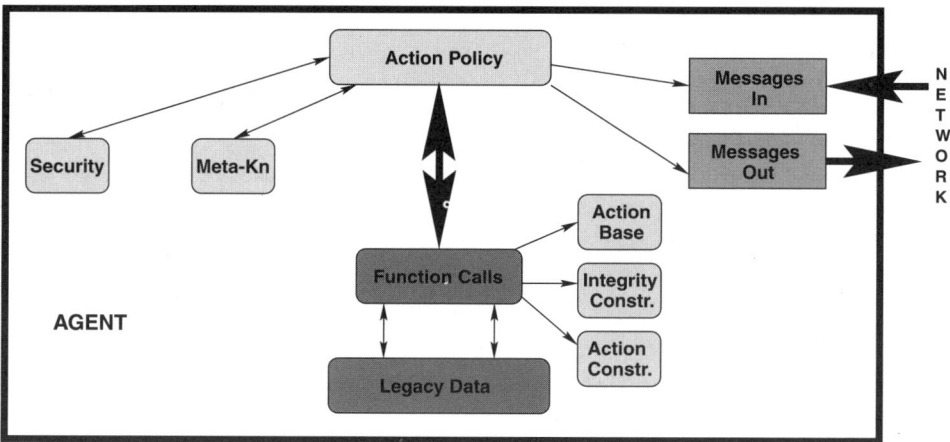

Figure 2.2
Basic Architecture of *IMPACT* Agents.

In order to illustrate the agent architecture described thus far, we now briefly revisit the STORE, CFIT, and CHAIN examples, and illustrate (briefly) how one of the agents in each of these scenarios may be captured within our agent architecture. However, as we have thus far not explicitly described languages for specifying service descriptions, metaknowledge, actions and action policies, etc., these examples will be informally described in English.

2.2.1 STORE Revisited

Consider the profiling agent used in the STORE example. This agent may have several services, two of which are listed below.

- *classify: user.*

This service may take as input, the social security number of a user, and provide as output, a classification of the user as a "low," "medium," "high," or "very high" spender.

- *provide: user-profile.*

This service also takes as input, the social security number of a user, and yields as output, a set of pairs of the form *(clothing,high), (appliances,low), (jewelry,high),* ... Unlike the service *classify: user*, the service *provide: user-profile* provides a more detailed classification of the user's spending habits.

In addition, the agent may support specific actions such as:

- *update* actions (that update user profiles) when more information becomes available about their purchases and

- *respond* actions that take a request (from another agent or human client) and give an answer to it.

The profiling agent may use, as an action policy, the rule that only agents created and owned by the department store may request all its profiling services. In addition, certain other agents not owned by the store, but who pay the store some money, may access the *classify: user* service. Of course, this is closely tied to the security requirements of this agent. The profiling agent may have an "empty" metaknowledge component, meaning that this agent does not perform any metareasoning about other agents and their beliefs.

2.2.2 CFIT Revisited

Now let us consider the autoPilot agent in the CFIT example. This agent may provide the following services;

- *maintain: course*

This service may take as input the current scheduled flight path of a plane, and try to maintain it throughout the flight, by returning a sequence of actions to be performed. Informally, this function merely examines the current flight path schedule, and "reads off" what actions are scheduled to be done at this point in time, and returns this set of actions.

- *adjust: course*

This service may take as input, a set of no-go areas from the terrain agent, and take appropriate action according to the plane's current location and its allocated flight path. Unlike the preceding function, it does not return a set of actions by reading it from the flight plan—rather, it creates a set of actions (i.e., it constructs a plan) to avoid an unexpected contingency.

- *return: control*

This service may take as input, the id of the requester and relinquish control of the plane to the requester if he or she is the pilot of the plane. This service may have no output.

- *create: plan(flight)*

This service may take as input, the GPS-based location of the plane, a set of "no-go" areas, and the plane's allocated flight path, and generate a flight plan for the plane.

Moreover, the autoPilot agent might support several specific actions, some of which could be the following;

- *collect* actions that collect GPS data from the on-board sensors and actuators as well as from the terrain agent,
- *compute* actions that compute the current location of the plane based on the collected GPS data,
- *climb* actions that climb by some specific amount per second to avoid no-go areas.

In addition, the autoPilot agent may have an action policy that determines the conditions under which it executes the above actions. For example, it may execute the *compute* action every 2 minutes (i.e. based on clock information), while it executes course information based on GPS data, terrain data, as well as data from on-board sensors. Moreover, the autoPilot agent might have to return control to the pilot whenever he requests so. The agent's security requirements might insist that the agent provides its flight plan and path only to the pilot of the plane. Furthermore, the metaknowledge component of the autoPilot agent may consist of its beliefs about the on-board sensors and actuators and the terrain agent. The autoPilot agent might reason about the plane's current location based on those beliefs and take appropriate actions. For example, if the autoPilot agent frequently receives course adjustment requests from a satellite agent, while the terrain agent and on-board sensors do not alert the autoPilot agent of its incorrect path, it may conclude that the satellite agent is an enemy trying to falsify the autoPilot agent. As is clear from the preceding discussion, the autoPilot agent may have to reason with uncertainty.

2.2.3 CHAIN Revisited

Let us consider the CHAIN example. Here, the supplier agent may provide a variety of services such as:

- *monitor: available-stock*

This service may take as input the amount and the name of the requested part, and then checks the ACCESS database to determine if the requested amount can be provided. It either returns the string "amount available" or "amount not available."

- *monitor: committed-stock*

This service may take as input the name of some part, and check an ACCESS database to see how much of that part is committed, and return as output the amount committed.

- *update: stock*

This service takes as input the name of a requested part and the amount requested. It first checks to see if the requested amount is available using the *monitor :committed-stock* function above. It then updates the available stock database, reducing the available amount by the amount requested. It also updates a "commitments" database, by adding the amount requested to the committed amount.

In addition, the supplier agent may support a set of specific actions, which might include the following:

- *update* actions that update the two ACCESS databases, and
- *respond* actions that take a part request and either confirm or reject the request.

The supplier agent's actions may be based on principles such as the following:

1. Parts may be ordered only by agents with whom the supplier agent has an existing contract.

2. Orders may be taken from agents that have a large outstanding payment balance, but such orders may trigger a *"We need you to make overdue payments before we ship your order"* message action to be executed.

Unlike other agents listed above, the supplier agent may have an empty metaknowledge component, as it may not perform any metareasoning about other agents and their beliefs.

2.3 Server Architecture

Consider the CHAIN example. It may well be the case that two "approved" supplier agents cannot provide a requested part that the plant agent needs to keep its production line running. In this case, the plant agent must locate new sources from which this part can be obtained. In an electronic setting, this means that there must be some *Yellow Pages Services* available. In this case, the `plant` agent can utilize this service and ask for identities of potential new supplier agents.

Broadly speaking, there are two general mechanisms for identifying service providers:

- In the first mechanism, the agent requesting or providing a service communicates with an *appropriate* yellow pages server. This approach first assumes the existence of a yellow pages server. Second, it assumes that the agent has a mechanism to identify which of several possible yellow pages servers is appropriate for its needs. Third, it assumes that somehow, the yellow pages server has information about agents and their services. Fourth, it assumes that all these agent services are described in some uniform language by the yellow pages server.
- In the second mechanism, the agent requesting or providing a service broadcasts this fact to all *appropriate* agents. This assumes that the agent knows who to broadcast this information to. Second, it assumes that all agents share a common language that supports this interaction.

The first approach places significant demands on the yellow pages server, but efficiently utilizes network resources and reduces load on agents (e.g., agents will not be flooded by unwanted messages). The second approach on the other hand makes fewer assumptions than the former, but freely uses network bandwidth, and hence, participating agents may be overwhelmed by the number of advertisements for services and requests for services sent to them.

In our effort, we have chosen to go with the first approach and we have taken it upon ourselves to provide all the infrastructural facilities that are needed so as to reduce unwanted message traffic and agent workload. This is accomplished by *IMPACT* Servers—in fact, an *IMPACT* Server is actually a collection of the following servers:

Registration Server: This server is mainly used by the creator of an agent to specify the services provided by it and who may use those services.

Yellow Pages Server: This server processes requests from agents to identify other agents that provide a desired service.

Thesaurus Server: This server receives requests when new agent services are being registered as well as when the yellow pages server is searching for agents providing a service.

Type Server: This server maintains a set of class hierarchies containing information about different data types used by different agents, and the inclusion relationship(s) between them.

We now describe these servers in greater detail.

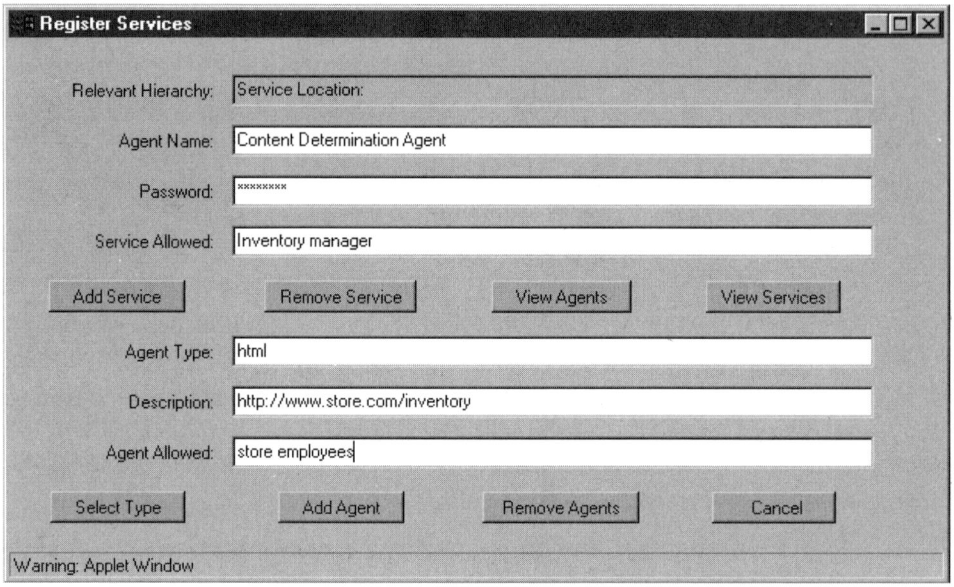

Figure 2.3
Agent/Service Registration Screen Dump.

2.3.1 Registration Server

When the creator of an agent wishes to deploy it, he *registers* the agent with an *IMPACT* server, using a *Registration Interface*. Figure 2.3 shows our prototype Java-based registration interface for registering a single agent. When registering an agent, the user specifies the services provided by that agent. A wide variety of languages may be used for this purpose—using straight English would be one such (extreme) example. Suppose that SDL (service description language) is the chosen one.

In this case, when an agent a wants to find another agent providing a service q_s expressed in SDL, we must *match* q_s with other service descriptions stored in the yellow pages, in order to find appropriate services. Efficiently doing this with free English descriptions and with q_s expressed in free flowing English is currently not feasible.

As a compromise, we have chosen to use *words* from English to describe services, but no free text is allowed. Instead, we assume in our framework that each service is named by a verb and a special structure called a noun-term. However, certain words in English are "similar" to others. For example, in the STORE example, the words *cup* and *mug* are similar, and a customer wanting coffee mugs will probably be interested in agents selling

Section 2.3 Server Architecture

coffee mugs as well as coffee cups. As a consequence, there is a need for data structures and algorithms to support such *similarity based* retrieval operations on service names. The Registration Server creates such data structures, and supports:

- *insertion* of new service names,
- *insertion* of data specifying that a given agent provides a service (and deletion of such information),
- *browsing* of these data structures.

As searching these data structures for *similarity based* retrieval operations performed by the yellow pages server is to be described in Section 2.3.4, we now proceed to some basic concepts needed before the above mentioned data structures can be described.

Hierarchies We assume that all agents use English words (including proper nouns) to express information about services. However, different multiagent applications may only use a small fragment of legitimate English words. For example, the CFIT example may use a vocabulary consisting of various flight and terrain related terminology—in contrast, the STORE example may not have words like *aileron* and *yaw* in its vocabulary.

Suppose Verbs is a set of verbs in English, and Nouns is a set of nouns in English. Note that these sets are not necessarily disjoint. For instance, in the CFIT example, *plan* may be both a verb and a noun. A *noun term* is either a noun or an expression of the form $n_1(n_2)$ where n_1, n_2 are both nouns. Thus for instance, if the nouns *flight, plan, route* are in the vocabulary of the CFIT example, then *flight, plan, route, flight(plan), plan(flight)* are (some) noun terms. We use the notation nt(Nouns) to denote the set of all syntactically valid noun terms generated by the set Nouns.

DEFINITION 2.3.1 (SERVICE NAME) If $v \in$ Verbs and $nt \in$ nt, then *v: nt* is called a *service name*.

If *create* is a verb in the vocabulary of the CFIT example, then *create: plan(flight)* is a service name. For that matter, so is *create: route*.

It is important to note that once we are given the sets Verbs and Nouns, the space of syntactically valid service names is uniquely determined. Of course, only a few of these service names will make sense for a given multiagent application. In most applications, the sets Verbs and Nouns evolve over time as more and more agents' services are registered. When the creator of an agent registers the agent with the *IMPACT* server, he might introduce new verbs and nouns which would enlarge the sets Verbs and Nouns. Table 2.1, Table 2.2

Table 2.1
Service List for the STORE example

AGENT	SERVICES
credit	*provide: information(credit)*
	provide: address
profiling	*provide: user-profile*
	classify: user
productDB	*provide: description(product)*
	identify: product
contentDetermin	*prepare: presentation(product)*
	determine: advertisement
	identify: items
interface	*present: presentation(product)*
	provide: information(product)
	provide: advertisement
saleNotification	*identify: user-profile*
	determine: items
	mail: brochure
	create: mail-list

Table 2.2
Service List for the CFIT example

AGENT	SERVICE
autoPilot	*maintain: course*
	adjust: course
	return: control
	create: plan(flight)
satellite	*broadcast: data(GPS)*
gps	*collect: data(GPS)*
	merge: data(GPS)
	create: information(GPS)
terrain	*generate: map(terrain)*
	determine: area(no-go)

and Table 2.3 on page 42 give a comprehensive list of the names of services offered by the agents in the STORE, CFIT and CHAIN examples.

Now consider the terrain agent used in the CFIT example. This agent provides a service called *generate: map(terrain)*. In particular, the terrain agent may provide this service to many agents in addition to agents in the CFIT example. Consider the following two situations:

1. Some agent on the network wants to find an agent providing a service *generate: map(ground)*. The words *ground* and *terrain* are synonyms, and hence, the CFIT terrain agent is a potential candidate agent providing the desired service. However, this can only be found by using a thesaurus, which we discuss later in Section 2.3.3.

2. A second possibility is that the above agent wants to find an agent providing a service called *generate: map(area)*. Certainly, the CFIT terrain agent above can provide terrain maps of areas. However, here, the word *area* is being specialized to a more specific word, *terrain*. We now specify how this kind of reasoning may be accomplished.

Suppose Σ is any set of English words, such that either all words in Σ are verbs, or all words in Σ are noun-terms. Furthermore, suppose $\sim$ is an arbitrary equivalence relation on Σ.

DEFINITION 2.3.2 (Σ-NODE) A Σ-*node* is any subset $N \subseteq \Sigma$ that is closed under $\sim$, i.e.

1. $x \in N \ \& \ y \in \Sigma \ \& \ y \sim x \Rightarrow y \in N$.
2. $x, y \in N \Rightarrow x \sim y$.

In other words, Σ-*nodes* are equivalence classes of Σ.

Observe that the empty set is always a trivial Σ-node, which will be of no interest to us.

Intuitively, as the reader can already see from Tables 2.1—2.3, service names are often specified by using verbs and noun terms. Suppose the $\sim$ relation denotes "semantic equivalence," i.e., if we consider two words w_1, w_2, saying that $w_1 \sim w_2$ means that these two words are considered semantically equivalent. If Σ is some vocabulary (of verbs or nouns), then a Σ-node is one that is closed under semantic equivalence. The first condition says that if two words are semantically equivalent, then they must label the same node. The second condition says that if two words label the same node, then they must be semantically equivalent. For example, in the case of the CFIT example, we would have *terrain* $\sim$ *ground*. However, *terrain* $\not\sim$ *area*.

It is easy to see, however, that in the context of maps, *terrain* is a specialization of *region*. Certainly, the phrase *terrain* refers to a specific aspect of a region. Terrain maps are maps (of a sort) of regions. This notion of specialization is captured through the definition of a Σ-Hierarchy given below.

DEFINITION 2.3.3 (Σ-HIERARCHY) A Σ-Hierarchy is a weighted, directed acyclic graph $\mathcal{SH} =_{def} (T, E, \wp)$ such that:

1. T is set of nonempty Σ-nodes;

2. if t_1 and t_2 are different Σ-nodes in T, then t_1 and t_2 are disjoint;

3. $\wp$ is a mapping from E to $\mathbb{Z}^+$ indicating a positive distance between two neighboring vertices.[2]

---

[2] We do not require $\wp$ to satisfy any metric axioms at this point in time.

Table 2.3
Service List for the CHAIN example

AGENT	SERVICE
plant	monitor: inventory update: inventory determine: amount(part) choose: supplier order: part monitor: performance(supplier) notify: supplier cancel: contract find: supplier
supplier	monitor: available-stock monitor: committed-stock update: stock
shipping	find: truck find: airplane prepare: schedule(shipping)
truck	provide: schedule(truck) manage: freight ship: freight
airplane	provide: freight manage: freight ship: freight

Figure 2.4 on the facing page and Figure 2.5 on page 44 provide hierarchies describing the three motivating examples in this book. In particular, Figure 2.4 describes a hierarchy on verbs, and Figure 2.5 provides a hierarchy on noun-terms.

Distances Given a Σ-Hierarchy $\mathcal{SH} =_{def} (T, E, \wp)$, the distance between two nodes, $w_1, w_2 \in T$, is defined as follows:

$$d_{\mathcal{SH}}(w_1, w_2) =_{def} \begin{cases} 0, & \text{if some } t \in T \text{ exists such that } w_1, w_2 \in t; \\ cost(p_{min}), & \text{if there is an undirected path in } \mathcal{SH} \text{ between} \\ & w_1, w_2 \text{ and } p_{min} \text{ is the least cost of such a path;} \\ \infty, & \text{otherwise.} \end{cases}$$

It is easy to see that given any Σ-hierarchy, $\mathcal{SH} =_{def} (T, E, \wp)$, the distance function, $d_{\mathcal{SH}}$ induced by it is well defined and satisfies the triangle inequality.

Example 2.3.1 (Distances in Verb and Noun-Term Hierarchies) Consider the verb and noun-term hierarchies in Figures 2.4 on the facing page and 2.5 on page 44 respectively. In these figures, the weights are shown on the arcs connecting nodes in the hierarchy. All edges with no explicitly marked weights are assumed to have 1 as their weight. Consider the terms

Verb Hierarchy

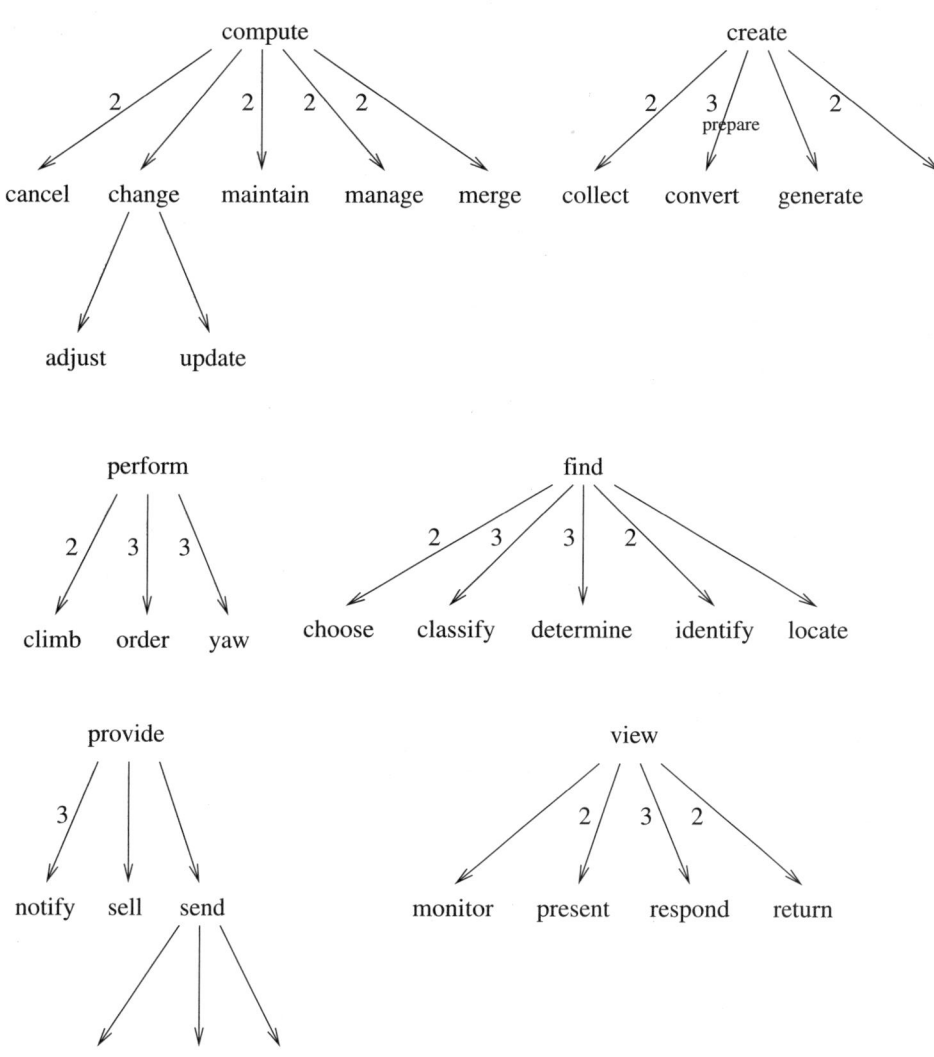

Figure 2.4
Example Verb Hierarchy (Missing Edge Labels are 1).

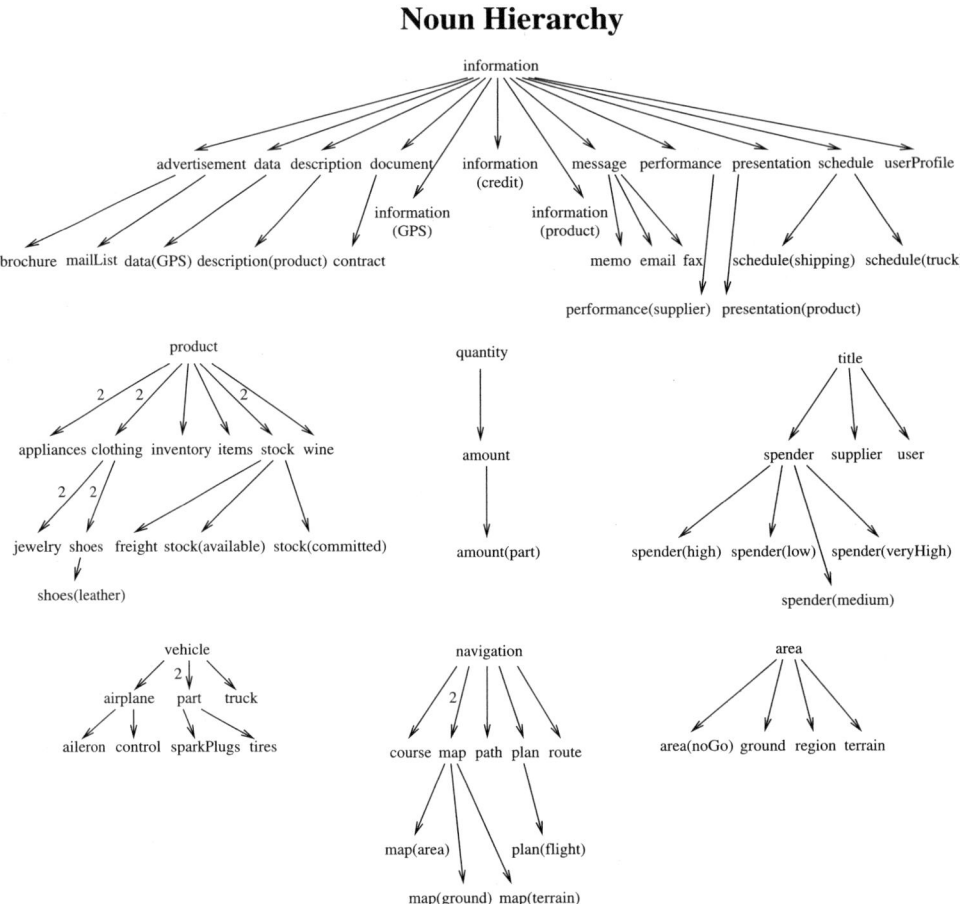

Figure 2.5
Example Noun-term Hierarchy.

compute and *adjust* in the verb hierarchy of Figure 2.4 on the preceding page. The distance between these two terms is given by

$d_{S\mathcal{H}} = cost(\text{compute,change,adjust}) = 2.$

Here, (compute,change,adjust) is the unique optimal path between compute and adjust. As another example, consider the terms *product* and *shoes(leather)* in the noun-term hierarchy of Figure 2.5. The distance between these two terms is given by

$d_{S\mathcal{H}} = cost(product, clothing, shoes, shoes(leather)) = 5.$

2.3.2 Steps in Registering an Agent

When the creator of an agent registers the agent, he interacts with the *IMPACT* server's *GUI* interface. Our current *IMPACT* server interface is a Java interface (Horstmann and Cornell 1997) which means that creators of agents can register their agents from any Java-enabled web browser. Figure 2.3 shows a screen shot of this interface.

Information about agents is maintained in an AgentTable, which contains the following fields:

agentName: Name of the agent.

passwd: Password used when registering the agent. Agent information can not be modified unless the correct password is supplied.

type: The type of information contained in the *descr* field (described below). Some valid types include HTML and English.

descr: A description of the agent. The format of this description depends on the *type* field mentioned above. For instance, if the type is HTML, this field's data will contain a URL. Alternatively, if the type is English, this field's data will contain a description of the agent in English, which can be displayed to users but which should not be parsed.

allowed: Indicates which groups of users are allowed to see information about the agent.

An agent designer goes through the following steps to add an agent:

1. *Specifying the name*: First, the agent designer must choose the name for his agent, as well as information on how other agents may connect to the agent. The designer may click the *View Agents* button to see descriptions for all agents currently in use. If the *Agent Name* or *Password* fields are given some values before clicking on *View Agents*, only agents matching the given name or using the given password will be displayed. Figure 2.3 on page 38 shows this interface.

2. *Security Conditions*: Once the agent designer has chosen a name, he should enter the desired values for *Agent Name*, *Password*, *Agent Type*, *Description*, and *Allowed*. These directly correspond to the fields of the AgentTable described above. For convenience, designers can use the *Select Type* button to choose an existing type from a pull-down menu.

3. *Registering*: Now, to register the agent, the designer should click on the *Add Agent* button. If the agent name is unique, the new agent is added to AgentTable. If the agent name was already in use and the supplied password matches the one in the AgentTable, the type, description, and allowed fields are updated.

Each agent in an AgentTable may provide a number of services. These are maintained in a ServiceTable which contains the following fields:

agentName: Name of the agent which provides a service. This name must match some name in AgentTable.

verbId: The unique identifier for a node in the verb hierarchy.

nounId: The unique identifier for a node in the noun-term hierarchy.

allowed: Indicates which groups of users are allowed to see information about the service. Thus, a service is only accessible to users who satisfy the conditions in both `AgentTable.allowed` and `ServiceTable.allowed`.

This design ensures that each service's verb and noun-term appear in their relevant hierarchies. An agent designer goes through the following steps when adding a service for her agent.

1. First, the agent designer must specify the name of the service. To do so, she may click the *View Services* button to see which services are currently in use. If the *Agent Name* field is given some value before clicking this button, only services for the agent matching the given name are returned.

Alternatively, she may browse the verb and noun-term hierarchies maintained by the *IMPACT* server, and/or query the hierarchy. For instance, if the agent designer wants to declare a service whose name is *update: stock*, she may want to check if one or more terms similar to *stock* are already in use. The noun term hierarchy may already contain terms such as *inventory* and in a case like this, the agent creator may wish to use this term instead of the term stock. Figure 2.6 on the facing page shows the agent browsing a hierarchy.

Hierarchies can be visualized by relating them to UNIX directory structures. For instance, "/a/b/c" indicates that node *c* is a child of node *b*, and node *b* is a child of root node *a*. In general, all root nodes can be considered children of a special node "/". For the verb hierarchy shown in Figure 2.6 on the next page, the Location field indicates the current node *n* while the listbox below this field gives the names and distances (from *n*) for all children of *n*. Here, if the user clicked on "classify", the Location field would contain "/find/classify" and the listbox would contain the names of "/find/classify"'s children. Alternatively, if the user clicked on "../" instead of "classify", the Location field would contain "/" and the listbox would contain the names of all the verb hierarchy root nodes. The noun-term hierarchy can be traversed in a similar way.

2. For each of the above services, the agent may wish to provide *security* conditions. This information tells the *IMPACT* server that the fact that the agent provides a service may only be disclosed to agents that satisfy the security conditions. For instance, in the CHAIN example, the fact that the `profiling` agent provides a *classify: user* service may be something that should be disclosed only to other agents owned by the department store in question and to employees of the department store.

Section 2.3   Server Architecture

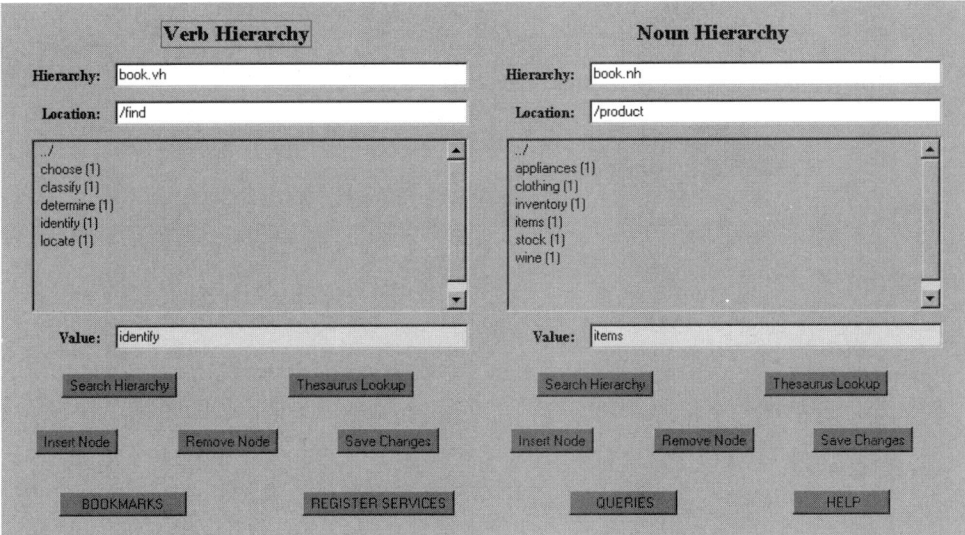

Figure 2.6
Hierarchy Browsing Screen Dump.

3. Finally, to add the service, the designer should fill in the *Agent Name* field and click on the *Add Service* button. The *IMPACT* server adds the new service to ServiceTable.

Note that *IMPACT* also allows services and agents to be removed if the user enters the appropriate values into the *Agent Name* and *Password* fields. When an agent is removed from AgentTable, all of its services are also removed from ServiceTable. To help prevent accidental erasure, a confirmation box is used to inform the user of all services which will be removed along with their agent.

2.3.3 Thesaurus Server

We have built a thesaurus server on top of a commercial thesaurus system (the *ThesDB* Thesaurus Engine from Wintertree Software). The thesaurus server allows the owner of a new agent to browse a thesaurus and find words similar to the ones he is using to describe services. This server supports only one type of operation invoked by external clients. The client provides a word as input, and requests all synonyms as output. The thesaurus server, in addition to providing synonyms as output, "marks" those synonyms that appear in one of the two hierarchies (verb, noun-term). See Figure 2.7 on the following page for an example.

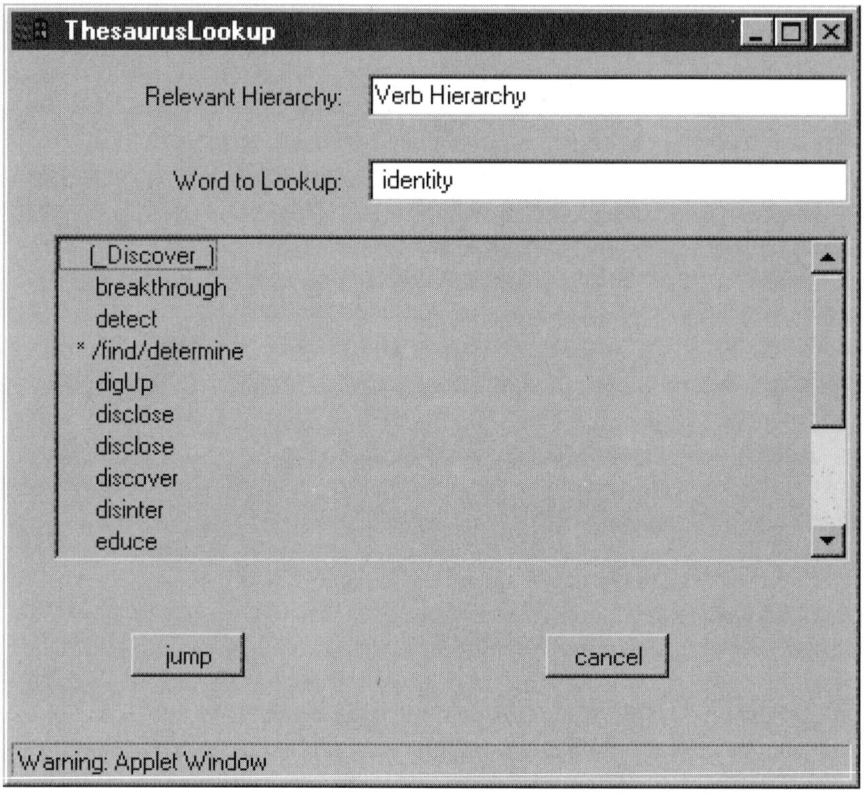

Figure 2.7
Thesaurus Screen Dump.

The thesaurus server can be accessed directly or through the registration server—in the latter case, a graphical user interface is available for human users.

2.3.4 Yellow Pages

At any given point in time, the *IMPACT* server receives zero, one or many requests from agents. We have described above the steps to be followed in registering an agent with the *IMPACT* server. The data structures created and managed by the registration server are used by the yellow pages server to provide *two* types of services.

Section 2.3   Server Architecture   49

Nearest Neighbor Retrievals: An agent a might send a request to the Yellow Pages Server requesting information on the agents that provide services that most "closely" match a service s_{req} that agent a is seeking. Furthermore, agent a might want the k "best" matches. If there is some underlying *metric* on the space of service descriptions, then we are interested in finding the agents that provide the k-nearest neighboring services with respect to the requested service, s_{req}. In Chapter 3, we will propose a formal service description language, and show that the notion of distance on hierarchies described in this chapter may be extended to a metric on service descriptions.

Range Retrievals: Alternatively, agent a might send a request to the Yellow Pages server requesting information on the agents that provide services that are within some "distance" of the requested service, s_{req}. In Chapter 3, we will show how this may be accomplished.

2.3.5 Synchronization Component

One problem with the use of *IMPACT* servers is that they may become a performance bottleneck. In order to avoid this, we allow multiple, mirrored copies of an *IMPACT* server to be deployed at different network sites. This solves the bottleneck problem, but raises the problem of consistency across the mirrored servers. The problem of replicated data management has been addressed by many researchers in the database community (Silberschatz, Korth, and Sudarshan 1997; Date 1995; Abbadi, Skeen, and Cristian 1985; Thomas 1979; Breibart and Korth 1997; Gray, Helland, O'Neil, and Shasha 1996; Holler 1981). Numerous algorithms have been proposed including primary copy, timestamping, majority voting, and quorum consensus. Except for timestamping algorithms, the others are based on distributed locking protocols and guarantee one-copy serializability (Abbadi, Skeen, and Cristian 1985). The number of messages exchanged in these algorithms is considerable. Moreover, one-copy serializability is not required in our system. As a result, we decided to deploy a version of the timestamping algorithms.

To ensure that all servers are accessing the same data, we have introduced a synchronization module. Users and agents do not access the synchronization module. Every time one copy of data structures maintained by an *IMPACT* server is updated, these updates are time-stamped and propagated to all the other servers. Each server incorporates the updates according to the time-stamps. If a server performs a local update before it should have incorporated a remote update, a rollback is performed as in classical databases (Silberschatz, Korth, and Sudarshan 1997).

Notice that the data structures of the *IMPACT* server are only updated when a new agent (or a new service) is added to an existing agent's service repertoire. As the use of existing agents and interactions between existing agents is typically much more frequent than such new agent/service introductions, this is not expected to place much burden on the system.

2.4 Related Work

During the last few years, there have been several attempts to define what an agent is—(Russell and Norvig 1995)[p. 33], (Wooldridge and Jennings 1995; Franklin and Graesser 1997; Hayes-Roth 1995; Etzioni and Weld 1995; Moulin and Chaib-Draa 1996; Foner 1993). For example, Oren Etzioni (Etzioni and Weld 1995) provide the following characterization of agents (Etzioni and Weld 1995):

Autonomy: An agent must be able to take initiative and exercise a non-trivial degree of control over its own actions. It needs to be goal-oriented, collaborative, and flexible, and to decide by itself when to act.

Temporal continuity: An agent is a continuously running process.

Communicability: An agent is able to engage in complex communication with other agents, including people.

Adaptivity: An agent automatically customizes itself to the preferences of its user and to changes in the environment.

We agree that the above characterizations are useful in describing *intelligent* agents. However, our definition of an agent is wider, and allows agents to have a wide range of intelligence—agents can be dumb (e.g., sensor agents), a bit more intelligent (e.g., databases and other data retrieval agents), or smarter (e.g., agents that learn and/or adapt, etc.), or even smarter (e.g., agents that perform a cycle of sophisticated learning and planning activities). For example, consider a database agent that provides valuable access to a database system. Such an agent may not satisfy the autonomy criterion listed above, but yet provides a useful service. Furthermore, we may have Java applets that perform a useful function—yet, such agents may not be adaptive. They may do one thing well, but may not really adapt much to the user(s) involved and/or the environment. In addition, we specify how a program P can be agentized. We believe our approach is the right way to go—requiring that all agents be "intelligent" according to the above criteria is too restrictive, and eliminates an extremely large percentage of useful programs in the world today. However, all agent infrastructures must be capable of deploying agents with the four properties mentioned above, and *IMPACT*'s architecture will support the creation of such smart agents.

Moulin and Chaib-Draa (1996) distinguish between artificial agents (software modules) and human agents (users). They propose that artificial agents should ideally possess several abilities: perception and interpretation of incoming data and messages, reasoning based upon their beliefs, decision making (goal selection, solving goal interactions, reasoning on intentions), planning, and the ability to execute plans including message passing. In this book we only discuss artificial agents and provide formal theories and software for building agents with the above capabilities. We also study additional agent capabilities such as service description and enforcing security policies.

There are two aspects to the development of agent architectures: what is the architecture of each agent and how do these architectures interconnect to form an overall multiagent framework? There are many approaches to the development of a single agent. These approaches were divided by Wooldrige and Jennings into three main categories (Wooldridge and Jennings 1995) (see also the discussion in Section 1.4):

Deliberative: A *deliberative agent architecture* is one which contains an explicitly represented, symbolic model of the world, and in which decisions (for example about what actions to perform) are made via logical (or at least pseudo-logical) reasoning, based on pattern matching and symbolic manipulations. Examples of such architecture include the Intelligent Resource-bounded Machine Architecture (*IRMA*) (Bratman, Israel, and Pollack 1988), *HOMER* (Vere and Bickmore 1990), Etzioni's softbots for *UNIX* environments (Etzioni, Lesh, and Segal 1994), Twok and Weld's information gathering agents (Twok and Weld 1996) and many others. The main criticism of this approach is that the computational complexity of symbol manipulation is very high and some key problems appear to be intractable.

Reactive: Such architectures are usually defined as those that do not include any kind of central symbolic world model and do not use any complex symbolic reasoning. One of the first architectures of this type is Brooks's *subsumption architecture* (Brooks 1986). Others include Rosenschein and Kaelbling's situated automata (Rosenschein 1985) and Maes's Agent Network Architecture (Maes 1989). These types of agents work efficiently when they are faced with 'routine' activities.

Hybrid: Several researchers have suggested that neither a completely deliberative nor a completely reactive approach is suitable for building agents. They use *hybrid* systems which attempt to combine the deliberate and the reactive approaches. Some examples include the *PRS* architecture (Georgeff and Lansky 1987), *TouringMachine* (Ferguson 1992) and *AIS* (Hayes-Roth 1995).

IMPACT is populated with different agents, possibly having different architectures of different types. The agent architecture proposed in this book is a hybrid architecture. As agents in *IMPACT* can be built on top of arbitrary pieces of code, it follows immediately that agents in *IMPACT* can be built on top of agents in other agent frameworks such as *PRS* architecture (Georgeff and Lansky 1987), *TouringMachine* (Ferguson 1992) and *AIS* (Hayes-Roth 1995).

The second aspect of developing agent architectures—how do agents interconnect to form an overall multiagent framework—has also been studied extensively. Bond and Gasser (Bond and Gasser 1988) divide multiagent systems into two main categories:

1. DPS (Distributed Problem Solving): This category considers how the work of solving a particular problem can be divided among several agents. Each agent is intelligent, but they all have a common goal and common preferences. DPS systems are described, for example, in (Smith and Davis 1983; Durfee 1988; Shehory and Kraus 1998).

2. MAS (Multi-Agent systems): coordinates intelligent behavior among a collection of autonomous intelligent agents. Each agent may have different goals and different interests, which may conflict with the interests of other agents in the system. MASs are discussed, for example, in (Sycara 1987; Rosenschein and Zlotkin 1994; Kraus, Wilkenfeld, and Zlotkin 1995).

These classes represent two extreme poles of the spectrum in multiagent research. Our research falls closer to the MAS pole, as we consider autonomous agents, possibly developed by different programmers or organizations. However, in our framework, sub-groups of agents (e.g., the agents in the supply chain example) may cooperate and form a DPS (sub)-system. A similar approach is taken in the *RETZINA* project (Sycara and Zeng 1996a) which is also a generic infrastructure for agent systems. However, in all current implementations of *RETZINA* agents are assumed to be cooperative.

3 Service Description Language

When an agent wishes to use a service, one of two situations may exist. In the first case, the agent knows which agent provides the desired service. The second case occurs when an agent does not know which agents, if any, provide the service it needs. In both cases, the agent needs to know what inputs the potential service provider agent needs in order to provide the service, and what outputs the service provider returns. This chapter presents *IMPACT*'s HTML-like Service Description Language (SDL), which is used by the agents to describe their services. It also describes in detail the *IMPACT* Yellow Pages Server, which provides matchmaking services to *IMPACT* agents.

3.1 Agent Service Description Language

The specification of a single service consists of the following components:

Service Name: This is a verb:*noun(noun)* expression describing the service which is defined in Definition 2.3.1 on page 39. For example, as discussed in Section 2.2.3, *monitor*: *available-stock* is the name of a service provided by the `supplier` agent in the CHAIN example.

Inputs: Services assume that the users of the service will provide zero or more inputs. The service description must include a specification of what inputs are expected and which of these inputs are mandatory. This specification must provide an "English" name for each input, as well as a semantic type for that input. For example, *Amount*: `Integer` specifies that we have an input called *Amount* of type `Integer` and *Part*: `PartName` specifies that we have an input called *Part* of type `PartName` (which could be an enumerated type).

Outputs: Each service must specify the outputs that it provides and each output is specified in the same way as an input.

Attributes: In addition, services may have attributes associated with them. Examples of such attributes include cost (for using the service), average response time for requests to that service, etc.

When an agent wishes to find agents that offer a desired service, it obtains the service name and identity of the agent involved from the yellow pages server. However, the rest of the description can be obtained directly from the agent that provides the service. This strategy is efficient as it reduces the load on the yellow pages server by distributing the workload to the agents.

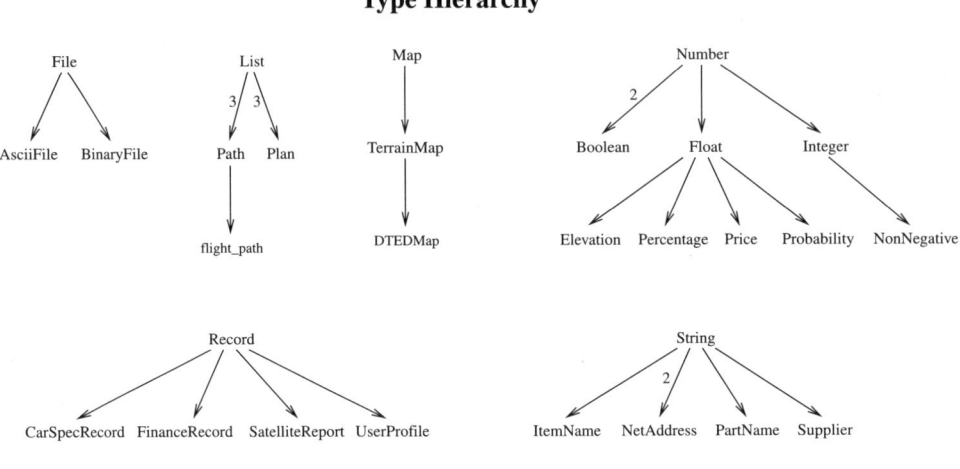

Figure 3.1
Example Type Hierarchy.

Before defining input specifications, we need to formally define types.

DEFINITION 3.1.1 (TYPE/TYPE HIERARCHY $(\mathcal{T}, \leq)$) A *type* τ is a set whose elements are called "values" of τ. The pair $(\mathcal{T}, \leq)$ is called a *type hierarchy* if $\mathcal{T}$ is a set of types and $\leq$ is a partial ordering on $\mathcal{T}$.

Figure 3.1 provides a hierarchy associated with the three motivating examples.

DEFINITION 3.1.2 (SET OF TYPE VARIABLES $V_\mathcal{T}$) Associated with any type hierarchy $(\mathcal{T}, \leq)$, is a set $V_\mathcal{T}$ of symbols called *type variables*.

Intuitively, a type variable ranges over the values of a given type. For instance, `PartName` may be a type variable ranging over strings. When specifying the inputs required to invoke a service, we need to specify variables and their associated types. This is done in the usual way, as defined below.

DEFINITION 3.1.3 (ITEMS $s : \tau$) If s is a variable ranging over objects of type τ, then $s : \tau$ is called an *item*.

Section 3.1   Agent Service Description Language   55

For example, *Part* : String, *Document* : AsciiFile, and *Addr* : NetAddress are all valid items if one assumes that the types String, AsciiFile and NetAddress are all well defined. As is common in most imperative programming languages, the syntactic object $s:\tau$ may be read as saying *"the variable s may assume values drawn from the type τ"*.

Each service requires zero, one, or more inputs. Some of these inputs are mandatory (i.e., the service cannot be provided if these inputs are not specified), while others are discretionary (they are not required for the service to be provided, but their provision may either increase the efficiency of the provided service, or the quality of the service). For example, the service *create* : *plan(flight)*, defined in the CFIT example, may require that the *location* and the *path* fields be filled, but may not require a *no_go* field to be filled in. This is captured in the following definition.

DEFINITION 3.1.4 (ITEM ATOM)   If $s:\tau$ is an item, then $\langle I \rangle s:\tau \langle \backslash I \rangle$ (resp. $\langle MI \rangle s:\tau \langle \backslash MI \rangle$) is called an *input* (resp. *mandatory input*) item atom, and $\langle O \rangle s:\tau \langle \backslash O \rangle$ is called an *output* item atom.

Each input item is either *mandatory* or not. For example, $\langle MI \rangle$*Location* : String$\langle \backslash MI \rangle$ is a mandatory input item atom, while $\langle I \rangle$*Nogo* : TerrainMap$\langle \backslash I \rangle$ is a non-mandatory input item atom. The following are all valid output item atoms: $\langle O \rangle$*Path1* : Path$\langle \backslash O \rangle$, $\langle O \rangle$*Specs* : CarSpecRecord$\langle \backslash O \rangle$ and $\langle O \rangle$*Financing_plan* : FinanceRecord$\langle \backslash O \rangle$.

DEFINITION 3.1.5 (SERVICE DESCRIPTION)   Let *sn* be a service name, $i_1, \ldots, i_n$ be input item atoms, $mi_1, \ldots, mi_k$ be mandatory input item atoms, and $o_1, \ldots, o_r$ be output item atoms. Then,

$\langle S \rangle$ *sn*
   $mi_1 \ldots mi_k$
   $i_1 \ldots i_n$
   $o_1 \ldots o_r$
$\langle \backslash S \rangle$

is called a *service description*.

We show below how the services offered by the agents in the three motivating examples— CHAIN, CFIT, and STORE—may be expressed within this framework. Prior to that, we define some convenient notation.

DEFINITION 3.1.6 (ITEM LIST)   If $s_1:\tau_1, \ldots, s_n:\tau_n$ are $n \geq 1$ items, then $\langle I \rangle s_1:\tau_1, \ldots, s_n:\tau_n \langle \backslash I \rangle$ is an *input item list*, which is a shorthand for $\langle I \rangle s_1:\tau_1 \langle \backslash I \rangle \cdots \langle I \rangle s_1:\tau_n \langle \backslash I \rangle$; also, $\langle MI \rangle s_1:\tau_1, \ldots, s_n:\tau_n \langle \backslash MI \rangle$ and $\langle O \rangle s_1:\tau_1, \ldots, s_n:\tau_n \langle \backslash O \rangle$ are *mandatory input item lists* and *output item lists*, respectively, which are shorthands for the items $\langle\text{MI}\rangle s_1 : \tau_1 \langle\backslash\text{MI}\rangle \cdots \langle\text{MI}\rangle s_l : \tau_n \langle\backslash\text{MI}\rangle$ and $\langle\text{O}\rangle s_l : \tau_1 \langle\backslash\text{O}\rangle \cdots \langle\text{O}\rangle s_l : \tau_n \langle\backslash\text{O}\rangle$, respectively.

3.1.1 STORE Revisited

The following are some service descriptions for the STORE Example:

$\langle\text{S}\rangle$ classify : *user*
  $\langle\text{MI}\rangle ssn : \texttt{String} \langle\backslash\text{MI}\rangle$
  $\langle\text{I}\rangle name : \texttt{String} \langle\backslash\text{I}\rangle$
  $\langle\text{O}\rangle class : \texttt{UserProfile} \langle\backslash\text{O}\rangle$
$\langle\backslash\text{S}\rangle$

This service may take as input, the name and the social security number of a user, and provide as output, a classification of the user as a "low," "medium," "high," or "very high," spender. The social security number is a mandatory input, whereas the name is optional as it can be uniquely determined from a person's social security number.

$\langle\text{S}\rangle$ provide : *information*
  $\langle\text{MI}\rangle Ssn : \texttt{String} \langle\backslash\text{MI}\rangle$
  $\langle\text{I}\rangle Name : \texttt{String} \langle\backslash\text{I}\rangle$
  $\langle\text{O}\rangle Credit\_info : \texttt{FinanceRecord} \langle\backslash\text{O}\rangle$
$\langle\backslash\text{S}\rangle$

This service takes as input the name and the social security number of a user. Once again, the social security number is a mandatory input whereas the name is optional. This service may provide the credit history (finance record) of the person as output.

3.1.2 CFIT Revisited

The following are some sample service descriptions for the CFIT example:

$\langle\text{S}\rangle$ create : *plan(flight)*
  $\langle\text{MI}\rangle Location : \texttt{SatelliteReport}, Flight\_route : \texttt{Path}, Nogo : \texttt{Map} \langle\backslash\text{MI}\rangle$
  $\langle\text{O}\rangle Plan : \texttt{Plan} \langle\backslash\text{O}\rangle$
$\langle\backslash\text{S}\rangle$

This service takes three mandatory inputs (the location of the plane, the allocated flight route of the plane, and a set of Nogo areas), and generates a modified flight path for the plane.

⟨S⟩ merge : *data(GPS)*

⟨MI⟩*Data* : `set_of_SatelliteReport`⟨\MI⟩
⟨O⟩*Merged_data* : `SatelliteReport`⟨\O⟩

⟨\S⟩

This service takes as mandatory input a set of Satellite Report GPS data from the `satellite` agents. It then merges this data to generate the output.

3.1.3 CHAIN Revisited

The following are some sample service descriptions for the CHAIN example:

⟨S⟩ monitor : *available_stock*

⟨MI⟩*Amount* : `Integer`, *Part_id* : `String`⟨\MI⟩
⟨I⟩*Name* : `String`⟨\I⟩
⟨O⟩*Status* : `String`⟨\O⟩

⟨\S⟩

This service takes the *Amount* and *Part_id* of the requested part as mandatory inputs, and the *name* of the requested part as an optional input. The *Name* of a *part* may be determined from its *Part_id*. This service returns as output the string `amount_available` or `amount_not_available`.

⟨S⟩ update : *stock*

⟨MI⟩*Dec_amount* : `Integer`, *Part_id* : `String`⟨\MI⟩
⟨I⟩*Name* : `String`⟨\I⟩
⟨O⟩*Success* : `Boolean`⟨\O⟩

⟨\S⟩

This service takes as input the *Dec_amount*, *Part_id*, and *Name* of the requested part (as in the previous example). Although *Dec_amount* and *Part_id* are mandatory inputs, *Name* is optional. This service updates the available stock database, reducing the available amount by *Dec_amount* units. The output value specifies whether the operation was successfully performed.

3.2 Metric of Service Descriptions

The yellow pages server processes requests from agents to identify other agents that provide a desired service using service names. For example, if there is an agent that offers the service sell : *cups* and another agent is looking for an agent offering the service sell : *mugs*, we would like the yellow pages server to match them. In order to do so, the server needs some metric on the space of service names. However, in the previous chapter we only defined distances on the verb hierarchy and on the noun-term hierarchy individually—no notion of distance has been proposed thus far between service names, i.e., between *pairs* of verbs and noun-terms. We now define what it means to *combine* two distance functions on two hierarchies.

DEFINITION 3.2.1 (COMPOSITE DISTANCE FUNCTION cd) Suppose we have two different sets of words Σ_1 and Σ_2 with Σ_1-hierarchy $\mathcal{SH}_1 =_{def} (T_1, E_1, \wp_1)$ and Σ_2-hierarchy $\mathcal{SH}_2 =_{def} (T_2, E_2, \wp_2)$. Let d_1, d_2 be the distance functions induced by $\mathcal{SH}_1, \mathcal{SH}_2$, respectively. Consider two pairs of words, $\langle w_1, w_1' \rangle, \langle w_2, w_2' \rangle \in \Sigma_1 \times \Sigma_2$. A *composite distance function* cd is any mapping from $(\Sigma_1 \times \Sigma_2) \times (\Sigma_1 \times \Sigma_2)$ to $\mathbb{Z}^+$ such that:

1. $\text{cd}(\langle w_1, w_1' \rangle, \langle w_2, w_2' \rangle) = \text{cd}(\langle w_2, w_2' \rangle, \langle w_1, w_1' \rangle)$ (Symmetry)
2. $\text{cd}(\langle w_1, w_1' \rangle, \langle w_1, w_1' \rangle) = 0$ (Ipso-distance)
3. If $d_1(w_1, w_2) \leq d_1(w_1, w_3)$, then
   $\text{cd}(\langle w_1, w_1' \rangle, \langle w_2, w_2' \rangle) \leq \text{cd}(\langle w_1, w_1' \rangle, \langle w_3, w_2' \rangle)$ (Expansion of d_1)
4. If $d_2(w_1', w_2') \leq d_2(w_1', w_3')$, then
   $\text{cd}(\langle w_1, w_1' \rangle, \langle w_2, w_2' \rangle) \leq \text{cd}(\langle w_1, w_1' \rangle, \langle w_2, w_3' \rangle)$ (Expansion of d_2)
5. $\text{cd}(\langle w_1, w_1' \rangle, \langle w_3, w_3' \rangle) \leq \text{cd}(\langle w_1, w_1' \rangle, \langle w_2, w_2' \rangle)$
   $+ \text{cd}(\langle w_2, w_2' \rangle, \langle w_3, w_3' \rangle)$ (Triangle Inequality).

A simple composite distance function is sum, the addition of two values.

It is easy to see that the third and the fourth items are not redundant. This is shown via the following example. Let Σ_1 and Σ_2 be two sets of words, each with at least three different words, and let $\sim_1$ and $\sim_2$ be empty. Suppose for every $w_1, w_2 \in \Sigma_1$ such that $w_1 \neq w_2$, we have $d_1(w_1, w_2) =_{def} 0.5$, and similarly for every $w_1', w_2' \in \Sigma_2$ such that $w_1' \neq w_2'$, we have $d_2(w_1', w_2') =_{def} 0.5$. We will choose two pairs of words $\langle \hat{w}_1, \hat{w}_1' \rangle, \langle \hat{w}_2, \hat{w}_2' \rangle \in \Sigma_1 \times \Sigma_2$ such that $\hat{w}_1 \neq \hat{w}_2$ and $\hat{w}_1' \neq \hat{w}_2'$ and will define $\text{cd}(\langle \hat{w}_1, \hat{w}_1' \rangle, \langle \hat{w}_2, \hat{w}_2' \rangle) =_{def} \text{cd}(\langle \hat{w}_2, \hat{w}_2' \rangle, \langle \hat{w}_1, \hat{w}_1' \rangle) =_{def} 1.2$. For every two other different pairs $\langle w_1, w_1' \rangle, \langle w_2, w_2' \rangle \in \Sigma_1 \times \Sigma_2$ such that $\langle w_1, w_1' \rangle \neq \langle \hat{w}_1, \hat{w}_1' \rangle$ or $\langle w_2, w_2' \rangle \neq \langle \hat{w}_2, \hat{w}_2' \rangle$, $\text{cd}(\langle w_1, w_1' \rangle, \langle w_2, w_2' \rangle) =_{def} 1$. Finally, for every $\langle w_1, w_1' \rangle \in \Sigma_1 \times \Sigma_2$ let $\text{cd}(\langle w_1, w_1' \rangle, \langle w_1, w_1' \rangle) =_{def} 0$. It is easy to see that the last item above is satisfied. However, choose any $w_3 \in \Sigma_1$ such that $w_3 \neq \hat{w}_1$ and $w_3 \neq \hat{w}_2$. From our definitions, $d_1(\hat{w}_1, \hat{w}_2) \leq d_1(\hat{w}_1, w_3)$. But $\text{cd}(\langle \hat{w}_1, \hat{w}_1' \rangle, \langle \hat{w}_2, \hat{w}_2' \rangle) > \text{cd}(\langle \hat{w}_1, \hat{w}_1' \rangle, \langle w_3, \hat{w}_2' \rangle)$. Thus, the third item above is not satisfied. Similarly, we can show that the fourth item is not satisfied.

Section 3.2   Metric of Service Descriptions   59

The last item in the above definition is also not redundant. This is shown via the following simple example. Suppose $\Sigma_1 =_{def} \{w_1, w_2\}$ where $w_1 \neq w_2$ and $\Sigma_2 =_{def} \{w'_1, w'_2\}$ where $w'_1 \neq w'_2$. We define cd as follows: $\text{cd}(\langle w_1, w'_1 \rangle, \langle w_2, w'_2 \rangle) =_{def} \text{cd}(\langle w_2, w'_2 \rangle, \langle w_1, w'_1 \rangle) =_{def} 1.5$; all other distances between any different pairs of words are 0.5. For example, $\text{cd}(\langle w_1, w'_1 \rangle, \langle w_1, w'_2 \rangle) =_{def} 0.5$. The distance between a pair of the same words is 0. It is easy to see that the last item above is not satisfied, i.e.,

$$\text{cd}(\langle w_1, w'_1 \rangle, \langle w_2, w'_2 \rangle) > \text{cd}(\langle w_1, w'_1 \rangle, \langle w_1, w'_2 \rangle) + \text{cd}(\langle w_1, w'_2 \rangle, \langle w_2, w'_2 \rangle).$$

Example 3.2.1 (Composite Distances)   Let d_1 and d_2 be distances defined as in Section 2.2 on the verb and noun-term hierarchies given in Figure 2.4 on page 43 and Figure 2.5 on page 44, respectively. In these figures, the weights are shown on the arcs connecting nodes in the hierarchy and all the other weights which are not explicitly shown are assumed to be 1. Moreover, let the composite distance function be defined as

$$\text{cd}(\langle w_1, w'_1 \rangle, \langle w_2, w'_2 \rangle) =_{def} d_1(w_1, w_2) + d_2(w'_1, w'_2).$$

Now consider the following two pairs: $\langle$provide, *information*$\rangle$ and $\langle$broadcast, *data(GPS)*$\rangle$. As can be seen from Figure 2.4 on page 43, the distance between provide and broadcast is

$$d_1(\text{provide, broadcast}) = 2,$$

as is the distance between *information* and *data(GPS)* (see Figure 2.5 on page 44). Thus, the composite distance between these two pairs is given by

$$\begin{aligned}\text{cd}(\langle\text{provide, }\textit{information}\rangle,\\ \langle\text{broadcast, }\textit{data(GPS)}\rangle) &= d_1(\text{provide, broadcast}) + d_2(\textit{information, data(GPS)})\\ &= 4.\end{aligned}$$

As another example, consider the pairs $\langle$identify, *items*$\rangle$ and $\langle$determine, *product*$\rangle$. In this case, as given by Figure 2.4 on page 43, the distance d_1 (identify, determine) between identify and determine is 5. And from Figure 2.5 on page 44, the distance between *items* and *product* is $d_2(\textit{items, product}) = 1$. Then, the composite distance between $\langle$identify, *items*$\rangle$ and $\langle$determine, *product*$\rangle$ will be the sum of their verb and nounterm distances, i.e., 6.

In Section 2.3 we defined the distance between two noun-terms when they appear in the noun-term hierarchy. However, when doing matchmaking, we may need to find the distance between two noun-terms that do not appear in the hierarchy. In particular, we may consider situations where we need to compare the distances between $n_1(n'_1)$ and $n_2(n'_2)$

where n_1, n'_1, n_2, n'_2 appear in the noun-term hierarchy, but $n_1(n'_1)$ and $n_2(n'_2)$ do not. In such a case we will use the composite distance function defined in Definition 3.2.1 on page 58 where both Σ_1 and Σ_2 are the noun-term hierarchies.

Another special case is computing the distance between $n_1(n_2)$ and n_1. For instance in the STORE example, what is the distance between *information* and *information(credit)*?

DEFINITION 3.2.2 (THE FUNCTION d_G) We interpret, n_1 as n_1(*general*), e.g., *information* as *information(general)*, and assume that a function denoted by d_G for computing the distance between any noun *n* and *general* is given to the system. The following is a possible function: Let *n* be a noun and let $w_1, \ldots, w_k$ be the weights of all the edges between the Noun-Term-node which includes *n* and any of its neighboring vertices. Then:

$$d_G(n, general) =_{def} max(w_1, \ldots, w_k).$$

The following example uses the hierarchies associated with the three motivating examples to compute d_G.

Example 3.2.2 (Distances) When *n* is the noun-term *map* or *navigation*, $d_G(n, general) = 2$ but when *n* is *plan* or *route*, $d_G(n, general) = 1$.

Consider a query which asks for *map(region)*. Which noun-term should we consider first? Although there is no noun-term in our hierarchy named *map(region)*, there are noun-terms for both *map* and *region*. Recall that $d_G(map, general) = 2$. If we can find a noun-term *n* with a distance of 2 or less from *map(region)*, we should start at *n*. Otherwise, we should start at *map*. In our current example, we should start at *map(area)* as *region* has a distance of 1 from *area* and so *map(area)* has a distance of $1 < 2$. However, if we were looking for *map(city)*, there is no noun-term with a distance of 2 or less so we should start at *map*.

We will use these definitions in the matchmaking process described in the next two sections.

3.3 Matchmaking as Nearest Neighbor Computations

In this section, we will present an algorithm, **find_nn**, to solve the *k*-nearest neighbor problem. Given a pair $\langle v, nt \rangle$ specifying a desired service, this algorithm will return a set of *k* agents that provide the most closely matching services.

Note 1 Throughout this chapter, we assume that if $n_1(n_2)$ is in a given hierarchy, then so is n_1.

Section 3.3 Matchmaking as Nearest Neighbor Computations

The most closely matching services are determined by examining:

- The verb hierarchy,
- the noun-term hierarchy, and
- the thesaurus.

Closeness between $\langle v, nt \rangle$ and another pair $\langle v', nt' \rangle$ is determined by using the distance functions associated with the verb and noun-term hierarchies, together with a composite distance function cd specified by the agent invoking the **find_nn** algorithm. The algorithm also uses the AgentTable and the ServiceTable described in Section 2.3, as well as the following internal data structures and/or subroutines:

Todo: This is a list of verb/noun-term pairs, which are extended by their distances from the verb/noun-term pair that is requested in the initial or recursive call to the **find_nn** function. The list is maintained in increasing order of distance, and is not necessarily complete.

ANSTABLE: This is a table consisting of at most k entries (k being the number of agents requested). At any given point in time during execution of the **find_nn** algorithm, *ANSTABLE* will contain the best answers found thus far, together with their distances from the requested service (v, nt). *ANSTABLE* will be maintained in increasing order w.r.t. this distance.

search_service_table: This function, given a verb/noun-term pair (V, NT) and an integer K, returns the set of all agents which provide the service $(V : NT)$; if their number exceeds K, it returns K of them, which are deliberatively chosen. (Different selection strategies are imaginable, e.g., random or order of appearance in the service table. We assume that a fixed such strategy is chosen, but do not discuss these issue further here.)

num_ans: This function merely keeps track of the number of answers in *ANSTABLE*.

next_nbr: This function takes as input the list *Todo* mentioned above and a pair (V, NT). Intuitively, *Todo* consists of verb/noun-term pairs that have not yet been relaxed. Suppose (V_1, NT_1) is the first verb/noun-term pair in this list. The *candidate-relaxation* of (V_1, NT_1), $cr(V_1, NT_1)$, is defined as follows:

1. If V' is an immediate neighbor of V_1 in the verb hierarchy, then (V', NT_1) is in $cr(V_1, NT_1)$.
2. If NT' is an immediate neighbor of NT_1 in the noun-term hierarchy, then (V_1, NT') is in $cr(V_1, NT_1)$.

The function *next_nbr* removes (V_1, NT_1) from the *Todo* list, and then inserts all members of $cr(V_1, NT_1)$ into the *Todo* list while maintaining the property that the *Todo* list is in ascending order w.r.t. distance from (V, NT). The function *next_nbr* returns as output the first member of the *Todo* list. If the *Todo* list is empty, it returns a special pair.

relax_thesaurus: This function is called when either V or NT of the specified service name do not appear in the corresponding hierarchy. It returns a pair that is "similar" to (V, NT) whose components do appear in the hierarchies.

The function accesses the thesaurus and the verb/noun-term hierarchies. When invoked with the input pair (V, NT), it uses the following procedure:

• If V is not in the verb hierarchy, then search the thesaurus for a verb V' that is in the verb hierarchy and is synonymous with V, and set V to V'.

• If NT is not in the noun-term hierarchy, then do the following:

– If NT is a single noun N, then search the thesaurus for a noun N' that is in the noun hierarchy and is synonymous with N. Set NT to N'.

– If NT is a noun-term $N1(N2)$ then do the following:

∗ If $N1$ is in the noun-term hierarchy let $N0 =_{def} N1$. Otherwise, search the thesaurus for a noun N' that is in the noun-term hierarchy and is synonymous with $N1$, and set $N0 =_{def} N'$. If $N0$ is still unassigned, return a special pair indicating an error.

∗ Let *ntList* be the set of all noun-terms of the form $N0(N')$ which occur in the noun-term hierarchy. If *ntList* is the empty set, set $NT =_{def} N0$.

∗ Otherwise, if $N2$ is in the noun-term hierarchy, let *adjOrigin* (adjective origin) be $N2$. Then, search the thesaurus for a noun N' that is in the noun-term hierarchy and is synonymous with $N2$ and set *adjOrigin* to N'. If no such N' exists, set $NT =_{def} N0$.

∗ Compute $cd(N0(N'), N0(adjOrigin))$ for each $N0(N')$ in *ntList*. Also, compute $cd(N0, N0(adjOrigin))$ using d_G.

∗ Let *nt* be a noun-term in *ntList* with the least distance to $N0(adjOrigin)$. If $cd(N0, N0(adjOrigin)) < cd(nt, N0(adjOrigin))$, set $NT =_{def} N0$. Otherwise, set $NT =_{def} nt$.

∗ If either V or NT after this step is still not in the verb or noun-term hierarchy, respectively, then return a pair indicating an error; otherwise, return the pair (V, NT).

Table 3.1 on the facing page contains part of a thesaurus built by making use of the commercial *ThesDB* Thesaurus Engine of Wintertree Software. Note that the synonyms shown are not the exhaustive list returned by *ThesDB*.

We are now ready to present Algorithm 3.3.1 on page 64.

Table 3.1
Example Thesaurus

Word	Synonyms
explore	inquire, examine, probe, investigate
vehicle	carrier, carriage, van, wagon, car, track
compute	approximate, calculate, deduce, estimate, evaluate
car(Japanese)	honda, nissan, mazda, toyota
scan	browse, glance, skim
car(American)	chevy, neon, dodge
title	license, entitlement, label, tag, designation
determine	ascertain, assure, confirm, findout, prove, certify, substantiate
appliance	apparatus, instrument, facility, equipment, device, machine, utensil, utility, tool
collect	acquire, bag, capture, clain, harvest, obtain
information	data, details, evidence, facts, advice, news, instruction, intelligence, knowledge, message
adjust	adapt, alter, change, deviate, modify, mutate, reform, transform
locate	discover, establish, find, place, position, situate
respond	answer, reply, acknowledge, expound, backfire, defend, retaliate
broadcast	advertise, announce, communicate, declare, disseminate, divulge, reveal, publish, report
stock	material, stuff, assets, capital, estate, property, category
provide	give, contribute, deliver, dispense, donate, lend, offer, present, supply, send, deploy, sell
identify	discover, detect, determine, find, recognize, realize, solve, unmask, designate, name, label
contract	agreement, acceptance, pledge, promise, affirmation, certification, assurance, oath

*Example 3.3.1 (*gps *Agent)* Consider the verb and noun-term hierarchies given in Figures 2.4 and 2.5, respectively, and the service table (Table 3.2 on page 65) and the thesaurus table (Table 3.1). Furthermore, suppose the composite distance function, cd, is the sum of the individual distance functions.

Suppose a gps agent in the CFIT example wants to find all agents who broadcast GPS data, or provide a similar service. In order to find such agents, it issues the call **find_nn**(broadcast, *data(GPS)*,5) to the *IMPACT YP* Server, thus limiting the output to five agents. The **find_nn** algorithm works then as follows. Initially, the pair $\langle V, NT \rangle$ is $\langle$broadcast, *data(GPS)*$\rangle$, and the list *Todo* contains $\langle \langle$broadcast, *data(GPS)*$\rangle, 0\rangle$ are created. Since $\langle$broadcast, *data(GPS)*$\rangle$

Algorithm 3.3.1 (find_nn)
find_nn(V:verb; NT:noun-term; K:integer)

(⋆ Find the K agents offering the services closest to $\langle V, NT \rangle$, and output them ⋆)
(⋆ with their distances; relax $\langle V, NT \rangle$ first, if it is not in the hierarchy.   ⋆)
(⋆ Output is either ANSTABLE (which contains a set of tuples of the form   ⋆)
(⋆ (agent name, service name, composite distance from $\langle V, NT \rangle$)) or ERROR ⋆)

1. *create*(*Todo*, *V*, *NT*);
2. *ClosedList* := *NIL*;
3. *ANSTABLE* := ∅;
4. **if** $\langle V, NT \rangle \in \Sigma_v \times \Sigma_{nt}$ **then**
5. { *done* := **false**;
6.   Sol := *search_service_table*(*V*, *NT*, *K*);
7.   **while** ¬*done* **do**
8.   { *insert*($\langle V, NT \rangle$, *ClosedList*);
9.   *insert*(Sol, *ANSTABLE*);
10. $n := num\_ans(ANSTABLE)$;
11.   **if** $n \geq K$ **then** *done* := **true**
12.   **else**
13.   { $\langle V', NT' \rangle := next\_nbr(Todo)$;
14.   **if** $error(V', NT') = $ **true then** *done* := **true**
15.   **else**
16.   { $\langle V, NT \rangle := \langle V', NT' \rangle$;
17.   Sol := *search_service_table*(*V*, *NT*, *K* − *n*);}
18.   }
19. }
20. }
21. **else** (⋆ search thesaurus ⋆)
22. { $\langle V', NT' \rangle := relax\_thesaurus(V, NT)$;
23.   **if** $error(V', NT') = $ **true then return** *ERROR*
24.   **else return** *find_nn*(*V'*, *NT'*, *K*);}
25. **return** *ANSTABLE*;
end.

belongs to $\Sigma_v \times \Sigma_{nt}$, we execute

search_service_table(broadcast, *data(GPS)*, **5**).

This assigns Sol the set {satellite1, satellite2, satellite6}, since, as can be seen from Table 3.2 on the facing page, these are the agents providing the service broadcast : *data(GPS)*.

Thus, during the first iteration of the while loop, ⟨broadcast, *data(GPS)*⟩ is added to *ClosedList*, and *ANSTABLE* is updated to the set

{(*satellite*1, 0), (*satellite*2, 0), (*satellite*6, 0)};

furthermore, $n := 3$ and thus ⟨broadcast, *data(GPS)*⟩ is relaxed by calling the function **next_nbr**, which returns ⟨broadcast, *data*⟩. The list *Todo* now contains the two entries ⟨⟨broadcast, *data*⟩, 1⟩ and ⟨⟨send, *data(GPS)*⟩, 1⟩.

Table 3.2
Example Service Table

Verb	Noun-term	Agent
broadcast	data(GPS)	satellite2
provide	information(credit)	credit3
broadcast	data(GPS)	satellite1
broadcast	data	satellite4
provide	information	news1
send	data(GPS)	satellite7
identify	items	contentDetermin2
ship	freight	truck1
provide	data(GPS)	satellite12
ship	product	shipping1
broadcast	information	satellite8
create	plan(flight)	autoPilot1
send	data(GPS)	satellite9
broadcast	data(GPS)	satellite6

The call **search_service_table**(broadcast,*data*,2) will return the singleton set {*satellite*4}, which provides the service broadcast : *data*. This result is inserted into *ANSTABLE* with its composite distance function value of 1. As we do not have five answers yet, the **next_nbr** function is called again. This call returns the verb/noun-term pair ⟨send, *data(GPS)*⟩. The subsequent call of **search_service_table**(send, *data(GPS)*,1) returns the singleton containing *satellite*7, which provides the service send : *data(GPS)*. Note that although *satellite*9 also provides the send : *data(GPS)* service, the **search_service_table** function chooses to return *satellite*7, because only one agent is requested for the result.

Now that there are five answers in the *ANSTABLE*, the **find_nn** function terminates by returning

(*satellite*1, 0), (*satellite*2, 0), (*satellite*6, 0), (*satellite*4, 1), (*satellite*7, 1).

Suppose $V \in \Sigma_v$ and $NT \in \Sigma_{nt}$. Also, let $\Sigma_v^V \subseteq \Sigma_v$ ($\Sigma_{nt}^{NT} \subseteq \Sigma_{nt}$) denote the set of all verbs (noun-terms) in our hierarchies whose distance from V (NT) is finite. Then in the worst case, **find_nn**(V, NT, K) will need $O(|\Sigma_v^V| \cdot |\Sigma_{nt}^{NT}| + K)$ time. Note however that if there are K services whose composite distance from ⟨V, NT⟩ is finite, then we can obtain a tighter bound. Specifically, let d_V (d_{NT}) be the maximum distance from a verb (noun-term) of one of these K services to V (NT). Furthermore, let $\Sigma_v^{d_V} \subseteq \Sigma_v^V$ ($\Sigma_{nt}^{d_{NT}} \subseteq \Sigma_{nt}^{NT}$) denote the set of all verbs (noun-terms) in our hierarchies whose distance from V (NT) is less than or equal to d_V (d_{NT}). Then in this case, **find_nn**(V, NT, K) will only need $O(|\Sigma_v^{d_V}| \cdot |\Sigma_{nt}^{d_{NT}}| + K)$ time.

3.4 Range Computations

The range search algorithm below allows the *IMPACT* server to answer queries of the form *"Find all agents that provide a service $vnt = \langle V', NT' \rangle$ which is within a distance D of a requested service $vnt = \langle V, NT \rangle$"*.

In the **range** algorithm below (Algorithm 3.4.1), *Todo* is a list of nodes to be processed, each of which is a service vnt' extended by its distance from the service vnt. The algorithm has two steps.

Step 1: The first step is the **while** loop. It finds all pairs $vnt^\star = \langle V^\star, NT^\star \rangle$ that are within the specified distance D from vnt. This step uses a procedure **expand** that behaves as follows: **expand**(vnt, vnt', D) first computes the set

$$\{vnt^\sharp \mid D' =_{def} \text{cd}(vnt^\sharp, vnt) \leq D, vnt^\sharp \in \textbf{cr}(vnt'), \langle vnt^\sharp, D' \rangle \notin RelaxList\}.$$

Algorithm 3.4.1 (Range)
range(V:verb; NT:noun-term; D:real)

(⋆ Find all agents offering a service within distance D to $\langle V, NT \rangle$ ⋆)
(⋆ Output is either an *ANSTABLE* or an *ERROR*   ⋆)

1. **if** $D < 0$ **then return** *ERROR*;
2. **if** $\langle V, NT \rangle \in \Sigma_v \times \Sigma_{nt}$ **then**
3. {*RelaxList* := NIL;
4. *Todo* := $\langle \langle V, NT \rangle, 0 \rangle$;
5. **while** *Todo* ≠ NIL **do**
6. {$\langle \langle V', NT' \rangle, D' \rangle :=$ *first element of Todo*;
7. insert $\langle \langle V', NT' \rangle, D' \rangle$ into *RelaxList*;
8. remove $\langle \langle V', NT' \rangle, D' \rangle$ from *Todo*;
9. expand $(\langle V, NT \rangle, \langle V', NT' \rangle, D)$;
10. }
11. **return** $\pi_{Agents,Dist}(RelaxList[\text{Verb} = V', NounTerm = NT']ServiceTable)$
12. }
13. **else**
14. {(⋆*search thesaurus* ⋆)
15. $\langle V', NT' \rangle :=$ *relax_thesaurus*(V, NT);
16. **if** *error*(V', NT') **then return** *ERROR*
17. **else return** *range*($V', NT', D - cd(\langle V, NT \rangle, \langle V', NT' \rangle)$);
18. }
end.

Section 3.4   Range Computations

Here, *RelaxList* contains the services which have already been considered. Then, **expand** inserts the elements of this set into *Todo*.

Step 2:   The second step executes a select operation on the Service Table, finding all agents that offer any of the service names identified in the first step. As in the **find_nn** algorithm, if V or NT are not in the relevant verb or noun-term hierarchies, algorithm **range** calls the **relax_thesaurus** procedure specified in the previous section to find a similar pair which belongs to them.

In Algorithm 3.4.1 on the facing page, the (equi-) join and projection operations from standard relational algebra are applied, in order to retrieve from the Service Table the agents providing the closest services collected in *RelaxList* (which is flattened to a relation).

Example 3.4.1 (Illustration of the Range Algorithm)   Consider the same noun-term and verb hierarchies in addition to the same Service Table and thesaurus from Example 3.3.1 on page 63. Also assume that the same composite distance function is employed. To see how the **range** algorithm works, consider the call *range*(broadcast, *data(GPS)*,2).

Initially, the *Todo* list contains the triple $\langle\langle$broadcast, *data(GPS)*$\rangle$, $0\rangle$ and the *RelaxList* is empty. During the first pass of the while loop, the $\langle\langle$broadcast, *data(GPS)*$\rangle$, $0\rangle$ triple is inserted into *RelaxList*. As the result of the first call to the **expand** procedure, the *Todo* list contains

$\langle\langle$broadcast, *data*$\rangle$, $1\rangle$, $\langle\langle$send, *data(GPS)*$\rangle$, $1\rangle$.

On the second pass, the *RelaxList* contains

$\langle\langle$broadcast, *data(GPS)*$\rangle$, $0\rangle$, $\langle\langle$broadcast, *data*$\rangle$, $1\rangle$

and the verb/noun-term pair $\langle$broadcast, *data*$\rangle$ is used in the **expand** function to find *candidate-relaxation* pairs. As a result of this call, the *Todo* list contains the following:

$\langle\langle$send, *data(GPS)*$\rangle$, $1\rangle$, $\langle\langle$broadcast, *information*$\rangle$, $2\rangle$, $\langle\langle$send, *data*$\rangle$, $2\rangle$.

After the third pass, the *RelaxList* and the *Todo* lists contain

$\langle\langle$broadcast, *data(GPS)*$\rangle$, $0\rangle$, $\langle\langle$broadcast, *data*$\rangle$, $1\rangle$, $\langle\langle$send, *data(GPS)*$\rangle$, $1\rangle$

and

$\langle\langle$broadcast, *information*$\rangle$, $2\rangle$, $\langle\langle$send, *data*$\rangle$, $2\rangle$,
$\langle\langle$mail, *data(GPS)*$\rangle$, $2\rangle$, $\langle\langle$ship, *data(GPS)*$\rangle$, $2\rangle$, $\langle\langle$provide, *data(GPS)*$\rangle$, $2\rangle$,

respectively. In the subsequent passes of the while loop, each verb/noun-term pair in the *Todo* list is copied to the *RelaxList* and relaxed one at a time, yielding no new pairs in the

Todo list. At the end of while loop, i.e., when all the pairs in the *Todo* list have been relaxed with the distance function constraint, then the resulting *RelaxList* contains the following:

$\langle\langle\text{broadcast}, data(GPS)\rangle, 0\rangle, \langle\langle\text{broadcast}, data\rangle, 1\rangle, \langle\langle\text{send}, data(GPS)\rangle, 1\rangle,$
$\langle\langle\text{broadcast}, information\rangle, 2\rangle, \langle\langle\text{send}, data\rangle, 2\rangle, \langle\langle\text{mail}, data(GPS)\rangle, 2\rangle,$
$\langle\langle\text{ship}, data(GPS)\rangle, 2\rangle, \langle\langle\text{provide}, data(GPS)\rangle, 2\rangle.$

Finally, the search on the Service Table results in the following agent list:

$\langle satellite1, 0\rangle, \langle satellite2, 0\rangle, \langle satellite6, 0\rangle,$
$\langle satellite4, 1\rangle, \langle satellite9, 1\rangle, \langle satellite7, 1\rangle, \langle satellite8, 1\rangle,$
$\langle satellite12, 2\rangle$

which is returned as the result of the call *range*(broadcast, *data(GPS)*,2).

Suppose $V \in \Sigma_v$ and $NT \in \Sigma_{nt}$. Also, let $vnt = \{\langle v, nt\rangle \mid v \in \Sigma_v \wedge nt \in \Sigma_{nt} \wedge cd(\langle v, nt\rangle, \langle V, NT\rangle) \leq D\}$ and let S be the set of all (agent name, $\langle v, nt\rangle$) pairs where $\langle v, nt\rangle \in vnt$. Then **range**($V, NT, D$) will need $O(|vnt| + |S|)$ time.

3.5 Simulation Evaluation

When evaluating the performance of the *IMPACT* yellow pages server, we need to consider two important parameters:

- the efficiency of finding *similar* services and
- the quality of the *matching* services provided as the output.

In order to evaluate efficiency, we ran a set of simulations on large hierarchies. We report on this in detail in the next section. For evaluating the quality of the matched services, we ran experiments with people who used the yellow pages services and were requested to specify whether the returned services are really *similar* and whether there are services in the system which are similar but were not found. We will report on these experiments in Subsection 3.5.2.

3.5.1 Performance Results

In this section, we report on experiments associated with our nearest neighbor and range query algorithms. We evaluated the performance of these algorithms as the number of nearest neighbors requested increased in number and as the range of the range query increased in size. In all cases, we used a *NASA* hierarchy consisting of 17,445 words (for experimental purposes, the same hierarchy was used as both a verb and a noun hierarchy, although the *IMPACT* prototype uses different hierarchies). Weights on all edges in the hierarchies were assumed to be 1 and the composite distance function was taken to be sum. The algorithms were implemented in C++ and the experiments were conducted on a Sun Sparc.

Figures 3.2 and 3.3 show the performance of the k nearest neighbor algorithm as k is increased from 1 to 20. For any given k we considered 100 queries, generated randomly. Figure 3.2 shows the average time taken for these 100 queries. Here, each timing starts immediately after a query is asked and ends when all results are returned. Notice that in some cases, even though k neighbors may be requested, we may only get back $k' < k$ answers. Figure 3.3 on the following page shows the average time per retrieved answer. As the reader will notice, the average time varied roughly between 0 and 1 second, and rose more or less linearly as k increased. However, when considering the average time per retrieved answer (Figure 3.3), we notice that the time taken is more or less constant, fluctuating near 0.2 seconds.

Figures 3.4 and 3.5 show the performance of the range query algorithm. Again, we ran 100 queries, and increased the range from 1 to 20 units. Figure 3.4 shows the average time taken for these 100 queries while Figure 3.5 shows the average time per retrieved answer. The average time per range query stays more or less constant at 1.6 seconds. This number is higher than in the case of k nearest neighbors, but is easily explained by the observation that the number of retrieved answers within r radial units may be significantly larger than r. The average time taken per retrieved answer for range queries is around 0.5 seconds. Note that in this experiment, for larger values of r, the number of answers returned did not increase with r. This was due to the small depth of the subtrees for the *NASA* hierarchy; after exhausting a subtree of a verb and noun-term hierarchy, the algorithm was able to determine that all remaining services must have an infinite distance from $\langle V, NT \rangle$.

3.5.2 Evaluating the Quality of Returned Matches

To help evaluate the quality of the returned service name matches, we conducted an experiment involving 35 participants. Here, we used a simple verb hierarchy (10 nodes), noun-term hierarchy (90 nodes), and ServiceTable (100 services). After an initial training phase, participants entered a precision phase where they were asked to perform 10 nearest neighbor and 10 range queries of their choice. After each query result, participants typed in a ranking between 0 (least satisfied) and 100 (most satisfied). Average satisfaction for nearest neighbor and range queries are shown in Figure 3.6. Notice that in general, precision decreased as the neighbor position (or composition distance) increased. The overall average precision for nearest neighbor and range queries were 46.04 and 39.22 respectively.

After completing the precision phase, participants started the recall phase. Here, they were allowed to view the ServiceTable (which up to this point was not available to them).

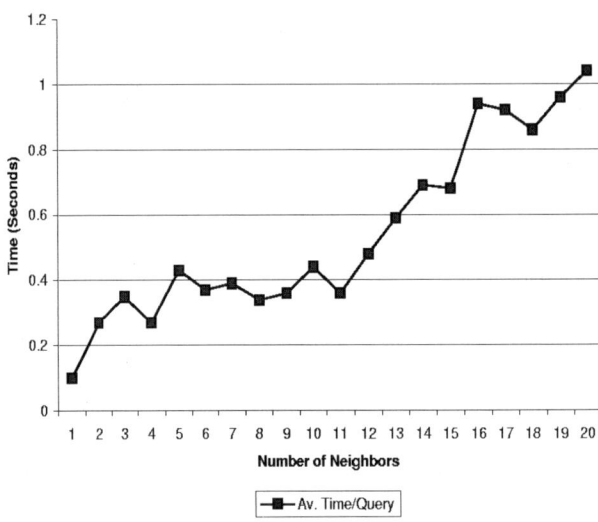

Figure 3.2
Performance of *k*-nearest neighbor algorithm: Average time per query.

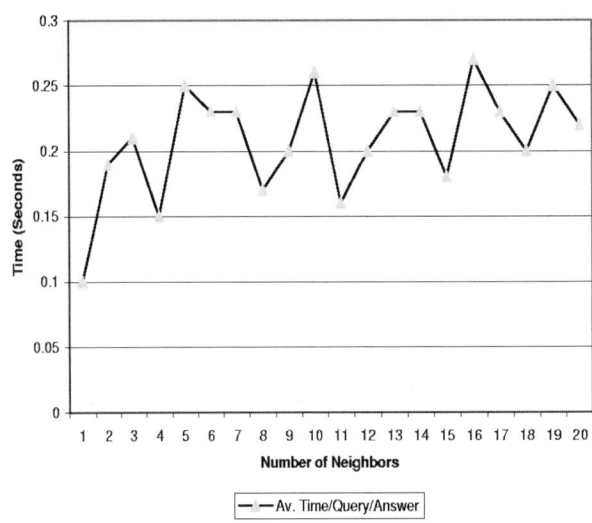

Figure 3.3
Performance of *k*-nearest neighbor algorithm: Average time per answer.

Section 3.5   Simulation Evaluation

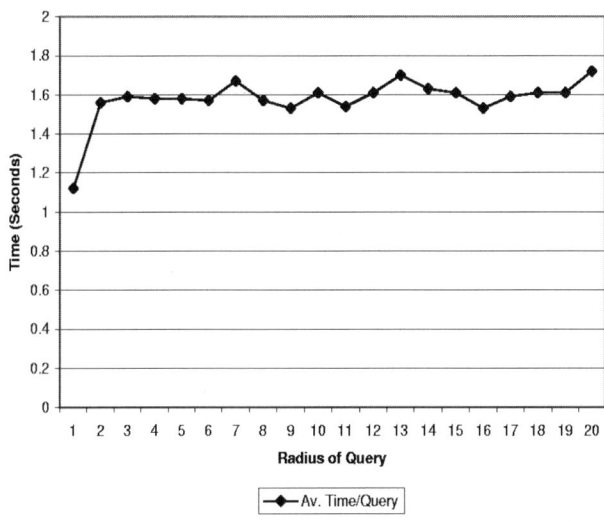

Figure 3.4
Performance of range query algorithm, Average time per query.

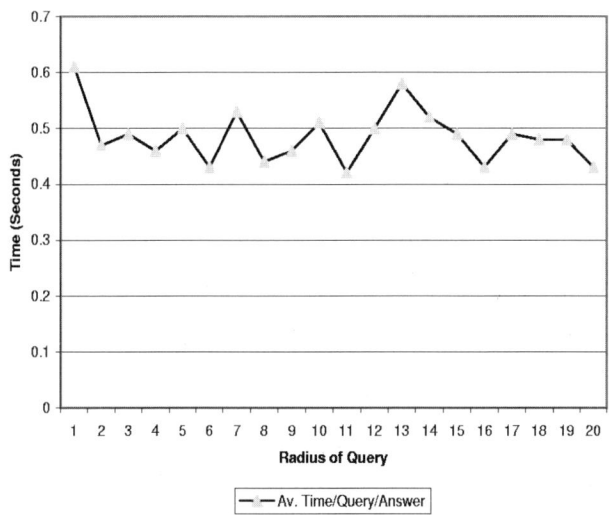

Figure 3.5
Performance of range query algorithm, Average time per answer.

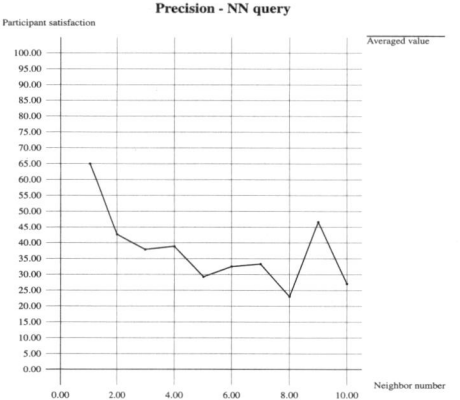 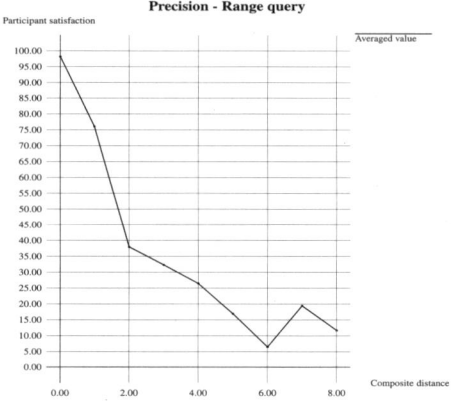

Precision for the k-nearest neighbor algorithm   Precision for the range algorithm

Figure 3.6
Experimental Results of Precision of our Algorithms.

Meanwhile, they were presented with text boxes containing the query answers they gave in the previous phase. After each answer, they were instructed to type in the name of all services in ServiceTable which did not appear as a query result but which should have been returned as an answer. The average number of these "suggested replacements" for nearest neighbor and range query answers are shown in Figure 3.7. The overall average number of suggested replacements for nearest neighbor and range query answers were 0.625 and 0.763 respectively. This implies that we obtained relatively good recall, and that we could get better precision by maintaining a more complete service table.

3.6 Related Work

Ontologies have long been part of research in *Artificial Intelligence*. For example, ontology-based thesauri have been an important part of research in Natural Language Processing (Bateman 1990). In the last few years, as the Web has evolved and the research on heterogeneous distributed systems has increased, ontologies have become increasingly important (Lenat 1995; Guha and Lenat 1994; Stoffel, Taylor, and Hendler 1997; Luke, Spector, Rager, and Hendler 1997; Campbell and Shapiro 1998). One of the main motivations for the development of ontologies is to support communication between multiple heterogeneous agents (Campbell and Shapiro 1998; Takeda, Iwata, Takaai, Sawada, and Nishida 1995) that use diverse vocabularies to specify common concepts.

Section 3.6   Related Work

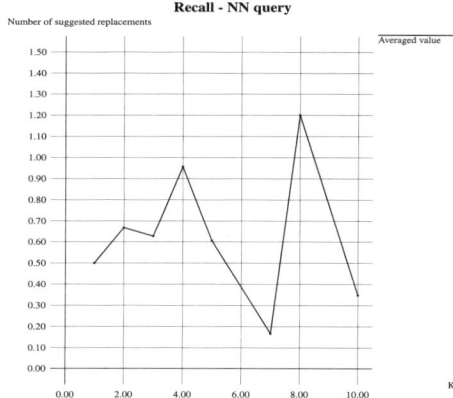 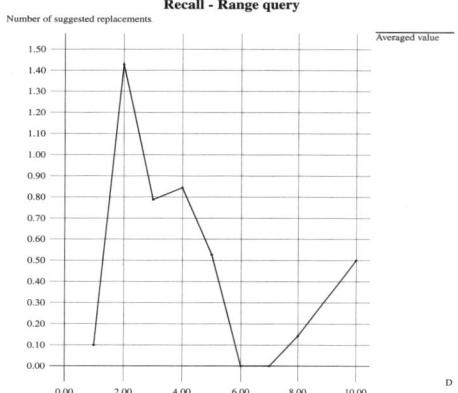

Recall for the *k*-nearest neighbor algorithm   Recall for the range algorithm (radius *D*)

Figure 3.7
Experimental Results of Recall of our Algorithms.

There are two main approaches to the development of ontologies: building a general large ontology (Lenat 1995) or developing a domain-specific ontology (Gruber and Olsen 1994). We have chosen an intermediate approach. Our hierarchies are not general ontologies. They are relatively simple and include verbs and noun-terms to describe agent services. They evolve over time: new verbs and noun-terms are added as more agents are registered. The verb and noun-term of any service *must* appear in the appropriate hierarchy. However, to complement these limited hierarchies, we use a general thesaurus while performing the matchmaking process.

Most of the ontologies and thesauri today are constructed by people (Frakes and Baeza-Yates 1992; Ushioda 1996). Recently however, methods were developed for automated construction of domain specific thesauri and ontologies (Dagan 1998). Our hierarchies are updated by the designers of agents when they register their agents and we use a commercial manually crafted thesaurus. This thesaurus may be replaced by a domain specific automated constructed thesaurus, given that there is a large corpus of documents in this domain.

There has been substantial work on "matchmaking" where agents advertise their services and matchmakers match an agent requesting a service with one (or more) agents that provide it, e.g., (Weinstein and Birmingham 1997; Kuokka and Harada 1996; Decker, Sycara, and Williamson 1997).[1] Two of the best known examples of this class of work are given below.

---

[1] There is also an interesting approach of using multiagent system to match and introduce users who share interests (Foner 1997).

Kuokka and Harada (1996) present the *SHADE* and *COINS* systems for matchmaking. *SHADE* uses logical rules to support matchmaking—the logic used is a subset of *KIF* and is very expressive. In contrast, *COINS* assumes that a message is a document (represented by a weighted term vector) and retrieves the "most similar" advertised services using the *SMART* algorithm of Salton and McGill (1983).

Decker, Sycara, and Williamson (1997) present matchmakers that store capability advertisements of different agents. They look for *exact* matches between requested services and retrieved services, and concentrate their efforts on architectures that support load balancing and protection of privacy of different agents.

Our effort differs from the above in the following ways: first, our service descriptions use a very simple, restricted language similar to HTML. By restricting our language, we are able to very clearly articulate what we mean by *similar* matches in terms of nearest neighbor and range queries, as well as provide very efficient algorithms (as demonstrated by our experiments) to implement these operations. Second, the user (or owner of an agent) can expand the underlying ontologies (verb, noun-term hierarchies) arbitrarily as needed, and we provide him software tools to do so. To date, we have explicitly encoded (in our language) service descriptions of over 60 well known independently developed programs available on the Web, and this number is increasing on a regular basis. However, we do not address issues such as load balancing which is addressed by Decker, Sycara, and Williamson (1997).

4 Accessing Legacy Data and Software

The design of data structures for an application depends fundamentally on the kind of data manipulated by that application, by the kinds of operations to be performed on the data, by the relative frequency of those operations, and by user communities' expectations on the performance of these different operations. Computer scientists design data structures and algorithms based on the above criteria, so as to efficiently support operations on the data structures. Under no circumstances should a definition of agents limit the choice of data structures and algorithms that an application designer must use.

Thus, the ability to build agents on top of arbitrary pieces of code is critical to the agent enterprise as a whole. For instance, in the CHAIN example, we might wish to build the supplier agents on top of an existing commercial relational DBMS system. Likewise, in the case of the terrain agent in the CFIT example, we might wish to build this agent on top of existing US military terrain reasoning software. In addition, there may be agents that are not built on top of a single piece of existing software, but which access a set of software packages. For instance, the Product Database agent productDB in the CHAIN example may access some file structures, as well as some databases.

In this chapter, we will define a single unified front-end to a set of disparate heterogeneous data sources and software packages, on top of which agents may be built. We will first start with an abstract definition of software code, and show how most packages may be viewed as instances of this abstract definition. An agent may be built on top of one or more such pieces of software code. We will introduce the concept of an agent state that describes what the agent's data structures are populated with at a given instant of time. Then we will introduce the concept of a code call condition which provides a generic query language that can span multiple abstractions of software code. We then introduce a specific code domain called a msgbox that can be used by different agents for messaging. Integrity constraints are then introduced as constraints that limit what the agent state might look like. We then show how the concept of a service description defined in Chapter 3 may be implemented via a concept called a service description program that uses the above concepts.

4.1 Software Code Abstractions

In this section, we focus on the *internal* data managed by the software code underlying an agent.

DEFINITION 4.1.1 (SOFTWARE CODE $\mathcal{S} = (\mathcal{T_S}, \mathcal{F_S}, \mathcal{C_S})$) We may characterize the code on top of which an agent is built as a triple $\mathcal{S} =_{def} (\mathcal{T_S}, \mathcal{F_S}, \mathcal{C_S})$ where:

1. $\mathcal{T_S}$ is the set of all data types managed by $\mathcal{S}$,

2. $\mathcal{F_S}$ is a set of predefined functions which makes access to the data objects managed by the agent available to external processes, and

3. $\mathcal{C_S}$ is a set of type composition operations. A type composition operator is a partial n-ary function c which takes as input types $\tau_1, \ldots, \tau_n$ and yields as output a type $c(\tau_1, \ldots, \tau_n)$. As c is a partial function, c may only be defined for certain arguments $\tau_1, \ldots, \tau_n$, i.e., c is not necessarily applicable on arbitrary types.

In other words, in the strict sense of object systems, $\mathcal{S}$ is definable as a collection (or hierarchy) of object classes in any standard object data management language such as *ODL* (Cattell et al. 1997). Almost all existing servers used in real systems, as well as most commercial packages available on the market are instances of the above definition. The same is true of commercial standards such as the Object Data Management Group's *ODMG* standard (Cattell et al. 1997), the *CORBA* framework (OMG 1998a; Siegal 1996) and Microsoft's COM/OLE (Microsoft 1999) (http://www.microsoft.com/com/comPapers.asp).

Intuitively, $\mathcal{T_S}$ is the set of all data types that are managed by the agent. $\mathcal{F_S}$ intuitively represents the set of all function calls supported by the package $\mathcal{S}$'s application programmer interface (*API*). $\mathcal{C_S}$ the set of ways of creating new data types from existing data types.

Given a software package $\mathcal{S}$, we use the notation $\mathcal{T_S^\star}$ to denote the *closure* of $\mathcal{T_S}$ under the operations in $\mathcal{C_S}$. In order to formally define this notion, we introduce the following definition.

DEFINITION 4.1.2 ($\mathcal{C_S}(\mathcal{T})$ AND $\mathcal{T_S^\star}$)

a) Given a set $\mathcal{T}$ of types, we define

$$\mathcal{C_S}(\mathcal{T}) =_{def} \mathcal{T} \cup \{\tau : \text{ there exists an } n\text{-ary composition operator } c \in \mathcal{C_S}$$
$$\text{and types } \tau_1, \ldots, \tau_n \in \mathcal{T} \text{ such that } c(\tau_1, \ldots, \tau_n) = \tau\}.$$

b) We define $\mathcal{T_S^\star}$ as follows:

$$\mathcal{T_S^0} =_{def} \mathcal{T_S},$$
$$\mathcal{T_S^{i+1}} =_{def} \mathcal{C_S}(\mathcal{T_S^i}),$$
$$\mathcal{T_S^\star} =_{def} \bigcup_{i \in \mathbb{N}} \mathcal{T_S^i}.$$

Intuitively, $\mathcal{T_S^\star}$ represents the set of all possible types that can be produced by repeatedly applying the composition operations in $\mathcal{C_S}$ on the base types in $\mathcal{T}$. Let us return to the CFIT,

CHAIN and STORE examples to see how some of the software packages within them may be captured by this definition.

4.1.1 CHAIN Revisited

Consider the two Supplier agents in the CHAIN example. Each of these agents may manage the set

$\mathcal{T}_S =_{def}$ {Integer, Location, String, Date, OrderLog, Stock}

of types. Here, OrderLog is a relation having the schema

(*client*/string, *amount*/Integer, *part_id*/String, *method*/String, *src*/Location, *dest*/Location, *pickup_st*/date, *pickup_et*/date),

while Stock is a relation having the schema (*amount*/Integer, *part_id*/String). Location is an enumerated type containing city names. In addition, $\mathcal{F}_S$ might consist of the functions:

- *monitorStock*(*Amount*/Integer, *Part_id*/String) of type String.
This function returns either amount_available or amount_not_available, which are status strings having the obvious meaning.
- *shipFreight*(*Amount*/Integer, *Part_id*/String, *method*/String, *Src*/Location, *Dest*/Location).
This function, when executed, updates the order log and logs information about the order, together with information on (i) the earliest time the order will be ready for shipping, and (ii) the latest time by which the order must be picked up by the shipping vendor. Notice that this does *not* mean that the shipment will in fact be picked up by the $airplane$ agent at that time. It just means that these are the constraints that will be used by the $supplier$ agent in its negotiations with the $shipping$ agent.
- *updateStock*(*Amount*/Integer, *Part_id*/String).
This function, when executed, updates the inventory of the Supplier. For example, if the supplier had 500 items of a particular part on hand, then the fact that 200 of these parts have been committed means that the stock has dropped to 300.

Finally, in this case, $\mathcal{C}_S$ might consist of the operations of projection of attributes of a relation and cartesian products of relations. Thus, $\mathcal{T}_S^*$ consists not only of all the above data types, but also of

1. sub-records of the above data types such as a relation having the schema (*amount*/Integer, *dest*/Location) derived from the OrderLog relation,
2. cartesian products of types, and
3. mixes involving the above two operations.

4.1.2 STORE Revisited

Consider the profiling agent in the STORE example. Here, the data types might consist of the set

$\mathcal{T}_S =_{def}$ {String, UserProfile},

while, $\mathcal{F}_S$ might contain the following function:

- *classifyUser(Ssn/*string*)* of type UserProfile.

This function takes as input, a person's social security number, and returns as output a value such as spender(high). The output type of this function is called UserProfile, which is an enumerated type consisting of spender(high) and similar strings.

Moreover, the credit agent might have the following data types;

$\mathcal{T}_S =_{def}$ {FinanceRecord, String},

and $\mathcal{F}_S$ might contain the following function:

- *provideCreditInfo(Ssn/*string*, DetailLevel/*string*)* of type FinanceRecord.

This function takes as input a person's social security number and a string high, medium, or low. It returns credit information about person *ssn* in a record of Type FinanceRecord, whose fields depend on the detail level requested.

Finally, let $\mathcal{C}_S$ be

$\{\pi_{f_1,\ldots,f_k}(\text{FinanceRecord}) : f_i, f_j \text{ are fields of FinanceRecord} \land i \neq j \Rightarrow f_i \neq f_j\}$.

Thus, in this example, $\mathcal{T}_S^*$ contains every type in $\mathcal{T}_S$ plus the FinanceRecord type which consists of all possible projections on the fields of type FinanceRecord. The type FinanceRecord is assumed to be a named type among these projections.

4.1.3 CFIT Revisited

Let us now consider the autoPilot agent and the gps agent in the CFIT example. Let the set of types by

$\mathcal{T}_S =_{def}$ {Map, Path, Plan, SatelliteReport}.

Here, the maps in question are a special class of maps called *DTED Digital Terrain Elevation Data* that specify the elevations of different regions of the world. (For financial reasons, our prototype implementation only uses *DTED* data for the continental United States—obtaining

Section 4.1   Software Code Abstractions   79

such data for the whole world is extremely expensive.) The type `SatelliteReport` may itself be a complex record type containing fields: `height` (height of ground), `sat_id` (identity of satellite providing the report), `dist` (current distance between the plane and the ground), and `2dloc` (current x, y location) which in turn has fields x and y.

Suppose the *autoPilot* agent's associated set of functions $\mathcal{F}_S$ contains:

- *createFlightPlan*(*Location*/`Map`, *Flight_route*/`Path`, *Nogo*/`Map`) of type `Plan`.

Intuitively, this function takes as input, the *actual* location of the plane, the flight path of the plane, and a map depicting *no_go* volumes. Intuitively, *no_go* volumes are regions of space where the plane is not supposed to fly. For example, a mountain, surrounded by an envelope of 1000 feet is an example of such a *no_go* volume. This functions returns as output a modified flight plan that avoids the *no_go* volumes.

Moroever, the $\mathcal{F}_S$ of the *gps* might contain the following function:

- *mergeGPSData*(*Data1*/`SatelliteReport`, *Data2*/`SatelliteReport`) of type `Satellite Report`.

This function takes as input satellite report data from two or more satellites, and merges them into a single report that can be used to pinpoint the location of the plane. Typically, this function would be iteratively used by the *gps* agent for this pinpointing to occur.

Let $\mathcal{C}_S$ be the singleton set

{list of `SatelliteReport`}.

Thus, $\mathcal{T}_S^*$ contains every type in $\mathcal{T}_S$, plus the type which consists of all lists of type `SatelliteReport`; for future reference, let us name this type `SatelliteReport`.

4.1.4   State of an Agent

At any given point t in time, the *state of an agent* will refer to a set $\mathcal{O}_S(t)$ of objects from the types $\mathcal{T}_S$, managed by its internal software code. An agent may change its state by taking an action—either triggered internally, or by processing a message received from another agent. Throughout this book we will assume that except for appending messages to an agent a's mailbox, another agent b cannot directly change a's state. However, it might do so indirectly by shipping the other agent a message issuing a change request. The precise definitions of messages and message management will be given in Section 4.3, while details of actions and action management will be described in Chapter 6.

4.2 Code Call Conditions

In this section, we introduce the reader to the important concept of a *code call atom*—this concept forms the basic syntactic object by which we may access multiple heterogeneous data sources. Before proceeding to this definition, we need to introduce some syntactic definitions.

Intuitively, code call conditions are logical expressions that access the data of heterogeneous software sources using the pre-existing external *API* (application program interface) function calls provided by the software package in question. In other words, the language of code-call conditions is layered on top of the physical data structures and implementation within a specific package.

4.2.1 Variables

Suppose we consider a body $S =_{def} (\mathcal{T}_S, \mathcal{F}_S, \mathcal{C}_S)$ of software code. Given any type $\tau \in \mathcal{T}_S$, we will assume that there is a set $root(\tau)$ of "root" variable symbols ranging over τ. Such "root" variables will be used in the construction of code calls.

However, consider a complex type τ, and suppose τ is a complex record type having fields $f_1, \ldots, f_n$. Then, for every variable of type τ, we require that $X.f_i$ be a variable of type τ_i where τ_i is the type of field f_i. In the same vein, if f_i itself has a sub-field g of type γ, then $X.f_i.g$ is a variable of type γ, and so on. The variables, $X.f_i$, $X.f_i.g$, etc. are called *path variables*. For any path variable Y of the form X.path, where X is a root variable, we refer to X as the root of Y, denoted by $root(Y)$; for technical convenience, $root(X)$, where X is a root variable, refers to itself. To see the distinction between root variables and path variables, let us return to the CFIT example.

Example 4.2.1 (CFIT Revisited) Let X be a (root) variable of type `SatelliteReport` denoting the current location of an airplane. Then X.2dloc, X.2dloc.x, X.2dloc.y, X.height, and X.dist are path variables. For each of the path variables Y, $root(Y) = X$. Here, X.2dloc.x, X.2dloc.y, and X.height are of type `Integer`, X.2dloc's type is a record of two `Integer` s, and X.dist is of type `NonNegative`.

DEFINITION 4.2.1 (VARIABLE ASSIGNMENT) An *assignment of objects to variables* is a set of equations of the form $V_1 := o_1, \ldots, V_k := o_k$ where the V_i's are variables (root or path) and the o_i's are objects—such an assignment is *legal*, if the types of objects and corresponding variables match.

We now return to the CFIT example to see an example assignment.

Example 4.2.2 (CFIT Revisited) A legal assignment may be

(X.height := 50, X.sat_id := iridium_17, X.dist := 25, X.2dloc.x := 3, X.2dloc.y := −4).

If the record is ordered as shown here, then we may abbreviate this assignment as (50, iridium_17, 25, ⟨3, −4⟩). Note however that

(X.height := 50, X.sat_id := iridium_17, X.dist := − 25, X.2dloc.x := 3, X.2dloc.y := −4)

would be illegal, because -25 is not a valid object for X.dist's type NonNegative.

4.2.2 Code Calls

A *code call* is a syntactic mechanism that allows a process (which may be an agent) to invoke an *API* function supported by a software package. First, we observe that an agent built on top of a piece, S, of software, may support several *API* functions, and it may or may not make all these functions available to other agents. Precisely which of these functions is made available is done through the *service description language.* We will describe briefly in Section 4.6 how service descriptions are linked with *API* function calls.

We now note that each such *API* function $f \in \mathcal{F}_S$ has a *signature*, specifying the types of inputs it takes, and the types of outputs it returns. This provides the basis for the following definition.

DEFINITION 4.2.2 (CODE CALL $S : f(d_1, \ldots, d_n)$) Suppose $S =_{def} (\mathcal{T}_S, \mathcal{F}_S, \mathcal{C}_S)$ is some software code and $f \in \mathcal{F}_S$ is a predefined function with n arguments, and $d_1, \ldots, d_n$ are objects or variables such that each d_i respects the type requirements of the i'th argument of f. Then,

$$S : f(d_1, \ldots, d_n)$$

is a *code call*. A code call is *ground* if all the d_i's are objects. We often switch between the software package S and the agent providing it. Therefore instead of writing $S : f(d_1, \ldots, d_n)$ where S is provided by agent a, we also write $a : f(d_1, \ldots, d_n)$.

In general, as we will see later, code calls are executable when they are ground. Thus, non-ground code calls must be *instantiated* prior to attempts to execute them. This makes sense—after all, most standard programming languages require that all input variables to a function or procedure be bound prior to invocation of that function or procedure.

Intuitively, the syntactic string $S : f(d_1, \ldots, d_n)$ may be read as: *execute function f as defined in package S on the arguments* $d_1, \ldots, d_n$.

Note 2 (Assumption on the Output Signature)   We will assume that the output signature of any code call is a set. There is no loss of generality in making this assumption—if a function does not return a set, but rather returns an atomic value, then that value can be coerced into a set anyway—by treating the value as shorthand for the singleton set containing just the value.

We now revisit our motivating examples to see some sample code calls.

Example 4.2.3 (CHAIN Revisited)   Here is a list of some sample code calls used by the supplier agents:

1. supplier : *monitorStock*(3, part_008).

This code call says that we should check whether 3 pieces of part_008 are available or not. Observe that the result of this call is either the singleton set {amount_available}, or the set {amount_not_available}.

2. supplier : *shipFreight*(3, part_008, truck, X, paris).

This code call says that we should create a pickup schedule for shipping 3 pieces of part_008 from location X to Paris by truck. Notice that until a value is specified for X, this code call cannot be executed. In contrast, the preceding code call is ground, and is executable.

Example 4.2.4 (STORE Revisited)   Here is a list of some sample code calls used in the STORE example, one used by the profiling agents, and other used by the credit agents:

1. profiling : *classifyUser*(123_45_6789).

This code call asks the profiling agent to classify the individual with social security number 123_45_6789.

2. credit : *provideCreditInfo*(123_45_6789, high).

This code call provides the finance records of the individual with social security number 123_45_6789. It requests high level of detail in this request, not just a crude summary of the person's credit history.

Observe that both code calls in this example are ground.

Example 4.2.5 (CFIT Revisited)   Here, GPS : *mergeGPSData*(S1, S2) is a code call which merges two pieces, S1 and S2, of satellite data, but the values of the two pieces are not stated. Thus, this call cannot be immediately executed.

4.2.3 Code Call Atoms

As we have already seen above, a code call executes an *API* function and returns as output a set of objects of the appropriate output type. Code-call atoms are *logical atoms* that are layered on top of code-calls. They are defined through the following inductive definition.

Section 4.2   Code Call Conditions

DEFINITION 4.2.3 (CODE CALL ATOM)   If *cc* is a code call, and X is either a variable symbol, or an object of the output type of *cc*, then

- **in**(X, cc),
- **not_in**(X, cc),

are called *code call atoms*. A code call atom is *ground* if no variable symbols occur anywhere in it.

Code call atoms, when evaluated, return boolean values, and thus may be thought of as special types of logical atoms. Intuitively, a code call atom of the form **in**(X, cc) succeeds just in case when X can be set to a pointer to one of the objects in the set of objects returned by executing the code call. In database terminology, X is a cursor on the result of executing the code call.

Likewise, a code call atom of the form **not_in**(X, cc) succeeds just in case X is not in the result set returned by cc (when X is an object), or when X cannot be made to point to one of the objects returned by executing the code call.

Note 3   The above definitions allow an agent to have a state described potentially by an infinite set of ground code call atoms. In Chapter 12, we will introduce the concept of a finiteness table that will deal with this problem.

Let us return to the code calls introduced earlier, and see how these code calls give rise to different code call atoms.

Example 4.2.6 (CHAIN Revisited)   Consider the following code call atoms associated with the supplier agents:

1. **in**(amount_available, supplier : *monitorStock*(3, part_008)).
This code call succeeds just in case the Supplier has 3 units of part_008 on stock.

2. **in**(X, supplier : *monitorStock*(3, part_008)).
This code call succeeds just in case there exists an X in the result of executing the code call shown here. In effect, X is a variable that can be bound to the status string returned by executing the code call supplier : *monitorStock*(3, part_008).

Example 4.2.7 (STORE Revisited)   Consider the following code call atoms associated with the profiling agent:

1. **not_in**(spender(low), profiling : *classifyUser*(U)). This code call succeeds just in case user U, whose identity must be instantiated prior to evaluation, is *not* classified as a low spender by the profiling agent.

2. **in**(X, profiling : *classifyUser*(123_45_6789)).

This code call computes the classification of the user with social security number 123_45_6789.

4.2.4 Code Call Conditions

Intuitively, a code call condition is nothing more than a conjunction of atomic code calls, with some additional syntax that "links" together variables occurring in the atomic code calls. The following definition expresses this intuition.

DEFINITION 4.2.4 (CODE CALL CONDITION) A *code call condition* is defined as follows:

1. Every code call atom is a code call condition.
2. If s and t are either variables or objects, then s = t is a code call condition.
3. If s and t are either integers/real valued objects, or are variables over the integers/reals, then s < t, s > t, s ≤ t, and s ≥ t are code call conditions.
4. If χ_1 and χ_2 are code call conditions, then χ_1 & χ_2 is a code call condition.

We refer to any code call condition of form 1.-3. as an *atomic* code call condition.

We now show how some of the code call atoms given earlier may be woven together into code call conditions.

Example 4.2.8 (CHAIN Revisited) Suppose a supplier agent is asked to ship 3 units of part_008. Our agent must first determine if 3 units are available. This can be done by using the following code call condition:

$\chi^{(1)}$: **in**(amount_available, supplier : *monitorStock*(3, part_008)).

The following is an equivalent way to ask the same query:

$\chi^{(2)}$: **in**(X, supplier : *monitorStock*(3, part_008)) & X = *amount_available*.

Now suppose that after shipping three units, we want to determine whether or not we should order more units of part_008. We decide to do so if the number of part_008s available (denoted by the variable U below) is less than the number of available part_009s (denoted by the variable V below). We can determine if this is the case by using the following code call condition:

$\chi^{(3)}$: **in**(amount_available, supplier : *monitorStock*(U, part_008)) &
    not_in(amount_available, supplier : *monitorStock*(U + 1, part_008)) &
    in(amount_available, supplier : *monitorStock*(V, part_009)) &
    not_in(amount_available, supplier : *monitorStock*(V + 1, part_009)) & U < V.

Observe that U and V must be assigned values before an evaluation of the respective code calls is possible.

Example 4.2.9 (STORE Revisited)   Suppose a STORE application is asked to send a brochure to all users who are not low spenders. First, the agent must generate a list of all target users. It can do so by asking the profiling agent to execute the following code call condition:

not_in(spender(low), profiling : *classifyUser*(X)).

After generating and sorting this list, we noticed that some users are listed twice. An investigation may reveal that some users are erroneously classified as both high and medium spenders. To create a list of all such users, we can use the following code call condition:

in(spender(medium), profiling : *classifyUser*(U)) &
in(spender(high), profiling : *classifyUser*(V))   & U = V.

Observe that this code call condition can be simplified by pushing through the equality U = V, so that we obtain the equivalent code call condition

in(spender(medium), profiling : *classifyUser*(U))   &
not_in(spender(high), profiling : *classifyUser*(U)).

Example 4.2.10 (CFIT Revisited)   Suppose we received GPS data from three satellites X1, X2, X3 and we wish to merge this data into one coherent satellite report X. Here, we could use the following code call condition:

in(Y, gps : *mergeGPSData*(X1, X2)) &
in(X, gps : *mergeGPSData*(Y, X3)).

We now wish to determine whether we would get the same results by only using data from satellites X1 and X2. If this is consistently true, we could cut costs using only two satellites instead of three. The following code call condition can be used to determine whether X3 is modifying the intermediate result Y:

in(Y, gps : *mergeGPSData*(X1, X2))   &
not_in(Y, gps : *mergeGPSData*(Y, X3)).

4.2.5   Safety

One aspect to keep in mind about code calls is that while code call syntax allows variables to appear in a code call, it is in general infeasible to evaluate a code call when it has uninstantiated variables. Thus, any time we attempt to actually execute a code call, we require that the code call must be fully instantiated. This motivates the definition of a *safe* code call below.

DEFINITION 4.2.5 (SAFE CODE CALL (CONDITION)) A code call $\mathcal{S} : f(\mathtt{d_1}, \ldots, \mathtt{d_n})$ is *safe* if and only if each $\mathtt{d_i}$ is ground. A code call condition $\chi_1 \& \ldots \& \chi_n$, $n \geq 1$, is *safe* if and only if there exists a permutation π of $\chi_1, \ldots, \chi_n$ such that for every $i = 1, \ldots, n$ the following holds:

1. If $\chi_{\pi(i)}$ is a comparison $\mathtt{s_1}\ op\ \mathtt{s_2}$, then

    1.1 at least one of $\mathtt{s_1}, \mathtt{s_2}$ is a constant or a variable X such that *root*(X) belongs to $RV_\pi(i) =_{def} \{root(\mathtt{Y}) \mid \exists j < i \text{ s.t. Y occurs in } \chi_{\pi(j)}\}$;

    1.2 if $\mathtt{s_i}$ is neither a constant nor a variable X such that $root(\mathtt{X}) \in RV_\pi(i)$, then $\mathtt{s_i}$ is a root variable.

2. If $\chi_{\pi(i)}$ is a code call atom of the form **in**($\mathtt{X}_{\pi(i)}, \mathtt{cc}_{\pi(i)}$) or **not_in**($\mathtt{X}_{\pi(i)}, \mathtt{cc}_{\pi(i)}$), then the root of each variable Y occurring in $\mathtt{cc}_{\pi(i)}$ belongs to $RV_\pi(i)$, and either $\mathtt{X}_{\pi(i)}$ is a root variable, or $root(\mathtt{X}_{\pi(i)})$ is from $RV_\pi(i)$.

Intuitively, a code call is safe, if we can reorder the code call atoms occurring in it in a way such that we can evaluate these atoms left to right, assuming that root variables are incrementally bound to objects.

Example 4.2.11 (CHAIN) Reconsider the three sample code call conditions $\chi^{(1)}$, $\chi^{(2)}$, and $\chi^{(3)}$ in Example 4.2.8. The cc conditions $\chi^{(1)}$ and $\chi^{(2)}$ are safe, but $\chi^{(3)}$ is unsafe, since there is no permutation of the atomic code call conditions which allows safety requirement 2 to be met for either U or V.

If code call condition χ is safe, then we can reorder the constituents $\chi_1, \ldots, \chi_n$ by a permutation π such that $\chi_{\pi(1)}, \ldots, \chi_{\pi(n)}$ can be evaluated without problems.

We next describe an algorithm which efficiently checks safety of a code call condition χ, and reorders the constituents χ_i in a suitable way in case that χ is safe. Before doing so, we need a notion of *relativized safe code call condition*.

DEFINITION 4.2.6 (SAFETY MODULO VARIABLES) Suppose χ is a code call condition, and **X** is any set of root variables. χ is said to be *safe modulo* **X** if and only if for an (arbitrary) assignment θ of objects to the variables in **X**, it is the case that $\chi\theta$ is safe.

Observe that an assignment of an object to a variable X implicitly assigns a value to all path variable X.f, X.f.g etc. Intuitively, a code call condition as actually written may be unsafe. However, it could be the intent that the code call condition only be invoked with certain arguments instantiated. If any such instantiation leads to a safe code call, then

Section 4.2   Code Call Conditions   87

the original code call is said to be safe modulo the arguments in question. The following example shows this situation.

Example 4.2.12 (CFIT Revisited) Recall that our first sample code call condition in Example 4.2.10 was

in(Y, gps : *mergeGPSData*(X1, X2)) &
in(X, gps : *mergeGPSData*(Y, X3)).

This code call condition is safe modulo {X1, X2, X3} but it is not safe modulo {X1, X2}. It is unsafe modulo {X1, X2} since neither of the two permutations of the two constituent atoms causes the variable X3 to be instantiated, irrespective of how X1, X2 may be instantiated.

The reader will easily observe that checking safety of a code call χ modulo variables **X** can be reduced to a call to a routine that checks for safety. This may be done as follows:

1. Find a constant (denoted c) that does not occur in χ.
Let $\theta =_{def} \{\mathbf{X} = \mathtt{c}\}$, i.e. every variable in **X** is set to c.
2. Check if $\chi\theta$ is safe.

Our algorithm for checking safety of a code call condition χ, **safe_ccc**, is described below.

Algorithm 4.2.1 (safe_ccc)
safe_ccc(χ : **code call condition; X: set of root variables**)

($\star$ input is a code call condition $\chi = \chi_1 \& \cdots \& \chi_n$; output is a proper reordering $\star$)
($\star$ $\chi' = \chi_{\pi(1)} \& \cdots \& \chi_{\pi(n)}$ if χ is safe modulo **X**; otherwise, the output is unsafe ; $\star$)

  1. $L := \chi_1, \ldots, \chi_n$;
  2. $\chi :=$ **true**;
  3. **while** L is not empty **do**
  4. {select all $\chi_{i_1}, \ldots, \chi_{i_m}$ from L such that χ_{i_j} is safe modulo **X**;
  5.   **if** $m = 0$ **then return** unsafe (*exit*);
  6.   **else**
  7.   {$\chi := \chi \& \chi_{i_1} \& \cdots \& \chi_{i_m}$;
  8.   remove $\chi_{i_1}, \ldots, \chi_{i_m}$ from L;
  9. $\mathbf{X} = \mathbf{X} \cup \{root(\mathtt{Y}) \mid \mathtt{Y}$ occurs in some $\chi_{i_1}, \ldots \chi_{i_m}\}$;
10. }
11. }
12. **return** χ';
end.

The theorem below establishes the correctness of the **safe_ccc** algorithm.

THEOREM 4.2.1 (SAFETY COMPUTATION) Suppose $\chi =_{def} \chi_1 \& \ldots \& \chi_n$ is a code call condition. Then, χ is safe modulo a set of root variables **X**, if and only if **safe_ccc**(χ, **X**) returns a reordering χ' of χ. Moreover, for any assignment θ to the variables in **X**, $\chi'\theta$ is a safe code call condition which can be evaluated left-to-right.

Proof Clearly, by construction of χ', we have that χ' is a safe code call condition modulo **X** (a suitable permutation for χ' is the identity). Thus, if the call of **safe_ccc**$(\chi, \mathbf{X})$ returns χ', then χ is safe modulo **X**, as a suitable permutation for π is given by the reordering of the constituents of χ realized in χ'.

On the other hand, suppose χ is safe modulo **X**. Then, some i from $1, \ldots, n$ must exist such that χ_i is safe modulo **X**. If, without loss of generality, $\chi_1, \ldots, \chi_k$ are all such χ_i, then it is easily seen that $\chi^{(1)} =_{def} \chi_{k+1} \& \cdots \& \chi_m$ must be safe modulo the variables $\mathbf{X}^{(1)} =_{def} \mathbf{X} \cup \{root(\mathtt{Y}) \mid \mathtt{Y} \text{ occurs in } \chi_1 \& \cdots \& \chi_k\}$. Employing an inductive argument, we obtain that the continuation of the computation succeeds for $L =_{def} \chi_{k+1}, \ldots, \chi_n$ modulo $\mathbf{X}^{(1)}$, and hence **safe_ccc**$(\chi, \mathbf{X})$ returns a reordered code call condition χ'. (The interested reader may observe that **safe_ccc** can be easily rewritten to a recursive algorithm.) Obviously, χ' is safe, and for any assignment θ to the variables in **X** (which are all root variables), the code call condition $\chi'\theta$ can be readily evaluated left-to-right. ∎

A straightforward implementation of **safe_ccc** runs in quadratic time, as the number of iterations is bounded by the number n of constituents χ_i of χ, and the body of the while loop can be executed in linear time. By using appropriate data structures, the algorithm can be implemented to run in overall linear time. Briefly, the method is to use cross reference lists of variable occurrences.

Observe that safety of a code call condition χ can be checked by calling **safe_ccc**$(\chi, \emptyset)$. Thus, checking the safety of χ, combined with a reordering of its constituents for left-to-right execution can be done very efficiently. The following example shows how the above algorithm works when applied to some of the code call conditions used in the CFIT Example.

Example 4.2.13 (CHAIN Example) Recall from Example 4.2.11 that $\chi^{(2)}$ in Example 4.2.8 was safe. We have $\chi^{(2)} = \chi_1 \& \chi_2$, where

χ_1 is **in**(X, supplier : *monitorStock*(3, part_008))

χ_2 is X = *amount_available*.

When we call **safe_ccc**$(\chi^{(2)}, \emptyset)$, then on the first iteration $m = 2$, $\chi_{i_1} = \chi_1$, and $\chi_{i_2} = \chi_2$. We add χ_{i_1} and χ_{i_2} to χ', remove them from L, and update **X**. Now, L is empty, and the algorithm correctly returns χ'. Notice that we would get the same answer even if we swapped χ_1 and χ_2.

Recall from Example 4.2.11 that $\chi^{(3)}$ in Example 4.2.8 was unsafe. We have $\chi^{(3)} = \chi_1 \& \chi_2 \& \chi_3 \& \chi_4 \& \chi_5$, where

Section 4.2   Code Call Conditions

χ_1 is **in**(amount_available, supplier : *monitorStock*(U, part_008)),

χ_2 is **not_in**(amount_available, supplier : *monitorStock*(U + 1, part_008)),

χ_3 is **in**(amount_available, supplier : *monitorStock*(V, part_009)),

χ_4 is **not_in**(amount_available, supplier : *monitorStock*(V + 1, part_009)), *and*

χ_5 is U < V.

When we run the **safe_ccc** algorithm, we get the following: On the first iteration, $m = 0$ since $\chi_1, \ldots, \chi_4$ are not safe (by condition 2 of Definition 4.2.5) and χ_5 is not safe (by condition 1 of Definition 4.2.5). Since $m = 0$, the algorithm correctly returns unsafe.

The following definition specifies what a *solution* of a code call condition is. Intuitively, code call conditions are evaluated against an agent state—if the state of the agent changes, the solution to a code call condition may also undergo a change.

DEFINITION 4.2.7 (CODE CALL SOLUTION)   Suppose χ is a code call condition involving the variables $\mathbf{X} =_{def} \{X_1, \ldots, X_n\}$, and suppose $\mathcal{S} =_{def} (\mathcal{T}_\mathcal{S}, \mathcal{F}_\mathcal{S}, \mathcal{C}_\mathcal{S})$ is some software code. A *solution* of χ w.r.t. $\mathcal{T}_\mathcal{S}$ in a state $\mathcal{O}_\mathcal{S}$ is a legal assignment of objects $o_1, \ldots, o_n$ to the variables $X_1, \ldots, X_n$, written as a compound equation $\mathbf{X} := \mathbf{o}$, such that the application of the assignment makes χ true in state $\mathcal{O}_\mathcal{S}$.

We denote by $\mathsf{Sol}(\chi)_{\mathcal{T}_\mathcal{S}, \mathcal{O}_\mathcal{S}}$ (omitting subscripts $\mathcal{O}_\mathcal{S}$ and $\mathcal{T}_\mathcal{S}$ when clear from the context), the set of all solutions of the code call condition χ in state $\mathcal{O}_\mathcal{S}$, and by $\mathcal{O}\_\mathsf{Sol}(\chi)_{\mathcal{T}_\mathcal{S}, \mathcal{O}_\mathcal{S}}$ (where subscripts are occasionally omitted) the set of all objects appearing in $\mathsf{Sol}(\chi)_{\mathcal{T}_\mathcal{S}, \mathcal{O}_\mathcal{S}}$

Example 4.2.14 (CHAIN Revisited)   Reconsider the code call condition $\chi^{(3)}$ given in Example 4.2.8:

in(amount_available, supplier : *monitorStock*(U, part_008))   &
not_in(amount_available, supplier : *monitorStock*(U + 1, part_008)) &
in(amount_available, supplier : *monitorStock*(V, part_009))   &
not_in(amount_available, supplier : *monitorStock*(V + 1, part_009)) & U < V.

Suppose there are n units of part_008 on stock and m units of part_009, where $n < m$. Then, $\mathsf{Sol}(\chi^{(3)})$ is the singleton set containing the assignment U := n, V := m. However, if $n \geq m$, then $\mathsf{Sol}(\chi^{(3)})$ is empty, since there are no satisfying assignments.

Example 4.2.15 (STORE Revisited)   Reconsider the code call condition given in Example 4.2.9.

$\chi =_{def}$ **not_in**(spender(low), profiling : *classifyUser*(X)).

Furthermore, let S be the set of all social security numbers of users who are not classified as low spenders. Then, $\mathsf{Sol}(\chi) = \{\mathtt{X} := \mathtt{s_i} \mid \mathtt{s_i} \in S\}$.

4.2.6 An Assumption

We are now ready to introduce an important assumption we make in our book. As the reader surely knows, most legacy programs that manipulate a certain data structure have existing code to insert and delete objects from that data structure.

*Note 4 (Assumption on the Existence of **ins**, **del** and **upd**)* Throughout this book, we assume that the set $\mathcal{F}_S$ associated with a software code package S contains three functions described below:

- A function **ins**$_S$, which takes as input a set of objects $\mathcal{O}$ manipulated by S, and a state $\mathcal{O}_S$, and returns a new state $\mathcal{O}'_S = $ **ins**$_S(\mathcal{O}, \mathcal{O}_S)$ which accomplishes the insertion of the objects in $\mathcal{O}$ into $\mathcal{O}_S$, i.e., **ins**$_S$ is an insertion routine.
- A function **del**$_S$, which takes as input a set of objects $\mathcal{O}$ manipulated by S and a state $\mathcal{O}_S$, and returns a new state $\mathcal{O}'_S =_{def}$ **del**$_S(\mathcal{O}, \mathcal{O}_S)$ which describes the deletion of the objects in $\mathcal{O}$ from $\mathcal{O}_S$, i.e., **del**$_S$ is a deletion routine.
- A function **upd**$_S$ which takes as input a data object o manipulated by S, a field f of object o, and a value v drawn from the domain of the type of field f of object o—this function changes the value of the f field of object o to v. (This function can usually be described in terms of the preceding two functions.)

In the above three functions, it is possible to specify the first argument, $\mathcal{O}$, through a code-call atom or a code-call condition involving a single variable. Intuitively, suppose we execute the function, **ins**$_{\texttt{FinanceRecord}}(\chi[\texttt{X}])$ where $\chi[\texttt{X}]$ is a code call condition involving the (sole) free variable X. This may be interpreted as the statement: "*Insert, using a* `FinanceRecord` *insertion routine, all objects* o *such that* $\chi[\texttt{X}]$ *is true w.r.t. the current agent state when* X := o". In such a case, the code call condition χ is used to identify the objects to be inserted, and the **ins**$_{\texttt{FinanceRecord}}$ function specifies the insertion routine to be used.

Assuming the existence of such insertion and deletion routines is very reasonable—almost all implementations of data structures in computer science include insertion and deletion routines!

As a single agent program may manage multiple data types $\tau_1, \ldots, \tau_n$, each with its own insertion routine **ins**$_{\tau_1}, \ldots,$ **ins**$_{\tau_n}$, respectively, it is often more convenient to associate with any agent a an insertion routine, **ins**$_a$, that exhibits the following behavior: given either a set $\mathcal{O}$ of objects (or a code call condition $\chi[\texttt{X}]$ of the above type), **ins**$_a(\chi[\texttt{X}], \mathcal{O}_S)$ is a generic *method* that selects which of the insertion routines **ins**$_{\tau_i}$, associated with the different data structures, should be invoked in order to accomplish the desired insertion. A similar comment applies to deletion as well. Throughout the rest of this book, we will assume that an insertion function **ins**$_a$ and a deletion function **del**$_a$ may be

Section 4.3   The Message Box Domain

associated with any agent a in this way. Where a is clear from context, we will drop the subscript.

At this point, we have briefly shown how the mechanism of code-calls and code-call conditions provides a unified syntax within which different software packages and databases may be accessed through their application programmer interfaces. All the above code call mechanisms have been implemented by us.

4.3 The Message Box Domain

Throughout this book, we will assume that each agent's associated software code includes a special type called Msgbox (short for message box). The message box is a buffer that may be filled (when it sends a message) or flushed (when it reads the message) by the agent. In addition, we assume the existence of an operating-systems level messaging protocol (e.g. *SOCKETS* or *TCP/IP* (Wilder 1993)) that can fill in (with incoming messages) or flush (when a message is physically sent off) this buffer.

The msgbox operates on objects of the form (i/o, "src", "dest", "message", "time"). The parameter i/o signifies an incoming or outgoing message respectively. The variable "src" specifies the originator of the message whereas "dest" specifies the destination. The "message" is a table consisting of triples of the form ("varName", "varType", "value") where "varName" is the name of the variable, "varType" is the type of the variable and the "value" is the value of the variable in string format. Finally, "time" denotes the time at which the message was sent.

We will assume that the agent has the following functions that are integral in managing this message box. Note that over the years, we expect a wide variety of messaging languages to be developed (examples of such messaging languages include *KQML* (Labrou and Finin 1997b) at a high level, and remote procedure calls at a much lower level). In order to provide maximal flexibility, we only specify below the *core* interface functions available on the Msgbox type. Note that this set of functions may be augmented by the addition of other functions on an agent by agent basis.

- *sendMessage*(<*source_agent*>, <*dest_gent*>, <*message*>): This causes a quintuple (o, "src", "dest", "message", "time") to be placed in Msgbox. The parameter o signifies an outgoing message. When the call *sendMessage*("src", "dest", "message") is executed, the state of Msgbox changes by the insertion of the above quintuple denoting the sending of a message from the source agent src to a given Destination agent dest involving the message body "message".

- *getMessage(<src>)*: This causes a collection of quintuples

(i, "src", "agent", "msg", "time")

to be read from Msgbox. The i signifies an incoming message. Note that all messages from the given source to the agent $agent$ whose message box is being examined, are returned by this operation. "time" denotes the time at which the message was received.

- *timedGetMessage(<op>, <valid>)*: This causes the collection of all quintuples tup of the form $tup =_{def}$ (i, <src>, <agent>, <message>, time) to be read from Msgbox, such that the comparison tup.time op $valid$ is true, where op is required to be any of the standard comparison operators $<, >, \leq, \geq,$ or $=$.

- *getVar(<mssgId>, <varName>)*: This functions searches through all the triples in the "message" to find the requested variable. First, it converts the variable from the string format given by the "value" into its corresponding data type which is given by "varType". If the requested variable is not in the message determined by the "MssgId", then an error string is returned.

Example 4.3.1 When the supplier agent needs to find a supplier for a part, it might send a request to the plant agent for its find_supplier action. In response to this request, the plant agent might send the following message to the supplier agent;

(o, plant, supplier, (Part_supplier, "string", $ps1$), 4:35 pm)

Note that the message body contains only the triple (part_supplier, "string", $ps1$) because the only variable returned is Part_supplier. Any subsequent invocation of the supplier agent's to the code call **in**(supplier, msgbox : *getVar*(Msg.Id, "Part_supplier")) will return the value ps1 in Part_supplier.

Agents interact with the external world through the Msgbox code—in particular, external agents may update agent a's Msgbox, thus introducing new objects to agent a's state, and triggering state changes which are not triggered by agent a.

Throughout this book, we will assume that every agent has as part of its state the specialized type Msgbox, together with the code calls on this type defined here. As an example, consider the following interactions between agents in the STORE example.

Example 4.3.2 (STORE Revisited) Suppose the profiling agent is asked to classify a user U with ssn S. To do this, the profiling agent may need to obtain credit information for U from the credit agent. The following actions may ensue:

1. The profiling agent sends the credit agent a message requesting S's credit information.

2. The credit agent reads this message and sends the profiling agent a reply.

3. The profiling agent reads this reply and uses it to generate an answer.

Now, we consider how this interaction can take place by using message boxes:

1. The profiling agent is asked to *classifyUser*(S). It generates a message M_1 of a particular format, e.g., a string "ask_provideCreditInfo_S_low," which encodes the request for S's credit information, and calls *sendMessage*(profiling, credit, M_1).

2. The credit agent either periodically calls *getMessage*(profiling) until M_1 arrives, or calls it triggered by the event that M_1 has arrived. By parsing M_1, it determines that it needs to execute *provideCreditInfo*(S, low) and send the result back to profiling. Depending on the result of the call, credit assembles a message M_2 encoding the FinanceRecord which was returned, or an error message. Here, we are assuming that the underlying OS level message protocol does not drop or reorder messages (if it did, we would have to include M_1 and M_1's *Time* in M_2's message). Next, the credit agent calls *sendMessage*(credit, profiling, M_2).

3. The profiling agent either periodically calls *getMessage*(credit) until M_2 arrives, or it is triggered by the arrival of M_2 and reads the message. By parsing M_2, it can determine what errors (if any) occurred or what the resulting finance_record was. Finally, the profiling agent can use the contents of M_2 to construct the UserProfile to be returned.

Suppose the credit agent *goes down* for a few hours but its message box remains functional. When the credit agent *starts up* again at 3:46:00pm 5/30/2001, it may want to only process messages sent in the last 5 minutes (all others may be regarded as obsolete). In this case, the credit agent may want to call the routine

timedGetMessage($\geq$, 3 : 41 : 00pm 5/30/2001).

4.4 Integrity Constraints

As we have already noted, at any given point t in time, each agent has an associated *agent state*. The state is a set of objects (of the types that the software code underlying the agent manages). Not all sets of such objects are *legal*. In this section, we will argue that only certain pieces of software code, namely those that satisfy certain *integrity constraints*, reflect permissible states. Agent integrity constraints specify properties that states of the agent must satisfy. The concept of an agent integrity constraint generalizes the concept of an integrity constraint studied in relational databases to the case of arbitrary data structures.

DEFINITION 4.4.1 (INTEGRITY CONSTRAINTS $\mathcal{IC}$) An *integrity constraint IC* is an expression of the form

$$\psi \Rightarrow \chi$$

where ψ is a safe code call condition, and χ is an atomic code call condition such that every root variable in χ occurs in ψ.

Note that the safety requirement on the precondition of an integrity constraint guarantees a mechanism to evaluate the precondition of an integrity constraint whose head is grounded.

The following examples show the integrity constraints that some of the agents associated with the motivating examples must satisfy.

Example 4.4.1 (CHAIN Revisited) The following integrity constraint says that the amount of part_008 available is at least as high as the sum of the number of part_001 available and the number of part_002 available:

IC_1 : **in**(amount_available, supplier : *monitorStock*(U, part_001)) &
  in(amount_available, supplier : *monitorStock*(V, part_002))
    $\Rightarrow$
  in(amount_available, supplier : *monitorStock*(U + V, part_008)).

The integrity constraint below says that at least three units of part_008 must always be available:

IC_2 : P = *part*_008 $\Rightarrow$ **in**(amount_available, supplier : *monitorStock*(3, P)).

Example 4.4.2 (STORE Revisited) The following integrity constraint says that the person with ssn 123_45_6789 is not a low spender:

IC_3 : S = 123_45_6789 $\Rightarrow$ **not_in**(spender(low), profiling : *classifyUser*(S)).

The integrity constraint below says that if a user is classified as a medium spender, then this user should not be classified as a high spender:

IC_4 : **in**(spender(medium), profiling : *classifyUser*(S)))
    $\Rightarrow$
  not_in(spender(high), profiling : *classifyUser*(S)).

Example 4.4.3 (CFIT Revisited) Recall that the type SatelliteReport (see 4.1.3 on page 78) comprises fields height, sat_id, dist, and 2dloc, where the last one is a record with fields x and y.

The following integrity constraint says that if report R stems from satellite sat_1, then the x coordinate of the current plane location must be positive:

IC_5 : R.sat_id = sat_1 $\Rightarrow$ R.2dloc.x $\geq$ 0.

The following integrity constraint says that if any satellite reports R1 and R2 contain the same coordinates, then they must contain the same height of the ground:

IC_6 : R1.2dloc.x = R2.2dloc.x & R1.2dloc.y = R2.2dloc.y
$$\Rightarrow$$
R1.height = R2.height

DEFINITION 4.4.2 (INTEGRITY CONSTRAINT SATISFACTION) A state $\mathcal{O}_S$ satisfies an integrity constraint *IC* of the form $\psi \Rightarrow \chi$, denoted $\mathcal{O}_S \models IC$, if for every legal assignment of objects from $\mathcal{O}_S$ to the variables in *IC*, either ψ is false or χ is true.

Let $\mathcal{IC}$ be a (finite) collection of integrity constraints *IC*, and let $\mathcal{O}_S$ be an agent state. We say that $\mathcal{O}_S$ satisfies $\mathcal{IC}$, denoted $\mathcal{O}_S \models \mathcal{IC}$, if and only if $\mathcal{O}_S$ satisfies every constraint $IC \in \mathcal{IC}$.

Let us revisit the integrity constraints associated with the STORE, CHAIN, and CFIT examples described above. The following examples illustrate the notion of *satisfaction* of these constraints.

Example 4.4.4 (CHAIN Revisited) Suppose two units each of part_001 and part_002 are available, and that five units of typepart_008 are in stock. Then, the first integrity constraint IC_1 of Example 4.4.1 is satisfied as both ψ and χ are true. IC_2 is not satisfied as ψ is true and χ is false.

Example 4.4.5 (STORE Revisited) Suppose the user with ssn 123_45_6789 is a low spender. Then the integrity constraint IC_3 of Example 4.4.2 is not satisfied as ψ is true and χ is false. However, IC_4 is satisfied as ψ is (vacuously) true and χ is true.

Example 4.4.6 (CFIT Revisited) Suppose R is the satellite report R = $\langle 50, 2, 25, \langle 4, -3 \rangle \rangle$, and this is the only report of satellite 2. Then, the integrity constraint IC_5 of Example 4.4.3 is satisfied as R.sat_id := 2, and as R.2dloc.x $\geq$ 0 is true.

Let R' := $\langle 45, 1, 25, \langle 4, -3 \rangle \rangle$ be another satellite report. Then, the integrity constraint IC_6 of Example 4.4.3 is not satisfied, as R1 := R and R2 := R', it is thus the case that ψ is true while χ is false.

4.5 Some Syntactic Sugar

In this section, we introduce two types of syntactic sugar that we use throughout this book. The first involves an **is**(,) predicate, while the second involves syntactic sugar to handle polymorphic functions. Neither of these syntactic extensions of the code call condition mechanism increase the expressive power of code call conditions, but do significantly increase the ease of expressing various conditions.

4.5.1 The is(,) Construct

We may extend the definition of a code call atom to say that if $\mathcal{S} : f(d_1, \ldots, d_n)$ is a code call, then **is**(X, $\mathcal{S} : f(d_1, \ldots, d_n)$) is a code-call atom such that X is the set of all objects returned by the function f. Thus, if f's output type is τ, i.e., f returns a set of objects of type τ, the variable X ranges over objects of type $\{\tau\}$.

Notice that **is**(X, $\mathcal{S} : f(d_1, \ldots, d_n)$) is in fact representable via an ordinary code call. Suppose we associate with f, a function f_{set} such that:

$$f_{set}(d_1, \ldots, d_n) =_{def} \{\{o \mid \mathbf{in}(o, \mathcal{S} : f(d_1, \ldots, d_n))\}\}.$$

In this case, $f_{set}(d_1, \ldots, d_n)$ always contains a single element—namely the set containing all answers of $f(d_1, \ldots, d_n)$. Thus, **is**(X, $\mathcal{S} : f(d_1, \ldots, d_n)$) is shorthand for the code call:

in(X, $\mathcal{S} : f_{set}(d_1, \ldots, d_n)$).

4.5.2 Polymorphic Code Calls

An important property to note is that in the real world, many *API* functions are polymorphic. For example, relational databases may be viewed as domains whose set of associated data types contain some "primitive" or "user defined" types, together with all record types constructible from these primitive types. However, expressing the relational algebra *functions* as domain functions is complex, as we shall see below.

Consider the function SELECT. When SELECT is applied to a relation, the output relation has the same schema as the input relation. That is, if we think of SELECT as a binary function taking as input, a condition (boolean expression) C and a relation R of type τ (or equivalently schema $(A_1, \ldots, A_n)$), then the output type of the resulting selection is also τ (i.e., $(A_1, \ldots, A_n)$).

Now consider the function PROJECT. This too is a binary function that takes as input, a set of attributes S, and a relation R of type τ (or schema $(A_1, \ldots, A_n)$). It returns as output, a relation of type τ' obtained by restricting the schema $(A_1, \ldots, A_n)$ to the attributes mentioned in S.

Section 4.5 Some Syntactic Sugar

Table 4.1
The **apply** Function

Operation	Argument 1	Argument 2
Selection	Boolean Expression	relation name
Projection	Set of attributes	relation name
Cartesian Product	relation name	relation name
Union	relation name	relation name
Intersection	relation name	relation name
Difference	relation name	relation name

In both the above cases, the type of the output of a relational operator is derived from the inputs of the relational operator. The reader can readily verify that the Cartesian Product operator concatenates the types of the two input relations involved, and the same holds for all other relational algebra operators.

As a consequence, we may think of the relational domain as consisting of a single higher order function called **apply**—this function takes as input, two arguments—a relational algebra operator, and a *list* of arguments to that operation. Table 4.1 describes this.

Suppose $\mathcal{BT}$ is a set of *base types* used in a relational database system—these may include not only the standard data types such as `char`, `integer`, `string`, etc. but also some set of user or application defined types. Let $\mathcal{BT}_s$ denote the smallest set satisfying the following conditions:

- Every type in $\mathcal{BT}$ is a type in $\mathcal{BT}_s$;
- For all integers $k \geq 1$, if $\tau_1, \tau_2, \ldots, \tau_k$ are in $\mathcal{BT}$, then $\tau_1 \times \tau_2, \ldots, \tau_k$ is in $\mathcal{BT}_s$.

Then the function **apply** is a mapping whose first argument is the union of the types in column 1 of the above table, and whose second argument is a list consisting of two parts—the first is any entry from the second column of the above table, while the third is any data type in $\mathcal{BT}_s$. The output type of **apply** may now be defined as follows.

We will often abuse notation in this book. Instead of writing

relation : **apply**(operation, [arguments])

we will often just write

relation : *operation*(arguments).

Similar methods may be used to encode the polymorphic behavior of functions in non-relational settings.

Table 4.2
Output Type of **apply**

Operation	List Element 1	List Element 2	Output Type
Selection	Condition	relation name	schema of relation
Projection	Set of attributes	relation name	Product of attribute types
Cartesian Product	relation name	relation name	$\tau_1 \times \tau_2$ where τ_i is the type of List Element i
Union	relation name	relation name	τ_1 where $\tau_1 = \tau_2$
Intersection	relation name	relation name	τ_1 where $\tau_1 = \tau_2$
Difference	relation name	relation name	τ_1 where $\tau_1 = \tau_2$

4.6 Linking Service Descriptions and Code Calls

In the preceding chapter, we said that each agent has an associated set of *service descriptions*. In this chapter, we have independently introduced the concept of a code call condition. We now briefly describe how these two concepts are *linked*.

DEFINITION 4.6.1 (SERVICE RULE) Suppose sn is the name of a service offered by an agent. Let $i_1, \ldots, i_k, mi_1, \ldots, mi_m$, and $o_1, \ldots, o_n$ be the inputs, mandatory inputs, and outputs of the service sn, respectively. A *service rule defining sn* is an expression of the form:

$$sn(i_1, \ldots, i_k, mi_1, \ldots, mi_m, o_1, \ldots, o_n) \leftarrow \chi$$

where χ is a code call condition that is safe modulo $mi_1, \ldots, mi_m$. In this case, χ is said to be the *body* of the above rule.

It is *important* to note that the body of a service rule consists of a code call condition that is safe with respect to the mandatory inputs of sn. This makes sense, because an agent requesting the service named sn must supply all mandatory inputs, and hence, the agent providing service sn must be able to execute the code call condition χ when only these mandatory inputs are specified. This is what the above definition accomplishes.

DEFINITION 4.6.2 (SERVICE DEFINITION PROGRAM sdp) Using the same notation as above, a *service definition program* (**sdp** for short) associated with service sn is a finite set of service rules defining sn.

Consider a service sn defined through a service definition program containing r rules. Let the body of the i'th rule be $\chi^{(i)}$. Suppose an agent specifies the mandatory inputs, i.e., an agent requesting this service specifies a substitution θ that assigns objects to each of the variables $mi_1, \ldots, mi_m$. In addition, the agent may specify a substitution δ for the discretionary inputs.

Then the service definition program treats the agent's request for service *sn* as described in algorithm **implement_service**.

Algorithm 4.6.1 (implement_service)
implement_service(P:sdp; μ:subs; δ:subst)

($\star$ P is a service definition program $\star$)
($\star$ μ is a substitution specifying values of all mandatory inputs $\star$)
($\star$ δ is a substitution specifying values of selected discretionary input variables $\star$)
($\star$ *Ans* (the output answer) is the result of evaluating P w.r.t. inputs μ and δ $\star$)

1. $Ans := \emptyset$; $Q := P$;
2. **while** $Q \neq \emptyset$ **do**
3. { select rule $r_i \in Q$;
4. $Q := Q \setminus \{r_i\}$;
5. $SOL := \text{Sol}((\chi)\mu\delta)$;
6. ($\star$ this returns a set of substitutions, one for each variable of *sn* $\star$)
7. ($\star$ that is not assigned an object by either of μ, δ $\star$)
8. restrict *SOL* to output variables;
9. $Ans := Ans \cup SOL$;
10. }
11. **return** *Ans*;
end.

4.7 Example Service Description Programs

We are now ready to see a few example sdp's from our three motivating examples. For each of these sdp's, we will see how services are processed by our system. Specifically, we make use of the *HERMES* Heterogeneous Reasoning and Mediator System implemented previously at the University of Maryland (Adali, Candan, Papakonstantinou, and Subrahmanian 1996). *HERMES* is a system that supports constructing *mediators*. The phrase mediator was originally introduced in Wiederhold (1993) to refer to a program that intregrated multiple databases. *HERMES* provides a platform for building mediators for different data/software integration applications. *HERMES* mediators consist of rules of the form

$A \leftarrow \chi \ \& \ B_1, \ \& \ldots \& \ B_n$

where $A, B_1, \ldots, B_n$ are atoms in classical logic (Lloyd 1987) and χ is a code call condition. Figure 4.1 on the following page shows a sample listing of *HERMES* mediators.

Example 4.7.1 (STORE Revisited) In *HERMES*, each sdp for the STORE example can be thought of as a predicate within the mediator for one of STORE's agents. Some sample

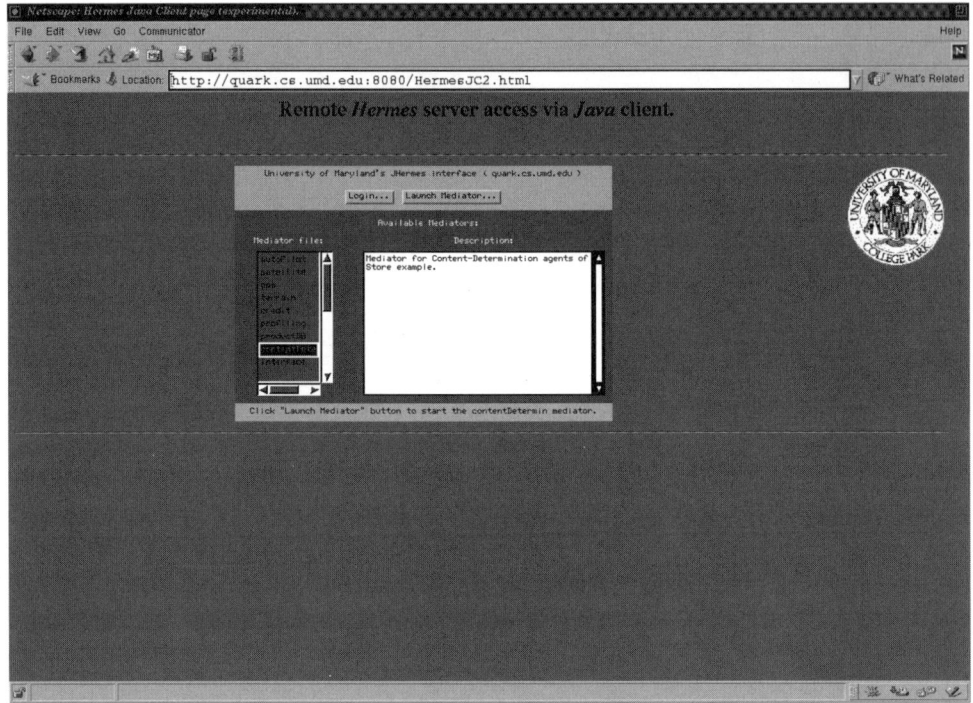

Figure 4.1
Sample *HERMES* mediators.

predicates, a sample query, and sample query results for the profiling agent are shown in Figures 4.2 on the next page and 4.3 on page 102. A sample sdp is:

goodSpender(⟨MI⟩*Category* : UserCat⟨\MI⟩
⟨O⟩*SSN* : ListOfStrings, *Class* : UserProfile⟨\O⟩)
←
in(SSN, profiling : *listUsers*(Category)) &
in(Class, profiling : *classifyUser*(SSN)) &
not_in(spender(low), general : *makeSet*(Class)).

A *HERMES* invocation of this sdp is shown in Figure 4.2. The query

goodSpender(corporateUsers, Ssn, Class)

Section 4.7   Example Service Description Programs   101

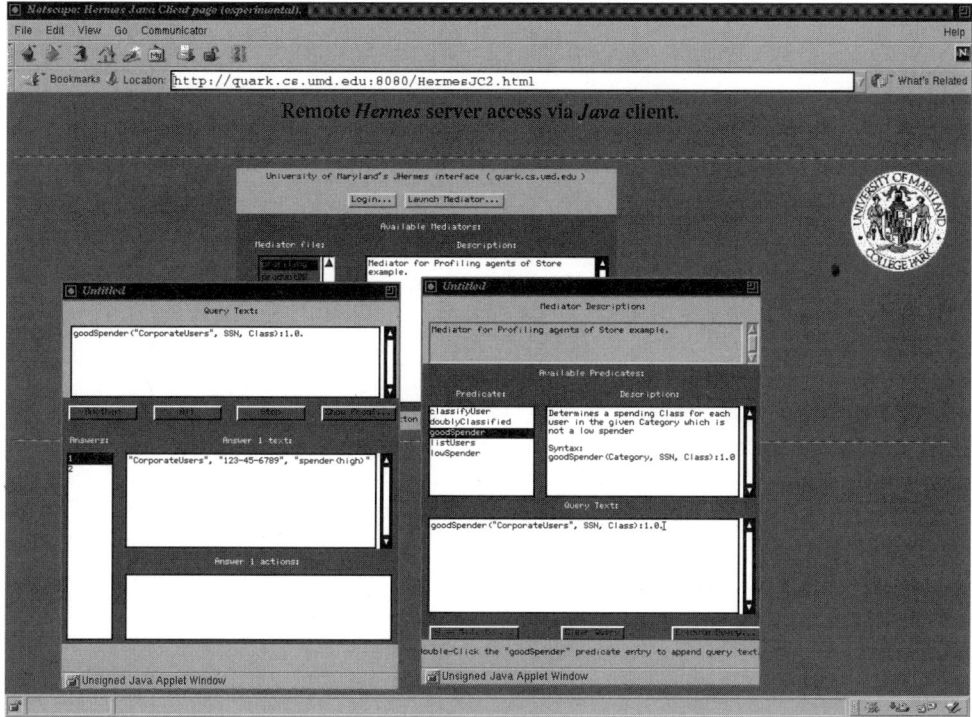

Figure 4.2
Sample query on the profiling agent's mediator (first result).

asks for the ssn and class of all corporate users who are not low spenders. First

profiling : *listUsers*(Category)

is invoked to return all ssn's for the given Category. For each ssn returned, we invoke

profiling : *classifyUser*(Ssn)

to determine the user's spending Class. Finally, we ensure that this Class is not spender(low). Note that as the second parameter of the **not_in** must be a set, we use the function general : *makeSet*(Class) to turn Class into a singleton set.

The two results for the query above are shown in Figures 4.2 and 4.3.

Now consider the following query on the same **sdp**:

goodSpender(corporateUsers, 123_45_6789, Class).

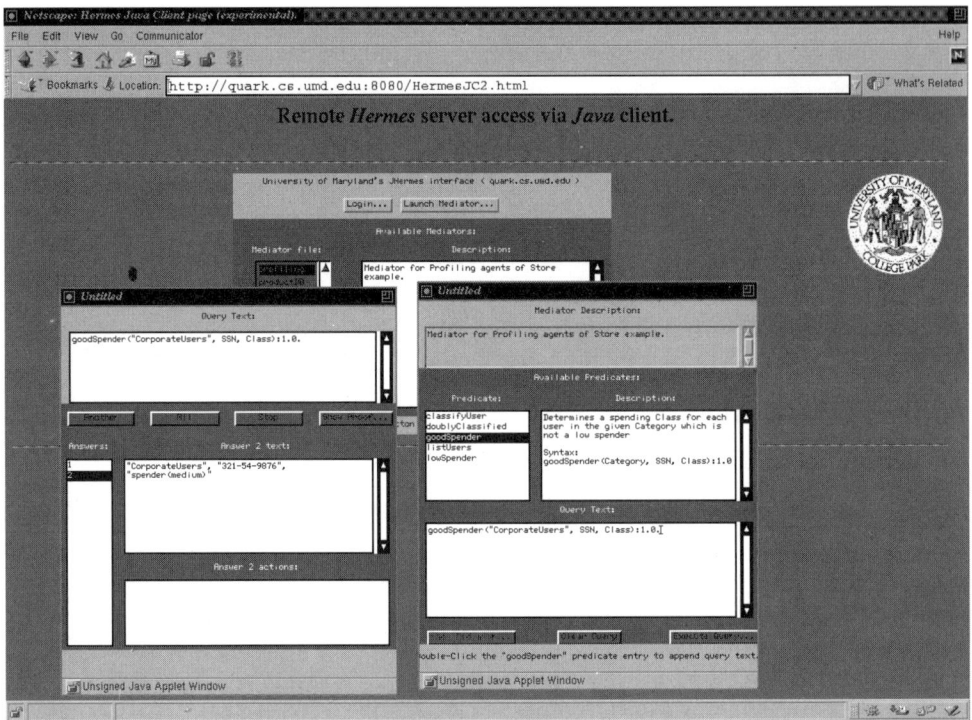

Figure 4.3
Sample Queries on goodSpender Predicate and profiling Agent's Mediator.

Here, as we are instantiating a value for ssn, the first **in** above is not satisfied by the ssn 321_54_9876, so we only retain one result for the entire query (i.e., the one shown in Figure 4.2).

Example 4.7.2 (CFIT Revisited) A sample query on the mediator for the autoPilot agent of the CFIT example is shown in Figure 4.4 on the next page. A sample sdp is:

tooLow($\langle$MI$\rangle$X: Integer, *CutOff*: Integer$\langle$\MI$\rangle$) $\leftarrow$ X.height < CutOff.
tooLow($\langle$MI$\rangle$X: Integer, *CutOff*: Integer$\langle$\MI$\rangle$) $\leftarrow$ X.dist < 50.

Here, the plane in satellite report X is too low if it is flying below the CutOff altitude or if its distance from the ground is less than 50 meters. In general, one can perform an OR by

Section 4.7 Example Service Description Programs 103

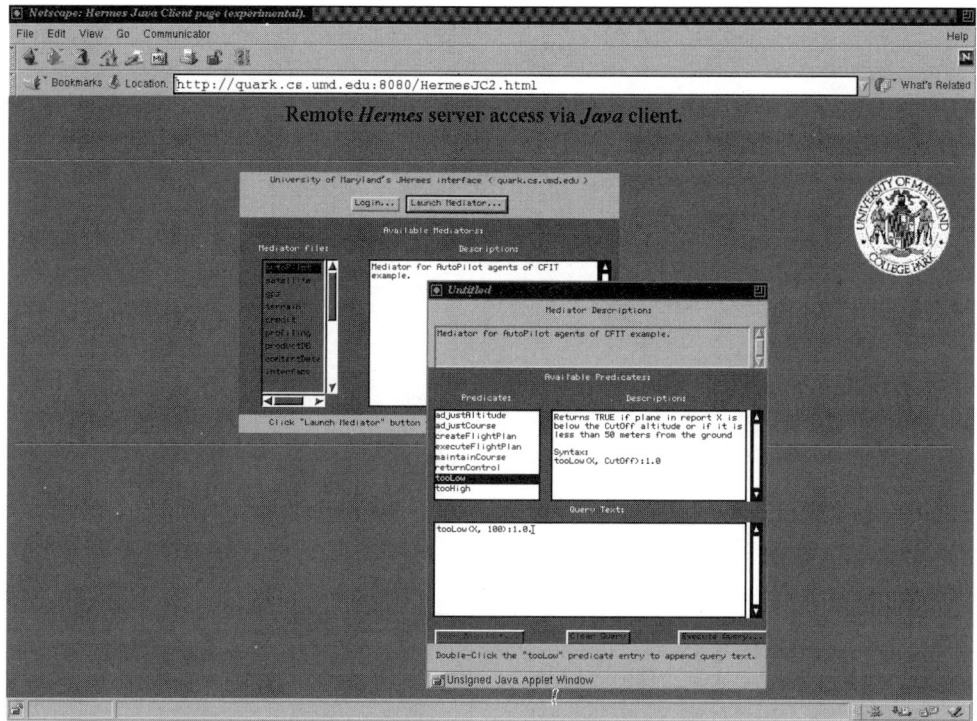

Figure 4.4
Sample query on the autoPilot agent's mediator.

defining two predicates with the same name and similar parameters. Suppose for instance that X.height := 100 and X.dist := 75. Then the query

tooLow(X, 110)

would evaluate to true as the first predicate is satisfied. However, *tooLow*(X, 90) evaluates to false as neither predicate is satisfied. Now if X.height := 100 and X.dist := 40, the same query *tooLow*(X, 90) would evaluate to true; even if the first predicate is not satisfied, the second one is satisfied. Finally, note that

tooLow(X, 170)

evaluates to true as both predicates are satisfied.

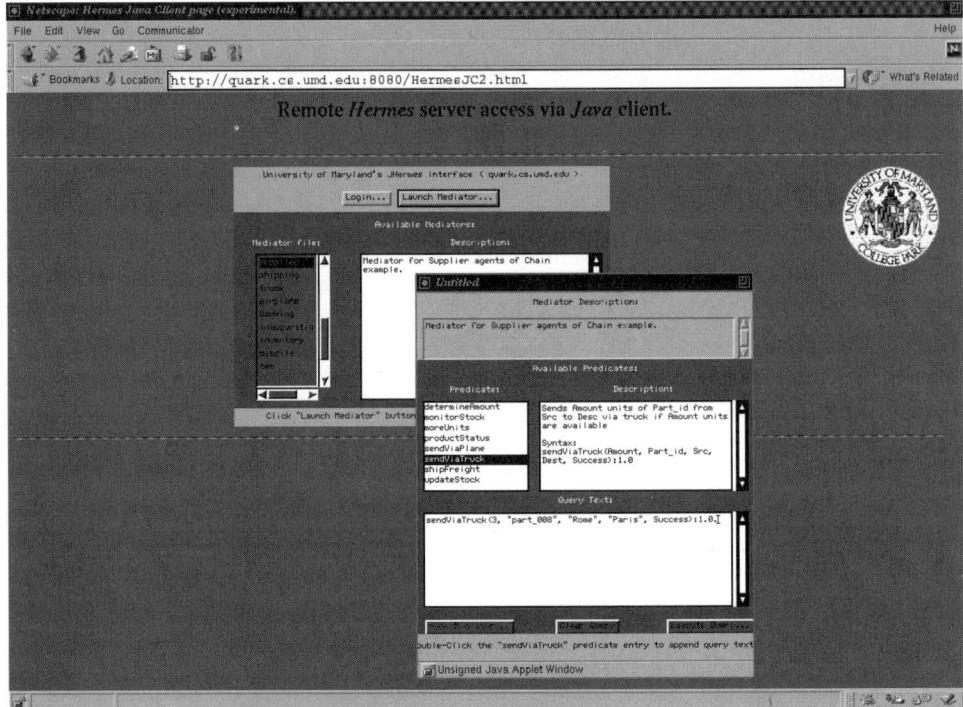

Figure 4.5
Sample query on the supplier agent's mediator.

Example 4.7.3 (CHAIN Revisited) A sample query on the mediator for the supplier agent of the CHAIN example is shown in Figure 4.5. A sample sdp is:

$sendViaTruck(\langle\text{MI}\rangle Amount:\texttt{Integer}, Part\_id:\texttt{String}\langle\backslash\text{MI}\rangle$
$\quad\quad\quad\langle\text{MI}\rangle Src:\texttt{String}, Dest:\texttt{String}\langle\backslash\text{MI}\rangle$
$\quad\quad\quad\langle\text{O}\rangle Success:\texttt{Boolean}\langle\backslash\text{O}\rangle)$
$\quad\quad\quad\leftarrow$
$\quad\quad\quad\textbf{in}(\texttt{amount\_available}, supplier:monitorStock(\texttt{Amount}, \texttt{Part\_id}))\ \&$
$\quad\quad\quad\textbf{in}(\texttt{Success}, supplier:shipFreight(\texttt{Amount}, \texttt{Part\_id}, \texttt{truck}, \texttt{Src}, \texttt{Dest})).$

Here, we ship Amount units of Part_id from Src to Dest via truck, if Amount units are available. If the call to *shipFreight* was successful, it will return **true**. If not enough units were available, then the entire sdp will not be satisfied. Finally, if enough units were available but they could not be shipped, Success will be set to **false**.

For instance, suppose 5 units of part_008 are available. Then the query

sendViaTruck(3, *part_008, rome, paris,* Success)

will be satisfied and Success will be **true**, if the shipping was possible. Note, however, that the query

sendViaTruck(7, *part_008, rome, paris,* Success)

will not be satisfied, as the first **in**(,) above was not satisfied and hence the second **in**(,) above was never called.

4.8 Related Work

In this section, we will briefly overview work on techniques to access heterogeneous data sources. Over the last decade, several approaches have been proposed to provide access to legacy data. Liu, Yan, and Ozsu (1997) classify large-scale interoperable distributed information delivery systems into two architectural classes: multidatabase management paradigm and mediator based paradigms. Multidatabase systems focus on providing access to a set of heterogeneous database and include *MULTIBASE* (Dayal 1983; Dayal and Hwang 1984), *Pegasus* (Ahmed, R., et al, 1991), *MIND* (Dogac, A., et al. 1996a; Dogac, A., et al. 1996b) and *IRO-DB* (Fankhauser, Finance, and Klas 1996). Furthermore, the importance of multidatabases is highlighted by commercial products, IBM's *DataJoiner* (Gupta and Lin 1994) and Microsoft's *OLE*-DB (Blakeley 1996; Blakeley and Pizzo 1998). Mediator based systems, on the other hand, focus on providing access to a set of diverse data sources, including non-database sources. These efforts include *HERMES* (Adali, Candan, Papakonstantinou, and Subrahmanian 1996), *TSIMMIS* (Chawathe, S., et al. 1994 Garcia-Molina, H., et al. 1997), *Garlic* (Carey, M. J., et al. 1995; Tork Roth, M., et al. 1996), DISCO (Tomasic, Raschid, and Valduriez 1998), *SIMS* (Arens, Chee, Hsu, and Knoblock 1993), *InfoSleuth* (Bayardo, R., et al. 1997) and *Carnot* (Woelk, Cannata, Huhns, Shen, and Tomlinson 1993).

HERMES (Adali, Candan, Papakonstantinou, and Subrahmanian 1996) integrates diverse data sources by modeling each source as a collection of domains. *HERMES* provides mediators that collect and combine information from a set of data sources.

The *TSIMMIS* project (Chawathe, S., et al. 1994 Garcia-Molina, H., et al. 1997) is a mediator system which provides an architecture and tools to access multiple heterogeneous information sources by translating source information into a common self-describing object-model, called *Object Exchange Model* (*OEM*). *TSIMMIS* supports rapid integration of heterogeneous information sources that may include both structured and unstructured data.

Integrated access to diverse information sources are achieved through a layer of source specific translators as well as mediators. Translators convert queries specified in the common model (*OEM*), into the native format of the underlying data source. Mediators collect information from informations sources, process and combine that information, and provide the results to an end-user or an application program. *TSIMMIS* does not aim to perform fully automated information integration that hides diversity from the user. *TSIMMIS* also has components that extract data from WWW and allow browsing of data sources over the Web.

Garlic (Carey, M. J., et al. 1995; Tork Roth, M., et al. 1996) is an ongoing project at IBM Almaden Research Center, which aims at integrating diverse data sources, including multimedia databases. It provides an object-oriented data model to express a unified schema which can be queried and manipulated by an object-oriented dialect of SQL. Data sources are integrated by means of wrappers, which participate in query processing, and translate information about data types and requests between Garlic's protocols and underlying repository's native protocols. *Garlic* aims at enabling the integration of data sources while maintaining the independence of data servers. The focus of *Garlic* is on extensibility and diverse data sources. *Garlic* is a query processor which optimizes and executes queries over diverse data sources.

DISCO (Tomasic, Raschid, and Valduriez 1998) is also a system that provides integration of heterogeneous data sources. The *DISCO* mediator data model is based on the ODMG-93 data model specification. It extends the *ODMG* ODL with two constructs: *extents* and *type mapping*. *DISCO* describes the set of queries using context-free grammars and uses a wrapper grammar to match queries. Query processing in *DISCO* is performed by cooperating between mediators and wrappers. Moreover, *DISCO* addresses the problem of executing a query when not all data sources are available.

SIMS (Arens, Chee, Hsu, and Knoblock 1993) is a broker and a mediator, that provides an interface between human users or application programs and the information sources to which they need access. It determines which data sources to use, how to obtain the desired information, how and where to temporarily store and manipulate data. *SIMS* employs *LOOM*, *LIM* and *KQML* as the technological infrastructure. *LOOM* serves as the knowledge representation system *SIMS* uses to describe the domain model and the contents of the information sources. In addition, *LOOM* is used to define a knowledge base that itself serves as an information source. *LOOM* provides both a language and an environment for constructing intelligent applications and provides some reasoning facilities. *LIM* (*LOOM* Interface Module) is used to mediate between *LOOM* and databases. *LIM* reads a database schema and uses it to build a *LOOM* representation of the database. *SIMS* employs *KQML* (Knowledge Query Manipulation Language) which is a language for agent-to-agent communications. *KQML* handles the interface protocols for transmitting queries, returning the appropriate information, and building the necessary structures.

The *Carnot* Project (Woelk, Cannata, Huhns, Shen, and Tomlinson 1993) is addressing the problem of logically unifying physically distributed, enterprise wide, heterogeneous information. *Carnot* provides a user with the means to navigate information efficiently and transparently, to update that information consistently, and to write applications easily for large, heterogeneous, distributed information systems. Communication services provide the user with a uniform method of interconnecting heterogeneous equipment and resources. These services implement and integrate various communication platforms that may occur within an enterprise. *Carnot* provides a declarative resource constraint base to build work flow scripts designed to carry out some business function. The Flex transaction model provides tools to specify intertask dependencies that exist in a workflow. *Carnot* enables the development and use of distributed, knowledge-based, communicating agents. The agents are high-performance expert systems that communicate and cooperate with each other, and with human agents, in solving problems. The agents interact by using Carnot's actor-based Extensible Services Switch (ESS) to manage their communications through *TCP/IP* and *OSI*. Thus, they can be located wherever appropriate within and among enterprises, in fact, anywhere that is reachable through the *Carnot* communication services. *Carnot* project developed semantic modeling techniques that enabled integration of static information resources and employed agents to provide interoperation among autonomous systems.

The goal of *InfoSleuth* (Bayardo et al. 1997) is to exploit and synthesize new technologies into a unified system that retrieves and processes information in an ever-changing network of information. *InfoSleuth* has its roots in the Carnot project which is specialized in integrating heterogeneous information sources. The problem addressed by *InfoSleuth* is the following; There is no formal control over the registration of new information sources, and applications tend to be developed without complete knowledge of the resources that will be available when they run. Federated database projects such as Carnot that do static data integration do not scale up and do not cope well with ever-changing environment. On the other hand, recent Web technologies are incapable of accessing information based on concepts, although they scale up. *InfoSleuth* integrates new technological developments such as agent technology, domain ontologies, brokerage, and internet computing, in support of mediated interoperation of data and services in a dynamic and open environment. Specialized agents that represent the users, the information resources, and the system itself cooperate to address the information processing requirements of the users, allowing easy, dynamic reconfiguration of system capabilities. Adding a new information source implies adding a new agent and advertising its capabilities. Ontologies give a concise, uniform, and declarative description of semantic information. Specialized broker agents semantically match information needs (specified in terms of some ontology) with currently available resources, so retrieval and update requests are only routed to relevant resources. Finally, Java and Java applets are used to provide users and administrators with system-independent user interfaces. *InfoSleuth* employs the following specialized agents; user agent, ontology agent, broker agent, resource agent, data analysis agent, task execution agent and monitor agent. Moreover, it uses *KQML* as the agent communication language. *InfoSleuth* also do not perform imprecise matching of services to requests.

The use of knowledge base in the above systems is to integrate the diverse data sources, i.e., they are mainly employed for semantic data integration. Moreover, none of these systems provides imprecise querying capabilities in terms of service brokering.

IMPACT agents require access to heterogeneous data sources. In this book, we employ *HERMES* (Adali, Candan, Papakonstantinou, and Subrahmanian 1996) as the underlying framework to access heterogeneous data sources. However, any of the mediator systems discussed in this section can be employed fairly easily. The only requirement is that they provide an *API* call to pose queries and an interface to retrieve the results of those queries.

One proposed solution to the problem of integrating a set of distributed, heterogeneous data sources is distributed object management (Ozsu, Dayal, and Valduries 1994; Manola, F., et al. 1992), which we discuss next.

4.8.1 Distributed Object Management

Manola, F., et al. (1992) state that modeling heterogeneous systems as a distributed set of objects provides an appropriate framework for interoperability. As objects communicate with each other using messages, they form a convenient mechanism to model heterogeneous autonomous distributed systems (Manola, F., et al. 1992). As each object's internals are hidden and accessed through its interface, this approach allows objects to interoperate with each other. (Ozsu, Dayal, and Valduries 1994) contains several papers that discuss various issues of distributed object management.

One important commercial standard enabling interoperability between heterogeneous systems is *OMG*'s Object Management Architecture (OMA), (Vinoski 1997; Soley and Stone 1995; OMG 1997). The Object Management Group (*OMG*) was founded as a non-profit organization with the aim of promoting theory and practice of object-oriented technology in software development. The main objective of *OMG* is to establish industry guidelines, create and popularize object management standards for application development based on existing technology. Furthermore, *OMG* plans to achieve this goal through the introduction of an architectural framework which contains detailed interface specifications which will drive the industry toward interoperable, reusable, and portable software components based on standard object-oriented interfaces.

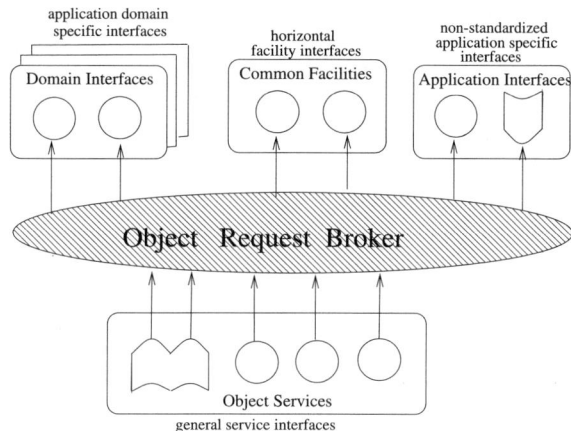

Figure 4.6
OMA Reference Model.

OMG defines the object management paradigm as the ability to encapsulate data and methods. This models the "real world" through representations of program components called *objects*. In this way, it is possible to encapsulate all legacy code within objects and represent legacy data sources as objects. Then, access to legacy data will be achieved through method invocations which are internally *API* calls of the underlying data source. This representation results in faster application development, easier maintenance, reduced program complexity, and reusable components.

OMG's OMA Reference Model, which has 5 main components (Soley and Stone 1995; OMG 1997), is given in Figure 4.6. The Object Request Broker (ORB) component of the Object Management Architecture is the communications heart of the standard. The *CORBA* component, which is discussed in greater detail below, will guarantee portability and interoperability of objects over a network of heterogeneous system.

The other four components are object interfaces, including (OMG 1998a):

Object Services: These are domain-independent interfaces that may be used by many different distributed object programs, (OMG 1998a). Object Services include life-cycle management of objects, such as delete, copy and create; management of object implementations; replication and archive management; security; transactions; query services; and many others. Two of the possibly most widely used services are the Naming Service and the Trading Service. Object Services will be discussed in Section 4.8.3.

Common Facilities: These are a set of generic application functions that can be configured to the requirements of a specific configuration.

Domain Interfaces: These interfaces are oriented towards specific application domains. For example, the Product Data Management Enablers is geared toward product data management.

Application Interfaces: are developed for specific applications.

All interfaces communicate through the ORB, and applications need only provide or use OMA-compliant interfaces to participate in the Object Management Architecture.

4.8.2 Common Object Request Broker Architecture (*CORBA*)

CORBA is the core communication mechanism which enables distributed objects to operate on each other. In *CORBA*, objects communicate with other objects via an *ORB*. Brokering involves target object location, message delivery, and method binding. In this model, clients send requests to the *ORB* asking for certain services to be performed by any server that can fulfill those needs. In *CORBA* only the *ORB* knows about the implementation details and actual locations of the components in the system. Clients and servers only need to know the interfaces of the components. All a *CORBA* client knows about the target object is its interface and its object reference. The interface determines the valid operations on a particular object. The structure of the *ORB* is given in Figure 4.7 (OMG 1998a).

Interfaces are defined using Interface Definition Language (*IDL*). An *IDL* interface declares a set of client accessible operations, exceptions, and typed attributes. *IDL* resembles

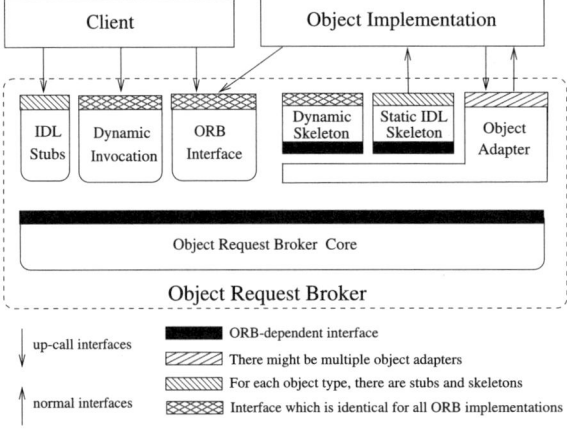

Figure 4.7
Structure of ORB.

a declarative subset of C++, but it is not a programming language. To use or implement an interface, the interface must be translated, or mapped, into corresponding elements of a particular programming language. Currently, *IDL* mappings to the C, C++, Smalltalk, COBOL, Ada and Java programming languages are available (OMG 1998a). We consider below, some example *IDL* definitions.

Example 4.8.1 (Interface Definitions for CHAIN, STORE and CFIT) The following are example interface definitions for the CHAIN, STORE, and CFIT examples respectively.

```
module CHAIN{
        struct date{
                short day;
                short month;
                short year;
        };
        struct orderLog{
                string client;
                short amount;
                string part_id;
                string method;
                Location src;
                Location dst;
                date pickup_st;
                date pickup_et;
        };
        exception UserException{
                string errMsg;
        };
        // supplier interface
        interface Supplier{
                void monitorStock(in short amount,
                                in string part_id,
                                out string status)
                        raises (UserException);
                void shipFreight(in short amount,
                                in string part_id,
                                in string method,
                                in Location src,
                                in Location dst)
```

```
                    raises (UserException);
                void updateStock(in short amount,
                                in string part_id)
                    raises (UserException);
        }; // end of supplier interface
}; // end of module CHAIN

module STORE{
        enum UserProfile{
                HIGH_SPENDER,
                LOW_SPENDER,
                AVERAGE_SEPENDER};
        exception UserException{
                string errMsg;
        };
        // profiling agent interface
        interface ProfilingAgent{
                void classifyUser(in string Ssn,
                                out Profile UserProfile)
                    raises (UserException);
                void provideUserProfile(in string Ssn,
                                out Profile UserProfile)
                    raises (UserException);
        }; // end of profiling agent interface
}; // end of module STORE

module CFIT{
        exception UserException{
            string errMsg;
        };
        // autoPilot agent interface
        interface autoPilot{
                void createFlightPlan(in Location SatelliteReport,
                                in Path flight_route,
                                in Map no_go,
                                out Plan flightPlan)
                    raises (UserException);
```

```
                void mergeGPSData(in SatReport data1,
                                 in SatReports data2,
                                 out SatReports mergedData)
                        raises (UserException);
        }; // end of autoPilot agent interface
}; // end of module CFIT
```

In *CORBA*, method invocations require exact matches between the requested service name, and the stored service name. On the other hand, in IMPACT servers, imprecise matching of the available services is provided via nearest neighbor and range queries. Another important difference is that one of the objectives of *CORBA* is to provide platform level independence by mapping clients requests to servers transparently. On the other hand, one focus of the IMPACT servers is to help agents seeking services to identify, using imprecise matching techniques, which other agents may be able to provide services "similar" to the requested service. Actual method invocation is not handled through IMPACT servers, rather agent-to-agent communication is encouraged.

CORBA does not assume a one-to-one relationship between clients and servers. Multiple servers can work with a single client or a single server can work with multiple clients. As stated previously, servers and clients find each other through the *ORB* rather than knowing directly about each other.

Hence, in *CORBA* only the *ORB* knows about the implementation details and actual locations of the components in the system. Clients and servers only know the interfaces of the components. The only means of communication is the requests and their responses in *CORBA* as shown in Figure 4.8 (OMG 1998a). In this way a distributed, heterogeneous environment becomes virtually local and homogeneous to the client. The changes in object implementation, or in object relocation has no effect on the clients.

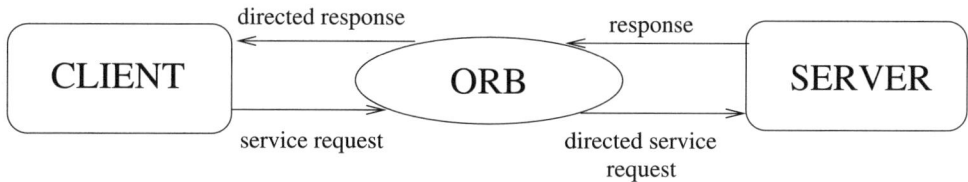

Figure 4.8
CORBA client/server interaction.

4.8.3 Object Services

Object Services are a collection of services that provide certain basic functions. Object Service components provide a generic environment in which single objects can perform their tasks. Standardization of Object Services leads to consistency over different applications. A specification of an Object Service contains a set of interfaces defined in *OMG IDL* and a description of service's behavior. A detailed discussion of CORBA Services is provided in (OMG 1998b). To summarize, Object Services include the following (OMG 1998b);

Naming Service: The Naming Service allows clients to find objects based on their names. A name is bound to an object relative to a naming context. Thus, name resolution consists of determining the object associated with the given naming context.

Event Service: The Event Service provides capabilities to handle asynchronous events, event notification and reliable event delivery. Moreover, both push and pull event delivery modes are supported, i.e., consumers either request events or suppliers notify consumers of the event.

Life Cycle Service: The Life Cycle Service provides conventions for creating, moving, deleting and copying objects. As *CORBA* supports distributed objects, it supports operations on objects that are in different locations. Standardization is achieved through an interface, defined by Life Cycle Service, for a generic factory that creates objects. Moreover, the Life Cycle Service defines an interface, namely *LifeCycleObject* to define remove, copy and move operations.

Persistent Object Service: The Persistent Object Service provides interfaces that can be used to retain the persistent state of objects. Although the object is still responsible for managing its state, it can delegate the actual work to the Persistent Object Service.

Transaction Service: The Transaction Service supports multiple transaction models, including flat and nested transaction models. Moreover, it supports interoperability between different programming models. Network interoperability is also supported, that is one transaction service may interoperate with a cooperative transaction service using different *ORB*s. The Transaction Service supports both system-managed and application-managed propagation. Finally, the Transaction Service can be implemented in a TP monitor environment.

Concurrency Control Service: The Concurrency Service helps objects coordinate concurrent access to shared resources. This is achieved through the use of locks. The Concurrency Service defines several lock modes. Moreover, it also defines Intention Locks that can be utilized for locking at multiple levels of granularity.

Relationship Service: With the help of the Relationship Service, entities and relationships can be explicitly represented. Entities are represented as *CORBA* objects, whereas the relationship interface can be extended to include relationship-specific attributes and operations. Moreover, *roles* can be defined, which represent *CORBA* objects in relationships.

Externalization Service: *Externalization* of an object refers to recording the internal object state to memory, disk, across the network, etc., whereas *internalization* refers to reading that information into a new object either in the same or different process. The Externalization Service defines the protocols for externalizing and internalizing objects.

Query Service: The Query Service allows users and objects to invoke queries on collections of other objects. Moreover, it allows indexing, and is based on existing standards, including SQL-92, OQL-93 and OQL-93 Basic.

Licensing Service: The Licensing Service provides mechanisms for producers to control the use of their property. The Licensing Service does not impose any business rules, thus producers need to implement business rules according to their needs.

Property Service: The Property Service allows dynamically associating named values with objects outside the static *IDL*-type system. It defines operations to create and manipulate sets of name-value pairs or name-value-mode triples.

Time Service: The Time Service provides current time with an error estimate, generates time-based events, computes the interval between two events and provides the order in which events occurred.

Security Service: The Security Service provides identification and authentication, authorization, access control and security auditing, security of communication between objects and administration of security information.

Object Trader Service: The Trading Service allows clients to find objects based on their properties. The Trading Service provides matchmaking services for objects. The service provider registers its service by invoking an export operation on the trader, and also passes the parameters needed by the service. A client can then invoke operations on advertised services by using an object reference which is carried by the export operation. The client issues an import operation on the trader who checks for appropriate service descriptions. There may be several trading objects within a single trading domain. Moreover, traders in different domains may be federated.

Object Collections Service: Collections are groups of objects that support specific behavior, such as sets, queues, stacks, lists, etc. The Collections Service provides mechanisms to create and manipulate such groups of objects.

4.8.4 COM/OLE

COM/OLE (Box 1998; Microsoft 1999) is Microsoft's alternative standard to *CORBA*. *COM* (Common Object Model) provides similar functionality to the *CORBA ORB*, whereas

OLE (Object Linking and Embedding) is the environment to componentize and handle compound documents. Microsoft (1999) defines *COM* as a software architecture that allows applications to be built from binary software components. The emphasis is on reusable software components.

COM objects are different from *CORBA* objects in that *COM* objects are not really "objects" in the common use of the term. (Liu, Yan, and Ozsu 1997) summarizes the differences between *CORBA* objects and *COM* objects: All *COM* objects support one interface and they do not have any identifiers or state. Moreover, no inheritance is defined among object classes. Finally, two definition languages are defined: IDL for defining interfaces and ODL for defining object types.

A client accesses *COM* objects through the interfaces defined for each object. Interface Function Tables provide the mapping between an interface definition and an interface mapping. Clients make use of these tables to locate particular implementations.

There are three types of *COM* servers: *in-process server*, *local server* and *remote server*. An *in-process server* shares the same address space with the client. A *local server* runs on the same machine but as a different process. Finally, a *remote server* runs on a separate machine as a separate process. The communication between a client and a *remote server* is achieved via DCE RPC. *COM* Servers provide a set of functions including encapsulation of a *COM* object, and a class factory, registration of the classes it supports, initialization of the *COM* library, verification of the compatibility of the library version with the object version, terminating itself when no client is active.

5 *IMPACT* Server Implementation

In Chapter 3, we have described the functions performed by an *IMPACT* server. In this chapter, we will provide a detailed description of how the *IMPACT* server is implemented. Readers who are not interested in the implementation can skip this entire chapter. Readers who only want a brief overview of the implementation can skip Section 5.2.

The architecture of the *IMPACT* server is shown in Figure 5.1 on the next page. It contains two major components: the *adminImpact* component, and the *dbImpact* component. The *adminImpact* and *dbImpact* components use Unix sockets and the *TCP/IP* protocol (Wilder 1993) to communicate with clients. For *dbImpact*, the client is usually *adminImpact*. For *adminImpact*, clients can be graphical user interfaces (*GUI*s) or agents requesting services from an *IMPACT* server. Users indirectly communicate with *adminImpact* by using a *Tcl/Tk* or *Java* based *GUI*. These *GUI*s hide client related details (like id numbers) from the user.

Intuitively, *dbImpact* contains several classes. Each class is responsible for providing a set of related services. For instance, the *hierClass* can be used to query/modify the *verb*, *noun-term*, or *dataType* hierarchies, the *thesClass* allows queries to a *thesaurus*, and the *tableClass* provides services for querying/updating an *agentTable* or *serviceTable*.

Before clients can use hierarchies, thesauri, or agent/service tables, these entities must be initialized. After invoking a class initialization service such as *hier_init*, *thes_init*, or *db_init*, *dbImpact* responds with an identification (id) number. This number can be used as a *handle* for accessing these resources. Information such as *type* and *owner* is associated with each handle.

This helps prevent clients from using the wrong type of handle in the wrong place or from illegally using another client's handles.

Clients can directly communicate with *dbImpact* servers. Alternatively, if a client wants to avoid the complexity of maintaining the id numbers discussed above, the client can indirectly communicate with a *dbImpact* server by talking to an *adminImpact* server. Here, client requests are processed in the following way:

1. First, a client sends a request to an *adminImpact* server. This request can use names (like `NASA_verb_hierarchy`) instead of id numbers (like "3") to refer to resources.

2. *adminImpact* translates these names into ids and sends the request to a *dbImpact* server.

3. After processing this request, the *dbImpact* server sends responses to the *adminImpact* server.

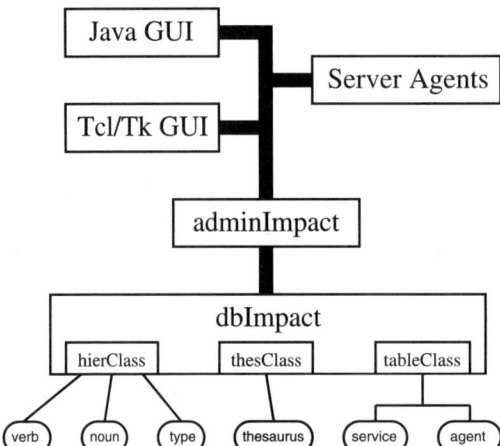

Figure 5.1
IMPACT server architecture.

4. The *adminImpact* server reads this response and updates its internal data structures if necessary.

5. Finally, the *adminImpact* server sends a (simplified) response to the client.

When an *adminImpact* or *dbImpact* server is started, a port is selected. Clients can then establish a connection by specifying the host name and port of a running server. Servers can handle multiple remote clients. Resource allocation to each client is carefully maintained so that memory can be freed if a connection is unexpectedly dropped.

Clients communicate with servers by sending request strings. The first word of these strings is always the name of the desired service. The remainder of these strings contains a space-separated list of arguments. After processing a request string, servers return a response string which begins with either Ok (indicating success), Error (indicating some error condition), or Exit (indicating that the connection should be dropped). If desired, servers can log all of these request/response strings.

When multiple requests arrive, servers put the strings for each request on a queue. These requests are then processed serially (one at a time). This simplifies the implementation of our operators.

For the remainder of this chapter, we shall begin by giving a brief description of the services offered by *dbImpact*. We shall then give the longer, more technical description for each service which includes information such as input parameters, output format, and examples. Finally, we shall consider how these services may be used to handle requests by an agent or a user.

5.1 Overview of *dbImpact* Services

This section provides a summary of the services offered by *dbImpact*. Note that all of these services are also provided by *adminImpact*.

1. Connection related services:

(a) *tcp_echo* echos back to the client every word it sent in its request. This service can be used for testing connections.

(b) *tcp_exit* informs the server that the client wants to disconnect. The server will respond with the Exit message.

2. Hierarchy creation, initialization, and termination (for using verb, noun-term, or dataType hierarchies):

(a) *hier_create* creates a new, blank hierarchy.

(b) *hier_init* initializes a hierarchy by reading its contents from a file.

(c) *hier_quit* frees memory associated with a hierarchy.

3. Hierarchy browsing/traversal (note that in our current implementation, hierarchies are stored as a forest of trees instead of a true DAG):

(a) *hier_firstId* returns the lowest numbered *nodeId* in a hierarchy. In the implementation, each node in a hierarchy is assigned a unique *nodeId* number.

(b) *hier_emptyId* returns **true** iff *nodeId* is empty (i.e., if the target node has been deleted).

(c) *hier_lastId* returns the highest numbered *nodeId* in a hierarchy. Clients can quickly scan every valid *nodeId* by processing all non-empty nodes between the first and last *nodeId*.

(d) *hier_getRoots* returns the *nodeId*s of all root nodes in a hierarchy.

(e) *hier_getKids* returns the *nodeId*s of all (immediate) children of a given node. It also returns the costs/distances to each of these nodes.

(f) *hier_getParent* returns the *nodeId* for the given node's parent (i.e., its immediate predecessor) or zero if the given node is a root node.

(g) *hier_search* returns the *nodeId*s for every node that matches a given search string. Wild card searches are supported.

4. Id/path conversions:

(a) *hier_getNames* returns the names associated with the given node. Usually, nodes will only have one name but we allow multiple names nonetheless.

(b) *hier_getPath* returns the *path* (from a root node) associated with the given node. For instance, when using our sample noun-term hierarchy, the *path* to the node named memo would be /information/message/memo.

(c) *hier_getNodeId* returns the *nodeId* associated with the given *path*. In other words, this service is the inverse of *hier_getPath*.

5. Hierarchy modification:

(a) *hier_insert* inserts a new node into a hierarchy. The new node becomes the child of a given node n (or a root node). For each child node n' of n (or for every root n'), the client can specify whether or not n' should become a child of the new node. Note that the client may also specify the distances to each node that will be adjacent to the newly inserted node.

(b) *hier_setCosts* allows clients to specify the distances between a node n and all nodes adjacent to n. By using this function, we can change edge weights without deleting and reinserting nodes.

(c) *hier_remove* removes a node n (but not its children) from a hierarchy. This service also ensures that for each $n_1, n_2 \neq n$ in the hierarchy, the distance between n_1 and n_2 is not changed.

(d) *hier_flush* flushes a hierarchy to disk. This is important because *hier_insert*, *hier_setCosts*, and *hier_remove* only modify the copy of the hierarchy which is located in memory.

6. Thesaurus functions:

(a) *thes_init* initializes a thesaurus so that it will use the given thesaurus file.

(b) *thes_quit* frees memory associated with a thesaurus.

(c) *thes_getCategories* returns the verb or noun categories associated with a given word w. Intuitively, each category represents a different meaning for w. Different categories will be returned when a client specifies different parts of speech.

(d) *thes_getSynonyms* returns a list of synonyms associated with the given category. Thus to get all synonyms of a word w, clients would first invoke *thes_getCategories* and then, for each answer returned, invoke *thes_getSynonyms*.

7. Db creation, initialization, and termination (for using agent/service tables):

(a) *db_create* creates new, blank, agents and service tables.

(b) *db_init* initializes a database connection.

(c) *db_quit* frees memory associated with a database connection.

Section 5.1   Overview of *dbImpact* Services   121

8. Hier-Db queries:

(a) *query_distance* returns the shortest distance between two nodes.

(b) *query_nn* runs the *find_nn*(v, nt, k) algorithm where v and nt are nodes in a verb and noun-term hierarchy. Here, the k nearest services to $\langle v, nt \rangle$ are returned.

(c) *query_range* runs the *range_nn*(v, nt, D) algorithm where v and nt are nodes in a verb and noun-term hierarchy. Here, all services whose composite distance from $\langle v, nt \rangle$ is less than or equal to D are returned.

(d) *query_findSource* takes a *verb* and a *noun-term* as input and returns as output the pair $\langle v, nt \rangle$ which most closely matches $\langle verb, noun\text{-}term \rangle$. We also require v and nt to appear in their respective hierarchies. Note that in order to satisfy these constraints, *query_findSource* may have to consult other services such as *hier_search*, *thes_getSynonyms*, *query_distance*, and so on. Once we determine v and nt, clients can use these as inputs to *query_nn* or *query_range*.

9. Db queries (viewing lists of *agent type*s, *agents*, or *services*):

(a) *db_getAgentTypes* returns a list of all *agent type*s which occur in an agent table. An *agent type* determines the format of an agent description *<agent_descr>*. Some sample *agent type*s include HTML, Hermes, and English. Here, *<agent_descr>* may be a URL, a function within a Hermes mediator, or an English description of an agent.

(b) *db_getAgents* returns information for all agents using a given password. If this password is ALL, information for all agents is returned. Here, an agent's information consists of its name, its allowed field, its agent type, and its agent descr.

(c) *db_getAgentInfo* returns information for the agent which matches a given name. This information has a format which is similar to the one of the output from *db_getAgents*.

(d) *db_getServices* returns information about all services which are offered by a given agent. This function can also be used to return all services offered by all agents. Service information consists of an agent name and *nodeId*s for the verb and noun-term used when registering the service.

(e) *db_getServicesToDelete* returns information for all services whose verb (or noun-term) uses a given *nodeId*. This can be used to determine which services have to be deleted if the *nodeId* node is removed from its hierarchy.

10. Db modification (adding/removing agents or services):

(a) *db_insertAgent* inserts the given agent tuple into an agent table.

(b) *db_removeAgent* removes a given agent from an agent table.

(c) *db_insertService* inserts the given service tuple into a service table.

(d) *db_removeService* removes a given service from a service table.

(e) *db_removeId* removes from a service table all services which would be returned by a similar call to *db_getServicesToDelete*.

(f) *db_removeAllServices* removes from a service table all services which would be returned by a similar call to *db_getServices*.

5.2 TCP/IP String Protocol for *IMPACT* servers

This section describes the format of the *TCP/IP* socket strings to be used by clients for communicating with *dbImpact*. The strings for *adminImpact* are similar except *hier_init*, *hier_quit*, *thes_init*, *thes_quit*, *db_init*, *db_quit*, <*agentTableName*>, <*serviceTableName*>, <*thesId*>, and <*dbId*> are omitted (*adminImpact* keeps this information hidden from its clients). In the notation we use to describe the *TCP/IP* socket strings, we will use the following notational conventions:

- "$\{<x>\}$" denotes a finite list of "$<x>$"s. We also use "$\{\{<x><y>\}\}$" to denote a finite list of the form $\{<x_1><y_1>\}\{<x_2><y_2>\}\{<x_3><y_3>\}\ldots$.
- *hier_*-functions are related to the verb, *noun*-term, or `dataType` hierarchies. <*hierId*> applies to one verb, *noun-term*, or `dataType` hierarchy. <*nodeId*> is the id number for a node in some <*hierId*> hierarchy. <*nodeCost*> is the cost to go from some <*nodeId*> node to its parent.
- "Db" functions are related to the `AgentTable` and `ServiceTable` relations:

— AgentTable(agentName[char 64], passwd[char 32], type[char 32], descr[char 256], allowed[char 64])

— ServiceTable(agentName[char 64], verbId[int], nounId[int], allowed[char 64])

- A search string <*searchStr*> must use one of the following forms:

— = ab (for nodes whose <*nodeName*>s exactly match ab),

— ab* (starting with ab),

— *ab (ending with ab),

— *ab* (containing the substring ab), or

— ab (shorthand for *ab*).

Section 5.2 *TCP/IP* String Protocol for *IMPACT* servers   123

A) Connection related services

A1: tcp_echo
DESCR: Echos back each word given as input
CLIENT: *tcp_echo* {<*word*>}
SERVER: (Ok {<*word*>}) | (Error <*errorString*>)
Ex.:   `tcp_echo hello world` ⤳ `Ok hello world`
Comm.:   Can be used to test connection. Must be called with at least one <*word*>.

A2: tcp_exit
DESCR: Informs the server that the client is disconnecting
CLIENT: *tcp_exit*
SERVER: Exit
Ex.:   `tcp_exit` ⤳ `Exit`
Comm.:   The *dbImpact* server will also send the "Exit" message before disconnecting clients (e.g., when *dbImpact* is shut down).

B) Hierarchy creation, initialization, and termination

B1: hier_create
DESCR: Creates a new, blank hierarchy called <*hierFileName*>
CLIENT: *hier_create* <*hierProvider*> <*hierFileName*>
SERVER: (Ok) | (Error <*errorString*>)
Ex.:   `hier_create ImpHier new.vh` ⤳ `Ok`
Comm.:   So far, the only valid <*hierProvider*> is "ImpHier".

B2: hier_init
DESCR: Initializes the <*hierId*> hierarchy by reading from <*hierFileName*>
CLIENT: *hier_init* <*hierProvider*> <*hierName*> <*hierFileName*>
SERVER: (Ok <*hierId*>) | (Error <*errorString*>)
Ex.:   `hier_init ImpHier verb ex.v`
            ⤳ `Error Could not open the 'ex.v' file`
Ex.:   `hier_init ImpHier verb Hier/ex.vh` ⤳ `Ok 7`
Ex.:   `hier_init ImpHier noun Hier/ex.nh` ⤳ `Ok 8`
Ex.:   `hier_init ImpHier dataType Hier/ex.th` ⤳ `Ok 9`

B3: hier_quit

DESCR: Frees memory used by the *<hierId>* hierarchy

CLIENT: *hier_quit <hierId>*

SERVER: (Ok) | (Error *<errorString>*)

Ex.: `hier_quit 7` ⤳ `Ok`

Ex.: `hier_quit 6`
⤳ `Error The value of 6 is not a valid hierId`

Comm.: Call *hier_quit* once for each *hier_init*.

C) Hierarchy browsing/traversal

C1: hier_firstId

DESCR: Returns the lowest numbered *<nodeId>* in *<hierId>* or zero if there are no nodes in the hierarchy

CLIENT: *hier_firstId <hierId>*

SERVER: (Ok *<nodeId>*) | (Error *<errorString>*)

Ex.: `hier_firstId 7` ⤳ `Ok 1`

C2: hier_emptyId

DESCR: Returns **true** iff *<nodeId>* is empty (i.e., if it has been deleted)

CLIENT: *hier_emptyId <hierId> <nodeId>*

SERVER: (Ok 0) | (Ok 1) | (Error *<errorString>*)

Ex.: `hier_emptyId 8 3` ⤳ `Ok 1`

Ex.: `hier_emptyId 8 4` ⤳ `Ok 0`

C3: hier_lastId

DESCR: Returns the highest numbered *<nodeId>* in *<hierId>* or zero if there are no nodes in the hierarchy

CLIENT: *hier_lastId <hierId>*

SERVER: (Ok *<nodeId>*) | (Error *<errorString>*)

Ex.: `hier_lastId 8` ⤳ `Ok 52`

Comm.: Clients can quickly scan every valid *<nodeId>* by processing all non-empty nodes between the first and last id

C4: hier_getRoots

DESCR: Returns the *<nodeId>*s for every root node in *<hierId>*

CLIENT: *hier_getRoots <hierId>*

Section 5.2   TCP/IP String Protocol for *IMPACT* servers   125

SERVER: (Ok <numFound> {<nodeId>}) | (Error <errorString>)
Ex.:   hier_getRoots 8 ↝ Ok 3 1 21 31

C5:   hier_getKids
DESCR: Returns the <nodeId>s for each immediate child of the given <nodeId>
CLIENT: hier_getKids <hierId> <nodeId>
SERVER: (Ok<numFound>{{<nodeId><nodeCost>}}) | (Error<errorString>)
Ex.:   hier_getKids 8 21 ↝ Ok 3 {22 1} {29 1} {30 1.5}

C6:   hier_getParent
DESCR: Returns the <nodeId> of the given <nodeId>'s parent or zero if the given
           <nodeId> is a root node
CLIENT: hier_getParent <hierId> <nodeId>
SERVER: (Ok <nodeId>) | (Error <errorString>)
Ex.:   hier_getParent 8 29 ↝ Ok 21
Ex.:   hier_getParent 8 21 ↝ Ok 0

C7:   hier_search
DESCR: Returns the <nodeId> of each node in <hierId> matching <searchStr>
CLIENT: hier_search <hierId> <searchStr>
SERVER: (Ok <numFound> {<nodeId>}) | (Error <errorString>)
Ex.:   hier_search 8 *Map ↝ Ok 2 7 19
Ex.:   hier_search 8 *MAp ↝ Ok 0

D) Id/path conversions

D1:   hier_getNames
DESCR: Returns the names associated with <nodeId>
CLIENT: hier_getNames <hierId> <nodeId>
SERVER: (Ok {<nodeName>}) | (Error <errorString>)
Ex.:   hier_getNames 8 3 ↝ Ok car(japanese)
Ex.:   hier_getNames 8 4 ↝ Ok Honda
Ex.:   hier_getNames 7 4 ↝ Ok explore investigate
Ex.:   hier_getNames 7 99 ↝ Error nodeId of 99 exceeds lastId

D2: hier_getPath

DESCR:	Returns the path (from a root node) associated with *<nodeId>*
CLIENT:	*hier_getPath <hierId> <nodeId>*
SERVER:	(Ok *<pathName>*)	(Error *<errorString>*)
Ex.:	hier_getPath 8 3 ⤳ Ok /vehicle/car/car(japanese)
Ex.:	hier_getPath 8 4 ⤳ Ok /vehicle/car/car(japanese)/honda
Ex.:	hier_getPath 8 4 ⤳ Ok /seek,search/explore,investigate

D3: hier_getNodeId

DESCR:	Returns the *<nodeId>* associated with *<pathName>* w.r.t. hier_getPath
CLIENT:	*hier_getNodeId <hierId> <pathName>*
SERVER:	(Ok *<nodeId>*)	(Error *<errorString>*)
Ex.:	hier_getNodeId 8 /vehicle/car/car(japanese) ⤳ Ok 3
Ex.:	hier_getNodeId 7 /seek,search/explore,investigate ⤳ Ok 4

E) Hier modification

E1: hier_insert

DESCR:	Inserts a new node called *<nodeName>*. The parent of this new node is specified by the first *<nodeId>* parameter below. The distance between this parameter and *<nodeName>* is specified by the first *<nodeCost>* below. If *<nodeName>* should be a root node, the first *<nodeId>* and *<nodeCost>* should be set to zero
CLIENT:	*hier_insert <hierId> <nodeName> <nodeId> <nodeCost> <childCount>* {{*<nodeId><nodeCost>*}}
SERVER:	(Ok *<nodeId>*)	(Error *<errorString>*)
Ex.:	hier_insert 8 bus 17 1 2 {22 4} {30 1.5} ⤳ Ok 53

E2: hier_setCosts

DESCR:	Sets the weights between the first *<nodeId>* below and its immediate children (the other *<nodeId>*s) to the given *<nodeCost>*s
CLIENT:	*hier_setCosts <hierId> <nodeId> <childCount>* {{*<nodeId><nodeCost>*}}
SERVER:	(Ok)	(Error *<errorString>*)

Ex.:   `hier_setCosts 8 53 2 {22 3} {30 1}` ↝ `Ok`
Comm.:   The costs for any unmentioned child nodes will not change

E3: hier_remove
DESCR: Removes <nodeId> (but not its children) from <hierId>
CLIENT: *hier_remove* <hierId> <nodeId>
SERVER: (Ok) | (Error <errorString>)
Ex.:   `hier_remove 8 53` ↝ `Ok`

E4: hier_flush
DESCR: Flushes the <hierId> hierarchy to disk
CLIENT: *hier_flush* <hierId>
SERVER: (Ok) | (Error <errorString>)
Ex.:   `hier_flush 8` ↝ `Ok`

F) Thesaurus functions

F1: thes_init
DESCR: Initializes the <thesId> thesaurus by using <thesaurusFileName>
CLIENT: *thes_init* <thesaurusProvider> <thesaurusFileName>
SERVER: (Ok <thesId>) | (Error <errorString>)
Ex.:   `thes_init ThesDB Thes/thesU.cth` ↝ `Ok 5`
Comm.:   So far, the only valid <thesaurusProvider> is "ThesDB"

F2: thes_quit
DESCR: Frees memory used by the <thesId> thesaurus
CLIENT: *thes_quit* <thesId>
SERVER: (Ok) | (Error <errorString>)
Ex.:   `thes_quit 5` ↝ `Ok`

F3: thes_getCategories
DESCR: Returns the verb or noun <category>s associated with <words>. Each category represents a different meaning for <words>
CLIENT: *thes_getCategories* <thesId> (verb | noun) "<words>"
SERVER: (Ok <numFound> {<category>}) | (Error <errorString>)

Ex.:	thes_getCategories 5 verb "place"
	↝ Ok 6 Attribute Install Locate Order Rank Situate
Ex.:	thes_getCategories 5 noun "place"
	↝ Ok 6 Location Place Precedence Rank Region Title
Comm.:	Categories returned depend on the selected part of speech

F4: thes_getSynonyms

DESCR:	Returns the synonyms associated with the given *<category>*
CLIENT:	*thes_getSynonyms <thesId>* (verb | noun) *<category>*
SERVER:	(Ok *<numFound>* {*<synonym>*})	(Error *<errorString>*)
Ex.:	thes_getSynonyms 5 verb Install ↝ Ok 9 buildIn connect initiate install instate locate place position setUp
Ex.:	thes_getSynonyms 5 noun Place ↝ Ok 13 arena campus circus floor forum ground habitat location place site spot stage station
Comm.:	The *<category>* should be a value returned by thes_getCategories

G) Db creation, initialization, and termination

G1: db_create

DESCR:	Creates new, blank, agent and service tables using the given names
CLIENT:	*db_create <databaseProvider> <agentTableName> <serviceTableName>*
SERVER:	(Ok)	(Error *<errorString>*)
Ex.:	db_create Oracle NewAgentTable NewServiceTable ↝ Ok
Comm.:	So far, the only valid *<databaseProvider>* is "Oracle"

G2: db_init

DESCR:	Initializes a (virtual) database connection
CLIENT:	*db_init <databaseProvider> <agentTableName> <serviceTableName>*
SERVER:	(Ok *<dbId>*)	(Error *<errorString>*)
Ex.:	db_init Oracle AgentTable ServiceTable ↝ Ok 6

G3: db_quit

DESCR:	Frees memory used by the *<dbId>* database connection
CLIENT:	*db_quit <dbId>*

SERVER: (Ok) | (Error <errorString>)
Ex.:   db_quit 6 ⤳ Ok

H) Hier-Db queries

H1: query_distance

DESCR: Returns the distance between the given <nodeId>s
CLIENT: query_distance <hierId> <nodeId> <nodeId>
SERVER: (Ok <cost>) | (Error <errorString>)
Ex.:   query_distance 8 1 15 ⤳ Ok 3.2
Ex.:   query_distance 8 1 16 ⤳ Error Infinite distance

H2: query_nn

DESCR: Returns the <k> nearest services/neighbors. The verb origin (VO) is given by the first <hierId> and <nodeId>. The noun-term origin (NO) is given by the second <hierId> and <nodeId> below. The query source is the pair (VO, NO).
CLIENT: query_nn <dbId> <hierId> <nodeId> <hierId> <nodeId> <k>
SERVER: (Ok <numFound> {{"<agentName>"<nodeId><nodeId><cost>}}) | (Error <errorString>)
Ex.:   query_nn 6 7 1 8 1 3
            ⤳ Ok 3 {"a1" 1 1 0} {"a2" 1 5 1} {"a 7" 9 10 3.4}
Comm.:   For the result, the first <nodeId> applies to the verb <hierId>, the second <nodeId> applies to the noun <hierId> hierarchy, and the <cost> is the composite distance from the query source

H3: query_range

DESCR: Returns all services whose composite distance from the query source is less than or equal to <maxCost>
CLIENT: query_range <dbId> <hierId> <nodeId> <hierId> <nodeId> <maxCost>
SERVER: (Ok <numFound> {{"<agentName>"<nodeId><nodeId><cost>}}) | (Error <errorString>)
Ex.:   query_range 6 7 1 8 1 2.5
            ⤳ Ok 2 {"a1" 1 1 0} {"a2" 1 5 1}
Comm.:   For parameter explanations, see the description of query_nn above.

H4: query_findSource

DESCR: Returns the query source which most closely matches the desired service (*<verb>*, *<nounTerm>*). If the *<verb>* or *<nounTerm>* does not appear in the given hierarchies, a search algorithm is used in conjunction with the *<thesId>* thesaurus

CLIENT: *query_findSource <thesId> <hierId> <verb> <hierId> <nounTerm>*

SERVER: (Ok *<nodeId>* *<nodeId>*) | (Error *<errorString>*)

Ex.: `query_findSource 5 7 rent 8 car(japanese)` ↝ `Ok 5 3`

Comm.: The returned *<nodeId>*s are usually passed by the client into query_nn and query_range as the query source.

I) Db queries (viewing lists of *agent Types*, *agents*, or *services*)

I1: db_getAgentTypes

DESCR: Returns a list of all *<agentType>* types in *<dbId>*'s AgentTable

CLIENT: *db_getAgentTypes <dbId>*

SERVER: (Ok {"*<agentType>*"}) | (Error *<errorString>*)

Ex.: `db_getAgentTypes 6` ↝ `Ok "HTML" "Hermes" "Desc"`

Comm.: *<agentType>* helps determine how to interpret *<agentDesc>*s below

I2: db_getAgents

DESCR: Returns information for all agents using *<agentPassword>*. If *<agentPassword>* is "ALL," info for all agents is returned

CLIENT: *db_getAgents <dbId>* "*<agentPassword>*"

SERVER: (Ok{{ "*<agentName>*" " *<agentAllowed>*" " *<agentType>*" " *<agentDesc>*"}}) | (Error *<errorString>*)

Ex.: `db_getAgents 6 "myPass"`
↝ `Ok {"agent1" "a" "HTML" "www.ag1.com"}`
`{"agent2" "a" "Desc" "At agent2, we provide..."}`

Comm.: If there is too much data to return, some results will be truncated and replaced by "...."

I3: db_getAgentInfo

DESCR: Returns the descriptive information for agent *<agentName>*

CLIENT: *db_getAgentInfo <dbId>* "*<agentName>*"

Section 5.2   TCP/IP String Protocol for *IMPACT* servers   131

SERVER: (Ok "*<agentName>*" " *<agentAllowed>*" " *<agentType>*" " *<agentDesc>*")
               | (Error *<errorString>*)
Ex.:   `db_getAgentInfo 6 "agent1"`
               ↝ `Ok "agent1" "a" "HTML" "www.ag1.com"`
Ex.:   `db_getAgentInfo 6 "a"`
               ↝ `Error Could not find the` *<agentName>* `agent`

I4: db_getServices
DESCR: Returns information for all services of agent *<agentName>*. If *<agentName>* is "ALL", info for all services is returned
CLIENT: *db_getServices <dbId> "<agentName>"*
SERVER: (Ok {{ "*<agentName>*" *<nodeId> <nodeId>*}})
               | (Error *<errorString>*)
Ex.:   `db_getServices 6 "a1"` ↝ `Ok {"a1" 1 1} {"a1" 9 9}`
Comm.:   The returned *<nodeId>*s are only relevant to the hierarchies used when inserting the returned services. If there is too much data to return, some results will be truncated and replaced by "...".

I5: db_getServicesToDelete
DESCR: Returns info for all services whose verb/noun-term use the given *<nodeId>*. Data associated with *<hierId>* is used to determine the relevant part of speech
CLIENT: *db_getServicesToDelete <dbId> <hierId> <nodeId>*
SERVER: (Ok {{ "*<agentName>*" *<nodeId> <nodeId>*}}) | (Error *<errorString>*)
Ex.:   `db_getServicesToDelete 6 7 10`
               ↝ `Ok {"a1" 10 1} {"a2" 10 5}`
Ex.:   `db_getServicesToDelete 6 8 10`
               ↝ `Ok {"a 7" 9 10}`
Comm.:   If there is too much data to return, some results will be truncated and replaced by "...".

J) Db modification (adding/removing agents or services)

J1: db_insertAgent
DESCR: Inserts the given tuple into *<dbId>*'s AgentTable
CLIENT: *db_insertAgent   <dbId>*   "*<agentName>*"   "*<agentPassword>*"
               "*<agentType>*" "*<agentDesc>*" " *<agentAllowed>*"

SERVER: (Ok) | (Error <*errorString*>)
Ex.: `db_insertAgent 6 "agent3" "myPass" "HTML" "www.ag2.com" "a"` ↝ `Ok`
Comm.: Modifies agent info if <*agentName*> already existed

J2: db_removeAgent
DESCR: Removes the <*agentName*> agent from <*dbId*>'s AgentTable
CLIENT: *db_removeAgent* <*dbId*> "<*agentName*>" "mvaragentPassword"
SERVER: (Ok) | (Error <*errorString*>)
Ex.: `db_removeAgent 6 "agent3" "myPass"` ↝ `Ok`
Ex.: `db_removeAgent 6 "agent3" "otherPass"` ↝ `Error Incorrect password`

J3: db_insertService
DESCR: Inserts given tuple into <*dbId*>'s ServiceTable
CLIENT: *db_insertService* <*dbId*> "<*agentName*>" "<*agentPassword*>" <*nodeId*> <*nodeId*>
SERVER: (Ok) | (Error <*errorString*>)
Ex.: `db_insertService 7 "a1" "myPass" 1 1` ↝ `Error Service already provided`
Ex.: `db_insertService 7 "a2" "myPass" 1 1` ↝ `Ok`
Comm.: The first <*nodeId*> above is for a verb, the second is for a noun

J4: db_removeService
DESCR: Removes the given service from <*dbId*>'s ServiceTable
CLIENT: *db_removeService* <*dbId*> "<*agentName*>" "<*agentPassword*>" <*nodeId*> <*nodeId*>
SERVER: (Ok) | (Error <*errorString*>)
Ex.: `db_removeService 7 "a2" "myPass" 1 1` ↝ `Ok`

J5: db_removeId
DESCR: Removes all services which would be returned by a call to "db_getServicesToDelete <*dbId*> <*hierId*> <*nodeId*>"
CLIENT: *db_removeId* <*dbId*> <*hierId*> <*nodeId*>
SERVER: (Ok) | (Error <*errorString*>)
Ex.: `db_removeId 6 7 1` ↝ `Ok`

J6: db_removeAllServices

DESCR: Removes all services which would be returned by a call to "db_getServices <*dbId*> <*agentName*>"

CLIENT: *db_removeAllServices* <*dbId*> "<*agentName*>" "<*agentPassword*>"

SERVER: (Ok) | (Error <*errorString*>)

Ex.: `db_removeAllServices 6 "a1" "myPass"` ⤳ Ok

5.3 Sample Client-Server Interactions

In this section, we provide some sample scenarios to help demonstrate how services are usually invoked. For each scenario, we present several linked Ex.s.

5.3.1 Traversing a Hierarchy

Example 5.3.1 (hier_getRoots) Suppose we want to browse the 'Hier/sample.vh' verb hierarchy. Then a *GUI* client should initialize this hierarchy and get the names for each root node. Our *GUI* client may interact with *dbImpact* in the following way:

`hier_init ImpHier verb Hier/sample.vh` ⤳ `Ok 2`

We use the "ImpHier" provider/class to initialize a "verb" hierarchy by using the "Hier/sample.vh" file. The "2" which is returned represents the id number for this hierarchy. Our subsequent commands will use this id number to refer to this hierarchy.

`hier_getRoots 2` ⤳ `Ok 3 1 9 14`

Here, we ask for the *nodeId*s of all root nodes in hierarchy number "2" (this "2" comes from the result returned by *hier_init*). We get back three ("3") *nodeId*s: "1," "9," and "14."

```
hier_getNames 2 1   ⤳ Ok compute
hier_getNames 2 9   ⤳ Ok create
hier_getNames 2 14  ⤳ Ok find
```

Here, we find that hierarchy "2" associates the names compute, create, and find with *nodeId*s "1," "9," and "14" respectively.

Example 5.3.2 (hier_getKids) The user now clicks on the "compute" entry. To show the children for this node, the client may execute the following requests:

`hier_getNodeId 2 /compute` ⤳ `Ok 1`

Here, we find that hierarchy "2" associates *nodeId* "1" with the node path "/compute."

`hier_getKids 2 1` ⤳ `Ok 3 {2 2} {3 1} {6 2}`

Here, *nodeId* "1" of hierarchy "2" has "3" children; their *nodeId*s are "2," "3," "6" and their distances from *nodeId* "1" are "2," "1," and "2" respectively.

`hier_getNames 2 2` ⤳ `Ok cancel`
`hier_getNames 2 3` ⤳ `Ok change`
`hier_getNames 2 6` ⤳ `Ok maintain`

Once again, in all requests we get the names for each *nodeId*.

Example 5.3.3 (hier_getKids again) The *GUI* indicates that the current hierarchy location is "/compute." The user now clicks on the "maintain" entry:

`hier_getNodeId 2 /compute/maintain` ⤳ `Ok 6`

As our current hierarchy location was "/compute," the full path for the "maintain" node is "/compute/maintain."

`hier_getKids 2 6` ⤳ `Ok 0`

Apparently, *nodeId* "6" (i.e., "maintain") is a leaf node because it has no ("0") children.

Example 5.3.4 (hier_getParent) The current hierarchy location becomes "/compute/maintain." Now, the user sees that this node has no children because the only available entry is "../". The user can click on this entry to go to the parent of "/compute/maintain":

`hier_getParent 2 6` ⤳ `Ok 1`

According to hierarchy "2," the node with *nodeId* "6" (i.e., "/compute/maintain") is a child of the node with *nodeId* "1" (i.e., "/compute").

5.3.2 Searching a Hierarchy

Example 5.3.5 (hier_search) Suppose we wanted to search the 'Hier/sample.vh' hierarchy for all nodes whose names begin with "co." Here, we may use the following commands:

`hier_init ImpHier verb Hier/sample.vh` ⤳ `Ok 2`

We initialize the verb hierarchy (assuming that it has not already been initialized).

```
hier_search 2 co*  ↝  Ok 2 1 10
```

Here, we are asking for all *nodeId*s in hierarchy "2" whose names match the pattern "co*." We find "2" matches: *nodeId*s "1" and "10."

```
hier_getPath 2 1   ↝  Ok /compute
hier_getPath 2 10  ↝  Ok /create/collect
```

Here, we find that hierarchy "2" associates the paths "/compute" and "/create/collect" with *nodeId*s "1" and "10" respectively. We use *hier_getPath* instead of *hier_getNames* so we can determine how to reach these nodes.

Example 5.3.6 (hier_search again) Suppose we were looking for a service that *"evaluates expressions."* Our first goal is to determine if evaluate appears in our verb hierarchy:

```
hier_search 2 =evaluate  ↝  Ok 0
```

We begin with an "=" in front of "evaluate" to indicate that we want an exact match (instead of "*evaluate*").

Example 5.3.7 (thes_getCategories) Although evaluate was not found, we may be able to find a synonym. First, we determine which categories (i.e., which *meanings*) are associated with evaluate:

```
thes_init ThesDB Thes/thesU.cth  ↝  Ok 4
```

Here, we use the "ThesDB" provider/class to initialize a thesaurus using the "Thes/thesU.cth" file. The "4" is the id number for this thesaurus which we will use in subsequent commands.

```
thes_getCategories 4 verb evaluate  ↝  Ok 3 Calculate Measure Think
```

We find that according to thesaurus "4," the word evaluate has three "verb" categories: "Calculate," "Measure," and "Think."

Example 5.3.8 (thes_getSynonyms) Now for each category, we determine the relevant synonyms and check to see if any of these are in our hierarchy:

```
thes_getSynonyms 4 verb Calculate
    ↝  Ok 6 assess calculate compute determine evaluate measure
```

Here, we see that the "verb" category "Calculate" has "6" synonyms: assess, calculate, compute, determine, evaluate, and measure.

```
hier_search 2 =assess     ⤳ Ok 0
hier_search 2 =calculate  ⤳ Ok 0
hier_search 2 =compute    ⤳ Ok 1 1
```

After two unsuccessful searches (where the number of matches was "0"), we finally find "1" node named "compute." This node has *nodeId* "1."

As compute is in our verb hierarchy, we change our service to "compute : *expressions*." A similar transformation can be performed on our noun-term *expressions*.

Example 5.3.9 (hier_lastId) Suppose that we want to use a search string consisting of an arbitrarily complex expression e which only our client can evaluate. Here, we will want to quickly get the node names for all (non-empty) nodes in our hierarchy. First, we determine the range of possible *nodeId*s:

```
hier_getFirstId 2  ⤳ Ok 1
hier_getLastId 2   ⤳ Ok 19
```

We find that hierarchy "2" uses *nodeId*s which are between "1" and "19" inclusive.

Example 5.3.10 (hier_emptyId) Then, for each *nodeId* i, we check if i is empty:

```
hier_emptyId 2 <i>  ⤳ Ok 0
```

The "0" (as opposed to a "1") indicates that node "i" is not empty.

Example 5.3.11 (hier_getPath) If the node i is empty, we skip it. Otherwise, we determine i's path name ($path(i)$):

```
hier_getPath 2 <i>  ⤳ Ok <path(i)>
```

Finally, the client displays $path(i)$ if it satisfies expression e.

5.3.3 Sample Hier-Db Queries

Example 5.3.12 (query_findSource) Suppose we wanted to find the two nearest services to evaluate : *area(*No_go*)*. We begin by determining the origin for this query:

Section 5.3   Sample Client-Server Interactions   137

```
hier_init ImpHier verb Hier/sample.vh  ↝  Ok 2
hier_init ImpHier noun Hier/sample.nh  ↝  Ok 3
thes_init ThesDB Thes/thesU.cth        ↝  Ok 4
```

At this point, we have initialized a verb hierarchy with id "2," a noun hierarchy with id "3," and a thesaurus with id "4."

```
query_findSource 4 2 evaluate 3 area(no_go)  ↝  Ok 1 2
```

According to thesaurus "4," the verb/noun-term pair ⟨*evaluate*, *area*(No_go)⟩ from verb/noun-term hierarchy ("2," "3") is closest to *nodeId* pair ("1," "2") where "1" is a *nodeId* in our verb hierarchy and "2" is a *nodeId* in our noun-term hierarchy.

```
hier_getPath 2 1  ↝  Ok /compute
hier_getPath 3 2  ↝  Ok /area/area(no_go)
```

Notice that the first *hier_getPath* is called on the verb hierarchy ("2"), while the second *hier_getPath* is called on the noun-term hierarchy ("3").

Example 5.3.13 (query_nn)   Next, we perform a nearest neighbor search from the given origin:

```
db_init Oracle AgentTable ServiceTable  ↝  Ok 5
```

Here, we use the "Oracle" provider/class to initialize the "AgentTable" and "ServiceTable" relations. The "5" is the id number for this pair of relations.

```
query_nn 5 2 1 3 2 2
    ↝ Ok 2 {"terrain_agent3" 1 2 0} {"satellite_agent5" 5 2 2}
```

Here, we are using our relations ("5") to perform a nearest neighbor query. Our query origin is the verb noun-term pair ⟨"1," "2"⟩ from verb/noun-term hierarchy ⟨"2," "3"⟩. The last input parameter indicates that we are looking for "2" answers. The first output parameter indicates that we found "2" answers: The first one is the agent named terrain_agent3 which offers a service whose verb/noun-term *nodeId* pair is ⟨"1," "2"⟩. This has a composite distance of "0" from our query origin ⟨"1," "2"⟩. The second answer is the agent named satellite_agent5 which offers a service with a verb/noun-term *nodeId* pair of ⟨"5," "2"⟩. This has a composite distance of "2" from our query origin ⟨"1," "2"⟩.

```
hier_getPath 2 5  ↝  Ok /compute/change/update
```

We use this command because we don't know which path in verb hierarchy "2" is associated with *nodeId* "5."

Example 5.3.14 (query_range)   Alternatively, if we wanted to determine all services within a composite distance of 2.5 from the same origin, we could use

```
query_range 5 2 1 3 2 2.5
```

The input and output parameters for *query_nn* and *query_range* are the same except for the last input parameter; for *query_nn*, this represents the desired number of answers but for *query_range*, this represents the maximum distance of an answer from the query source.

5.3.4 Registering Agents and Services

Suppose we wanted to add a $saleNotification$ agent which performs services like "*mail* : *brochures*" and "*create* : *mail-list*." To add this agent, a user would fill in the *agent name*, *password*, *agentType*, *description*, and *allowed fields*.

Example 5.3.15 (db_getAgentInfo)   Originally, we consider calling this agent the "sales notifier." Lets see if this agent name is already in use:

```
db_init Oracle AgentTable ServiceTable ⤳ Ok 5
db_getAgentInfo 5 "sales notifier" ⤳
 Ok "sales notifier" "XYZ salespeople" "English"
   "XYZ's sales notification agent"
```

The result indicates that there is an agent known as "sales notifier" which can be accessed by "XYZ salespeople." An "English" description for the agent is "XYZ's sales notification agent."

Example 5.3.16 (db_getAgents)   Apparently, our name has been taken. Lets try "SNA" instead:

```
db_getAgentInfo 5 "SNA" ⤳ Error Could not find the <agentName> agent
```

Section 5.3   Sample Client-Server Interactions   139

Fortunately, the name is available. We decide to use the name "SNA" with password "pass4SNA." In the future though, we may want to first use the *GUI*'s "View Agents" button to see which agents are currently registered with the system. The implementation of this button may use the following:

`db_getAgents 5 "ALL"`

The "ALL" here indicates that we want information on all agents, not just those who use a given password.

Example 5.3.17 (db_getAgentTypes)   Now, we must decide on an agentType. Instead of creating a new type, we use the "Select Type" pull-down menu to choose the "HTML" type. Clients can determine the contents for this menu by invoking

`db_getAgentTypes 5  ⇝  Ok "English" "French" "HTML" "Hermes"`

In this Ex., the user would have four choices.

Example 5.3.18 (db_insertAgent)   Next, we fill in our URL "http://www.sna.org" for the description and "SNA_advertisers" for the allowed field. Finally, we click on the "Add Agent" button which sends the following command to a *dbImpact* server:

`db_insertAgent 5 "SNA" "pass4SNA" "HTML" "http://www.sna.org" "SNA_advertisers"  ⇝  Ok`

Here, we are inserting an agent named "SNA" with password "pass4SNA." Our *agentType* is "HTML" because our *agentDesc* description is a URL: "http://www.sna.org." We allow this agent to be viewed by all "SNA_advertisers."

To add a service $v:nt$ to our agent, start by traversing the verb and noun-term hierarchies until the current hierarchy locations become v and nt respectively. Then, click on "Register Services." Next, make sure that the "Agent Name" and "Password" fields are filled with "SNA" and "pass4SNA" respectively. Finally, click on "Add Service." If the agent name exists, the password is correct. If the service does not already exist, then $v:nt$ will be added.

Example 5.3.19 (db_insertService)   For instance, when we add the service "mail: brochure," the client may perform the following commands:

```
hier_init ImpHier verb Hier/sample.vh ⇝ Ok 2
hier_init ImpHier noun Hier/sample.nh ⇝ Ok 3
hier_getNodeId 2 /mail ⇝ Ok 13
hier_getNodeId 3 /information/advertisement/brochure ⇝ Ok 8
```

We use *hier_getNodeId* to get the *nodeId*s for the verb mail and the noun-term *brochure*. We use these *nodeId*s to specify our service in the following statement:

```
db_insertService 5 SNA pass4SNA 13 8 ⇝ Ok
```

Here, we are indicating that agent "SNA" with password "pass4SNA" offers the ⟨13, 8⟩ service, i.e., ⟨mail, *brochure*⟩.

6 Agent Programs

In Chapter 4, we described a *code call* mechanism that allows us to build agents "on top" of arbitrary data structures. This is because the vast majority of useful software applications out there in the market were developed prior to the ongoing interest in agents. Furthermore, even in the future, different data structures will prove to be necessary for different applications, and for such packages to meaningfully interoperate with other such packages, we need to *agentize* them.

In this chapter, we will set up the basic infrastructure that decides how an agent will or should *act*. For instance, in the CFIT example, the satellite agent "wakes up" every Δt units of time, broadcasts a location report, and goes back to "sleep" for another Δt seconds. In contrast, in the case of the truck agent in the CHAIN example, the agent's work is initiated by receipt of a message from another agent that requires truck resources. In the STORE example, the credit agent may treat different agents differently, providing appropriate responses to authorized agents, and denying service to other agents. In each of these cases, the agent is making a decision on how to respond to changes in its environment (e.g., receipt of a message, ticking of the clock, etc.). Different agents use different policies to make such decisions. Yet, the creator or administrator of an agent will want his agent to adhere to certain principles—he must set up *behavioral guidelines* that his agent must obey. These guidelines will, in all likelihood, state that the agent is obliged to take certain actions under certain circumstances, and that it is forbidden from taking certain actions under other circumstances. In some cases, it may have discretion about what actions to take. The main aim of this chapter is to define a language called *Agent Programs*, by using which the individual deploying an agent may specify what actions the agent must take, and the rules governing the execution of these actions.

6.1 Agent Decision Architecture

The basic decisionmaking structures used by an agent are shown in Figure 6.1. Later, in Chapters 7, 9, and 10, we will expand this significantly to include *beliefs* (about other agents), *uncertainty*, and *security* concerns. These basic decisionmaking structures include the following components:

Underlying Software Code: This consists of the basic set of data structures and legacy code on top of which the agent is built. It is accessed through the code-call mechanism

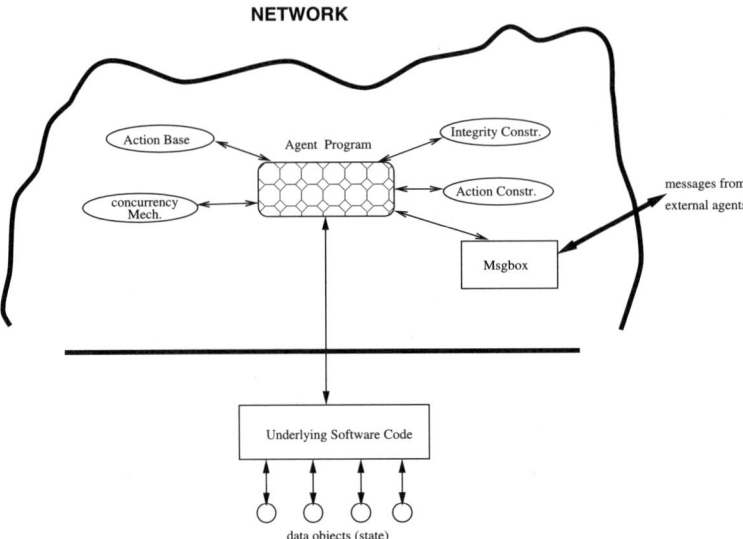

Figure 6.1
Agent Decision Architecture.

formalized in Chapter 4. At any given point t of time, there is a finite set of objects associated with each data type managed by the agent. The set of all such objects, across all the data types managed by the software code, is called the *state of the agent* at time t. Clearly, the state of the agent varies with time. Without loss of generality, we will assume that each agent's legacy code includes the "message box" described in Section 4.3.

Integrity Constraints: The agent has an associated finite set, $\mathcal{IC}$, of integrity constraints. These integrity constraints reflect the expectations, on the part of the designer of the agent, that the state of the agent must satisfy.

Actions: Each agent has an associated set of *actions*. An action is implemented by a body of code implemented in any suitable imperative (or declarative) programming language. The agent reasons about actions via a set of preconditions and effects defining the conditions an agent state must satisfy for the action to be considered executable, and the new state that results from such an execution. We assume that the preconditions and effects associated with an action correctly specify the behavior of the code implementing the action. The syntax and informal semantics of actions, as well as their sequential and concurrent execution, is described in Section 6.2.

Action Constraints: In certain cases, the creator of the agent may wish to prevent the agent from concurrently executing certain actions even though it may be feasible for the agent to take them. Action constraints are user constrained specifications stating the conditions under which actions may not be concurrently executed. Action constraints are described in Section 6.3.

Agent Programs: Finally, an agent program is a set of rules, in a language to be defined in Section 6.4, that an agent's creator might use to specify the principles according to which the agent behaves, and the policies governing what actions the agent takes, from among a possible plethora of possible actions. In short, the agent program associated with an agent encodes the "do's and dont's" of the agent.

6.2 Action Base

In this section, we will introduce the concept of an action and describe how the effects of actions are implemented. In most work in AI (Nilsson 1980; Genesereth and Nilsson 1987; Russell and Norvig 1995) and logical approaches to action (Baral and Lobo 1996), it is assumed that states are sets of ground logical atoms. In the fertile area of active databases, it is assumed that states reflect the content of a relational database. However, neither of these two approaches is adequate for our purpose because the state of an agent which uses the software code $\mathcal{S} = (\mathcal{T}_\mathcal{S}, \mathcal{F}_\mathcal{S}, \mathcal{C}_\mathcal{S})$ is described by the set $\mathcal{O}_\mathcal{S}$. The data objects in $\mathcal{O}_\mathcal{S}$ *could* be logical atoms (as is assumed in most AI settings), or they *could* be relational tuples (as is assumed in active databases), but in all likelihood, the objects manipulated by $\mathcal{S}$ are much more complex, structured data types.

DEFINITION 6.2.1 (ACTION; ACTION ATOM) An *action* α consists of six components:

Name: A name, usually written $\alpha(X_1, \ldots, X_n)$, where the X_i's are root variables.

Schema: A schema, usually written as $(\tau_1, \ldots, \tau_n)$, of types. Intuitively, this says that the variable X_i must be of type τ_i, for all $1 \leq i \leq n$.

Action Code: This is a body of code that executes the action.

Pre: A code-call condition χ, called the *precondition* of the action, denoted by $Pre(\alpha)$, which must be *safe modulo the variables* $X_1, \ldots, X_n$;

Add: a set $Add(\alpha)$ of code-call conditions;

Del: a set $Del(\alpha)$ of code-call conditions.

An *action atom* is a formula $\alpha(t_1, \ldots, t_n)$, where t_i is a term, i.e., an object or a variable, of type τ_i, for all $i = 1, \ldots, n$.

It is important to note that there is a big distinction between our definition of an action, and the classical definition of an action in AI (Genesereth and Nilsson 1987; Nilsson 1980). Here are the differences.

Item	Classical AI	Our framework
Agent State	Set of logical atoms	Arbitrary data structures
Precondition	Logical formula	Code call condition
Add/delete list	set of ground atoms	Code call condition
Action Implementation	Via add list and delete list	Via arbitrary program code
Action Reasoning	Via add list and delete list	Via add list and delete list

A more subtle difference is that in classical AI, states are *physically modified* by unioning the current state with items in the add list, and then deleting items in the delete list. In contrast, the add-list and the delete-list in our framework plays no role whatsoever in the physical implementation of the action. The action is implemented by its associated action code. The agent uses the preconditions, add list, and the delete list to reason about what is true/false in the new state.

Given any action, we may associate with it an automaton modeling a transition system as follows. The state space of the automaton is the set of all possible (perhaps infinitely many) states of the agent in question. The states in which the precondition of the action are false have no outgoing edges in the automaton. There is an edge (transition) from one state to another if the first state satisfies the precondition of the action, and the second state results from the execution of the action in the first state.

Note 5 Throughout this book, we assume that the precondition, add and delete lists associated with an action, correctly describe the behavior of the action code associated with the action.

Let us now consider some examples of actions and their associated descriptions in specific domains. Obviously, the code implementing these actions is not listed below.

Example 6.2.1 (CHAIN Revisited) Suppose the supplier agent of the CHAIN example has an action called *update_stockDB* which is used to process orders placed by other agents.

Name: *update_stockDB*(Part_id, Amount, Company)

Schema: (String, Integer, String)

Pre: in(X, supplier : *select*('uncommitted', id, =, Part_id)) & X.amount > Amount.

Del: in(X, supplier : *select*('uncommitted', id, =, Part_id)) &
in(Y, supplier : *select*('committed', id, =, Part_id))

Add: in($\langle$part_id, X.amount $-$ Amount$\rangle$,
supplier: *select*(*'uncommitted'*, id, =, Part_id))&
in($\langle$part_id, Y.amount $+$ Amount$\rangle$,
supplier: *select*(*'committed'*, id, =, Part_id))

This action updates the two ACCESS databases for *uncommitted* and *committed* stock. The supplier agent should first make sure that the amount requested is available by consulting the *uncommitted* stock database. Then, the supplier agent updates the *uncommitted* stock database to reduce the amount requested and then adds a new entry to the *committed* stock database for the requesting company.

Example 6.2.2 (CFIT Revisited) Suppose the autoPilot agent in the CFIT example has the following action for computing the current location of the plane:

Name: *compute_currentLocation*(Report)

Schema: (SatelliteReport)

Pre: in(Report, msgbox: *getVar*(Msg.Id, "Report"))

Del: in(OldLocation, autoPilot: *location*()).

Add: in(OldLocation, autoPilot: *location*())&
in(FlightRoute, autoPilot: *getFlightRoute*())&
in(Velocity, autoPilot: *velocity*())&
in(NewLocation, autoPilot : *calculateLocation*(OldLocation, FlightRoute, Velocity))

This action requires a satellite report which is produced by the gps agent by merging the GPS Data. Then, it computes the current location of the plane based on this report as well as the allocated flight route of the plane.

Example 6.2.3 (STORE Example Revisited) The profiling agent might have the following action:

Name: *update_highProfile*(Ssn, Name, Profile)

Schema: (String, String, UserProfile)

Pre: in(spender(high), profiling: *classifyUser*(Ssn))

Del: in($\langle$Ssn, Name, OldProfile$\rangle$, profiling: *all*(*'highProfile'*))

Add: in($\langle$Ssn, Name, Profile$\rangle$, profiling: *all*(*'highProfile'*))

This action updates the user profiles of those users who are high spenders. In order to determine the high spenders, it first invokes the *classifyUser* code call. After obtaining the target list of users, it updates entries of those users in the profile database. The profiling agent may also have similar actions for low and medium spenders.

In our framework, we assume that any explicit state change initiated by an agent is an action. For example, *sending messages* and *reading messages* are actions. Similarly, *making an update* to an internal data structure is an action. *Performing a computation* on the internal data structures of an agent is also an action (as the result of the computation in most cases is returned by modifying the agent's state).

Example 6.2.4 (Java Agents) In today's world, the word "agent" is often considered (in certain non-AI communities) to be synonymous with Java applets. What is unique about an applet is that it is *mobile*. A Java applet hosted on machine H can "move" across the network to a target machine T, and execute its operations there. The actions taken by a Java agent agentID, may be captured within our framework as follows.

Name: *exec*(Op, Host, Target, ArgumentList), which says *"Execute the operation* Op *on the list* ArgumentList *of arguments located at the* Target *address by moving there from the* Host *address."*

Pre: in(Host, java : *location*(Agent-id)) &
in(ok, security : *authorize*(Agent-id, Op, Target, ArgumentList)).

This says that the Java implementation recognizes that the agent in question is currently at the Host machine and that the security system of the remote machine authorizes the agent to download itself on the target and execute its action.

Add/Del: This consists of whatever insertions and deletions must be done to data in the Host's workspace.

We are now ready to define an action base. Intuitively, each agent has an associated action base, consisting of actions that it can perform on its object state.

DEFINITION 6.2.2 (ACTION BASE) An *action base*, $\mathcal{AB}$, is any finite collection of actions.

The following definition shows what it means to execute an action in a given state.

DEFINITION 6.2.3 $((\theta, \gamma)$-EXECUTABILITY) Let $\alpha(\vec{X})$ be an action, and let $\mathcal{S} =_{def} (\mathcal{T}_S, \mathcal{F}_S, \mathcal{C}_S)$ be an underlying software code accessible to the agent. A ground instance $\alpha(\vec{X})\theta$ of $\alpha(\vec{X})$ is said to be *executable* in state $\mathcal{O}_S$, if, by definition, there exists a solution γ of $Pre(\alpha(\vec{X}))\theta$ w.r.t. $\mathcal{O}_S$. In this case, $\alpha(\vec{X})$ is said to be (θ, γ)-*executable* in state $\mathcal{O}_S$, and $(\alpha(\vec{X}), \theta, \gamma)$ is a feasible *execution triple* for $\mathcal{O}_S$. By $\Theta\Gamma(\alpha(\vec{X}), \mathcal{O}_S)$ we denote the set of all pairs (θ, γ) such that $(\alpha(\vec{X}), \theta, \gamma)$ is a feasible execution triple in state $\mathcal{O}_S$.

Intuitively, in $\alpha(\vec{X})$, the substitution θ causes all variables in $\vec{X}$ to be grounded. However, it is entirely possible that the precondition of α has occurrences of other free variables not occurring in $\vec{X}$. Appropriate ground values for these variables are given by solutions of $Pre(\alpha(\vec{X})\theta)$ with respect to the current state $\mathcal{O}_S$. These variables can be viewed as "hidden parameters" in the action specification, whose value is of less interest for an action to be executed.

The following definition tells us what the result of (θ, γ)-execution is.

DEFINITION 6.2.4 (ACTION EXECUTION)   Suppose $(\alpha(\vec{X}), \theta, \gamma)$ is a feasible execution triple in state $\mathcal{O}_S$. Then the *result* of executing $\alpha(\vec{X})$ w.r.t. (θ, γ) is given by the state

$$\text{apply}((\alpha(\vec{X}), \theta, \gamma), \mathcal{O}_S) = \textbf{ins}(\mathcal{O}_{add}, \textbf{del}(\mathcal{O}_{del}, \mathcal{O}_S)),$$

where $\mathcal{O}_{add} = \mathcal{O}\_Sol(Add(\alpha(\vec{X})\theta)\gamma)$ and $\mathcal{O}_{del} = \mathcal{O}\_Sol(Del(\alpha(\vec{X})\theta)\gamma)$; i.e., the state that results if first all objects in solutions of call conditions from $Del(\alpha(\vec{X})\theta)\gamma$ on $\mathcal{O}_S$ are removed, and then all objects in solutions of call conditions from $Add(\alpha(\vec{X})\theta))\gamma$ on $\mathcal{O}_S$ are inserted.

We reiterate here the fact that the above definition assumes that the execution of the action code leads to a state which is described precisely by apply $((\alpha(\vec{X}), \theta, \gamma), \mathcal{O}_S)$—otherwise, the specification of the action code provided by its associated precondition and add lists are incorrect.

Furthermore, observe that in the above definition, we do not pay attention to integrity constraints. Possible violation of such constraints owing to the execution of an action will be handled later (Section 6.5.1) in the definition of the semantics of agent programs that we are going to develop, and will of course prevent integrity-violating actions from being executed on the current agent state.

While we have stated above what it means to execute a feasible execution triple on an agent state $\mathcal{O}_S$, there remains the possibility that many different execution triples are feasible on a given state, which may stem from different actions $\alpha(\vec{X})$ and $\alpha(\vec{X}')$, or even from the same grounded action $\alpha(\vec{X})\theta$. Thus, in general, we have a set AS of feasible execution triples that should be executed. It is natural to assume that AS is the set of all feasible execution triples. However, it is perfectly imaginable that only a subset of all feasible execution triples should be executed. For example, if only one from many solutions γ is selected—in a well-defined way—such that $(\alpha(\vec{X}), \theta, \gamma)$ is feasible, for a grounded action $\alpha(\vec{X})\theta$; we do not discuss this any further here.

6.2.1   Concurrent Execution of Actions

Suppose then we wish to simultaneously execute a set of (not necessarily all) feasible execution triples AS. There are many ways to define this.

DEFINITION 6.2.5 (CONCURRENCY NOTION)   A *notion of concurrency* is a function, **conc**, that takes as input, an object state, $\mathcal{O}_S$, and a set of execution triples AS, and returns as output, a single new execution triple such that if $AS = \{\alpha\}$ is a singleton action, then **conc**$(\mathcal{O}_S, AS_i) = \alpha$.

Intuitively, the above definition says that a notion of concurrency is a black box—it takes a set of actions to be executed concurrently as input, together with a state, and produces as output, a single action to be executed in the state (if possible). The single action produced represents a "merge" of the individual actions, and may not be explicitly present in the agent's action base, but rather is a composite action constructed dynamically. It is entirely possible that this single "merged" action is not executable in the state, thus indicating that the action in question is unexecutable. The condition on singleton $AS = \{\alpha\}$ in the above definition says that concurrent execution of a single action yields the same action.

Of course, the concept of a notion of concurrency is very broad, and can have numerous instances, some of which are more intuitive than others. We will present three alternative notions of concurrency that fall within this general description.

DEFINITION 6.2.6 (WEAKLY-CONCURRENT EXECUTION) Suppose AS is a set of feasible execution triples in the agent state $\mathcal{O}_S$. The *weakly concurrent execution of AS in $\mathcal{O}_S$*, is defined to be the agent state

$$\text{apply}(AS, \mathcal{O}_S) =_{def} \text{ins}(\mathcal{O}_{add}, \text{del}(\mathcal{O}_{del}, \mathcal{O}_S)),$$

where

$$\mathcal{O}_{add} =_{def} \bigcup_{(\alpha(\vec{X}), \theta, \gamma) \in AS} \mathcal{O}\_Sol(Add(\alpha(\vec{X})\theta)\gamma),$$

$$\mathcal{O}_{del} =_{def} \bigcup_{(\alpha(\vec{X}), \theta, \gamma) \in AS} \mathcal{O}\_Sol(Del(\alpha(\vec{X})\theta)\gamma).$$

For any set A of actions, the execution of A on $\mathcal{O}_S$ is the execution of the set

$$\{(\alpha(\vec{X}), \theta, \gamma) \mid \alpha(\vec{t}) \in AS, \; \alpha(\vec{X})\theta = \alpha(\vec{t})\theta \text{ ground}, (\theta, \gamma) \in \Theta\Gamma(\alpha(\vec{X}))\}$$

of all feasible execution triples stemming from some grounded action in AS, and apply $(A, \mathcal{O}_S)$ denotes the resulting state.

As the reader will note, this is a definition which does everything in parallel—it first does all deletions and then all insertions. While weakly concurrent executions work just fine when the set A of actions involve no "conflicts," they are problematic when the actions in A compete for resources.

Section 6.2 Action Base

Example 6.2.5 (CHAIN Revisited)   Consider the following set of action executions:

update_stockDB(widget5, 250, companyA),
update_stockDB(widget10, 100, companyB),
update_stockDB(widget5, 500, companyB).

Furthermore, suppose the uncommitted stock database contains the three tuples ⟨widget5, 1000⟩, ⟨widget10, 500⟩ and ⟨widget15, 1500⟩, and the committed stock database contains the tuples ⟨widget5, 2000⟩, ⟨widget10, 900⟩ and ⟨widget15, 1500⟩. Weak concurrent execution of these actions will attempt to execute an action, having the delete list

in(X, supplier : *select*(*'uncommitted'*, id, =, widget5)),

in(Y, supplier : *select*(*'committed'*, id, =, widget5)),

in(X, supplier : *select*(*'uncommitted'*, id, =, widget10)),

in(Y, supplier : *select*(*'committed'*, id, =, widget10)).

It is important to note that even though we should have two "copies" each of the first two code calls above, one copy suffices, because weak concurrent executions considers the union of the delete lists and the union of the add list. Likewise, this action has the add list

in(⟨widget5, 750⟩, supplier : *select*(*'uncommitted'*, id, =, widget5)),

in(⟨widget5, 500⟩, supplier : *select*(*'uncommitted'*, id, =, widget5)),

in(⟨widget5, 2250⟩, supplier : *select*(*'committed'*, id, =, widget5)),

in(⟨widget5, 2500⟩, supplier : *select*(*'committed'*, id, =, widget5)).

in(⟨widget10, 400⟩, supplier : *select*(*'uncommitted'*, id, =, widget10)),

in(⟨widget10, 1000⟩, supplier : *select*(*'committed'*, id, =, widget10)).

We see that the above executions lead to an intuitively inconsistent state in which the committed stock database claims that the number of committed items of widget 5 is both 2250 and 2500!

Thus, *before* attempting to perform a weakly concurrent execution of a set of actions, we must ensure that the set of actions satisfy some consistency criteria, otherwise there is a danger of doing something absurd.

The following definition, called *sequential-concurrent execution*, (or *S*-concurrent execution for short) removes some, but not all of these problems, and in turn, introduces some new problem. In effect, it says that a set of actions is S-concurrently executable, just if there is some way of ordering the actions so that they can be sequentially executed.

DEFINITION 6.2.7 (SEQUENTIAL-CONCURRENT EXECUTION) Suppose we have a set $AS =_{def} \{(\alpha_i(\vec{X}_i, \theta_i, \gamma_i)) \mid 1 \leq i \leq n\}$ of feasible execution triples on an agent state $\mathcal{O}_S$. Then, AS is said to be S-concurrently executable in state $\mathcal{O}_S$, if, by definition, there exists a permutation π of AS and a sequence of states $\mathcal{O}_S^0, \ldots, \mathcal{O}_S^n$ such that:

- $\mathcal{O}_S^0 = \mathcal{O}_S$ and
- for all $1 \leq i \leq n$, the action $\alpha_{\pi(i)}(\vec{X}_{\pi(i)})$ is $(\theta_{\pi(i)}, \gamma_{\pi(i)})$-executable in the state $\mathcal{O}_S^{i-1}$, and $\mathcal{O}_S^i = \text{apply}((\vec{X}_{\pi(i)}, \theta_{\pi(i)}, \gamma_{\pi(i)}), \mathcal{O}_S^{i-1})$.

In this case, AS is said to be π-executable, and $\mathcal{O}_S^n$ is the *final state resulting from the execution $AS[\pi]$*.

A set ACS of actions is S-concurrently executable on the agent state $\mathcal{O}_S$, if the set $\{(\alpha(\vec{X}), \theta, \gamma) \mid \alpha(\vec{t}) \in \text{it ACS}, \alpha(\vec{X})\theta = \alpha(\vec{t})\theta \text{ ground}, (\theta, \gamma) \in \Theta\Gamma(\alpha(\vec{X}))\}$ is S-concurrently executable on $\mathcal{O}_S$.

S-concurrent executions eliminate the problems of consistency that plague the weakly concurrent executions. For instance, in the case of Example 6.2.5, S-concurrent executions yield sensible results. However, this also introduces two weaknesses:

1. We would like to *deterministically* predict the result of executing a set of actions concurrently. Weakly-concurrent executions allow such predictions, but S-concurrent ones do not.

2. The problem of checking whether a set of feasible execution triples is S-concurrently executable is NP-hard (see below), and this intractability occurs even in very simple settings.

The notion of *full-concurrent execution* (F-concurrent execution given below), removes the first of these problems, but not the second. It removes the first problem by saying that a set of feasible execution triples is F-concurrently executable, precisely if each and every sequence of triples from this set is serially executable and the results of each of these serial executions is identical.

DEFINITION 6.2.8 (FULL-CONCURRENT EXECUTION) Suppose we have a set $AS =_{def} \{(\alpha_i(\vec{X}_i, \theta_i, \gamma_i)) \mid 1 \leq i \leq n\}$ of feasible execution triples and an agent state $\mathcal{O}_S$. Then, AS is said to be F-concurrently executable in state $\mathcal{O}_S$, if and only if the following holds:

1. For every permutation π, AS is π-executable.

2. For any two permutations π_1, π_2 of AS, the final states $AS[\pi_1]$ and $AS[\pi_2]$, respectively, which result from the executions are identical.

A set *ACS* of actions is F-concurrently executable on the agent state $\mathcal{O}_S$, if the set

$$\{(\alpha(\vec{X}), \theta, \gamma) \mid \alpha(\vec{t}) \in ACS, \alpha(\vec{X})\theta = \alpha(\vec{t})\theta \text{ ground}, (\theta, \gamma) \in \Theta\Gamma(\alpha(\vec{X}))\},$$

is F-concurrently executable on $\mathcal{O}_S$.

The following example shows how F-concurrent executions avoid the problems mentioned above.

Example 6.2.6 (CHAIN example revisited)   Let us return to the situation raised in Example 6.2.5. The following set of action executions are F-concurrently executable:

update_stockDB(widget5, 250, companyA),
update_stockDB(widget10, 100, companyB),
update_stockDB(widget15, 500, companyB).

Further assume that the uncommitted stock database contains the same tuples as in Example 6.2.5 on page 149. This set of action executions is F-concurrently executable on this state of the supplier agent, because any permutation of these three actions will result in the same final agent state. That is, whatever the execution sequence is, the resulting uncommitted stock database will contain the following tuples: ⟨widget5, 750⟩, ⟨widget10, 400⟩ and ⟨widget15, 1000⟩.

6.2.2 Complexity of Concurrent Execution

The following result specifies the complexity of weakly concurrent executability, S-concurrent executability, and F-concurrent executability of a set of feasible execution triples. In general, it shows that only weakly concurrent executability is tractable, while the other notions are intractable.

For deriving this result, we assume that we have a set of feasible execution triples AS to be executed on a given state $\mathcal{O}_S$, such that following operations are possible in polynomial time:

1. testing whether the grounded precondition $Pre(\alpha(\vec{X}))\theta\gamma$ for any triple $(\alpha(\vec{X}), \theta, \gamma) \in AS$ is satisfied in an agent state $\mathcal{O}_S$;

2. determining all objects in solutions of $Add(\alpha(\vec{X})\theta\gamma)$ and in $Del(\alpha(\vec{X})\theta\gamma)$ on an agent state, as well as insertion/deletion of objects from an agent state;

3. construction of all objects that may be involved in the state and intermediate states evolving from execution of AS on $\mathcal{O}_S$ under any permutation π.

Such a setting applies e.g., in the case where the agent state is a collection of ground facts, which is maintained under the domain closure axiom.

THEOREM 6.2.1   Let $AS =_{def} \{(\alpha_1, \theta_1, \gamma_1), \ldots, (\alpha_n, \theta_n, \gamma_n)\}$ be a given set of feasible execution triples $(\alpha_i, \theta_i, \gamma_i)$ on a given agent state $\mathcal{O}_S$. Then, under the previous assumptions, testing whether AS is S-concurrently executable is co-NP-complete.

Proof   The problem is NP, since we can guess an appropriate permutation π and check in polynomial time whether AS is π-feasible. Indeed, by our assumptions we can always evaluate the precondition $Pre(\alpha(\vec{X}_{\pi(i)})\theta_{\pi(i)}\gamma_{\pi(i)})$ in polynomial time on $\mathcal{O}_S^i$, and we can construct the state $\mathcal{O}_S^{i+1}$ in polynomial time from $\mathcal{O}_S^i$, for all $i = 0, \ldots, n-1$; overall, this is possible in polynomial time.

To show NP-hardness, we provide a reduction from a restriction of the satisfiability problem (SAT). Recall that SAT is the following problem: given a formula $\phi = \bigwedge_{i=1}^m C_i$ which is the conjunction of propositional clauses C_i such that each clause C_i is a disjunction $C_i = L_{i,1} \vee \cdots \vee L_{i,k_i}$ of literals over propositional atoms $X = \{x_1, \ldots, x_n\}$, decide whether ϕ is satisfiable. It is a well-known that SAT is co-NP-complete problem. This remains true if we assume that each clause C_i contains three literals, and either the literals $L_{i,1}$, $L_{i,2}$, $L_{i,3}$ are all positive, or they are all negative; this restriction is known as monotone 3SAT (M3SAT) (Garey and Johnson 1979).

We now transform M3SAT into the S-concurrent execution problem, for a setting where the software code S provides access to a relational database $\mathcal{DB}$ and an agent state $\mathcal{O}_S$ is a relational database instance D.

Let I be an instance of M3SAT, consisting of clauses $C_1, \ldots, C_m$ over variables $x_1, \ldots, x_n$, such that each C_i is either positive or negative.

The database $\mathcal{DB}$ has four relations:

1. VAL(*Var,BV*), which stores a Boolean value for each variable;
2. SV(*Var*), which intuitively holds the variables which have assigned a value;
3. SAT(*C*) which intuitively stores the clauses which are satisfied;
4. the 0-ary relation INIT.

The initial database $\mathcal{D}$ holds all possible tuples, in particular, both tuples $(x_i, 0)$ and $(x_i, 1)$ are in VAL for every atom x_i. This will ensure that every execution triple in AS is feasible.

The execution triples in AS are designed such that a feasible schedule must have the following phases:

Initialization: An action *init* must be executed here, which clears all relations except VAL.

Choice: In this phase, for each atom x_i a truth value is chosen by removing from VAL either $(x_i, 0)$ (which sets x_i to 1), or $(x_i, 1)$ (which sets x_i to 0).

Checking: In this phase, it is checked for every single clause C_i independently whether C_i is satisfied.

Success: In this phase, the single tests for the C_i are combined; if the result is positive, i.e., the assignment selected in the choice phase satisfies every C_i, then a success action *sat* is executed which enables to gracefully execute the remaining actions.

Clearance: In this phase, which is entered only if the Success phase had a positive result, all remaining actions which have not been executed so far are taken. Moreover, we add an action which completely clears the database, such that every feasible permutation π leads to the empty database.

The actions and their descriptions are given in the following table:

Phase	Action	Precondition
Init	*init*	INIT
Choice	$set_1(X)$	$VAL(X, 1) \wedge VAL(X, 0)$
	$set_0(X)$	$VAL(X, 1) \wedge VAL(X, 0)$
Checking	$check_{i,j}$	$SV(x_1) \wedge \cdots \wedge SV(x_n) \wedge At_{i,j}$
Success	*sat*	$SAT(c_1) \wedge \cdots \wedge SAT(c_m)$
Clearance	*clear*	$\emptyset$

Phase	Action	Add Set	Delete Set
Init	*init*	$\emptyset$	{SV(V), SAT(C), INIT}
Choice	$set_1(X)$	{SV(X)}	{INIT, VAL(X, 0)}
	$set_0(X)$	{SV(X)}	{INIT, VAL(X, 1)}
Checking	$check_{i,j}$	{SAT(c_i)}	{INIT}
Success	*sat*	{VAL(x_i, 0), VAL(x_i, 1) | $i = 1, \ldots, n$}	{INIT}
Clearance	*clear*	$\emptyset$	all relations

Here $At_{i,j} = VAL(x_k, 1)$ if the j-th literal of clause C_i is x_k, and $At_{i,j} = VAL(x_k, 0)$ if it is $\neg x_k$.

Observe that all variables in the preconditions of the above actions α are action parameters. Thus, γ is void in every solution of $Pre(\alpha(\vec{X})\theta)$, and thus for every $\alpha(\vec{X})$ and θ at most one feasible triple $(\alpha(\vec{X}), \theta, \gamma)$ may exist, in which γ is void; we hence write simply $\alpha(\vec{X})\theta$ for this triple. Let the set *ACS* be as follows:

$ACS =_{def} \{set_1(x_i), set_0(x_i) \mid 1 \leq i \leq n\} \cup$

$\{check_{i,j} \mid 1 \leq i \leq m, 1 \leq j \leq 3\} \cup \{init, clear, sat\}.$

Notice the following observations on a feasible permutation π for *ACS*:

- *init* must be executed first, i.e., $\alpha_{\pi(1)} = init$, and *clear* must be executed as the last action.
- Clause checking can only be done after some choice action $set_v(x_i)$, $v \in \{0, 1\}$, has occurred, for every $i = 1, \ldots, n$.

- In the choice phase, execution of at most one of the actions $set_1(x_i)$, $set_0(x_i)$ is possible, for every $i = 1, \ldots, n$.
- Success is only possible, if for each clause C_i at least one action $check_{i,j}$ has been executed.
- After the Success phase, first every remaining action $set_v(x_i)$ can be executed, then all remaining actions $check_{i,j}$ are possible, and finally *clear* can be done.

It is the case that AS is S-concurrently executable, i.e., there exists some permutation π such that AS is π-feasible, *if and only if* I is a Yes-Instance of M3SAT. ∎

Remark 1 The construction can be extended so to obtain a fixed action base $\mathcal{AB}$ such that the set AS in the construction is an instance of $\mathcal{AB}$. This involves the addition of further relations to the schema describing the clauses in I, and using an ordering on the domain elements. Moreover, strict typing of the values occurring in the relations is possible.

THEOREM 6.2.2 Let $AS =_{def} \{(\alpha_1, \theta_1, \gamma_1), \ldots, (\alpha_n, \theta_n, \gamma_n)\}$ be a given set of feasible execution triples $(\alpha_i, \theta_i, \gamma_i)$ on a given agent state $\mathcal{O}_S$. Then, under the previous assumptions, testing whether AS is F-concurrently executable is co-NP-complete.

Proof The problem is in co-NP, since we can guess permutations π and π' such that either $AS[\pi] = \alpha_{\pi(1)}, \ldots, \alpha_{\pi(n)}$ or $AS[\pi'] = \alpha_{\pi'(1)}, \ldots, \alpha_{\pi'(n)}$ is not feasible, or $AS[\pi]$ and $AS[\pi']$ yield a different result. By our assumptions, the guess for π and π' can be verified in polynomial time (cf. proof of Theorem 6.2.1).

To show that the problem is co-NP-hard, we consider the case where S is a relational database $\mathcal{D}$ and an agent state $\mathcal{O}_S$ is a relational database instance D.

We reduce the complement of M3SAT to F-concurrent executability checking. Let I be an instance of M3SAT, consisting of at least one positive clause and at least one negative clause. Here, each clause is supposed to have three (not necessarily different) literals.

Let I' be the instance of I which results if every positive clause is made negative and vice versa, and if every atom x_i is replaced by x_{n+i}. Clearly, I' is a Yes-instance if and only if I is a Yes-instance, if and only if $I \cup I'$ is satisfied by some truth assignment to $x_1, \ldots, x_{2n}$ in which x_i has the opposite value to the value of x_{n+i}, for every $i = 1, \ldots, n$.

The relational database D we construct has four relations:

- POS (V_1, V_2, V_3) and NEG (V_1, V_2, V_3), which serve for storing the positive and negative clauses of $I \cup I'$, respectively,
- VAL *(Var, BV)*, which stores a truth value assignment to the variables, s.t. variable x_i is true if $(x_i, 1) \in$ VAL, and x_i is false if $(x_i, 0) \in$ VAL, for every $i = 1, \ldots, 2n$, and
- a 0-ary relation UNSAT.

Section 6.2   Action Base   155

The initial database D contains the relations POS and NEG storing the clauses of $I \cup I'$, the relation VAL which holds the tuples $(x_i, 0)$ and $(x_{n+i}, 1)$, for every $i = 1, \ldots, n$ and the relation UNSAT is empty.

The action base contains the actions $switch(X, Y)$ and $eval$, where

$switch$: $Pre(switch(X, Y)) = \emptyset$,
$\quad\quad\quad Add(switch(X, Y)) = \{\text{VAL}(X, 1), \text{VAL}(Y, 0)\}$,
$\quad\quad\quad Del(switch(X, Y)) = \{\text{VAL}(X, 0), \text{VAL}(Y, 1)\}$;

$eval$: $Pre(eval) =$
$$\left\{ \begin{array}{l} \exists V_1, V_2, V_3.\text{POS}(V_1, V_2, V_3) \wedge \text{VAL}(V_1, 0) \wedge \text{VAL}(V_2, 0) \wedge \text{VAL}(V_3, 0) \\ \wedge \\ \exists V_1, V_2, V_3.\text{NEG}(V_1, V_2, V_3) \wedge \text{VAL}(V_1, 1) \wedge \text{VAL}(V_2, 1) \wedge \text{VAL}(V_3, 1) \end{array} \right\}$$
$\quad\quad\, Add(eval) = \{\text{UNSAT}\}$,
$\quad\quad\, Del(eval) = \emptyset$.

Observe that like in the proof of Theorem 6.2.1, all unbound variables in preconditions of actions are action parameters; we thus write analogously $(\alpha(\vec{X})\theta)$ for $(\alpha(\vec{X}), \theta, \gamma)$ where γ is void.

The set AS of execution triples is

$AS = \{switch(x_i, x_{n+i}) \mid 1 \leq i \leq n\} \cup \{eval\}$.

Intuitively, a switch action $switch(x_i, x_{n+i})$ flips the value of x_i from 0 to 1 and the value from x_{n+i} from 1 to 0. The $eval$ action checks whether for the truth assignment to $x_1, \ldots, x_{2n}$ given in the database, there is some positive clause and some negative clause that are both violated.

For any permutation π on AS, the actions $\alpha_{\pi(j)}$ scheduled before $\alpha_{\pi(i)} = eval$ flip the values of some variables; notice that flipping x_i is simultaneously done with flipping x_{n+i}. The precondition $Pre(eval)$ is true, precisely if there exists some positive clause P and some negative clause N in $I \cup I'$ which are both violated; this is equivalent to the property that the current assignment σ stored in D does not satisfy I.

To see this, if P is from I, then I is not satisfied by σ, and if P is from I', then there is a corresponding negative clause $N(P)$ in I such that $N(P)$ is not satisfied. On the other hand, if σ does not satisfy I, then there exists either a positive clause $P \in I$ or a negative clause $N \in I$ which is not satisfied, and thus the corresponding negative clause $N(P) \in I'$ (resp. positive clause $P(N) \in I'$) is not satisfied by σ; this means $Pre(eval)$ is true.

Clearly, all actions in AS are executable on the initial database DB, and every feasible permutation $AS[\pi]$ yields the same resulting database. Hence, it follows that AS is F-concurrently executable, if and only if I is a Yes-Instance. This proves the result.

Note that we can derive AS from a simple fixed program, if we store the pairs x_i, x_{n+i} in a separate relation. The result then immediately extends to the data complexity of a collection of feasible execution triples. ∎

Remark 2 The F-concurrent execution problem in the above database setting is polynomial, if the precondition is a conjunction of literals and there are no free (existential) variables in it. Then the condition amounts to the following property. Let ACS be a set of action execution triples, and denote by $pre^+(\alpha)$ (resp., $pre^-(\alpha)$) the positive (resp., negated) ground atoms in the precondition of α, for any action α. Moreover, let $Add\downarrow(\alpha)$ and $Del\downarrow(\alpha)$ be the ground instances of the atoms in $Add(\alpha)$ and $Del(\alpha)$ over the database, respectively.

(i) $Add\downarrow(\alpha) \cap Pre^-(\beta) = \emptyset$, for every actions $\alpha, \beta \in ACS$ such that $\alpha \neq \beta$;

(ii) $Del\downarrow(\alpha) \cap (Pre^+(\beta) \cup Add\downarrow(\beta)) = \emptyset$, for every $\alpha, \beta \in AS$ such that $\alpha \neq \beta$;

(iii) $Add\downarrow(\alpha) \cap Del\downarrow(\alpha) = \emptyset$, for every $\alpha \in AS$.

(Condition (iii) is actually not needed, but avoids philosophical problems.) An alternative, less conservative approach would be to limit change by α to the atoms not in $Add\downarrow(\alpha)$ $\cap Del\downarrow(\alpha)$.

Thus, of the three kinds of concurrency we have introduced in this section, the only one that is polynomial is the concept of *weak concurrency*.

Note 6 Throughout the rest of this book, we will assume that the developer of an agent has chosen some notion, **conc**, of concurrent action execution for his agent. This may vary from one agent to another, but each agent uses a single notion of concurrency. Thus, when talking of an agent a, the phrase "AS is concurrently executable" is to be considered to be synonymous with the phrase "AS is concurrently executable w.r.t. the notion of concurrency used by agent a."

Our implementation of the work described in this chapter allows the designer of an agent to select a notion of concurrency from an existing menu of options. In addition, new concurrency notions may also be added to this menu.

6.3 Action Constraints

In the preceding section, we have explained what it means for a set of actions to be concurrently executable with respect to a notion of concurrency, **conc**. In addition to the notion of concurrency selected by an agent's designer, the designer may want to explicitly state that certain actions cannot be concurrently executed (perhaps under some conditions).

Section 6.3   Action Constraints   157

DEFINITION 6.3.1 (ACTION CONSTRAINT)   An action constraint *AC* has the syntactic form:

$$\{\alpha_1(\vec{X}_1), \ldots, \alpha_k(\vec{X}_k)\} \hookleftarrow \chi \tag{6.1}$$

where $\alpha_1(\vec{X}_1), \ldots, \alpha_k(\vec{X}_k)$ are action names, and χ is a code call condition.

The above constraint says that if condition χ is true, then the actions $\alpha_1(\vec{X}_1), \ldots, \alpha_k(\vec{X}_k)$ are not concurrently executable. Examples of such action constraints, drawn from our motivating examples, are given below.

Example 6.3.1 (CHAIN Example Revisited)   The following are some action constraints for the supplier agent of CHAIN example:

{*update_stockDB*(Part_id1, Amount1, Company1),
update_stockDB(Part_id2, Amount2, Company2)} $\hookleftarrow$
$$\text{Part\_id1} = \text{Part\_id2} \ \&$$
$$\textbf{in}(X, \text{supplier} : select('uncommitted', \text{id}, =, \text{Part\_id1})) \ \&$$
$$\text{X.amount} < \text{Amount1} + \text{Amount2} \ \&$$
$$\text{Company1} \neq \text{Company2}.$$

{*respond_request*(Part_id1, Amount1, Company1),
respond_request(Part_id2, Amount2, Company2)} $\hookleftarrow$ Part_id1 = Part_id2 &
$$\text{Company1} \neq \text{Company2}.$$

The first constraint states that if the two update_stockDB actions update the same Part_id and the total amount available is less than the sum of the requested amounts, then these actions cannot be concurrently executable. The second constraint states that if two companies request the same Part_id, then the supplier agent does not respond to them concurrently. That is, the supplier agent processes requests one at a time.

Example 6.3.2 (CFIT Example Revisited)   The following is an action constraint for the autoPilot agent:

{*compute_currentLocation*(Report),
adjust_course(No_go, FlightRoute, CurrentLocation)} $\hookleftarrow$

This action constraint states that the actions *compute_currentLocation* and *adjust_course* may never be executed concurrently. This is because the *adjust_course* action requires the current location of the plane as input, and the *compute_currentLocation* action computes the required input.

The following example shows an action constraint for the gps agent:

$\{collect\_data(\texttt{Satellite}), merge\_data(\texttt{Satellite1}, \texttt{Satellite2})\} \hookleftarrow$
$$\texttt{Satellite} = \texttt{Satellite1}.$$
$\{collect\_data(\texttt{Satellite}), merge\_data(\texttt{Satellite1}, \texttt{Satellite2})\} \hookleftarrow$
$$\texttt{Satellite} = \texttt{Satellite2}.$$

These two action constraints state that the gps agent cannot concurrently execute the action merge_data and collect_data, if the satellite it is collecting data from is one of the satellites whose data it is merging.

Example 6.3.3 (STORE Example Revisited) The following are some action constraints for the profiling agent in the STORE example:

$\{update\_highProfile(\texttt{Ssn1}, \texttt{Name1}, \texttt{profile}), update\_lowProfile(\texttt{Ssn2}, \texttt{Name2}, \texttt{profile})\} \hookleftarrow$
$$\textbf{in}(spender(high), profiling : classifyUser(\texttt{Ssn1}))$$
$$\texttt{Ssn1} = \texttt{Ssn2} \ \& \ \texttt{Name1} = \texttt{Name2}$$
$\{update\_userProfile(\texttt{Ssn1}, \texttt{Name1}, \texttt{Profile}), classify\_user(\texttt{Ssn2}, \texttt{Name2})\} \hookleftarrow$
$$\texttt{Ssn1} = \texttt{Ssn2} \ \& \ \texttt{Name1} = \texttt{Name2}$$

The first action states that if the user is classified as a high spender, then the profiling agent cannot execute *update_highProfile* and *update_lowProfile* concurrently. In contrast, the second action constraint states that the profiling agent cannot classify a user profile if it is currently updating the profile of that user.

DEFINITION 6.3.2 (ACTION CONSTRAINT SATISFACTION) A set S of ground actions satisfies an action constraint AC as in (6.1) on a state $\mathcal{O}_S$, denoted $S, \mathcal{O}_S \models AC$, if there is no legal assignment θ of objects in $\mathcal{O}_S$ to the variables in $\mathcal{AC}$ such that $\chi\theta$ is true and $\{\alpha_1(\vec{X})\theta, \ldots, \alpha_k(\vec{X})\theta\} \subseteq S$ holds (i.e., no concurrent execution of actions excluded by AC is included in S). We say that S *satisfies* a set $\mathcal{AC}$ of actions constraints on $\mathcal{O}_S$, denoted $S, \mathcal{O}_S \models \mathcal{AC}$, if $S, \mathcal{O}_S \models AC$ for every $AC \in \mathcal{AC}$.

Clearly, action constraint satisfaction is *hereditary* w.r.t. the set of actions involved, i.e., $S, \mathcal{O}_S \models \mathcal{AC}$ implies that $S', \mathcal{O}_S \models \mathcal{AC}$, for every $S' \subseteq S$.

Example 6.3.4 (STORE Example Revisited) Suppose our state consists of the three uncommitted stock database tuples given in Example 6.2.5 on page 149 and let $\mathcal{AC}$ be the first action constraint given in Example 6.3.1 on the preceding page. Then if S_1 consists of

update_stockDB(widget5, 250, companyA),
update_stockDB(widget10, 100, companyB),
update_stockDB(widget5, 500, companyB)

and S_2 consists of

update_stockDB(widget5, 750, companyA),
update_stockDB(widget10, 100, companyB),
update_stockDB(widget5, 500, companyB),

S_1 satisfies $\mathcal{AC}$ but S_2 does not because (Part_id1 = Part_id2 = widget5), only X.amount = 1000 units of this part are available, and (Amount1 + Amount2) = (750 + 500) $\geq$ 1000.

6.4 Agent Programs: Syntax

Thus far, we have introduced the following important concepts:

Software Code Calls: this provides a single framework within which the interoperation of diverse pieces of software may be accomplished;

Software/Agent states: this describes exactly what data objects are being managed by a software package at a given point in time;

Integrity Constraints: this specifies exactly which software states are "valid" or "legal";

Action Base: this is a set of actions that an agent can physically execute (if the preconditions of the action are satisfied by the software state);

Concurrency Notion: this is a function that merges together a set of actions an agent is attempting to execute into a single, coherent action;

Action Constraints: this specifies whether a certain set of actions is incompatible.

However, in general, an agent must have an associated "action" policy or action strategy. In certain applications, an agent may be *obliged* to take certain actions when the agent's state satisfies certain conditions. For example, an agent monitoring a nuclear power plant may be obliged to execute a *shutdown* action when some dangerous conditions are noticed. In other cases, an agent may be explicitly forbidden to take certain actions—for instance, agents may be forbidden from satisfying requests for information on US advanced air fighters from Libyan nationals.

In this section, we introduce the concept of *Agent Programs*—programs that specify what an agent must do (in a given state), what an agent must not do, and what an agent is permitted to do, and how the agent can actually select a set of actions to perform that honor its permissions, obligations, and restrictions. Agent Programs are declarative in nature, and have a rich semantics that will be discussed in Section 6.5.

DEFINITION 6.4.1 (ACTION STATUS ATOM) Suppose $\alpha(\vec{t})$ is an action atom, where $\vec{t}$ is a vector of terms (variables or objects) matching the type schema of α. Then, the formulas $\mathbf{P}(\alpha(\vec{t}))$, $\mathbf{F}(\alpha(\vec{t}))$, $\mathbf{O}(\alpha(\vec{t}))$, $\mathbf{W}(\alpha(\vec{t}))$, and $\mathbf{Do}\,(\alpha(\vec{t}))$ are *action status atoms*. The set $AS = \{\mathbf{P}, \mathbf{F}, \mathbf{O}, \mathbf{W}, \mathbf{Do}\,\}$ is called the action status set.

We will often abuse notation and omit parentheses in action status atoms, writing $\mathbf{P}\alpha(\vec{t})$ instead of $\mathbf{P}(\alpha(\vec{t}))$, and so on.

An action status atom has the following intuitive meaning (a more detailed description of the precise reading of these atoms will be provided later in Section 6.5.2):

- $\mathbf{P}\alpha$ means that the agent is permitted to take action α;
- $\mathbf{F}\alpha$ means that the agent is forbidden from taking α;
- $\mathbf{O}\alpha$ means that the agent is obliged to take action α;
- $\mathbf{W}\alpha$ means that obligation to take action α is waived; and,
- $\mathbf{Do}\,\alpha$ means that the agent does take action α.

Notice that the operators $\mathbf{P}, \mathbf{F}, \mathbf{O}$, and $\mathbf{W}$ have been extensively studied in the area of deontic logic (Meyer and Wieringa 1993; Åquist 1984). Moreover, the operator $\mathbf{Do}$ is in the spirit of the "praxiological" operator $E_a A$ (Kanger 1972), which informally means that "agent a sees to it that A is the case" (Meyer and Wieringa 1993, p. 292).

DEFINITION 6.4.2 (ACTION RULE) An *action rule* (*rule*, for short) is a clause r of the form

$$A \leftarrow L_1, \ldots, L_n \tag{6.2}$$

where A is an action status atom, and each of $L_1, \ldots, L_n$ is either an action status atom, or a code call atom, each of which may be preceded by a negation sign ($\neg$).

DEFINITION 6.4.3 (SAFETY) We require that each rule r be *safe* in the sense that:

1. $B_{cc}(r)$ is safe modulo the root variables occurring explicitly in $B_{as}^+(r)$, and
2. the root of each variable in r occurs in $B_{cc}(r) \cup B_{as}^+(r)$.

All variables in a rule r are implicitly universally quantified at the front of the rule. A rule is *positive*, if no negation sign occurs in front of an action status atom in its body.

For any rule r of the form (6.2), we denote by $H(r)$, the atom in the head of r, and by $B(r)$, the collection of literals in the body; by $B^-(r)$ we denote the negative literals in $B(r)$, and by $B^+(r)$ the positive literals in $B(r)$. Moreover, by $\neg.B^-(r)$ we denote the atoms of the negative literals in $B^-(r)$. Finally, the index *as* (resp., *cc*) for any of these sets denotes restriction to the literals involving action status atoms (resp., code call atoms).

Section 6.4   Agent Programs: Syntax   161

DEFINITION 6.4.4 (AGENT PROGRAM)   An *agent program* $\mathcal{P}$ is a finite collection of rules. An agent program $\mathcal{P}$ is *positive* if all its rules are positive.

We are now ready to provide several examples of agent programs associated with our three motivating examples.

Example 6.4.1 (CHAIN Example Revisited)   The supplier agent may use the agent program shown below. In the following rules, the supplier agent makes use of the message box to get various variables it needs as described in Chapter 4. In order to extract variables, the supplier agent invokes the code call getVar of the message box domain.

r1:   **F** *update_stockDB*(Part_id, Amount_requested, Company) ←
        O *process_request*(Msg.Id, Agent),
        in(Amount_requested, msgbox : *getVar*(Msg.Id, "Amount_requested")),
        in(Part_id, msgbox : *getVar*(Msg.Id, "Part_id")),
        in(Company, msgbox : *getVar*(Msg.Id, "Company")),
        in(amount_not_available, supplier : *monitorStock*(Amount_requested, Part_id))

This rule ensures that we cannot invoke update_stockDB when Amount_requested exceeds the amount available.

r2:   **F** *update_stockDB*(Part_id1, Amount_requested1, Company1) ←
        O *process_request*(Msg.Id1, Agent1),
        O *process_request*(Msg.Id2, Agent2),
        in(Amount_requested1, msgbox : *getVar*(Msg.Id1, "Amount_requested1")),
        in(Amount_requested2, msgbox : *getVar*(Msg.Id2, "Amount_requested2")),
        in(Part_id1, msgbox : *getVar*(Msg.Id1, "Part_id1")),
        in(Part_id2, msgbox : *getVar*(Msg.Id2, "Part_id2")),
        in(Company1, msgbox : *getVar*(Msg.Id1, "Company1")),
        in(Company2, msgbox : *getVar*(Msg.Id2, "Company2")),
        =(Part_id1, Part_id2),
        Do *update_stockDB*(Part_id2, Amount_requested2, Company2),
        =(Amount_requested,   Amount_requested1 + Amount_requested2),
        in(amount_not_available, supplier : *monitorStock*(Amount_requested, Part_id))
        Company1 $\neq$ Company2

This rule ensures that we do not invoke update_stockDB for Amount_requested1 units of Part_id1 when the Amount_requested1 exceeds the amount that will be available after our agent finishes the update_stockDB action for Amount_requested2 units of Part_id2.

r3:   **O** *order_part*(Part_id, amount_to_order) ←
        O *process_request*(Msg.Id, Agent),

in(Amount_requested, msgbox : *getVar*(Msg.Id, "Amount_requested")),
in(Part_id, msgbox : *getVar*(Msg.Id, "Part_id")),
in(supplies_too_low, supplier : *too_low_threshold*(Part_id)),
in(amount_not_available, supplier : *monitorStock*(supplies_too_low, Part_id),)

If our supply for Part_id falls below the supplies_too_low threshold, then we are obliged to order amount_to_order more units for this part. Note that amount_to_order and supplies_too_low represent integer constants.

r4: **P** *order_part*(Part_id, amount_to_order) ←
   O *process_request*(Msg.Id, Agent),
   in(Amount_requested, msgbox : *getVar*(Msg.Id, "Amount_requested")),
   in(Part_id, msgbox : *getVar*(Msg.Id, "Part_id")),
   in(supplies_low, supplier : *low_threshold*(Part_id)),
   in(amount_not_available, supplier : *monitorStock*(supplies_low, Part_id)),

If our supply for Part_id falls below the supplies_low threshold, then we may order amount_to_order more units for this part. When supplies_low > supplies_too_low, we may use rule r4 to reduce the number of times we need to invoke rule R3. Note that amount_to_order and supplies_too_low represent integer constants.

r5: **W** *order_part*(Part_id, amount_to_order) ←
   O *process_request*(Msg.Id, Agent),
   in(Amount_requested, msgbox : *getVar*(Msg.Id, "Amount_requested")),
   in(Part_id, msgbox : *getVar*(Msg.Id, "Part_id")),
   in(supplies_low, supplier : *low_threshold*(Part_id)),
   in(amount_not_available, supplier : *monitorStock*(supplies_low, Part_id)),
   in(part_discontinued, supplier : *productStatus*(Part_id))

If the part Part_id has been discontinued, we are not obliged to order amount_to_order more units of the part when supplies fall below our supplies_too_low threshold (i.e., when rule R3 is fired).

r6: **O** *request*("plant", "find:supplier") ←
   O *process_request*(Msg.Id, Agent),
   in(Amount_requested, msgbox : *getVar*(Msg.Id, "Amount_requested")),
   in(Part_id, msgbox : *getVar*(Msg.Id, "Part_id")),
   Do *order_part*(Part_id, Amount_requested)

If we decide to order Amount_requested units of part Part_id, request the plant agent's find : *supplier* service to determine if there is a supplier which can provide Amount_requested units of Part_id. Note that the supplier agent does not know how the plant agent decides upon which manufacturing plant to use.

r7: **O** *request*("shipping", "prepare:schedule(shipping)") ←
  O *process_request*(Msg.Id, Agent),
  O *process_request*((Msg.Id1, Agent1),
  =(Agent1, plant),
  in(Amount_requested, msgbox: *getVar*(Msg.Id, "Amount_requested")),
  in(Part_id, msgbox: *getVar*(Msg.Id, "Part_id")),
  in(Part_supplier, msgbox: *getVar*(Msg.Id1, "Part_supplier")),
  Do *order_part*(Part_id, Amount_requested),

If we decide to order Amount_requested units of part Part_id, we must also use the shipping agent's *prepare : schedule(shipping)* service to determine how and when the requested Amount_requested units can be shipped to us from the Part_supplier which is determined by the plant agent. Part_supplier is extracted from a message sent from the plant agent in response to the supplier agent's request to the find : *supplier* service.

r8: **O** *process_request*(Msg.Id, Agent) ←
  in(Msg, msgbox: *getAllMsgs*()),
  =(Agent, Msg.Source),

This rule says that the agent is obliged to process all requests in its message box from other agents. This does not mean that it will respond positively to a request.

r9: **O** *delete_msg*(Msg.Id) ←
  Do *process_request*(Msg.Id, Agent)

This rule says that the agent deletes all messages that it has processed from its message box.

Example 6.4.2 (CFIT Example Revisited) The agent program used by the autoPilot agent may use the following rules in its agent program. The same methods used in the Example 6.4.1 apply here too.

r1: **F** *maintain_course*(No_go, Flight_route, Current_location) ←
  O *process_request*(Msg.Id, terrain),
  in(No_go, msgbox: *getVar*(Msg.Id, "No_go")),
  in(Current_location, autoPilot: *location*()),
  in(Flight_route, autoPilot: *getFlightRoute*()),
  Do *adjust_course*(No_go, Flight_route, Current_location)

After receiving the No_go regions from the terrain agent, if the autoPilot agent decides to adjust_course, it is no longer allowed to perform the maintain_course action. Note that the autoPilot agent maintains the local variables Flight_route and Current_location.

r2: **F** *adjust_course*(No_go, Flight_route, Current_location) ←
    O *process_request*(Msg.Id, terrain),
    in(No_go, msgbox : *getVar*(Msg.Id, "No_go")),
    in(Current_location, autoPilot : *location*()),
    in(Flight_route, autoPilot : *getFlightRoute*()),
    Do *maintain_course*(No_go, Flight_route, Current_location)

If the agent has decided to maintain_course, it is no longer allowed to perform the adjust_course action.

r3: **O** *return_control*() ←
    in(manual_override, autoPilot : *pilotStatus*(pilot_message))

If the pilot wants to disengage the auto-pilot, manual control should be returned.

r4: **P** *compute_currentLocation*(Report) ←
    O *process_request*(Msg.Id, terrain),
    in(No_go, msgbox : *getVar*(Msg.Id, "No_go")),
    in(Report, msgbox : *getVar*(Msg.Id, "Report")),
    in(Current_location, autoPilot : *location*()),
    in(Flight_route, autoPilot : *getFlightRoute*()),
    Do *adjust_course*(No_go, Flight_route, Current_location)

If the agent decides to adjust_course, it may invoke compute_currentLocation in order to update its estimate for Current_location.

r5: **O** *create_flight_plan*(No_go, Flight_route, Current_location) ←
    O *process_request*(Msg.Id, terrain),
    in(No_go, msgbox : *getVar*(Msg.Id, "No_go")),
    in(Current_location, autoPilot : *location*()),
    in(Flight_route, autoPilot : *getFlightRoute*()),
    Do *adjust_course*(No_go, Flight_route, Current_location)

If the agent decides to adjust_course, it must create a flight plan which avoids the No_go regions received from the terrain agent. The No_go regions are specified by the terrain agent's determine : *area(no-go)* service.

r6: **O** *execute_flight_plan*(Flight_route) ←
    O *process_request*(Msg.Id, terrain),
    in(No_go, msgbox : *getVar*(Msg.Id, "No_go")),
    in(Current_location, autoPilot : *location*()),
    in(Flight_route, autoPilot : *getFlightRoute*()),
    Do *adjust_course*(No_go, Flight_route, Current_location)

Once a flight plan (i.e., Flight_route) has been generated, we can execute this plan by invoking the *execute_flight_plan* action.

r7: **O** *process_request*(Msg.Id, Agent) ←
  in(Msg, msgbox : *getAllMsgs*()),
  =(Agent,Msg.Source)

This rule says that the agent is obliged to process all requests in its message box. This does not mean that it will respond positively to a request. Note that the autoPilot agent may receive messages from different agents, for example the terrain agent and the gps agent.

r8: **O** *delete_msg*(Msg.Id) ←
  Do *process_request*(Msg.Id, Agent)

This rule says that the agent deletes all messages that it has processed from its message box.

Example 6.4.3 (STORE Example Revisited)   The agent program used by the profiling agent may use the following rules in its agent program. The same methods used in Example 6.4.1 apply here too.

r1: **F** *update_highProfile*(Ssn, Name, Profile) ←
  Do *process_request*(Msg.Id, Agent),
  in(Ssn, msgbox : *getVar*(Msg.Id, "Ssn")),
  in(Name, msgbox : *getVar*(Msg.Id, "Name")),
  in(Profile, msgbox : *getVar*(Msg.Id, "Profile")),
  in(spender(low), profiling : *classifyUser*(Ssn))

If a user is classified as spender(low), then we may not use *update_highProfile* to update their profile.

r2: **F** *update_highProfile*(Ssn, Name, Profile) ←
  Do *process_request*(Msg.Id, Agent),
  in(Ssn, msgbox : *getVar*(Msg.Id, "Ssn")),
  in(Name, msgbox : *getVar*(Msg.Id, "Name")),
  in(Profile, msgbox : *getVar*(Msg.Id, "Profile")),
  in(spender(medium), profiling : *classifyUser*(Ssn))

If a user is classified as spender(medium), then we may not use *update_highProfile* to update their profile. If the only other user classification is spender(high), then rules r1 and r2 together specify that only users which are high spenders can have their profiles modified by the update_highProfile action.

r3: **P** *request*("credit", "provide:information(credit)") ←
  Do *process_request*(Msg.Id, Agent),
  in(Ssn, msgbox : *getVar*(Msg.Id, "Ssn")),
  in(Name, msgbox : *getVar*(Msg.Id, "Name")),
  Do *classify_user*(Ssn, Name)

If the agent needs to classify a user, it can easily request the credit agent's provide : *information(credit)* service to help decide which classification to use.

r4: **P** *request*("credit", "provide:address") ←
  Do *process_request*(Msg.Id, Agent),
  in(Ssn, msgbox : *getVar*(Msg.Id, "Ssn")),
  in(Name, msgbox : *getVar*(Msg.Id, "Name")),
  Do *classify_user*(Ssn, Name)

If the agent needs to classify a user, it may also request the credit agent's provide : *address* service to get further information about the customer.

r5: **O** *update_highProfile*(Ssn, Name, RiskProfile) ←
  Do *process_request*(Msg.Id, Agent),
  =(Agent, credit),
  in(Ssn, msgbox : *getVar*(Msg.Id, "Ssn")),
  in(Name, msgbox : *getVar*(Msg.Id, "Name")),
  in(RiskProfile, msgbox : *getVar*(Msg.Id, "RiskProfile")),
  in(spender(high), profiling : *classifyUser*(Ssn))

If a high spending customer overdrafts a check, update this user's information to reflect the fact that she has a risky profile. Note that the set of customers who overdraft a check is determined from a message from the credit agent.

r6: **O** *inform_sale_notifier*(Ssn, Name, Profile) ←
  Do *process_request*(Msg.Id, Agent),
  in(Ssn, msgbox : *getVar*(Msg.Id, "Ssn")),
  in(Name, msgbox : *getVar*(Msg.Id, "Name")),
  in(Profile, msgbox : *getVar*(Msg.Id, "Profile")),
  Do *update_highProfile*(Ssn, Name, Profile),
  =(Profile, riskProfile)

If a high spending customer acquires a riskProfile, notify the saleNotification agent. After this notification, the saleNotification agent may decide to defer the production of expensive brochures for this customer until his/her credit is in better standing.

r7: **W** *inform_sale_notifier*(Ssn, Name, Profile) ←
  Do *process_request*(Msg.Id, Agent),

Section 6.4   Agent Programs: Syntax   167

>   **Do** *process_request*((Msg.Id1, Agent1),
>   =(Agent, saleNotification),
>   **in**(Ssn, msgbox : *getVar*(Msg.Id, "Ssn")),
>   **in**(Name, msgbox : *getVar*(Msg.Id, "Name")),
>   **in**(Profile, msgbox : *getVar*(Msg.Id, "Profile")),
>   **in**(offseason, msgbox : *getVar*(Msg.Id1, "offseason")),
>   **Do** *update_highProfile*(Ssn, Name, Profile)

If we are in the offseason (e.g., if it is summer and we are dealing with winter coats), then there is no need to call *inform_sale_notifier* whenever we invoke *update_highProfile*.

r8:   **O** *process_request*(Msg.Id, Agent) ←
  in(Msg, msgbox : *getAllMsgs*()),
  =(Agent,Msg.Source)

This rule says that the agent is obliged to process all requests in its message box. This does not mean that it will respond positively to the request. Note that the profiling agent can receive messages from different agents, such as the credit agent and the saleNotification agent.

r9:   **O** *delete_msg*(Msg.Id) ←
  Do *process_request*(Msg.Id, Agent)

This rule says that the agent deletes all messages that it has processed from its message box.

Before proceeding to discuss the formal semantics of agent programs, we quickly revisit the architecture of an agent's decisionmaking component shown in Figure 6.1 on page 142.

1. Every agent manages a set of data types through a set of well-defined *methods*.

2. These data types and methods include a message box data structure, with associated manipulation algorithms described in Chapter 4.

3. At a given point *t* in time, the state of an agent reflects the set of data items the agent currently has access to—these data items must all be of one of the data types alluded to above.

4. At time *t*, the agent may receive a set of *new* messages—these new messages constitute a *change* to the state of the agent.

5. The aforementioned changes may *trigger* one or more rules in the agent's associated agent program to become true. Based on the selected semantics for agent programs (to be described in Section 6.5), the agent makes a decision on what actions to actually perform, in keeping with the rules governing its behavior encoded in its associated Agent Program. This computation is made by executing a program called *ComputeSem* which computes the semantics of the agent.

Algorithm 6.4.1 (Agent-Decision-Cycle)
Agent-Decision-Cycle(Curr: agent_state;
$\quad\quad\quad\quad\quad\quad$ $\mathcal{IC}$**: integrity constraint set;**
$\quad\quad\quad\quad\quad\quad$ $\mathcal{AC}$**: action constraint set;**
$\quad\quad\quad\quad\quad\quad$ $\mathcal{AB}$ **: action base;**
$\quad\quad\quad\quad\quad\quad$ **conc: notion of concurrency;**
$\quad\quad\quad\quad\quad\quad$ **Newmsg: set of messages)**
1. **while true do**
2. { $DoSet := ComputeSem(\ Curr, \mathcal{IC}, \mathcal{AC}, \mathcal{AB},$ **conc**, $Newmsg)$;
   ($\star$ find a set of actions to execute based on messages received $\star$)
3. $\quad Curr :=$ result of executing the single action **conc**($DoSet$); }
end.

---

6. The actions that are supposed to be performed according to the above mentioned semantics are then concurrently executed, using the notion of concurrency, **conc**, selected by the agent's designer. The agent's state may (possibly) change as a consequence of the performance of such actions. In addition, the message box of other agents may also change.

7. The cycle continues perpetually.

In view of the above discussion, every agent's behavior can be encoded through the *Agent Decision Cycle* Algorithm (Algorithm 6.4.1).

Before we conclude this section, we outline a simple example to illustrate the above behavior.

Example 6.4.4 (Clock-Driven Actions) Let us consider a very simple agent in the STORE scenario, that sends a message at 10 pm every day to the sales manager of the store, summarizing the total value of merchandise sold on that day. This behavior may be modeled in terms of a clock agent, and a salesMonitor agent (which will interact with other agents). At 10 pm every day, the clock agent sends a message to the salesMonitor agent saying it is 10 pm, together with the current date. This is an *update* to the state of salesMonitor which causes the salesMonitor to execute an action called *sendsales*(Today). This causes the desired message to be sent to the Sales Manager.

In general, an agent takes actions based on its current state, which in turn, is affected by the receipt of messages from other agents. The Agent Decision Cycle is illustrated in the context of our three motivating examples below.

Example 6.4.5 (CHAIN Example Revisited) Consider the agent program for the supplier agent given in Example 6.4.1 on page 161.

1. Each time we sell supplies, our agent consults rules r1 and r2 to ensure that the amount requested never exceeds the amount available, even if the requests are coming from multiple companies. If two concurrent requests for the same part are considered by the supplier of Example 6.4.1 on page 161, and if both these requests can be individually (but not jointly) satisfied, then our current example non-deterministically satisfies one. The agent program in question does not adopt any preference strategies.

2. If we do not replenish our supplies, rule r4 will fire when our supply of part Part_id falls below the supplies_low threshold. Our agent is now allowed to order more supplies. If more supplies are not ordered, rule r3 will eventually fire when our supply of part Part_id falls below the supplies_too_low threshold. The agent is now obliged to order more parts. This obligation can be waived, however, if part Part_id has been discontinued (see rule r5).

3. When we order parts, rule r6 will fire. Here, the supplier agent consults the plant agent to determine which supplier to use. Once an appropriate supplier has been found, the supplier agent asks the shipping agent to provide a shipping schedule (rule r7) so the ordered parts can be delivered.

It is easy to see, from rules (r8) and (r9) that the same message requesting parts will not be considered twice. Rule (r9) ensures that once a message is processed, it is deleted from the message box.

Example 6.4.6 (CFIT Example Revisited) Consider the agent program for the autoPilot agent given in Example 6.4.2 on page 163.

1. We alternate between the maintain_course and adjust_course actions (while obeying rules r1 and r2) until control is returned to the pilot (rule r3).

2. Suppose our autoPilot agent discovers that by following its current course, it may fly into a mountain. Here, the *adjust_course* action will be invoked. By rule r4, the agent may now call *compute_currentLocation* to get a better idea of the plane's position.

3. The current estimate for the plane's position will now be used by the terrain agent to determine which areas are No_go (see rule r5). Furthermore, rule r5 indicates that a flight plan (Flight_route) which avoids these No_go areas should be generated.

4. Finally, our agent will invoke *execute_flight_plan* (by rule r6) to actually maneuver the plane out of harm's way by using Flight_route.

Example 6.4.7 (STORE Example Revisited) Consider the agent program for the profiling agent given in Example 6.4.3 on page 165.

1. We begin by classifying the spending profile for a user. To do this, we may consult the credit agent by using its services such as provide : *information(credit)* (by rule r3) or provide : *address* (by rule r4).

2. If this classification indicates that our user has a low or medium spending profile, we do not worry about updating the user's profile (see rules r1 and r2).

3. Suppose our user is a high spender who overdrafts a check. When this occurs, the credit agent will send a message to our profiling agent. By rule r5, the profiling agent will now classify our user with a riskProfile.

4. Once a user obtains this profile, the profiling agent may send (by rule r6) a message to the saleNotification agent so the latter agent can take whatever actions it deems necessary. Note however that this message will not be sent if the profiling agent knows that the saleNotification agent is not receiving messages. By rule r7, this situation may occur during the off-season.

Example 6.4.8 (CFIT Example: Multiagent Interaction) The reader may be wondering exactly how the agents in a multiagent application interact with one another. In this example, we provide a discussion of how this happens in a microcosm of the CFIT example. Appendix A of this book contains the full working code for agents in the CFIT example.

Consider the autoPilot agent in the CFIT example. Every Δ units of time, the autoPilot agent receives a message from a clock agent. This message includes a "Wake" request telling the autoPilot agent to wake up.

The agent program associated with autoPilot causes the *wake* action to be executed, which in turn triggers other actions. These include:

• Executing an action *sendMessage*(autoPilot, gps, <*service_request*>) where the service request <*service_request*> of the gps agent is requesting the current location of the plane.

• The gps agent executes its *getAllMsgs* and retrieves the message sent by the autoPilot agent.

• The decision program of the gps agent executes this request and also executes the action *sendMessage*(gps, autoPilot, <*answer*>) where <*answer*> is the answer to the request made by the autoPilot agent.

• The autoPilot agent executes the *getAllMsgs* action and retrieves the message sent by the gps agent.

• The decision program of the autoPilot agent checks to see if the location of the plane sent by the GPS is where the flight plan says the plane should be. If yes, it executes the action *sleep* and goes to sleep for another Δ units of time. If not, it executes the action

sendMessage(autoPilot, terrain, <*request*>)

where <*request*> requests the terrain agent to send the elevation of the plane at its current location (as determined by the GPS agents) as well as send the No_go areas.

- The terrain agent executes its *getAllMsgs* action and retrieves the message sent by the autoPilot agent.
- The decision program of the terrain agent executes this request and also executes the action *sendMessage*(terrain, autoPilot, Ans) where Ans is the answer to the request made by the autoPilot Agent.
- The autoPilot agent executes the *getAllMsgs* action and retrieves the message sent by the terrain agent.
- It then executes its *replan* action with the new terrain (correct) location of the plan and the terrain "No go" areas.

6.5 Agent Programs: Semantics

If an agent uses an agent program $\mathcal{P}$, the question that the agent must answer, over and over again is: *What is the set of all action status atoms of the form* **Do** α *that are true with respect to* $\mathcal{P}$*, the current state,* $\mathcal{O}_S$*, the underlying set* $\mathcal{AC}$ *of action constraints, and the set* $\mathcal{IC}$ *of underlying integrity constraints on agent states?* This defines the set of actions that the agent must execute concurrently. In this section, we will provide a series of successively more refined semantics for action programs that answers this question.

In Section 6.5.1, we will introduce the concept of a feasible status set. Feasible status sets do not by themselves constitute a semantics for agent programs, but they form the *basic construct* upon which all our semantics will be built.

In Section 6.5.2, we will define the semantics of Agent Programs to be those feasible status sets that are deemed to satisfy certain rationality requirements. In Section 6.5.4, we add a further requirement—the semantics of an agent program $\mathcal{P}$ is characterized by a subset of rational status sets—those that satisfy an additional *reasonable*-ness condition. This is further refined in Section 6.5.6, where two alternative policies for selecting the "right" reasonable status sets are provided. As feasible status sets may allow certain actions to be neither permitted nor forbidden, we introduce the notation of a complete status set in Section 6.5.6. Two policies are allowed—one of these policies is akin to the closed world assumption in databases (Reiter 1978) (all actions that are not explicitly permitted are forbidden) and the other is akin to the open world assumption (all actions that are not explicitly forbidden are allowed).

All the preceding semantics describe ways of syntactically selecting one or more feasible status sets as somehow being the "right" feasible status sets. For example, all rational status sets are feasible status sets, but not vice-versa. Reasonable status sets are also feasible status sets (and in fact rational status sets) but not vice-versa. The same applies to the other types of status sets. In Section 6.5.7, we use numerical cost measures to select status sets. Given a semantics Sem where

Sem ∈ {Feasible, Rational, Reasonable, F-preferential, P-preferential, Weak Rational},

Section 6.5.7 shows how to associate a "cost" with each Sem-status set. An optimal Sem-status set is one which minimizes cost. A status set's cost may be defined in terms of (1) the cost of performing the **Do** actions in that status set, and/or (2) the "badness" value of the state that results, and/or (3) a mix of the previous two criteria. Section 6.5.7 will define these expressions formally.

Figure 6.2 captures the relationship between these different semantic structures. The definition of Sem-status sets is layered on top of the definitions of the other semantics—hence, to avoid clutter, we do not include them in this figure.

6.5.1 Feasible Status Sets

In this section, we will introduce the important concept of a feasible status set. While feasible status sets do not per se constitute the desired semantics for agent programs in general, every semantics we define for Agent Programs will build upon this basic definition.

Intuitively, a feasible status set consists of assertions about the status of actions, such that these assertions are compatible with (but are not necessarily forced to be true by) the rules of the agent program and the underlying action and integrity constraints.

In what follows, we assume the existence of a body of software code $S = (\mathcal{T}_S, \mathcal{F}_S, \mathcal{C}_S)$, an action base $\mathcal{AB}$, and action and integrity constraints $\mathcal{AC}$ and $\mathcal{IC}$, respectively, in the background. The first concept we introduce are status sets.

DEFINITION 6.5.1 (STATUS SET) A *status set* is any set S of ground action status atoms over S. For any operator Op ∈ {**P, Do, F, O, W**}, we denote by Op(S) the set Op(S) = $\{\alpha \mid \text{Op}(\alpha) \in S\}$.

Informally, a status set S represents information about the status of ground actions. If some atom Op(α) occurs in S, then this means that the status Op is true for α. For example, **Do** (α), **F**(β) ∈ S means that action α will be taken by the agent, while action β is forbidden. Of course, not every status set is meaningful. For example, if both **F**(α) and **P**(α) are in S, then S is intuitively inconsistent, since α can not be simultaneously permitted and forbidden. In order to characterize the meaningful status sets, we introduce the concepts of deontic and action consistency.

Section 6.5   Agent Programs: Semantics

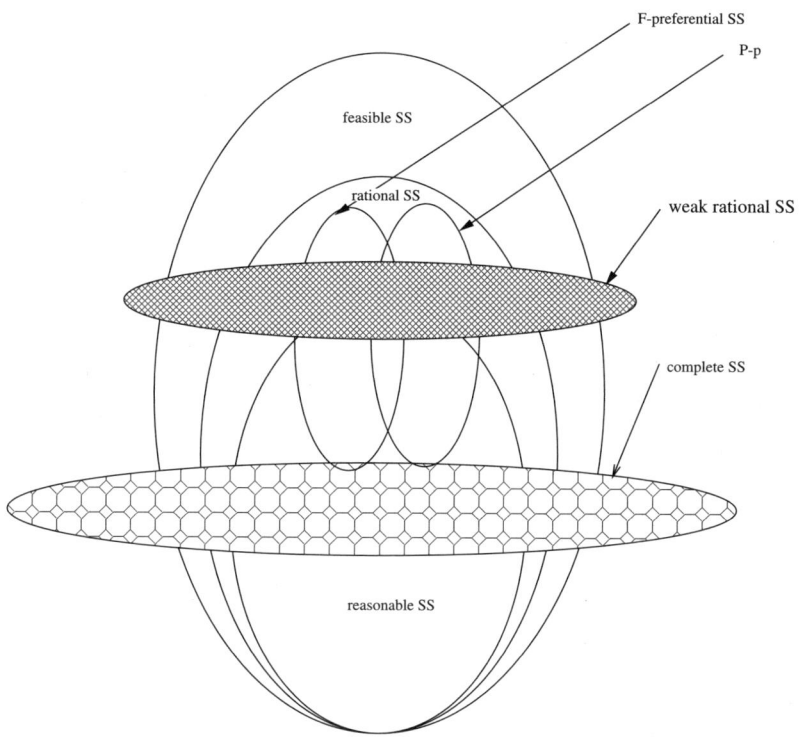

Figure 6.2
Relationship between different Status Sets (SS).

DEFINITION 6.5.2 (DEONTIC AND ACTION CONSISTENCY)   A status set S is called *deontically consistent*, *if* it satisfies the following rules for any ground action α:

- If $\mathbf{O}\alpha \in S$, then $\mathbf{W}\alpha \notin S$
- If $\mathbf{P}\alpha \in S$, then $\mathbf{F}\alpha \notin S$
- If $\mathbf{P}\alpha \in S$, then $\mathcal{O}_S \models \exists^* Pre(\alpha)$, where $\exists^* Pre(\alpha)$ denotes the existential closure of $Pre(\alpha)$, i.e., all free variables in $Pre(\alpha)$ are governed by an existential quantifier. This condition means that the action α is in fact executable in the state $\mathcal{O}_S$.

A status set S is called *action consistent*, if $S, \mathcal{O}_S \models \mathcal{AC}$ holds.

Besides consistency, we also wish that the presence of certain atoms in S entails the presence of other atoms in S. For example, if $\mathbf{O}\alpha$ is in S, then we expect that $\mathbf{P}\alpha$ is also in S, and if $\mathbf{O}\alpha$ is in S, then we would like to have $\mathbf{Do}\,\alpha$ in S. This is captured by the concept of deontic and action closure.

DEFINITION 6.5.3 (DEONTIC AND ACTION CLOSURE)   The *deontic closure* of a status S, denoted **D-Cl**(S), is the closure of S under the rule

If **O**$\alpha \in S$, then **P**$\alpha \in S$,

where α is any ground action. We say that S is *deontically closed*, if $S = $ **D-Cl**(S) holds.

The *action closure* of a status set S, denoted **A-Cl**(S), is the closure of S under the rules

If **O**$\alpha \in S$, then **Do**$\alpha \in S$,

If **Do**$\alpha \in S$, then **P**$\alpha \in S$,

where α is any ground action. We say that a status S is action-closed, if $S = $ **A-Cl**(S) holds.

The following straightforward results shows that status sets that are action-closed are also deontically closed, i.e.,

PROPOSITION 6.5.1   Suppose S is a status set. Then,

1. **A-Cl**$(S) = S$ implies **D-Cl**$(S) = S$
2. **D-Cl**$(S) \subseteq$ **A-Cl**(S), for all S.

Proof

1. Suppose **A-Cl**$(S) = S$. It is immediate from the definition of **D-Cl**$_h(t)$ at $S \subseteq$ **D-Cl**(S). So suppose Op$(\alpha) \in$ **D-Cl**(S). There are two cases—either Op $=$ **P** or Op $\neq$ **P**.

  If Op $=$ **P**, then either Op(α) is in S (in which case we are done), or Op$(\alpha) \in$ **D-Cl**$(S) - S$—this must be because **O**$\alpha \in S$. Therefore, as $S = $ **A-Cl**(S), we know by the first rule defining **A-Cl**(S) that **Do**$\alpha \in$ **A-Cl**(S) and by the second rule defining **A-Cl**(S), we know that **P**$\alpha \in$ **A-Cl**$(S) = S$.

  If Op $\neq$ **P**, by definition of **D-Cl**(S), we know that Op$(\alpha) \in S$ because **D-Cl**(S) is constructed only by adding status atoms of the form **P**α to S.

2. Suppose Op$(\alpha) \in$ **D-Cl**(S). If Op$(\alpha) \in S$, then it follows immediately by definition that Op$(\alpha) \in$ **A-Cl**(S), so assume Op$(\alpha) \notin S$. Then Op $=$ **P**, and **P**$\alpha \in S$ means that **O**$\alpha \in S$. By the same two rules defining **A-Cl**(S) (see argument in case 1 above), it follows that **P**$\alpha \in$ **A-Cl**(S).

A status set S which is consistent and closed is certainly a meaningful assignment of a status to each ground action. Note that we may have ground actions α that do not occur anywhere within a status set—this means that no commitment about the status of α has been made. The following definition specifies how we may "close" up a status set under the rules expressed by an agent program P.

DEFINITION 6.5.4 (OPERATOR **App**$_{\mathcal{P},\mathcal{O}_S}(S)$)   Suppose $\mathcal{P}$ is an agent program, and $\mathcal{O}_S$ is an agent state. Then, **App**$_{\mathcal{P},\mathcal{O}_S}(S)$ is defined to be the set of all ground action status atoms A

such that there exists a rule in P having a ground instance of the form $r : A \leftarrow L_1, \ldots, L_n$ such that

1. $B^+_{as}(r) \subseteq S$ and $\neg.B^-_{as}(r) \cap S = \emptyset$, and
2. every code call $\chi \in B^+_{cc}(r)$ succeeds in $\mathcal{O}_S$, and
3. every code call $\chi \in \neg.B^-_{cc}(r)$ does not succeed in $\mathcal{O}_S$, and
4. for every atom $\mathsf{Op}(\alpha) \in B^+(r) \cup \{A\}$ such that $\mathsf{Op} \in \{\mathbf{P}, \mathbf{O}, \mathbf{Do}\}$, the action α is executable in state $\mathcal{O}_S$.

Note that part (4) of the above definition only applies to the "positive" modes $\mathbf{P}, \mathbf{O}, \mathbf{Do}$. It does not apply to atoms of the form $\mathbf{F}\alpha$ as such actions are not executed, nor does it apply to atoms of the form $\mathbf{W}\alpha$, because execution of an action might be (vacuously) waived, if its prerequisites are not fulfilled.

Our approach is to base the semantics of agent programs on consistent and closed status sets. However, we have to take into account the rules of the program as well as integrity constraints. This leads us to the notion of a feasible status set.

DEFINITION 6.5.5 (FEASIBLE STATUS SET) Let $\mathcal{P}$ be an agent program and let $\mathcal{O}_S$ be an agent state. Then, a status set S is a *feasible status set* for $\mathcal{P}$ on $\mathcal{O}_S$, if the following conditions hold:

(S1) (closure under the program rules) $\mathbf{App}_{\mathcal{P},\mathcal{O}_S}(S) \subseteq S$;

(S2) (deontic and action consistency) S is deontically and action consistent;

(S3) (deontic and action closure) S is action closed and deontically closed;

(S4) (state consistency) $\mathcal{O}'_S \models \mathcal{IC}$, where $\mathcal{O}'_S = \mathrm{apply}(\mathbf{Do}\,(S), \mathcal{O}_S)$ is the state which results after taking all actions in $\mathbf{Do}\,(S)$ on the state $\mathcal{O}_S$ (using **conc**).

Notice that condition (S2) is hereditary, i.e., if a status set S satisfies (S2), then any subset $S' \subseteq S$ satisfies (S2) as well.

In general, there are action programs that have zero, one or several feasible status sets. This is illustrated through the following examples.

Example 6.5.1 (CHAIN example revisited)   Let us consider a simple agent program containing just the rule (r4) of Example 6.4.1, together with rule (r8) and (r9) that manage the message box.

r4: **P** *order_part*(Part_id, amount_to_order) ←
  O *process_request*(Msg.Id, Agent),
  in(Amount_requested, msgbox : *getVar*(Msg.Id, "Amount_requested")),
  in(Part_id, msgbox : *getVar*(Msg.Id, "Part_id")),
  in(supplies_low, supplier : *low_threshold*(Part_id)),
  in(amount_not_available, supplier : *monitorStock*(supplies_low, Part_id)),

Suppose the current state of the agent supplier is such that the number of items of a certain part say (p50) falls below the supplies_low threshold for that part. Suppose the company making the request is zzz_corp, and the Amount_requested is 50, and the amount_to_order is 2000. In this case, this agent program will have multiple feasible status sets. Some feasible status sets will contain **P***order_part*(p50, 2000) but will not contain **Do** *order_part*(p50, 2000). However, other feasible status sets will contain both **P***order_part*(p50, 2000) and **Do** *order_part*(p50, 2000).

Example 6.5.2 (CHAIN example revisited) On the other hand, suppose our agent program contains rules (r3), (r8) and (r9) of Example 6.4.1, and suppose that for all parts, the amount of the part in stock is above the too_low_threshold amount. Further, suppose our agent program contains the rule

F *order_part*(Part_id, Amount_requested) ←
  O *process_request*(Msg.Id, Agent),
  in(Amount_requested, msgbox : *getVar*(Msg.Id, "Amount_requested")),
  in(Part_id, msgbox : *getVar*(Msg.Id, "Part_id")),
  ¬**O** *order_part*(Part_id, Amount_requested).

In this case, for all parts, we are forbidden from placing an order. Hence, this agent program has only one feasible status set in that respect, viz. that which contains status atoms of the form

F *order_part*(Part_id, Amount_requested)

together with relevant message processing action status atoms.

Example 6.5.3 The following (artificial) example shows that some agent programs may have no feasible status sets at all.

Pα ←

Fα ←

Clearly, if the current object state allows α to be executable, then no status set can satisfy both the closure under program rules requirement, and the deontic consistency requirement.

The following are immediate consequences of the definition of a feasible status set, which confirm that it appropriately captures a "possible" set of actions dictated by an agent program that is consistent with the obligations and restrictions on the agent program.

PROPOSITION 6.5.2 (PROPERTIES OF FEASIBLE STATUS SETS) Let S be a feasible status set. Then,

1. If $\mathbf{Do}\,\alpha \in S$, then $\mathcal{O}_S \models Pre(\alpha)$;
2. If $\mathbf{P}\alpha \notin S$, then $\mathbf{Do}\,\alpha \notin S$;
3. If $\mathbf{O}\alpha \in S$, then $\mathcal{O}_S \models Pre(\alpha)$;
4. If $\mathbf{O}\alpha \in S$, then $\mathbf{F}\alpha \notin S$.

Proof

1. Suppose $\mathbf{Do}\,\alpha \in S$. Then, as S is feasible, we know that $S = \mathbf{A\text{-}Cl}(S)$, and hence $\mathbf{P}\alpha \in S$. As S is feasible, and hence deontically consistent, the third condition of deontic consistency specifies that α's precondition is true in state $\mathcal{O}_S$.
2. This follows immediately because as S is feasible, we have $S = \mathbf{A\text{-}Cl}(S)$. The second condition defining $\mathbf{A\text{-}Cl}(S)$, when written in contrapositive form, states that $\mathbf{P}\alpha \notin S$ implies that $\mathbf{Do}\,\alpha \notin S$.
3. As S is feasible, $S = \mathbf{A\text{-}Cl}(S)$. The first condition specifying $\mathbf{A\text{-}Cl}(S)$ allows us to infer that $\mathbf{O}\alpha \in S$ implies that $\mathbf{Do}\,\alpha \in S$. The result follows immediately from part (1) of this theorem.
4. From the above argument, as $S = \mathbf{A\text{-}Cl}(S)$, we can conclude that $\mathbf{O}\alpha \in S$ implies that $\mathbf{P}\alpha \in S$. By the deontic consistency requirement, $\mathbf{F}\alpha \notin S$.

The reader may be tempted to believe that Condition 4 in Definition 6.5.4 is redundant. However, as the following agent program $\mathcal{P}$ amply demonstrates, this is not the case.

Example 6.5.4 Consider the agent program $\mathcal{P}$ given by:

$\mathbf{P}\alpha \leftarrow$

Assume that α is not executable in state $\mathcal{O}_S$. Then, under the current definition, no feasible status set S contains $\mathbf{P}\alpha$; e.g., $S = \emptyset$ is a feasible status set. If we drop condition 4 from Definition 6.5.4, then no feasible status set S exists, as $\mathbf{P}\alpha$ must be contained in every such S, which then violates deontic consistency.

6.5.2 Rational Status Sets

Intuitively, a feasible status set describes a set of status atoms that are compatible with the state of the software, the obligations and restrictions imposed on the agent by its associated agent program, and the deontic consistency requirements. Nevertheless, we note that feasible status sets may include **Do**ing actions that are not strictly necessary.

Example 6.5.5 (Expanded CHAIN Example)   Let us return to the example feasible status sets we saw in Example 6.5.1. In this case, this agent program had multiple feasible status sets. Some feasible status sets will contain **P**$order\_part$(p50, 2000) but will not contain **Do** $order\_part$(p50, 2000). However, other feasible status sets will contain both **P** $order\_part$(p50, 2000) and **Do** $order\_part$(p50, 2000). It is immediately apparent that we do not want *both* action status atoms **P** $order\_part$(p50, 2000) and **Do** $order\_part$(p50, 2000) to be present in feasible status sets: there is no good reason to in fact perform the action $order\_part$(p50, 2000) (the agent program in question does not mandate that **Do** $order\_part$(p50, 2000) be true).

The notion of a rational status set is postulated to accommodate this kind of reasoning. It is based on the principle that each action which is executed should be sufficiently "grounded" or "justified" by the agent program. That is, there should be evidence from the rules of the agent program that a certain action must be executed. For example, it seems unacceptable that an action α is executed, if α does not occur in any rule of the agent program at all.

This way, we also have to make sure that execution of an action must not be driven by the need to preserve the consistency of the agent's state. Rather, the integrity constraints should serve to prevent executions which appear to be rational if no integrity constraints were present. This motivates the following formal notion of groundedness.

DEFINITION 6.5.6 (GROUNDEDNESS; RATIONAL STATUS SET)   A status set S is *grounded*, if there exists no status set $S' \neq S$ such that $S' \subseteq S$ and S' satisfies conditions $(S1)$–$(S3)$ of a feasible status set.

A status set S is a *rational status set*, if S is a feasible status set and S is grounded.

Notice that if S is a feasible status set, then every $S' \subseteq S$ satisfies the condition $(S2)$ of feasibility. Therefore, the requirement of $(S2)$ for S' in the definition of groundedness is redundant. However, it seems more natural to have this condition included in the definition of groundedness. Moreover, if we did not have hereditary action consistency, then inclusion of action consistency would be indispensable.

Example 6.5.6 (Expanded CHAIN Example Continued)   Returning to Example 6.5.5, it is immediately apparent that all feasible status sets that contain both **P**$order\_part$(P, N) and **Do** $order\_part$(P, N) are not rational, while those that only contain **P**$order\_part$(P, N) satisfy rationality.

Observe that the definition of groundedness does not include condition (S4) of a feasible status set. A moment of reflection will show that omitting this condition is indeed appropriate. Recall that the integrity constraints must be maintained when the current agent state is changed into a new one. If we were to include the condition (S4) in groundedness, it may happen that the agent is forced to execute some actions which the program does not mention, just in order to maintain the integrity constraints. The following example illustrates this point.

If we go back to the example the agent program of Example 6.5.2, we observe that this program always has a unique rational status set, independent of the state of the agent. This is no accident. In fact, as will be shown below, *positive* programs enjoy the desirable property that if they have any rational status set at all, then they have a unique rational status set. In other words, they can have at most one rational status set. Observe that this property does not hold for non-positive agent programs in general.

It is possible to give a characterization of the unique rational status set in terms of a fixpoint operator, akin to the least fixpoint of logic programs (Lloyd 1987; Apt 1990). For that, we define for every positive program $\mathcal{P}$ and agent state $\mathcal{O}_S$ an operator $\mathbf{T}_{\mathcal{P},\mathcal{O}_S}$ that maps a status set S to another status set.

DEFINITION 6.5.7 ($\mathbf{T}_{\mathcal{P},\mathcal{O}_S}$ OPERATOR) Suppose $\mathcal{P}$ is an agent program and $\mathcal{O}_S$ an agent state. Then, for any status set S,

$$\mathbf{T}_{\mathcal{P},\mathcal{O}_S}(S) = \mathbf{App}_{\mathcal{P},\mathcal{O}_S}(S) \cup \mathbf{D\text{-}Cl}(S) \cup \mathbf{A\text{-}Cl}(S).$$

Note that as $\mathbf{D\text{-}Cl}(S) \subseteq \mathbf{A\text{-}Cl}(S)$, we may equivalently write this as

$$\mathbf{T}_{\mathcal{P},\mathcal{O}_S}(S) = \mathbf{App}_{\mathcal{P},\mathcal{O}_S}(S) \cup \mathbf{A\text{-}Cl}(S).$$

The following property of feasible status sets is easily seen.

LEMMA 6.5.1 Let $\mathcal{P}$ be an agent program, let $\mathcal{O}_S$ be any agent state, and let S be any status set. If S satisfies (S1) and (S3) of feasibility, then S is pre-fixpoint of $\mathbf{T}_{\mathcal{P},\mathcal{O}_S}$, i.e., $\mathbf{T}_{\mathcal{P},\mathcal{O}_S}(S) \subseteq S$.

Proof Suppose $\mathsf{Op}(\alpha) \in \mathbf{T}_{\mathcal{P},\mathcal{O}_S}(S) = \mathbf{App}_{\mathcal{P},\mathcal{O}_S}(S) \cup \mathbf{A\text{-}Cl}(S)$. Then either $\mathsf{Op}(\alpha) \in \mathbf{App}_{\mathcal{P},\mathcal{O}_S}(S)$ or $\mathsf{Op}(\alpha) \in \mathbf{A\text{-}Cl}(S)$. By condition (S1) defining a feasible status set, we know that $\mathbf{App}_{\mathcal{P},\mathcal{O}_S}(S) \subseteq S$. By condition (S3), $S = \mathbf{A\text{-}Cl}(S)$ and hence, $\mathbf{A\text{-}Cl}(S) \subseteq S$. Therefore, $\mathbf{T}_{\mathcal{P},\mathcal{O}_S}(S) \subseteq S$. ∎

Clearly, if the program $\mathcal{P}$ is positive, then $\mathbf{T}_{\mathcal{P},\mathcal{O}_S}$ is a monotone operator, i.e., $S \subseteq S'$ implies $\mathbf{T}_{\mathcal{P},\mathcal{O}_S}(S) \subseteq \mathbf{T}_{\mathcal{P},\mathcal{O}_S}(S')$, and hence, it has a least fixpoint $lfp(\mathbf{T}_{\mathcal{P},\mathcal{O}_S})$. Moreover, since $\mathbf{T}_{\mathcal{P},\mathcal{O}_S}$ is in fact continuous, i.e., $\mathbf{T}_{\mathcal{P},\mathcal{O}_S}(\bigcup_{i=0}^{\infty} S_0) = \bigcup_{i=0}^{\infty} \mathbf{T}_{\mathcal{P},\mathcal{O}_S}(S_i)$ for any chain

$S_0 \subseteq S_1 \subseteq S_2 \subseteq \cdots$ of status sets, the least fixpoint is given by

$$lfp(\mathbf{T}_{\mathcal{P},\mathcal{O}_S}) = \bigcup_{i=0}^{\infty} \mathbf{T}^i_{\mathcal{P},\mathcal{O}_S},$$

where $\mathbf{T}^0_{\mathcal{P},\mathcal{O}_S} = \emptyset$ and $\mathbf{T}^{i+1}_{\mathcal{P},\mathcal{O}_S} = \mathbf{T}_{\mathcal{P},\mathcal{O}_S}(\mathbf{T}^i_{\mathcal{P},\mathcal{O}_S})$, for all $i \geq 0$ see e.g., (Lloyd 1987; Apt 1990). We then have the following result.

THEOREM 6.5.1   Let $\mathcal{P}$ be a positive agent program, and let $\mathcal{O}_S$ be an agent state. Then, S is a rational status set of $\mathcal{P}$ on $\mathcal{O}_S$, if and only if $S = lfp(\mathbf{T}_{\mathcal{P},\mathcal{O}_S})$ and S is a feasible status set.

Proof   ($\Rightarrow$) Suppose $S = lfp(\mathbf{T}_{\mathcal{P},\mathcal{O}_S})$ a rational status set of $\mathcal{P}$ on $\mathcal{O}_S$. Then, S is feasible by definition of rational status set. By Lemma 6.5.1, S is a pre-fixpoint of $\mathbf{T}_{\mathcal{P},\mathcal{O}_S}$. Since $\mathbf{T}_{\mathcal{P},\mathcal{O}_S}$ is monotone, it has by the Knaster-Tarski Theorem a least pre-fixpoint, which coincides with $lfp(\mathbf{T}_{\mathcal{P},\mathcal{O}_S})$ (Apt 1990; Lloyd 1987). Thus, $lfp(\mathbf{T}_{\mathcal{P},\mathcal{O}_S}) \subseteq S$. Clearly, $lfp(\mathbf{T}_{\mathcal{P},\mathcal{O}_S})$ satisfies (S1) and (S3); moreover, $lfp(\mathbf{T}_{\mathcal{P},\mathcal{O}_S})$ satisfies (S2), as S satisfies (S2) and this property is hereditary. By the definition of rational status set, it follows $lfp(\mathbf{T}_{\mathcal{P},\mathcal{O}_S}) = S$.

($\Leftarrow$) Suppose $S = lfp(\mathbf{T}_{\mathcal{P},\mathcal{O}_S})$ is a feasible status set. Since every status set S' which satisfies (S1)–(S3) is a pre-fixpoint of $\mathbf{T}_{\mathcal{P},\mathcal{O}_S}$ and $lfp(\mathbf{T}_{\mathcal{P},\mathcal{O}_S})$ is the least prefix point, $S' \subseteq S$ implies $S = S'$. It follows that S is rational. ∎

Notice that in case of a positive program, $lfp(\mathbf{T}_{\mathcal{P},\mathcal{O}_S})$ always satisfies the conditions (S1) and (S3) of a feasible status set (i.e., all closure conditions), and thus is a rational status set if it satisfies (S2) and (S4), i.e., the consistency criteria. The uniqueness of the rational status set is immediate from the previous theorem.

COROLLARY 1   Let $\mathcal{P}$ be a positive agent program. Then, on every agent state $\mathcal{O}_S$, the rational status set of $\mathcal{P}$ (if one exists) is unique, i.e., if S, S' are rational status sets for $\mathcal{P}$ on $\mathcal{O}_S$, then $S = S'$.

Example 6.5.7 (CHAIN example revisited)   Let us return to the agent program described in Example 6.5.5. Let us augment this example with a new action, fax_order. Suppose we augment our agent program of Example 6.5.5 with the two rules

Do *fax_order*(company1, Part_id, Amount_requested) ←
    O *process_request*(Msg.Id, Agent),
    in(Amount_requested, msgbox: *getVar*(Msg.Id, "Amount_requested")),
    in(Part_id, msgbox: *getVar*(Msg.Id, "Part_id")),
    Do *order_part*(Part_id, Amount_requested),
    ¬ **Do** *fax_order*(company2, Part_id, Amount_requested).

P *fax_order*(company2, Part_id, Amount_requested) ←
    O*process_request*(Msg.Id, Agent),
    in(Amount_requested, msgbox: *getVar*(Msg.Id, "Amount_requested")),
    in(Part_id, msgbox: *getVar*(Msg.Id, "Part_id")),
    Do *order_part*(Part_id, Amount_requested),
    =(Part_id,p50).

It is now easy to see that there are two rational status sets—one of which contains the status atom **Do***fax_order*(company1, Part_id, 2000) and the other **Do***fax_order*(company2, Part_id, 2000). Thus, the introduction of negated status atoms in rule bodies leads to this potential problem.

As shown by Example 6.5.7 Corollary 1 is no longer true in the presence of negated action status atoms. We postpone the discussion about the existence of a unique rational status set at this point, as we introduce a stronger concept than rational status sets below for which this discussion is more appropriate. Nonetheless, we note the following property on the existence of a (not necessarily unique) rational status set.

PROPOSITION 6.5.3 Let $\mathcal{P}$ be an agent program. If $\mathcal{IC} = \emptyset$, then $\mathcal{P}$ has a rational status set *if and only if* $\mathcal{P}$ has a feasible status set.

Proof By definition of rationality, we know that if S is a rational status set of $\mathcal{P}$ then it must be a feasible status set as well.

Suppose $\mathcal{P}$ has a feasible status set. Then the set of all feasible status sets of $\mathcal{P}$ on $\mathcal{O}_S$ has a non-empty set of inclusion-minimal elements. Indeed, from the grounding of the agent program, we can remove all rules which violate the conditions 2.-4. of the operator $\mathbf{App}_{\mathcal{P},\mathcal{O}_S}(S)$, and can remove literals involving code calls from the remaining rules. Moreover, the deontic and action closure conditions can be incorporated into the program via rules. Thus, we end up with a set T of propositional clauses, whose models are feasible status sets of $\mathcal{P}$. Since $\mathcal{P}$ has a feasible status set, T has a model, i.e., an assignment to the propositional atoms which satisfies all clauses in T. Now, each satisfiable set of clauses in a countable language possesses at least one minimal model (w.r.t. inclusion, i.w., a $\subseteq$-minimal set of atoms is assigned the value **true**); this can be shown applying the same technique which proves that every such set of clauses can be extended to a maximal satisfiable set of clauses. Thus, T has at least one minimal model. As easily seen, any such model is a minimal feasible status set of $\mathcal{P}$.

Suppose now S' is one of the minimal feasible status sets of $\mathcal{P}$ on $\mathcal{O}_S$. Then (as we show below) S' is grounded, and hence a rational status set.

To show that S' is grounded, we need to show that S' satisfies conditions (S1)–(S3) of the definition of feasible status set—this is true because S' is feasible. In addition, we need to show that no strict subset $S^\star$ of S satisfies conditions (S1)–(S3).

Suppose there is a strict subset $S^\star$ of S satisfying conditions (S1)–(S3). Then, as $\mathcal{IC} = \emptyset$, $S^\star$ also satisfies condition (S4) of the definition of feasibility, and hence $S^\star$ is a feasible status set. But this contradicts the inclusion minimality of S', and hence, we may infer that S' has no strict subset $S^\star$ of S satisfying conditions (S1)–(S3). Thus, S' is grounded, and we are done. ∎

The following result follows immediately from the proof of Proposition 6.5.3.

COROLLARY 2   Let $\mathcal{P}$ be an agent program and suppose $\mathcal{IC} = \emptyset$. Then, S is a rational status set of $\mathcal{P}$ if and only if S is an inclusion-minimal feasible status set of $\mathcal{P}$.

Moreover, we remark at this point that the unique rational status set of a positive program (if it exists) can be computed in polynomial time, if we adopt reasonable underlying assumptions (see Chapter 11, Section 11.4.1).

6.5.3 Reading of Rational Status Sets

We are now ready to return to the question "*Exactly how should we read the atoms* $\mathsf{Op}(\alpha)$ *for* $\mathsf{Op} \in \{\mathbf{P}, \mathbf{F}, \mathbf{W}, \mathbf{O}, \mathbf{Do}\}$ *appearing in a rational status set?*" In Section 6.4, we had promised a discussion of this issue. It appears that the reading:

$\mathsf{Op}(\alpha) \equiv$ "It is the case that α is Op^*"

where Op^* is the proper verb corresponding to operator Op (forbidden, permitted, etc), is *not* the one which is expressed inherently by rational status sets. Rather, a status atom in a rational status set should be more appropriately interpreted as follows:

$\mathsf{Op}(\alpha) \equiv$ "It is <u>derivable</u> that α should be Op^*."

where "derivable"—without giving a precise definition here—means that $\mathsf{Op}(\alpha)$ is obtained from the rules of the agent program and the deontic axioms, under reasonable assumptions about the status of actions; the groundedness property of the rational status set ensures that the adopted assumptions are as conservative as possible.

Furthermore, a literal $\neg\mathsf{Op}(\alpha)$ in a program should be interpreted as:

$\neg\mathsf{Op}(\alpha) \equiv$ "It is not derivable that α should be Op^*."

It is important to emphasize that there is no reason to view a rational status set as an ideally rational agent's three-valued model of a two-valued reality, in which each action is

Section 6.5   Agent Programs: Semantics

either forbidden or permitted. For example, the agent program

$\mathbf{P}\alpha \leftarrow$
$\mathbf{F}\alpha \leftarrow \mathbf{P}\beta$
$\mathbf{F}\alpha \leftarrow \mathbf{F}\beta$

has a unique rational status set, namely $S = \{\mathbf{P}\alpha\}$. A possible objection against this rational status set (which arises naturally from similar arguments in logic programming with incomplete information) is the following.

1. β is either forbidden or permitted.
2. In either of these two cases, α is forbidden.
3. Therefore, the rational status set $S = \{\mathbf{P}\alpha\}$ is "wrong."

"Complete" status sets, defined in Section 6.5.6 remedy this problem.

This brings us back to our interpretation of $\mathsf{Op}(\alpha)$. The fallacy in the above argument is the implicit equivalence assumed to hold between the statement "β is either forbidden or permitted" and the statement $\mathbf{P}\beta \vee \mathbf{F}\beta$. The latter statement is read "It is either derivable that β is permitted, or it is derivable that β is forbidden" which is certainly very different from the former statement.

In addition, we believe that deontic logic is different from the setting of reasoning with incomplete information because the true state of affairs need not be one in which the status of every particular action is decided. In fact, the status may be open—and it may even be impossible to refine it without arriving at inconsistency. For example, this applies to the legal domain, which is one of the most fertile application areas of deontic logic.

6.5.4 Reasonable Status Sets

A more serious attack against rational status sets, stemming from past research in nonmonotonic logic programming is that for agent programs with negation, the semantics of rational status sets allows logical contraposition of the program rules. For example, consider the following program:

$\mathbf{Do}(\alpha) \leftarrow \neg \mathbf{Do}(\beta).$

This program has two rational status sets: $S_1 = \{\mathbf{Do}(\alpha), \mathbf{P}(\alpha)\}$, and $S_2 = \{\mathbf{Do}(\beta), \mathbf{P}(\beta)\}$. The second rational status set is obtained by applying the contrapositive of the rule:

$\mathbf{Do}(\beta) \leftarrow \neg \mathbf{Do}(\alpha)$

However, the second rational set seems less intuitive than the first as there is no explicit rule in the above program that justifies the derivation of this $\mathbf{Do}(\beta)$.

This observation leads us to the following remarks. First, in the area of logic programming and knowledge representation, the meaning of negation in rules has been extensively discussed and there is broad consensus in that area that contraposition is a proof principle which should not be applied: rather, derivation should be constructive from rules. These observations led to the wellknown stable model semantics for logic programs due to Gelfond and Lifschitz (1988), which in turn was shown to have strong equivalences with the classical nonmonotonic reasoning paradigms such as default logic (Reiter 1980) and auto-epistemic logic (Moore 1985b) see (Gelfond and Lifschitz 1991; Marek and Truszczyński 1993), as well as numerical reasoning paradigms such as linear programming and integer programming (Bell, Nerode, Ng, and Subrahmanian 1994; Bell, Nerode, Ng, and Subrahmanian 1996).

Second, the presence of derivation by contraposition may have a detrimental effect on the complexity of programs, since it inherently simulates disjunction. Therefore, it is advisable to have a mechanism which cuts down possible rational status sets in an effective and appealing way, so that negation can be used without introducing high computational cost.

For these reasons, we introduce the concept of a *reasonable status set*. The reader should note that if he really does want to use contraposition, then he should choose the rational status set approach, rather than the reasonable status set approach.

DEFINITION 6.5.8 (REASONABLE STATUS SET) Let $\mathcal{P}$ be an agent program, let $\mathcal{O}_S$ be an agent state, and let S be a status set.

1. If $\mathcal{P}$ is a positive agent program, then S is a *reasonable status set* for $\mathcal{P}$ on $\mathcal{O}_S$, if and only if S is a rational status set for $\mathcal{P}$ on $\mathcal{O}_S$.

2. The reduct of $\mathcal{P}$ w.r.t. S and $\mathcal{O}_S$, denoted by $red^S(\mathcal{P}, \mathcal{O}_S)$, is the program which is obtained from the ground instances of the rules in $\mathcal{P}$ over $\mathcal{O}_S$ as follows.

(a) First, remove every rule r such that $B_{as}^-(r) \cap S \neq \emptyset$;

(b) Remove all atoms in $B_{as}^-(r)$ from the remaining rules.

Then S is a *reasonable status set* for $\mathcal{P}$ w.r.t. $\mathcal{O}_S$, if it is a reasonable status set of the program $red^S(\mathcal{P}, \mathcal{O}_S)$ with respect to $\mathcal{O}_S$.

Let us quickly revisit our motivating examples to see why reasonable status sets reflect an improvement on rational status sets.

Example 6.5.8 (CHAIN example revisited) Let us return to the case of the agent program presented in Example 6.5.7. Here we have two rational status sets, one containing **Do** *fax_order*(company1,p50, 500), while the other contains **Do** *fax_order*(company2, p50,500).

Section 6.5 Agent Programs: Semantics

According to the above definition, only the rational status set that contains the status atom **Do** fax_order(company1, p50, 500) is reasonable. The reason is that the first rule listed explicitly in Example 6.5.7 says that if we do not infer **Do** fax_order(company2, p50, 500), then we should infer **Do** fax_order(company1, p50, 500), thus implicitly providing higher priority to the rational status set containing **Do** fax_order(company1, p50, 500).

A more simplistic example is presented below.

Example 6.5.9 For the program $\mathcal{P}$:

Do $\beta \leftarrow \neg$**Do** α,

the reduct of $\mathcal{P}$ w.r.t. $S = \{$**Do** $\beta,$ **P**$\beta\}$ on agent state $\mathcal{O}_S$ is the program

Do $\beta \leftarrow$.

Clearly, S is the unique reasonable status set of $red^S(\mathcal{P}, \mathcal{O}_S)$, and hence S is a reasonable status set of $\mathcal{P}$.

The use of reasonable status sets also has some benefits with respect to knowledge representation. For example, the rule

Do $\alpha \leftarrow \neg$**F**α \hfill (6.3)

says that action α is executed by default, unless it is explicitly forbidden (provided, of course, that its precondition succeeds). This default representation is possible because under the reasonable status set approach, the rule itself can not be used to derive **F**α, which is inappropriate for a default rule.

This benefit does not accrue when using rational status sets because the single rule has two rational status sets: $S_1 = \{$**Do** $(\alpha),$ **P**$\alpha\}$ and $S_2 = \{$**F**$\alpha\}$. If we adopt reasonable status sets, however, then only S_1 remains and α is executed. If rational status sets are used, then the decision about whether α is executed depends on the choice between S_1 and S_2. (Notice that if the agent would execute those actions α such that **Do** (α) appears in all rational status sets, then no action is taken here. However, such an approach is not meaningful in general, and will lead to conflicts with integrity constraints.)

The definition of reasonable status sets does not introduce a completely orthogonal type of status set. Rather, it prunes out some rational status sets. This is shown by the following property.

PROPOSITION 6.5.4 Let $\mathcal{P}$ be an agent program and $\mathcal{O}_S$ an agent state. Then, every reasonable status set of $\mathcal{P}$ on $\mathcal{O}_S$ is a rational status set of $\mathcal{P}$ on $\mathcal{O}_S$.

Proof In order to show that a reasonable status set S of $\mathcal{P}$ is a rational status of $\mathcal{P}$, we have to verify (1) that S is a feasible status set and (2) that S is grounded.

Since S is a reasonable status set of $\mathcal{P}$, it is a rational status set of $\mathcal{P}' = red^S(\mathcal{P}, \mathcal{O}_S)$, i.e., a feasible and grounded status set of $\mathcal{P}'$. Since the conditions $(S2)$–$(S4)$ of the definition of feasible status set depend only on S and $\mathcal{O}_S$ but not on the program, this means that for showing (1) it remains to check that $(S1)$ (closure under the program rules) is satisfied.

Let thus r be a ground instance of a rule from $\mathcal{P}$. Suppose the body $B(r)$ of r satisfies the conditions 1.–4. of $(S1)$. Then, by the definition of $red^S(\mathcal{P}, \mathcal{O}_S)$, we have that the reduct of the rule r, obtained by removing all literals of $B^-_{as}(r)$ from the body, is in $\mathcal{P}'$. Since S is closed under the rules of $\mathcal{P}'$, we have $H(r) \in S$. Thus, S is closed under the rules of $\mathcal{P}$, and hence $(S1)$ is satisfied. As a consequence, (1) holds.

For (2), we suppose S is not grounded, i.e., that some smaller $S' \subset S$ satisfies $(S1)$–$(S3)$ for $\mathcal{P}$, and derive a contradiction. If S' satisfies $(S1)$ for $\mathcal{P}$, then S' satisfies $(S1)$ for $\mathcal{P}'$. For, if r is a rule from $\mathcal{P}'$ such that 1.–4. of $(S1)$ hold for S', then there is a ground rule r' of $\mathcal{P}$ such that r is obtained from r' in the construction of $red^S(\mathcal{P}, \mathcal{O}_S)$ and, as easily seen, 1.–4. of $(S1)$ hold for S'. Since S' satisfies $(S1)$ for $\mathcal{P}$, we have $H(r) \in S'$. It follows that S' satisfies $(S1)$ for $\mathcal{P}'$. Furthermore, since $(S2)$ and $(S3)$ do no depend on the program, also $(S2)$ and $(S3)$ are satisfied for S' w.r.t. $\mathcal{P}'$. This means that S is not a rational status set of $\mathcal{P}'$, which is the desired contradiction.

Thus, (1) and (2) hold, which proves the result. ∎

In Chapter 12, we define a syntactically restricted class of agent programs called *regular agent programs* that are guaranteed to have at least one reasonable status set. Existence of reasonable status sets cannot always be guaranteed because (as we have seen), some programs may have no feasible status sets.

6.5.5 Violating Obligations: Weak Rational Status Sets

Thus far, we have adopted a semantics of agent programs which followed the principle that actions which the agent is obliged to take are actually executed, i.e., the rule

If $\mathbf{O}\alpha$ *is true, then* $\mathbf{Do}\,\alpha$ *is true* (6.4)

is strictly obeyed. This is known as *regimentation* (Krogh 1995), and reflects the ideal behavior of an agent in a normative system.

However, the essence of deontism is in capturing what *should* be done in a specific situation, rather than what *finally is to be* done under any circumstances (Åquist 1984; Meyer and Wieringa 1993; Hansson 1994). Taking this view, the operator $\mathbf{O}\alpha$ is a suggestion for what should be done; it may be well the case, that in a given situation, an obligation $\mathbf{O}\alpha$ is true, but α is not executed as it would be impossible (due of a violation of some action constraints), or lead to inconsistency. Such a behavior, e.g., in the legal domain, is a violation of a normative codex, which will be sanctioned in some way.

Example 6.5.10 (Conflicting Obligations) Suppose an agent A is obliged to serve requests of other agents A_1 and A_2, represented by facts $\mathbf{O}(serve(A_1))$ and $\mathbf{O}(serve(A_2))$, respectively, but there is an action constraint which states that no two service requests can be satisfied simultaneously. This scenario is described by the program $\mathcal{P}$:

$\mathbf{O}(serve(A_1)) \leftarrow$

$\mathbf{O}(serve(A_2)) \leftarrow$

and the action constraint

$AC : \{serve(A_1), serve(A_2)\} \hookleftarrow \mathbf{true}$.

The program $\mathcal{P}$ has no rational status set (and even no feasible status set exists). The reason is that not both obligations can be followed without raising an inconsistency, given by a violation of the action constraint AC.

Thus, in the above example, the program is inconsistent and the agent does not take any action. In reality, however, we would expect that the agent serves at least one of the requests, thus only violating one of the obligations. The issue of which request the agent should select for service may depend on additional information—e.g., priority information, or penalties for each of the requests. In absence of any further directives, however, the agent may arbitrarily choose one of the requests.

This example and the sketched desired behavior of the agent prompts us to introduce another generalization of our approach, to a semantics for agent programs which takes into account possible violations of the regimentation rule (6.4) in order to reach a valid status set. An important issue at this point is which obligations an agent may violate, and how to proceed if different alternatives exist. We assume in the following that no additional information about obligations and their violations is given, and develop our approach on this basis. Weak rational status sets introduced below allow obligations to be "dropped" when conflicts arise. Later, Section 6.5.7 discusses how to build more complex structures involving cost/benefit information on top of weak rational status sets.

Our intent is to generalize the rational status set approach gracefully, and similarly the reasonable status set approach. That is, in the case where a program $\mathcal{P}$ has a rational status set on an agent state $\mathcal{O}_S$, then this status set (resp., the collection of all such status sets) should be the meaning of the program. On the other hand, if no rational status set exists, then we are looking for possible violations of obligations which make it possible to have such a status set. In this step, we apply Occam's Razor and violate the set of obligations as little as possible; i.e., we adopt a status set S which is rational, if a set Ob of rules $\mathbf{O}\alpha \Rightarrow \mathbf{Do}\,\alpha$ is disposed, and such that no similar status set S' for some disposal set Ob' exists which is a proper subset of Ob. We formalize this intuition next in the concept of weak rational (resp., reasonable) status set.

DEFINITION 6.5.9 (RELATIVIZED ACTION CLOSURE) Let S be a status set, and let A be a set of ground actions. Then, the action closure of S under regimentation relativized to A, denoted $\mathbf{A\text{-}Cl}_A(S)$, is the closure of S under the rules

If $\mathbf{O}\alpha \in S$ then $\mathbf{Do}\,\alpha \in S$, for any ground action $\alpha \in A$ (6.5)

If $\mathbf{Do}\beta \in S$, then $\mathbf{P}\beta \in S$, for any ground action β.   (6.6)

A set S is action closed under regimentation relativized to A, if $S = \mathbf{A\text{-}Cl}_A(S)$ holds.

Notice that $\mathbf{A\text{-}Cl}(\cdot) = \mathbf{A\text{-}Cl}_{GA}(\cdot)$, where GA is the set of all ground actions. Using the concept of relativized action closure, we define weak versions of feasible (resp., rational, reasonable) status sets.

DEFINITION 6.5.10 (RELATIVIZED STATUS SETS) Let $\mathcal{P}$ be a program, let $\mathcal{O}_S$ be an agent state, and let A be a set of ground actions. Then, a status set S is A-feasible (resp., A-rational, A-reasonable), if S satisfies the condition of feasible (resp., rational, reasonable) status set, where the action closure $\mathbf{A\text{-}Cl}(\cdot)$ is replaced by the relativized action closure $\mathbf{A\text{-}Cl}_A(\cdot)$ (but $\mathbf{D\text{-}Cl}(\cdot)$ remains unchanged).

DEFINITION 6.5.11 (WEAK RATIONAL, REASONABLE STATUS SETS) A status set S is weak rational (resp., weak reasonable), if there exists an A such that S is A-rational (resp., A-reasonable) and there are no $A' \neq A$ and S' such that $A \subseteq A'$ and S' is an A'-rational (resp., A'-reasonable) status set.

An immediate consequence of this definition is the following.

COROLLARY 3 Let $\mathcal{P}$ be an agent program. If $\mathcal{P}$ has a rational (resp., reasonable) status set on an agent state $\mathcal{O}_S$, then the weak rational (resp., weak reasonable) status sets of $\mathcal{P}$ on $\mathcal{O}_S$ coincide with the rational (resp., reasonable) status sets of $\mathcal{P}$ on $\mathcal{O}_S$.

Thus, the concept of weak rational (resp., reasonable) status set is a conservative extension of rational (resp., reasonable) status set as desired.

Example 6.5.11 (Conflicting Obligations—Continued) The program $\mathcal{P}$ has two weak rational status sets, namely

$W_1 = \{\mathbf{O}(serve(A_1)), \mathbf{O}(serve(A_2)), \mathbf{P}(serve(A_1)), \mathbf{P}(serve(A_2)), \mathbf{Do}\,(serve(A_1))\},$

$W_2 = \{\mathbf{O}(serve(A_1)), \mathbf{O}(serve(A_2)), \mathbf{P}(serve(A_1)), \mathbf{P}(serve(A_2)), \mathbf{Do}\,(serve(A_2))\}.$

The set W_1 is a $\{serve(A_1)\}$-rational status set, while symmetrically W_2 is a $\{serve(A_2)\}$-rational status set. Both W_1 and W_2 are also weak reasonable status sets of $\mathcal{P}$.

As the previous example shows, even a positive agent program may have more than one weak rational status set. Moreover, in other scenarios, no weak rational status set exists. To cure the first problem, one could impose a total preference ordering on the weak rational status sets. The second problem needs a more sophisticated treatment that is not straightforward; after all, the presence of some conflicts which can not be avoided by violating obligations indicates that there is a major problem, and we must question whether the agent program $\mathcal{P}$ is properly stated.

By generalizing the definitions in Section 6.5.2, it is possible to characterize the weak rational status sets of a positive agent program $\mathcal{P}$ using a fixpoint operator.

DEFINITION 6.5.12 (OPERATOR $\mathbf{T}_{\mathcal{P},\mathcal{O}_S,A}$) Suppose $\mathcal{P}$ is an agent program, $\mathcal{O}_S$ an agent state, and A is a set of ground actions. Then, for any S status set S,

$$\mathbf{T}_{\mathcal{P},\mathcal{O}_S,A}(S) = \mathbf{App}_{\mathcal{P},\mathcal{O}_S}(S) \cup \mathbf{D\text{-}Cl}(S) \cup \mathbf{A\text{-}Cl}_A(S).$$

Note that with respect to $\mathbf{T}_{\mathcal{P},\mathcal{O}_S}(S)$, the action closure $\mathbf{A\text{-}Cl}(\cdot)$ is replaced by the relatived action closure $\mathbf{A\text{-}Cl}_A(\cdot)$; however, $\mathbf{D\text{-}Cl}(S)$ may not be dropped, since $\mathbf{D\text{-}Cl}(S)$ is in general not contained in $\mathbf{A\text{-}Cl}_A(S)$.

Clearly, also $\mathbf{T}_{\mathcal{P},\mathcal{O}_S,A}$ is monotone and continuous if $\mathcal{P}$ is positive, and hence has a least fixpoint $lfp(\mathbf{T}_{\mathcal{P},\mathcal{O}_S,A}) = \bigcup_{i=0}^{\infty} \mathbf{T}^i_{\mathcal{P},\mathcal{O}_S,A}$ where $\mathbf{T}^0_{\mathcal{P},\mathcal{O}_S,A} = \emptyset$ and $\mathbf{T}^{i+1}_{\mathcal{P},\mathcal{O}_S,A} = \mathbf{T}_{\mathcal{P},\mathcal{O}_S,A}(\mathbf{T}^i_{\mathcal{P},\mathcal{O}_S,A})$, for all $i \geq 0$.

The following characterization of A-rational status sets is then obtained.

THEOREM 6.5.2 Let $\mathcal{P}$ be a positive agent program, let A be a set of ground actions, and let $\mathcal{O}_S$ be an agent state. Then, a status set S is an A-rational status set of $\mathcal{P}$ on $\mathcal{O}_S$, if and only if $S = lfp(\mathbf{T}_{\mathcal{P},\mathcal{O}_S,A})$ and S is an A-feasible status set.

Proof The proof is analogous to the proof of Theorem 6.5.4; observe that any status set S' which satisfies the conditions $(S1)$ and $(S3)$ of A-relativized feasibility, is a pre-fixpoint of $\mathbf{T}_{\mathcal{P},\mathcal{O}_S,A}$. ∎

From the previous theorem, we obtain the following result.

THEOREM 6.5.3 Let $\mathcal{P}$ be a positive agent program, and let $\mathcal{O}_S$ be an agent state. Then, a status set S is a weak rational status set of $\mathcal{P}$ on $\mathcal{O}_S$, if and only if $S = lfp(\mathbf{T}_{\mathcal{P},\mathcal{O}_S,A})$ and S is A-feasible for some maximal A w.r.t. inclusion.

Proof S is weak rational, if and only if S is A-rational for some A such that for every $A' \neq A$ such that $A \subseteq A'$, no A'-rational status set exists. This is equivalent to the fact that A is a maximal set of ground actions such that some A-rational status sets exist. By

Theorem 6.5.2, a status set S is A-rational if and only if $S = lfp(\mathbf{T}_{\mathcal{P},\mathcal{O}_S,A})$ and S is A-feasible; the result follows. ∎

In general, this criterion does not enable efficient recognition of a weak rational status set (which is, in fact, intractable). The status set S for A in the theorem is unique, and can be detailed as follows.

DEFINITION 6.5.13 ($A(S)$)   For any status set S, we use $A(S)$ to denote the set $\mathbf{Do}\,(S) \cup \{\alpha \mid \alpha \notin \mathbf{O}(S)\}$.

PROPOSITION 6.5.5   Let $\mathcal{P}$ be any agent program, and let $\mathcal{O}_S$ be any agent state. Suppose a status set S is A-feasible for some A. Then, S is $A(S)$-feasible, and $A \subseteq A(S)$, i.e., $A(S)$ is the unique maximal set of ground actions A such that S is A-feasible.

Proof   Clearly, S is $A(S)$-feasible. Suppose that $A(S)$ is not the unique maximal set A such that S is A-feasible. Then, there exists a set $A' \neq A(S)$ and a ground action $\alpha \in A' \setminus A(S)$ such that S is A'-feasible. From the definition of $A(S)$, it follows $\mathbf{O}\alpha \in S$ and $\mathbf{Do}\,\alpha \notin S$; since the rule $\mathbf{O}\alpha \Rightarrow \mathbf{Do}\,\alpha$ applies w.r.t. A', it follows $\mathbf{Do}\,\alpha \in S$, which is a contradiction. ∎

Thus, if S is a weak rational status set, then $A = A(S)$ is the unique maximal set such that S is A-feasible. From Theorem 6.5.3, we obtain the following corollary.

COROLLARY 4   Let S_1, S_2 be weak rational status set of a positive agent program $\mathcal{P}$ on an agent state $\mathcal{O}_S$. Then, $\mathbf{O}(S_1) = \mathbf{O}(S_2)$ implies $S_1 = S_2$.

As a consequence, for every choice of a maximal set of obligations which can be obeyed, the resulting weak rational status set is uniquely determined when $\mathcal{P}$ is positive. This means that the commitment to a set of obligations does not introduce further ambiguities about the status of actions, which is a desired feature of the semantics.

It is easy to see that the operator $\mathbf{T}_{\mathcal{P},\mathcal{O}_S,A}$ is monotone in A, i.e., enjoys the following property.

PROPOSITION 6.5.6   Let $\mathcal{P}$ be a positive agent program, let $\mathcal{O}_S$ be an agent state, and let A_1, A_2 be sets of ground actions such that $A_1 \subseteq A_2$. Then, for any status set S, $\mathbf{T}_{\mathcal{P},\mathcal{O}_S,A_1}(S) \subseteq \mathbf{T}_{\mathcal{P},\mathcal{O}_S,A_2}(S)$ holds, and $lfp(\mathbf{T}_{\mathcal{P},\mathcal{O}_S,A_1}) \subseteq lfp(\mathbf{T}_{\mathcal{P},\mathcal{O}_S,A_2})$.

For the case where no integrity constraints are present, we obtain the following result from Theorem 6.5.3 and Proposition 6.5.5.

THEOREM 6.5.4   Let $\mathcal{P}$ be a positive agent program, where $\mathcal{IC} = \emptyset$, and let $\mathcal{O}_S$ be an agent state. Then, a status set S is a weak rational status set of $\mathcal{P}$ on $\mathcal{O}_S$, if and only if (i) $S = lfp(\mathbf{T}_{\mathcal{P},\mathcal{O}_S,A})$ and S is A-feasible for $A = A(S)$, and (ii) for each ground action $\alpha \notin A(S)$, the status set $S_{A'} = lfp(\mathbf{T}_{\mathcal{P},\mathcal{O}_S,A'})$ is not A'-feasible, where $A' = A(S) \cup \{\alpha\}$.

Proof

($\Rightarrow$): If S is weak rational, then (*i*) follows from Theorem 6.5.3 and Proposition 6.5.5. Suppose for some A' in (*ii*), $S_{A'} = lfp(\mathbf{T}_{\mathcal{P},\mathcal{O}_S,A'})$ is A'-feasible. Then, by Theorem 6.5.2, the set $S_{A'}$ is A'-rational, which contradicts that S is a weak rational status set.

($\Leftarrow$): Suppose (*i*) and (*ii*) hold. Then, by Theorem 6.5.2, S is A-rational. Suppose S is not a weak rational status set; hence some $A' \neq A$ exists, $A \subseteq A'$, for which some A'-rational status set S' exists. Since property (*S2*) of the feasibility condition is hereditary, it follows from Proposition 6.5.6 that for every $A'' \subseteq A'$ the status set $S_{A''} = lfp(\mathbf{T}_{\mathcal{P},\mathcal{O}_S,A''})$ satisfies (*S2*). Moreover, $S_{A''}$ satisfies (*S1*) and (*S3*). Since $\mathcal{IC} = \emptyset$, we have that $S_{A''}$ is A''-feasible. Let $\alpha \in A' \setminus A$ and set $A'' = A \cup \{\alpha\}$. This raises a contradiction to (*ii*). Consequently, an A' as hypothesized does not exist, which proves that S is weak rational. ■

We remark at this point that for a fixed program $\mathcal{P}$, this criterion implies that under suitable conditions, there is a polynomial time algorithm for the recognition of a weak rational status set when no integrity constraints are present. As we will see later in Section 11.4.1, deciding whether some weak rational status set exists and actually computing one is then possible in polynomial time.

6.5.6 Preferred and Complete Status Sets

In this section, we study what happens when we consider three classes of rational status sets.

• A rational status set S is F-preferred if there is no other rational status set whose set of forbidden atoms is a strict subset of S's set of forbidden atoms. Intuitively, such status sets are *permissive*—most things are allowed unless explicitly forbidden.

• A rational status set S is P-preferred if there is no other rational status set whose set of permitted atoms is a strict subset of S's set of permitted atoms. Intuitively, such status sets are *dictatorial*—most things are allowed unless explicitly permitted.

• The notion of a status set does not insist that for each action α, either $\mathbf{P}\alpha$ or $\mathbf{F}\alpha$ be in S. However, for any action α, either α must be permitted or must be forbidden. Complete status sets insist that this additional condition be satisfied.

Preference As we have briefly mentioned in the previous section, it may be desirable to use a preference policy for pruning among the status sets. In particular, the issue whether an action should be considered forbidden or allowed is highly relevant.

It appears that there is no straightforward solution to this problem, and that in fact different approaches to using defaults are plausible. For example, the following two are suggestive:

Weak Preference: The first approach takes the view that an action should, if possible, be considered as being not forbidden. According to this view, status sets are preferred in which the set of forbidden actions is small. Note that owing to the three-valued nature of the status of an action in a status set (which can be forbidden, permitted, or neither), this does not necessarily mean that the part of explicitly permitted actions in a preferred action set is large. This policy is thus a weak default about the status of an action.

Strong preference: Another approach is to enforce a deontic completion about whether actions are permitted or forbidden, and to request that in an action set, every action is either forbidden or permitted, and such that permission is preferred over forbiddance. This approach requires a redefinition of the notion of a grounded consistent action set, however (keep the permission and forbidden-parts fixed). It amounts to a kind of strong default rule that actions which are not forbidden are explicitly permitted.

These two approaches attempt to treat forbidden actions. Of course, one could foster approaches which symmetrically aim at permitted actions, and implement (weak or strong) *default rules* about such actions. Likewise, default rules for other status operators may be designed. Which approach is in fact appropriate, or even a mixed use of different default for different actions, may depend on the particular application domain. In the following, we take a closer look at weak defaults rules on forbidden actions.

It would be useful if rules like

$$\mathbf{Do}(\alpha) \leftarrow \neg \mathbf{F}\alpha$$

may be stated in an agent program, with the intuitive reading that action α is executed by default, unless it is explicitly forbidden (provided, of course, that its precondition succeeds).

This single rule has two feasible status sets that are grounded: $A_1 = \{\mathbf{Do}(\alpha), \mathbf{P}\alpha\}$ and $A_2 = \{\mathbf{F}\alpha\}$. Under the policy that by default, actions which are not explicitly forbidden are considered to be permitted, A_1 is preferred over A_2 and α is executed. If no such default policy is taken, then no set is preferred over the other, and it depends on the choice between A_1 and A_2, whether α is executed. (If the agent executes those actions α such that $\mathbf{Do}(\alpha)$ appears in all rational status sets, then no action is taken here.) Adopting the view that actions should not be considered forbidden unless explicitly stated motivates the following definition.

DEFINITION 6.5.14 (F-PREFERENCE) A set S of action status atoms is F-*preferred*, if S is a rational status set, and there exists no other rational status set S' which has a smaller forbidden part than S, i.e., $\mathbf{F}(S') \subset \mathbf{F}(S)$ holds.

Example 6.5.12 Consider the simple program

$\mathbf{P}(\gamma) \leftarrow \neg \mathbf{P}\beta$

$\mathbf{F}(\alpha) \leftarrow \mathbf{P}\beta$

$\mathbf{Do}\,(\beta) \leftarrow \mathbf{P}\beta$

It is easy to see that both $\{\mathbf{P}\gamma\}$ and $\{\mathbf{P}(\beta), \mathbf{Do}\,(\beta), \mathbf{F}(\alpha)\}$ are rational status sets of this agent program. However, $\{\mathbf{P}\gamma\}$ is F-preferential, as the set of status atoms of the form $\mathbf{F}(\cdot)$ in it is empty, while this is not the case with $\{\mathbf{P}(\beta), \mathbf{Do}\,(\beta), \mathbf{F}(\alpha)\}$.

Dual to F-preference, we can define preference for P. Intuitively, F-preference amounts to a "brave" principle from the view of action permission, while P-preference amounts to a "cautious" one. Both F- and P-preference are the extremal instances of a more general preference scheme, which allows to put individual preference on each action α from the action base.

Complete Status Sets The preceding examples show that there may well be feasible status sets in which there is an action α such that α is neither forbidden nor permitted.

It may be desirable, however, that this issue is resolved in a status set which is acceptable for the user; that is, either $\mathbf{P}\alpha$ or $\mathbf{F}\alpha$ is contained in the status set. This may apply to some particular actions α, as well as to all actions in the extremal case.

Our framework for agent programs is rich enough to handle this issue in the language in a natural, simple way. Namely, by including a rule

$\mathbf{F}\alpha \leftarrow \neg \mathbf{P}\alpha$

in a program, we can ensure that every feasible (and thus rational) status set includes either $\mathbf{F}\alpha$ or $\mathbf{P}\alpha$; we call this rule the *F/P-completion rule of α*. For an agent program $\mathcal{P}$, we denote by $Comp_{F/P}(\mathcal{P})$ the augmentation of $\mathcal{P}$ by the F/P-completion rules for all actions α in the action base.

Call a status set S *F/P-complete*, if for every ground action α, either $\mathbf{P}\alpha \in S$, or $\mathbf{F}\alpha \in S$. Then, we have the following immediate property.

PROPOSITION 6.5.7 Let $\mathcal{P}$ be an agent program. Then, every feasible status set S of $Comp_{F/P} \times (\mathcal{P})$ is F/P-complete.

Example 6.5.13 The program

$\mathbf{P}\alpha \leftarrow$

$\mathbf{F}\alpha \leftarrow \mathbf{P}\beta$

$\mathbf{F}\alpha \leftarrow \mathbf{F}\beta$

has a unique rational status set. However, the program $Comp_{F/P}(\mathcal{P})$ has no feasible status set, and thus also no rational status set.

This is intuitive, if we adopt the view that the status of each action being permitted or forbidden is complete, since there is no way to adopt either $\mathbf{P}\beta$ or $\mathbf{F}\beta$ without raising an inconsistency.

Example 6.5.14 Consider the program $\mathcal{P}_1$:

$\mathbf{Do}\,(\alpha) \leftarrow \neg \mathbf{F}\alpha.$

Here, we have two rational status sets, namely $S_1 = \{\mathbf{Do}\,(\alpha), \mathbf{P}\alpha\}$ and $S_2 = \{\mathbf{F}\alpha\}$. Both are F/P-complete, and are the rational status sets of $Comp_{P/F}$.

On the other hand, the program $\mathcal{P}_2$:

$\mathbf{Do}\,(\alpha) \leftarrow \mathbf{P}\alpha,$

has the unique rational status set $S = \{\}$, while its F/P-completion has the two rational status sets S_1 and S_2 from above. Thus, under F/P-completion semantics, the programs $\mathcal{P}_1$ and $\mathcal{P}_2$ are equivalent.

In fact, the following property holds.

PROPOSITION 6.5.8   Let $\mathcal{P}_1$ and $\mathcal{P}_2$ be ground agent programs and $\mathcal{O}_S$ a state, such that $\mathcal{P}_2$ results by replacing in $\mathcal{P}_1$ all literals $\mathsf{Op}(\alpha)$ (resp., $\neg\,\mathsf{Op}(\alpha)$) occurring in rules bodies, where $Op \in \{\mathbf{P}, \mathbf{F}\}$, by $\neg\,\overline{\mathsf{Op}}(\alpha)$ (resp., $\neg\,\overline{\mathsf{Op}}(\alpha)$) and $\overline{\mathsf{Op}}$ is the deontic status opposite to Op. Then, $Comp_{P/F}(\mathcal{P}_1)$ and $Comp_{P/F}(\mathcal{P}_2)$ have the same sets of feasible status sets.

Hence, under F/P-completion, $\neg\mathbf{F}$ amounts to $\mathbf{P}$ and similarly $\neg\mathbf{P}$ to $\mathbf{F}$.

Further completion rules can be used to reach a complete state on other status information as well. For example, a completion with respect to obligation/waiving can be reached by means of rules

$\mathbf{W}\alpha \leftarrow \neg \mathbf{O}\alpha$

for actions α. Such completion rules are in fact necessary, in order to ensure that the rational status sets can be completed to a two-valued deontic "model" of the program. Applying F/P-completion does not suffice for this purpose, as shown by the following example.

Example 6.5.15   Consider the program $\mathcal{P}$:

$\mathbf{P}\alpha \leftarrow$

$\mathbf{F}\alpha \leftarrow \mathbf{O}\beta$

$\mathbf{F}\alpha \leftarrow \mathbf{W}\beta$

The set $S = \{\mathbf{P}\alpha, \mathbf{P}\beta\}$ is a feasible status of $Comp_{F/P}(\mathcal{P})$. However, S cannot be completed to a deontic model of $\mathcal{P}$, in which $\mathbf{O}\beta$ and $\mathbf{W}\alpha$ are true or false, respectively, and such that the deontic axiom $\mathbf{W}\alpha \leftrightarrow \neg\mathbf{O}\alpha$ is satisfied.

6.5.7 Optimal Status Sets

Thus far, we have discussed the following semantics for agent programs, described as specialized status sets:

feasible, rational, reasonable, weak rational, F-preferential, P-preferential, and complete status sets.

Let Sem be a variable over any of these semantics. The developer of an agent should choose a semantics Sem in keeping with the philosophical and epistemic principles he wishes his agent to uphold.

However, in the real world, many choices are made based on the cost of a certain course of action, as well as the benefits gained by adopting that course of action. For example, if we consider the CHAIN example, it is quite likely that Suppliers 1 and 2 charge two different prices for the item that the plant agent wishes to order. Furthermore, as the two suppliers are likely to be located at different sites, transportation costs are also likely to vary. If one supplier can supply the entire quantity required, the plant agent will in all likelihood, select the one whose total cost (cost of items plus transportation) is lower. Note that this cost is being described in terms of the costs of the actions being executed in a status set.

However, yet another parameter that needs to be taken into account is the desirability of the final state that results by executing the Do-actions in a Sem-status set. For example, the time at which the supplies will arrive at the company is certainly pertinent, but is not accounted for by the cost parameters listed above. If supplier2 will provide the supplies one day before supplier1, then the plant agent may well choose to go with supplier1, even if supplier2's overall cost is lower.

What the preceding discussion suggests is that we associate with any Sem-status set, a notion of a cost, and that this cost must take into account the set of Do-status atoms in the status set, and the final state that results. This motivates our definition of a cost function.

DEFINITION 6.5.15 (COST FUNCTION) Suppose $\mathcal{S} = (\mathcal{T}_\mathcal{S}, \mathcal{F}_\mathcal{S}, \mathcal{C}_\mathcal{S})$ is a body of software code, and States is the set of all possible states associated with this body of code. Let $\mathcal{AB}$ be the action base. A *cost function*, cf, is a mapping from (States $\times 2^{\mathcal{AB}}$) to the non-negative real numbers such that:

$$[(\forall s_1, s_2)(\forall A) \text{ cf}(s_1, A) = \text{cf}(s_2, A)] \rightarrow [(\forall s)(\forall A, A')(A \subseteq A' \rightarrow \text{cf}(s, A) \leq \text{cf}(s, A'))].$$

The precondition of the above implication basically reflects state independence. A cost function is *state-independent* if for any set A of actions, and any two arbitrarily chosen states s_1, s_2, the cost function returns the same value for $\text{cf}(s_1, A)$ and $\text{cf}(s_2, A)$. State-independence implies that the cost function's values are only affected by the actions taken, i.e., by the set of actions A.

The above axiom says that for cf to be a cost function, if it is state-independent, then the values it returns must monotonically increase as the set of actions is enlarged (i.e., as more actions are taken).

One might wonder whether cost functions should satisfy the stronger condition:

(∗) $(\forall s)(\forall A, A'). A \subseteq A' \rightarrow \text{cf}(s, A) \leq \text{cf}(s, A')$.

The answer is "no"—to see why, consider the situation where executing the actions in A is cheaper than executing the actions in A', but this is offset by the fact that the state obtained by executing the actions in A' is less desirable than the state obtained by executing the actions in A.

Alternatively, one might wonder whether cost functions should satisfy the condition:

(∗∗) $(\forall s_1, s_2)(\forall A). s_1 \subseteq s_2 \rightarrow \text{cf}(s_1, A) \leq \text{cf}(s_2, A)$.

Again, the answer is no. Executing all actions in A in state s_1 may lead to a more desirable state than doing so in state s_2. As an example on the lighter side, consider the action *enter*(room). State s_1 is empty, state $s_2 = \{\textbf{in}(room, python)\}$. Clearly, $s_1 \subseteq s_2$. For most of us, executing the action *enter*(room) in state s_1 is vastly preferable to executing the action *enter*(room) in state s_2.

However, even though not all cost functions should be required to satisfy (∗) and (∗∗), there will certainly be applications where either (∗) and/or (∗∗) are satisfied. In such cases, it may turn out to be computationally beneficial to take advantage of properties (∗) and (∗∗) when computing optimal Sem-status sets defined below.

DEFINITION 6.5.16 (WEAK/STRONG MONOTONIC COST FUNCTIONS) A cost function is said to be weakly monotonic, if, by definition, it satisfies condition (∗) above. It is strongly monotonic, if, by definition, it satisfies both conditions (∗) and (∗∗).

We are now ready to come to the definition of optimal status sets.

DEFINITION 6.5.17 (OPTIMAL Sem-STATUS SET) Suppose $\mathcal{S} = (\mathcal{T}_S, \mathcal{F}_S, \mathcal{C}_S)$ is a body of software code, and $\mathcal{O}_S$ is the current state. A Sem-status set X is said to be *optimal with respect to cost function* cf *if* there is no other Sem-status set Y such that

$\text{cf}(\mathcal{O}_S, \{\textbf{Do}\,\alpha \in Y\}) < \text{cf}(\mathcal{O}_S, \{\textbf{Do}\,\alpha \in X\})$.

Note that the above definition induces different notions of status set, depending on what Sem is taken to be.

6.6 Relationship with Logic Programming and Nonmonotonic Logic

Thus far in this chapter, we have introduced several semantics for agent programs. In this section, we will show that these semantics for agent programs are specifically tied to well known semantics for logic programs. In particular, we will show that three major semantics for logic programs may be "embedded" within the concept of agent programs.

- First, we will exhibit a transformation, called AG, that takes an arbitrary logic program P as input and produces as output an agent program, and empty sets of action constraints and integrity constraints. We will show that the (Herbrand) models of P are in a 1-1 correspondence with the feasible status sets of AG(P), if they are projected to their **P**-parts.
- Second, we will show that the minimal Herbrand models of P are in a 1-1 correspondence with the rational status sets of AG(P). This automatically implies, by results of Marek and Subrahmanian (1992), the existence of a 1-1 correspondence between supported models of P, rational status sets of AG(P), weak extensions of a default theory associated with P as defined by Marek and Subrahmanian (1992), and expansions of an auto-epistemic theory associated with P. Similar equivalences also exist between rational status sets and disjunctive logic programs (Lobo et al. 1992).
- Third, we show that the stable models of P are in a 1-1 correspondence with the reasonable status sets of AG(P). As a consequence of known results due to Marek and Truszczyński (1993), it follows immediately that there is a 1-1 correspondence between reasonable status sets and extensions of default logic theories associated with P.

Throughout this section, we assume the reader is familiar with standard logic program terminology as described by Apt (1990) and Lloyd (1987) and terminology of nonmonotonic logic programming (Marek and Truszczyński 1993; Brewka et al. 1997; Dix 1995; Brewka and Dix 1999).

6.6.1 Feasible Status Sets and Models of Logic Programs

In this subsection, we describe a transformation AG that takes as input, a logic program P, and produces as output:

1. an action base, all of whose actions have a void (tautologous) precondition, an empty $Add(\cdot)$, and an empty $Del(\cdot)$;

2. an agent program $\mathsf{AG}(P)$; and,

3. empty sets of action and integrity constraints.

As all components other than the agent program produced by $\mathsf{AG}(P)$ are empty, we will abuse notation slightly and use $\mathsf{AG}(P)$ to denote the agent program produced by AG.

For each ground instance of a rule r in P of the form

$a \leftarrow b_1, \ldots, b_m, \neg c_1, \ldots, \neg c_n$

insert the rule

$$\mathbf{P}(a) \leftarrow \mathbf{P}(b_1), \ldots, \mathbf{P}(b_m), \neg \mathbf{P}(c_1), \ldots, \neg \mathbf{P}(c_n) \tag{6.7}$$

in $\mathsf{AG}(P)$. Here, the atoms a, b_i, and c_j of P are viewed as names of actions, each of which has an empty scheme and empty $Add(\cdot)$ and del-sets. It is important to note that the only types of status atoms that occur in $\mathsf{AG}(P)$ are of the form $\mathbf{P}(\cdot)$.

Example 6.6.1 Consider the logic program containing the two rules:

$a \leftarrow$
$b \leftarrow a, \neg c.$

The $\mathsf{AG}(P)$ is the agent program:

$\mathbf{P}(a) \leftarrow$
$\mathbf{P}(b) \leftarrow \mathbf{P}(a), \neg \mathbf{P}(c).$

We observe that the logic program has three models. These are given by:

$M_1 = \{a, b\}$
$M_2 = \{a, c\}$
$M_3 = \{a, b, c\}$

$\mathsf{AG}(P)$ happens to have more than three feasible status sets. These are given by:

$F_1 = \{\mathbf{P}(a), \mathbf{P}(b)\}.$
$F_2 = \{\mathbf{P}(a), \mathbf{P}(b), \mathbf{Do}\,(a)\}.$
$F_3 = \{\mathbf{P}(a), \mathbf{P}(b), \mathbf{Do}\,(b)\}.$
$F_4 = \{\mathbf{P}(a), \mathbf{P}(b), \mathbf{Do}\,(a), \mathbf{Do}\,(b)\}.$
$F_5 = \{\mathbf{P}(a), \mathbf{P}(c)\}.$
$F_6 = \{\mathbf{P}(a), \mathbf{P}(c), \mathbf{Do}\,(a)\}.$
$F_7 = \{\mathbf{P}(a), \mathbf{P}(c), \mathbf{Do}\,(c)\}.$
$F_8 = \{\mathbf{P}(a), \mathbf{P}(c), \mathbf{Do}\,(a), \mathbf{Do}\,(c)\}.$
$F_9 = \{\mathbf{P}(a), \mathbf{P}(b), \mathbf{P}(c)\}.$

$F_{10} = \{\mathbf{P}(a), \mathbf{P}(b), \mathbf{P}(c), \mathbf{Do}\,(a)\}.$
$F_{11} = \{\mathbf{P}(a), \mathbf{P}(b), \mathbf{P}(c), \mathbf{Do}\,(b)\}.$
$F_{12} = \{\mathbf{P}(a), \mathbf{P}(b), \mathbf{P}(c), \mathbf{Do}\,(c)\}.$
$F_{13} = \{\mathbf{P}(a), \mathbf{P}(b), \mathbf{P}(c), \mathbf{Do}\,(a), \mathbf{Do}\,(b)\}.$
$F_{14} = \{\mathbf{P}(a), \mathbf{P}(b), \mathbf{P}(c), \mathbf{Do}\,(a), \mathbf{Do}\,(c)\}.$
$F_{15} = \{\mathbf{P}(a), \mathbf{P}(b), \mathbf{P}(c), \mathbf{Do}\,(b), \mathbf{Do}\,(c)\}.$
$F_{16} = \{\mathbf{P}(a), \mathbf{P}(b), \mathbf{P}(c), \mathbf{Do}\,(a), \mathbf{Do}\,(b), \mathbf{Do}\,(c)\}.$

Many further feasible status sets exist, if we take atoms with the other modalities **F**, **O** and **W** into account.

However, when we examine the above sixteen and all other feasible status sets, and if we ignore the **Do** atoms in them, we find only three feasible status sets, viz. F_1, F_5 and F_9. The reader will easily note that the feasible status sets F_2, F_3, F_4 reflect different ways of determining which actions that are permitted in F_1 should actually be done. The same observation holds with regard to F_5 and the feasible status sets F_6, F_7, F_8. Likewise, the feasible status sets $F_{10}, \ldots, F_{17}$ are derived from F_9 in the same way.

The reader will note that in this example, M_1, M_2, M_3 stand in one one correspondence to the projections of $F_1, \ldots, F_{16}$ with respect to the modality **P**, i.e., M_1, M_2, M_3 stand in 1-1 correspondence with F_1, F_5, and F_9.

The following result shows, conclusively, that this is no accident.

PROPOSITION 6.6.1 There exists a 1-1 correspondence between the models of P and the **P**-projection of the feasible status sets of $\mathsf{AG}(P)$, i.e.,

1. If M is a model of the program P, then $A_M = \{\mathbf{P}(a) \mid a \in M\}$ is a feasible status set of $\mathsf{AG}(P)$.

2. If A is a feasible status set of $\mathsf{AG}(P)$, then $M_A = \{a \mid \mathbf{P}(a) \in A, a \text{ occurs in } P\}$ is a model of P.

Proof (1) Suppose M is a model of the program P. To show that A_M is a feasible status set of $\mathcal{P}(P)$, we need to show that A_M satisfies conditions $(S1)$–$(S4)$ in the definition of a feasible status set.

$(S1)$ Suppose r is a ground instance of a rule in $\mathsf{AG}(P)$ whose body is true w.r.t. A_M. Rule r must be one of the form $\mathbf{P}a \leftarrow \mathbf{P}b_1, \ldots, \mathbf{P}b_m, \neg \mathbf{P}c_1, \ldots, \mathbf{P}c_m$. Then $\{\mathbf{P}(b_1), \ldots, \mathbf{P}(b_m)\} \subseteq A_M$ and $\{\mathbf{P}(c_1), \ldots, \mathbf{P}(c_n)\} \cap A_M = \emptyset$. By definition of A_M, it follows that $\{a_1, \ldots, a_m\} \subseteq M$. By definition of A_M we have $\{c_1, \ldots, c_n\} \cap M = \emptyset$. As M is a model of P, $a \in M$, and hence, by definition of A_M, $\mathbf{P}(a) \in A_M$.

Thus, A_M satisfies condition $(S1)$ in the definition of feasible status set.

(*S2*) It is easy to see that the conditions defining deontic and action consistency (Definition 6.5.2) are satisfied. The reason is that by definition, A_M only contains atoms of the form $\mathbf{P}(\cdot)$ and hence, the first two bullets of Definition 6.5.2 are immediately true. The third bullet of Definition 6.5.2 is satisfied because all actions in $\mathsf{AG}(P)$ have an empty precondition, and hence, the consequent of the implication in the third bullet is immediately true. The action consistency requirement is satisfied trivially as $\mathsf{AG}(P)$ contains no action constraints.

(*S3*) The deontic and action closure requirements stated in Definition 6.5.3 are trivially satisfied because A_M contains no status atoms of the form $\mathbf{O}(\cdot)$ or $\mathbf{Do}(\cdot)$.

(*S4*) As $\mathsf{AG}(P)$ contains no integrity constraints, it follows immediately that the state consistency requirement is satisfied by A_M.

This completes the proof of (1) of the theorem.

(2) Suppose A is a feasible status set of $\mathsf{AG}(P)$ and M_A satisfies the body of a ground instance r of a rule in P. Let rule r be of the form

$$a \leftarrow b_1, \ldots, b_m, \neg c_1, \ldots, \neg c_n.$$

As $\{b_1, \ldots, b_m\} \subseteq M_A$, we must, by definition, have $\{\mathbf{P}(b_1), \ldots, \mathbf{P}(b_m)\} \subseteq M_A$. As $\{c_1, \ldots, c_n\} \cap M_A = \emptyset$, we must, by definition, have $A \cap \{\mathbf{P}(c_1), \ldots, \mathbf{P}(c_n)\} = \emptyset$. By construction of $\mathsf{AG}(P)$, we have the rule

$$\mathbf{P}(a) \leftarrow \mathbf{P}(b_1), \ldots, \mathbf{P}(b_m), \neg\mathbf{P}(c_1), \ldots, \neg\mathbf{P}(c_n)$$

in $\mathsf{AG}(P)$. As A is a feasible status set, it must satisfy axiom (*S1*). Hence, $\mathbf{P}(a) \in A$, which implies that $a \in M_A$. This completes the proof. ■

6.6.2 Rational Status Sets and Minimal Models of Logic Programs

If we return to Example 6.6.1, we will notice that the logic program P shown there has two minimal Herbrand models, corresponding to M_1, M_2 respectively, and the feasible status sets, F_1, F_5 correspond to the rational status sets of $\mathsf{AG}(P)$. Intuitively, minimal Herbrand models of a logic program select models of P that are inclusion-minimal, while rational status sets select feasible status sets that are also inclusion-minimal. As there is a 1-1 correspondence between models of P and the $\mathbf{P}$-parts of the feasible status sets of $\mathsf{AG}(P)$, it follows immediately that the inclusion minimal elements should also be in 1-1 correspondence. The following result is in fact an immediate corollary of Proposition 6.6.1 and establishes this 1-1 correspondence.

PROPOSITION 6.6.2 There exists a 1-1 correspondence between the minimal models of P and the rational status sets of $\mathsf{AG}(P)$, i.e.

1. If M is a minimal model of the program P, then $A_M = \{\mathbf{P}(a) \mid a \in M\}$ is a rational status set of $\mathcal{P}(P)$.

2. If A is a rational status set of $\mathsf{AG}(P)$, then $M_A = \{a \mid \mathbf{P}(a) \in A, a \text{ occurs in } P\}$ is a minimal model of P.

When taken in conjunction with results of Lobo and Subrahmanian (1992), the above result implies that there exists a translation T, given in (Lobo and Subrahmanian 1992), such that the rational status sets of $\mathsf{AG}(P)$ correspond exactly to the extensions of a pre-requisite free normal default theory $T(P)$.

6.6.3 Reasonable Status Sets and Stable Semantics

In this section, we show that the reasonable status sets of $\mathsf{AG}(P)$ correspond to the stable models of P. Before stating this main result formally, let us return to the case of Example 6.6.1.

Example 6.6.2 It is easy to see that the logic program P of Example 6.6.1 has exactly one stable model, viz. M_1. It is easy to see that $\mathsf{AG}(P)$ program has a unique reasonable status set, viz. $RS_1 = \{\mathbf{P}(a), \mathbf{P}(b)\}$. As Proposition 6.6.3 below will show, this is not an accident.

The following result explicitly states this.

PROPOSITION 6.6.3 There exists a 1-1 correspondence between the stable models of P and the reasonable status sets of $\mathsf{AG}(P)$, i.e.,

1. If M is a stable model of the program P, then $A_M = \{\mathbf{P}(a) \mid a \in M\}$ is a reasonable status set of $\mathsf{AG}(P)$.

2. If A is a reasonable status set of $\mathcal{P}(P)$, then $M_A = \{a \mid \mathbf{P}(a) \in A, a \text{ occurs in } P\}$ is a stable model of P.

Proof We show part (1). Part (2) is proved by an analogous (and somewhat simpler) reasoning. Suppose M is a stable model of P. Then let $Q = red^{A_M}(\mathsf{AG}(P), \emptyset)$ be the agent program obtained as the reduct of $\mathsf{AG}(P)$ w.r.t. A_M and the empty object state. To show that A_M is a reasonable status set of $\mathsf{AG}(P)$, we need to show that A_M is a rational status set of Q. For this we need to show that each of the conditions $(S1)$–$(S4)$ is true for A_M with respect to Q, and that A_M is an inclusion-minimal set satisfying this condition.

$(S1)$ Consider a rule r in Q of the form

$\mathbf{P}(a) \leftarrow \mathbf{P}(b_1), \ldots, \mathbf{P}(b_m)$

such that $\{\mathbf{P}(b_1), \ldots, \mathbf{P}(b_m)\} \subseteq A_M$. By definition, $\{b_1, \ldots, b_m\} \subseteq M$. As $r \in Q$, there must exist a rule r' in $\mathsf{AG}(P)$ of the form

$$\mathbf{P}(a) \leftarrow \mathbf{P}(b_1), \ldots, \mathbf{P}(b_m), \neg\mathbf{P}(c_1), \ldots, \neg\mathbf{P}(c_n)$$

such that $\{\mathbf{P}(c_1), \ldots, \mathbf{P}(c_n)\} \cap A_M = \emptyset$. This means that there is a rule $r^\star$ in P of the form

$$a \leftarrow b_1, \ldots, b_m, \neg c_1, \ldots, \neg c_n$$

such that $\{c_1, \ldots, c_n\} \cap M = \emptyset$. Thus as M satisfies the body of $r^\star$ and as M is a stable model of P (and hence a model of P), $a \in M$ which implies that $\mathbf{P}(a) \in A_M$. This part of the proof is completed.

(S2)   The first bullet in the definition of deontic consistency is immediately satisfied as A_M contains no status atoms of the form $\mathbf{W}(\cdot)$. The second bullet in the definition of deontic consistency is immediately satisfied as A_M contains no status atoms of the form $\mathbf{F}(\cdot)$. The third one in the definition of deontic consistency is immediately satisfied as all actions have an empty precondition, which is vacuously true. The action consistency requirement is immediately satisfied as the set $\mathcal{AC}$ of action constraints produced by AG is empty.

(S3) A_M is deontically closed because, by definition, A_M contains no status atoms of the form $\mathbf{O}(\cdot)$. A_M is action-closed because A_M contains no status atoms of the form $\mathbf{O}(\cdot), \mathbf{Do}(\cdot)$.

(S4) A_M satisfies the state consistency property because the set $\mathcal{IC}$ of integrity constraints produced by AG is empty.

At this point, we have shown that A_M is a feasible status set of Q. To establish that it is a rational status set of Q, we need to show that it is inclusion-minimal. Suppose not. Then there exists a set $S \subset A_M$ such that S is a feasible status set of Q. Let $S^\star = \{a \mid \mathbf{P}(a) \in S\}$. It is straightforward to show that $S^\star$ is a stable model of P. But then $S^\star \subset M$, which is a contradiction, as no stable model of any logic program can be a strict subset of another stable model (Marek and Subrahmanian 1992). ∎

It is important to observe that by this correspondence, we obtain alternative proofs for the complexity results on reasonable status sets in Chapter 11. This is because the complexity results known for non-monotonic logic programs with stable model semantics (Marek and Truszczyński 1991; Marek and Truszczyński 1993) directly imply the above results.

6.6.4 Discussion

Thus far, in this section, we have shown that given any logic program P, we can convert P into an agent program, $\mathsf{AG}(P)$, (together with associated action base and empty sets of integrity constraints and action constraints) such that:

1. The **P**-parts of feasible status sets are in 1-1 correspondence with the models of P;
2. Rational status sets are in 1-1 correspondence with the minimal models of P;
3. Reasonable status sets are in 1-1 correspondence with the stable models of P.

The above results, when taken in conjunction with known results linking logic programs and nonmonotonic reasoning, provide connections with wellknown nonmonotonic logics as well. For example, the following results are well known:

• Marek and Truszczyński (1993) prove 1-1 correspondences between stable models of logic programs and extensions of default logic theories.

• Marek and Subrahmanian (1992) and Marek and Truszczyński (1993) prove 1-1 correspondences between stable models of logic programs and appropriate types of expansions of auto-epistemic theories.

• Lobo and Subrahmanian (1992) prove 1-1 correspondences between minimal models of logic programs, and extensions of prerequisite-free normal default logic theories.

• Ben-Eliyahu and Dechter (1994) prove that stable models and minimal models of logic programs may be viewed as models of a suitable logical theory.

An important topic that we have not addressed here is whether there exists a transformation $\wp$ that takes as input an agent state, action base, an agent program, a set of integrity constraints, and a set of action constraints, and produces as output a logic program such that the above equivalences hold. This is somewhat complicated to do because the use of arbitrary agent states over arbitrary data structures means that classical model semantics, minimal model semantics, and stable semantics cannot be used directly. Rather, the notion of models over arbitrary data structures introduced by Lu, Nerode, and Subrahmanian (1996) must be used. For this reason, we defer this to further work.

However, we remark that for feasible and rational status sets, no 1-1 correspondence to the models and minimal models, respectively, of a polynomial-time constructible logic program similar as above is possible in general: An agent program may lack a feasible or rational status set (even in absence of integrity constraints), while a logic program always has some model and minimal model. In Chapter 11, we will show that existence of a feasible as well as a rational status set for an agent program is co-NP-hard, even for agent programs without integrity constraints. Furthermore, it is wellknown that computing a model (resp., minimal model) of a logic program is in FNP (resp., FNP//log). Hence, it is not possible to polynomially reduce the $F\Sigma_2^P$-hard computation of a rational status set of a general agent program to the computation of a model (resp., minimal model) of a polynomial time-constructible logic program, unless the polynomial hierarchy collapses, which is considered to be very unlikely. In particular, no polynomial-time constructible logic program exists whose minimal models correspond 1-1 to the rational status sets of a general agent program. Observe that from the complexity side, a 1-1 correspondence between reasonable status sets of an agent program and the stable models of a polynomial-time constructible logic program is not excluded; in fact, a rather natural translation seems feasible.

6.7 Related Work

6.7.1 Agent Programming Frameworks

Shoham (1993) was perhaps the first to propose an explicit programming language for agents, based on object oriented concepts, and based on the concept of an agent state. In Shoham's approach, an *"agent is an entity whose state is viewed as consisting of mental components such as beliefs, capabilities, choices, and commitments"* (Shoham 1993). He proposes a language, *Agent-0*, for agent programming, that provides a mechanism to express actions, time, and obligations. *Agent-0* is a simple, yet powerful language. There are several differences between our approach and Shoham's. Our language builds on top of arbitrary data structures, whereas Shoham's language is more or less logical (though it uses a LISP-like syntax). For us, states are instantiations of data structures managed by the program code associated with agents, while for Shoham, the agent state consists of beliefs, capabilities, choices, and commitments. This allows Shoham to focus on reasoning about beliefs (e.g., agent a knows that agent b knows that agent a has no money), whereas our focus is on decision making on top of arbitrary data structures. Clearly both paradigms are needed for successfully building an agent.

Closely related to Shoham's work is that of Hindriks et al. (1997) where an agent programming language based on *BDI*-agents is presented (*BDI* stands for *"Belief, Desires, Intentionality"*). They proceed upon the assumptions that an agent language must have the ability for updating belief and goals and, for practical reasoning finding means to achieve goals. Hindriks et al. (1997) argue that *"Now, to program an agent is to specify its initial mental state, the semantics of the basic actions the agent can perform, and to write a set of practical reasoning rules"* (Hindriks et al. 1997, p. 211).

In our framework, as decision layers can (in principle) be embedded on top of arbitrary pieces of software code, representations of beliefs and goals such as those developed by researchers in "reasoning about beliefs" can be easily incorporated as modules into those data structures, though we have not focused on this part. We do not *insist* that all agents have an a priori goal. For instance, consider an ACCESS database agent. This agent has no real goal that requires AI planning, unless one considers the fact that it should respond to user queries as a goal. Practical reasoning is achieved in our system because each agent processes an explicit call through a *method* used to process that call. In contrast to the framework in (Hindriks et al. 1997), for us, an initial state is any set of (instantiated) data types—they assume this is a set of logical atoms. Likewise, practical reasoning rules for us are implemented as methods (or code-calls), but the decision about which of these actions is to be taken is represented through rules.

ConGolog (Giacomo et al. 1997) is a logic programming language for concurrent execution of actions. *ConGolog* creates static plans from a set of goals and primitive actions. *ConGolog* is built on the framework of Cohen and Levesque (1990a) who develop a logic of rational agents based on intentionality using speech acts as a starting point. Their work has subsequently been used for a variety of other multiagent frameworks—we do not go into these extensions here, as they are not directly related to our effort.

In general, the approach in this chapter builds upon the approaches of Shoham (1993) and Hindriks et al. (1997) in the following sense: first, we agree with these earlier approaches that the behavior of agents should be encoded through an agent program, and second, that actions taken by agents should modify agent states. However, we differ from these approaches in the following sense. First, our notion of an agent state is built on top of arbitrary data structures, rather than on top of states represented in logic. As a consequence, our approach complements the work of Shoham (1993) and Hindriks et al. (1997) where they focus on logical representations of agent state, describing beliefs, capabilities, commitments, and goals. In addition, (Shoham 1993) describes temporal action scheduling which our language does not currently support, though ongoing work will extend it to do so. If these modes of reasoning can be expressed as data structures, then the notion of agent proposed here can benefit from the contributions in Shoham (1993) and Hindriks et al. (1997). Second, we propose a set of increasingly more satisfying declarative (epistemic) formal semantics for our work. Hindriks, de Boer, van der Hock and Meyer (1997) propose an elegant proof theoretic operational semantics. Our semantics has the advantage of being neatly related to existing wellunderstood semantics for logic programs. Third, we analyze the tradeoffs between adopting an epistemically satisfying semantics and the computational complexity of these semantics. The results also contain algorithmic approaches to computing these semantics.

6.7.2 Deontic Logic

In many applications, the administrators of an application have certain legal obligations (that is, they are required to take certain actions), as well as certain restrictions (that is, they are forbidden to take certain actions) if certain conditions are true. However, not all actions are either forbidden or obligatory. The vast majority of actions fall within a "gray" area—they are permitted, but neither obligatory or forbidden. In the field of databases, no active database system was available that provides a formal semantics for obligatory, permitted, and forbidden actions. Our approach in this chapter subsumes a formal semantics for such actions in databases, building on top of classical deontic logic syntax (Åquist 1984; Meyer and (Wieringa 1993).

We have added to deontic logic as well in several ways: first, we have introduced the **Do** operator which standard deontic logic does not contain. Second, classical deontic logic does not account for interference between multiple actions (i.e., do actions α, β have mutually inconsistent effects, or can actions α, β be simultaneously executed), while our framework takes into account both effects of actions, and provides different notions of concurrent executability. Third, our framework also allows nonmonotonic inference through the negation operator in rule bodies—this nonmonotonic negation operator does not occur in classical deontic logic model theory. The need for non-monotonic operators has been well argued by Reiter (1980). Last, but not least, the semantics of classical deontic logic is given in terms of a classical Hintikka-Kripke style model theory. Owing to the introduction of the new features described above, and because most deontic logic model theory leads to one or another deontic paradox, we chose to develop an alternative semantics that incorporates nonmonotonicity, concurrent actions, and the **Do** operator proposing the concepts of feasible, rational, and reasonable status sets, and their variants, through which many desirable deontic desiderata (e.g., regimentation, relaxing obligations when they cannot be satisfied) can be incorporated. Precisely how various other deontic assumptions can be captured within our semantics remains to be worked out.

The approach of Hindriks et al. (1997) is based on such logics and has already been discussed. Dignum and Conte (1997) have used deontic logic extensively to develop methods for goal formation—in our framework, goal formation is one of several actions that an agent can take. Thus, we can specifically gain from the work of Dignum and Conte (1997) through explicitly plugging in such a framework as an action called *form-goals* implemented through the elegant work they report.

6.7.3 Agent Decision Making Frameworks

There has been a significant amount of work on agent decision making. Rosenschein (1985) was perhaps the first to say that agents act according to states, and which actions they take are determined by rules of the form "When P is true of the state of the environment, then the agent should take action A." As the reader can easily see, our framework builds upon this intuitive idea, though (i) our notion of state is defined very generally and (ii) agent programs have a richer set of rules than those listed above. Rosenschein and Kaelbling (1995) extend this framework to provide a basis for such actions in terms of situated automata theory.

Bratman et al. (1988) define the *IRMA* system which uses similar ideas to generate plans. In their framework, different possible courses of actions (plans) are generated based on the agent's intentions. These plans are then evaluated to determine which ones are consistent and optimal with respect to achieving these intentions.

Verharen, Dignum, and Bos (1997) present a language-action approach to agent decision making, which has some similarities to our effort. However, they do not develop any formal semantics for their work, and their language for agent programs uses a linguistic rather than a logical approach. Schoppers and Shapiro (1997) describe techniques to design agents that optimize objective functions—such objective functions are similar to the cost functions we have described.

One effort that is close to ours is the approach of Singh (1997). Like us, he is concerned about heterogeneity in agents, and he develops a theory of agent interactions through workflow diagrams. Intuitively, in this framework, an agent is viewed as a finite state automaton. It is well known that finite state automata can be easily encoded in logic. This makes our framework somewhat more general than Singh's, which explicitly encodes automata (hard to do when an agent has hundreds of *ground* actions it can take). Sycara and Zeng (1996b) provide a coordinated search methodology for multiple agents. Haddadi (1995) develops a declarative theory of interactions as do Rao and Georgeff (1991) and Coradeschi and Karlsson (1997) build agents for air traffic simulation.

There has been extensive work on negotiation in multiagent systems, based on the initial idea of contract nets, due to Smith and Davis (1983). In this paradigm, an agent seeking a service invites bids from other agents and selects the bid that most closely matches its own. Schwartz and Kraus (1997) present a model of agent decision making where one agent invites bids (this is an action!) and others evaluate the bids (another action) and respond; this kind of behavior is encodable through agent programs together with underlying data structures. This body of work is complementary to ours: an agent negotiates by taking certain actions in accordance with its negotiation strategy, while we provide the "hooks" to include such actions within our framework, but do not explicitly study how the negotiation actions are performed, as this has been well done by others (Smith and Davis 1983; Schwartz and Kraus 1997).

Coalition formation mechanisms, where agents dynamically team up with other agents, has been intensely studied by many researchers, e.g., (Shehory et al. 1997; Sandholm and Lesser 1995; Wooldridge and Jennings 1997). Determining which agents to team with is a sort of decision making capability. d'Inverno et al. (1997) present a framework for dMARS based on the BDI model. Like us, they assume a state space, and the fact that actions cause state transitions. Labrou and Finin (1997b) develop the semantics of KQML, but do not explicitly present an action language.

6.7.4 Reasoning about Actions

Several works (Gelfond and Lifschitz 1993; Baral and Gelfond 1993; Baral and Gelfond 1994; Baral et al. 1995) have addressed the problem of modeling the logic of actions by means of logic programming languages. In this section, we briefly address these, one by one.

Gelfond and Lifschitz (1993) propose a logic programming language called $\mathcal{A}$, in which users may express knowledge about actions and their effects. This framework was later extended by Baral, Gelfond and others in a series of appealing papers (Baral and Gelfond 1994; Baral et al. 1995; Baldoni et al. 1998a; Baldoni et al. 1998b). The language $\mathcal{A}$ allows users to make statements of the form

f **after** $a_1, \ldots, a_m$
  initially f
a **causes** f **if** $p_1, \ldots, p_n$.

Intuitively, the first statement says that executing actions $a_1, \ldots, a_m$ makes f true (afterwards). Likewise, the second statement says f was true in the initial state, and the third statement describes the effect of a on f if certain preconditions are satisfied.

The key differences between our approach, and this genre of work are the following.

1. First and foremost, our approach applies to heterogeneous data sources, while this body of work assumes all data is stored in the form of logical atoms.

2. Second, the modalities for determining what is permitted, what is forbidden, what is obligatory, what is done, are not treated in the above body of work.

3. Third, in our approach, we use the semantics to determine which set of firable actions (in a state) must actually be fired, and this policy of *choosing* such sets of actions in accordance with the policies expressed in an agent program and the underlying integrity constraints is different from what is done in (Gelfond and Lifschitz 1993; Baral and Gelfond 1994; Baral et al. 1995; Baldoni et al. 1998a; Baldoni et al. 1998b).

7 Meta Agent Programs

In this chapter we extend our framework considerably by allowing agents to *reason* about other agents based on the beliefs they hold. We introduce certain *belief data structures* that an agent needs to maintain and introduce *meta agent program* as an extension of agent programs introduced in the previous chapter. We also extend the semantics of *agent programs* to semantics of *meta agent programs*. Finally, we show how meta agent programs can be implemented via agent programs by *encoding beliefs into extended code calls*.

In contrast to the previous chapters we do not consider all three examples CFIT, STORE and CHAIN. The reason is that adding meta-reasoning capabilities to the STORE or CHAIN example would seem rather artificial. Instead, we extend our CFIT example and use this scenario extensively throughout this chapter.

7.1 Extending CFIT by Route and Maneuver Planning

We extend our CFIT example by replacing the original plane by a helicopter that operates together with other helicopters in the air and certain tanks at the surface. Thus we consider tasks that are important in route and maneuver planning over free terrain.

A simplified version of such an application that deals with meta-reasoning by agents is shown in Figure 7.1 and is described below. This example, referred to as the CFIT* example (because it extends our earlier CFIT example) will provide a unifying theme throughout this chapter, and will be used to illustrate the various definitions we introduce.

Our application involves tracking enemy vehicles on the battlefield, and attempting to predict what these enemy agents are likely to do in the future, based on metaknowledge that we have about them.

A set of enemy vehicle agents: These agents (mostly tanks) move across free terrain, and their movements are determined by a program that the other agents listed below do not have access to (though they may have beliefs about this program). A detailed description is given in Subsection A.4.1.

A terrain route planning agent, terrain, which was already introduced in Chapter 1 (see Table 2.2). Here we extend the terrain agent so that it also provides a flight path computation service for helicopters, through which it plans a flight, given an origin, a destination, and a set of constraints specifying the height at which the helicopters wish to fly. The terrain route planning agent is built on top of an existing *US ARMY Route*

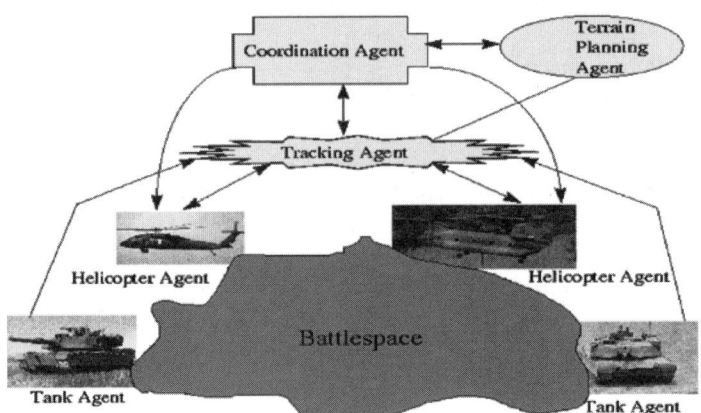

Figure 7.1
Agents in of CFIT* Example.

planning software package developed at the *Topographic and Engineering Center* (Benton and Subrahmanian 1994). The code calls and actions associated with terrain are described in Subsection A.4.2.

A tracking agent, which takes as input, a *DTED* (Digital Terrain Elevation Data) map, an id assigned to an enemy agent, and a time point. It produces as output, the location of the enemy agent at the given point in time (if known) as well as its best guess of what kind of enemy the agent is. Section A.4.3 provides full details.

A coordination agent, that keeps track of current friendly assets. This agent receives input and ships requests to the other agents with a view to determining exactly what target(s) the enemy columns may be attempting to strike, as well as determining how to nullify the oncoming convoy. The situation is complicated by the fact that the agent may have a hard time determining what the intended attack target is. It may be further complicated by uncertainty about what kind of vehicle the enemy is using—depending upon the type of vehicle used, different routes may be designated as optimal by the terrain route planning agent. Section A.4.4 provides a detailed description.

A set of helicopter agents, that may receive instructions from the coordination agent about when and where to attack the enemy vehicles. When such instructions are received, the helicopter agents contact the terrain route planning agent, and request a flight path. Such a flight path uses terrain elevation information (to ensure that the helicopter does not fly into the side of a mountain). We refer the reader to Subsection A.4.5 for a complete description.

The aim of all agents above (except for the enemy agents) is to attack and nullify the enemy attacking force. To do this, the coordination agent sends requests for information and analyses to the other friendly agents, as well as instructions to them specifying actions they must take. It is important to note that the coordination agent's actions are based on its *beliefs* about what the enemy is likely to do. These beliefs include:

• *Beliefs about the type of enemy vehicle.* Each enemy vehicle has an associated type—for example, one vehicle may be a T-80 tank, the other may be a T-72 tank. However, the coordination agent may not precisely know the type of a given enemy vehicle, because of inaccurate and/or uncertain identification made by the sensing agent. At any point in time, it holds some beliefs about the identity of enemy vehicle.

• *Beliefs about intentions of enemy vehicle.* The coordination agent must try to guess what the enemy's target is. Suppose the tracking agent starts tracking a given enemy agent at time t_0, and the current time is t_{now}. Then the tracking agent can provide information about the location of this agent at each instant between time t_0 and time t_{now}. Let ℓ_i denote the location of one such enemy agent at time t_i, $0 \leq i \leq now$. The coordination agent believes that the enemy agent is trying to target one of its assets $A_1, \ldots, A_k$, but does not know which one. It may ask the terrain agent to plan a route from ℓ_0 to each of the locations of $A_1, \ldots, A_k$, and may decide that the intended target is the location whose associated route most closely matches the observed initial route taken by the enemy agent between times t_0 and t_{now}.

• *Changing beliefs with time.* As the enemy agent continues along its route, the coordination agent may be forced to revise its beliefs, as it becomes apparent that the actual route being taken by the enemy vehicle is inconsistent with the expected route. Furthermore, as time proceeds, sensing data provided by the tracking agent may cause the coordination agent to revise its beliefs about the enemy vehicle type. As the terrain agent plans routes based on the type of enemy vehicle being considered, this may cause changes in the predictions made by the terrain agent.

• *Beliefs about the enemy agent's reasoning.* The coordination agent may also hold some beliefs about the enemy agents' reasoning capabilities (see the *Belief-Semantics Table* in Definition 7.2.4 on page 217). For instance, with a relatively unsophisticated and disorganized enemy whose command and control facilities have been destroyed, it may believe that the enemy does not know what moves friendly forces are making. However, in the case of an enemy with viable/strong operational command and control facilities, it may believe that the enemy does have information on the moves made by friendly forces—in this case, additional actions to mislead the enemy may be required.

A detailed description of all agents and their actions will be given in the Section A.4.

7.2 Belief Language and Data Structures

In this section, we introduce the important notion of a *belief atom*. Belief atoms express the beliefs of one agent a about what holds in another agent's, say b's, state. They will be used later in Definition 7.2.7 on page 225 to define the notion of a *meta agent program*, which is central to this chapter. When an agent a reasons about another agent b, it must have some beliefs about b's underlying action base (*what actions can b take?*), b's action program (*how will b reason?*) etc. These beliefs will be discussed later in more depth.

In this section, we will describe the belief language that is used by *IMPACT* agents. In particular, our definitions proceed as follows:

1. We first describe in Subsection 7.2.1 a hierarchy of belief languages of increasing complexity as we go "up" the hierarchy.

2. We then define in Subsection 7.2.2 an intermediate structure called a *basic belief table*. Intuitively, a basic belief table maintained by agent a contains information about the beliefs a has about the states of other agents, as well as a itself. It also includes a's belief about action status atoms that are adopted by other agents.

3. Each agent also has some beliefs about how other agents reason about beliefs. As the same syntactic language fragment can admit many different semantics, the agent maintains a *Belief Semantics Table*, describing its perceptions of the semantics used by other agents to reason about beliefs (Subsection 7.2.3).

4. We then extend in Subsection 7.2.4 the concept of a basic belief table to a *belief table*. Intuitively, a belief table is obtained by adding an extra column to the basic belief table—the reason for separating these two definitions is that the new column may refer to conditions on the columns of basic belief tables. Intuitively, belief tables contain statements of the form *If condition ϕ is true, then agent a believes ψ* where ψ is a condition about some agent b's state, or about the actions that agent b might take.

It is important to note that assuming additional datatypes as part of our underlying software package has strong implications on the possible code calls as introduced in Definition 4.2.2 on page 81: the more datatypes we have, the more types of code calls can be formulated in our language. We will introduce in Definition 7.3.5 on page 229 a precise notion of the set of *extended code calls*.

7.2.1 Belief Language Hierarchy

We are now ready to start defining the beliefs that agent a may hold about the code calls agent b can perform. These code calls determine the code call conditions that may or may

Section 7.2   Belief Language and Data Structures

not hold in agent b's state. Let us denote this by the belief atom

$\mathcal{B}_a(b, \chi)$

which represents one of the beliefs of agent a about what holds in the state of agent b. In that case, agent a must have beliefs about agent b's software package $\mathcal{S}^b$: the code call condition χ has to be contained in $\mathcal{S}^b$. We will collect all the beliefs that an agent a has about another agent b in a set $\Gamma^a(b)$ (see Definition 7.3.4 on page 229).

From now on we will refer to code call conditions satisfying the latter property as *compatible code call conditions*. We will use the same term for action atoms: *compatible action atoms* of agent a with respect to agent b, are those action atoms in the action base that a believes agent b holds. We also assume that the structure of such an action contained in b's base (as believed by a) is defined in $\Gamma^a(b)$. This means that the *schema*, the *set of preconditions*, the *add-list* and the *delete-list* are uniquely determined.

DEFINITION 7.2.1 (BELIEF ATOM/LITERAL, $\mathcal{B}At_1(a, b)$, $\mathcal{B}Lit_1(a, A)$)   Let a, b be agents in A. Then we define the set $\mathcal{B}At_1(a, b)$ of a-belief atoms about b of level 1 as follows:

1. If χ is a compatible code call condition of a with respect to b, then $\mathcal{B}_a(b, \chi)$ is a *belief atom*.

2. For $Op \in \{\mathbf{O}, \mathbf{W}, \mathbf{P}, \mathbf{F}, \mathbf{Do}\}$: if $\alpha(\vec{t})$ is a compatible action atom of agent a with respect to b, then $\mathcal{B}_a(b, Op\, \alpha(\vec{t}))$ is a *belief atom*.

If $\mathcal{B}_a(b, \chi)$ is a belief atom, then $\mathcal{B}_a(b, \chi)$ and $\neg \mathcal{B}_a(b, \chi)$ are called *belief literals of level 1*, the corresponding set is denoted by $\mathcal{B}Lit_1(a, b)$.

Let

$$\mathcal{B}At_1(a, A) =_{def} \bigcup_{b \in A} \mathcal{B}At_1(a, b) \quad \text{and} \quad \mathcal{B}Lit_1(a, A) =_{def} \bigcup_{b \in A} \mathcal{B}Lit_1(a, b)$$

be the set of all a-belief atoms (resp. belief literals) relative to A. This reflects the idea that agent a can have beliefs about many agents in A, not just about a single one.

Here are a couple of belief atoms from our CFIT* example:

Example 7.2.1 (Belief Atoms In CFIT)*

- $\mathcal{B}_{heli1}(tank1, \mathbf{in}(pos1, tank1 : getPos()))$
This belief atom says that the agent, heli1 believes that agent tank1's current state indicates that tank1's current position is pos1.

- $\mathcal{B}_{heli1}(tank1, \mathbf{F}attack(pos1, pos2))$
This belief atom says that the agent, heli1 believes that agent tank1's current state indicates that it is forbidden for tank1 to attack from pos1 to pos2.

- $\mathcal{B}_{\text{heli3}}(\text{tank1}, \mathbf{O}\mathit{drive}(\text{pos1}, \text{pos2}, 35))$

This belief atom says that the agent, heli3 believes that agent tank1's current state makes it obligatory for tank1 to drive from location pos1 to pos2 at 35 miles per hour.

It is important to note that these are *beliefs* held by agents heli1 and heli3, respectively. Any of them could be an incorrect belief.

Thus far, we have not allowed for nested beliefs. The language $\mathcal{B}\text{Lit}_1(a, A)$ does not allow agent a to have beliefs of the form *"Agent b believes that agent c's state contains code call condition χ,"* i.e., agent a cannot express beliefs it has about the beliefs of another agent.

The next definition introduces nested beliefs and also a general *belief language*. We introduce the following notation: for a given set X of formulae we denote by $\mathbf{Cl}_{\{\&, \neg\}}(X)$ the set of all conjunctions consisting of elements of X or their negations: $x_1 \wedge \neg x_2 \wedge \ldots \wedge x_n$, where $x_i \in X$. We emphasize that this does not correspond to the usual closure of X under & and $\neg$: in particular, it does not allow us to formulate disjunctions, if X consists of atoms.

DEFINITION 7.2.2 (NESTED BELIEFS $\mathcal{B}\text{Lit}_i(a, b)$, BELIEF LANGUAGE $\mathcal{BL}_i^a$) In the following let $a, b \in A$. We want to define $\mathcal{BL}_i^a$, the *belief language of agent a of level i*. This is done recursively as follows.

i ≤ 1: In accordance with Definition 7.2.1 on the page before (where we already defined $\mathcal{B}\text{At}_1(a, b)$) we denote by $\mathcal{B}\text{At}_0(a, b)$ as well as by $\mathcal{B}\text{Lit}_0(a, b)$

$\{\phi \mid \phi$ is a compatible code call condition or action atom$\}$

the flat set of code call conditions or action atoms—no belief atoms are allowed. Furthermore, we define

$\mathcal{BL}_0(a, b) =_{def} \mathcal{B}\text{At}_0(a, b)$
$\mathcal{BL}_1(a, b) =_{def} \mathbf{Cl}_{\{\&, \neg\}}(\mathcal{B}\text{At}_1(a, b))$,

i.e., the set of formulae $\mathcal{B}\text{At}_0(a, b)$, resp. the of all conjunctions of belief literals from $\mathcal{B}\text{At}_1(a, b)$. We call

$\mathcal{BL}_0^a =_{def} \bigcup_{b \in A} \mathcal{BL}_0(a, b)$
$\mathcal{BL}_1^a =_{def} \mathbf{Cl}_{\{\&, \neg\}}\left(\bigcup_{b \in A} \mathcal{BL}_1(a, b)\right)$

the *belief languages of agent a of level 0, resp. of level 1*.

i > 1: To define nested belief literals we set for $i > 1$

$\mathcal{B}\text{At}_i(a, b) =_{def} \{\mathcal{B}_a(b, \beta) \mid \beta \in \mathcal{B}\text{At}_{i-1}(b, A)\}$,
$\mathcal{B}\text{Lit}_i(a, b) =_{def} \{(\neg)\mathcal{B}_a(b, \beta) \mid \beta \in \mathcal{B}\text{At}_{i-1}(b, A)\}$.

This finishes the recursive definition of $\mathcal{B}\text{Lit}_i(a, b)$.

The definition of the *belief language of agent* a *of level* i can now be given directly:

$$\mathcal{BL}_i^a =_{def} \mathbf{Cl}_{\{\&,\neg\}} \left(\bigcup_{b \in A} \mathcal{BL}_i(a, b) \right) \qquad (7.1)$$

where

$$\mathcal{BL}_i(a, b) =_{def} \mathbf{Cl}_{\{\&,\neg\}}(\mathcal{BAt}_i(a, b)).$$

Finally we define the maximal belief language an agent a can have:

$$\mathcal{BL}_\infty^a =_{def} \mathbf{Cl}_{\{\&,\neg\}} \left(\bigcup_{i=0}^{\infty} \mathcal{BL}_i^a \right). \qquad (7.2)$$

Formulae in this language are also called *general belief formulae*.

We will later also use the following definitions:

1. $\mathcal{BAt}_i(a, A) =_{def} \cup_{b \in A} \mathcal{BAt}_i(a, b)$ is called the set of belief atoms of depth i.
2. $\mathcal{BLit}_i(a, A) =_{def} \cup_{b \in A} \mathcal{BLit}_i(a, b)$ is called the set of belief literals of depth i.
3. We define

$$\mathcal{BAt}_\infty(a, A) =_{def} \bigcup_{i=0}^{\infty} \mathcal{BAt}_i(a, A), \qquad \mathcal{BLit}_\infty(a, A) =_{def} \bigcup_{i=0}^{\infty} \mathcal{BLit}_i(a, A).$$

At first sight the last definition looks overly complicated. The reason is that every agent keeps track of only its *own* beliefs, not those of other agents (we will see later in Lemma 3 on page 220 that an agent may be able to simulate another agent's state). This means that a nested belief atom of the form $\mathcal{B}_a(b, \mathcal{B}_c(d, \chi))$ does not make sense (because $b \neq c$) and is not allowed in the above definition.

Note also that the closure under $\{\&, \neg\}$ in Equation (7.1) allows us to use conjunctions with respect to different agents $\mathcal{B}_a(b, \chi) \wedge \mathcal{B}_a(c, \chi')$. The closure in Equation (7.2) allows us to also use different nested levels of beliefs, like $\mathcal{B}_a(b, \chi) \wedge \mathcal{B}_a(c, \mathcal{B}_c(d, \chi'))$. However, for most practical applications this additional freedom seems not to be necessary. We discuss this point again in Lemma 3 on page 220.

Here are some belief formulae from the CFIT* example (see Section 7.1 or Appendix A.4):

Example 7.2.2 (Belief Formulae for CFIT)* The following are belief formulae from $\mathcal{BL}_1^{heli1}$, $\mathcal{BL}_2^{tank1}$ and $\mathcal{BL}_3^{coord}$.

- $\mathcal{B}_{heli1}(tank1, \mathbf{in}(pos1, tank1 : \textit{getPosition}()))$.
  This formula is in $\mathcal{BL}_1^{heli1}$. It says that agent heli1 believes that agent tank1's current state indicates that tank1's current position is pos1.

- $\mathcal{B}_{\text{tank1}}(\text{heli1}, \mathcal{B}_{\text{heli1}}(\text{tank1}, \textbf{in}(\text{pos1}, \text{tank1} : \textit{getPosition}()))).$
This formula is in $\mathcal{BL}_2^{\text{tank1}}$. It says that agent tank1 believes that agent heli1 believes that agent tank1's current position is pos1.

- $\mathcal{B}_{\text{coord}}(\text{tank1}, \mathcal{B}_{\text{tank1}}(\text{heli1}, \mathcal{B}_{\text{heli1}}(\text{tank2}, \textbf{in}(\text{pos2}, \text{tank2} : \textit{getPosition}())))).$
This formula is in $\mathcal{BL}_3^{\text{coord}}$. It says that agent coord believes that agent tank1 believes that heli1 believes that agent tank2's current position is pos2.

However, the following formula does not belong to any of the above belief languages:

$\mathcal{B}_{\text{tank1}}(\text{heli1}, \mathcal{B}_{\text{tank1}}(\text{tank1}, \textbf{in}(\text{pos1}, \text{tank} : \textit{getPosition}()))).$

The reason for this is because in heli1's state there can be no beliefs belonging to tank1.

7.2.2 Basic Belief Table

We now describe how the agent keeps track of its beliefs about other agents and how these beliefs can be updated. The easiest way to structure a set of beliefs is to view it as a relational database structure. The notion of a basic belief table provides the starting point for defining how an agent maintains beliefs about other agents.

DEFINITION 7.2.3 (BASIC BELIEF TABLE **BBT**^a) Every agent a has an associated *basic belief table* **BBT**^a which is a set of pairs

$\langle h, \phi \rangle$

where $h \in A$ and $\phi \in \mathcal{BL}_i^h$, $i \in \mathbb{N}$.

For example, if the entry $\langle b, \mathcal{B}_b(a, \chi) \rangle$ is in the table **BBT**^a, then this intuitively means that agent a believes that agent b has the code call condition χ among its own beliefs about agent a. Here $\phi \in \mathcal{BL}_1^b$.

*Example 7.2.3 (Basic Belief Table for CFIT*Agents)* We define suitable basic belief tables for agent tank1 (Table 7.1) and heli1 (Table 7.2 on the next page).

Table 7.1
A Basic Belief Table for agent tank1

Agent	Formula
heli1	$\textbf{in}(\text{pos1}, \text{heli1} : \textit{getPosition}())$
heli2	$\mathcal{B}_{\text{heli2}}(\text{tank1}, \textbf{in}(\text{pos1}, \text{tank1} : \textit{getPosition}()))$
tank2	$\mathcal{B}_{\text{tank2}}(\text{heli1}, \mathcal{B}_{\text{heli1}}(\text{tank1}, \textbf{in}(\text{pos3}, \text{tank1} : \textit{getPosition}())))$

Table 7.2
A Basic Belief Table for agent heli1

Agent	Formula
heli2	**in**(pos2, heli2 : *getPosition*())
tank1	**in**(pos1, tank1 : *getPosition*())
tank1	$\mathcal{B}_{\text{tank1}}(\text{heli1}, \textbf{in}(\text{pos1}, \text{heli1} : \textit{getPosition}()))$
tank2	$\mathcal{B}_{\text{tank2}}(\text{tank1}, \mathcal{B}_{\text{tank1}}(\text{heli1}, \textbf{in}(\text{pos4}, \text{heli1} : \textit{getPosition}())))$

These tables indicate that tank1 and heli1 work closely together and know their positions. Both believe that the other knows about both positions. tank1 also believes that tank2 believes that in heli2's state, tank1 is in position pos3 (which is actually wrong).

heli1 thinks that tank2 believes that tank1 believes that heli1 is in position pos4, which is also wrong.

What kind of operations should we support on belief tables? We distinguish between two different types:

1. For a given agent h, other than a, we may want to select all entries in the table having h as first argument.

2. For a given belief formula ϕ, we may be interested in all those entries, whose second argument "implies" (w.r.t. some underlying definition of entailment) the given formula ϕ.

The latter point motivates us to consider more general relations between belief formulae with respect to an epistemic background theory. This will extend the expressibility and usefulness of our overall framework. For example the background theory can contain certain epistemic axioms about beliefs or even certain inference rules and the relation between belief formulae can be the entailment relation with respect to the chosen background theory.

7.2.3 Belief Semantics Table

Agent a may associate different background theories with different agents: it may assume that agent h reasons according to semantics $\mathcal{BSem}_h^a$ and assumes that agent h' adopts a stronger semantics $\mathcal{BSem}_{h'}^a$. We will store the information in a separate relational data structure:

DEFINITION 7.2.4 (BELIEF SEMANTICS TABLE **BSemT**^{a} OF AGENT a) Every agent a has an associated *belief semantics table* **BSemT**^{a} which is a set of pairs

$\langle h, \mathcal{BSem}_h^a \rangle$

where $h \in A$, $BSem_h^a$ is a belief semantics over $\mathcal{BL}_i^h$ and $i \in \mathbb{N}$ is fixed. In addition we require at most one entry per agent h. Hence, $BSem_h^a$ determines an entailment relation

$$\phi \models_{BSem_h^a} \psi$$

between belief formulae $\phi, \psi \in \mathcal{BL}_i^h$. We also assume the existence of the following function (which constitutes an extended code call, see Definition 7.3.5 on page 229) over **BSemT^a**:

BSemT^a : select (agent, =, h),

which selects all entries corresponding to a specific agent $h \in A$.

Example 7.2.4 (Belief Semantics Tables for CFIT Agents)* We briefly describe what suitable Belief Semantics Table for heli1 and tank1 may look like. We have to define entailment relations $BSem_{tank2}^{tank1}$, $BSem_{heli1}^{tank1}$, $BSem_{heli2}^{tank1}$, and $BSem_{tank1}^{heli1}$, $BSem_{tank2}^{heli1}$, $BSem_{heli2}^{heli1}$. For simplicity we restrict these entailment relations to belief formulae of level at most 1, i.e., $\mathcal{BL}_1^h$.

1. $BSem_{tank1}^{heli1}$: The smallest entailment relation satisfying the schema

$$\mathcal{B}_{tank1}(tank1.1, \chi) \to \chi.$$

This says that heli1 believes that all beliefs of tank1 about tank1.1 are actually true: tank1 knows all about tank1.1.

2. $BSem_{tank2}^{heli1}$: The smallest entailment relation satisfying the schema

$$\mathcal{B}_{tank2}(tank2.1, \chi) \to \chi.$$

This says that heli1 believes that all beliefs of tank2 about tank2.1 are actually true: tank2 knows all about tank2.1.

3. $BSem_{heli1}^{tank1}$: The smallest entailment relation satisfying the schema

$$\mathcal{B}_{heli1}(tank1, \chi) \to \chi.$$

This says that tank1 believes that if heli1 believes in χ for tank1, then this is true (heli1 knows all about tank1. An instance of χ is **in**(pos1, tank1 : *getPosition*()).

4. $BSem_{heli2}^{tank1}$: The smallest entailment relation satisfying the schema

$$\mathcal{B}_{heli2}(tank2, \chi) \wedge \mathcal{B}_{heli2}(tank2.1, \chi) \to \chi.$$

This says that tank1 believes that if heli2 believes that χ is true both for tank2 and tank2.1 then this is actually true.

The notion of a semantics used in the belief semantics table is very general: it can be an arbitrary relation on $\mathcal{BL}_i^h \times \mathcal{BL}_i^h$. We briefly illustrate (1) *which sort of semantics can be expressed* and (2) *how our framework can be suitably restricted for practical applications.*

The following two simple axioms that can be built into a semantics, show the generality and flexibility of our framework:

(1) $\mathcal{B}_{h_2}(h, \chi) \Rightarrow \mathcal{B}_{h_2}(h', \chi)$
(2) $\mathcal{B}_{h_2}(h, \chi) \Rightarrow \chi$

The first axiom refers to different agents h, h' while the second combines different *levels* of belief atoms: see Equations 7.1 on page 215 and 7.2 on page 215 and the discussion after Definition 7.2.2 on page 214. In many applications, however, such axioms will not occur: $h = h'$ is fixed and the axioms operate on the same level i of belief formulae.

Thus it makes sense to consider simplified versions of semantics that are easy to implement and to handle. In fact, given the results of Eiter, Subrahmanian, and Rogers (1999) and the various semantics Sem for agent programs (i.e., with no belief atoms), we now show how such a semantics Sem naturally induces a semantics $BSem_h^a$ for use in a belief semantics table. These semantics can be implemented and handled as built-ins. Entries in **BSemT^a** then have the form

$\langle h_1, \text{Sem}_{feas} \rangle$
$\langle h_2, \text{Sem}_{rat} \rangle$
$\langle h_3, \text{Sem}_{reas} \rangle$

meaning that agent a believes that the agents h_i behave according to the indicated semantics, which are well understood for agent programs without beliefs.

The idea is to use the semantics Sem of the action program $\mathcal{P}^a(b)$ (that a believes b to have) for the evaluation of the belief formulae. However, this is a bit complicated by the fact that the computation of the semantics depends on various other parameters like the *state* and the *action* and *integrity constraints*.

Before stating the definition, we recall that a semantics Sem is a set of action status sets which depend on (1) an action program, (2) a set of action constraints, (3) a set of integrity constraints, and, finally, (4) the current state. The notation $\text{Sem}_h(\mathcal{P})$ only reflects the influence of (1) but (2)–(4) are equally important. For example, when the belief table contains the entry $\langle h_1, \chi \rangle$ where χ is a code call condition, χ is a belief of a about h_1's state. χ is therefore a condition on the state of h_1. In contrast, an entry $\langle h_1, \text{Op}\,\alpha(\vec{t}) \rangle$, where $\text{Op}\,\alpha(\vec{t})$ is an action atom, is a belief of a on the actions that h_1 holds. Consequently action atoms can be seen as conditions on h_1's action program.

In the following remark, we show how to define belief semantics defined on belief languages of level 0 and 1. But belief formulae contain *both* code call conditions and action atoms and those are, as just discussed, evaluated in different domains. Therefore for a formula ϕ that is a *conjunction* of code call conditions (ccc's for short) and action atoms, we let

$\text{CCC}(\phi)$ be the conjunction of all ccc's occuring in ϕ,
$\text{ACT}(\phi)$ be the conjunction of all action atoms occuring in ϕ.

This remark is not a precise statement that can be proved or disproved but rather a *methodology* of how to incorporate the agent semantics in our framework.

Remark 3 (Sem for Agent Programs induces $BSem_h^a$) Let Sem be the *reasonable, rational* or *feasible* semantics for agent programs (i.e., not containing beliefs). Suppose agent a believes that agent h reasons according to Sem. Let $\mathcal{P}(h)$ be the agent program of h and $\mathcal{O}(h)$, $\mathcal{AC}(h)$ and $\mathcal{IC}(h)$ the state, action constraints and integrity constraints of h. Then there is a basic belief table **BSemT^a** and a belief semantics $BSem_h^a$ induced by Sem such that

- a believes in h's state, and
- a believes in all actions taken by h with respect to Sem and $\mathcal{P}(h)$.

More generally: let $i \in \mathbb{N}$ and suppose agent a believes that agent h_1 believes that agent h_2 believes that... believes that agent h_{i-1} acts according to $\mathcal{P}^a(\sigma)$ (where $\sigma =_{def} [h_1, h_2, \ldots, h_{i-1}]$) and state $\mathcal{O}(\sigma)^1$. Then there is a basic belief table **BSemT^a** and a belief semantics $BSem_\sigma^a$ induced by Sem on a suitably restricted subset of $\mathcal{BL}_1^h \times \mathcal{BL}_1^h$ such that

- a believes in h_{i-1}'s state, and
- a believes in all actions taken by h_{i-1} with respect to Sem and $\mathcal{P}(\sigma)$.

The reason that the above statement is not amenable to a proof or disproof is the part *Suppose agent a believes that agent h reasons according to* Sem. It is intuitively clear what this means, about the precise meaning is given by "the proof" that follows.

Justification of Remark. We define a belief semantics $BSem_h^a$ on $\mathcal{BL}_0^h \times \mathcal{BL}_0^h$ with respect to a state $\mathcal{O}$, $\mathcal{AC}$, and $\mathcal{IC}$ as follows:

$$\phi \models_{BSem_h^a} \psi \text{ by } \begin{cases} 1.\ \text{ACT}(\psi) \in \text{Sem}_h(\mathcal{P}^a(h) \cup \{\text{ACT}(\phi)\}) \text{ wrt. the state } \mathcal{O} \cup \text{CCC}(\phi). \\ 2.\ \mathcal{O} \cup \text{CCC}(\phi) \models \text{CCC}(\psi). \\ 3.\ \mathcal{AC} \text{ are satisfied wrt. enlarged program } \mathcal{P}^a(h) \cup \{\text{ACT}(\phi)\}. \\ 4.\ \mathcal{O} \cup \text{CCC}(\phi) \models \mathcal{IC} \end{cases}$$

We now define a belief semantics $BSem_h^a$ on $\mathcal{BL}_1^h \times \mathcal{BL}_1^h$ with respect to a state $\mathcal{O}$, $\mathcal{AC}$, and $\mathcal{IC}$ as follows.

---

[1] See Definition 7.3.4 on page 229 and Definition 7.3.2 on page 227 for a detailed introduction of these concepts.

Section 7.2   Belief Language and Data Structures   221

1. We restrict, as already discussed, to entailment relations that operate on the *same* level of beliefs. For level 0 we just defined such a relation.

2. For level 1 beliefs we also restrict to those that contain the same agent as first component: $\{\mathcal{B}_h(c, \phi) \mid \phi$ is a code call condition or an action atom$\}$.

3. For a belief formula ϕ of level 1 which has the form $\mathcal{B}_h(c, \phi_1) \wedge \cdots \wedge \mathcal{B}_h(c, \phi_n)$ we let

$$\text{CCC}(\phi) =_{def} \text{CCC}(\phi_1) \wedge \cdots \wedge \text{CCC}(\phi_n)$$

and

$$\text{ACT}(\phi) =_{def} \text{ACT}(\phi_1) \wedge \cdots \wedge \text{ACT}(\phi_n).$$

4. We define:

$$\phi \models_{BSem_h^a} \psi \text{ by } \begin{cases} 1.\ \text{ACT}(\psi) \in \text{Sem}_c(\mathcal{P}^a([h, c]) \cup \{\text{ACT}(\phi)\}) \text{ wrt. } \mathcal{O} \cup \text{CCC}(\phi). \\ 2.\ \mathcal{O} \cup \text{CCC}(\phi) \models \text{CCC}(\psi). \\ 3.\ \mathcal{AC} \text{ are satisfied wrt. enlarged program } \mathcal{P}^a([h, c]) \cup \{\text{ACT}(\phi)\}. \\ 4.\ \mathcal{O} \cup \text{CCC}(\phi) \models \mathcal{IC} \end{cases}$$

The notation $\mathcal{P}^a([h, c])$ denotes the program that a believes h to believe about c. The sequences σ will be introduced in Definition 7.3.2 on page 227. ∎

7.2.4   Belief Tables

We are now ready to give the full definition of a belief table.

DEFINITION 7.2.5 (BELIEF TABLE $\mathbf{BT}^a$)   Every agent a has an associated *belief table* $\mathbf{BT}^a$, which consists of triples

$$\langle h, \phi, \chi_B \rangle$$

where $h \in A$, $\phi \in \mathcal{BL}_i^h$ and $\chi_B \in \mathcal{BCond}^a(h)$ is a *belief condition of* a to be defined below (see Definition 7.2.6 on page 223).

We identify that part of $\mathbf{BT}^a$ where the third entries are empty (or, equivalently, *true*) with the basic belief table introduced in Definition 7.2.3 on page 216. Thus, every belief table induces a (possibly empty) basic belief table.

We also assume the existence of the following two functions over $\mathbf{BT}^a$:

$\mathbf{BT}^a$: proj-select (agent, $=$, h)

which selects all entries of **BT**^{a} of the form $\langle h, \phi, \textbf{true} \rangle$ (i.e., corresponding to a specific agent $h \in A$ and having the third entry empty) and projects them on the first two arguments, and

BT^a : B-proj-select (r, h, ϕ)

for all $r \in \mathcal{R} =_{def} \{\Rightarrow, \Leftarrow, -\}$ and for all belief formulae $\phi \in \mathcal{BL}_\infty^h$. This function selects all entries of **BT**^{a} of the form $\langle h, \psi, \textbf{true} \rangle$ that contain a belief formula ψ which is in relation r to ϕ with respect to the semantics $\mathcal{B}Sem_h^a$ as specified in the belief semantics table **BSemT**^{a} and projects them on the first two arguments.

For example, if we choose $\Rightarrow \in \mathcal{R}$ as the relation r then

$$(\psi \Rightarrow \phi) \in \mathcal{B}Sem_h^a$$

or, equivalently, $\models_{\mathcal{B}Sem_h^a} (\psi \Rightarrow \phi)$ says ϕ is entailed by ψ relative to semantics $\mathcal{B}Sem_h^a$.

The reader may well ask about whether belief update function should also be included. In fact, belief updating is an *action* that may be included in an agent, should the agent developer deem it necessary for his agent. Such an action can be implemented using any standard belief updating algorithm proposed in the literature.

We emphasize the fact that although the two introduced project-select functions are defined on the full belief table **BT**^{a}, they can be thought of as operating on the induced basic belief table **BBT**^{a}, which results from **BT**^{a} by projection on the first two arguments of those triples where the third entry is empty.

Why do we require that **BT**^{a} : proj-select (agent, =, h) selects only those triples where the third entry is **true**? The reason is that when we evaluate the belief condition (to ensure compatibility in Definition 7.3.14 on page 237) we do this recursively and thus end with triples having the third entry **true**. We could have, of course, added another argument to the function which allows us to specify the third entry.

In the last definition we introduced the notion of a belief table but we did not yet specify the third entry in it, the *belief condition*. The role of such a belief condition is to extend the expressiveness of the basic belief table by restricting the applicability to particular states, namely those satisfying the belief condition. Intuitively, $\langle b, \phi, \chi_B \rangle$ means that

Agent a believes that ϕ is true in agent b's state, if the condition χ_B holds.

Note that agent a can only reason about his own state, which *contains* (through the belief table **BT**^{a} and the belief semantics table **BSemT**^{a}) his beliefs as well as his underlying epistemic theory about other agent's states.

BT^a and **BSemT**^{a}, taken together, *simulate* agent b's state as believed by agent a.

Note 7 There is considerable work on modal multiagent logics where agent a has beliefs about agent b and so on. In general, in such logics, each agent has an associated belief theory about another agent. This is consistent with our view. Given an agent b, agent a's base-beliefs about b consists of the set of all formulas ϕ such that there is a row r in $\mathbf{BT}^a$ with r.Agent $= b$ and r.Condition $=$ **true** and r.Formula $= \phi$. Agent a's total set of beliefs about agent b is the set of all formulas derivable from its base beliefs using the semantics that agent a believes agent b is using—which is contained in $\mathbf{BSemT}^a$.

A belief condition χ_B that occurs in an entry $\langle b, \phi, \chi_B \rangle$ must therefore be evaluated in what agent a believes is agent b's state. This is important because the code call conditions must be compatible and therefore not only depend on agent a but also on agent b.

DEFINITION 7.2.6 (BELIEF CONDITIONS $\mathcal{B}Cond^a(h)$) The set $\mathcal{B}Cond^a(h)$ of belief conditions of agent a is defined inductively as follows:

1. Every code call condition χ of agent a compatible with agent h is in $\mathcal{B}Cond^a(h)$.

2. If X is an entry in the basic belief table (or, equivalently the projection of an entry of the belief table $\mathbf{BT}^a$ on the first two arguments) or a variable over basic belief table tuples, then

in(X, $\mathbf{BT}^a$: proj-select (agent, $=, h$))

is in $\mathcal{B}Cond^a(h)$.

3. If X is an entry in the basic belief table or a variable over such entries, $r \in \mathcal{R}, \phi \in \mathcal{BL}_i^a$ and $h \in A$ then

in(X, $\mathbf{BT}^a$: B-proj-select (r, h, ϕ))

is in $\mathcal{B}Cond^a(h)$.

4. If χ is in $\mathcal{B}Cond^a(h)$, then so is $\neg \chi$.
5. If χ is in $\mathcal{B}Cond^a(h)$, then so is $\exists X \chi$.
6. If χ and χ' are in $\mathcal{B}Cond^a(h)$, then so is $\chi \& \chi'$.

As belief conditions corresponding to step 1. above will be checked in what agent a believes agent b's state is, we introduce the following notation:

- h_part(χ) $=_{def}$ the subconjunction of χ consisting of all code call conditions

  not involving $\mathbf{BT}^a$,

- a_part(χ) $=_{def}$ the subconjunction of χ consisting of all code call conditions

  that involve $\mathbf{BT}^a$.

Table 7.3
A Belief Table for agent tank1

Agent	Formula	Condition
heli1	**in**(pos1, heli1 : *getPosition*())	**true**
heli2	$\mathcal{B}_{\text{heli2}}(\text{tank1}, \textbf{in}(\text{pos1}, \text{tank1} : \textit{getPosition}()))$	$\mathcal{B}cond_1^{\text{tank1}}$
tank2	$\mathcal{B}_{\text{tank2}}(\text{heli1}, \mathcal{B}_{\text{heli1}}(\text{tank1}, \textbf{in}(\text{pos3}, \text{tank1} : \textit{getPosition}())))$	$\mathcal{B}cond_2^{\text{tank1}}$

Note that h_part(χ) consists of conditions that have to be checked in what a believes agent h's state is, while a_part(χ) refers to the belief tables of agent a. Similarly, for other agent b, c, d we have the notion of b_part(χ), c_part(χ) and d_part(χ).

Example 7.2.5 (Belief Table for CFIT Agents Revisited)* We now consider Table 7.3 and extend our basic belief tables for agent tank1 (Table 7.1 on page 216) and heli1 (Table 7.2 on page 217). Let $\mathcal{B}cond_1^{\text{tank1}}$ be the code call condition **in**(pos1, tank1 : *getPosition*()) and define $\mathcal{B}cond_2^{\text{tank1}}$ by

in($\langle$heli1, belief atom$\rangle$, **BT**^{a} : proj-select (agent, =, heli1)),

where

belief atom $=_{\textit{def}} \mathcal{B}_{\text{heli1}}(\text{tank1}, \textbf{in}(\text{pos3}, \text{tank1} : \textit{getPosition}()))$.

The first row in the table says that tank1 unconditionally believes that in heli1's state the position for heli1 is pos1.

The second row in the belief table above, says that tank1 believes that if tank1's position is pos1, heli2 believes that in tank1's state the position of tank1 is pos1.

The third row in the belief table says that if tank1 believes heli1 believes that tank1's position is pos3, then tank2 believes heli1 believes tank1's position is pos3.

The table for heli1 is as shown in Table 7.4 on the next page, where $\mathcal{B}cond_1^{\text{heli1}}$ stands for

in(pos2, heli2 : *getPosition*())

and $\mathcal{B}cond_2^{\text{tank1}}$ is defined by

in($\langle$tank1, belief atom$\rangle$, **BT**^{a} : proj-select (agent, =, tank1)),

where

belief atom $=_{\textit{def}} \mathcal{B}_{\text{tank1}}(\text{heli1}, \textbf{in}(\text{pos4}, \text{heli1} : \textit{getPosition}()))$.

We are now in a position to formally express a meta agent program, i.e., a program which formalizes the actions and the circumstances under which an agent a will execute

Section 7.2   Belief Language and Data Structures   225

Table 7.4
A Belief Table for agent heli1

Agent	Formula	Condition
heli2	**in**(pos2, heli2 : *getPosition*())	**true**
tank1	**in**(pos1, tank1 : *getPosition*())	**true**
tank1	$\mathcal{B}_{\text{tank1}}(\text{heli1}, \mathbf{in}(\text{pos1}, \text{heli1} : getPosition()))$	$\mathcal{B}cond_1^{\text{heli1}}$
tank2	$\mathcal{B}_{\text{tank2}}(\text{tank1}, \mathcal{B}_{\text{tank1}}(\text{heli1}, \mathbf{in}(\text{pos4}, \text{heli1} : getPosition())))$	$\mathcal{B}cond_2^{\text{heli1}}$

these actions based not only on its own state but also on its beliefs about other agent's states.

DEFINITION 7.2.7 (META AGENT PROGRAM (map) $\mathcal{BP}$)   A *meta agent rule*, (mar for short), for agent a is an expression r of the form

$$A \leftarrow L_1, \ldots, L_n \tag{7.3}$$

where A is an action status atom, and each of $L_1, \ldots, L_n$ is either a code call literal, an action literal or a belief literal from $\mathcal{B}\text{Lit}_\infty(a, A)$.

A *meta agent program*, (map for short), for agent a is a finite set $\mathcal{BP}$ of meta agent rules for a.

Note that belief atoms are not allowed in the head of rules. Thus a meta agent program does not define beliefs: it only uses them to derive action status atoms. Beliefs are solely defined by the belief data structures (belief table and through the belief semantics table).

Example 7.2.6 (map's For CFIT*-Agents)   Let heli1's meta agent program be as follows:

P *attack*(P1, P2) ← $\mathcal{B}_{\text{heli1}}(\text{tank1}, \mathbf{in}(\text{P2}, \text{tank1} : getPos()))$,

        P *fly*(P1, P3, A, S),

        P *attack*(P3, P2).

where *attack*(P1, P2) is an action which means attack position P2 from position P1. heli1's program says heli1 can attack position P2 from P1 if heli1 believes tank1 is in position P2, heli1 can fly from P1 to another position P3 at altitude A and speed S, and heli1 can attack position P2 from P3.

Let tank1's meta agent program be as follows:

O *attack*(P1, P2) ← **O** *driveRoute*([P0, P1, P2, P3], S),

        $\mathcal{B}_{\text{tank1}}(\text{tank2}, \mathbf{in}(\text{P2}, \text{tank2} : getPos()))$.

If tank1 must drive through a point where it believes tank2 is, it must attack tank2.

From now on we assume that the software package $\mathcal{S}^a = (\mathcal{T}_\mathcal{S}^a, \mathcal{F}_\mathcal{S}^a)$ of each agent a contains as distinguished data types

1. the belief table **BT**^{a}, and
2. the belief semantics table **BSemT**^{a},

as well as the corresponding functions

BT^a : B-proj-select (r, h, ϕ) and **BSemT**^{a} : select (agent, =, h).

7.3 Meta-Agent Programs: Semantics

It remains to define the *semantics* of meta agent programs. As in the case of agent programs without any metaknowledge (presented in the previous chapter), the basic notion upon which more sophisticated semantics will be based, is the notion of a *feasible status set* for a given meta agent program $\mathcal{BP}$. In order to do this we first have to introduce the notion of a *belief status set*, the counterpart of a status set for a meta agent program.

DEFINITION 7.3.1 (BELIEF STATUS SET $\mathcal{BS}$)   A belief status set $\mathcal{BS}$ of agent a, also written $\mathcal{BS}(a)$, is a set consisting of two kinds of elements:

- ground action status atoms over $\mathcal{S}^a$ and
- belief atoms from $\mathcal{BAt}_\infty(a, A)$ of level greater or equal to 1.

The reason that we do not allow belief atoms of level 0 is to avoid having code call conditions in our set. Such conditions are not implied by the underlying map (only action status atoms are allowed in the heads of rules). Moreover, in the agent programs without beliefs (which we want to extend) they are not allowed as well (see Definition 6.5.1 on page 172).

We note that such a set must be determined in accordance with

1. the map $\mathcal{BP}$ of agent a,
2. the current state $\mathcal{O}$ of a,
3. the underlying set of action and integrity constraints of a.

In contrast to agent programs without beliefs we now have to cope with all agents about which a holds certain beliefs. Even if the map $\mathcal{BP}$ does not contain nested beliefs (which are allowed), the belief table **BT**^{a} may and, by the belief semantics table **BSemT**^{a}, such nested beliefs may imply (trigger) other beliefs. Thus we cannot restrict ourselves to belief atoms of level 1.

Any belief status set BS of agent a induces, in a natural way, for any agent $b \in A$, two sorts of sets: the *state* and the various *action status sets* that agent a believes other agents b to hold or those that a believes other agents b to hold about other agents c. To easily formalize the latter conditions, we introduce the notion of a sequence:

DEFINITION 7.3.2 (SEQUENCE $\sigma, [\rho]$ OF AGENTS) A sequence σ of agents from A is defined inductively as follows:

1. The empty sequence [] is a sequence.
2. If $a \in A$ and $[\rho]$ is a sequence, then $[a], [-a], [a, \rho], [\rho, a]$ are sequences.

We use both σ and $[\rho]$ to refer to an arbitrary sequence.

The overall intuition of the formula $\mathcal{B}_a(b, \mathcal{B}_b(c, \mathcal{B}_c(d, \chi)))$ is that if we keep agent a in mind, then agent a believes in a code call condition of type $[b, c, d]$, i.e., a ccc that b believes that c believes that it holds in d's state.

We also say sometimes "σ's state" and refer to the code call conditions that are true in what a believes that b believes ... where $[a, b, \ldots] = \sigma$.

DEFINITION 7.3.3 (INDUCED STATUS SET $\Pi_b^{\text{action}}(BS)$ AND STATE $\Pi_b^{\text{state}}(BS)$ Let a, b be agents and $\mathcal{BP}$ a map of a. Every belief status set BS of an agent a induces the following two sets describing a's beliefs about b's actions and b's state

$\prod_b^{\text{action}}(BS) =_{def} \{\text{Op}\,\alpha(\vec{t}) \mid \mathcal{B}_a(b, \text{Op}\,\alpha(\vec{t})) \in BS, \text{ where Op} \in \{\mathbf{O}, \mathbf{W}, \mathbf{P}, \mathbf{F}, \mathbf{Do}\}\}$

$\prod_b^{\text{state}}(BS) =_{def} \{\chi \mid \mathcal{B}_a(b, \chi) \in BS \text{ and } \chi \text{ is a code call condition}\}$

Now assume that agent a believes in BS. Then $\Pi_b^{\text{state}}(BS)$ formalizes the state of agent b as believed by agent a. Similarly, $\Pi_b^{\text{action}}(BS)$ represents the action status set of agent b as believed by agent a.

For any sequence σ, BS induces the following two sets:

$\prod_\sigma^{\text{action}}(BS)$ describing a's belief about actions corresponding to σ

$\prod_\sigma^{\text{state}}(BS)$ describing a's belief about the state corresponding to σ,

depending on the depth of the belief atoms occuring in $\mathcal{BP}$.

The formal definition of $\Pi_\sigma^{\text{action}}(BS)$ and $\Pi_\sigma^{\text{state}}(BS)$ is by induction on the structure of σ. As it should be clear, we avoid this technical definition. Instead we shortly illustrate the case for $\sigma = [b, c]$. Then

$\prod_{[b,c]}^{\text{action}}(BS) =_{def} \{\text{Op}\alpha(\vec{t}) \mid \mathcal{B}_a(b, \mathcal{B}_b(c, \text{Op}\alpha(\vec{t}))) \in BS\}$

$\prod_{[b,c]}^{\text{state}}(BS) =_{def} \{\chi \mid \mathcal{B}_a(b, \mathcal{B}_b(c, \chi)) \in BS\}$.

It is important to note that for any sequence, σ of agents, $\Pi_\sigma^{\text{action}}(\mathcal{BS})$ is a set of action status atoms. Likewise, $\Pi_\sigma^{\text{state}}(\mathcal{BS})$ is a set of code call conditions that do *not* involve beliefs. For the empty sequence [], we identify $\Pi_{[]}^{\text{action}}(\mathcal{BS})$ (resp. $\Pi_{[]}^{\text{state}}(\mathcal{BS})$) with a's own action status set (resp. a's own state) as defined by the subset of $\mathcal{BS}$ not involving belief atoms.

Example 7.3.1 (Belief Status Sets for CFIT*-Agents) We consider the map of heli1 given in Example 7.2.6 on page 225

$\mathcal{BS}(\text{heli}1) =_{def}$ {**P** *fly*(pointA, pointB, 10000, 200),
  O *fly*(pointA, pointB, 10000, 200),
  $\mathcal{B}_{\text{heli}1}$(heli2, **P***fly*(PointA, PointB, 10000, 200)),
  $\mathcal{B}_{\text{heli}1}$(heli2, **in**(pos, heli2 : *getPos*())),
  $\mathcal{B}_{\text{heli}1}$(heli2, $\mathcal{B}_{\text{heli}2}$(tank1, **in**(pos, tank1 : *getPos*())))
  $\mathcal{B}_{\text{heli}1}$(heli2, $\mathcal{B}_{\text{heli}2}$(tank1, **P***drive*(pointX, pointY, 40)))}

This belief status set is for heli1 and it says:

1. It is possible to fly from pointA to pointB at an altitude of 10000 feet and a speed of 200 knots.

2. It is obligatory to fly from pointA to pointB at an altitude of 10000 feet and a speed of 200 knots.

3. heli1 believes that in heli2's state it is possible to fly from pointA to pointB at 10000 feet and 200 knots.

4. heli1 believes that in heli2's state the position of heli2 is pos.

5. heli1 believes heli2 believes that tank1's position is pos.

6. heli1 believes heli2 believes that in tank1's state it is possible to drive from pointX to pointY at 40 miles per hour.

We then have:

$\Pi_{\text{heli}2}^{\text{action}}(\mathcal{BS}(\text{heli}1)) = \{\mathbf{P}\textit{fly}(\text{pointA}, \text{pointB}, 10000, 200)\}$

$\Pi_{\text{heli}2}^{\text{state}}(\mathcal{BS}(\text{heli}1)) = \{\mathbf{in}(\text{pos}, \text{heli}2 : \textit{getPos}())\}$

$\Pi_{[\text{heli}2,\text{tank}1]}^{\text{action}}(\mathcal{BS}(\text{heli}1)) = \{\mathbf{P}\textit{drive}(\text{pointX}, \text{pointY}, 40)\}$

$\Pi_{[\text{heli}2,\text{tank}1]}^{\text{state}}(\mathcal{BS}(\text{heli}1)) = \{\mathbf{in}(\text{pos}, \text{tank}1 : \textit{getPos}())\}$

These sets formalize the following:

- $\Pi_{\text{heli}2}^{\text{action}}(\mathcal{BS}(\text{heli}1))$ describes heli1's beliefs about heli2's actions and it says that it is possible to fly from pointA to pointB at 10000 feet and 200 knots.

- $\Pi^{\text{state}}_{\text{heli2}}(\mathcal{BS}(\text{heli1}))$ describes heli1's beliefs about heli2's state and it says that its position is pos.
- $\Pi^{\text{action}}_{[\text{heli2,tank1}]}(\mathcal{BS}(\text{heli1}))$ describes heli1's beliefs about heli2's beliefs about tank1's actions, and it says that it is possible to drive from pointX to pointY at 40 miles per hour.
- $\Pi^{\text{state}}_{[\text{heli2,tank1}]}(\mathcal{BS}(\text{heli1}))$ describes heli1's beliefs about heli2's beliefs about tank1's state, and it says that its position is pos.

Obviously for a to make a guess about agent b's behaviour, agent a not only needs a belief table and a belief semantics table, but a also needs to guess about b's action base, action program as well as the action and integrity constraints used by b. This is very much like having a guess about b's software package which we motivated and illustrated just before Definition 7.2.1 on page 213 (see the notion of *compatible* code call condition). For notational convenience and better readability we merge all these ingredients into a set $\Gamma^a(b)$.

DEFINITION 7.3.4 ($\Gamma^a(b)$, Info(a))   For agents a, b $\in$ A, we denote by $\Gamma^a(b)$ the following list of all beliefs that agent a holds about another agent b: the software package $\mathcal{S}^a(b)$, the *action base* $\mathcal{AB}^a(b)$, the *action program* $\mathcal{P}^a(b)$, the *integrity constraints* $\mathcal{IC}^a(b)$ and the *action constraints* $\mathcal{AC}^a(b)$. $\Gamma^a(b)$ may also contain these objects for sequences $\sigma = [b, c]$ instead of b: we use therefore also the notation $\Gamma^a([b, c])$. $\Gamma^a(\sigma)$ represents a's beliefs about b's beliefs about c.

In addition, given an agent a, we will often use the notation Info(a) to denote the software package $\mathcal{S}^a$, the action base $\mathcal{AB}$, the action program $\mathcal{P}$, the integrity constraints $\mathcal{IC}$ and action constraints $\mathcal{AC}$ used by agent a. Thus we define Info(a) $=_{def} \Gamma^{[]}(a)$.

Note that although not all of these functions will be refered to explicitly in the rest of this chapter, they are important. Often we do not explicitly mention the set of underlying action constraints, integrity constraints, action base or the software package that agent a believes agent b to have (or that agent a believes w.r.t. a sequence σ), just for simplifying the notation.

The set $\boldsymbol{\Gamma}^a(b)$ is very important and therefore we introduce the corresponding software code calls, thereby extending our original package $\mathcal{S}$.

DEFINITION 7.3.5 (EXTENDED CODE CALLS, $\mathcal{S}^{\text{EXT}}$)   Given an agent a, we will from now on distinguish (if it is not immediately clear from context) between *basic* and *extended* code calls respectively code call conditions. The basic code calls refer to the package $\mathcal{S}$, while the latter refer to the extended software package which also contains

1. the following function of the belief table:

(a) a : *belief_table*(), which returns the full belief table of agent a, as a set of triples $\langle h, \phi, \chi_\mathcal{B} \rangle$,

2. the following functions of the belief semantics table:

(b) $a : belief\_sem\_table()$, which returns the full belief semantics table, as a set of pairs $\langle h, \mathcal{BS}em_h^a \rangle$,

(c) $a : bel\_semantics(h, \phi, \psi)$, which returns **true** when $\phi \models_{\mathcal{BS}em_h^a} \psi$ and **false** otherwise.

3. the following functions, which implement for every sequence σ the beliefs of agent a about σ as described in $\Gamma^a(\sigma)$:

(d) $a : software\_package(\sigma)$, which returns the set $\mathcal{S}^a(\sigma)$,

(e) $a : action\_base(\sigma)$, which returns the set $\mathcal{AB}^a(\sigma)$,

(f) $a : action\_program(\sigma)$, which returns the set $\mathcal{P}^a(\sigma)$,

(g) $a : integrity\_constraints(\sigma)$, which returns the set $\mathcal{IC}^a(\sigma)$

(h) $a : action\_constraints(\sigma)$, which returns the set $\mathcal{AC}^a(\sigma)$,

4. the following functions which simulate the state of another agent b or a sequence σ,

(i) $a : bel\_ccc\_act(\sigma)$, which returns all the code call conditions and action status atoms that a believes are true in σ's state. We write these objects in the form "**in**(,)"(resp. "**Op** α" for action status atoms) in order to distinguish them from those that have to be checked in a's state.

(j) $a : not\_bel\_ccc\_act(\sigma)$, which returns all the code call conditions and action status atoms that a does not believe to be true in $\sigma's$ state.

We also write $\mathcal{S}^{\text{ext}}$ for this extended software package and distinguish it from the original $\mathcal{S}$ from which we started.

The functions introduced in the previous definition will be used in the definition of the mapping $\mathfrak{Trans}$ and the formulation of the properties corresponding to belief table and belief semantics compatibility (see Diagram 7.4). They also play a role in the formulation of our main Theorem 7.4.1 (although we often avoid explicitly mentioning integrity constraints, action constraints, the action base, and the whole software package when we consider an agent's state).

7.3.1 Feasible Belief Status Sets

Consider now an agent a with associated structures, Info(a). Suppose $\mathcal{BS}$ is an arbitrary status set. We would like to first identify the conditions that determine whether it "makes sense" for agent a to hold the set of beliefs prescribed by $\mathcal{BS}$. In particular, agent a must use some epistemically well justified criteria to hold a set, $\mathcal{BS}$, of beliefs. In this section, we introduce the concept of a *feasible belief status set*. Intuitively, $\mathcal{BS}$ is feasible *if and only if* it satisfies two types of conditions—conditions on the agent a, and conditions on the beliefs of agent a about other agents b or sequences σ.

Conditions on agent a:

1. Deontic and action consistency: $\mathcal{BS}$ must not contain any inconsistencies. For example, $\mathcal{BS}$ may not contain action status atoms, $\mathbf{O}\alpha$ and $\mathbf{F}\alpha$ as these two action status atoms are mutually incompatible. Similarly, the set of actions taken by agent a must not violate any action constraints, i.e., if Todo = $\{\alpha \mid \mathbf{Do}\ \alpha \in \mathcal{BS}\}$, then for each ground instance of an action constraint of the form ActSet $\hookleftarrow \chi$, either χ is false in the current agent state, or ActSet $\not\subseteq$ Todo.

2. Deontic and action closure: This condition says that $\mathcal{BS}$ must be closed under the deontic operations. For example, if $\mathbf{O}\alpha \in \mathcal{BS}$, then $\mathbf{P}\alpha \in \mathcal{BS}$, and so on.

3. Closure under rules of $\mathcal{BP}$: Furthermore, if we have a rule in $\mathcal{BP}$ having a ground instance whose body's code-call conditions are all true in the current agent state, and whose action status atoms and belief literals are true in $\mathcal{BS}$, then the head of that (ground) rule must be in $\mathcal{BS}$.

4. State consistency: Suppose we concurrently execute all actions in the set Todo. Then the new state that results must be consistent with the integrity constraints associated with agent a.

Conditions on beliefs of agent a about other agents b:

5. Local Coherence: This condition requires that for any agent b, every induced status set $\Pi_b^{\text{action}}(\mathcal{BS})$ is feasible (in the original sense) with respect to the induced state $\Pi_b^{\text{state}}(\mathcal{BS})$ and action program $\mathcal{P}^a(b)$. Furthermore a similar condition must hold for any sequence σ instead of just b.

6. Compatibility with BT^a: We have to ensure that (1) all belief atoms of the basic belief table are contained in $\mathcal{BS}$ and that (2) whenever a belief condition is true, then the corresponding belief formula is true in $\mathcal{BS}$.

7. Compatibility with BSemT^a: If $\langle b, \mathcal{BS}em_b^a \rangle$ is an entry in **BSemT^a**, we have to ensure that b's induced state is closed under the semantics $\mathcal{BS}em_b^a$.

We are now ready to formalize the above 7 basic conditions through a sequence of definitions.

DEFINITION 7.3.6 (DEONTIC/ACTION CONSISTENCY) A belief status set $\mathcal{BS}$ held by agent a is said to be *deontically consistent, if, by definition,* it satisfies the following rules for any ground action α and any sequence σ of agents (including the empty sequence):

1. If $\mathbf{O}\alpha \in \Pi_\sigma^{\text{action}}(\mathcal{BS})$, then $\mathbf{W}\alpha \notin \Pi_\sigma^{\text{action}}(\mathcal{BS})$.
2. If $\mathbf{P}\alpha \in \Pi_\sigma^{\text{action}}(\mathcal{BS})$, then $\mathbf{F}\alpha \notin \Pi_\sigma^{\text{action}}(\mathcal{BS})$.
3. If $\mathbf{P}\alpha \in \Pi_\sigma^{\text{action}}(\mathcal{BS})$, then $\Pi_\sigma^{\text{state}}(\mathcal{BS}) \models Pre(\alpha)$ (i.e., α is executable in $\Pi_\sigma^{\text{state}}(\mathcal{BS})$).

A belief status set $\mathcal{BS}$ is called *action consistent*, if and only if for every ground action instance, ActSet $\hookleftarrow \chi$, of an action constraint in $\mathcal{AC}$, either χ is false in state $\mathcal{O}$ or $\mathcal{BS} \cap \{\mathbf{Do}\,\alpha \mid \alpha \in \text{ActSet}\} = \emptyset$.

Intuitively, the requirement of deontic consistency ensures that belief sets are internally consistent and do not have conflicts about whether an action should or should not be taken by agent $\mathfrak{a}$. Action consistency ensures that the agent cannot violate action constraints.

At this point, the reader may wonder why we need to ensure that deontic/action consistency requirements also apply to *sequences* of agents rather than to just agent $\mathfrak{a}$ by itself. The reason is that if we replaced all occurrences of σ in the preceding definition by the empty sequence [], i.e., we just look at $\mathfrak{a}$'s own action status set, then we may still encounter *deontic inconsistencies nested within beliefs*. For example, agent $\mathfrak{a}$'s belief set could contain both $\mathcal{B}_\mathfrak{a}(\mathfrak{b}, \mathbf{O}\alpha)$ and $\mathcal{B}_\mathfrak{a}(\mathfrak{b}, \mathbf{F}\alpha)$. In this case, agent $\mathfrak{a}$ believes that action α is both forbidden and obligatory for agent $\mathfrak{b}$—a state of affairs that is clearly inconsistent. It is to rule out such scenarios that we have defined deontic and action consistency as above.

The following definition specifies what it means for a belief status set to be deontically closed.

DEFINITION 7.3.7 (DEONTICALLY CLOSED BELIEF STATUS SET) Suppose $\mathcal{BS}$ is a belief status set held by agent $\mathfrak{a}$. $\mathcal{BS}$ is said to be deontically closed if and only if the following two conditions hold:

if $\mathbf{O}\alpha \in \prod_\sigma^{\text{action}}(\mathcal{BS})$ then $\mathbf{P}\alpha \in \prod_\sigma^{\text{action}}(\mathcal{BS})$,

where α is any ground action and σ is any sequence of agents. We say that $\mathcal{BS}$ is *deontically closed if, by definition, $\mathcal{BS} = \mathbf{D}\text{-}\mathbf{Cl}(\mathcal{BS})$.

Intuitively, $\mathcal{BS}$ is deontically closed if for every agent sequence σ, if agent $\mathfrak{a}$ believes that action α is obligatory w.r.t. sequence σ, then $\mathfrak{a}$ must also believe that α is permitted w.r.t. σ. The following lemma establishes that given any belief status set, there exists a unique minimal (w.r.t. set inclusion) superset of it that is deontically closed.

LEMMA 7.3.1 Suppose $\mathcal{BS}$ is a belief status set held by agent $\mathfrak{a}$. Then there is a belief status set denoted $\mathbf{D}\text{-}\mathbf{Cl}(\mathcal{BS})$ such that:

1. $\mathcal{BS} \subseteq \mathbf{D}\text{-}\mathbf{Cl}(\mathcal{BS})$ and
2. $\mathbf{D}\text{-}\mathbf{Cl}(\mathcal{BS})$ is deontically closed and
3. Every other deontically closed superset of $\mathcal{BS}$ is a superset of $\mathbf{D}\text{-}\mathbf{Cl}(\mathcal{BS})$.

Proof First note that the set of all ground status atoms satisfies conditions (1) and (2) above. So all we have to show is that such a minimal extension of $\mathcal{BS}$ exists. Let us define a sequence $\mathcal{BS}_i$, where $\mathcal{BS}_0 =_{def} \mathcal{BS}$ and

$\mathcal{BS}_{i+1} =_{def} \mathcal{BS}_i \cup \{\mathcal{B}_a(b, \mathbf{P}\alpha) \mid \mathcal{B}_a(b, \mathbf{O}\alpha) \in \mathcal{BS}_i\}$.

Obviously, $\cup \mathcal{BS}_i$ is a minimal extension of $\mathcal{BS}$ as required in the statement. The general case for arbitrary sequences σ instead of just [b] is analogous. ∎

The unique minimal status set that is a superset of $\mathcal{BS}$ and which is deontically closed is called the deontic closure of $\mathcal{BS}$.

DEFINITION 7.3.8 (DEONTIC CLOSURE **D-Cl**($\mathcal{BS}$)) Suppose $\mathcal{BS}$ is a belief status set held by agent a. The *deontic closure* of $\mathcal{BS}$, denoted **D-Cl**($\mathcal{BS}$), is the smallest superset of $\mathcal{BS}$ that is deontically closed.

Just as in the case of deontically closed sets, a belief status set is said to be action closed *if, by definition,* whenever agent a believes action α is obligatory for some agent sequence, then it must also believe that that agent sequence will do it. Furthermore, if it believes action α is done by some agent sequence, then it must also believe that that agent sequence is permitted to do it.

DEFINITION 7.3.9 (ACTION CLOSED BELIEF STATUS SET) Suppose $\mathcal{BS}$ is a belief status set held by agent a. $\mathcal{BS}$ is said to be *action closed* iff the following conditions hold:

1. if $\mathbf{O}\alpha \in \Pi_\sigma^{\text{action}}(\mathcal{BS})$, then $\mathbf{Do}\ \alpha \in \Pi_\sigma^{\text{action}}(\mathcal{BS})$,
2. if $\mathbf{Do}\ \alpha \in \Pi_\sigma^{\text{action}}(\mathcal{BS})$, then $\mathbf{P}\alpha \in \Pi_\sigma^{\text{action}}(\mathcal{BS})$,

As in the case of deontically closed belief status sets, if $\mathcal{BS}$ is any belief status set, there is a unique minimal (w.r.t. set inclusion) superset of $\mathcal{BS}$ which is action closed. This is the gist of the following lemma.

LEMMA 7.3.2 Suppose $\mathcal{BS}$ is a belief status set held by agent a. Then there is a unique belief status set, denoted **A-Cl**($\mathcal{BS}$), such that:

1. $\mathcal{BS} \subseteq \mathbf{A\text{-}Cl}(\mathcal{BS})$ and
2. **A-Cl**($\mathcal{BS}$) is action closed and
3. There is no strict subset of **A-Cl**($\mathcal{BS}$) satisfying the preceding two conditions.

Proof We have to show that such a minimal extension of $\mathcal{BS}$ exists and follow the proof of the last lemma. We define a sequence $\mathcal{BS}_i$, where $\mathcal{BS}_0 =_{def} \mathcal{BS}$ and

$\mathcal{BS}_{i+1} =_{def} \mathcal{BS}_i \cup \{\mathcal{B}_a(b, \mathbf{P}\alpha) \mid \mathcal{B}_a(b, \mathbf{Do}\ \alpha) \in \mathcal{BS}_i\}$
$\cup \{\mathcal{B}_a(b, \mathbf{Do}\ \alpha) \mid \mathcal{B}_a(b, \mathbf{O}\alpha) \in \mathcal{BS}_i\}$.

Obviously, $\bigcup \mathcal{BS}_i$ is a minimal extension of $\mathcal{BS}$ as required in the statement. As in the previous lemma, the general case for arbitrary sequences σ instead of just [b] is analogous. ∎

In view of the above theorem, we call **A-Cl**($\mathcal{BS}$) the *action closure* of $\mathcal{BS}$.

DEFINITION 7.3.10 (ACTION CLOSURE **A-Cl**($\mathcal{BS}$))   Suppose $\mathcal{BS}$ is a belief status set held by agent $\mathfrak{a}$. The *action closure* of $\mathcal{BS}$, denoted **A-Cl**($\mathcal{BS}$), is the smallest superset of $\mathcal{BS}$ that is action closed.

We are now ready to start defining the notion of closure of a belief status set, $\mathcal{BS}$, under the rules of a map, $\mathcal{BP}$. First, we define an operator, **App**$_{\mathcal{BP},\mathcal{O}}(\mathcal{BS})$ that takes as input, a belief status set, $\mathcal{BS}$, and produces as output, another belief status set, obtained by applying the rules in $\mathcal{BP}$ with respect to the state $\mathcal{O}$ once.

DEFINITION 7.3.11 (OPERATOR **App**$_{\mathcal{BP},\mathcal{O}}(\mathcal{BS})$)   Suppose $\mathcal{BP}$ is a map, and $\mathcal{O}$ is an agent state. Then, **App**$_{\mathcal{BP},\mathcal{O}}(\mathcal{BS})$ is defined to be the set of all ground action status atoms A such that there exists a rule in $\mathcal{BP}$ having a ground instance of the form $r : A \leftarrow L_1, \ldots, L_n$, which we denote by

$$A \leftarrow B_{cc}^+(r) \cup B_{cc}^-(r) \cup B_{\text{other}}^+(r) \cup B_{\text{other}}^-(r)$$

(in order to distinguish between positive/negative occurrences of code call atoms and non-code call atoms, i.e., action status literals and belief literals) such that:

1. $B_{\text{other}}^+(r) \subseteq \mathcal{BS}$ and $\neg.B_{\text{other}}^-(r) \cap \mathcal{BS} = \emptyset$, and
2. every code call $\chi \in B_{cc}^+(r)$ succeeds in $\mathcal{O}$, and
3. every code call $\chi \in \neg.B_{cc}^-(r)$ does not succeed in $\mathcal{O}$, and
4. for every atom $\mathsf{Op}(\alpha) \in B^+(r) \cup \{A\}$ such that $\mathsf{Op} \in \{\mathbf{P}, \mathbf{O}, \mathbf{Do}\}$, the action α is executable in state $\mathcal{O}$.

Intuitively, the operator **App**$_{\mathcal{BP},\mathcal{O}}(\mathcal{BS})$ closes $\mathcal{BS}$ by applying all rules of the map $\mathcal{BP}$ once. The following example shows how this operator works, using our familiar CFIT* example.

Example 7.3.2 (**App**$_{\mathcal{BP},\mathcal{O}}(\mathcal{BS})$ *for* CFIT*)   We continue with Example 7.2.6 on page 225 and consider the following belief status set for heli1:

$\mathcal{BS}_1(\text{heli1}) =_{def} \{\mathcal{B}_{\text{heli1}}(\text{tank1}, \text{in}(\text{pointB}, \text{tank1} : getPos())),$
$\qquad\qquad \mathbf{P}\, fly(\text{pointA}, \text{pointC}, 5000, 100), \mathbf{P}\, attack(\text{pointC}, \text{pointB})\}$

Then **App**$_{\mathcal{BP},\mathcal{O}}(\mathcal{BS}_1(\text{heli1})) = \{\mathbf{P}\, attack(\text{pointA}, \text{pointB})\}$.

Note that no belief atoms are present, because the definition of **App** only specifies program rule heads and we cannot have belief atoms in rule heads. Also, the atoms **P** *fly*(pointA, pointC, 5000, 100) and **P** *attack*(pointC, pointB) were not preserved because there are no rules to support them.

DEFINITION 7.3.12 (PROGRAM CLOSURE) A belief status set, $\mathcal{BS}$, is said to be *closed* with respect to a map, $\mathcal{BP}$, and an agent state, $\mathcal{O}$, if, by definition, $\mathbf{App}_{\mathcal{BP},\mathcal{O}}(\mathcal{BS}) = \{\mathrm{Op}\,\alpha \mid \mathrm{Op}\,\alpha \in \mathcal{BS}$ where $\mathrm{Op} \in \{\mathbf{O}, \mathbf{W}, \mathbf{P}, \mathbf{F}, \mathbf{Do}\}\}$.

Intuitively, this definition says that when we restrict $\mathcal{BS}$ to the action status atoms associated with agent a, then the set of action status atoms that the map, $\mathcal{BP}$, makes true in the current state, is equal to the set of action status atoms already true in $\mathcal{BS}$. The following example builds upon the previous one, and explains why certain belief status sets, $\mathcal{BS}$, satisfy the program closure condition, while others do not.

In the preceding example the belief status set $\mathcal{BS}_1(\mathtt{heli1})$ does not satisfy the program closure property because $\mathbf{App}_{\mathcal{BP},\mathcal{O}}(\mathcal{BS}_1(\mathtt{heli1}))$ is not equal to

$\{\mathrm{Op}\,\alpha \mid \mathrm{Op}\,\alpha \in \mathcal{BS}\} = \{\mathbf{P}\mathit{fly}(\mathtt{pointA}, \mathtt{pointC}, 5000, 100), \mathbf{P}\mathit{attack}(\mathtt{pointC}, \mathtt{pointB})\}$.

However, supose we add the following two rules to heli1's program:

P *fly*(pointA, pointC, 5000, 100) ←

P *attack*(pointC, pointB) ←

In this case, the belief status set $\mathcal{BS}_2(\mathtt{heli1})$ satisfies the program closure rule:

$\mathcal{BS}_2(\mathtt{heli1}) =_{def} \{\mathcal{B}_{\mathtt{heli1}}(\mathtt{tank1}, \mathbf{in}(\mathtt{pointB}, \mathtt{tank}: \mathit{getPos}())),$
$\qquad\qquad \mathbf{P}\mathit{fly}(\mathtt{pointA}, \mathtt{pointC}, 5000, 100),$
$\qquad\qquad \mathbf{P}\mathit{attack}(\mathtt{pointC}, \mathtt{pointB}),$
$\qquad\qquad \mathbf{P}\mathit{attack}(\mathtt{pointA}, \mathtt{pointB})\}$.

Then $\mathbf{App}_{\mathcal{BP},\mathcal{O}}(\mathcal{BS}_2(\mathtt{heli1}))$ is given by the three action status atoms

P*attack*(pointA, pointB),
P*attack*(pointC, pointB),
P*fly*(pointA, pointC, 5000, 100).

At this point, we have finished describing the requirements on agent a that must be true. In addition, we must specify conditions on the *beliefs* that agent a holds about other agents, b. To some extent, this has already been done in the definitions of deontic and action consistency/closure. However, more coherent conditions need to be articulated. The first of these is the fact that the beliefs held by agent a about another agent b must be coherent. For instance, if a believes that it is obligatory for agent b to do action α, then a must also believe that b will do α. Other, similar conditions also apply. This condition may be expressed through the following definition.

DEFINITION 7.3.13 (LOCAL COHERENCE) A belief status set, $\mathcal{BS}$, held by agent a is said to be *locally coherent w.r.t. a sequence, σ of agents if, by definition,* the induced status set $\Pi^{\text{action}}_\sigma(\mathcal{BS})$ is feasible in the sense of Chapter 6 and (Eiter, Subrahmanian, and Rogers 1999) with respect to the induced state $\Pi^{\text{state}}_\sigma(\mathcal{BS})$ and agent program $\mathcal{P}^a(\sigma)$.

$\mathcal{BS}$ is said to be *locally coherent if, by definition,* $\mathcal{BS}$ is coherent with respect to all sequences, σ, of agents.

The above definition makes explicit reference to the definition of feasible status set, provided by (Eiter, Subrahmanian, and Rogers 1999). It is important to note that $\Pi^{\text{action}}_\sigma(\mathcal{BS})$ is a set of action status atoms, and that $\Pi^{\text{state}}_\sigma(\mathcal{BS})$ involves no belief literals, and $\mathcal{P}^a(\sigma)$ is an *agent program* with no belief modalities, as defined in Definition 6.4.4 on page 161. Here are a few examples of what it means for a belief status set held by agent a to be locally coherent.

Example 7.3.3 (Local Coherence) Let

$\mathcal{BS}(\text{heli2}) =_{def} \{\mathcal{B}_{\text{heli2}}(\text{heli1}, \mathbf{P})fly(\text{PointA}, \text{PointB}, 1000, 100),$
$\qquad\qquad\qquad \mathcal{B}_{\text{heli2}}(\text{heli1}, \mathbf{in}(100, \text{heli1}: getSpeed())),$
$\qquad\qquad\qquad \mathcal{B}_{\text{heli2}}(\text{heli1}, \mathbf{in}(1000, \text{heli1}: getAltitude()))\}$

and let heli1's program as believed by heli2 (we denote it by $\mathcal{P}^{\text{heli2}}(\text{heli1})$) be:

$\mathbf{P}fly(\text{X}, \text{Y}, \text{A}, \text{S}) \leftarrow \mathbf{in}(\text{S}, \text{heli1}: getSpeed()), \mathbf{in}(\text{A}, \text{heli1}: getAltitude()).$

The set $\mathcal{BS}(\text{heli2})$ is locally coherent w.r.t. the sequence (heli2). Notice that:

$\Pi^{\text{action}}_{\text{heli1}}(\mathcal{BS}(\text{heli2})) =_{def} \{\mathbf{P}fly(\text{PointA}, \text{PointB}, 1000, 100)\}$

is feasible with respect to:

$\Pi^{\text{state}}_{\text{heli1}}(\mathcal{BS}(\text{heli2})) = \{\mathbf{in}(100, \text{heli1}: getSpeed()), \mathbf{in}(1000, \text{heli1}: getAltitude())\}.$

Let

$\mathcal{BS}(\text{tank1}) =_{def} \{\mathcal{B}_{\text{tank1}}(\text{heli2}, \mathcal{B}_{\text{heli2}}(\text{heli1}, \mathbf{P}fly(\text{PointA}, \text{PointB}, 1000, 100))),$
$\qquad\qquad\qquad \mathcal{B}_{\text{tank1}}(\text{heli2}, \mathcal{B}_{\text{heli2}}(\text{heli1}, \mathbf{in}(100, \text{heli1}: getSpeed())))$,
$\qquad\qquad\qquad \mathcal{B}_{\text{tank1}}(\text{heli2}, \mathcal{B}_{\text{heli2}}(\text{heli1}, \mathbf{in}(1000, \text{heli1}: getAltitude()))))\}$

and let the $\mathcal{P}^{\text{tank1}}([\text{heli2}, \text{heli1}])$ be the program tank1 believes heli2 believes heli1 has:

$\mathbf{P}fly(\text{X}, \text{Y}, \text{A}, \text{S}) \leftarrow \mathbf{in}(\text{S}, \text{heli1}: getSpeed()), \mathbf{in}(\text{A}, \text{heli1}: getAltitude()).$

Then $\mathcal{BS}(\text{tank1})$ is locally coherent w.r.t. the sequence [heli2,heli1]. Just like in the previous example: $\Pi^{\text{action}}_{[\text{heli2,heli1}]}(\mathcal{BS}(\text{tank1})) = \{\mathbf{P}\textit{fly}(\text{PointA, PointB, 1000, 100})\}$ is feasible with respect to:

$$\Pi^{\text{state}}_{[\text{heli2,heli1}]}(\mathcal{BS}(\text{tank1}))$$
$$= \{\mathbf{in}(100, \text{heli1}: \textit{getSpeed}()), \mathbf{in}(1000, \text{heli1}: \textit{getAltitude}())\}.$$

In addition to being locally coherent, for a belief status set to be considered feasible, we need to ensure that it does not ignore the contents of the belief table of agent a. This may be encoded through the following condition.

DEFINITION 7.3.14 (COMPATIBILITY WITH $\mathbf{BT}^a$)   Suppose $\langle h, \phi, \chi_B \rangle$ is in $\mathbf{BT}^a$. $\mathcal{BS}$ is said to be *compatible* with $\langle h, \phi, \chi_B \rangle$ *if, by definition,* either

1. $h\_\text{part}(\chi_B)$ is false w.r.t. $\pi^{\text{state}}_h(\mathcal{BS})$ or $a\_\text{part}(\chi_B)$ is false w.r.t. a's state $\mathcal{O_S}$.
2. ϕ is a code call condition or an action status atom and $\mathcal{B}_a(h, \phi) \in \mathcal{BS}$.

$\mathcal{BS}$ is said to be *compatible* with $\mathbf{BT}^a$ *if, by definition,* it is compatible with all tuples in $\mathbf{BT}^a$.

Intuitively, this condition says that if a row in the belief table of agent a has a "true" condition, then agent a must hold the corresponding belief about the agent h in question. The following example illustrates this concept of compatibility.

Example 7.3.4 (Compatibility)   We continue with Table 7.3 on page 224. We define

$\mathcal{BS}(\text{tank1}) =_{\textit{def}} \{\mathcal{B}_{\text{tank1}}(\text{heli1}, \mathbf{in}(\text{pos1}, \text{heli1}: \textit{getPosition}()))\}.$

$\mathcal{BS}(\text{tank1})$ is compatible with $\mathbf{BT}^a$.

However, the following belief set is not compatible with the given belief table:

$\mathcal{BS}(\text{tank1}) = \{\mathbf{in}(\text{pos1}, \text{tank1}: \textit{getPosition}())\}.$

This is because there is a true condition in the first row of the table but the belief set does not contain

$\mathcal{B}_{\text{tank1}}(\text{heli1}, \mathbf{in}(\text{pos1}, \text{heli1}: \textit{getPosition}()))$

according to the definition of compatibility.

The last condition in defining feasible belief status sets is that for any agent b, the beliefs agent a holds about agent b must be closed under the notion of entailment that agent a thinks agent b uses.

DEFINITION 7.3.15 (COMPATIBILITY WITH **BSemT**^{a})   Suppose $\langle b, BSem_b^a \rangle$ is an entry in **BSemT**^{a}, and suppose BS is a belief status set. Let $BS[b] = \{\chi \mid \mathcal{B}_a(b, \chi) \in BS\}$. BS is said to be *compatible* with $\langle b, BSem_b^a \rangle$ *if, by definition,*

$\{\chi' \mid BS[b] \models_{Sem_b^a} \chi'\} \subseteq BS.$

BS is said to be *compatible* with **BSemT**^{a} iff BS is compatible with every entry in **BSemT**^{a}.

The last property we need is the consistency of the belief table and the belief semantics table.

DEFINITION 7.3.16 (BELIEF CONSISTENCY)   We require that a belief status set is consistent with respect to beliefs hold by agent a about other agents, i.e., that it does not contain a belief atom φ and its negation $\neg\varphi$. Such a set is called belief-consistent wrt. agent a.

We are now ready to define feasible belief status sets.

DEFINITION 7.3.17 (FEASIBLE BELIEF STATUS SET)   A belief status set, BS held by agent a, is said to be *feasible* with respect to a meta-agent program, BP, an agent state, $\mathcal{O}$, and a set $\mathcal{IC}$ of integrity constraints, and a set $\mathcal{AC}$ of action constraints *if, by definition,* BS satisfies our 7 conditions stated above (deontically and action consistent, deontically and action closed, closed under the map BP's rules, state consistent, locally coherent, compatible with **BT**^{a}, compatible with **BSemT**^{a} and belief-consistent).

Example 7.3.5 (Feasible Belief Status Sets)   Let the map of heli1 be the following;

r1:   **P** *attack*(P1, P2) ← $\mathcal{B}_{heli1}$(tank1, **in**(P2, tank1 : *getPos*())),
    P *fly*(P1, P3, A, S),
    P *attack*(P3, P2).

r2:   **O** *attack*(P1, P2) ← *flyRoute*([P0, P1, P2, P3], S),
    $\mathcal{B}_{heli1}$(tank1, **in**(P2, tank1 : *getPos*())).

r3:   **P** *attack*(pos3, pos1) ←

r4:   **P** *fly*(pos0, pos3, 5000, 100) ←

Let the set of $\mathcal{IC}$ be given as;

in(S, heli : *getSpeed*()) & $S <$ MaxSpeed

in(A, heli : *getAltitude*()) & $A <$ MaxAltitude

and suppose the set $\mathcal{AC}$ contains the following action constraints:

$\{attack(P1, P2), attack(P3, P4)\} \hookleftarrow P1 = P3 \;\&\; P2 \neq P4$

Let

$$\mathcal{BS}(\mathrm{heli1}) =_{def} \{\mathcal{B}_{\mathrm{heli1}}(\mathrm{tank1}, \mathbf{in}(\mathrm{pos1}, \mathrm{tank1}: \mathit{getPos}())),$$
$$\mathcal{B}_{\mathrm{heli1}}(\mathrm{heli2}, \mathbf{in}(\mathrm{pos2}, \mathrm{heli2}: \mathit{getPos}())),$$
$$\mathbf{P}\mathit{fly}(\mathrm{pos0}, \mathrm{pos3}, 5000, 100),$$
$$\mathcal{B}_{\mathrm{heli1}}(\mathrm{heli2}, \mathbf{P}\mathit{fly}(\mathrm{pos0}, \mathrm{pos1}, 10000, 200)),$$
$$\mathcal{B}_{\mathrm{heli1}}(\mathrm{heli2}, \mathbf{in}(200, \mathrm{heli2}: \mathit{getSpeed}())),$$
$$\mathcal{B}_{\mathrm{heli1}}(\mathrm{heli2}, \mathbf{in}(10000, \mathrm{heli2}: \mathit{getAltitude}())),$$
$$\mathbf{P}\mathit{attack}(\mathrm{pos3}, \mathrm{pos1}),$$
$$\mathbf{P}\mathit{attack}(\mathrm{pos0}, \mathrm{pos1})\}.$$

Then, we have

$$\prod\nolimits_{\mathrm{heli2}}^{\mathrm{action}} (\mathcal{BS}(\mathrm{heli1})) = \{\mathbf{P}\mathit{fly}(\mathrm{pos0}, \mathrm{pos1}, 10000, 200)\}$$

$$\prod\nolimits_{\mathrm{heli2}}^{\mathrm{state}} (\mathcal{BS}(\mathrm{heli1})) = \{\mathbf{in}(200, \mathrm{heli2}: \mathit{getSpeed}()), \mathbf{in}(10000, \mathrm{heli2}: \mathit{getAltitude}())\}$$

$$\prod\nolimits_{\mathrm{tank1}}^{\mathrm{state}} (\mathcal{BS}(\mathrm{heli1})) = \{\mathbf{in}(\mathrm{pos1}, \mathrm{tank1}: \mathit{getPos}())\}$$

Let the belief table of heli1 be Table 7.4 on page 225. Finally let $\mathcal{P}^{\mathrm{heli1}}(\mathrm{heli2})$ be:

$\mathbf{P}\mathit{fly}(\mathrm{X}, \mathrm{Y}, \mathrm{A}, \mathrm{S}) \leftarrow \mathbf{in}(\mathrm{S}, \mathrm{heli2}: \mathit{getSpeed}()), \mathbf{in}(\mathrm{A}, \mathrm{heli2}: \mathit{getAltitude}()).$

Then, the belief status set $\mathcal{BS}(\mathrm{heli1})$ is feasible with respect to the above map, $\mathcal{AC}$ and $\mathcal{IC}$. Note that $\mathcal{BS}(\mathrm{heli1})$ satisfies all of the 7 conditions. It is deontically and action consistent, because $\mathcal{BS}(\mathrm{heli1})$ does not contain any inconsistencies; although $\mathbf{P}\mathit{fly}(\mathrm{pos0}, \mathrm{pos3}, 5000, 100)$ is in $\mathcal{BS}(\mathrm{heli1})$, the action status atom $\mathbf{F}\mathit{fly}(\mathrm{pos0}, \mathrm{pos3}, 5000, 100)$ is not.

$\mathcal{BS}(\mathrm{heli1})$ is deontically and action closed beacuse $\Pi_{\mathrm{heli2}}^{\mathrm{action}}(\mathcal{BS}(\mathrm{heli1}))$ does not contain any inconsistency. It is closed under the map. Note that the set $\mathbf{App}_{\mathcal{BP},\mathcal{O}}(\mathcal{BS}_2(\mathrm{heli1}))$ is given by

$\{\mathbf{P}\mathit{attack}(\mathrm{pos0}, \mathrm{pos1}), \mathbf{P}\mathit{attack}(\mathrm{pos3}, \mathrm{pos1}), \mathbf{P}\mathit{fly}(\mathrm{pos0}, \mathrm{pos3}, 5000, 100)\}.$

$\mathcal{BS}(\mathrm{heli1})$ is locally coherent with respect to the sequence $[\mathrm{heli2}]$. Note that

$$\prod\nolimits_{\mathrm{heli2}}^{\mathrm{action}} (\mathcal{BS}(\mathrm{heli1})) = \{\mathbf{P}\mathit{fly}(\mathrm{pos0}, \mathrm{pos1}, 10000, 200)\}$$

is feasible with respect to

$$\prod\nolimits_{\mathrm{heli2}}^{\mathrm{state}} (\mathcal{BS}(\mathrm{heli1})) = \{\mathbf{in}(200, \mathrm{heli2}: \mathit{getSpeed}()), \mathbf{in}(10000, \mathrm{heli2}: \mathit{getAltitude}())\}$$

$\mathcal{BS}(\text{heli1})$ is also locally coherent with respect to the sequence [tank1] as $\Pi_{\text{tank1}}^{\text{action}} \times (\mathcal{BS}(\text{heli1})) = \emptyset$.

$\mathcal{BS}(\text{heli1})$ is compatible with $\mathbf{BT}^{\text{heli1}}$. The following belief status set is also feasible:

$\mathcal{BS}_1(\text{heli1}) =_{def} \{ \mathcal{B}_{\text{heli1}}(\text{tank1}, \mathbf{in}(\text{pos1}, \text{tank1}: getPos())),$
$\qquad \mathcal{B}_{\text{heli1}}(\text{heli2}, \mathbf{in}(\text{pos2}, \text{heli2}: getPos())),$
$\qquad \mathbf{P}\!fly(\text{pos0}, \text{pos3}, 5000, 100),$
$\qquad \mathbf{P}\!flyRoute([\text{point1}, \text{point2}, \text{point3}, \text{point4}], S),$
$\qquad \mathcal{B}_{\text{heli1}}(\text{heli2}, \mathbf{P}\!fly(\text{pos0}, \text{pos1}, 10000, 200)),$
$\qquad \mathcal{B}_{\text{heli1}}(\text{heli2}, \mathbf{in}(200, \text{heli2}: getSpeed())),$
$\qquad \mathcal{B}_{\text{heli1}}(\text{heli2}, \mathbf{in}(10000, \text{heli2}: getAltitude())),$
$\qquad \mathbf{P}attack(\text{pos3}, \text{pos1}),$
$\qquad \mathbf{P}attack(\text{pos0}, \text{pos1})\}.$

Now consider the following belief status set for heli1, with the same map, belief table, $\mathcal{AC}$ and $\mathcal{IC}$.

$\mathcal{BS}_2(\text{heli1}) =_{def} \{ \mathcal{B}_{\text{heli1}}(\text{tank1}, \mathbf{in}(\text{pos1}, \text{tank1}: getPos())),$
$\qquad \mathbf{P}\!fly(\text{pos0}, \text{pos3}, 5000, 100),$
$\qquad \mathcal{B}_{\text{heli1}}(\text{heli2}, \mathbf{P}\!fly(\text{pos0}, \text{pos1}, 10000, 200)),$
$\qquad \mathcal{B}_{\text{heli1}}(\text{heli2}, \mathbf{in}(200, \text{heli2}: getSpeed())),$
$\qquad \mathcal{B}_{\text{heli1}}(\text{heli2}, \mathbf{in}(10000, \text{heli2}: getAltitude())),$
$\qquad \mathbf{P}attack(\text{pos3}, \text{pos1}),$
$\qquad \mathbf{P}attack(\text{pos0}, \text{pos1})\}.$

$\mathcal{BS}_2(\text{heli1})$ is not feasible because it is not compatible with $\mathbf{BT}^{\text{heli1}}$. Because $\mathcal{BS}_2(\text{heli1})$ does not contain $\mathcal{B}_{\text{heli1}}(\text{heli2}, \mathbf{in}(\text{pos2}, \text{heli1}: getPos()))$.

The following belief status set of heli1 is also not feasible:

$\mathcal{BS}_3(\text{heli1}) =_{def} \{ \mathcal{B}_{\text{heli1}}(\text{tank1}, \mathbf{in}(\text{pos1}, \text{tank1}: getPos())),$
$\qquad \mathcal{B}_{\text{heli1}}(\text{heli2}, \mathbf{in}(\text{pos2}, \text{heli2}: getPos())),$
$\qquad \mathbf{P}\!fly(\text{pos0}, \text{pos3}, 5000, 100),$
$\qquad \mathcal{B}_{\text{heli1}}(\text{heli2}, \mathbf{P}\!fly(\text{pos0}, \text{pos1}, 10000, 200)),$
$\qquad \mathcal{B}_{\text{heli1}}(\text{heli2}, \mathbf{in}(200, \text{heli2}: getSpeed())),$
$\qquad \mathcal{B}_{\text{heli1}}(\text{heli2}, \mathbf{in}(10000, \text{heli2}: getAltitude()))\}.$

The reason is that it is not closed under the map $\mathcal{BP}$'s rules, as

$\mathbf{App}_{\mathcal{BP},\mathcal{O}}(\mathcal{BS}_3(\text{heli1})) = \{\mathbf{P}attack(\text{pos0}, \text{pos1})\}.$

Finally, the following belief status set is also not feasible:

$BS_4(\text{heli1}) =_{def} \{\mathcal{B}_{\text{heli1}}(\text{tank1}, \textbf{in}(\text{pos1}, \text{tank1}: getPos())),$
$\qquad\qquad\mathcal{B}_{\text{heli1}}(\text{heli2}, \textbf{in}(\text{pos2}, \text{heli2}: getPos())),$
$\qquad\qquad\textbf{P}fly(\text{pos0}, \text{pos3}, 5000, 100),$
$\qquad\qquad\textbf{F}fly(\text{pos0}, \text{pos3}, 5000, 100),$
$\qquad\qquad\mathcal{B}_{\text{heli1}}(\text{heli2}, \textbf{P}fly(\text{pos0}, \text{pos1}, 10000, 200)),$
$\qquad\qquad\mathcal{B}_{\text{heli1}}(\text{heli2}, \textbf{in}(200, \text{heli2}: getSpeed())),$
$\qquad\qquad\mathcal{B}_{\text{heli1}}(\text{heli2}, \textbf{in}(10000, \text{heli2}: getAltitude())),$
$\qquad\qquad\textbf{P}attack(\text{pos3}, \text{pos1}),$
$\qquad\qquad\textbf{P}attack(\text{pos0}, \text{pos1})\}.$

It is not deontically consistent as for $\alpha = fly(\text{pos0}, \text{pos3}, 5000, 100)$ both $\textbf{P}\alpha$ and $\textbf{F}\alpha$ are in $BS_4(\text{heli1})$.

7.3.2 Rational Belief Status Sets

The notion of a rational belief status set is a useful strengthening of feasible belief status sets. The idea is that all executed actions should be *grounded* or *justified* by the meta agent program. As a simple example, consider a feasible belief status set and add a $\textbf{Do}\alpha$ atom for an action α that does not occur in any rule of the program or in the action and integrity constraints at all. It is immediate that this new set still is a feasible belief status set, although not a minimal one: there is no reason to believe in $\textbf{Do}\alpha$. Rational sets rule out such non-minimal status sets:

DEFINITION 7.3.18 (GROUNDEDNESS; RATIONAL BELIEF STATUS SET) A belief status set BS which is locally coherent, compatible with $\textbf{BT}^a$, and compatible with $\textbf{BSemT}^a$ is *grounded*, if there exists no belief status set BS' strictly contained in BS ($BS' \subset BS$) such that BS' satisfies the following 3 conditions of a feasible belief status set as given in Definition 7.3.17 on page 238: deontically and action consistent, deontically and action closed, closed under the map BP's rules.

A belief status set BS is a *rational status set*, if BS is a feasible belief status set and BS is grounded.

If we compare this last definition with the original definition of a belief status set (Definition 7.3.17 on page 238), the reader will note that only the state consistency is not explicitly required while minimizing BS'. In contrast, the local coherence and the two compatibility conditions are required and do not guide the minimization process. If state consistency were *added* to the minimization policy, then an agent would be forced to execute actions in order to satisfy the integrity constraints. However, such actions may not be mentioned at all by the program, and thus it seems unreasonable to execute them. Of course, the state consistency is guaranteed, because we check groundedness only for *feasible* belief status sets.

7.3.3 Reasonable Belief Status Sets

As shown in Eiter, Subrahmanian, and Rogers (1999) for programs without beliefs, rational belief status sets allow the arbitrary contraposition of rules, which is often not intended. For example the program consisting of the simple rule

Do $(\alpha) \leftarrow \neg$**Do** (β)

has two rational belief status sets: $S_1 = \{$**Do** $(\alpha),$ **P** $(\alpha)\}$, and $S_2 = \{$**Do** $(\beta),$ **P**$(\beta)\}$. The second one seems less intuitive because there is no rule in the program to justify deriving **Do** (β).

This leads, in analogy to Eiter, Subrahmanian, and Rogers (1999) to the following notion:

DEFINITION 7.3.19 (REASONABLE BELIEF STATUS SET) Let $\mathcal{BP}$ be an agent program, let $\mathcal{O}_S$ be an agent state, and let $\mathcal{BS}$ be a belief status set.

1. If $\mathcal{BP}$ is a positive meta agent program, then $\mathcal{BS}$ is a *reasonable belief status set* for $\mathcal{P}$ on $\mathcal{O}_S$, *if, by definition*, $\mathcal{BS}$ is a rational belief status set for $\mathcal{P}$ on $\mathcal{O}_S$.

2. The reduct of $\mathcal{BP}$ w.r.t. $\mathcal{BS}$ and $\mathcal{O}_S$, denoted by $\text{red}^{\mathcal{BS}}(\mathcal{BP}, \mathcal{O}_S)$, is the program which is obtained from the ground instances of the rules in $\mathcal{BP}$ over $\mathcal{O}_S$ as follows.

a. First, remove every rule r such that $B_{\text{other}}^{-}(r) \cap \mathcal{BS} \neq \emptyset$;

b. Remove all atoms in $B_{\text{other}}^{-}(r)$ from the remaining rules.

Then $\mathcal{BS}$ is a *reasonable belief status set* for $\mathcal{BP}$ w.r.t. $\mathcal{O}_S$, if it is a reasonable belief status set of the (positive) meta agent program $\text{red}^{\mathcal{BS}}(\mathcal{BP}, \mathcal{O}_S)$ with respect to $\mathcal{O}_S$.

7.4 How to Implement Meta-Agent Programs?

Meta-Agent Programs significantly extend agent programs by allowing to reason about beliefs. But within the *IMPACT*-platform developed at the University of Maryland, agent programs have been already efficiently implemented and thus the question arises if we can take advantage of this work. In fact, as we will show in this section, this can be done by

1. *transforming meta agent programs into agent programs*, and
2. *taking advantage of extended code calls $\mathcal{S}^{ext}$ as introduced in Definition 7.3.5 on page 229.*

The first step is a source-to-source transformation: the belief atoms in a meta agent program are replaced by suitable code calls to the new datastructures. We also note that the second step is indispensable, as every agent dealing with meta agent programs needs to deal with *Belief Tables*, *Belief Semantics Tables* and some functions operating on them.

Let us illustrate the transformation with the following simplified example. Recall that we already introduced *extended* code call conditions in Definition 7.3.5 on page 229: those also involve the new datatypes (belief- and belief semantics tables). Suppose the belief table does not contain any belief conditions (i.e., it coincides with its basic belief table). Then if χ is any code call condition of agent c, the extended code call atom

in($\langle$c, χ, **true**$\rangle$, $a : belief\_table$())

corresponds to the belief atom

$\mathcal{B}_a(c, \chi)$.

However, this does not mean that we can just replace the latter expression by the former. The problem is that beliefs need not neccessarily be stored in the belief table. They can also be triggered by entries in the belief table and/or in the belief semantics table. In fact, this was why we explicitly formulated condition 7 on compatibility with the belief semantics table. Also if the third entry in the belief table, the belief condition, is present, then the first two entries of this triple specify a belief that must hold. Therefore we will use the additional function

$a : bel\_ccc\_act(\sigma)$,

which was introduced in Definition 7.3.5 on page 229 and thus *implement* belief atoms with extended code calls:

in("χ", $a : bel\_ccc\_act(c)$)

What happens if the formula χ is not a code call, but again a belief formula, say $\mathcal{B}_c(d, \chi')$? An expression of the form **in**($\mathcal{B}_c(d, \chi')$, $a : bel\_ccc\_act(c)$) is not a wellformed formula in our framework (recall that $a : bel\_ccc\_act(\sigma)$ returns a set of code call conditions and action status atoms but no belief formulae). In fact, even if it were, it would not help in reducing the belief atoms to something involving only extended code calls. Here is where the inductive definition of $\mathfrak{Trans}$ comes in. We map

$\mathcal{B}_a(c, \mathcal{B}_c(d, \chi'))$

to

in("χ'", $a : bel\_ccc\_act([c, d])$).

Our main theorem in this section states that there is indeed a uniform transformation $\mathfrak{Trans}$ from arbitrary meta agent programs (which can also contain nested beliefs) to agent programs such that the semantics are preserved:

$$\mathsf{Sem}(\mathcal{BP}) = \mathsf{Sem}(\mathfrak{Trans}(\mathcal{BP})) \tag{7.4}$$

where Sem is either the *feasible*, *rational* or *reasonable* belief status set semantics.

DEFINITION 7.4.1 ($\mathfrak{Trans}$)   For an agent $\mathfrak{a}$, we defined in Definition 7.2.2 on page 214 the maximal belief language $\mathcal{BL}_\infty^\mathfrak{a}$. We define the mapping

$\mathfrak{Trans} : \mathcal{BL}_\infty^\mathfrak{a} \to$ Code Call Conditions of $\mathcal{S}^{\mathrm{ext}}$

by induction on the structure of belief literals:

Level 0:   If *bel_lit* is a code call condition or an action status atom, then $\mathfrak{Trans}(\mathit{bel\_lit}) =_{\mathit{def}}$ *bel_lit*.

Level 1:   If *bel_lit* has the form $(\neg)\mathcal{B}_\mathfrak{a}(\mathfrak{b}, \phi)$ where ϕ is a code call condition or an action status atom, then

1. $\mathfrak{Trans}(\mathcal{B}_\mathfrak{a}(\mathfrak{b}, \phi)) \mapsto \mathbf{in}(\text{"}\phi\text{"}, \mathfrak{a} : \mathit{bel\_ccc\_act}(\mathfrak{b}))$,
2. $\mathfrak{Trans}(\neg\mathcal{B}_\mathfrak{a}(\mathfrak{b}, \phi)) \mapsto \mathbf{in}(\text{"}\phi\text{"}, \mathfrak{a} : \mathit{bel\_ccc\_act}(\mathfrak{b}))$,

Level $n + 1$:   If *bel_lit* has the form $(\neg)\mathcal{B}_\mathfrak{a}(\mathfrak{b}, \phi)$ where ϕ is of level n, then we define $\mathfrak{Trans}(\mathcal{B}_\mathfrak{a}(\mathfrak{b}, \phi))$ by

$\mathbf{in}(\text{"}\chi\text{"}, \mathfrak{a} : \mathit{bel\_ccc\_act}([\mathfrak{b}, \rho]))$ if $\mathfrak{Trans}(\phi) = \mathbf{in}(\text{"}\chi\text{"}, \mathfrak{a} : \mathit{bel\_ccc\_act}(\rho))$

and we define $\mathfrak{Trans}(\neg\mathcal{B}_\mathfrak{a}(\mathfrak{b}, \phi))$ by

$\mathbf{in}(\text{"}\chi\text{"}, \mathfrak{a} : \mathit{bel\_ccc\_act}([\mathfrak{b}, \rho]))$ if $\mathfrak{Trans}(\phi) = \mathbf{in}(\text{"}\chi\text{"}, \mathfrak{a} : \mathit{bel\_ccc\_act}(\rho))$

Linear Extension to $\mathcal{BL}_\infty^\mathfrak{a}$:   Up to now $\mathfrak{Trans}$ is only defined on belief literals, not for arbitrary belief formulae (which can be arbitrary conjunctions of belief literals (see Definition 7.2.2 on page 214)).

However we can easily extend $\mathfrak{Trans}$ as follows:

$\mathfrak{Trans}(\mathrm{bel\_lit}_1 \wedge \ldots \wedge \mathrm{bel\_lit}_n) = \mathfrak{Trans}(\mathrm{bel\_lit}_1) \wedge \ldots \wedge \mathfrak{Trans}(\mathrm{bel\_lit}_n)$.

For a belief status set $\mathcal{BS}$ we denote by $\mathfrak{Trans}^{\mathrm{action}}(\mathcal{BS})$ the subset of all action status atoms in $\mathcal{BS}$. This is exactly the status set as defined in Definition 6.5.1 on page 172 for agent programs without beliefs.

Section 7.4   How to Implement Meta-Agent Programs?   245

For a belief status set $\mathcal{BS}$ and an agent $b \in A$, we also define:

$\mathfrak{Trans}^{\text{state}}(\mathcal{BS}, b) =_{def} \{\chi \mid \mathcal{B}_a(b, \chi) \in \mathcal{BS}$ and χ is a code call condition$\}$
$\mathfrak{Trans}^{\text{action}}(\mathcal{BS}, b) =_{def} \{\mathsf{Op}\,\alpha(\vec{t}) \mid \mathcal{B}_a(b, \mathsf{Op}\,\alpha(\vec{t})) \in \mathcal{BS}$, where $\mathsf{Op} \in \{\mathbf{O}, \mathbf{W}, \mathbf{P}, \mathbf{F}, \mathbf{Do}\}\}$.

As in Definition 7.3.3 on page 227, these definitions are easily extended to arbitrary sequences σ instead of just b.

This transformation $\mathfrak{Trans}$ maps all belief literals into extended code call conditions and will be used in the following to map any set containing belief literals (like belief status sets or meta agent programs) into one without belief literals but containing extended code calls. Also $\mathfrak{Trans}$ can be easily applied to $\mathcal{BP}$:

$\mathfrak{Trans}(\mathcal{BP})$: this is the program $\mathcal{BP}$ where all ocurrences of belief literals bel_lit have been replaced by $\mathfrak{Trans}$(bel_lit).

Thus $\mathfrak{Trans}$ naturally defines an agent program without beliefs and thus we can use an existing implementation for agent programs to compute them.

Although the mapping $\mathfrak{Trans}$ is very simple, some more work is needed in order to get the above claimed equivalence result. Namely, in the definition of a feasible belief status set we have explicitly required the compatibility with the belief table and the belief semantics table (see Definitions 7.3.14 on page 237 and 7.3.15 on page 238). If we use $\mathfrak{Trans}$ to get rid of all belief atoms in a belief status set by transforming them into code calls, then we need to formulate similar conditions in terms of code calls. Otherwise we can not expect a strong equivalence result to hold. The following picture may help to clarify the problem:

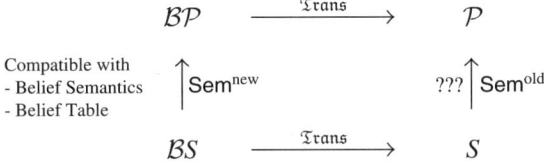

It will be easy to show that if the conditions on the left side are fulfilled, and $\mathcal{BS}$ belongs to the semantics Sem of $\mathcal{BP}$, then S belongs to the semantics Sem of $\mathcal{P}$. But in order to reduce the semantics of meta agent programs to those of agent programs we must also have the converse, namely that all S's of $\mathcal{P}$ on the right hand side are induced by $\mathcal{BS}$'s on the left hand side. Such a result can only hold if we have corresponding conditions (indicated by "???" in the above diagram) on the right hand side.

The way we solve this problem is

1. to extend the original set of integrity constraints $\mathcal{IC}$ by a new constraint which expresses the compatibility with the belief semantics table using the new functions now available in $\mathcal{S}^{\text{ext}}$,

2. to add a new condition (which can not be expressed as an integrity constraint) which ensures the compatibility with the belief table.

As to 1. we denote by $\mathcal{IC}^{\text{ext}}$ the set $\mathcal{IC}$ of original integrity constraints augmented with the following extended integrity constraints (one for each agent $b \in A$):

$\mathbf{in}(\langle b, \mathcal{BSem}_b^a \rangle a : belief\_sem\_table())$ &
$\mathbf{in}("\chi", a : bel\_ccc\_act(b))$ &
$\mathbf{in}(\mathbf{true}, a : bel\_semantics(b, "\chi", "\chi'"))$
$\Rightarrow$
$\mathbf{in}("\chi'", a : bel\_ccc\_act(b))$.

Note that we assume for ease of notation that the formulae χ, χ' are just code call conditions. In general, they can be arbitrary belief formulae (as determined by $\mathcal{BSem}_b^a$). In this case, we have to take their transformation as provided by $\mathfrak{Trans}$. To be more precise, we have to add the constraints:

$\mathbf{in}(\langle b, \mathcal{BSem}_b^a \rangle a : belief\_sem\_table())$ &
$\mathbf{in}(\mathbf{true}, a : bel\_semantics(b, "\chi", "\chi'"))$ &
$\mathfrak{Trans}(\chi)$
$\Rightarrow$
$\mathfrak{Trans}(\chi')$

As to 2. we require the following condition

Closure: Let the state $\mathcal{O}_{\mathcal{S}^{\text{ext}}}$ satisfy $\mathbf{in}(\langle b, \phi, \chi_B \rangle, a : belief\_table())$ as well as $a\_part(\chi_B)$ and let $\mathfrak{Trans}^{\text{state}}(\mathcal{BS}, b)$ satisfy $b\_part(\chi_B)$. Let further ϕ be a code call condition or an action status atom,

1. If ϕ is a code call condition or an action status atom, then $\mathcal{O}_{\mathcal{S}^{\text{ext}}}$ satisfies the code call atom $\mathbf{in}(\phi, a : bel\_ccc\_act(b))$.

2. If ϕ is of the form $\mathcal{B}_b(c, \phi')$, where ϕ' is a code call condition or an action status atom, then $\mathcal{O}_{\mathcal{S}^{\text{ext}}}$ satisfies $\mathbf{in}("\phi'", a : bel\_ccc\_act([b, c]))$.

3. More generally, if ϕ is a nested belief atom, then we can associate with this atom a sequence $[\rho]$ (as introduced in Definition 7.3.2 on page 227) and we require that $\mathcal{O}_{\mathcal{S}^{\text{ext}}}$ satisfies $\mathbf{in}("\phi'", a : bel\_ccc\_act([\rho]))$.

Thus we end up with the following picture:

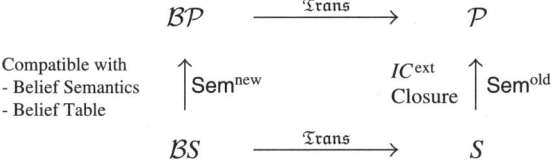

The following theorem and its corollaries make the statement (7.4 on page 244) precise.

THEOREM 7.4.1 (IMPLEMENTING BELIEF PROGRAMS BY AGENT PROGRAMS)   Let $\mathcal{BP}$ be a meta agent program, $a \in A$, $\mathcal{O}_{\mathcal{S}\text{ext}}$ a state of agent a, $\mathcal{IC}$ a set of integrity constraints, and $\mathcal{AC}$ a set of action constraints for a.

If $\mathcal{BS}$ is a feasible belief status set of agent a wrt. $\mathcal{BP}$, $\mathcal{O}_{\mathcal{S}\text{ext}}$, $\mathcal{IC}$ and $\mathcal{AC}$, then

1. $\mathfrak{Trans}^{\text{action}}(\mathcal{BS})$ is a feasible status set of $\mathfrak{Trans}(\mathcal{BP})$ wrt. $\mathcal{O}_{\mathcal{S}\text{ext}}$ and $\mathcal{IC}^{\text{ext}}$. In addition $\mathcal{O}_{\mathcal{S}\text{ext}}$ satisfies **Closure**.

2. for all sequences σ: $\mathfrak{Trans}^{\text{action}}(\mathcal{BS}, \sigma)$ is a feasible status set wrt. the set of code call conditions $\mathfrak{Trans}^{\text{state}}(\mathcal{BS}, \sigma)$ and $\mathcal{P}^a(\sigma)$, where $\mathbf{in}(\mathcal{P}^a(\sigma), a : action\_program(\sigma))$ is true in $\mathcal{O}_{\mathcal{S}\text{ext}}$.

Moreover, every feasible status set of $\mathfrak{Trans}(\mathcal{BP})$ for a state $\mathcal{O}_{\mathcal{S}\text{ext}}$ and $\mathcal{IC}^{\text{ext}}$ where $\mathcal{O}_{\mathcal{S}\text{ext}}$ satisfies **Closure** is obtained in that way.

Proof   We first show 1. and 2. Let $\mathcal{BS}$ be a feasible belief status set of agent a wrt. $\mathcal{BP}$, $\mathcal{O}_{\mathcal{S}\text{ext}}$, $\mathcal{IC}$ and $\mathcal{AC}$. $\mathfrak{Trans}^{\text{action}}(\mathcal{BS})$ is certainly a status set of $\mathfrak{Trans}(\mathcal{BP})$: it consists just of certain action status atoms for $\mathfrak{Trans}(\mathcal{BP})$. To check feasibility of this set, we have to check *(1) closure under program rules*, *(2) deontic and action consistency*, *(3) deontic and action closure* and *(4) state consistency*. But all these properties are immediate from the corresponding conditions for $\mathcal{BS}$ (see **S1** of Definition 6.5.5 on page 175 for *(1)*, Definition 6.5.2 on page 173 for *(2)*, Lemmas 6.5.3 on page 174 and 6.5.3 on page 174 for *(3)*, state consistency is analogously to *(4)* defined, and note that $\mathfrak{Trans}^{\text{action}}(\mathcal{BS}, \sigma)$ and $\mathfrak{Trans}^{\text{state}}(\mathcal{BS}, \sigma)$ correspond to $\Pi^{\text{action}}_\sigma(\mathcal{BS})$ and $\Pi^{\text{state}}_\sigma(\mathcal{BS}))$.

Why is $\mathcal{IC}^{\text{ext}}$ true and why does $\mathcal{O}_{\mathcal{S}\text{ext}}$ satisfy **Closure**? $\mathcal{IC}^{\text{ext}}$ follows by the *belief semantics compatibility* condition and **Closure** by the *belief table compatibility*.

The condition 2. is implied by *local coherence*.

Now we have to prove the converse, namely that every feasible status set of $\mathfrak{Trans}(\mathcal{BP})$ for a state $\mathcal{O}_{\mathcal{S}\text{ext}}$ and $\mathcal{IC}^{\text{ext}}$ where $\mathcal{O}_{\mathcal{S}\text{ext}}$ satisfies **Closure** is obtained in that way. Let S be such a feasible status set. Then we reconstruct $\mathcal{BS}^{\text{new}}$ using the code calls $a : bel\_ccc\_act([\rho])$.

Whenever $\mathcal{O}_{\mathcal{S}\text{ext}}$ satisfies a code call atom

in("χ", $\mathfrak{a}$: $bel\_ccc\_act([b, \rho])$)

where "χ" is a code call atom of the form "**in**(ϕ, : ())" or an action status atom, then we add $\mathcal{B}_{\mathfrak{a}}(b, \chi)$ to $\mathcal{BS}^{\text{new}}$. Whenever $\mathcal{O}_{\mathcal{S}\text{ext}}$ satisfies a code call atom

in("χ", $\mathfrak{a}$: $not\_bel\_ccc\_act([b, \rho])$)

where "χ" is a code call atom of the form "**in**(ϕ, : ())" or an action status atom, then we add $\neg\mathcal{B}_{\mathfrak{a}}(b, \chi)$ to $\mathcal{BS}^{\text{new}}$.

Note that because of the **Closure** condition, such code call atoms must hold and satisfy (if retransformed to belief formulae) the belief table compatibilty condition. By construction, $\mathcal{BS}^{\text{new}}$ is a status set and the feasibility is guaranteed by the feasiblity of S and the conditions we have just mentioned. ∎

COROLLARY 5 ($\mathfrak{Trans}(\mathcal{BP})$ IS INVARIANT UNDER RATIONAL AND REAS. SEMANTICS) If $\mathcal{BS}$ is a rational (resp. reasonable) belief status set of agent $\mathfrak{a}$ wrt. $\mathcal{BP}$, $\mathcal{O}_{\mathcal{S}\text{ext}}$, $\mathcal{IC}$ and $\mathcal{AC}$, then

1. $\mathfrak{Trans}^{\text{action}}(\mathcal{BS})$ is a *rational* (resp. *reasonable*) status set of $\mathfrak{Trans}(\mathcal{BP})$ wrt. $\mathcal{O}_{\mathcal{S}\text{ext}}$ satisfying **Closure** and wrt. $\mathcal{IC}^{\text{ext}}$,

2. for all sequences σ: $\mathfrak{Trans}^{\text{action}}(\mathcal{BS}, \sigma)$ is a rational (resp. reasonable) status set wrt. the set of code call conditions $\mathfrak{Trans}^{\text{state}}(\mathcal{BS}, \sigma)$ and $\mathcal{P}^{\mathfrak{a}}(\sigma)$, where **in**($\mathcal{P}^{\mathfrak{a}}(\sigma)$,)$\mathfrak{a}$: $action\_program(\sigma)$) is true in $\mathcal{O}_{\mathcal{S}\text{ext}}$.

Moreover, every *rational* (resp. *reasonable*) status set of $\mathfrak{Trans}(\mathcal{BP})$ for a state $\mathcal{O}_{\mathcal{S}\text{ext}}$ and $\mathcal{IC}^{\text{ext}}$ where $\mathcal{O}_{\mathcal{S}\text{ext}}$ satisfies **Closure** is obtained in that way.

Proof We distinguish between rational and reasonable status sets. As the latter are based on the former we first consider rational sets.

Rational: Using Theorem 7.4.1 on the preceding page, it only remains to prove that every $\mathcal{BS}$ which is locally coherent, compatible with **BT**$^{\mathfrak{a}}$ and with **BSemT**$^{\mathfrak{a}}$ satisfies:

$\mathcal{BS}$ is grounded wrt. $\mathcal{BP}$ *if and only if* $\mathfrak{Trans}(\mathcal{BS})$ is grounded wrt. $\mathfrak{Trans}(\mathcal{BP})$.

This equivalence is easily shown by comparing the operators given in Definition 7.3.11 on page 234 for programs with beliefs and Definition 6.5.4 on page 174 for programs without. Note that the transformation $\mathfrak{Trans}$ ensures that all belief literals of $\mathcal{BP}$ are transformed into extended code call conditions and these code call conditions are taken care of by our conditions (**Closure** and $\mathcal{IC}^{\text{ext}}$). A detailed inspection shows that every application of

$\mathbf{App}_{\mathcal{BP},\mathcal{O}_S}(\mathcal{BS})$ corresponds exactly to an application of $\mathbf{App}_{\mathfrak{Trans}(\mathcal{BP}),\mathcal{O}_{S\text{ext}}}(\mathfrak{Trans}(\mathcal{BS}))$ and thus the result follows.

Reasonable: Here we have to show that applying $\mathfrak{Trans}()$ is compatible with the reduction operation:

$$\mathfrak{Trans}(\text{red}^{\mathcal{BS}}(\mathcal{BP},\mathcal{O}_{S\text{ext}})) = \text{red}^{\mathfrak{Trans}(\mathcal{BS})}(\mathfrak{Trans}(\mathcal{BP}),\mathcal{O}_{S\text{ext}}).$$

The result then follows immediately by the definition of reasonable status sets, which are based on rational sets for positive programs. The problem is therefore reduced to the former case.

That the condition above holds follows immediately be the very definition of red. As we have a one-one correspondence between the body atoms of $\mathcal{BP}$ and those of $\mathfrak{Trans}(\mathcal{BP})$, a rule in $\mathcal{BP}$ is removed *if and only if* the corresponding rule in $\mathfrak{Trans}(\mathcal{BP})$ is removed. ∎

7.5 Related Work

In this chapter, we have provided a framework within which an agent may reason about the beliefs it has about other agents' states, beliefs and possible actions. Our framework builds upon classical logic programming results. As there has been considerable work on these areas, we try to relate our work with the most relevant of these works. We do not explicitly relate ordinary agent programs Eiter, Subrahmanian, and Rogers (1999) with other agent systems, as that has been done in great detail in Chapter 6 on page 141 and in Eiter, Subrahmanian, and Rogers (1999). Rather, we focus primarily on meta-reasoning capabilities of agents and compare maps with meta reasoning capabilities of other agent frameworks.

Kowalski and Sadri (1998) have developed an agent architecture that uses logical rules expressed in Horn clause-like syntax, to encode agent behavior—both rational and reactive. The reactive agent rules are of the form

$\alpha \leftarrow \text{condition}$

where α is an action, and the condition in the body of the rule is a logical condition. Rationality is captured through integrity constraints. In the current language of (Kowalski and Sadri 1998), there seems to be no obvious support for meta-reasoning, though no doubt it could be encoded in, via some use of the metalogical *demo* predicate (Kowalski 1995).

Schroeder, de Almeida Mora, and Pereira (1997) have shown how extended logic programming may be used to specify the behavior of a diagnostic agent. They propose an architecture that supports cooperation between multiple diagnostic agents. Issues of interest arise when conflicting diagnoses are hypothesized by different agents. Their architecture consists of a knowledge base implemented by an extended logic program (Alferes and Pereira 1996), and inference machine that embodies the *REVISE* algorithm (Damasio, Nejdl, and Pereira 1994) for eliminating contradictions, and a control layer. No meta-reasoning issues are brought up explicitly in this work.

Concurrently with our effort, Martelli, Mascardi, and Zini (1998, Martelli, Mascardi, and Zini (1997) have developed a logic programming based framework called CaseLP that may be used to implement multiagent applications by building on top of existing software. As in our work, agents have states, and states are changed by the agents' actions, and the behavior of an agent is encoded through rules. No meta-reasoning issues are brought up explicitly in this work.

Morgenstern (1990) was one of the first to propose a formal extension of auto-epistemic logic to deal with multiagent reasoning. She extended auto-epistemic logic (Moore 1985b) with belief modalities indexed by agent names. She proposed a concept of expansions for such theories.

The *Procedural Reasoning System* (*PRS*) is one of the best known multiagent construction system that implements BDI agents (BDI stands for "Belief, Desires, Intentionality") (d'Inverno, Kinny, Luck, and Wooldridge 1997). This framework has led to several interesting applications including a practical, deployed application called *OASIS* for air traffic control in Sydney, Australia. The theory of *PRS* is captured through a logic based development, in (Rao and Georgeff 1991).

Gmytrasiewicz and Durfee (1992) have developed a logic of knowledge and belief to model multiagent coordination. Their framework permits an agent to reason not only about the world and its own actions, but also to simulate and model the behavior of other agents in the environment. In a separate paper (Gmytrasiewicz, Durfee, and Wehe. 1991), they show how one agent can reason with a probabilistic view of the behavior of other agents so as to achieve coordination. This is good work.

There are some significant differences between our work and theirs. First, we focus on agents that are built on top of arbitrary data structures. Second, our agent meta-reasoning language is very general—an agent can decide, for instance, that it will reason only with level 1 nested beliefs—and hence, our framework allows different agents to pick the level of belief reasoning appropriate for them. Third, our action framework is very general as well, and meta-reasoning with *permitted*, *obligatory* and *forbidden* actions is novel. Fourth, our framework allows an agent to "plug in" different estimates of the semantics used by other agents.

Researchers in the distributed knowledge community have also conducted extensive research into how one agent reasons about its beliefs about other agents (and their beliefs). Fagin and Vardi (1986) present a multiagent modal logic where knowledge modalities are indexed by agent names. They provide a semantics for message passing in such an environment. However, their work is quite different from ours.

8 Temporal Agent Programs

In Chapter 6, we have described the important concept of an *agent program* and provided a set of semantics for agent programs based on the concept of a *status set* semantics. Once the designer of an agent has selected the type Sem of semantics he would like his agent to use, the agent continuously executes a cycle as shown in Figure 8.1 (cf. Algorithm 6.4.1):

However, the reader will notice that once an agent finishes computing a status set S, it *immediately* executes **conc**(*DoSet*) where *DoSet* is the set of all actions of the form $\{\alpha \mid \mathbf{Do}\,\alpha \in S\}$. This may not always be desirable—for instance, the agent may want to make commitments *now* to perform certain actions in the *future*.

The *syntax* of agent programs described in Chapter 6 suffers from three major shortcomings which we describe below, and these shortcomings also extend to the *semantics* of agent programs.

Temporal Extents of Actions: In practice, actions have a *temporal extent*. To see why actions may have temporal extents, consider the CHAIN and CFIT examples. In the CHAIN example, the truck agent may execute the *drive*(boston, chicago) action. Clearly, this action has a nontrivial temporal extent during which many other events can occur. Similarly, in the case of the autoPilot agent in the CFIT example, when the action *adjustAltitude* (35000) requires the plane to adjust its altitude to 35,000 feet, this action takes some time to perform.

Scheduling Actions: In addition, the designer of an agent may wish to schedule actions to be executed in the *future*. To see why, consider the STORE example. It may be a legal requirement that every time the credit agent provides a credit report on a customer, that customer must be notified within 10 days. Furthermore, all customers must receive annual reports from the credit agent about his/her credit summary for the year. These annual reports are required to be mailed by February 15 of every year.

Reasoning about the Past: Last, but not least, the designer of an agent may wish to take actions (or schedule actions) based on *what has happened in the past*. For example, the credit agent in the STORE example may execute the action *terminateCredit* for a customer who has not responded to three previous actions taken by the credit agent asking him to make an overdue payment.

In order to address these three problems, we will extend the notion of an agent program to that of a *temporal agent program* $\mathcal{TP}$ (tap for short). A tap allows the designer of an

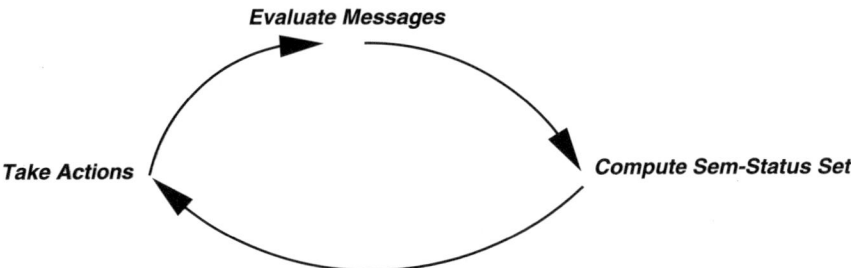

Figure 8.1
Cycle for Agent Reasoning.

agent to specify temporal aspects of actions and states. For simplicity, we assume in this chapter that time points are represented by non-negative integers and the time line extends infinitely far into the future.[1]

The organization of this chapter is as follows. In Section 8.1, we will describe the important concept of a *temporal action*. Then, in Section 8.2, we will define the syntax of taps. In Section 8.3, we will extend the notion of feasible status sets, rational status sets, and reasonable status sets introduced in Chapter 6, to taps. In Section 8.6 we provide an application of taps to handle strategic negotiations described in the literature. In Section 8.8, we will describe how taps are related to other existing formalisms for temporal agent reasoning.

Remark 4 Throughout this chapter, we will assume that the structure of time is modeled by the set of natural numbers $\mathbb{N}$. Every agent has an initial "start" time 0, which usually denotes the time of deployment of the agent. We assume a distinguished integer valued variable X_{now} which is instantiated to the current time (this can be done by adding the code call **in**(X_{now}, $agent : current\_time$())).

We also use t_{now} as a metavariable over time (natural numbers). The reader should note that although the concept of a temporal agent program does not depend on a particular time instance, the semantics of such a program, the temporal feasible status set, will be computed later **at a fixed instant of time**. We use t_{now} as an index for all concepts that depend on this particular time. This reflects the fact that the state of an agent, $\mathcal{O}$, is considered a snapshot at a particular time instance. The semantics of a program must change over time, because, as time goes by, the agent state changes and therefore rules of the program may apply later that did not before.

---

[1] The time unit depends on the specific application, e.g., minutes, hours, days, weeks, and we will not discuss it here.

There is a wide variety of literature, such as (Koubarakis 1994; Ladkin 1986; Ladkin 1987; Leban, McDonald, and Forster 1986; Niezette and Stevenne 1992) showing how time units (e.g., weeks, months, years, decades, etc.) may be represented and manipulated when the natural numbers are assumed to represent time. Hence, in this book, when we refer to a time point such as *Jan. 11, 1998*, we will assume the existence of a mapping from such a representation of time, to the natural numbers, and vice versa.

8.1 Actions with Temporal Duration

Recall, from Definition 6.2.1 of Chapter 6, that an action has five components. These components include the *name* of the action, the *schema* of the action, the *preconditions* required to execute the action, an *add-list* for the action, and *delete-list* for the action.

We would like to provide, in this chapter, an extension of this general definition, to handle the possibility that an action has a *duration* or *temporal extent*. Let us return to our initial example of the autoPilot, drawn from the CFIT example. Suppose the current altitude of the plane is 20,000 feet, the current velocity of the plane is 1000 feet per minute, and the plane executes the action *adjustAltitude*(35000) specifying that it is going to adjust the altitude to 35,000 feet starting now. If the airplane's climb angle is 5 degrees, then it is easy to see (by elementary geometry, see Figure 8.2) that in one minute, the plane will gain $1000 \sin(5)$ feet in height. Thus, if our lowest measure of temporal granularity is "minute" then the plane will reach the altitude of 35,000 feet in

$$\left\lceil \frac{35000 - 20000}{1000 \sin(5)} \right\rceil$$

minutes. In general, at the end of minute i, where

$$0 \leq i \leq \left\lceil \frac{35000 - 20000}{1000 \sin(5)} \right\rceil$$

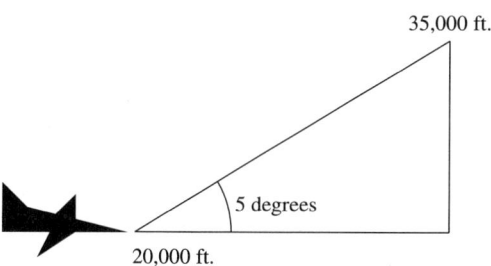

Figure 8.2
autoPilot's "Climb" Action.

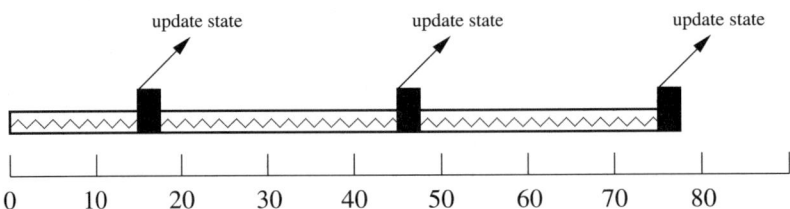

Figure 8.3
Checkpoints of an Action.

the altitude of the plane will be given by the formula

$20000 + (1000 \sin(5) \times i)$.

While this reasoning is trivial from a geometric point of view, it does provide some important guidance on what a definition of a timed-action must look like.

1. First, the definition of a timed action must specify the total amount of time it takes for the action to be "completed."

2. Second, the definition of a timed action must specify exactly how the state of the agent changes *while* the action is being executed. Most traditional AI planning frameworks (Nilsson 1980) assume that an action's effects are realized only *after* the entire action is successfully executed.

A further complication arises when we consider the truck agent in the CHAIN example, when the truck agent is executing the action *drive*(boston, chicago, i90). Unlike the case of the autoPilot agent, there may be no easy "formula" that allows us to specify where the truck is at a given instant of time, and furthermore, there *may* be no need to know that the truck has moved one mile further west along Interstate I-90 since the last report. The designer of the truck agent may be satisfied with knowing the location of the truck every 30 minutes.

Thus, the notion of a *timed action* should allow the designer of an agent to specify the preconditions of an action, as well as *intermediate effects* that the action has prior to completion. Thus, a *timed action* should have some *checkpoints* and intermediate effects could be incorporated within the agent state at these *checkpoints*. For example, Figure 8.3 shows a simple case where an action has a duration of 75 units of time and the action starts being taken at time 0. The action causes the state of the world to continuously change during this time interval. However, the designer of the agent executing this action has specified (using the mechanism described below) that the effects of this action need to be incorporated as updates to the state at times 15, 45 and 75.

8.1.1 Checkpoints

It is important to note that it is the *agent designer's responsibility* to specify checkpoints in a manner that satisfies his application's needs. If he needs to incorporate intermediate effects on a millisecond by millisecond basis, his checkpoints should be spaced out at each millisecond (assuming the time unit is not larger than a millisecond). If on the other hand, the designer of the truck agent feels that checkpoints are needed on an hourly basis (assuming the time unit of the time line is not larger than an hour), then he has implicitly decided that incorporating the effects of the *drive* action on an hourly basis is good enough for his application—thus, the decision of what checkpoints to use is entirely made on an application by application basis, and we would like our definition of a timed action to support such checkpoint articulation by an agent designer.

In addition, an agent designer may specify checkpoints by referring to *absolute* time, or he may specify checkpoints by referring to *relative* time. For example, in the STORE example, an absolute checkpoint may say that the action *check_credit* must be executed at 3 am every morning. This is an absolute checkpoint. In contrast, an agent designer associated with the *climb* action of a plane may specify a *relative* checkpoint, requiring that the height of the plane be updated every 30 seconds after it has started to climb.

DEFINITION 8.1.1 (CHECKPOINT EXPRESSIONS rel: $\{X \mid \chi\}$, abs: $\{X \mid \chi\}$) A *checkpoint expression* is defined as follows:

- If $i \in \mathbb{N}$ is a positive integer, then rel: $\{i\}$ and abs: $\{i\}$ are checkpoint expressions.
- If χ is a code call condition involving a non-negative, integer-valued variable X, then rel: $\{X \mid \chi\}$ and abs: $\{X \mid \chi\}$ are *checkpoint expressions*.

We distinguish between checkpoint expressions and actual checkpoints: the latter are time points specified by checkpoint expressions (see below).

We will also use $\{chk\}$ as a metavariable for arbitrary checkpoint expressions, both relative and absolute ones.

A designer of an agent can use absolute time points and relative time points to specify the checkpoints. abs: $\{i\}$ and abs: $\{X \mid \chi\}$ specify *absolute* time points. Intuitively, when we associate the checkpoint expression abs: $\{X \mid \chi\}$ with an action α, then this says that *every* member of the set

$\{X\theta \mid \theta$ is a solution of χ w.r.t. the current object state $\mathcal{O}_S\}$

is a checkpoint for α. When we associate abs: $\{i\}$ with an action then this says that i itself (viewed as an absolute time point) is a checkpoint.

Alternatively, associating the checkpoint expression rel: $\{i\}$ with action α says that checkpointing must be done every i units of time *from the start time of* α. If rel: $\{X \mid \chi\}$ is associated with an action, then this says that for *every* member d of the set

$\{X\theta \mid \theta \text{ is a solution of } \chi \text{ w.r.t. the current object state } \mathcal{O}_S\}$

checkpointing must be done every d units of time *from the start time of α on*. The following are simple checkpoint expressions.

- rel:{100}.

This says that a checkpoint occurs at the time of the start of the action, 100 units later, 200 units later, and so on.

- abs:{T | **in**(T, clock:*time*()) & **in**(0, math:*remainder*(T, 100)) & T > 5000}.

This says that a checkpoint occurs at absolute times 5000, 5100, 5200, and so on.

Note that by this definition, checkpoints associated with an action α that are just integers with a prefix "rel" denote *relative* times but not absolute time points. So we have to distinguish between the time point "100" (which can occur in a nontrivial checkpoint expression) and the relative time "100" denoting a sequence of time points of the form

$t^\alpha_{\text{start}}, \; t^\alpha_{\text{start}} + 100, \; t^\alpha_{\text{start}} + 200, \ldots$

where t^α_{start} is the starting time of performing α.

Example 8.1.1 The following are some example checkpoint expressions from our STORE, CFIT, and CHAIN examples;

- The autoPilot agent in the CFIT example may use the following checkpoint expression; rel:{30}, to create checkpoints every 30 seconds.
- The credit agent of the STORE example may use the following checkpoint expression:

abs:{ X_{now} | **in**(X_{now}, clock:*time*()) & **in**(Overdue, credit:*checkCredit*(Ssn, Name))&
  > (Overdue, 0)   & **in**(0, math:*remainder*(X_{now}, 10))
}.

This checkpoint expression tells that checkpoints occur at the time X_{now} when there is a customer with an overdue payment credit.

- The truck agent in the CHAIN example may use the checkpoint expression rel:{60}, to create checkpoints every hour, assuming that the time unit is a minute.

8.1.2 Timed Actions

DEFINITION 8.1.2 (TIMED EFFECT TRIPLE $\langle\{chk\}, Add, Del\rangle$)   A *timed effect triple* is a triple of the form $\langle\{chk\}, Add, Del\rangle$ where $\{chk\}$ is a checkpoint expression, and *Add* and *Del* are add lists and delete lists.

Intuitively, when we associate a triple of the form $\langle \{chk\}, Add, Del \rangle$ with an action α, we are effectively saying that the contents of the *Add-* and *Del-* lists are used to update the state of the agent at every time point specified in $\{chk\}$.

A couple of simple timed effect triples are shown below.

- $\langle \text{rel}: \{100\}, Add_1, Del_1 \rangle$ where Add_1 and Del_1 are add and delete lists. This timed effect triples says that every 100 units of time, the state should be updated by incorporating the code calls in Add_1 and Del_1.

- $\langle \text{abs}: \{X_{now} \mid \textbf{in}(X_{now}, \text{clock}: time()) \,\&\, \textbf{in}(0, \text{math}: rem.(X_{now}, 100)) \,\&\, X_{now} > 5000\},$ $Add_2, Del_2 \rangle$ says that at times 5000, 5100, 5200, and so on, the state should be updated by incorporating the code calls in Add_2 and Del_2.

Example 8.1.2 (Timed Effect Triples) The following are some example timed effect triples associated with our **STORE**, **CFIT**, and **CHAIN** examples;

- The autoPilot agent may employ the following timed effect triple to update the altitude of the plane every 30 seconds;

1st arg: rel : $\{30\}$
2nd arg: $\{\textbf{in}(\texttt{NewAltitude}, \text{plane}: altitude(X_{now}))\}$
3rd arg: $\{\textbf{in}(\texttt{OldAltitude}, \text{plane}: altitude(X_{now} - 30))\}$

- The credit agent may use the following timed effect triple to notify a customer whose credit has an overdue payment every 10 days;

1st arg: rel : $\{X_{now} \mid \textbf{in}(X_{now}, \text{clock}: time()) \,\&\,$
$\qquad\qquad\quad \textbf{in}(\texttt{Overdue}, \text{credit}: checkCredit(\texttt{Ssn}, \texttt{Name})) \&$
$\qquad\qquad\quad > (\texttt{Overdue}, 0) \,\&\, \textbf{in}(0, \text{math}: remainder(X_{now}, 10))$
$\qquad\qquad\}$

2nd arg: $\{\textbf{in}(\langle \texttt{Name}, \texttt{Ssn}, X_{now} \rangle, \text{credit}: customer\_to\_be\_notified()) \&$
$\qquad\quad\;\textbf{in}(X_{now}, \text{clock}: time())$
$\qquad\quad\;\}$

3rd arg: $\{\}$

The truck agent may employ the following timed effect triple to update its current location every hour, assuming that the time unit is a minute;

1st arg: rel: $\{60\}$
2nd arg: $\{\textbf{in}(\texttt{NewPosition}, \text{truck}: location(X_{now}))\}$
3rd arg: $\{\textbf{in}(\texttt{OldPosition}, \text{truck}: location(X_{now} - 60))\}$

We are now ready to define the concept of a timed action—an action whose effects are incorporated into a state at the checkpoints specified by the designer of the agent.

DEFINITION 8.1.3 (TIMED ACTION)   A *timed action* α consists of five components:

Name: A name, usually written $\alpha(X_1, \ldots, X_n)$, where the X_i's are root variables.

Schema: A schema, usually written as $(\tau_1, \ldots, \tau_n)$, of types. Intuitively, this says that the variable X_i must be of type τ_i, for all $1 \leq i \leq n$.

Pre: A code-call condition χ, called the *precondition* of the action, denoted by $Pre(\alpha)$ ($Pre(\alpha)$ must be *safe modulo the variables* $X_1, \ldots, X_n$);

Dur: A checkpoint expression $\{chk\}$. Depending on the current object state, this expression determines a *duration* duration$(\alpha) \in \mathbb{N}$ of α. duration(α) is not used as an absolute time point but as a duration (length of a time interval).

Tet: A set **Tet**(α) of timed effect triples such that if $\langle\{chk\}, Add, Del\rangle$ and $\langle\{chk\}', Add', Del'\rangle$ are in **Tet**(α), then $\{chk\}$ and $\{chk\}'$ have no common solution w.r.t. any object state. The set **Tet**(α) together with **Dur**(α) determines the set of checkpoints checkpoints(α) for action α (as defined below).

Intuitively, if α is an action that we start executing at t^α_{start}, then **Dur**(α) specifies how to compute the duration duration(α) of α, and **Tet**(α) specifies how to compute all the checkpoints associated with action α. It is important to note that **Dur**(α) and **Tet**(α) may not specify the duration and checkpoint times explicitly (even if the associated checkpoints are of the form abs : $\{X \mid \chi\}$, i.e., absolute times). These are computed as follows:

- If **Dur**(α) is of the form rel: $\{i\}$, then the duration duration(α) of execution is i. If **Dur**(α) is of the form abs: $\{X \mid \chi\}$ or rel: $\{X \mid \chi\}$, it is possible that χ may have many solutions, with different solutions assigning different values to X. In this case, the duration of execution of an action is given by

$$\text{duration}(\alpha) = \min \left\{ \left\|X\theta - t^\alpha_{\text{start}}\right\| \;\middle|\; \theta \text{ is a solution of } \chi \text{ w.r.t. } \mathcal{O}_S \text{ at time } t^\alpha_{\text{start}} \right.$$
$$\left. \text{and } X\theta \gneq t^\alpha_{\text{start}} \right\}.$$

Intuitively, the above definition says that we find solutions to χ which are greater to t^α_{start}. Of such solutions, we pick the smallest—the duration of α is from α's start time, to the time point chosen in this way.

- Once the duration duration(α) of the execution is fixed, the set of checkpoints checkpoints(α) is the union of the following sets

$$\{X\theta \mid \langle \text{abs}:\{X \mid \chi\}, Add, Del\rangle \in \textbf{Tet}(\alpha) \text{ and } \theta \text{ is a solution of } \chi, X\theta > t^\alpha_{\text{start}}$$
$$\text{and } \|X\theta - t^\alpha_{\text{start}}\| \leq \text{duration}(\alpha)\}$$

and

$$\{i \mid \langle \text{abs}:\{i\}, Add, Del\rangle \in \textbf{Tet}(\alpha), i > t^\alpha_{\text{start}} \text{ and } \|i - t^\alpha_{\text{start}}\| \leq \text{duration}(\alpha)\}$$

and

$$\{t^\alpha_{\text{start}} + i \times j \mid \langle \text{rel}:\{i\}, Add, Del\rangle \in \textbf{Tet}(\alpha) \text{ and } i, j \in \mathbb{N}, i, j > 0$$
$$\text{with } t^\alpha_{\text{start}} + i \times j \leq \text{duration}(\alpha)\}$$

and

$$\{t^\alpha_{\text{start}} + i \times X\theta \mid \langle \text{rel}:\{X \mid \chi\}, Add, Del\rangle \in \textbf{Tet}(\alpha) \text{ and } \theta \text{ is a solution of } \chi$$
$$\text{and } i > 0 \text{ is an integer and } \|t^\alpha_{\text{start}} + i \times X\theta\| \leq \text{duration}(\alpha)\}.$$

In other words, even though **Tet**(α) may imply the existence of infinitely many checkpoints, only those that occur at or before the end of the scheduled completion of execution of the action α are considered to be valid checkpoints.

Let us return to the sample scenario of an aircraft climbing from 20,000 feet to 35,000 feet at a climb angle of 5 degrees and a speed of 1000 feet per minute. In this case, the corresponding action *climb*(CurHt, ToHt, Angle, Speed) may be described via the following components:

Name: *climb*(CurHt, ToHt, Angle, Speed)

Schema: (Integer, Integer, Angle, Integer)

Pre: **in**(CurHt, $plane:altitude(X_{\text{now}})$)

Dur: rel:$\{X \mid \textbf{in}(X, math:compute(\frac{\text{ToHt}-\text{CurHt}}{\text{Speed}\times\sin(\text{Angle})}))\}$

Tet: $\{\langle\text{rel}:\{4\}, Add, Del\rangle\}$ where:

– *Del*: **in**(Y, $plane:altitude(X_{\text{now}} - 4)$)

– *Add*: **in**(X, $plane:altitude(X_{\text{now}})$)

The **Tet** part says that we update the altitude of the plane every 4 units of time until it will reach its top height, i.e., during $\frac{\text{ToHt}-\text{CurHt}}{\text{Speed}\times\sin(\text{Angle})}$ minutes from the time it had started climbing.

We now present some examples of timed actions used by agents in our STORE, CFIT, and CHAIN examples.

Example 8.1.3 (STORE Revisited) The action *monitorCredit*(Ssn, Name) of the credit agent may be described as follows;

- **Name:** *monitorCredit*(Ssn, Name)
- **Schema:** (String, String)
- **Pre: in**(overdue, credit : *checkCredit*(Ssn, Name)) & > (Overdue, 0)
- **Dur:** rel : {30}
- **Tet:**

1st arg: rel : $\{X_{now} \mid $ **in**$(X_{now},$ clock : *time*()) &
$\qquad\qquad\qquad$ **in**(Overdue, credit : *checkCredit*(Ssn, Name))&
$\qquad\qquad\qquad$ > (Overdue, 0) & **in**(0, math : *remainder*(X_{now}, 10))
$\qquad\qquad$ }

2nd arg: $\qquad$ {**in**($\langle$Name, Ssn, $X_{now}\rangle$, credit : *customer_to_be_notified*())&
$\qquad\qquad\qquad$ **in**(X_{now}, clock : *time*())}
$\qquad\qquad$ }

3rd arg: $\qquad$ {}

Whenever there is a customer with an overdue payment, the credit agent executes the *monitorCredit* timed action. The *monitorCredit* is executed for 30 days, and a notification is sent to the customer every 10 days.

Example 8.1.4 (CHAIN Revisited) The action *drive*(FromCity, ToCity) of the truck agent may be described with the following components;

- **Name:** *drive*(FromCity, ToCity)
- **Schema:** (String, String)
- **Pre:**
- **Dur:** rel : {72}
- **Tet:**

1st arg: rel : {2}
2nd arg: {**in**(NewPosition, truck : *location*(X_{now}))}
3rd arg: {**in**(OldPosition, truck : *location*($X_{now} - 2$))}

The truck agent executes the *drive* timed action for 72 hours, and its location is updated every two hours.

8.2 Syntax of Taps

In this section, we develop the formal syntax of taps, and explain their semantics *informally*. Section 8.3 will describe the semantics of taps formally. We first define the notion of a *temporal annotation*.

DEFINITION 8.2.1 (TEMPORAL ANNOTATIONS $[tai_1, tai_2]$) We first define *temporal annotation items* tai.

1. Every integer is a temporal annotation item.
2. The distinguished integer valued variable X_{now} is a temporal annotation item.
3. Every integer valued variable is a temporal annotation item.
4. If $tai_1, \ldots, tai_n$ are temporal annotation items, and $b_1, \ldots, b_n$ are integers (positive or negative), then $(b_1 tai_1 + \cdots + b_n tai_n)$ is a temporal annotation item.

We are now ready to define the notion of a *temporal annotation*.

- If tai_1, tai_2 are annotation items, then $[tai_1, tai_2]$ is a temporal annotation.

Intuitively, a temporal annotation whose variables are instantiated defines a set of time points. For example:

- $[2, 5]$ is a temporal annotation item describing the set of time points between 2 and 5 (inclusive).
- $[2, 3X + 4Y]$ is a temporal annotation item. When $X := 2, Y := 3$, this defines the set of time points between 2 and 18.
- $[X + Y, X + 4y]$ is a temporal annotation item. When $X := 2, Y := 3$, this defines the set of time points between 5 and 18.
- $[X + 4Y, X - Y]$ is a temporal annotation item. When $X := 2, Y := 3$, this defines the empty set of time points.
- $[X_{now}, X_{now} + 5]$ is a temporal annotation item. When $X_{now} := 10$, this specifies the set of time points between 10 and 15.
- $[X_{now} - 5, X_{now} + 5]$ is a temporal annotation item. When $X_{now} := 10$, this specifies the set of time points between 5 and 15; when $X_{now} := 3$ this specifies the set of time points between 0 and 8.

8.2.1 Temporal Action State Conjuncts

Next, we define the concept of an *action state condition* that looks exactly like the body of a rule in an (ordinary) agent program. This is a simple piece of syntax that serves as an intermediate semantical construct.

DEFINITION 8.2.2 (ACTION STATE CONDITION) If χ is a code call condition, and $L_1, \ldots, L_n$ are action status atoms (see Definition 6.4.1 on page 160), then $(\chi \ \& \ L_1 \ \& \ \ldots \ \& \ L_n)$ is called an *action state condition*. Note that according to this definition, negated action status atoms do not occur in an action state condition.

In order to say that an action state condition is true now, we define a *temporal action state conjunct* below.

DEFINITION 8.2.3 (TEMPORAL ACTION STATE CONJUNCT) If ρ is an action state condition, and ta is a temporal annotation, then ρ : ta is called a *temporal action state conjunct*. We also denote it by tasc.

Intuitively, when ρ : ta is ground, we may read this as "ρ is true at some point in ta". For example, the following are simple tascs.

- **in**(X, supplier : *select*('*uncommitted*', id, =, part_10)) & X.amount > 500 : [5, 9].
Intuitively, this tasc is true if at some point in time t_i between times 5 and 9 (inclusive), it is the case that the supplier had over 500 pieces of part_10 available.

- **in**(X, supplier : *select*('*uncommitted*', id, =, part_10)) & X.amount > 500 : [X_{now} − 10, X_{now}].
Intuitively, this tasc is true if at some point in time t_i in the last 10 time units, the supplier in question had over 500 pieces of part_10 available.

- **in**(X, supplier : *select*('*uncommitted*', id, =, part_10)) & X.amount > 500 &
  Do *shipped*(["xyz-corp.", part_10, Amount) & Amount > 100 : [X_{now} − 10, X_{now}].
Intuitively, this tasc is true if at some point in time t_i in the last 10 time units, the supplier in question had over 500 pieces of part_10 available and over 100 items were shipped by the supplier to "xyz-corp." at time t_i.

Examples of tascs associated with the STORE and CFIT examples are given below.

*Example 8.2.1 (*STORE *Revisited)* Here are some example tascs associated with the STORE example;

- **not_in**(spender(low), profiling : *classifyUser*(Ssn)) : [X_{now} − 15, X_{now}]
This tasc is true if it is the case that the user, whose social security number is Ssn, has not been classified as a *low* spender at some time point t_i in the last 15 days, assuming that the time unit is a day.

- **in**(spender(high), profiling : *classifyUser*(Ssn)) : [9, 29]

This tasc is true if at some point t_i between times 9 and 29 (inclusive), it is the case that the profiling agent has classified the user, whose social security number is Ssn, as a "high" spender.

Example 8.2.2 (CFIT Revisited) The following are some example tascs associated with the CFIT example;

- **in**(Y, gps : *mergeGPSData*(X1, X2)) & **in**(X, gps : *mergeGPSData*(Y, X3)) : [6, 10]

This tasc is true if the gps agent has received GPS data from satellites X1, X2 and X3 and merged these data into one coherent satellite report X at some point t_i between times 6 and 10.

- **in**(X, satellite1 : *broadcastGPSData*()) : [X$_{now}$ − 5, X$_{now}$]

This tasc is true if at some time point t_i in the last 5 seconds, it is the case that satellite1 agent has broadcasted GPS data report X.

8.2.2 Definition of Temporal Agent Programs

DEFINITION 8.2.4 (TEMPORAL AGENT RULE/PROGRAM $\mathcal{TP}$) A *temporal agent rule* is an expression of the form:

$$\text{Op}\,\alpha : [\text{tai}_1, \text{tai}_2] \leftarrow \rho_1 : \text{ta}_1 \,\&\, \cdots \,\&\, \rho_n : \text{ta}_n \qquad (8.1)$$

where Op $\in$ {**P**, **Do**, **F**, **O**, **W**}, and ρ_1 : ta$_1$, ..., ρ_n : ta$_n$ are tascs.

A *temporal agent program* is a finite set of temporal agent rules.

As in Prolog, throughout this chapter, we will often replace the "&" sign by a ",". Intuitively, a temporal agent rule of the form shown in (8.1) above, when ground, may be interpreted as:
Intuitive Reading of Temporal Agent Rule (First Cut)
"If ρ_1 was true at some time point in the interval ta$_1$ *and ... and ρ_n was true at some time point in the interval* ta$_n$, *then* Op α *should be true at some time point in the interval* [tai$_1$, tai$_2$]*".*

The formal interpretation is somewhat more involved—we will present below a few simple example taps, and then provide a more precise reading of the above rule.

For example, consider the simple rule used by the autoPilot agent in the CFIT example. This agent may be required to execute a climb action within 3 units of time of receiving a message instructing it to climb. This can be encoded by the following simple temporal agent rule.

Do *climb*CurHt, ToHt, Angle, Speed : [X$_{now}$, X$_{now}$ + 3] ← body where body denotes

in(M, msgbox : *all*()) & = (M.body.call, "*climb*(CurHt, ToHt, Angle, Speed)" : [X $_{now}$, X $_{now}$].

Examples of detailed taps associated with the STORE, CFIT, and CHAIN examples are shown below.

Example 8.2.3 (CFIT Revisited) The autoPilot agent may employ the following temporal agent program;

r1: **F***maintain_course*(No_go, Flight_route, Current_location) : [X $_{now}$, X $_{now}$] ←
    Do *adjust_course*(No_go, Flight_route, Current_location) : [X $_{now}$, X $_{now}$]

If the autoPilot agent decides to adjust_course, it is no longer allowed to perform the maintain_course action.

r2: **O***return_control*() : [X $_{now}$, X $_{now}$ + 10] ←
    in(manual_override, autoPilot : *pilotStatus*(Pilot_message)) : [X $_{now}$, X $_{now}$]

If the pilot wants to disengage the auto-pilot, manual control should be returned within the next 10 seconds, assuming that the unit of time is a second.

r3: **Do** *climb*(CurHt, ToHt, Angle, Speed) : [X $_{now}$, X $_{now}$ + 15] ←
    O*process_request*(Msg.Id, Agent),
    = (Msg.body.call, "*climb*(CurHt, ToHt, Angle, Speed)" : [X $_{now}$, X $_{now}$]

If the autoPilot agent receives a message instructing it to climb, it executes the climb action within the next 15 second.

r4: **P***compute_currentLocation*(Report) : [X $_{now}$, X $_{now}$ + 5] ←
    Do *adjust_course*(No_go, Flight_route, Current_location) : [X $_{now}$, X $_{now}$]

If the autoPilot agent decides to execute the *adjust_course* action, it may invoke the action *compute_currentLocation* within the next 5 seconds to update its estimate for Current_location.

r5: **O***create_flight_plan*(No_go, Flight_route, Current_location) : [X $_{now}$, X $_{now}$ + 3] ←
    O*process_request*(Msg.Id, Agent), = (Agent, terrain),
    in(No_go, msgbox : *getVar*(Msg.Id, "No_go")),
    Do *adjust_course*(No_go, Flight_route, Current_location) : [X $_{now}$, X $_{now}$]

If the autoPilot agent receives the No_go areas from the terrain agent and decides to adjust_course, then it must create a flight plan avoiding No_go regions in 3 seconds.

Section 8.2   Syntax of Taps

r6: **O***execute_flight_plan*(Flight_route):[$X_{now}, X_{now} + 20$] ←
  Do *adjust_course*(No_go, Flight_route, Current_location):[X_{now}, X_{now}]

When the autoPilot agent generates a new Flight_route, it is obliged to execute the flight plan for 20 seconds.

Example 8.2.4 (STORE Revisited) The credit agent may use the following temporal agent program.

r1: **Do** *notifyCustomer*(Ssn, Name):[X_{now}, X_{now}] ←
  in(Overdue, credit:*checkCredit*(Ssn, Name)), > (Overdue, 0),
  in(T, clock:*time*()), **in**(0, math:*remainder*(T, 15)):[X_{now}, X_{now}]

The credit agent sends a notice every 15 days to a customer who has an overdue payment until he pays his bill (i.e., Overdue = 0).

r2: **O***notifyCustomer*(Ssn, Name):[$X_{now}, X_{now} + 10$] ←
  Do *provideCreditReport*(Ssn, Name):[X_{now}, X_{now}]

Every time the credit agent provides a credit report of a customer, it is required to notify the customer within 10 days.

r3: **O***checkCredit*(all):[X_{now}, X_{now}] ←
  in(T, clock:*time*()), = (T, "12am"):[X_{now}, X_{now}]

The credit agent is obliged to check all credit files at 12 am every day.

r4: **O***provideCreditInfo*(Ssn, Name):[$X_{now}, X_{now} + 1$] ←
  Do *process_request*(*Msg.Id*, Agent), = (Agent, profiling),
  = (Msg.body.call, "*provideCreditInfo*(Ssn, Name)"):[X_{now}, X_{now}]

The credit agent has to process the profiling agent's credit information request within a day.

Example 8.2.5 (CHAIN Revisited) The supplier agent may use the following temporal agent program;

r1: **O***order_part*(Part_id, Amount_to_order):[$X_{now}, X_{now} + 5$] ←
  O*process_request*(*Msg.Id*, Agent),
  in(Part_id, msgbox:*getVar*(Msg.Id, "Part_id")),
  in(supplies_too_low, supplier:*too_low_threshold*(Part_id)),
  in(amount_not_avail, supplier:*monitorStock*(supplies_too_low, Part_id)):[X_{now}, X_{now}]

If our supply for Part_id falls below the supplies_too_low threshold, then we are obliged to order amount_to_order more units for this part. Note that amount_to_order and supplies_too_low represent integer constants, and amount_not_available is status string constant.

r2:   **O**request(plant, find : *supplier*):[X$_{now}$, X$_{now}$ + 2]   ←
   Oprocess_request(*Msg.Id*, Agent),
   in(Amount_requested, msgbox : *getVar*(Msg.Id, "Amount_requested")),
   in(Part_id, msgbox : *getVar*(Msg.Id, "Part_id")),
   Do *order_part*(Part_id, Amount_requested):[X$_{now}$, X$_{now}$]

If we decide to order Amount_requested units of part Part_id now, we need to use the plant agent's find:*supplier* service within the next 2 hours to determine if there is a supplier which can provide Amount_requested units of Part_id.

r3:   **O**request(shipping, prepare : *schedule(shipping)*):[X$_{now}$, X$_{now}$ + 10]   ←
   Oprocess_request(*Msg.Id*, Agent),
   Oprocess_request(*Msg.Id1*, Agent1), = (Agent1, plant),
   in(Amount_requested, msgbox : *getVar*(Msg.Id, "Amount_requested")),
   in(Part_id, msgbox : *getVar*(Msg.Id, "Part_id")),
   in(Part_supplier, msgbox : *getVar*(Msg.Id1, "Part_supplier")),
   Do *order_part*(Part_id, Amount_requested):[X$_{now}$, X$_{now}$]

If we decide to order Amount_requested units of part Part_id, we must also use the shipping agent's prepare:*schedule(shipping)* service within the next 10 hours.

r4:   **O***delete_msg*(*Msg.Id*):[X$_{now}$, X$_{now}$]   ←
   Do *process_request*(*Msg.Id*, Agent):[X$_{now}$, X$_{now}$].

This rule says that the agent immediately deletes all messages that it has processed from its message box.

The intuitive reading of the rule (8.1) is not precisely correct, and the reason for this is that it is possible for the body of a temporal agent rule to become true *now*, but which was not true before. Thus, we may be obliged by such a rule to do something in the past—something that is clearly infeasible. The following example rule says that if today's paper shows the price of *IBM* stock to be over 400, then we are obliged to sell it yesterday.

Do *sell_stock*(ibm):[X$_{now}$ − 1, X$_{now}$ − 1] ← **in**(X, stock : *quote*(ibm)) & X ≥ 400:[X$_{now}$, X$_{now}$].

Suppose the price of *IBM* stock yesterday was 390, but today it is 410, and we are reasoning temporally at the level of days. Then this rule did not have a true precondition yesterday, and hence there was no need to sell *IBM* stock. However, the body of this rule is true today, and the rule says that we should sell the *IBM* stock yesterday—something that is clearly impossible to do now!

Section 8.3   Semantics of Taps

In addition, in order to take actions based on temporal data, past states of the world, as well as an archive of past actions need to be maintained. The informal interpretation of a rule therefore needs to refer to a history of the past. We may now re-interpret the temporal agent rule

$$\mathsf{Op}\,\alpha : [\mathsf{tai}_1, \mathsf{tai}_2] \leftarrow \rho_1 : \mathsf{ta}_1 \,\&\, \ldots \,\&\, \rho_n : \mathsf{ta}_n$$

as follows:

Intuitive Reading of Temporal Agent Rule (Second Cut)
"If for all $1 \leq i \leq n$, there exists a time point t_i such that ρ_i is true at time t_i and such that $t_i \leq \mathsf{t}_{\mathsf{now}}$ (i.e., t_i is now or is in the past) and $t_i \in \mathsf{ta}_i$ (i.e., t_i is true at one of the designated time points), then $\mathsf{Op}\,\alpha$ is true at some point $t \geq \mathsf{t}_{\mathsf{now}}$ (i.e., now or in the future) such that $\mathsf{tai}_1 \leq t \leq \mathsf{tai}_2$."

In other words, the antecedent of a rule always refers to *past or current states of the world, and past action status atoms*, and the obligations, permissions, forbidden actions that are implied by rules apply to the *future*. Note that this framework is completely compatible with basing actions on *predictions* about the future, because such predictions are made *now* and hence are statements about the future in the current state!

In the next section, we will give a formal semantics for taps, which extends the semantics of agent programs.

8.3   Semantics of Taps

In this section, we provide a formal semantics for taps—we have already explained their informal semantics in the last section.

Recall our assumption that time points are represented by the natural numbers. In classical temporal logics, a temporal interpretation associates a set of ground atoms with each time point. In our framework, things are somewhat more complex. This is because at any given point t in time, certain things are true in an agent's state, and certain action status atoms are true as well. Thus, we will introduce *two* temporal structures:

1. a *temporal status set*, which captures actions, and
2. a *history*.

Figure 8.4 illustrates this concept.

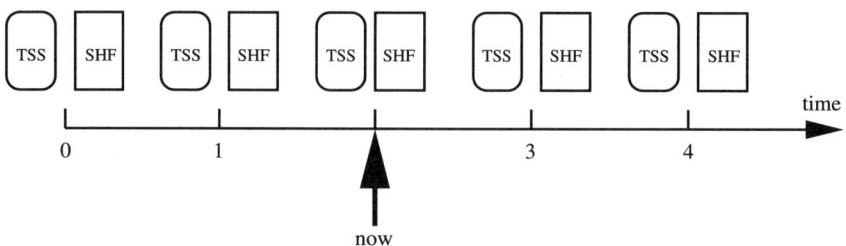

Figure 8.4
Temporal Status Set and State History Function (SHF) Over Time.

8.3.1 Temporal Status Set

DEFINITION 8.3.1 (TEMPORAL STATUS SET $TS_{t_{now}}$) A temporal status set $TS_{t_{now}}$ at time t_{now} is a mapping from natural numbers to ordinary status sets:

$$TS_{t_{now}} : \mathbb{N} \longrightarrow \{S \mid S \text{ is a status set}\}.$$

Intuitively, if $TS_{t_{now}}(3) = \{\mathbf{O}\alpha, \mathbf{Do}\,\alpha, \mathbf{P}\alpha, \mathbf{F}\beta\}$, then this means that according to the temporal status set $TS_{t_{now}}$, at time instant 3, α is obligatory/done/permitted, while β is forbidden. Similarly, if $TS_{t_{now}}(4) = \{\mathbf{P}\alpha\}$ then this means that according to the temporal status set $TS_{t_{now}}$, at time 4, α is permitted.

DEFINITION 8.3.2 (STATE HISTORY FUNCTION $\text{hist}_{t_{now}}$) A *state history function* $\text{hist}_{t_{now}}$ at a time t_{now} is a partial function from $\mathbb{N}$ to agent states

$$\text{hist}_{t_{now}} : \mathbb{N} \longrightarrow \{\mathcal{O}_S \mid \mathcal{O}_S \text{ is an agent state}\}$$

such that $\text{hist}_{t_{now}}(t_{now})$ is always defined, and for all $i > t_{now}$, $\text{hist}_{t_{now}}(i)$ is undefined.

Notice that the definition of state history does not *require* that an agent stores the entire past. For many agent applications, storing the entire past may be neither necessary nor desirable. The definition of state history function above merely requires that the agent stores the agent state of the current time. In addition, the agent cannot store its state in the future. Even though an agent can *schedule* actions in the future, and even though an agent can have *beliefs about the future*, it cannot be sure about what its state will be in the future. Thus, the designer of an agent may make decisions such as those given below:

1. He may decide to store no past information at all. In this case, $\text{hist}_{t_{now}}(i)$ is defined *if and only if $i = t_{now}$*.

Section 8.3   Semantics of Taps

2. He may decide to store information only about the past i units of time. This means that he stores the agent's state at times $t_{now}, (t_{now} - 1), \ldots, (t_{now} - i)$, i.e., $\text{hist}_{t_{now}}$ is defined for the following arguments: $\text{hist}_{t_{now}}(t_{now}), \text{hist}_{t_{now}}(t_{now} - 1), \ldots, \text{hist}_{t_{now}}(t_{now} - i)$ are defined.

3. He may decide to store, in addition to the current state, the history every five time units. That is $\text{hist}_{t_{now}}(t_{now})$ is defined and also for every i, $0 \leq i \leq t_{now}$, if $i \mod 5 = 0$, $\text{hist}_{t_{now}}(i)$ is defined. Such an agent may be specified by an agent designer when he believes that maintaining some past snapshots is adequate, instead of all past snapshots.

Suppose we are now given a temporal status set $TS_{t_{now}}$ and a state history function, $\text{hist}_{t_{now}}$. We define below, what it means for a triple consisting of $TS_{t_{now}}$, $\text{hist}_{t_{now}}$ and the current time, t_{now}, to *satisfy* a tap.

DEFINITION 8.3.3 (SATISFACTION, CLOSURE OF $TS_{t_{now}}$ UNDER tap RULES)   Suppose t_{now} is any integer. We present below, an inductive definition of satisfaction of formulas by $\langle TS_{t_{now}}, \text{hist}_{t_{now}}, t_{now} \rangle$;

1. $\langle TS_{t_{now}}, \text{hist}_{t_{now}}, t_{now} \rangle \models_{temp}^{\mathcal{O}} \chi \& L_1 \& \ldots \& L_n : [\text{tai}_1, \text{tai}_2]$ where $\chi \& L_1 \& \ldots \& L_n : [\text{tai}_1, \text{tai}_2]$ is ground *if, by definition,* there is an integer i, $\text{tai}_1 \leq i \leq \text{tai}_2$ such that $\text{hist}_{t_{now}}(i)$ is defined and χ is true in the agent state $\text{hist}_{t_{now}}(i)$ and $\{L_1, \ldots, L_n\} \subseteq TS_{t_{now}}(i)$. In this case, i is said to *witness* the truth of this tasc.

2. $\langle TS_{t_{now}}, \text{hist}_{t_{now}}, t_{now} \rangle \models_{temp}^{\mathcal{O}}$ Op $\alpha : [\text{tai}_1, \text{tai}_2] \leftarrow \rho_1 : \text{ta}_1 \& \ldots \& \rho_n : \text{ta}_n$ (where rule 8.2 is ground) *if, by definition,* either:

  (a) there exists an $1 \leq i \leq n$ such that for all $t_i \leq t_{now}$ and $t_i \in \text{ta}_i$, t_i is not a witness to the truth of $\rho_i : \text{ta}_i$ by $\langle TS_{t_{now}}, \text{hist}_{t_{now}}, t_{now} \rangle$, or
  (b) there exists a $t_j \geq t_{now}$ such that $t_j \in [\text{tai}_1, \text{tai}_2]$ and Op $\alpha \in TS_{t_{now}}(t_j)$.

3. $\langle TS_{t_{now}}, \text{hist}_{t_{now}}, t_{now} \rangle \models_{temp}^{\mathcal{O}} (\forall x)\phi$ *if, by definition,* $\langle TS_{t_{now}}, \text{hist}_{t_{now}}, t_{now} \rangle \models_{temp}^{\mathcal{O}} \phi[x/s]$ for all ground terms s.[2]

4. $\langle TS_{t_{now}}, \text{hist}_{t_{now}}, t_{now} \rangle \models_{temp}^{\mathcal{O}} (\exists x)\phi$ *if, by definition,* $\langle TS_{t_{now}}, \text{hist}_{t_{now}}, t_{now} \rangle \models_{temp}^{\mathcal{O}} \phi[x/s]$ for some ground term s.

5. $\langle TS_{t_{now}}, \text{hist}_{t_{now}}, t_{now} \rangle \models_{temp}^{\mathcal{O}} \mathcal{TP}$ where $\mathcal{TP}$ is a tap *if, by definition,* for each temporal agent rule (tar) $r \in \mathcal{TP}$: $\langle TS_{t_{now}}, \text{hist}_{t_{now}}, t_{now} \rangle \models_{temp}^{\mathcal{O}} r$.

The definition of satisfaction by $\langle TS_{t_{now}}, \text{hist}_{t_{now}}, t_{now} \rangle$ is complex. In particular, item (2) in the above definition has subtle aspects to it. Thus, let us consider a very simple example of the working of the definition of satisfaction.

---
[2] Here $\phi[x/s]$ denotes the replacement of all free occurrences of x in ϕ by ground term s.

Example 8.3.1 Suppose we consider the following very simple table, describing a temporal status set, $\mathcal{T}S_{t_{now}}$.

i	$\mathcal{T}_{t_{now}} S(i)$
0	{**P**α_1, **O**α_2, **Do**α_2, **P**α_2, **F**α_3}
1	{**O**α_2, **Do**α_2, **P**α_2}
2	{**P**α_3, **Do**α_3}
$i \geq 3$	{**F**α_1, **O**α_2, **P**α_4}

Suppose we also consider the very simple table describing the state of this agent—for the sake of simplicity, this agent has only one code call.

i	hist$_{t_{now}}(i)$
0	**in**(a, d:$f()$)
1	**in**(a, d:$f()$), **in**(b, d:$f()$)
2	**in**(b, d:$f()$)
3	**in**(a, d:$f()$), **in**(c, d:$f()$)

Suppose $t_{now} = 3$. Let us examine some simple formulas and see whether $\langle \mathcal{T}S_{t_{now}}, \text{hist}_{t_{now}}, t_{now}\rangle$ satisfies these formulas.

- **in**(a, d:$f()$) & **in**(b, d:$f()$) : [$t_{now} - 3, t_{now}$].
This formula is satisfied by $\langle \mathcal{T}S_{t_{now}}, \text{hist}_{t_{now}}, t_{now}\rangle$ because $i = 1$ is a witness to the satisfaction of this formula.

- **in**(a, d:$f()$) & **in**(b, d:$f()$) & **Do**α_2) : [$t_{now} - 3, t_{now}$].
This formula is satisfied by $\langle \mathcal{T}S_{t_{now}}, \text{hist}_{t_{now}}, t_{now}\rangle$ because $i = 1$ is a witness to the satisfaction of this formula. Notice that at time 1, the action status atom **Do**$\alpha_2 \in \mathcal{T}S_{t_{now}}(1)$ and the other **in**(,) atoms are also true in the agent state at time 1.

- **in**(a, d:$f()$) & **in**(b, d:$f()$) & **Do**α_3 : [$t_{now} - 3, t_{now} - 3$].
This formula is not satisfied by $\langle \mathcal{T}S_{t_{now}}, \text{hist}_{t_{now}}, t_{now}\rangle$ because the action status atom **Do**$\alpha_3 \notin \mathcal{T}S_{t_{now}}(0)$.

- The rule

Doα_4 : [t_{now}, t_{now}] $\leftarrow$ **in**(a, d:$f()$) & **in**(b, d:$f()$) & **Do**α_3 : [$t_{now} - 3, t_{now} - 3$]

is satisfied by $\langle \mathcal{T}S_{t_{now}}, \text{hist}_{t_{now}}, t_{now}\rangle$ because its antecedent is not satisfied via a witness $i \leq t_{now}$ by $\langle \mathcal{T}S_{t_{now}}, \text{hist}_{t_{now}}, t_{now}\rangle$.

Section 8.3 Semantics of Taps

- The rule

$\mathbf{F}\alpha_1 : [t_{now}, t_{now} + 3] \leftarrow \mathbf{in}(a, d:f()) \& \mathbf{in}(b, d:f()) \& \mathbf{Do}\,\alpha_2 : [t_{now} - 3, t_{now}]$

is satisfied by $\langle \mathcal{T}S_{t_{now}}, \text{hist}_{t_{now}}, t_{now}\rangle$ because its antecedent is satisfied by it (witness $i = 1 < t_{now}$) and its consequent is true at a future time instant, viz. at time $3 \geq t_{now}$.

- Consider the following tap

  – $\mathbf{F}\alpha_1 : [t_{now}, t_{now} + 2] \leftarrow \mathbf{in}(a, d:f()) \& \mathbf{in}(c, d:f()) : [t_{now}, t_{now}]$
  – $\mathbf{P}\alpha_3 : [t_{now}, t_{now}] \leftarrow \mathbf{in}(b, d:f()) \& \mathbf{in}(c, d:f()) \& \mathbf{Do}\,\alpha_1 : [t_{now} - 2, t_{now}]$
  – $\mathbf{O}\alpha_2 : [t_{now}, t_{now} + 4] \leftarrow \mathbf{in}(a, d:f()) \& \mathbf{P}\alpha_1 : [t_{now} - 3, t_{now}]$

This tap is satisfied by $\langle \mathcal{T}S_{t_{now}}, \text{hist}_{t_{now}}, t_{now}\rangle$ as all of the temporal agent rules are satisfied. The first rule is satisfied by $\langle \mathcal{T}S_{t_{now}}, \text{hist}_{t_{now}}, t_{now}\rangle$, because its antecedent is satisfied by a witness $i = 3 \leq t_{now}$, and its consequent is satisfied as $\mathbf{F}\alpha_1 \in \mathcal{T}S_{t_{now}}(i \geq 3)$. The second rule is satisfied by $\langle \mathcal{T}S_{t_{now}}, \text{hist}_{t_{now}}, t_{now}\rangle$, since its antecedent is not satisfied as $\mathbf{Do}\,\alpha_1 \notin \mathcal{T}S_{t_{now}}(i \leq t_{now})$. Finally, the third rule is satisfied by $\langle \mathcal{T}S_{t_{now}}, \text{hist}_{t_{now}}, t_{now}\rangle$, because its antecedent is satisfied via a witness $i = 0 \leq t_{now}$ and its consequent is satisfied because $\mathbf{O}\alpha_2 \in \mathcal{T}S_{t_{now}}(i \geq 3)$.

- The following tap is satisfied by $\langle \mathcal{T}S_{t_{now}}, \text{hist}_{t_{now}}, t_{now}\rangle$ since all three of the temporal agent rules are satisfied.

  – $\mathbf{F}\alpha_1 : [t_{now}, t_{now}] \leftarrow \mathbf{in}(a, d:f()) \& \mathbf{O}\alpha_2 : [t_{now} - 2, t_{now}]$
  – $\mathbf{P}\alpha_4 : [t_{now}, t_{now} + 5] \leftarrow \mathbf{in}(b, d:f()) \& \mathbf{P}\alpha_3 : [t_{now} - 2, t_{now}]$
  – $\mathbf{O}\alpha_3 : [t_{now}, t_{now}] \leftarrow \mathbf{in}(c, d:f()) \& \mathbf{P}\alpha_3 : [t_{now} - 3, t_{now}]$

The first rule is satisfied by $\langle \mathcal{T}S_{t_{now}}, \text{hist}_{t_{now}}, t_{now}\rangle$ since its antecedent is satisfied via a witness $i = 1 \leq t_{now}$ and its consequent is satisfied as $\mathbf{F}\alpha_1 \in \mathcal{T}S_{t_{now}}(i \geq 3)$. The second rule is satisfied as its antecedent is satisfied via the witness $i = 2 \leq t_{now}$ and $\mathbf{P}\alpha_4 \in \mathcal{T}S_{t_{now}}(i \geq 3)$. Lastly, the third rule is also satisfied by $\langle \mathcal{T}S_{t_{now}}, \text{hist}_{t_{now}}, t_{now}\rangle$ because its antecedent is not satisfied as there is no witness i such that $\mathbf{in}(c, d:f())$ is true in $\text{hist}_{t_{now}}(i)$ and $\mathbf{P}\alpha_3 \in \mathcal{T}S_{t_{now}}(i)$.

In general, an agent has the ability to keep track not only of its state history, but also its action history—that is, at time t_{now}, the agent may know what obligations it had in the past, what actions it took in the past, etc. As an action in the present or in the future cannot affect the state of the world or the actions take in the past, it is important that every agent's temporal status sets be compatible with the past. However, as in the history component, a designer of an agent may decide not to store all the obligations, actions etc of the past. The following two definitions capture these concepts.

DEFINITION 8.3.4 (ACTION HISTORY) An *action history* $\text{acthist}_{t_{now}}$ for an agent is a partial function from $\mathbb{N}$ to status sets:

$\text{acthist}_{t_{now}} : \mathbb{N} \longrightarrow \{S \mid S \text{ is a status set}\}.$

Intuitively, an action history specifies not only what an agent has done in the past, but also what an agent is *obliged/permitted* to or *forbidden from* doing in the future. In this respect, an action history is different from a state history. Here is an example of an action history:

i	$\text{acthist}_2(i)$
0	$\{\mathbf{P}\alpha_1, \mathbf{O}\alpha_2, \mathbf{Do}\,\alpha_2, \mathbf{P}\alpha_2, \mathbf{F}\alpha_3\}$
1	$\{\mathbf{O}\alpha_2, \mathbf{Do}\,\alpha_2, \mathbf{P}\alpha_2\}$
2	$\{\mathbf{P}\alpha_3, \mathbf{Do}\,\alpha_3\}$
3	$\{\mathbf{F}\alpha_3\}$
4	$\{\mathbf{O}\alpha_1, \mathbf{Do}\,\alpha_1\}$
$i \geq 5$	$\{\mathbf{F}\alpha_1\}$

If the current time is $t_{now} = 2$, then this tells us that the agent is forbidden from doing α_3 at time 3 and is obliged to do action α_1 at time 4. What this means is that when this agent receives new requests from other agents at time 3, it must consider the fact that it is forbidden from doing α_3 at time 3 and doing α_4 at time 4, i.e., it must find a new temporal status set, based on commitments made in the past (even if these commitments involve the future). The new temporal status set, in turn, may add more commitments or forbidden actions to the future and the $\text{acthist}_{t_{now}}$ with respect to t_{now} and the future may be changed.

Intuitively, an action history specifies the *intention* of an agent, as far as its future actions are concerned. For example, according to the above example, at time 3, the agent *intends* to $\mathbf{Do}\,\alpha_3$, even though it is not obliged to do so. An external event at time 3 may well cause it to change its mind.

DEFINITION 8.3.5 (HISTORY-COMPATIBLE TEMPORAL STATUS SET) Suppose the current time is t_{now} and $\text{acthist}_{t_{now}}(\cdot)$ denotes the action history of an agent, and suppose $\mathcal{T}S_{t_{now}}$ is a temporal status set. $\mathcal{T}S_{t_{now}}$ is said to be *action history-compatible* at time t_{now} *if, by definition,* for all $i < t_{now}$, if $\text{acthist}_{t_{now}}(i)$ is defined, then $\mathcal{T}S_{t_{now}}(i) = \text{acthist}_{t_{now}}(i)$, and for all $i \geq t_{now}$, if $\text{acthist}_{t_{now}}(i)$ is defined, then $\text{acthist}_{t_{now}}(i) \subseteq \mathcal{T}S_{t_{now}}(i)$.

In other words, all temporal status sets should be consistent with the past history of actions taken by the agent and with commitments to do things in the future that were made in the past by the agent.

Example 8.3.2 For instance, if $t_{now} = 2$, the temporal status set from Example 8.3.1 is not history-compatible with our sample action history since $\text{acthist}_{t_{now}}(3)$ is not a subset of

$\mathcal{TS}_{t_{now}}(3)$. Note however that if $\mathcal{TS}_{t_{now}}(3) = \mathcal{TS}_{t_{now}}(4) = \{\mathbf{O}\alpha_1, \mathbf{Do}\,\alpha_1, \mathbf{F}\alpha_3\}$, then $\mathcal{TS}_{t_{now}}$ would be history-compatible with our sample action history at time $t_{now} = 2$.

As we have seen earlier in Chapter 6, it is immediately apparent that given a temporal agent program, and a state/action history associated with that tap, temporal status sets must satisfy some "feasibility" requirements in order for them to be considered to represent the semantics of the tap in question. We are now ready to address the issue of what constitutes a feasible temporal status set.

8.3.2 Feasible Temporal Status Sets

Let us consider an agent a that uses a temporal agent program tap to determine what actions it should take, and when it should take these actions. Let the current time be t_{now} and suppose $\text{hist}_{t_{now}}(\cdot)$, $\text{acthist}_{t_{now}}(\cdot)$ represent the state and action histories associated with this agent at time t_{now}.

DEFINITION 8.3.6 (TEMPORAL DEONTIC CONSISTENCY) $\mathcal{TS}_{t_{now}}$ is said to be *temporally deontically consistent* at time t_{now} *if, by definition,* for all time points i, $\mathcal{TS}_{t_{now}}(i)$ is deontically consistent.[3]

Thus, if $\mathcal{TS}_{t_{now}}(4) = \{\mathbf{Do}\,\alpha, \mathbf{F}\alpha\}$, then $\mathcal{TS}_{t_{now}}$ cannot be deontically consistent.

DEFINITION 8.3.7 (TEMPORAL DEONTIC/ACTION CLOSURE) $\mathcal{TS}_{t_{now}}$ is said to be *temporally deontically closed* at time t_{now} *if, by definition,* for all time points i, $\mathbf{D\text{-}Cl}(\mathcal{TS}_{t_{now}}(i)) = \mathcal{TS}_{t_{now}}(i)$. (Recall that $\mathbf{D\text{-}Cl}(S)$ is defined in Definition 6.5.3 on page 174).

$\mathcal{TS}_{t_{now}}$ is said to be *temporally action closed* at time t_{now} *if, by definition,* for all time points i, $\mathbf{A\text{-}Cl}(\mathcal{TS}_{t_{now}}(i)) = \mathcal{TS}_{t_{now}}(i)$. (Recall that $\mathbf{A\text{-}Cl}(S)$ is defined in Definition 6.5.3 on page 174).

DEFINITION 8.3.8 (ACTION CONSISTENCY) $\mathcal{TS}_{t_{now}}$ is said to be *temporally action consistent* at time t_{now} *if, by definition,* for all time points i such that $\text{acthist}_{t_{now}}(i)$ and $\text{hist}_{t_{now}}(i)$ are defined, $\mathbf{Do}_i = \{\mathbf{Do}\,\alpha \mid \mathbf{Do}\,\alpha \in \mathcal{TS}_{t_{now}}(i)\}$ satisfies the action constraints with respect to the agent state $\text{hist}_{t_{now}}(i)$.[4]

It is important to note in the above definition that action consistency is only checked with respect to time points for which the agent designer chose to save the agent state.

Example 8.3.3 Let action constraint $AC = \{\alpha_2, \alpha_3\} \hookleftarrow$. Furthermore, let $t_{now} = 3$, let $\text{hist}_{t_{now}}$ be the state history function from Example 8.3.1, and let $\mathcal{TS}_{t_{now}}$ be similar to the temporal status set from Example 8.3.1 except $\mathcal{TS}_{t_{now}}(4) = \{\mathbf{F}\alpha_1, \mathbf{Do}\,\alpha_2, \mathbf{Do}\,\alpha_3\}$. Then

---

[3] Recall that deontic consistency of a set of action status atoms (such as $\mathcal{TS}_{t_{now}}(i)$) is defined in Chapter 6.
[4] Note that for $i = t_{now}$ both $\text{acthist}_{t_{now}}(i)$ and $\text{hist}_{t_{now}}(i)$ are defined.

$\mathcal{TS}_{t_{now}}$ is temporally action consistent since for all time points $i \leq 3$, $\mathbf{Do}_i$ satisfies AC w.r.t. $\mathrm{hist}_{t_{now}}(i)$. Note that although $\mathbf{Do}_4$ does not satisfy AC, this does not alter the outcome since $\mathrm{hist}_{t_{now}}(4)$ is not defined.

Our next notion is *Checkpoint Consistency*. This condition, relative to a *temporal status set* $\mathcal{TS}_{t_{now}}$, formalizes that *the execution of an action can be consistently done along the checkpoints*, i.e., updating the *Add* and *Del* lists during execution along the checkpoints is consistent.

DEFINITION 8.3.9 (CHECKPOINT CONSISTENCY) $\mathcal{TS}_{t_{now}}$ is said to be *checkpoint consistent* at time t_{now} *if, by definition,* for all actions α that are

1. currently being executed, i.e., $t^\alpha_{start} < t_{now}$ and $t^\alpha_{start} + \mathrm{duration}(\alpha) \geq t_{now}$,
2. and have checkpoints in the future, i.e., $\mathrm{checkpoints}(\alpha) \cap \{i \mid i \geq t_{now}\} \neq \emptyset$,

the following holds:

the new state that results from updating state $\mathrm{hist}_{t_{now}}(t^\alpha_{start})$ by concurrently executing the action

conc($\{$ **Tet**$_i(\alpha) \mid $ **Do** $\alpha \in \mathcal{TS}_{t_{now}}(i)$ and $i \in \mathrm{checkpoints}(\alpha)\}$)

satisfies the integrity constraints $\mathcal{IC}$.

Here, **Tet**$_i(\alpha)$ denotes the action (non-timed) which has an empty precondition, and whose *add* and *del* lists are as stated in **Tet**(α).

It is important to note that every time a checkpoint is encountered, we must ensure that all integrity constraints are satisfied. This means that at every checkpoint, we must ensure that the concurrent execution of all actions of the form **Do** α at that time point does not lead to a state which is inconsistent.

Thus, suppose **Do** $\alpha \in \mathrm{acthist}_{t_{now}}(5)$ and $\mathrm{duration}(\alpha) = 9$ and checkpoints occur at times 8, 11 and 14. Note that $\mathrm{hist}_{t_{now}}(i)$ is undefined for all $i > 5$. Thus, at time 8, we check if the result of updating $\mathrm{hist}_{t_{now}}(5)$ by the add/delete lists associated with the checkpoint 8 satisfies the integrity constraints. At time 11, we again check if the result of updating $\mathrm{hist}_{t_{now}}(5)$ by the add/delete lists associated with the checkpoint 11 satisfies the integrity constraints. The same is done at time 14.

The last requirement is that of *state consistency*. We have to make sure that at all time points i, the state obtained by applying all **Do** actions satisfies the integrity constraints.

DEFINITION 8.3.10 (STATE CONSISTENCY) $TS_{t_{now}}$ is said to be *state consistent at time* t_{now} *if, by definition,* for all $i \leq t_{now}$: the state obtained from $hist_{t_{now}}(i)$ by concurrently applying all **Do** actions contained in $TS_{t_{now}}(i)$ satisfies the integrity constraints $\mathcal{IC}$.

DEFINITION 8.3.11 (FEASIBLE TEMPORAL STATUS SET) Suppose the current time is t_{now} and $hist_{t_{now}}$, $acthist_{t_{now}}$ are the state/action history respectively. Further suppose that $\mathcal{IC}$, $\mathcal{AC}$ are sets of integrity constraints and actions constraints, respectively. $TS_{t_{now}}$ is said to be a *feasible temporal status set* with respect to the above parameters *if, by definition,*

(1) $TS_{t_{now}}$ is closed under the rules of $\mathcal{TP}$
(2) $TS_{t_{now}}$ is temporally deontically and action consistent at time t_{now},
(3) $TS_{t_{now}}$ is temporally deontically and action closed at time t_{now},
(4) $TS_{t_{now}}$ is checkpoint consistent at time t_{now},
(5) $TS_{t_{now}}$ is state consistent at time t_{now},
(6) $TS_{t_{now}}$ is history compatible at time t_{now}.

DEFINITION 8.3.12 (FINITARY FEASIBLE TEMPORAL STATUS SET) A feasible temporal status set $TS_{t_{now}}$ is said to be *finitary if, by definition,* $\{i \mid TS_{t_{now}}(i) \neq \emptyset\}$ is finite.

Intuitively, a finitary feasible temporal status set is one that makes commitments for only finitely many future time points (the past is always finite as our model of time is the natural numbers). This is consistent with the way most real life agents behave. No human being makes commitments infinitely into the future, and it is hard to think of a practically useful software agent with such longevity.

Example 8.3.4 Consider the following temporal agent program $\mathcal{TP}$:

r1: **O***return_control*() : $[X_{now}, X_{now} + 5]$ ←
  in(manual_override, autoPilot : *pilotStatus*(Pilot_message))&
  O*process_request*(Msg.Id, Agent) : $[X_{now}, X_{now}]$

r2: **O***process_request*(Msg.Id, Agent) : $[X_{now}, X_{now} + 2]$ ←
  in(Msg, msgbox : *getAllMsgs*()), = (Agent, Msg.Source) : $[X_{now}, X_{now}]$

r3: **O***delete_msg*(Msg.Id) : $[X_{now}, X_{now} + 1]$ ←
  Do *process_request*(Msg.Id, Agent) : $[X_{now}, X_{now}]$

Here, if a pilot wants to disengage the auto-pilot, he/she can do so by sending a message to the message box. After this message is processed, it will be deleted and the *return_control* action will be invoked. This action eventually ensures that manual control is actually restored to the pilot, i.e., **in**(manual_override, autoPilot : *pilotStatus*(Pilot_message)) . Specifically, the *return_control()* action has a **Dur** of rel:{3} and a **Tet** of {⟨rel:{1}, *Add*, *Del*⟩} where

- *Del* is **in**(automatic, autoPilot:*pilotStatus*(Pilot_message)) and
- *Add* is **in**(manual_override, autoPilot:*pilotStatus*(Pilot_message))

The key idea is that the switch from automatic to manual_override control is not instantaneous. For simplicity, we'll assume that the *process_request* and *delete_msg* actions have negligible durations.

Let $\mathcal{IC}$ contain one integrity constraint: **in**($Status_1$, autoPilot:*pilotStatus* (Pilot_message))& $\neq$ ($Status_1, Status_2$) $\Rightarrow$ **not_in**($Status_2$, autoPilot:*pilotStatus*())Pilot_message. Intuitively, this indicates that only one flight control status will be accurate at any single point in time.

Let α_1, α_2, and α_3 denote the following actions: *return_control()*, *process_request* (Msg.Id, Agent), and *delete_msg*(Msg.Id). Thus, the following action constraint indicates that we can not process and delete a message at the same time: $AC = \{\alpha_2, \alpha_3\} \hookleftarrow$. Let $\mathcal{AC} = \{AC\}$ and let $t_{now} = 4$. We are now ready to provide a sample state history (hist$_{t_{now}}$), action history (acthist$_{t_{now}}$), and feasible temporal status set ($TS_{t_{now}}$).

i	hist$_{t_{now}}(i)$
0	**in**(automatic, autoPilot:*pilotStatus*(Pilot_message))
1	**in**(automatic, autoPilot:*pilotStatus*(Pilot_message)), **in**(m_1, msgbox:*getAllMsgs*())
2	**in**(automatic, autoPilot:*pilotStatus*(Pilot_message)), **in**(m_1, msgbox:*getAllMsgs*())
3	**in**(automatic, autoPilot:*pilotStatus*(Pilot_message)), **in**(m_1, msgbox:*getAllMsgs*())
4	**in**(semi_automatic, autoPilot:*pilotStatus*(Pilot_message))

Note that eventually, we would expect hist$_{t_{now}}(5)$ to contain **in**(semi_manual, autoPilot:*pilotStatus*(Pilot_message)) and hist$_{t_{now}}(6)$ to contain **in**(manual_override, autoPilot:*pilotStatus*(Pilot_message)).

i	acthist$_{t_{now}}(i)$
0	{**P**α_2}
1	{**P**α_2}
2	{**P**α_2, **O**α_2, **Do**α_2}
3	{**P**α_3, **O**α_3, **Do**α_3, **P**α_1, **O**α_1, **Do**α_1}
4	{**P**α_1, **O**α_1, **Do**α_1}
5	{**P**α_1, **O**α_1}

Section 8.3 Semantics of Taps

i	$TS_{t_{now}}(i)$
0	$\{\mathbf{P}\alpha_2\}$
1	$\{\mathbf{P}\alpha_2\}$
2	$\{\mathbf{P}\alpha_2, \mathbf{O}\alpha_2, \mathbf{Do}\,\alpha_2\}$
3	$\{\mathbf{P}\alpha_3, \mathbf{O}\alpha_3, \mathbf{Do}\,\alpha_3, \mathbf{P}\alpha_1, \mathbf{O}\alpha_1, \mathbf{Do}\,\alpha_1\}$
4	$\{\mathbf{P}\alpha_1, \mathbf{O}\alpha_1, \mathbf{Do}\,\alpha_1\}$
5	$\{\mathbf{P}\alpha_1, \mathbf{O}\alpha_1, \mathbf{Do}\,\alpha_1\}$

$TS_{t_{now}}$ is temporally deontically consistent since no actions have preconditions and since for each $TS_{t_{now}}(i)$, there are no forbidden or withdrawn actions. $TS_{t_{now}}$ is temporally action closed (and hence, temporally deontically closed) since for each $TS_{t_{now}}(i)$ where $\mathbf{O}\alpha_j \in TS_{t_{now}}(i)$, $\mathbf{Do}\,\alpha_j \in TS_{t_{now}}(i)$ and $\mathbf{P}\alpha_j \in TS_{t_{now}}(i)$. $TS_{t_{now}}$ is temporally action consistent since there is no $\mathbf{Do}_i$ where $\mathbf{Do}\,\alpha_2, \mathbf{Do}\,\alpha_3 \in \mathbf{Do}_i$. $TS_{t_{now}}$ is checkpoint consistent since the only relevant action, α_1, never violates the integrity constraints in $\mathcal{IC}$. Finally, the reader may easily verify that $TS_{t_{now}}$ is closed under the rules in $\mathcal{TP}$.

Notice that after time 3 in the example above, we no longer permit action α_2 (i.e., we do not process any more messages). This behavior can be changed by defining $\mathrm{hist}'_{t_{now}}$, $\mathrm{acthist}'_{t_{now}}$, and $TS'_{t_{now}}$ in the following way: For each $0 \leq i \leq 4$, let $\mathrm{hist}'_{t_{now}}(i) = \mathrm{hist}_{t_{now}}(i)$. Then for each $0 \leq i \leq 3$, let $\mathrm{acthist}'_{t_{now}}(i) = \mathrm{acthist}_{t_{now}}(i)$ and let $TS'_{t_{now}}(i) = TS_{t_{now}}(i)$. Finally for each $4 \leq i \leq 7$, let $\mathrm{acthist}'_{t_{now}}(i) = (\mathrm{acthist}_{t_{now}}(i) \cup \mathbf{P}\alpha_2)$ and let $TS'_{t_{now}}(i) = (TS_{t_{now}}(i) \cup \mathbf{P}\alpha_2)$. Note that $TS'_{t_{now}}$ is also a feasible temporal status set.

8.3.3 Rational Temporal Status Sets

Our last notion is that of a rational feasible temporal status set. Feasible status sets may contain **Do**ing actions that are not strictly necessary.

The reason is that in Definition 8.3.12 we did not require the set to be *minimal*. Minimal sets do not contain superfluous action status atoms: each such atom is grounded.

DEFINITION 8.3.13 (RATIONAL FEASIBLE TEMPORAL STATUS SET) A temporal status set $TS_{t_{now}}$ is *grounded*, if there exists no temporal status set $TS'_{t_{now}} \neq TS_{t_{now}}$ such that $TS'_{t_{now}} \subseteq TS_{t_{now}}$ and $TS'_{t_{now}}$ satisfies conditions (1)–(4) of a feasible temporal status set.

A temporal status set $TS_{t_{now}}$ is a *rational temporal status set*, if $TS_{t_{now}}$ is a feasible status set and $TS_{t_{now}}$ is grounded.

Notice that if is $TS_{t_{now}}$ a feasible status set, then every $TS'_{t_{now}} \subseteq TS_{t_{now}}$ satisfies the condition (2) of feasibility. Therefore, the requirement of (2) for $TS'_{t_{now}}$ in the definition of groundedness is redundant. However, it seems more natural to have this condition included in the definition of groundedness. Moreover, if we did not have hereditary action consistency, then inclusion of action consistency would be indispensable.

Example 8.3.5 Recall that in Example 8.3.4, we found that $TS'_{t_{now}}$ is a feasible temporal status set (w.r.t. the t_{now}, $hist'_{t_{now}}$, $acthist'_{t_{now}}$, $\mathcal{IC}$, and $\mathcal{AC}$ we defined in that example). For each $0 \leq i \leq 4$, let $TS''_{t_{now}}(i) = TS'_{t_{now}}(i)$ and for each $4 \leq i \leq 7$, let $TS''_{t_{now}}(i) = (TS'_{t_{now}}(i) \cup \{\mathbf{O}\alpha_2, \mathbf{Do}\,\alpha_2\})$. Then $TS''_{t_{now}}$ is also a feasible temporal status set (w.r.t. the parameters above) but it is not a rational feasible temporal status set since $TS'_{t_{now}} \subseteq TS''_{t_{now}}$ and $TS'_{t_{now}}$ is a feasible temporal status set.

8.4 Compact Representation of Temporal Status Sets

Representing a temporal feasible status set explicitly is difficult because of the fact that in the worst case, for every time point i, we must specify $TS_{t_{now}}(i)$. To ameliorate this problem, we describe below, a *constrained representation* of temporal feasible status sets.

DEFINITION 8.4.1 (TEMPORAL INTERVAL CONSTRAINT tic) An *atomic temporal interval constraint* is an expression of the form $\ell \leq t \leq u$ where t is a variable ranging over natural numbers, and ℓ, u are natural numbers.

Temporal Interval Constraints are inductively defined as follows:

1. Atomic temporal interval constraints are temporal interval constraints.

2. If tic_1, tic_2 are temporal interval constraints involving the same variable t, then ($tic_1 \vee tic_2$), (tic_1 & tic_2) and $\neg tic_1$ are temporal interval constraints.

For example, ($5 \leq t \leq 10$) is an atomic temporal interval constraint. So is ($50 \leq t \leq 60$). In addition, ($5 \leq t \leq 10$) $\vee$ ($50 \leq t \leq 60$) and ($5 \leq t \leq 10$) & ($50 \leq t \leq 60$) are temporal interval constraints.

As the concepts of constraints and solutions of constraints with variables ranging over the natural numbers is well known and well studied in the literature (Cormen, Leiserson, and Rivest 1989), we will not repeat those concepts here.

DEFINITION 8.4.2 (INTERVAL CONSTRAINT ANNOTATED STATUS ATOM) If tic is a temporal interval constraint, and $\mathbf{Op}\,\alpha$ is an action status atom, then $\mathbf{Op}\,\alpha$: tic is an interval constraint annotated status atom.

Intuitively, the interval constraint annotated status atom $\mathbf{Op}\,\alpha$: tic may be read as "$\mathbf{Op}\,\alpha$ *is known to be true at all time points that are solutions of* tic." For example, $\mathbf{O}\,\alpha$: ($500 \leq t \leq 6000$) says that some agent is obliged to do α at times $500, 501, \ldots, 6000$. Notice that one single statement allows us to *implicitly* represent the obligation of this agent to do α at 5,501 time instances! Clearly, this interval constraint annotated status atom is a succinct representation of the following

DEFINITION 8.4.3 (INTERVAL CONSTRAINT TEMPORAL STATUS SET ic-$\mathcal{T}S$) An *interval constraint temporal status set*, denoted ic-$\mathcal{T}S$, is a set of interval constraint annotated status atoms.

It is likewise easy to see that an interval constraint temporal status set is a very succinct representation of a status set. The status set represented by an interval constraint temporal status set ic-$\mathcal{T}S$ is defined through the following definition.

DEFINITION 8.4.4 (TEMPORAL STATUS SET ASSOCIATED WITH ic-$\mathcal{T}S$) Suppose ic-$\mathcal{T}S$ is an interval constraint temporal status set. The associated temporal status set $\mathcal{T}S_{t_{now}}$ is defined as follows.

$\mathcal{T}S_{t_{now}}(i) =_{def} \{$Op $\alpha \mid$ there is an interval constraint annotated status atom
Op α : tic in ic-$\mathcal{T}S$ such that i is a solution of tic$\}$

It is easy to see that all finitary temporal status sets can be represented via interval constraint temporal status sets. The following example shows an interval constraint temporal status set.

Example 8.4.1 Recall that in Example 8.3.4, we defined a (finitary) feasible temporal status set $\mathcal{T}S'_{t_{now}}$. Its corresponding interval constraint temporal status set has the following description:

$\{$Op α_1 : $(3 \leq t \leq 5) \mid$ Op $\in \{\mathbf{P}, \mathbf{O}, \mathbf{Do}\}\} \cup$
$\{\mathbf{P} \alpha_2$: $((0 \leq t \leq 2) \vee (4 \leq t \leq 7))\} \cup$
$\{$Op α_2 : $(2 \leq t \leq 2) \mid$ Op $\in \{\mathbf{O}, \mathbf{Do}\}\} \cup$
$\{$Op α_3 : $(3 \leq t \leq 3) \mid$ Op $\in \{\mathbf{P}, \mathbf{O}, \mathbf{Do}\}\}$

We will abuse notation and use ic-$\mathcal{T}C$ and its associated $\mathcal{T}S_{t_{now}}$ interchangeably. In particular, we will use ic-$\mathcal{T}C(i)$ instead of $\mathcal{T}S_{t_{now}}(i)$.

8.5 Computing Feasible Temporal Status Sets

In this section, we will provide a simple iterative fixpoint algorithm to compute a feasible temporal status set.

Suppose the current time, t_{now} and the histories, $hist_{t_{now}}(\cdot)$ and $acthist_{t_{now}}(\cdot)$ are arbitrary, but fixed. How can we compute a temporal feasible status set? A close look at Definition 8.3.11 gives the following insights:

1. The history compatibility requirement already determines the $\mathcal{T}S_{t_{now}}(i)$ for $i < t_{now}$.
2. The checkpoint consistency puts constraints on the $\mathcal{T}S_{t_{now}}(i)$ for $i \leq t_{now}$.

3. The state consistency requirement is either fulfilled for $i < t_{now}$ or not. If it is not fulfilled, there is no feasible temporal status set at all. If it is fulfilled, then this requirement adds an additional restriction on $TS_{t_{now}}(t_{now})$.

4. The important part lies in condition (1) of Definition 8.3.11: closure under the rules. Obviously we can evaluate the bodies of all rules containing temporal annotations [tai_1, tai_2] with $tai_2 < t_{now}$, because they are fixed (see 1. above). If the body of such a rule is true, we have to fulfill the head of the rule. If $Op\, \alpha$: [tai_1, tai_2] is such a head, the status atom $Op\, \alpha$ must be contained in a $TS_{t_{now}}(i)$ with $tai_1 \leq i \leq tai_2$ and $t_{now} \leq i$.

The problem is therefore to compute the set $TS_{t_{now}}(t_{now})$! Adding more and more action status atoms to $TS_{t_{now}}(t_{now})$ leads to more and more program rules that evaluate to true!

But also putting an action status atom $\mathbf{Do}\ \beta$ in one of the $TS_{t_{now}}(i)$ where $i > t_{now}$ influences the set $TS_{t_{now}}(t_{now})$! Suppose that the constraints stated by checkpoint consistency are satisfied, so that $\mathbf{Do}\ \beta$ can be put into $TS_{t_{now}}(t_{now} + 1)$. As these constraints never ever change, $\mathbf{Do}\ \beta$ can stay there. But later we might be forced to make $\mathbf{F}\,\beta$: [$t_{now}, t_{now} + 1$] true. The fact that not both $\mathbf{F}\,\beta$ and $\mathbf{Do}\ \beta$ can be contained in $TS_{t_{now}}(t_{now} + 1)$ (deontic consistency) forces us to include $\mathbf{F}\,\beta$ into $TS_{t_{now}}(t_{now})$.

Therefore we have to *delay* even the action status atoms for the $TS_{t_{now}}(i)$ for $i > t_{now}$. This introduces an inherent *non-determinism* into the construction of a feasible status set.

8.5.1 Fixpoint Operator and Choice Function

We associate with $\mathcal{TP}$, an operator $\mathsf{TPT}_{\mathcal{TP}}$ that maps interval constraint temporal status sets to interval constraint temporal status sets. In order to define this operator, we need some intermediate definitions.

DEFINITION 8.5.1 (OPERATOR $\mathbf{App}_{\mathcal{TP},\mathcal{O}}$(ic-$\mathcal{TS}$) AND CHOICE FUNCTION Choice) Suppose $\mathcal{TP}$ is an agent program, $\mathcal{O}$ is an agent state and ic-$\mathcal{TS}$ is an interval constraint temporal status set. Then, $\mathbf{App}_{\mathcal{TP},\mathcal{O}}$(ic-$\mathcal{TS}$) is defined to be the set of all existentially quantified interval constraint annotated status atoms of the form $Op\, \alpha : \exists t (tai_1 \leq t \leq tai_2)$ such that there exists a ground instance of a rule r in $\mathcal{TP}$ with head $Op\, \alpha$: [tai_1, tai_2] satisfying

the body of this rule r is satisfied by $\langle TS_{t_{now}}, hist_{t_{now}}, t_{now}\rangle$ wrt. ic-$\mathcal{TS}$ (see (1) of Definition 8.3.3),

The set $\mathbf{App}_{\mathcal{TP},\mathcal{O}}$(ic-$\mathcal{TS}$) may include existentially quantified atoms that are already satisfied and thus contained in some $TS_{t_{now}}(i)$. Those atoms need not to be taken into account. But all other atoms have have to be satisfied. How can we assign them to the $TS_{t_{now}}(i)$? There is an inherent nondeterminism in this assignment and therefore we introduce a Choice Function Choice which takes as input the current interval constraint temporal status set ic-TS, the set $\mathbf{App}_{TP,O}$(ic-TS) and produces a new ic-TS_{new} such that

(1) ic-$TS(i)$ = ic-$TS_{new}(i)$ for $i < t_{now}$,

(2) if Op $\alpha : \exists t$ (tai$_1 \leq t \leq$ tai$_2$) $\in \mathbf{App}_{TP,O}$(ic-TS) then there is a t with tai$_1 \leq t \leq$ tai$_2$ and $t \geq t_{now}$ such that Op $\alpha \in$ ic-$TS_{new}(t)$.

(3) the constraints given by checkpoint-consistency are satisfied,

(4) ic-TS_{new} is temporal deontic consistent (this applies to all $i > t_{now}$) and action consistent (this applies to $i = t_{now}$),

(5) if Op $\alpha \in$ ic-$TS_{new}(t_{now})$ where Op $\in \{\mathbf{P}, \mathbf{O}, \mathbf{Do}\}$, then α is executable in the current state hist$_{t_{now}}(t_{now})$. Here we denote by ic-$TS(i)$ the set $TS_{t_{now}}(i)$ according to Definition 8.4.4.

The choice function Choice in the last definition can be realized so that it systematically tries to fulfill the existentially quantified status atoms by choosing for each status atom Op $\alpha : \exists t$ (tai$_1 \leq t \leq$ tai$_2$) the *least* possible ic-$TS(t)$ (i.e., starting with t_{now}) and adding the atom to it. If it is not possible to find such a mapping, we define the value of Choice to be "no solution". If this happens, then the ic-TS we started with cannot be extended to a feasible temporal status set and therefore has to be changed.

Choice can be easily realized to directly modify (the representation of) the interval constraint temporal status ic-TS with which we started: adding a status atom Opα to ic-$TS(i_0)$ means to modify one of the tic's of the Op $\alpha :$ tic $\in$ ic-TS. Such a modification can be the addition of an atomic temporal interval constraint (i.e., adding a new disjunct $\ldots \vee t_0 \leq t \leq t_0$) or it can lead to a simplification of constraints: for example if we have $t_0 - 1 \leq t < t_0$ & $t_0 + 1 \leq t < t_0 + 5$ and add $\ldots \vee t_0 \leq t \leq t_0$ we end up with $t_0 - 1 \leq t < t_0 + 5$.

Example 8.5.1 Consider the feasible temporal status set $TS'_{t_{now}}$ defined in Example 8.3.4 and shown in Example 8.4.1. Here, at time 3, we do not permit both α_2 and α_3 because of action constraint $AC = \{\alpha_2, \alpha_3\} \hookleftarrow$. If we remove AC from $\mathcal{AC}$, then we can add $\mathbf{P}\alpha_2 : (3 \leq t \leq 3)$ to $TS'_{t_{now}}$. In this case, its corresponding interval constraint temporal status set will have the following description:

{Op$\alpha_1 : (3 \leq t \leq 5) \mid$ Op $\in \{\mathbf{P}, \mathbf{O}, \mathbf{Do}\}\} \cup$
{$\mathbf{P}\alpha_2 : (0 \leq t \leq 7)\} \cup$
{Op$\alpha_2 : (2 \leq t \leq 2) \mid$ Op $\in \{\mathbf{O}, \mathbf{Do}\}\} \cup$
{Op$\alpha_3 : (3 \leq t \leq 3) \mid$ Op $\in \{\mathbf{P}, \mathbf{O}, \mathbf{Do}\}\}$

Note that Part (5) of the above definition only applies to the current state (at time t_{now}) and to "positive" modes $\mathbf{P}, \mathbf{O}, \mathbf{Do}$. It does not apply to atoms of the form $\mathbf{F}\alpha$ as such actions are not executed, nor does it apply to atoms of the form $\mathbf{W}\alpha$, because execution of an action might be (vacuously) waived, if its prerequisites are not fulfilled.

Intuitively, the last definition extends the set ic-$\mathcal{T}S$ by adding those action status atoms that are obtained by letting the rules of the program fire once. This means: we evaluate the bodies of all program rules with respect to ic-$\mathcal{T}S$ and obtain

1. with $\mathbf{App}_{\mathcal{TP},\mathcal{O}}$(ic-$\mathcal{T}S$) all existentially quantified action status atoms that have to be contained in one of the ic-$\mathcal{T}S(i)$,

2. with Choice a systematic procedure to actually include all action status atoms obtained in 1. in such a way, that checkpoint, deontic and action consistency as well as state consistency are satisfied.

As we are interested in *feasible* temporal status sets, we also have to make sure that our sets are deontically and action closed. Therefore we have to add to the set ic-$\mathcal{T}S$ its deontic and action closure. This is very easy: the only thing to do is to add for each interval constraint status atom of the form $\mathbf{O}\alpha$: tic the new atom $\mathbf{P}\alpha$: tic (we call this $\mathbf{D}\text{-}\mathbf{Cl}$(ic-$\mathcal{T}S$)). To ensure action consistency, we have to add $\mathbf{Do}\alpha$: tic (if $\mathbf{O}\alpha$: tic $\in$ ic-$\mathcal{T}S$) and $\mathbf{P}\alpha$: tic (if $\mathbf{Do}\alpha$: tic $\in$ ic-$\mathcal{T}S$): this closure is denoted by $\mathbf{A}\text{-}\mathbf{Cl}$(ic-$\mathcal{T}S$).

In addition, we want that a feasible set is not only closed under *one* application of the program rules, but under arbitrary many such applications. This leads us to the following operator:

DEFINITION 8.5.2 (TPT$_{\mathcal{TP}}$ OPERATOR) Suppose $\mathcal{TP}$ is a temporal agent program and $\mathcal{O}$ an agent state. Then, for any interval constraint status set ic-$\mathcal{T}S$, we define the following operator mapping interval constraint temporal status sets into themselves:

$$\text{TPT}_{\mathcal{TP}}(\text{ic-}\mathcal{T}S) = \text{Choice}(\mathbf{App}_{\mathcal{TP},\mathcal{O}}(\text{ic-}\mathcal{T}S), \text{ic-}\mathcal{T}S) \cup \mathbf{D}\text{-}\mathbf{Cl}(\text{ic-}\mathcal{T}S) \cup \mathbf{A}\text{-}\mathbf{Cl}(\text{ic-}\mathcal{T}S).$$

Note that as $\mathbf{D}\text{-}\mathbf{Cl}$(ic-$\mathcal{T}S$) $\subseteq \mathbf{A}\text{-}\mathbf{Cl}$(ic-$\mathcal{T}S$), we may equivalently write this as

$$\text{TPT}_{\mathcal{TP}}(\text{ic-}\mathcal{T}S) = \text{Choice}(\mathbf{App}_{\mathcal{TP},\mathcal{O}}(\text{ic-}\mathcal{T}S), \text{ic-}\mathcal{T}S) \cup \mathbf{A}\text{-}\mathbf{Cl}(\text{ic-}\mathcal{T}S).$$

8.5.2 Properties of TPT$_{\mathcal{TP}}$ and Choice

The following property of temporal feasible status sets is easily seen.

LEMMA 8.5.1 Let $\mathcal{TP}$ be a temporal agent program, let $\mathcal{O}$ be any agent state, and let ic-$\mathcal{T}S$ be any interval constraint temporal status set. If ic-$\mathcal{T}S$ satisfies (1) and (2) of feasibility (Definition 8.3.11), then there is a choice function Choice such that ic-$\mathcal{T}S$ is a pre-fixpoint of TPT$_{\mathcal{TP}}$, i.e., TPT$_{\mathcal{TP}}$(ic-$\mathcal{T}S$) $\subseteq$ ic-$\mathcal{T}S$.

Proof The condition (1) immediately gives us a definition of the choice function Choice. Suppose $\text{Op}(\alpha) \in \text{TPT}_{\mathcal{TP}}(S) = \text{Choice}(\mathbf{App}_{\mathcal{TP},\mathcal{O}}(\text{ic-}\mathcal{T}S), \text{ic-}\mathcal{T}S) \cup \mathbf{A}\text{-}\mathbf{Cl}(\text{ic-}\mathcal{T}S)$. Then either Op($\alpha$) stems from $\mathbf{App}_{\mathcal{TP},\mathcal{O}}$(ic-$\mathcal{T}S$) or from $\mathbf{A\text{-}Cl}$(ic-$\mathcal{T}S$). By condition (1) defining a feasible temporal status set, we know that Op(α) $\in$ ic-$\mathcal{T}S$. By condition (3), ic-$\mathcal{T}S$ = $\mathbf{A\text{-}Cl}$(ic-$\mathcal{T}S$) and hence, $\mathbf{A\text{-}Cl}$(ic-$\mathcal{T}S$) $\subseteq$ ic-$\mathcal{T}S$. Therefore, TPT$_{\mathcal{TP}}$(ic-$\mathcal{T}S$) $\subseteq$ ic-$\mathcal{T}S$. ∎

Clearly, if the program $\mathcal{TP}$ is positive, and Choice never takes the value "no solution" then TPT$_{\mathcal{TP}}$ is a monotone operator, i.e., $S \subseteq S'$ implies TPT$_{\mathcal{TP}}(S) \subseteq$ TPT$_{\mathcal{TP}}(S')$, and hence, it has a least fixpoint lfp(TPT$_{\mathcal{TP}}$). Moreover, since TPT$_{\mathcal{TP}}$ is in fact continuous under these assumptions, i.e., TPT$_{\mathcal{TP}}(\bigcup_{i=0}^{\infty} S_0) = \bigcup_{i=0}^{\infty}$ TPT$_{\mathcal{TP}}(S_i)$ for any chain $S_0 \subseteq S_1 \subseteq S_2 \subseteq \cdots$ of status sets, the least fixpoint is given by

$$\mathit{lfp}(\mathsf{TPT}_{\mathcal{TP}}) = \bigcup_{i=0}^{\infty} \mathsf{TPT}_{\mathcal{TP}}^{i},$$

where TPT$_{\mathcal{TP}}^{0}$ = $\emptyset$ and TPT$_{\mathcal{TP}}^{i+1}$ = TPT$_{\mathcal{TP}}$(TPT$_{\mathcal{TP}}^{i}$), for all $i \geq 0$ (see e.g., (Lloyd 1987; Apt 1990)).

Note that different choice functions Choice may lead to different feasible temporal status sets. Moreover, if during the iteration of TPT$_{\mathcal{TP}}$ the value of Choice is "no solution", then we have to backtrack to the last iteration and modify Choice. A fair implementation of Choice (i.e., in such a way that all possible choice functions are considered) ensures that if there exists a rational temporal status set at all, it will be constructed eventually. We then have the following result.

THEOREM 8.5.1 Let $\mathcal{TP}$ be a positive agent program, and let $\mathcal{O}$ be an agent state. Then, ic-$\mathcal{T}S$ is a rational temporal status set of $\mathcal{TP}$ on $\mathcal{O}$, *if and only if* there is a choice function Choice such that ic-$\mathcal{T}S$ = lfp(TPT$_{\mathcal{TP}}$) and ic-$\mathcal{T}S$ is a feasible temporal status set.

Proof ($\Rightarrow$) Suppose ic-$\mathcal{T}S$ is a rational status set of $\mathcal{TP}$ on $\mathcal{O}$. Then, ic-$\mathcal{T}S$ is feasible by definition of rational status set. The existence of Choice is obvious: because of the closure under the rules, all Op α : tic are satisfied and each such Op α is contained in one $\mathcal{TS}_{t_{\text{now}}}(i)$ as determined by ic-$\mathcal{T}S$. We choose Choice in accordance with ic-$\mathcal{T}S$. We also use the observations made in the beginning of Section 8.5 to initialize ic-$\mathcal{T}S$.

By Lemma 8.5.1, ic-$\mathcal{T}S$ is a pre-fixpoint of TPT$_{\mathcal{TP}}$. Since TPT$_{\mathcal{TP}}$ is monotone, by the Knaster-Tarski Theorem it has a least pre-fixpoint, which coincides with lfp(TPT$_{\mathcal{TP}}$) (cf. (Apt 1990; Lloyd 1987)). Thus, lfp(TPT$_{\mathcal{TP}}$) $\subseteq$ ic-$\mathcal{T}S$. Clearly, lfp(TPT$_{\mathcal{TP}}$) satisfies (1) and (3); moreover, lfp(TPT$_{\mathcal{TP}}$) satisfies (2), as ic-$\mathcal{T}S$ satisfies (2) and this property is hereditary. By the definition of rational status set, it follows lfp(TPT$_{\mathcal{TP}}$) = ic-$\mathcal{T}S$.

($\Leftarrow$) Suppose Choice exists such that ic-$\mathcal{T}S$ = lfp(TPT$_{\mathcal{TP}}$) is a feasible status set. Since every status set ic-$\mathcal{T}S'$ which satisfies (1)–(3) is a pre-fixpoint of TPT$_{\mathcal{TP}}$ and lfp(TPT$_{\mathcal{TP}}$) is the least prefix point, ic-$\mathcal{T}S' \subseteq$ ic-$\mathcal{T}S$ implies ic-$\mathcal{T}S$ = ic-$\mathcal{T}S'$. It follows that ic-$\mathcal{T}S$ is rational. ∎

Notice that in case of a positive program, $\mathit{lfp}(\mathsf{TPT}_{\mathcal{TP}})$, if it exists, always satisfies the conditions (1) and (3) of a feasible status set (i.e., all closure conditions), and thus is a rational status set if it satisfies (2) and (4), i.e., the consistency criteria. The uniqueness of the rational status set is immediate from the previous theorem with respect to a given Choice function.

COROLLARY 6 Let $\mathcal{TP}$ be a positive temporal agent program. Then, on every agent state $\mathcal{O}$, the rational temporal status set of $\mathcal{TP}$ (if one exists) is uniquely determined by the choice function Choice, i.e., if ic-$\mathcal{T}S$, ic-$\mathcal{T}S'$ are rational temporal status sets for $\mathcal{TP}$ on $\mathcal{O}$ with respect to the same choice function Choice, then ic-$\mathcal{T}S$ = ic-$\mathcal{T}S'$.

However, there may exist different choice functions that lead to different rational temporal status sets. In addition, a rational temporal status set need not exist at all.

8.6 An Application of Tap: Strategic Negotiations

Consider an extension of the CHAIN example, where there are several suppliers, each located in a different geographical area. Each supplier stores items which can be supplied to clients both in its geographical area, as well as other areas. It is not beneficial for a given supplier to store all the items which may be needed by its clients (because of space constraints, storage, maintenance and other inventory related costs). Rather, if a supplier does not have an item in stock, it may ask another supplier for the item, and then provide the item to its customer. The needs of each client change dynamically over time, and furthermore, new clients may be acquired, and old clients may take their business elsewhere. Every three months, the suppliers decide where to store each item.

Each supplier in the group is independent and has its own commercial interests, but would like to cooperate with other suppliers in order to make more items available to its clients while minimizing its costs. For each supplier, the goal is to optimize his "bottom" line profits. This is done by maximizing the profits from its customers, as well as payments made by other suppliers who need to order items from it. The costs it encounters are storage costs for the items stored locally, as well as delivery costs for obtaining items stored by a different supplier. Delivery costs depend on the distance between the suppliers. When another supplier requests an item stored locally, the supplier has some small cost for handling the request. All costs depend on the demands of clients in different geographical areas. The suppliers have some statistical estimates of projected demands over the next three months.

As each supplier has its own preferences regarding possible locations of items, its interests may conflict with the interests of other suppliers. In (Schwartz and Kraus 1997) it was shown that it is beneficial to use the model of alternating offers, in which all agents negotiate to

Section 8.6   An Application of Tap: Strategic Negotiations   285

reach an agreement which specifies the location of *all* the relevant items.[5] An agent may opt out of the negotiations and choose to store all the items it may need locally.

The protocol proposed in (Schwartz and Kraus 1997) consists of two phases. In the first phase, each supplier will search for an allocation of the items, using any search algorithm and resources it has. All the agents will simultaneously broadcast their findings to the other agents at the end of the phase, and the one with the highest sum designated as the allocation which will be used in the second phase.

In the second phase the protocol of alternative offers will be used. This involves several iterations until an agreement is reached. During even time periods, one agent makes an offer, and in the next time period each of the other agents may either accept the offer, reject it, or opt out of the negotiation. If an offer is accepted by all agents, then the negotiation ends, and this offer is implemented. If at least one of the agents opts out of the negotiation, then each supplier stores all the items it needs. If no agent has chosen "Opt," but at least one of the agents has rejected the offer, the negotiation proceeds to the next time period, another agent makes a counter-offer, the other agents respond, and so on.

The details of the strategies that are in perfect-equilibrium are specified in (Schwartz and Kraus 1997). We demonstrate here how a designer of an agent can program these negotiations in *IMPACT*. As the time of the negotiations plays an important role in strategic-model of negotiations, we need to use the tap framework which enables us to express the time dependent actions taken by the agent.

We assume that there are *number_agents* agents (where *number_agents* > 2) who are numbered 0, 1, 2, . . . , *number_agents* − 1, and that the program specified below is for agent i. Furthermore, we assume that each agent has an evaluation function V^i representing its preferences. It is a function from the set of possible allocations to the real numbers. We denote by $\mathcal{V}$, the set of evaluation functions of all the agents.

We associate with each agent, a specialized package called search that supports a function, *findAlloc* which gets as input a set of *Items* to be located, the valuation functions of the agents and a maximization criteria (e.g., *max_sum*) and which returns an allocation that is better for all agents than opting out those opting and attempts to maximize the given criteria. It was recommended in (Schwartz and Kraus 1997) that this function will use the random restart hill-climbing algorithm (Minton, Johnston, Philips, and Laird 1992).

We associate with each agent, a specialized package called schedule that supports the code calls listed below that determine the status of the negotiations.

- schedule : *firstPhase*() → Time

---

[5] The problem considered in (Schwartz and Kraus 1997) was that of data allocation in multi-servers environment.

firstPhase returns the time point in the first phase in which the agents need to broadcast possible allocations.

- schedule : *secondPhase*(Time) → Boolean

secondPhase gets as an input, a time point and returns **true** if it belongs to the second phase of the interaction.

- schedule : *endNego*(Messages) → Boolean

endNego gets as an input a set of answers or an offer or an empty set and return **true** if the negotiations ends and **false** otherwise.

The *msgbox* package has already been discussed in Section 4.3. Here we extend it by adding the following code calls to it.

- msgbox : *gatherAnswers*(NumAgents, Time) → SetofAnswers

gatherAnswers gets as input a number of agents and a time point and returns the answers sent by these agents at the specified time point.

- msgbox : *gatherProposals*(NumAgents, Time) → SetofProposals

gatherProposals gets as input a number of agents and a time point and returns the proposals made by these number of agents at the specified time point (possibly, including the proposal of agent i).

- msgbox : *doneBroadcast*(Time) → Boolean

doneBroadcast gets as input a time point, and returns **true** if the agent has broadcast the required answer at this time period and false otherwise.

In order to be able to perform the code call *gatherAnswers*, the agent needs to perform the action *processAnswers*.

r1: **O***broadcast*(Prop):[X_{now}, X_{now}] ←
　　　in(Prop, search : *findAlloc*(Items, $\mathcal{V}$, max_sum)),
　　　in(X_{now}, schedule : *firstPhase*()):[X_{now}, X_{now}]

In the first phase the agent must broadcast to all the agents the allocation it found.

r2: **O***broadcast*(Offer):[X_{now}, X_{now}] ←
　　　Do *processAnswers*():[$X_{now} - 1$, $X_{now} - 1$],
　　　in(X2, msgbox : *gatherAnswers*(number_agents $- 1$, $X_{now} - 1$)),
　　　in(**false**, schedule : *endNego*(X2)),
　　　in(T1, schedule : *firstPhase*()),
　　　in(X1, msgbox : *gatherProposals*(number_agents, T1)),
　　　in(Offer, math : *max*(X1, $\mathcal{V}$, max_sum)),
　　　in(**true**, schedule : *secondPhase*(X_{now})),

Section 8.6   An Application of Tap: Strategic Negotiations

       in(0, math : *remainder*(X_{now}, 2)),
       in(i, math : *remainder*($X_{now}/2$, number_agents)) : [X_{now}, X_{now}]

If the second phase of the interaction has been reached, and the negotiations have not ended in the preceding time period, then the agent whose turn it is to make an offer is obliged to make an offer. The offer is the one that maximizes the sum of the utilities of the agents among the allocations obtained in the first phase of the interactions. These proposals are gathered using the *gatherProposals* function. The desired proposal is determined using the *max* function.

Thus, in the protocol described above, offers are made only in even time periods. Therefore, the agent is obliged to broadcast a proposal only when the time period is even. In particular, agent *i* should make offers in time periods, $2i$, $2(i + agents\_number)$, $2(i + 2 \times agents\_number)$, etc.

The agent doesn't need to send a proposal if the negotiation ends. This is determined by processing the answers of the previous time period which is gathered using the *gatherAnswers* code call.

r3:   **O***broadcast*("yes") : [X_{now}, X_{now}] ←
        Do *processAnswers*() : [$X_{now} - 1$, $X_{now} - 1$],
        in(Offer1, msgbox : *gatherProposals*(1, $X_{now} - 1$)),
        in(**false**, schedule : *endNego*(Offer1)),
        in(T1, schedule : *firstPhase*()),
        in(X1, msgbox : *gatherProposals*(number_agents, T1)),
        in(Offer2, math : *max*(X1, $\mathcal{V}$, max_sum)), = (Offer2, Offer1),
        in(**true**, schedule : *secondPhase*(X_{now})),
        in(1, math : *remainder*(X_{now}, 2)),
        not_in(i, math : *remainder*(($X_{now} - 1)/2$, number_agents)) : [X_{now}, X_{now}]

The agent will answer yes if it received a proposal which maximizes the sum among the proposals received in the first phase. Answers are given only in odd time points and an agent *i* should answer only when it wasn't its turn to make an offer, i.e., if the remainder of the the division of ($X_{now} - 1)/2$ by *number_agents* is not *i*. This is relevant only if the negotiations haven't ended yet, i.e., the code call *endNego* returns **false**, given the offer made in the previous time point (i.e., Offer1).

As in rule r2, in order to identify the proposal that maximizes the sum, the proposals of the first phase are gathered using the *gatherProposals* code call and the one that maximizes the sum criteria is determined using the code call *max*. In addition, to find the offer that was made in the previous time point *gatherProposals* with arguments 1 and $X_{now} - 1$ is used and the result is in Offer1. If both offers are the same, then it should accept the offer.

r4: **O***opt*: [X $_{now}$, X $_{now}$] ←
  Do *processAnswers*(): [X $_{now}$ − 1, X $_{now}$ − 1],
  in(Offer1, msgbox : *gatherProposals*(1, X $_{now}$ − 1)),
  in(false, schedule : *endNego*(Offer1)),
  in(T1, schedule : *firstPhase*()),
  in(X1, msgbox : *gatherProposals*(number_agents, T1)),
  in(Offer2, math : *max*(X1, $\mathcal{V}$, max_sum)), ≠ (Offer2, Offer1),
  in(true, schedule : *secondPhase*(X $_{now}$)),
  in(1, math : *remainder*(X $_{now}$, 2)),
  not_in(i, math : *remainder*((X $_{now}$ − 1)/2, number_agents)) : [X $_{now}$, X $_{now}$]

The agent will opt out of the negotiations if it received a proposal which does not maximize the sum among the proposals received in the first phase. The only difference between r4 and r3 is that Offer1 is equal to Offer2 in r3, and thus the agents should accept the offer. In r4 Offer1 is not equal to Offer2 and according to the specifications of the strategies that are in equilibrium, it should opt out of the negotiation.

r5: **F***processAnswers*(): [$T1, T1$] ←
  in(false, msgbox : *doneBroadcast*(T1)) : [X $_{now}$, X $_{now}$]

An agent is forbidden to read the answer of other agents before it broadcast its answers.

r6: **O***processAnswers*(): [X $_{now}$, X $_{now}$] ←
  in(1, math : *remainder*(X $_{now}$, 2)) : [X $_{now}$, X $_{now}$]

An agent is obliged to process the answers it obtained from other agents.

8.7 An Application of Tap: Delivery Agents in Contract Net Environments

In this section, we show how agent programs may be used to simulate a contract net problem. We consider the problem described in (Sandholm 1993) where there are several companies each having a set of geographically dispersed *dispatch centers* which ship the companies' products to other locations.

Each dispatch center is responsible for the deliveries initiated by certain factories and has a certain number of vehicles to take care of deliveries. The geographical operation areas of the dispatch centers overlap considerably. This enables several centers to handle a given delivery. Every delivery has to be included in the route of some vehicle. The problem of each dispatch center is to find routes for its vehicles minimizing its transportation costs and maximizing its benefits.

Sandholm (1993) suggests that in solving this problem, each dispatch center—represented by one agent—first solves its local routing problem. After that, an agent can potentially negotiate with other dispatch agents to take on some of their deliveries or to let them take on some of its deliveries for a dynamically negotiated fee. Sandholm presents a formalization of a bidding and awarding decision process. This formalization is based on marginal cost calculations. Here we will demonstrate how to program such agents in *IMPACT*. We will use the term "center" and its associated agent interchangeably.

We will use several specialized packages and functions in building such agents. The optimizer package provides functions to compute prices, costs, etc. and for identifying deliveries that can be sub-contracted to other centers. It includes the following code calls:

- optimizer:*findDelivery*() → Delivery

findDelivery chooses deliveries (from the deliveries handled by the center) which will be announced to other centers in order to get bids from them. In Sandholm's implementation, deliveries were chosen randomly from the deliveries whose destination lies in another center's main operation area.

- optimizer:*maxPrice*(Del) → Real

maxPrice gets as input a delivery and returns the maximum price of the announcement (i.e., the maximum price the agent is willing to pay). It uses a heuristic approximation of the marginal cost saved if the delivery is removed from the routing solution of the agent. An example of such a heuristic is described in (Sandholm 1993).

- optimizer:*price*(Del) → Real

price gets as an input a delivery and returns the price that the delivery would cost if done by this server.

- optimizer:*feasible*(Del) → Boolean

feasible gets as input a delivery and returns **true** if it is feasible for the agent to perform the delivery, given its current and pending commitments.

- optimizer:*getTime*(Del) → Time

getTime gets a delivery as an input and returns the time until which the agent is willing to accept bids for an announcement for this delivery.

- optimizer:*gatherAnnounceExpired*(Time) → ListofAnnouncements

gatherAnnounceExpired gets a time point and finds the announcements whose waiting time have expired.

- optimizer:*sentBid*(Id) → Boolean

sentBid gets as input an announcement Id and returns **true** if the agent has already sent a bid for this announcement and **false** otherwise.

- optimizer : *verifyAward*(A) → Boolean

verifyAward gets as input an award and returns **true** if the details of the award are the same as in the bid sent by the agent.

- optimizer : *annTime*(Time) → Boolean

annTime gets as input a time point and returns **true** if the agent should consider sending announcements in the specified time point.

- optimizer : *bidTime*(Time) → Boolean

annTime gets as input a time point and returns **true** if the agent should consider sending bids in the specified time point.

The gis package includes functions which provide information on the geographical locations of the dispatch centers. Such a package could well be any commercial geographic information system. The gis package supports the following code call:

- gis : *centers_located*(Del) → ListofCenters

centers_located gets as input a delivery and returns centers (other than the agent's center) whose associated operations area cover the destination of the delivery.

The msgbox package is extended with the following code calls:

- msgbox : *getId*() → String

getId provides a unique name for an announcement. It could be implemented as a combination of the agent's identification number and a counter which is increased each time *getId* is called.

- msgbox : *gatherAnnounce*(Time) → ListofAnnouncements

gatherAnnounce gets as an input a time point and returns announcements which were received from other agents and their expiration time is before the specified time. The fields of an announcement are: its identification number (Id), the delivery (Del), the sender (Center), the expiration time (Time) and the maximal price (C_max).

- msgbox : *gatherBids*(Id) → ListofBids

gatherBids gets an identification number of an announcement and returns all bids that were sent as a response to the specified announcement.

- msgbox : *gatherAwards*() → ListofAnnouncements

gatherAwards returns all the awarding messages the agent received.

The following is the agent program that solves the contract net problem.

r1:   **O** *send_ann*(Center, Id, Del, C_max, Time):[X_{now}, X_{now}] ←
  in(**true**, optimizer : *annTime*(X_{now})),

Section 8.7 An Application of Tap: Delivery Agents in Contract Net Environments

        in(Del, optimizer : *findDelivery*()),
        in(Center, gis : *centers_located*(Del)),
        in(C_max, optimizer : *maxPrice*(Del)),
        in(Time, optimizer : *getTime*(Del)),
        in(Id, msgbox : *getId*()) : [X_{now}, X_{now}]

An agent should consider sending announcements if the optimizer indicates (using *annTime*) that X_{now} is an appropriate time for doing so. In these time points, an agent is obliged to send an announcement for the deliveries chosen by the optimizer to all the centers whose operation areas include the destination of the delivery. The delivery is chosen by the optimizer, who also computes the maximal price the agent is willing to pay.

r2:   **O** *send_bid*(A.Center, A.Id, A.Del, C_bid) : [X_{now}, X_{now}] ←
        in(**true**, optimizer : *bidTime*(X_{now})),
        in(A, msgbox : *gatherAnnounce*(X_{now})),
        in(**false**, optimizer : *sentBid*(A.Id)),
        in(**true**, optimizer : *feasible*(A.delivery)),
        in(C_bid, optimizer : *price*(A.Del)) , <(C_bid, A.C_max) : [X_{now}, X_{now}]

The agent considers announcements received from other agents. It first verifies that the time of the announcement hasn't passed. Then it verifies that performing the delivery of the announcement is feasible given its other commitments. Finally, it determines the bidding price using the *price* function. If this price it lower than the maximal price the announcer is willing to pay, then it is obliged to send the bid.

r3:   **O** *send_award*(B2.Center, B2.Id) : [X_{now}, X_{now}] ←
        in(A, optimizer : *gatherAnnounceExpired*(X_{now})),
        is(B1, msgbox : *gatherBids*(A.Id)),
        in(B2, math : *min*(B1)), <(B2.price, A.C_max)
        Do *delete*(A.Del) : [X_{now}, X_{now}]

When the time of an announcement has expired, the agent is determining the identity of the successful bidder. These announcements are identified by *gatherAnnounceExpired*. The agent awards the delivery to the center which offers the lowest bid, given that this bid is lower than the maximal price the agent is willing to pay. All the bids are gathered by the *gatherBids* function and *min* returns the one with the minimal price. In addition, the delivery of the announcement is removed from the current deliveries of the center.

r4:   **O** *send_reject*(B2.Center, B2.Id) : [X_{now}, X_{now}] ←
        in(A, optimizer : *gatherAnnounceExpired*(X_{now})),

is(B1, msgbox: *gatherBids*(A.Id)),
in(B2, math: *max*(B1)), >(B2.price,B.C_max):[X_{now}, X_{now}]

This rule indicates a situation when no award is made. It occurs when the minimal bid is higher than the maximal price the agent is willing to pay. Most of the conditions are the same as in rule r4, except for B.price > C_max.

r5:   **O** *send_reject*(B3.Center, B3.Id):[X_{now}, X_{now}] ←
     in(A, optimizer: *gatherAnnounceExpired*(X_{now})),
     is(B1, msgbox: *gatherBids*(A.Id)),
     in(B2, math: *min*(B1)),
     in(B3, msgbox: *gatherBids*(A.Id)), ≠(B2,B3):[X_{now}, X_{now}]

The agent is obliged to send rejection messages to all unsuccessful bidders. The conditions involved are similar to these of r3. The difference is that the bid (B3) is different from the minimal one (B2).

r6:   **O** *indicate*(A.Center, A.Id, A.Del, C_bid):[X_{now}, X_{now}] ←
     Do *send_bid*(A.Center, A.Id, A.Del, C_bid):[X_{now}, X_{now}]

The agent must keep the details of its bids. It will be used to verify the correctness of the details of awards.

r7:   **O** *add*(A.del):[X_{now}, X_{now}] ←
     in(A, msgbox: *gatherAwards*(X_{now})),
     in(**false**, optimizer: *verifyAward*(A)):[X_{now}, X_{now}]

The agent must add a delivery of an award it received for one of its bids to its schedule, given that the details specified in the award are the same as in the bid sent by the agent. Note that in this system bids are binding.

8.8 Related Work

Actions and time have been extensively studied by many researchers in several areas of computing (e.g., (Manna and Pnueli 1992; Haddawy 1991; Ginsberg and Smith 1987; Morgenstern 1988; Allen 1984; Lamport 1994; Nirkhe, Kraus, Perlis, and Miller 1997; Dean and McDermott 1987; McDermott 1982; Rabinovich 1998), and (Singh 1998)). We present here the main differences between others' work and ours, and discuss work that combines time with deontic operators. Surveys of research on temporal reasoning include (Benthem 1991; Benthem 1995; Baker and Shoham 1995; Lee, Tannock, and Williams 1993; Vila 1994; Alur and Henzinger 1992; Chittaro and Montanari 1998).

- One of the main differences between our approach and the temporal logics approach is that we allow the history to be partially specified but in their approach, the entire history is defined for any time period. Allowing the history to be partially defined is needed when modeling bounded agents, as in this book.

- In our model, time can be expressed explicitly (as in, for example, (Thomas, Shoham, Schwartz, and Kraus 1991)). We do not use the modal temporal logic approach where time periods cannot be expressed in the language.

- We use a simple interval based temporal logic (Allen 1984), and introduce a mechanism for specifying intermediate effects of an action. We focus on the semantics of temporal agent programs which specify the commitments of the agents. We do not have modal operators associated with time but only with the obligations, permissions, etc. of an agent. Other interval temporal logics (e.g., (Halpern and Shoham 1991; Allen and Ferguson 1994; Artale and Franconi 1998)) were developed for describing complex plans and/or the study of appropriate semantics and their complexity for interval based temporal logics.

- We presented a temporal interval constraint language in order to provide a compact way to represent temporal feasible status sets. Other attempts to use constraints to simplify temporal reasoning include Dechter, Meiri, and Pearl (1991) who were one of the first to apply general purpose constraint solving techniques (such as the Floyd-Warshall shortest path algorithm) to reason about temporal relationships, and Koehler and Treinen (1995) that use a translation of their interval-based temporal logic (LLP) into constraint logic (CPL) to obtain an efficient deduction system.

- Most traditional AI planning frameworks assume that an action's effects are realized only after the entire action is successfully executed (Hendler, Tate, and Drummond 1990; Hendler and McDermott 1995). We proposed a mechanism that allows an agent designer to specify intermediate effects.

Several researchers have combined logics of commitments and actions with time.

Cohen and Levesque (1990a) and Cohen and Levesque (1990b) define the notion of persistence goals (P-GOAL). They assume that if an agent has a P-GOAL toward a proposition, then the agent believes that this proposition is not true now, but that it will be true at some time in the future. The agent will drop a persistent goal only if it comes to believe that it is true or that it is impossible. In their logic, time doesn't explicitly appear in the proposition; thus, they cannot express a P-GOAL toward propositions that will be true at some specific time in the future or consider situations where a proposition is true now, but which the agent believes will become false later and therefore has a P-GOAL to make it true again after it becomes false. They do not have any notion of agent programs. Their logic is used for abstract specifications of agents behavior.

Sonenberg, Tidhar, Werner, Kinny, Ljungberg, and Rao (1992) use a similar approach to that of Cohen and Levesque. However, they provide detailed specifications of various plan-constructs that may be used in the development of collaborative agents. (Shoham 1993)'s Agents0 has programs with commitments and a very simple mechanism to express time points.

Fiadeiro and Maibaum (1991) provide a complex temporal semantics to the deontic concepts of permission and obligation in order to be able to reason about the temporal properties of systems whose behavior has been specified in a deontic way. They are interested in the normative behavior of a system, while we focus on decision making of agents over time.

Horty (1996) proposes an analysis of what an agent ought to do. It is based on a loose parallel between action in indeterministic time (branching time) and choice under uncertainty, as it is studied in decision theory. Intuitively, a particular preference ordering is adapted from a study of choice under uncertainty; it is then proposed that an agent ought to see to it that A occurs whenever the agent has an available action which guarantees the truth of A, and which is not dominated by another action that does not guarantee the truth of A. The obligations of our agents are influenced by their programs and we do not use decision theory. An agent's obligations is determined using its status set and we provide a language for writing agents program with time.

Dignum and Kuiper (1997), and Dignum, Weigand, and Verharen (1996) combine temporal logic with deontic logic. Their semantics is based on Kripke models with implicit time while ours is based on status sets where time can be explicitly expressed. They focus on modeling deadlines and we focus on programming agents. They admit that automatic reasoning with specifications written in their language is not yet possible.

Kraus, Sycara, and Evenchik (1998) presented a logical model of the mental states of agents based on a representation of beliefs, desires, intentions, and goals and use it as the basis for the development of automated negotiators. As in our model, they also use explicit time structures and their modal operators G (for goal), *Int* (for intention), and *Do* have some similarities to our obligation, permission and do operators. However, their semantics is very different from ours. They use a *minimal structures* Chellas (1980) style semantics for each of their modal operators which leads to a set of axioms that are not appropriate for our agents. In addition, they require a fully specified history and use a discrete "point-based" representation of time, while we use an interval-based representation of discrete time.

9 Probabilistic Agent Programs

Thus far, we have assumed that all agents reason with a complete and certain view of the world. However, in most real world applications, agents have only a partial, and often uncertain view of what is true in the world.

For example, consider the CFIT* example described in Chapter 7. In this example, the tracking agent is keeping track of the locations of enemy vehicles over time. Any such endeavor is fraught with uncertainty—the tracking agent may not have the ability to conduct surveillance on a specific enemy vehicle when, for instance, the vehicle's location is occluded from the tracking agent's sensors. This is an example of *positional* uncertainty. Likewise, in the case of the CHAIN example, the plant agent may know that a certain purchase was sent sometime during the first week of June 1998, but is not sure about the exact date on which it was sent—this *temporal uncertainty* may affect the planning performed by this agent.

In general, uncertainty in an agent's reasoning occurs due to the following *basic* phenomena:

- *The agent is uncertain about its state.*

Throughout this book, we have assumed that agents are certain about their state, i.e. if a code-call of the form $a : f(d_1, \ldots, d_n)$ is executed, a *definite answer* results. If the set $\{o_1, \ldots, o_k\}$ of objects is returned, then each of these objects is definitely in the result. However, consider our tracking agent in the CFIT* example—when identifying an object through visual imagery, it may return the fact that object o is a T-72 tank with 70–80% probability and a T-80 tank with 20–30% probability. Thus, if we were to execute a code-call of the form $tracking : findobjects(image1)$, the answer described above is difficult to express in our current framework—returning a set containing triples of the form $\{(t72, 0.7, 0.8), (t80, 0.2, 0.3)\}$ would be incorrect because this does not capture the intuition that the object is either a T-72 or a T-80, but not both.

- *The agent is uncertain about when some of its actions will have effects.*

In Chapter 8, we have provided a detailed definition of how actions can have effects over time, and how such delayed effects can be modeled through the mechanism of checkpoints. However, there are a wide range of applications in which we cannot be sure of when an action's effects will be realized. For instance, consider the case where an action of the form $Fly(\text{boston}, \text{chicago}, \text{flightnum})$ is executed at time t. Even if we know the arrival and departure times of the flight in question, there is some uncertainty about exactly when this action will be completed. The airline in question may have statistical data showing a probability distribution over a possible space of completion times.

• *The agent is uncertain about its beliefs about another agent's state.*

This kind of uncertainty arises, for instance, in the CFIT* example where, as seen in Example 7.2.2 on page 215, we may have a situation where heli1 is not sure where agent tank1 is currently located—here, heli1 may believe that agent tank1 is located at some point along a stretch of highway with a certain probability distribution. In this case, heli1 needs to take this uncertainty into account when determining whether to fire at the enemy tank.

• *The agent is uncertain about its beliefs about another agent's actions.*

This kind of uncertainty arises when one agent is unsure about what another agent will do—what are the other agent's obligations, permissions, etc. For example, the heli1 agent may not be certain about the speed at which a given enemy vehicle can move over a certain kind of terrain. Thus, it may hypothesize that the enemy tank1 agent will execute one of the actions **Do** *Drive*(pos1, pos2, 35), ..., **Do** *Drive*(pos1, pos2, 50), with an associated probability distribution over these potential actions.

This is not intended to be a complete and comprehensive list of why agents may need to deal with uncertainty—rather, it represents a small set of core reasons for needing to deal with uncertainty.

In this chapter, we will comprehensively address the first kind of uncertainty described above, and we will briefly indicate how we can deal with the other types of uncertainty.

Before going into our technical development, a further note is in order. Uncertainty has been modeled in many different ways. Fuzzy sets (Zadeh 1965; Baldwin 1987; Dubois and Prade 1988; Dubois and Prade 1989), Bayesian networks (Pearl 1988), possibilistic logic (Dubois and Prade 1991; Dubois, Land, and Prade 1991; Dubois, Lang, and Prade 1994; Dubois and Prade 1995) and probabilities (Nilsson 1986; Emden 1986; Fagin and Halpern 1989; Fagin, Halpern, and Megiddo 1990; Guntzer, Kiessling, and Thone 1991; Kiessling, Thone, and Guntzer 1992; Ng and Subrahmanian 1993b; Ng and Subrahmanian 1993a; Lakshmanan and Sadri 1994a; Lakshmanan and Sadri 1994b; Ng and Subrahmanian 1995; Zaniolo, Ceri, Faloutsos, Snodgrass, Subrahmanian, and Zicari 1997; Lakshmanan and Shiri 1999) are four leading candidates for reasoning about uncertain domains. Of all these, there is little doubt that probability theory remains the most widely studied. As a consequence, we have chosen to develop a *probabilistic* theory of agent reasoning in uncertain domains. The others represent rich alternative avenues for exploration in the future.

9.1 Probabilistic Code Calls

Consider a code call of the form $a{:}_{RV}fd_1,\ldots,d_n$. This code call returns as output, some set of objects $o_1,\ldots,o_k$ each of type τ where τ is the output type of f. By returning o_i as an output object, we are declaring that in an agent state $\mathcal{O}$, $o_i \in a{:}_{RV}f(d_1,\ldots,d_n)$. Uncertainty arises when we do not know what objects are in the set $a{:}_{RV}f(d_1,\ldots,d_n)$.

For instance, in the CFIT* example, the tracking agent, when invoked with the code call tracking:*findobjects*(image1), may wish to report that a T-72 tank is definitely in the image, and another tank, either a T-72 (70–80% probability) or a T-80 (20–30% probability), is in the image. The current output type of the code call tracking:*findobjects*(image1) does not allow this to be returned. The problem is that instead of returning a set of objects, in this case, we need to return a set of *random variables* (see (Ross 1997)) in the strict sense of probability theory. Furthermore, these random variables need to have the same type as the code call's output type.

DEFINITION 9.1.1 (RANDOM VARIABLE OF TYPE τ) A *random variable* of type τ is a finite set **RV** of objects of type τ, together with a probability distribution $\wp$ that assigns real numbers in the unit interval [0, 1] to members of **RV** such that $\Sigma_{o \in \mathbf{RV}} \wp(o) \leq 1$.

It is important to note that in classical probability theory (Ross 1997), random variables satisfy a stronger requirement that $\Sigma_{o \in \mathbf{RV}} \wp(o) = 1$. However, in many real life situations, a probability distribution may have missing pieces, which explains why we have chosen a weaker definition.

Let us see how this notion of a random variable is pertinent to our CFIT* example.

Example 9.1.1 (CFIT Example Revisited)* For example, consider the CFIT* example, and suppose we have a tank as shown in Figure 9.1 on the following page. In this case, the tracking agent may not know the precise location of the tank because some time may have elapsed since the last surveillance report at which this tank was observed. Based on its projections, it may know that the tank is somewhere between markers 11 and 15 on a particular road. It may assume that the probability of exactly which point it is at is uniformly distributed over these points. Hence, given any of these five points, there is a 20% probability that the tank is at that point.

DEFINITION 9.1.2 (PROBABILISTIC CODE CALL $a{:}_{RV}f(d_1,\ldots,d_n)$) Suppose $a{:}f(d_1,\ldots,d_n)$ is a code call where f's output type is τ. A *probabilistic code call* associated with $a{:}f(d_1,\ldots,d_n)$ when executed on state $\mathcal{O}$ returns as output, a set of random variables of type τ. To distinguish this code call from the original code call, we denote it by $a{:}_{RV}f(d_1,\ldots,d_n)$.

298   Chapter 9   Probabilistic Agent Programs

Figure 9.1
Example of Random Variable in CFIT* Example.

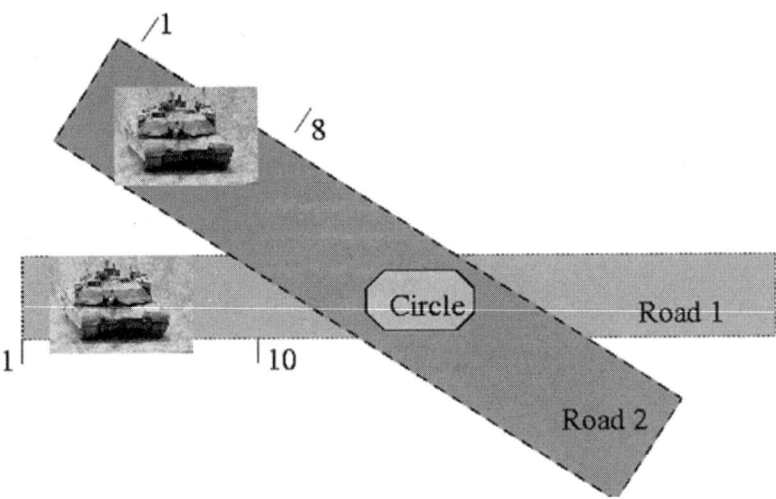

Figure 9.2
Example of Probabilistic code calls in CFIT* Example.

The following example illustrates the use of probabilistic code calls.

Example 9.1.2 (CFIT Example Revisited)*   Let us extend Example 9.1.1 on the page before to the situation shown in Figure 9.2. Here, two vehicles are moving on two intersecting roads. The traffic circle is at location 12 on both roads. Suppose we know that the tank on road 1 (tank1) is somewhere between locations 1 and 10 (with a uniform distribution) and tank2 on road 2 is somewhere between locations 1 and 8 (with a uniform distribution as well).

Suppose we can execute a code call that answers the query "Find all vehicles within 6 units of the traffic circle." Clearly both tank1 and tank2 *may* be within 6 units of the circle. The probability that tank1 is within 6 units of the circle is the probability that tank1 is at one of locations 6, 7, 8, 9, 10, which equals 0.5. Similarly, the probability that tank2 is within 6 units of the circle is the probability that tank2 is at one of locations 6, 7, 8 which is 0.375.

Therefore, the answer to this probabilistic code call should contain two random variables[1]

$\langle\{\text{tank1}\}, 0.5\rangle, \langle\{\text{tank2}\}, 0.375\rangle$.

It is important to note that probabilistic code calls and ordinary code calls have the same syntax—however, the results they return may be different. The former returns a set of random variables of type τ, while the latter returns a set of objects of type τ.

Let us see how the above definition of a probabilistic code call may be extended to probabilistic code call atoms. Syntactically, a probabilistic code call atom is exactly like a code call atom—however, as a probabilistic code call returns a set of *random variables*, probabilistic code call atoms are true or false with some probability. Let us consider some simple examples before providing formal definitions.

Example 9.1.3 (CFIT* Example Revisited) Let us return to the case of Example 9.1.2 on the preceding page. Consider the code-call atom **in**(X, χ) where χ is the code call "Find all vehicles within 6 units of the traffic circle" described in Example 9.1.2. Clearly, **in**(tank1, χ) should be true with 50% probability and **in**(tank2, χ) should be true with 37.5% probability because of the reasoning in Example 9.1.2.

However, as the following example shows, this kind of reasoning may very quickly lead to problems.

Example 9.1.4 (Combining Probabilities I) Suppose we consider a code call χ containing the following two random variables.

$\mathbf{RV}_1 = \langle\{a, b\}, \wp_1\rangle$

$\mathbf{RV}_2 = \langle\{b, c\}, \wp_2\rangle$

Suppose $\wp_1(a) = 0.9$, $\wp_1(b) = 0.1$, $\wp_2(b) = 0.8$, $\wp_2(c) = 0.1$. What is the probability that b is in the result of the code call χ?

---

[1] Distinguish this from the following *one* random variable: $\langle\{\text{tank1}, \text{tank2}\}, \wp\rangle$.

Answering this question is problematic. The reason is that we are told that there are at most two objects returned by χ. One of these objects is either a or b, and the other is either b or c. This leads to four possibilities, depending on which of these is true. The situation is further complicated because in some cases, knowing that the first object is b may preclude the second object from being b—this would occur, for instance, if χ examines photographs each containing two different people and provides identifications for each. a, b and c may be potential id's of such people returned by the image processing program. In such cases, the same person can never be pictured with himself or herself.

Of course, in other cases, there may be no reason to believe that knowing the value of one of two objects tells us anything about the value of the second object. For example if we replace people with colored cubes (with a denoting amber cubes, b black, and c cyan), there is no reason to believe that two identical black cubes cannot be pictured next to each other.

The source of the problem above is that of *disjunctive information*. The object b could be in the result of executing the code call χ in one of two ways—because of the first random variable, or because of the second.

There are two ways around this problem. Thus far in this book, we have assumed that all code calls return *sets* of objects, not multisets. Under this interpretation, the scenario in Example 9.1.4 on the preceding page has another *hidden* constraint which says that if the first random variable is known to have a value, then the other random variable cannot have the same value.

The other scenario would be to argue that the reasoning in Example 9.1.4 is incorrect—that if two objects are completely identical, then they must be the same. This means that if we have two distinct black cubes, then these two black cubes must be *distinguishable* from one another via some property such as their location in the photo, or *Id*s assigned to them must be distinct. This is in fact quite reasonable: it is the *extensionality principle* which dates back to Leibniz.

In either of these two cases, it is reasonable to assume that every code call returns a set of random variables that have no overlap. This is formalized in the next definition.

DEFINITION 9.1.3 (COHERENT PROBABILISTIC CODE CALL)   Consider a probabilistic code call that returns a set of random variables of type τ. This probabilistic code call is said to be *coherent if, by definition,* whenever $\langle X_1, \wp_1 \rangle$, $\langle X_2, \wp_2 \rangle$ are distinct random variables in the set of output random variables, then $X_1 \cap X_2 = \emptyset$.

Throughout the rest of this chapter, we will assume that only coherent probabilistic code calls are considered. Thus, the expression "probabilistic code call" will in fact denote "coherent probabilistic code call."

Section 9.1   Probabilistic Code Calls

DEFINITION 9.1.4 (PROBABILISTIC CODE CALL ATOM)   Suppose $a{:}_{\mathbf{RV}}f(d_1,\ldots,d_n)$ is a ground probabilistic code call and suppose o is an object of the output type of this code call w.r.t. agent state $\mathcal{O}$. Suppose $[\ell, u]$ is a closed subinterval of the unit interval $[0, 1]$. We define below, what it means for o to *probabilistically satisfy* a code call atom.

- $o \models_{\mathcal{O}}^{[\ell,u]} \mathbf{in}(X, a{:}_{\mathbf{RV}}f(d_1,\ldots,d_n))$
if, by definition, $(Y, \wp)$ is a random variable contained in $a{:}_{\mathbf{RV}}f(d_1,\ldots,d_n)$ when evaluated w.r.t. $\mathcal{O}$ and $o \in Y$ and $\ell \leq \wp(o) \leq u$.

- $o \models_{\mathcal{O}}^{[\ell,u]} \mathbf{not\_in}(X, a{:}_{\mathbf{RV}}f(d_1,\ldots,d_n))$
if, by definition, for all random variables $(Y, \wp)$ contained in $a{:}_{\mathbf{RV}}f(d_1,\ldots,d_n)$ when evaluated w.r.t. $\mathcal{O}$, either $o \notin Y$ or $\wp(o) \notin [\ell, u]$.

As in Definition 4.2.4 on page 84, we define the important notion of probabilistic code call conditions.

DEFINITION 9.1.5 (PROBABILISTIC CODE CALL CONDITION)   A *probabilistic code call condition* is defined as follows:

1. Every probabilistic code call atom is a probabilistic code call condition.

2. If s and t are either variables or objects, then s = t is a probabilistic code call condition.

3. If s and t are either integers/real valued objects, or are variables over the integers/reals, then s < t, s > t, s ≤ t, and s ≥ t are probabilistic code call conditions.

4. If χ_1 and χ_2 are probabilistic code call conditions, then χ_1 & χ_2 is a probabilistic code call condition.

We refer to any probabilistic code call condition of form 1.-3. as an *atomic* probabilistic code call condition.

Extending the above definition of satisfaction of probabilistic code call atoms to the case of *probabilistic code call conditions* is much more problematic. The reason is that the scenario outlined in Example 9.1.4 has been "made to go away" only partly by the assumption of coherence made above. To see why, consider the simple example given below.

Example 9.1.5 (Combining Probabilities I)   Suppose the tracking agent is examining a surveillance photo showing an enemy tank. A marking on the side of the tank indicates it is either a T-72 or a T-80 tank. The construction of the gun turret indicates either a type A1 or a type A2 turret. The tracking agent has two code calls—tracking:$_{\mathbf{RV}}$ *marking*(image) and tracking:$_{\mathbf{RV}}$ *turret*(image) both of which extract marking and turret information for the same image. The first code call returns one random variable $\{t72, t80\}$ with probabilities

30% and 70% respectively. The second code call also returns one random variable $\{a1, a2\}$ with probabilities 40% and 60% respectively. What is the probability that the code call condition

in(t72, tracking:$_{\mathbf{RV}}$ *marking*(image)) & **in**(a2, tracking:$_{\mathbf{RV}}$ *turret*(image))

is true?

The answer to this question depends very much upon the knowledge we have (if any) about the dependencies between the identification of a tank as a T-72 or a T-80, and the type of gun turret on these. Some example scenarios are:

1. *We may know that all T-72's have type A1 gun turrets, and all T-80's have type A2 gun turrets.*
In this case, the probability of this code call condition being true is 0.

2. *We may know that gun turret types are independent of the type of tank.*
In this case, the probability of this code call condition being true is $0.3 \times 0.6 = 0.18$.

3. *We may be ignorant of the the dependencies between gun turret types and tank types.*
In this case, as argued by (Boole 1854), we cannot return a point probability—rather, only an *interval* can be established for the probability that the above code call is true. In general, Boole's result says that if we are ignorant about the relationship between two events, then all we can say(Ng and Subrahmanian 1993b) is that $\mathbf{Prob}(e_1 \wedge e_2)$ lies in the interval:

$[\max(0, \mathbf{Prob}(e_1) + \mathbf{Prob}(e_2) - 1), \min(\mathbf{Prob}(e_1), \mathbf{Prob}(e_2)).]$

Applying this formula to the above case, we conclude that the probability of the above code call condition lies somewhere in the interval $[0, 0.3]$. Boole's reasoning has been extensively used for probabilistic reasoning under conditions of ignorance (Nilsson 1986; Fagin, Halpern, and Megiddo 1990; Ng and Subrahmanian 1993b; Ng and Subrahmanian 1995).

This motivates our definition of a *conjunction strategy*, first introduced by Lakshmanan, Leone, Ross, and Subrahmanian (1997), and later used in logic programming by Dekhtyar and Subrahmanian (1996).

DEFINITION 9.1.6 (PROBABILISTIC CONJUNCTION STRATEGY $\otimes$) Let events e_1 and e_2 have probabilistic intervals $[L_1, U_1]$ and $[L_2, U_2]$ respectively. Then a *probabilistic conjunction strategy* is a binary operation $\otimes$ which uses this information to compute the probabilistic interval $[L, U]$ for event $(e_1 \wedge e_2)$. When the events involved are clear from context, we use "$[L, U] = [L_1, U_1] \otimes [L_2, U_2]$" to denote "$(e_1 \wedge e_2, [L, U]) = (e_1, [L_1, U_1]) \otimes (e_2, [L_2, U_2])$." Every conjunctive strategy must conform to the following postulates of probabilistic conjunction:

1. *Bottomline*: $([L_1, U_1] \otimes [L_2, U_2]) \leq [\min(L_1, L_2), \min(U_1, U_2)]$.
2. *Ignorance*: $([L_1, U_1] \otimes [L_2, U_2]) \subseteq [\max(0, L_1 + L_2 - 1), \min(U_1, U_2)]$.
3. *Identity*: When $(e_1 \wedge e_2)$ is consistent and $[L_2, U_2] = [1, 1]$, $([L_1, U_1] \otimes [L_2, U_2]) = [L_1, U_1]$.
4. *Annihilator*: $([L_1, U_1] \otimes [0, 0]) = [0, 0]$.
5. *Commutativity*: $([L_1, U_1] \otimes [L_2, U_2]) = ([L_2, U_2] \otimes [L_1, U_1])$.
6. *Associativity*: $(([L_1, U_1] \otimes [L_2, U_2]) \otimes [L_3, U_3]) = ([L_1, U_1] \otimes ([L_2, U_2] \otimes [L_3, U_3]))$.
7. *Monotonicity*: $([L_1, U_1] \otimes [L_2, U_2]) \leq ([L_1, U_1] \otimes [L_3, U_3])$ if $[L_2, U_2] \leq [L_3, U_3]$.

The following are some sample conjunctive strategies:

- Use the $\otimes_{ig}$ (ignorance) operator when we do not know the dependencies between e_1 and e_2. $([L_1, U_1] \otimes_{ig} [L_2, U_2]) \equiv [\max(0, L_1 + L_2 - 1), \min(U_1, U_2)]$.
- Use the $\otimes_{pc}$ (positive correlation) operator when the overlap between e_1 and e_2 is maximal. $([L_1, U_1] \otimes_{pc} [L_2, U_2]) \equiv [\min(L_1, L_2), \min(U_1, U_2)]$.
- Use the $\otimes_{nc}$ (negative correlation) operator when the overlap between e_1 and e_2 is minimal. $([L_1, U_1] \otimes_{nc} [L_2, U_2]) \equiv [\max(0, L_1 + L_2 - 1), \max(0, U_1 + U_2 - 1)]$.
- Use the $\otimes_{in}$ (independence) operator when e_1 and e_2 are independent. $([L_1, U_1] \otimes_{in} [L_2, U_2]) = [L_1 \cdot L_2, U_1 \cdot U_2]$.

9.2 Probabilistic Agent Programs: Syntax

With this background in mind, we are now ready to define the syntax of a probabilistic agent program, or pap for short. This syntax will build upon the well studied *annotated logic paradigm* proposed by(Subrahmanian 1987), and later studied extensively (Kifer and Subrahmanian 1992; Ng and Subrahmanian 1993b; Ng and Subrahmanian 1993a).

9.2.1 Annotation Syntax

We will assume the existence of an *annotation language* $\mathbf{L}^{ann}$—the constant symbols of $\mathbf{L}^{ann}$ are the real numbers in the unit interval $[0, 1]$. In addition, $\mathbf{L}^{ann}$ contains a finite set of function symbols, each with an associated arity, and a (possibly infinite) set of variable symbols, ranging over the unit interval $[0, 1]$. All function symbols are *pre-interpreted* in the sense that associated with each function symbol f of arity k is a fixed function from $[0, 1]^k$ to $[0, 1]$.

DEFINITION 9.2.1 (ANNOTATION ITEM)   We define annotation items inductively as follows:

- Every constant and every variable of $\mathbf{L}^{ann}$ is an annotation item.
- If f is an annotation function of arity n and $ai_1, \ldots, ai_n$ are annotation items, then $f(ai_1, \ldots, ai_n)$ is an annotation item.

An annotation item is *ground* if no annotation variables occur in it.

Thus, for example, $0, 0.9, (V+0.9), (V+0.9)^2$ are all annotation items if V is a variable in $\mathbf{L}^{ann}$ and "+", "*" are annotation functions of arity 2.

DEFINITION 9.2.2 (ANNOTATION $[ai_1, ai_2]$)   If ai_1, ai_2 are annotation items, then $[ai_1, ai_2]$ is an *annotation*. If ai_1, ai_2 are both ground, then $[ai_1, ai_2]$ is a *ground annotation*.

For example, $[0, 0.4], [0.7, 0.9], [0.1, \frac{V}{2}], [\frac{V}{4}, \frac{V}{2}]$ are all annotations. The annotation $[0.1, \frac{V}{2}]$ denotes an interval only when a value in $[0, 1]$ is assigned to the variable V.

DEFINITION 9.2.3 (ANNOTATED CODE CALL CONDITION $\chi : \langle [ai_1, ai_2] \otimes \rangle$)   If χ is a probabilistic code call condition, $\otimes$ is a conjunction strategy, and $[ai_1, ai_2]$ is an annotation, then $\chi : \langle [ai_1, ai_2] \otimes \rangle$ is an *annotated code call condition*. $\chi : \langle [ai_1, ai_2], \otimes \rangle$ is *ground* if there are no variables in either χ or in $[ai_1, ai_2]$.

Intuitively, a ground annotated code call condition says that the probability (under conjunction strategy $\otimes$) of the χ being true lies in the interval defined by $[ai_1, ai_2]$.

Example 9.2.1 (Sample Annotated Code Calls)   Consider the code calls described in Example 9.1.5 on page 301. These can be written as annotated code calls in the following way:

- **in**(t72, tracking:$_{\mathbf{RV}}$ *marking*(image)) : $\langle [0.3, 0.3], \otimes_{ig} \rangle$
- **in**(a2, tracking:$_{\mathbf{RV}}$ *turret*(image)) : $\langle [0.7, 0.7], \otimes_{ig} \rangle$
- **in**(t72, tracking:$_{\mathbf{RV}}$ *marking*(image)) & **in**(a2, tracking:$_{\mathbf{RV}}$ *turret*(image)) : $\langle [0, 0.3], \otimes_{ig} \rangle$

The definition of a *probabilistic action rule* is exactly like the definition of an action rule (Equation 6.2 on page 160) in Chapter 6, except that we now allow annotated code calls to occur in the body of a rule.

DEFINITION 9.2.4 (PROBABILISTIC AGENT PROGRAMS $\mathcal{PP}$)   Suppose Γ is a conjunction of annotated code calls, and $A, L_1, \ldots, L_n$ are action status atoms. Then

$$A \leftarrow \Gamma, L_1, \ldots, L_n \tag{9.1}$$

is a *probabilistic action rule*.

Section 9.2   Probabilistic Agent Programs: Syntax   305

Finally a *probabilistic agent program* is a finite set of probabilistic action rules.

Example 9.2.2 (Sample pap*)*   The following are some sample probabilistic action rules from a pap for the CFIT* example.

r1:   **P** *compute_currentLocation*(report) ←
  in(Current_Location, autoPilot:$_{\mathbf{RV}}$ *location*()),
  Current_Location.Z < 200 : $\langle [0.1, 1], \otimes_{ig} \rangle$

If the probability than the plane is below 200 meters is greater than or equal to 0.1, then the agent is allowed to update its estimate of the plane's current location.

r2:   **O** *compute_currentLocation*(report) ←
  in(Current_Location, autoPilot:$_{\mathbf{RV}}$ *location*()) ,
  Current_Location.Z < 200 : $\langle [0.5, 1], \otimes_{ig} \rangle$

If the probability than the plane is below 200 meters is greater than or equal to 0.5, then the agent is also obliged to update its estimate of the plane's current location.

r3:   **F** *compute_currentLocation*(report) ←
  in(stealth_mode, autoPilot:$_{\mathbf{RV}}$ *planeStatus*()) : $\langle [1, 1], \otimes_{ig} \rangle$

If the plane is in stealth mode, the agent may not compute the plane's current location (since doing so may trigger enemy radars).

r4:   **Do** *warn_pilot*(sensor_malfunction, altimeter) ←
  not_in(stealth_mode, autoPilot:$_{\mathbf{RV}}$ *planeStatus*()) : $\langle [1, 1], \otimes_{ig} \rangle$,
  F *compute_currentLocation*(report)

If the plane is not in stealth mode and, for some reason, our agent is not allowed (or able) to compute the plane's current location, then warn the pilot of a possible sensor malfunction.

r5:   **O** *warn_pilot*(enemy_detected, X) ←
  O *process_request*(Msg.Id, tracking),
  in(enemy_detected, msgbox : *getVar*(Msg.Id, "enemy_detected")),
  in(X, msgbox : *getVar*(Msg.Id, "X")),
  in(ListOfNeutralizedAgents, msgbox : *getVar*(Msg.Id, "ListOfNeutralizedAgents")),
  not_in(X, ListOfNeutralizedAgents)

If the tracking agent detects a surface-to-air missile battery (with probability 0.2 or higher), then our agent is obliged to warn the pilot that an enemy has been detected.

r6:   **W** *warn_pilot*(enemy_detected, X) ←
  O *process_request*(Msg.Id, tracking),
  in(enemy_detected, msgbox : *getVar*(Msg.Id, "enemy_det ected")),
  in(X, msgbox : *getVar*(Msg.Id, "X")),

in(ListOfNeutralizedAgents, msgbox:*getVar*(Msg.Id, "ListOfNeutralizedAgents")),
in(X, ListOfNeutralizedAgents)

If the tracking agent detects a surface-to-air missile battery but we are sure that this threat has already been neutralized, then our agent is not required to notify the pilot of the battery's presence.

r7: **Do** *signal_base*(enemy_detected, X) ←
  not_in(stealth_mode, autoPilot:$_{RV}$ *planeStatus*()) : $\langle [1, 1], \otimes_{ig} \rangle$,
  Do *warn_pilot*(enemy_detected, X)

If the pilot is warned of enemy presence, and the plane is not in stealth mode, send an alert signal to the coordinating base as well.

9.3 Probabilistic Agent Programs: Semantics

In the preceding section, we have defined the syntax of paps, and informally described their semantics. In this section, we will formally extend the concept of a *feasible status set S* (Definition 6.5.5 on page 175) to *feasible probabilistic status sets* $\mathcal{PS}$.

Recall that for a status set $\mathcal{PS}$ to be feasible in the sense of Definition 6.5.5, four broad properties must be satisfied:

- Closure under the program rules;
- Deontic and action consistency;
- Deontic and action closure;
- State consistency

In the rest of this section, we show how these four defining characteristics may be extended to the probabilistic case. When doing so, we will observe that various problems arise that need to be addressed. However, the first thing we need to do is to define what it means for an agent state to satisfy an annotated code call—this definition will be critical in the definition of a feasible probabilistic status set.

Although syntactically the notion of a probabilistic status set is the same as in the non-probabilistic case, namely a set of action status atoms, we introduce the following notation to emphasize that the code calls ocurring in the status atoms are in fact *probabilistic* code calls.

DEFINITION 9.3.1 (PROBABILISTIC STATUS SET $\mathcal{PS}$) A *probabilistic status set* is any set $\mathcal{PS}$ of ground probabilistic action status atoms over $\mathcal{S}$. For any operator $\mathsf{Op} \in \{\mathbf{P}, \mathbf{Do}, \mathbf{F}, \mathbf{O}, \mathbf{W}\}$, we denote by $\mathsf{Op}(\mathcal{PS})$ the set $\mathsf{Op}(\mathcal{PS}) = \{\alpha \mid \mathsf{Op}(\alpha) \in \mathcal{PS}\}$.

9.3.1 Satisfaction of Annotated Formulae

In this section, we define what it means for an agent state to satisfy an annotated code call condition. This will be needed several times in this chapter—for example, in order to define what it means for a state to satisfy an integrity constraint, and/or what it means for a state to satisfy the body of a probabilistic action rule.

The first important definition we need specifies when an agent state satisfies a ground annotated code call.

DEFINITION 9.3.2 (SATISFYING AN ANNOTATED CODE CALL CONDITION) Suppose $\mathcal{O}$ is an agent state, and suppose $\chi : \langle [ai_1, ai_2], \otimes \rangle$ is a ground annotated code call condition. $\mathcal{O}$ is said to *satisfy* $\chi : \langle [ai_1, ai_2], \otimes \rangle$, denoted $\mathcal{O} \models^{[ai_1, ai_2]} \chi : \langle [ai_1, ai_2], \otimes \rangle$, *if, by definition,* one of the following cases holds:

- χ is of the form $o = o$ (where o is an object),
- χ is of the form $r_1 < r_2$, where r_1, r_2 are real numbers (or integers) such that r_1 is less than r_2,
- χ is of the form **in**(X, a:$_{\mathbf{RV}}f(d_1, \ldots, d_n)$) and $o \models_{\mathcal{O}}^{[ai_1, ai_2]}$ **in**(X, a:$_{\mathbf{RV}}f(d_1, \ldots, d_n)$),
- χ is of the form **not_in**(o, a:$_{\mathbf{RV}}f(d_1, \ldots, d_n)$) and $o \models_{\mathcal{O}}^{[ai_1, ai_2]}$ **not_in**(X, a:$_{\mathbf{RV}}f \times (d_1, \ldots, d_n)$),
- χ is of the form $\chi_1 \wedge \chi_2$ and $[\ell_1, u_1], [\ell_2, u_2]$ are the tightest intervals such that $\mathcal{O} \models^{[\ell_1, u_1]} \chi_1$ and $\mathcal{O} \models^{[\ell_2, u_2]} \chi_2$ and $[ai_1, ai_2] \supseteq [\ell_1, u_1] \otimes [\ell_2, u_2]$.

$\mathcal{O}$ is said to *satisfy* a non-ground annotated code call $\chi : \langle [ai_1, ai_2], \otimes \rangle$, *if, by definition,* $\mathcal{O}$ satisfies all ground instances of $\chi : \langle [ai_1, ai_2], \otimes \rangle$.

Below, we present some simple examples of satisfaction of annotated code calls by agent states.

Example 9.3.1 (Satisfaction of Annotated Code Calls) Let χ_5 denote the annotated code call in rule r5 of Example 9.2.2 on page 305 and suppose that **in**(X, tracking :$_{\mathbf{RV}}getListOfAgents$()) returns either agent a_1 or agent a_2. If agent state $\mathcal{O}$ indicates that a_1 is either a sam_battery (with probability 0.3) or a tank (with probability 0.7), and a_2 is either a sam_battery (with probability 0.4) or a tank (with probability 0.6), then $\mathcal{O} \models^{[0.2,1]} \chi_5$. Note however that if agent state $\mathcal{O}$ indicates that a_1 is either a sam_battery (with probability 0.1) or a tank (with probability 0.9), then $\mathcal{O} \not\models^{[0.2,1]} \chi_5$ since here, $\mathcal{O}$ does not satisfy all ground instances of χ_5.

9.3.2 Closure and $\mathbf{App}_{\mathcal{PP},\mathcal{O}_S}(\mathcal{PS})$

Suppose we consider a probabilistic status set $\mathcal{PS}$. Given a probabilistic agent program $\mathcal{PP}$, we can associate with it, an operator $\mathbf{App}_{\mathcal{PP},\mathcal{O}_S}(\mathcal{PS})$ that maps probabilistic status sets to probabilistic status sets.

DEFINITION 9.3.3 (OPERATOR $\mathbf{App}_{\mathcal{PP},\mathcal{O}_S}(\mathcal{PS})$)   Suppose $\mathcal{PP}$ is a probabilistic agent program, $\mathcal{O}_S$ is an agent state, and $\mathcal{PS}$ is a probabilistic status set. Then

$\mathbf{App}_{\mathcal{PP},\mathcal{O}_S}(\mathcal{PS}) = \{\mathsf{Op}\,\alpha \mid \mathsf{Op}\,\alpha$ is the head of a ground instance of a rule r in $\mathcal{PP}$ satisfying the 4 conditions below$\}$

1. $B_{as}^{+}(r) \subseteq \mathcal{PS}$ and $\neg.B_{as}^{-}(r) \cap \mathcal{PS} = \emptyset$, and
2. For every annotated code call condition $\chi : \langle [\mathsf{ai}_1, \mathsf{ai}_2], \otimes \rangle$ in the body of r, it is the case that $\mathcal{O}_S \models^{[\mathsf{ai}_1,\mathsf{ai}_2]} \chi : \langle [\mathsf{ai}_1, \mathsf{ai}_2], \otimes \rangle$ and
3. if $\mathsf{Op} \in \{\mathbf{P}, \mathbf{O}, \mathbf{Do}\}$, then $\mathcal{O}_S \models^{[1,1]} Pre(\alpha)$ and
4. for every action status atom of the form $\mathsf{Op}\,\beta$ in $B_{as}^{+}(r)$ such that $\mathsf{Op} \in \{\mathbf{P}, \mathbf{O}, \mathbf{Do}\}$, $\mathcal{O}_S \models^{[1,1]} Pre(\beta)$.

It is important to observe that the last two clauses in the definition of operator $\mathbf{App}_{\mathcal{PP},\mathcal{O}_S}(\mathcal{PS})$ distinguish it from the case of the operator $\mathbf{App}_{\mathcal{P},\mathcal{O}_S}(S)$ used in ordinary agent programs as defined in Chapter 6 (Definition 6.5.4 on page 174). The last clause in the above definition says that if the annotated code call condition in the body of a probabilistic action rule is true, and if we know with 100% certainty that the preconditions of all actions β such that either $\mathbf{P}\beta$, $\mathbf{O}\beta$ or $\mathbf{Do}\,\beta$ occurs in the body of the rule are true in our (uncertain agent state), then the agent can fire the rule. Of course, the third clause in the above definition says that for the rule to fire, we must further be certain that if $\mathsf{Op}\,\alpha$ is in the head of the rule for $\mathsf{Op} \in \{\mathbf{P}, \mathbf{O}, \mathbf{Do}\}$, then the precondition of this rule must also be true.

In short, we are assuming that the agent cannot perform an action without being 100% certain that the precondition of that action is true in the current state. Knowing that the precondition of an action *may* be true in the current state does not allow the agent to attempt the action. *An agent cannot do something unless it knows for sure that it can do it.*

This is an important new wrinkle that occurs when we deal with uncertainty in an agent's state—the agent may not know whether an action in its repertoire is in fact executable, because the state of the agent is itself uncertain. The following examples show how the CFIT* example may be applicable to the case of such agents.

Example 9.3.2 (Operator $\mathbf{App}_{\mathcal{PP},\mathcal{O}_S}(\mathcal{PS})$)   Let $\mathcal{PP}$ contain only rule r5 from Example 9.2.2 on page 305, let χ_5 denote the annotated code call given in Example 9.3.1 on page 307, and let $\mathcal{PS} = \emptyset$. Then

$$\mathbf{O}\textit{warn\_pilot}(\texttt{enemy\_detected}, \texttt{x}) \in \mathbf{App}_{\mathcal{PP},\mathcal{O}_S}(\mathcal{PS})$$
$$\textit{if and only if}$$
$$\mathcal{O}_S \models^{[0.2,1]} \chi_5 \quad \text{and} \quad \mathcal{O}_S \models^{[1,1]} \textit{Pre}(\textit{warn\_pilot}(\texttt{enemy\_detected}, \texttt{x})).$$

Thus if a precondition for *warn_pilot* is that the communication channel must be at least 80% secure, then $\mathbf{O}\textit{warn\_pilot}(\texttt{enemy\_detected}, \texttt{x})$ will not appear in $\mathbf{App}_{\mathcal{PP},\mathcal{O}_S}(\mathcal{PS})$ if this requirement is not met.

9.3.3 Deontic/Action Consistency/Closure

In this section, we extend the concept of deontic and action consistency (Definition 6.5.2 on page 173) introduced earlier in Chapter 6 to the case of probabilistic agent programs.

DEFINITION 9.3.4 (DEONTIC AND ACTION CONSISTENCY)   A probabilistic status set $\mathcal{PS}$ is called *deontically consistent* with respect to an agent state $\mathcal{O}$ *if, by definition*, it satisfies the following rules for any ground action α:

- If $\mathbf{O}\alpha \in \mathcal{PS}$, then $\mathbf{W}\alpha \notin \mathcal{PS}$.
- If $\mathbf{P}\alpha \in \mathcal{PS}$, then $\mathbf{F}\alpha \notin \mathcal{PS}$.
- If $\mathbf{P}\alpha \in \mathcal{PS}$, then $\mathcal{O} \models^{[1,1]} \textit{Pre}(\alpha)$.

A probabilistic status set $\mathcal{PS}$ is called *action consistent* with respect to an agent state $\mathcal{O}$ *if, by definition*, for every action constraint of the form

$$\{\alpha_1(\vec{X}_1), \ldots, \alpha_k(\vec{X}_k)\} \hookleftarrow \chi \tag{9.2}$$

either $\mathcal{O} \not\models^{[1,1]} \chi$ or $\{\alpha_1(\vec{X}_1), \ldots, \alpha_k(\vec{X}_k)\} \not\subseteq \mathcal{PS}$.

As the reader can see, the concept of a probabilistic status set being deontically consistent is similar to the non-probabilistic case—we emphasize that in both cases, all permitted actions must have preconditions that are true with 100% probability in the state. Likewise, the concept of action consistency is also the same—if the precondition of an action constraint is true with 100% probability, then the set of actions in the head of the action constraint cannot be concurrently executed. Below, we use the CFIT* example to illustrate the concept of deontic and action consistency.

Example 9.3.3 (Deontic and Action Consistency)   Consider the probabilistic agent program from Example 9.2.2 on page 305 and suppose that our agent's plane is in stealth mode and its current altitude is less than 200 meters with probability 0.3. Then probabilistic action rules r1, r3 will fire and produce a probabilistic status set $\mathcal{PS}$ consisting of **P***compute_currentLocation*(report), **F***compute_currentLocation*(report) which is not deontically consistent.

Let action constraint $AC = warn\_pilot(X_1, X_2), warn\_pilot(X_3, X_4) \leftarrow (X_1 \neq X_3)$. This indicates that we can only send the pilot one warning message at a time. Consider the pap in Example 9.2.2 and suppose that our agent's plane is not in stealth mode and is not allowed to compute its current location. Also suppose that at the same time, the tracking agent detects a surface-to-air missile battery which has not been neutralized. Then rules r4, r5 will fire and may produce a probabilistic status set $\mathcal{PS}$ consisting of status atoms **Do** *warn_pilot*(enemy_detected, x), **Do** *warn_pilot*(sensor_malfunction, altimeter), **O***warn_pilot*(enemy_detected, x), which is deontically consistent but is not action consistent w.r.t. AC.

The deontic and action closure of a status $\mathcal{PS}$ is defined in exactly the same way (Definition 6.5.3 on page 174) as in the non-probabilistic case.

9.3.4 Probabilistic Feasible Status Sets

The last requirement in defining a feasible probabilistic status set is to ensure that the new state that results after concurrently executing a set of actions is consistent with the integrity constraints.

We say that an agent state $\mathcal{O}$ *satisfies* an integrity constraint having the form

$$\psi \Rightarrow \chi$$

if, by definition, either $\mathcal{O} \not\models^{[1,1]} \psi$ or $\mathcal{O} \models^{[1,1]} \chi$.

DEFINITION 9.3.5 (PROBABILISTIC STATE CONSISTENCY) We say that a probabilistic status set $\mathcal{PS}$ is *probabilistic state consistent* w.r.t. state $\mathcal{O}$ *if, by definition,* the new state, $\mathcal{O}'_S =$ apply(**Do** ($\mathcal{PS}$), $\mathcal{O}_S$) obtained after concurrently executing all actions of the form **Do** $\alpha \in \mathcal{PS}$ satisfies all integrity constraints.

The following example illustrates the notion of state consistency.

Example 9.3.4 (State Consistency) Let integrity constraint $IC =$ **in**(Current_Location, autoPilot:$_{RV}$*location* $\Rightarrow$ (Current_Location.Z > 100). This indicates that the plane's altitude must remain above 100 meters. Here, if $\mathcal{PS} = \{$**Do** *decrease_altitude*(5)$\}$ (i.e., an action which decreases the plane's altitude by 5 meters) and the plane's current altitude is not above 105 meters, then $\mathcal{PS}$ is not state consistent.

We have now shown how the four elements of the definition of feasible status set may be extended to the case of probabilistic agent programs.

Section 9.3   Probabilistic Agent Programs: Semantics   311

DEFINITION 9.3.6 (FEASIBLE PROBABILISTIC STATUS SET)   Let $\mathcal{PP}$ be an agent program and let $\mathcal{O}_S$ be an agent state. Then, a probabilistic status set $\mathcal{PS}$ is a *feasible probabilistic status set* for $\mathcal{PP}$ on $\mathcal{O}_S$, if the following conditions hold:

($\mathcal{PS}$ 1): $\mathbf{App}_{\mathcal{PP},\mathcal{O}_S}(\mathcal{PS}) \subseteq \mathcal{PS}$ (closure under the program rules);

($\mathcal{PS}$ 2): $\mathcal{PS}$ is deontically and action consistent (deontic and action consistency);

($\mathcal{PS}$ 3): $\mathcal{PS}$ is action closed and deontically closed (deontic and action closure);

($\mathcal{PS}$ 4): $\mathcal{PS}$ is state consistent(state consistency).

The following example uses the CFIT* example to illustrate the notion of feasible probabilistic status sets.

Example 9.3.5 (Feasible Probabilistic Status Set)   Consider the pap in Example 9.2.2 and suppose that our agent's plane is not in stealth mode and its current altitude is less than 200 meters with probability 0.7. Then rules r1, r2 will fire and produce a probabilistic status set $\mathcal{PS}_1 = \{\mathbf{P}compute\_currentLocation(\texttt{report}), \mathbf{O}compute\_currentLocation(\texttt{report})\}$. Here, $\mathcal{PS}_1$ is not feasible since it is not action closed. Note however that $\mathcal{PS}_2 = \mathcal{PS}_1 \cup \{\mathbf{Do}\,compute\_currentLocation(\texttt{report})\}$ is a feasible probabilistic status set.

9.3.5   Rational Probabilistic Status Sets

The extension of the concept of a rational probabilistic status set of ordinary agent programs to the case of probabilistic agent programs is straightforward, as illustrated by the following definition.

DEFINITION 9.3.7 (GROUNDEDNESS; RATIONAL PROBABILISTIC STATUS SET)   A probabilistic status set $\mathcal{PS}$ is *grounded*, if there exists no probabilistic status set $\mathcal{PS}' \neq \mathcal{PS}$ such that $\mathcal{PS}' \subseteq \mathcal{PS}$ and $\mathcal{PS}'$ satisfies conditions ($\mathcal{PS}$1)–($\mathcal{PS}$3) of a feasible probabilistic status set.

A probabilistic status set $\mathcal{PS}$ is a *rational probabilistic status set*, if $\mathcal{PS}$ is a feasible probabilistic status set and $\mathcal{PS}$ is grounded.

Note that this definition of a rational probabilistic status set is identical to that in the case of ordinary agent programs—the only difference is that the relevant conditions in the definition of a feasible probabilistic status set have been changed.

9.3.6   Reasonable Probabilistic Status Sets

As was the case for rational status sets, the notion of a reasonable status set extends immediately to probabilistic agent programs.

DEFINITION 9.3.8 (REASONABLE PROBABILISTIC STATUS SET) Let $\mathcal{PP}$ be a probabilistic agent program, let $\mathcal{O}_S$ be an agent state, and let $\mathcal{PS}$ be a probabilistic status set.

1. If $\mathcal{PP}$ is a positive probabilistic agent program, then $\mathcal{PS}$ is a *reasonable probabilistic status set* for $\mathcal{PP}$ on $\mathcal{O}_S$, if, by definition, $\mathcal{PS}$ is a rational probabilistic status set for $\mathcal{PP}$ on $\mathcal{O}_S$.

2. The reduct of $\mathcal{PP}$ w.r.t. $\mathcal{PS}$ and $\mathcal{O}_S$, denoted by $red^P S(\mathcal{PP}, \mathcal{O}_S)$, is the program which is obtained from the ground instances of the rules in $\mathcal{PP}$ over $\mathcal{O}_S$ as follows.

(a) First, remove every rule r such that $B_{as}^{-}(r) \cap \mathcal{PS} \neq \emptyset$;

(b) Remove all atoms in $B_{as}^{-}(r)$ from the remaining rules.

Then $\mathcal{PS}$ is a *reasonable probabilistic status set* for $\mathcal{PP}$ w.r.t. $\mathcal{O}_S$, if it is a reasonable probabilistic status set of the program $red^P S(\mathcal{PP}, \mathcal{O}_S)$ with respect to $\mathcal{O}_S$.

9.3.7 Relations between Feasible, Rational and Reasonable Status Sets

It is immediate from the very definitions—as in Chapter 6—that rational probabilistic status sets are feasible. In fact, most of the results in Chapter 6 either translate literally to probabilistic status sets or they can be easily adapted. As an example, we consider the following analog of Proposition 6.5.2 on page 177.

PROPOSITION 9.3.1 (PROPERTIES OF FEASIBLE STATUS SETS) Let $\mathcal{PS}$ be a feasible probabilistic status set. Then,

1. If $\mathbf{Do}\,(\alpha) \in \mathcal{PS}$, then $\mathcal{O}_S \models^{[1,1]} Pre(\alpha)$;
2. If $\mathbf{P}\alpha \notin \mathcal{PS}$, then $\mathbf{Do}\,(\alpha) \notin \mathcal{PS}$;
3. If $\mathbf{O}\alpha \in \mathcal{PS}$, then $\mathcal{O}_S \models^{[1,1]} Pre(\alpha)$;
4. If $\mathbf{O}\alpha \in \mathcal{PS}$, then $\mathbf{F}\alpha \notin \mathcal{PS}$.

Proof

1. Suppose $\mathbf{Do}\,\alpha \in \mathcal{PS}$. Then, as $\mathcal{PS}$ is feasible, we know that $\mathcal{PS} = \mathbf{A\text{-}Cl}(\mathcal{PS})$, and hence $\mathbf{P}\alpha \in \mathcal{PS}$. As $\mathcal{PS}$ is feasible, and hence deontically consistent, the third condition of deontic consistency specifies that α's precondition is true in state $\mathcal{O}_S$.

2. This follows immediately because as $\mathcal{PS}$ is feasible, we have $\mathcal{PS} = \mathbf{A\text{-}Cl}(\mathcal{PS})$. The second condition defining $\mathbf{A\text{-}Cl}(\mathcal{PS})$, when written in contrapositive form, states that $\mathbf{P}\alpha \notin \mathcal{PS}$ implies that $\mathbf{Do}\,\alpha \notin \mathcal{PS}$.

3. As $\mathcal{PS}$ is feasible, $\mathcal{PS} = \mathbf{A\text{-}Cl}(\mathcal{PS})$. The first condition specifying $\mathbf{A\text{-}Cl}(\mathcal{PS})$ allows us to infer that $\mathbf{O}\alpha \in \mathcal{PS}$ implies that $\mathbf{Do}\,\alpha \in \mathcal{PS}$. The result follows immediately from part (1) of this proposition.

4. From the above argument, as $\mathcal{PS} = \mathbf{A\text{-}Cl}(\mathcal{PS})$, we can conclude that $\mathbf{O}\alpha \in \mathcal{PS}$ implies that $\mathbf{P}\alpha \in \mathcal{PS}$. By the deontic consistency requirement, $\mathbf{F}\alpha \notin \mathcal{PS}$.

The next theorem shows that reasonable probabilistic status sets are stronger than rational probabilistic status sets.

PROPOSITION 9.3.2 (REASONABLE STATUS SETS ARE RATIONAL)   Let $\mathcal{PP}$ be a probabilistic agent program and $\mathcal{O}_S$ an agent state. Then, every reasonable probabilistic status set of $\mathcal{PP}$ on $\mathcal{O}_S$ is a rational probabilistic status set of $\mathcal{PP}$ on $\mathcal{O}_S$.

Proof   In order to show that a reasonable probabilistic status set $\mathcal{PS}$ of $\mathcal{PP}$ is a rational status of $\mathcal{PP}$, we have to verify (1) that $\mathcal{PS}$ is a feasible probabilistic status set and (2) that $\mathcal{PS}$ is grounded.

Since $\mathcal{PS}$ is a reasonable probabilistic status set of $\mathcal{PP}$, it is a rational probabilistic status set of $\mathcal{PP}' = red^P S(\mathcal{PP}, \mathcal{O}_S)$, i.e., a feasible and grounded probabilistic status set of $\mathcal{PP}'$. Since the conditions $(\mathcal{PS}2)$–$(\mathcal{PS}4)$ of the definition of feasible probabilistic status set depend only on $\mathcal{PS}$ and $\mathcal{O}_S$ but not on the program, this means that for showing (1) it remains to check that $(\mathcal{PS}1)$ (closure under the program rules) is satisfied.

Let thus r be a ground instance of a rule from $\mathcal{PP}$. Suppose the body $B(r)$ of r satisfies the conditions 1.–4. of $(\mathcal{PS}1)$. Then, by the definition of $red^P S(\mathcal{PP}, \mathcal{O}_S)$, we have that the reduct of the rule r, obtained by removing all literals of $B_{as}^-(r)$ from the body, is in $\mathcal{PP}'$. Since $\mathcal{PS}$ is closed under the rules of $\mathcal{PP}'$, we have $H(r) \in \mathcal{PS}$. Thus, $\mathcal{PS}$ is closed under the rules of $\mathcal{PP}$, and hence $(\mathcal{PS}1)$ is satisfied. As a consequence, (1) holds.

For (2), we suppose $\mathcal{PS}$ is not grounded, i.e., that some smaller $\mathcal{PS}' \subset \mathcal{PS}$ satisfies $(\mathcal{PS}1)$–$(\mathcal{PS}3)$ for $\mathcal{PP}$, and derive a contradiction. If $\mathcal{PS}'$ satisfies $(\mathcal{PS}1)$ for $\mathcal{PP}$, then $\mathcal{PS}'$ satisfies $(\mathcal{PS}1)$ for $\mathcal{PP}'$. For, if r is a rule from $\mathcal{PP}'$ such that 1.–4. of $(\mathcal{PS}1)$ hold for $\mathcal{PS}'$, then there is a ground rule r' of $\mathcal{PP}$ such that r is obtained from r' in the construction of $red^P S(\mathcal{PP}, \mathcal{O}_S)$ and, as easily seen, 1.–4. of $(\mathcal{PS}1)$ hold for $\mathcal{PS}'$. Since $\mathcal{PS}'$ satisfies $(\mathcal{PS}1)$ for $\mathcal{PP}$, we have $H(r) \in \mathcal{PS}'$. It follows that $\mathcal{PS}'$ satisfies $(\mathcal{PS}1)$ for $\mathcal{PP}'$. Furthermore, since $(\mathcal{PS}2)$ and $(\mathcal{PS}3)$ do no depend on the program, also $(\mathcal{PS}2)$ and $(\mathcal{PS}3)$ are satisfied for $\mathcal{PS}'$ w.r.t. $\mathcal{PP}'$. This means that $\mathcal{PS}$ is not a rational probabilistic status set of $\mathcal{PP}'$, which is the desired contradiction.

Thus, (1) and (2) hold, which proves the result.   ∎

Again as in Chapter 6 we define for every program $\mathcal{PP}$ and agent state $\mathcal{O}_S$ an operator $\mathbf{T}_{\mathcal{PP},\mathcal{O}_S}$ which maps a probabilistic status set $\mathcal{PS}$ to another status set.

DEFINITION 9.3.9 ($\mathbf{T}_{\mathcal{PP},\mathcal{O}_S}$ OPERATOR)   Suppose $\mathcal{PP}$ is a probabilistic agent program and $\mathcal{O}_S$ an agent state. Then, for any probabilistic status set $\mathcal{PS}$,

$$\mathbf{T}_{\mathcal{PP},\mathcal{O}_S}(\mathcal{PS}) = \mathbf{App}_{\mathcal{PP},\mathcal{O}_S}(\mathcal{PS}) \cup \mathbf{D\text{-}Cl}(\mathcal{PS}) \cup \mathbf{A\text{-}Cl}(\mathcal{PS}).$$

Note that as $\mathbf{D\text{-}Cl}(\mathcal{PS}) \subseteq \mathbf{A\text{-}Cl}(\mathcal{PS})$, we may equivalently write this as

$$\mathbf{T}_{\mathcal{PP},\mathcal{O}_S}(\mathcal{PS}) = \mathbf{App}_{\mathcal{PP},\mathcal{O}_S}(\mathcal{PS}) \cup \mathbf{A\text{-}Cl}(\mathcal{PS}).$$

The following property of feasible probabilistic status sets is easily seen.

LEMMA 9.3.1 ($\mathcal{PS}$ AS PREFIXPOINT OF $\mathbf{T}_{\mathcal{PP},\mathcal{O}_S}$)   Let $\mathcal{PP}$ be a probabilistic agent program, let $\mathcal{O}_S$ be any agent state, and let $\mathcal{PS}$ be any probabilistic status set. If $\mathcal{PS}$ satisfies ($\mathcal{PS}1$) and ($\mathcal{PS}3$) of feasibility, then $\mathcal{PS}$ is pre-fixpoint of $\mathbf{T}_{\mathcal{PP},\mathcal{O}_S}$, i.e., $\mathbf{T}_{\mathcal{PP},\mathcal{O}_S}(\mathcal{PS}) \subseteq \mathcal{PS}$.

Proof   Suppose $\mathsf{Op}(\alpha) \in \mathbf{T}_{\mathcal{PP},\mathcal{O}_S}(\mathcal{PS}) = \mathbf{App}_{\mathcal{PP},\mathcal{O}_S}(\mathcal{PS}) \cup \mathbf{A\text{-}Cl}(\mathcal{PS})$. Then we have either $\mathsf{Op}(\alpha) \in \mathbf{App}_{\mathcal{PP},\mathcal{O}_S}(\mathcal{PS})$ or $\mathsf{Op}(\alpha) \in \mathbf{A\text{-}Cl}(\mathcal{PS})$. By condition ($\mathcal{PS}1$) defining a feasible probabilistic status set, we know that $\mathbf{App}_{\mathcal{PP},\mathcal{O}_S}(\mathcal{PS}) \subseteq \mathcal{PS}$. By condition ($\mathcal{PS}3$), $\mathcal{PS} = \mathbf{A\text{-}Cl}(\mathcal{PS})$ and hence, $\mathbf{A\text{-}Cl}(\mathcal{PS}) \subseteq \mathcal{PS}$. Therefore, $\mathbf{T}_{\mathcal{PP},\mathcal{O}_S}(\mathcal{PS}) \subseteq \mathcal{PS}$.   ∎

In the next two sections we will consider *positive* probabilistic programs because our $\mathbf{T}_{\mathcal{PP},\mathcal{O}_S}$ operator has nice properties for this important class of programs. But before restricting to positive programs, we mention the following analog to Proposition 6.5.3 on page 181.

PROPOSITION 9.3.3 (EXISTENCE OF RATIONAL PROBABILISTIC STATUS SETS)   Let $\mathcal{PP}$ be a probabilistic agent program. If $\mathcal{IC} = \emptyset$, then $\mathcal{PP}$ has a rational probabilistic status set *if and only if* $\mathcal{PP}$ has a feasible probabilistic status set.

Proof   By definition of rationality, we know that if $\mathcal{PS}$ is a rational status set of $\mathcal{PP}$ then it must be a feasible probabilistic status set as well.

Suppose $\mathcal{PP}$ has a feasible probabilistic status set. Then the set of all feasible probabilistic status sets of $\mathcal{PP}$ on $\mathcal{O}_S$ has a non-empty set of inclusion-minimal elements. Indeed, from the grounding of the probabilistic agent program, we can remove all rules which violate the conditions 2.–4. of the operator $\mathbf{App}_{\mathcal{PP},\mathcal{O}_S}(\mathcal{PS})$, and can remove literals involving code calls from the remaining rules. Moreover, the deontic and action closure conditions can be incorporated into the program via rules. Thus, we end up with a set T of propositional clauses, whose models are feasible probabilistic status sets of $\mathcal{PP}$. Since $\mathcal{PP}$ has a feasible probabilistic status set, T has a model, i.e., an assignment to the propositional atoms which satisfies all clauses in T. Now, each satisfiable set of clauses in a countable language possesses at least one minimal model (w.r.t. inclusion, i.w., a $\subseteq$-minimal set of atoms is assigned the value **true**); this can be shown applying the same technique which proves that every such set of clauses can be extended to a maximal satisfiable set of clauses. Thus, T has at least one minimal model. As easily seen, any such model is a minimal feasible probabilistic status set of $\mathcal{PP}$.

Suppose now $\mathcal{PS}'$ is one of the minimal feasible probabilistic status sets of $\mathcal{PP}$ on $\mathcal{O}_S$. Then (as we show below) $\mathcal{PS}'$ is grounded, and hence a rational probabilistic status set.

To show that $\mathcal{PS}'$ is grounded, we need to show that $\mathcal{PS}'$ satisfies conditions ($\mathcal{PS}1$)–($\mathcal{PS}3$) of the definition of feasible probabilistic status set—this is true because $\mathcal{PS}'$ is feasible. In addition, we need to show that no strict subset $\mathcal{PS}^\star$ of $\mathcal{PS}$ satisfies conditions ($\mathcal{PS}1$)–($\mathcal{PS}3$).

Suppose there is a strict subset $\mathcal{PS}^\star$ of $\mathcal{PS}$ satisfying conditions ($\mathcal{PS}1$)–($\mathcal{PS}3$). Then, as $\mathcal{IC} = \emptyset$, $\mathcal{PS}^\star$ also satisfies condition ($\mathcal{PS}4$) of the definition of feasibility, and hence $\mathcal{PS}^\star$ is a feasible probabilistic status set. But this contradicts the inclusion minimality of $\mathcal{PS}'$, and hence, we may infer that $\mathcal{PS}'$ has no strict subset $\mathcal{PS}^\star$ of $\mathcal{PS}$ satisfying conditions ($\mathcal{PS}1$)–($\mathcal{PS}3$). Thus, $\mathcal{PS}'$ is grounded, and we are done. ∎

COROLLARY 7 (CHARACTERIZATION OF RATIONAL PROBABILISTIC STATUS SETS) Let $\mathcal{PP}$ be a probabilistic agent program and suppose $\mathcal{IC} = \emptyset$. Then: $\mathcal{PS}$ is a rational probabilistic status set of $\mathcal{PP}$ if and only if $\mathcal{PS}$ is an inclusion-minimal feasible probabilistic status set of $\mathcal{PP}$.

9.4 Computing Probabilistic Status Sets of Positive paps

In this section, we develop a formal fixpoint theory for paps—in particular, given any positive pap $\mathcal{PP}$, we show how to associate with it, a fixpoint operator that maps probabilistic status sets and associated agent states to probabilistic status sets. We will then use this fixpoint operator to define a polynomial time procedure to compute reasonable probabilistic status sets of positive paps.

DEFINITION 9.4.1 (OPERATOR $\mathbf{T}_{\mathcal{PP},\mathcal{O}_S}$) We define $\mathbf{T}_{\mathcal{PP},\mathcal{O}_S}$ in accordance with Definitions 9.3.3 on page 308 and 9.3.9 on the facing page.

$$\mathbf{T}_{\mathcal{PP},\mathcal{O}_S}(\mathcal{PS}) = \mathbf{A\text{-}Cl}(\mathbf{App}_{\mathcal{PP},\mathcal{O}_S}(\mathcal{PS})),$$

where

$\mathbf{App}_{\mathcal{PP},\mathcal{O}_S}(\mathcal{PS}) =_{def} \{\mathsf{Op}\,\alpha \mid \mathsf{Op}\,\alpha \leftarrow \Gamma, L_1, \ldots, L_n$ is a ground instance of a probabilistic agent rule in $\mathcal{PP}$ and $\mathcal{O} \models^{[1,1]} \Gamma$ and $\{L_1, \ldots, L_n\} \subseteq \mathcal{PS}$ and for every atom $\mathsf{Op}'(\beta) \in \{L_1, \ldots, L_n\} \cup \{\mathsf{Op}(\alpha)\}$ such that $\mathsf{Op}' \in \{\mathbf{P}, \mathbf{O}, \mathbf{Do}\}$, the action β is executable in state $\mathcal{O}_S$.$\}$

Intuitively, the operator $\mathbf{T}_{\mathcal{PP},\mathcal{O}_S}$ takes as input a probabilistic status set $\mathcal{PS}$ and the current agent state. It returns as output, a new probabilistic status set derivable from the current

---

Algorithm 9.4.1 ($\mathbf{T}_{\mathcal{PP},\mathcal{O}_S}$ Computation for Positive paps**)**
Compute-$\mathbf{T}_{\mathcal{PP},\mathcal{O}_S}(\mathcal{O}_S$: agent state, $\mathcal{PS}$: probabilistic status set)

($\star$ the probabilistic agent program $\mathcal{PP}$ is positive; $\star$)
($\star$ **Input:** an agent state $\mathcal{O}_S$, and a prob. status set $\mathcal{PS}$ $\star$)
($\star$ **Output:** a deontically and action consistent set $\mathbf{T}_{\mathcal{PP},\mathcal{O}_S}(\mathcal{PS})$ (if existent) $\star$)
($\star$ or *"no consistent set exists"* $\star$)

1. $X = \mathcal{PS}$;
2.   **for each** rule $r \in \mathcal{PP}$
3.   **for each** ground instance $r\theta$ of r
4.   **if** $r\theta = \mathbf{Op}\,\alpha \leftarrow \Gamma, L_1, \ldots, L_n$ **and**
              $\mathcal{O}_S \models^{[1,1]} \chi$ and $\{L_1, \ldots, L_n\} \subseteq \mathcal{PS}$ **and**
              for every atom $\mathbf{Op}'(\beta) \in \{L_1, \ldots, L_n\} \cup \{\mathbf{Op}(\alpha)\}$
              such that $\mathbf{Op}' \in \{\mathbf{P}, \mathbf{O}, \mathbf{Do}\}$: $\mathcal{O}_S \models^{[1,1]} Pre(\beta)$
5.   **then** $X := X \cup \mathbf{A\text{-}Cl}(\{\mathbf{Op}\,\alpha\})$,
6.   **if** X contains $(\mathbf{O}\alpha$ and $\mathbf{W}\alpha)$ or $(\mathbf{P}\alpha$ and $\mathbf{F}\alpha)$
7.   **then Return** *"no consistent set exists"*.
8.   Return X.
end.

---

probabilistic status set using two steps:

1. Closure under program rules,
2. Closure under deontic modalities.

In addition, it is checked that only those action status atoms in the body are used for building the new probabilistic status set, which can be executed in the current state. Computationally, we may compute the operator $\mathbf{T}_{\mathcal{PP},\mathcal{O}_S}$ as follows:

The following examples demonstrate the behavior of the $\mathbf{T}_{\mathcal{PP},\mathcal{O}_S}$ operator on our motivating examples.

Example 9.4.1 (Computation of $\mathbf{T}_{\mathcal{PP},\mathcal{O}_S}$) Let agent program $\mathcal{PP}$ be the pap given in Example 9.2.2 on page 305, let agent state $\mathcal{O}_S$ indicate that our agent's plane is in stealth mode and is at an altitude below 200 meters with probability 0.80, and let $\mathcal{PS} = \emptyset$. Then Compute-$\mathbf{T}_{\mathcal{PP},\mathcal{O}_S}$ will operate in the following way:

Initally, $X = \emptyset$.

After r1, $X = \{\mathbf{P}\textit{compute\_currentLocation}(\texttt{report})\}$.

After r2, $X = \{\mathbf{P}\textit{compute\_currentLocation}(\texttt{report}),$
$\mathbf{O}\textit{compute\_currentLocation}(\texttt{report}), \mathbf{Do}\,\textit{compute\_currentLocation}(\texttt{report})\}$.

After r3, $X = \{\mathbf{P}\textit{compute\_currentLocation}(\texttt{report}),$
$\mathbf{O}\textit{compute\_currentLocation}(\texttt{report}), \mathbf{Do}\,\textit{compute\_currentLocation}(\texttt{report}),$

F*compute_currentLocation*(report)}.

After r4–r7, X will not change.

Note that since X is not deontically consistent, Compute-$\mathbf{T}_{\mathcal{PP},\mathcal{O}_S}$ will return *"no consistent set exists"*.

Now let $\mathcal{PP}$ be the pap in Example 9.2.2, let $\mathcal{O}_S$ indicate that our agent's plane is not in stealth mode and is at an altitude below 200 meters with probability 0.30, and let

$\mathcal{PS} = \{\mathbf{F}compute\_currentLocation(\texttt{report})\}$.

Then Compute-$\mathbf{T}_{\mathcal{PP},\mathcal{O}_S}$ will operate in the following way:

Initally, $X = \emptyset$.

After r1, $X = \{\mathbf{P}compute\_currentLocation(\texttt{report})\}$.

After r2–r3, X will not change.

After r4, $X = \{\mathbf{P}compute\_currentLocation(\texttt{report})$,
Do *warn_pilot*(sensor_malfunction, altimeter)}.

After r4–r7, X will not change.

Finally, Compute-$\mathbf{T}_{\mathcal{PP},\mathcal{O}_S}$ will return the value of X given above.

In order to compute a reasonable probabilistic status set of a positive pap $\mathcal{PP}$, all we need to do is to iteratively apply the $\mathbf{T}_{\mathcal{PP},\mathcal{O}_S}$ operator till we find that the status set remains unchanged by the application of this operator.

At this point, we merely need to check if the resulting set satisfies the conditions for feasibility. In order to describe this process, we first need to define the iteration of the $\mathbf{T}_{\mathcal{PP},\mathcal{O}_S}$ operator.

$\mathbf{T}^0_{\mathcal{PP},\mathcal{O}_S} = \emptyset$.
$\mathbf{T}^{i+1}_{\mathcal{PP},\mathcal{O}_S} = \mathbf{T}_{\mathcal{PP},\mathcal{O}_S}(\mathbf{T}^i_{\mathcal{PP},\mathcal{O}_S})$.
$\mathbf{T}^{\omega}_{\mathcal{PP},\mathcal{O}_S} = \bigcup_{i=0}^{\infty} \mathbf{T}^i_{\mathcal{PP},\mathcal{O}_S}$.

Example 9.4.2 (Iterations of $\mathbf{T}_{\mathcal{PP},\mathcal{O}_S}$) Let $\mathcal{PP}$ be the pap given in Example 9.2.2 on page 305. Furthermore, let $\mathcal{O}_S$ indicate that a_1 is a sam_battery (with probability 0.3), a_2 is a sam_battery (with probability 0.6), a_2 has been neutralized, and our agent's plane is not in stealth mode. Then $\mathbf{T}^0_{\mathcal{PP},\mathcal{O}_S} = \emptyset$ and

$\mathbf{T}^1_{\mathcal{PP},\mathcal{O}_S} = \{\mathbf{O}warn\_pilot(\texttt{enemy\_detected}, a_1), \quad \mathbf{Do}\,warn\_pilot(\texttt{enemy\_detected}, a_1),$
$\qquad\qquad \mathbf{P}warn\_pilot(\texttt{enemy\_detected}, a_1), \quad \mathbf{O}warn\_pilot(\texttt{enemy\_detected}, a_2),$

Do *warn_pilot*(enemy_detected, a_2), **P***warn_pilot*(enemy_detected, a_2),
W*warn_pilot*(enemy_detected, a_2)}

by rules r5–r6 of $\mathcal{PP}$. Note that after removing conflicting modalities,

$\mathbf{T}^1_{\mathcal{PP},\mathcal{O}_S}$ = {**O***warn_pilot*(enemy_detected, a_1), **Do** *warn_pilot*(enemy_detected, a_1),
P*warn_pilot*(enemy_detected, a_1)}.

Now by rule r7,

$\mathbf{T}^2_{\mathcal{PP},\mathcal{O}_S}$ = {**O***warn_pilot*(enemy_detected, a_1), **Do** *warn_pilot*(enemy_detected, a_1),
P*warn_pilot*(enemy_detected, a_1), **Do** *signal_base*(enemy_detected, a_1),
P*signal_base*(enemy_detected, a_1)}.

Note that $\mathbf{T}^3_{\mathcal{PP},\mathcal{O}_S} = \mathbf{T}^2_{\mathcal{PP},\mathcal{O}_S}$, $\mathbf{T}^4_{\mathcal{PP},\mathcal{O}_S} = \mathbf{T}^3_{\mathcal{PP},\mathcal{O}_S}$, etc.

The following theorem guarantees that $\mathbf{T}_{\mathcal{PP},\mathcal{O}_S}$ has a unique least fixpoint.

LEMMA 9.4.1 (MONOTONICITY AND CONTINUITY OF $\mathbf{T}_{\mathcal{PP},\mathcal{O}_S}$) Suppose $\mathcal{PP}$ is a positive pap. Then the operator $\mathbf{T}_{\mathcal{PP},\mathcal{O}_S}$ is monotone and continuous, i.e.,

1. $\mathcal{PS}_1 \subseteq \mathcal{PS}_2 \Rightarrow \mathbf{T}_{\mathcal{PP},\mathcal{O}_S}(\mathcal{PS}_1) \subseteq \mathbf{T}_{\mathcal{PP},\mathcal{O}_S}(\mathcal{PS}_2)$,

2. $\mathbf{T}^\omega_{\mathcal{PP},\mathcal{O}_S}$ is a fixpoint of $\mathbf{T}_{\mathcal{PP},\mathcal{O}_S}$. Moreover, it is the least fixpoint of $\mathbf{T}_{\mathcal{PP},\mathcal{O}_S}$.

Proof The monotonicity property is trivial. Part 2. follows from the stronger property of *continuity*, i.e.,

$$\mathbf{T}_{\mathcal{PP},\mathcal{O}_S}\left(\bigcup_{i=0}^{\infty} \mathcal{PS}_0\right) = \bigcup_{i=0}^{\infty} \mathbf{T}_{\mathcal{PP},\mathcal{O}_S}(\mathcal{PS}_i)$$

for any chain $\mathcal{PS}_0 \subseteq \mathcal{PS}_1 \subseteq \mathcal{PS}_2 \subseteq \cdots$ of probabilistic status sets, which is also immediate (see e.g., (Lloyd 1987; Apt 1990)). ∎

For example, if we return to the example paps used in this chapter, we notice that their associated $\mathbf{T}_{\mathcal{PP},\mathcal{O}_S}$ operator's fixpoint is as shown below.

Example 9.4.3 (Fixpoints of $\mathbf{T}_{\mathcal{PP},\mathcal{O}_S}$) Consider the iterations of $\mathbf{T}_{\mathcal{PP},\mathcal{O}_S}$ given in Example 9.4.2 on the page before. Here, we showed that $\mathbf{T}^3_{\mathcal{PP},\mathcal{O}_S} = \mathbf{T}^2_{\mathcal{PP},\mathcal{O}_S}$. Thus, $\mathbf{T}^2_{\mathcal{PP},\mathcal{O}_S}$ is a fixpoint for $\mathbf{T}_{\mathcal{PP},\mathcal{O}_S}$. Note that since $\mathbf{T}^4_{\mathcal{PP},\mathcal{O}_S} = \mathbf{T}^3_{\mathcal{PP},\mathcal{O}_S}$, $\mathbf{T}^4_{\mathcal{PP},\mathcal{O}_S}$ is also a fixpoint for $\mathbf{T}_{\mathcal{PP},\mathcal{O}_S}$. However, since $\mathbf{T}^1_{\mathcal{PP},\mathcal{O}_S} \neq \mathbf{T}^2_{\mathcal{PP},\mathcal{O}_S} = \mathbf{T}^3_{\mathcal{PP},\mathcal{O}_S}$, $\mathbf{T}^2_{\mathcal{PP},\mathcal{O}_S}$ is the least fixpoint for $\mathbf{T}_{\mathcal{PP},\mathcal{O}_S}$.

The following results tell us that Lemma 9.3.1, which holds for arbitrary programs, can be strengthened to the case of positive probabilistic programs as follows.

THEOREM 9.4.1 (RATIONAL PROBABILISTIC STATUS SETS AS LEAST FIXPOINTS) Let $\mathcal{PP}$ be a positive probabilistic agent program, and let $\mathcal{O}_S$ be an agent state. Then, $\mathcal{PS}$ is a rational probabilistic status set of $\mathcal{PP}$ on $\mathcal{O}_S$, *if and only if* $\mathcal{PS} = lfp(\mathbf{T}_{\mathcal{PP},\mathcal{O}_S})$ and $\mathcal{PS}$ is a feasible probabilistic status set. Recall that *lfp* stands for least fixpoint.

Proof ($\Rightarrow$) Suppose $\mathcal{PS} = lfp(\mathbf{T}_{\mathcal{P},\mathcal{O}_S})$ a rational probabilistic status set of $\mathcal{PP}$ on $\mathcal{O}_S$. Then, $\mathcal{PS}$ is feasible by definition of rational probabilistic status set. By Lemma 9.3.1, $\mathcal{PS}$ is a pre-fixpoint of $\mathbf{T}_{\mathcal{PP},\mathcal{O}_S}$. Since $\mathbf{T}_{\mathcal{PP},\mathcal{O}_S}$ is monotone, it has by the Knaster-Tarski Theorem a least pre-fixpoint, which coincides with $lfp(\mathbf{T}_{\mathcal{P},\mathcal{O}_S})P$ (see (Apt 1990; Lloyd 1987)). Thus, $lfp(\mathbf{T}_{\mathcal{PP},\mathcal{O}_S}) \subseteq \mathcal{PS}$. Clearly, $lfp(\mathbf{T}_{\mathcal{PP},\mathcal{O}_S})$ satisfies ($\mathcal{PS}$1) and ($\mathcal{PS}$3); moreover, $lfp(\mathbf{T}_{\mathcal{PP},\mathcal{O}_S})$ satisfies ($\mathcal{PS}$2), as $\mathcal{PS}$ satisfies ($\mathcal{PS}$2) and this property is hereditary. By the definition of rational probabilistic status set, it follows $lfp(\mathbf{T}_{\mathcal{PP},\mathcal{O}_S}) = \mathcal{PS}$.

($\Leftarrow$) Suppose $\mathcal{PS} = lfp(\mathbf{T}_{\mathcal{P},\mathcal{O}_S})P$ is a feasible probabilistic status set. Since every probabilistic status set $\mathcal{PS}'$ which satisfies ($\mathcal{PS}$1)–($\mathcal{PS}$3) is a pre-fixpoint of $\mathbf{T}_{\mathcal{PP},\mathcal{O}_S}$ and $lfp(\mathbf{T}_{\mathcal{PP},\mathcal{O}_S})$ is the least prefix point, $\mathcal{PS}' \subseteq \mathcal{PS}$ implies $\mathcal{PS} = \mathcal{PS}'$. It follows that $\mathcal{PS}$ is rational. ∎

Notice that in case of positive programs, $lfp(\mathbf{T}_{\mathcal{PP},\mathcal{O}_S})$ always satisfies the conditions ($\mathcal{PS}$1) and ($\mathcal{PS}$3) of a feasible probabilistic status set (i.e., all closure conditions), and thus is a rational probabilistic status set if it satisfies ($\mathcal{PS}$2) and ($\mathcal{PS}$4), i.e., the consistency criteria. The uniqueness of the rational probabilistic status set is immediate from the previous theorem.

COROLLARY 8 Let $\mathcal{PP}$ be a positive probabilistic agent program. Then, on every agent state $\mathcal{O}_S$, the rational probabilistic status set of $\mathcal{PP}$ (if one exists) is unique, i.e., if $\mathcal{PS}, \mathcal{PS}'$ are rational probabilistic status sets for $\mathcal{PP}$ on $\mathcal{O}_S$, then $\mathcal{PS} = \mathcal{PS}'$.

As a consequence of the above Theorem 9.4.1 gives us a concrete method to compute reasonable probabilistic status sets (note that for positive probabilistic programs they coincide with rational sets).

The above algorithm is based on Theorem 9.4.1 and the remark that for positive probabilistic programs reasonable probabilistic status sets coincide with rational sets. It is easy to see that the **while** loop of the algorithm can be executed in polynomial time (data-complexity). The checks to determine if X satisfies the three conditions at the end of the algorithm are each polynomial time checks (assuming the existence of a polynomial oracle to compute code call conditions). We therefore get:

THEOREM 9.4.2 (POLYNOMIAL DATA COMPLEXITY) The algorithm given above for computing reasonable probabilistic status sets of positive paps has polynomial data-complexity.

The following example walks the reader through the detailed working of this algorithm on the motivating example pap introduced earlier on in this chapter.

Example 9.4.4 (Compute-$T_{\mathcal{PP},\mathcal{O}_S}$) Let $\mathcal{PP}$ and $\mathcal{O}_S$ be the pap and agent state given in Example 9.4.2 on page 317, let *IC* be the integrity constraint given in Example 9.3.4 on page 310, and let *AC* be the action constraint given in Example 9.3.3 on page 309. Then Compute-$T_{\mathcal{PP},\mathcal{O}_S}(\mathcal{O}_S, \mathcal{PP})$ will operate in the following way: Initially, *change* = **true** and $X = T^0_{\mathcal{PP},\mathcal{O}_S}$. Then $newX = T^1_{\mathcal{PP},\mathcal{O}_S} \neq X$ so $X = T^1_{\mathcal{PP},\mathcal{O}_S}$ and we remain in the loop. Now, $newX = T^2_{\mathcal{PP},\mathcal{O}_S} \neq X$ so $X = T^2_{\mathcal{PP},\mathcal{O}_S}$ and we stay in the loop. Next, $newX = T^3_{\mathcal{PP},\mathcal{O}_S} = X$ so *change* = **false** and we exit the loop. Finally, since the preconditions for each **Do** $\alpha \in X$ is 100% satisfied and since none of our integrity or action constraints are violated, the algorithm returns X.

9.5 Agent Programs are Probabilistic Agent Programs

In this chapter we have extended not only the notion of an agent program, but also the underlying notion of a code call. Code calls are now arbitrary random variables and one might ask if and how this new notion contains the original one. It turns out that not only are agent programs a special case of paps but also the computational procedures given above reduce in the presence of certain knowledge to the ones described in Chapter 6. Let us make our claims more precise.

Algorithm 9.4.2 (Reasonable Prob. Status Set Computation for Positive paps**)**
Compute-*lfp* ($T_{\mathcal{PP},\mathcal{O}_S}$): **agent state,** $\mathcal{PP}$: **probabilistic agent program**

($\star$ the probabilistic agent program $\mathcal{PP}$ is positive; $\star$)
($\star$ **Input:** an agent state $\mathcal{O}_S$, and a pap $\mathcal{PP}$ $\star$)
($\star$ **Output:** a reasonable probabilistic status set $\star$)

1. *change* := **true**; $X := \emptyset$;
2. **while** *change* **do**
3. $newX = $ **Compute-**$T_{\mathcal{PP},\mathcal{O}_S}(X)$;
4. **if** $newX := $ "*no consistent set exists*"
5. **then return** no reasonable prob. status set exists.
6. **if** $X \neq newX$ **then** $X := newX$
7. **else** *change* := **false**.
8. **end while;**
9. **if** X satisfies all the following conditions
10. • **Do** $\alpha \in X \Rightarrow \mathcal{O} \models^{[1,1]} Pre(\alpha)$;
11. • The new state obtained by executing **conc**({**Do** α | **Do** $\alpha \in X$}
12.   satisfies the integrity constraints;
13. • {**Do** α | **Do** $\alpha \in X$} satisfies the action constraints.
14. **then return** X
15. **else return** no reasonable prob. status set exists.
end.

DEFINITION 9.5.1 (AGENT PROGRAMS AS INSTANCES OF paps)   Let $\mathcal{PP}$ be a probabilistic agent program, $\mathcal{PS}$ a probabilistic status set and $\mathcal{O}$ a probabilistic agent state. Assume further that all random variables associated with these notions do not contain any uncertainty, i.e., each random variable **RV** has the form

$\langle \{\text{object}_{\mathbf{RV}}\}, 1 \rangle.$

Thus each random variable returns back exactly one object with probability 1 (of course, diferent random variables return in general different objects). Under this condition we can define the following mappings

Red$_1(\cdot)$**,** which maps every probabilistic code call of the form $\langle \{o\}, 1 \rangle$ to o:

$\text{Red}_1(\langle \{o_{\mathbf{RV}}\}, 1 \rangle) = o.$

Red$_2(\cdot)$**,** which maps annotated code call conditions to code call conditions by simply removing the annotations and the conjunction strategy:

$\text{Red}_2(\chi : \langle [\text{ai}_1, \text{ai}_2], \otimes \rangle) = \chi.$

We can easily extend $\text{Red}_2(\cdot)$ to a mapping from arbitrary conjunctions of annotated code calls to conjunctions of code calls.

Red$_3(\cdot)$**,** which maps every probabilistic agent program to a non-probabilistic agent program: it clearly suffices to define $\text{Red}_3(\cdot)$ on probabilistic agent rules. This is done as follows

$\text{Red}_3(A \leftarrow \Gamma, L_1, \ldots, L_n) = A \leftarrow \text{Red}_2(\Gamma), L_1, \ldots, L_n.$

Under the assumption stated in the last definition, the following theorem holds.

THEOREM 9.5.1 (SEMANTICS OF AGENT PROGRAMS AS AN INSTANCE OF paps)   We assume that all random variables have the form

$\langle \{\text{object}_{\mathbf{RV}}\}, 1 \rangle.$

Then the following holds: ($\chi : \langle [\text{ai}_1, \text{ai}_2], \otimes \rangle$ is a ground annotated code call condition, $\mathcal{O}_\mathcal{S}$ an agent state)

Satisfaction: the satisfaction relations coincide, i.e.,

$\mathcal{O} \models^{[\text{ai}_1, \text{ai}_2]} \chi : \langle [\text{ai}_1, \text{ai}_2], \otimes \rangle$ *if and only if* $\mathcal{O} \models \text{Red}_2(\chi : \langle [\text{ai}_1, \text{ai}_2], \otimes \rangle).$

App-Operators: the App-Operators coincide, i.e.,

$\mathbf{App}_{\text{Red}_3(\mathcal{PP}), \mathcal{O}_\mathcal{S}}(\mathcal{PS}) = \mathbf{App}_{\mathcal{PP}, \mathcal{O}_\mathcal{S}}(\mathcal{PS}),$

where the operator on the left hand side is the one introduced in Definition 6.5.4 on page 174.

Feasibility: Feasible probabilistic status sets coincide with feasible status sets under our reductions, i.e., $\mathcal{PS}$ is a feasible probabilistic status set w.r.t. $\mathcal{PP}$ *if and only if* $\mathcal{PS}$ is a feasible status set w.r.t. $\text{Red}_3(\mathcal{PP})$.

Rational: Rational probabilistic status sets coincide with rational status sets under our reductions, i.e., $\mathcal{PS}$ is a rational probabilistic status set w.r.t. $\mathcal{PP}$ *if and only if* $\mathcal{PS}$ is a rational status set w.r.t. $\text{Red}_3(\mathcal{PP})$.

Reasonable: Reasonable probabilistic status sets coincide with reasonable status sets under our reductions, i.e., $\mathcal{PS}$ is a reasonable probabilistic status set w.r.t. $\mathcal{PP}$ *if and only if* $\mathcal{PS}$ is a reasonable status set w.r.t. $\text{Red}_3(\mathcal{PP})$.

Computation of Status Sets: The computations of probabilistic status sets given in Algorithms 9.4.1 on page 316 and 9.4.2 on page 320 for a pap $\mathcal{PP}$ reduce to the computation of status sets for $\text{Red}_3(\mathcal{PP})$.

Proof The first two statements are immediate. Feasibility requires to check the conditions ($\mathcal{PS}1$)–($\mathcal{PS}4$) and therefore reduces to the first two statements. Rational and reasonable status sets are completely analogous.

That our algorithms reduce to the non-probabilistic case under our general assumption is trivial: the difference is only the satisfaction relation $\models^{[1,1]}$ which, by the first statement, coincides with $\models$. ∎

9.6 Extensions to Other Causes of Uncertainty

Thus far, the framework for handling uncertainty that we have proposed is simplistic in many respects. First of all, it does not handle temporal uncertainty. Second, it does not handle uncertainty in the agent's beliefs about the states of other agents. Third, it does not handle uncertainty in the agent's beliefs about the actions of other agents. In this section, we will discuss how we may extend the above uncertainty paradigm to handle these modes of uncertainty.

9.6.1 Probabilities over Action Effect Times

In Chapter 8, we have described the concept of a *checkpoint* in cases where actions have durations. In such a case, uncertainty can arise in the following ways. First, the duration of an action may itself be uncertain. For instance, we may know that in the CFIT example, it will take 45–60 minutes for tank1 to reach the traffic circle from its current location. We may further have a probability distribution telling us that the probability that tank1 will reach the circle in exactly 45 minutes is 0.1, the probability that it will reach in 46 minutes is 0.08, the probability that it will reach in 47 minutes is 0.075, and so on. In other words, the probability distribution is a random variable.

In order to accommodate actions with uncertain durations, reconsider the concept of a timed action α given in Definition 8.1.3 on page 258. Here, instead of **Dur**(α) being a checkpoint expression, we instead specify **Dur**(α) via:

- A pair of checkpoint expressions $\langle \{chk\}_1, \{chk\}_2 \rangle$. If $\{chk\}_i$ is of the form rel: $\{t_i\}$, then $\{chk\}_i$ denotes the time point t_i—if it is of the form abs: $\{X \mid \chi\}$ or rel: $\{X \mid \chi\}$, then $\{chk\}_i$ denotes the expression duration(α) defined immediately after Definition 8.1.3 on page 258.

  In this case, the pair of checkpoint expressions $\langle \{chk\}_1, \{chk\}_2 \rangle$ denotes the *set of all time points lying between and including the time points denoted by* $\{chk\}_1$ *and* $\{chk\}_2$. We use **Int**($\{chk\}_1, \{chk\}_2$) to denote this interval of time points.

- A *probability distribution* $\wp^t$ on the above set of time points such that

$$\sum_{t \in \mathbf{Int}(\{chk\}_1, \{chk\}_2)} \wp^t(t) \leq 1.$$

Based on this, it is possible to extend the definition of a temporal feasible status set (Definition 8.3.11 on page 275) so that for any given time point t, we associate with t, a *set* of possible agent states, and a *set* of possible sets of action status atoms true at that time point. The detailed description of temporal probabilistic agent reasoning is deferred for future work.

9.6.2 Probabilities over Beliefs about Other Agents

Recall that in Chapter 7, we introduced two important data structures that allow an agent to reason about other agents' states and actions. These data structures are:

- The belief table, and
- The belief semantics table.

The belief table of an agent a consists (cf. Definition 7.2.5 on page 221) of a set of triples of the form

$\langle h, \phi, \chi_B \rangle$

where $h \in A$, $\phi \in \mathcal{BL}_i^h$ and $\chi_B \in \mathcal{BCond}^a(h)$ is a *belief condition of* a. Intuitively, this triple says that if the condition χ_B is true in agent a's state, then a believes that condition ϕ is true w.r.t. agent h's state.

As the beliefs of an agent about another agent's state may be uncertain, we would like to be able to make statements of the form

If condition χ_B is true, then agent a believes that one of $\{\phi_1, \ldots, \phi_k\}$ is true with $\mathbf{Prob}_a$ being a probability distribution (perhaps incomplete) over $\{\phi_1, \ldots, \phi_k\}$.

This leads to the following definition.

DEFINITION 9.6.1 (PROBABILISTIC BELIEF TABLE) Every agent a has an associated *probabilistic belief table* $\mathbf{PBT}^a$, which consists of quadruples

$$\langle h, \Phi, \mathbf{Prob}_\Phi, \chi_B \rangle$$

where $h \in A$, Φ is a set of formulas from $\mathcal{BL}_i^h$, $\mathbf{Prob}_\Phi$ is a probability distribution on Φ such that $\Sigma_{\phi \in \Phi} \mathbf{Prob}_\Phi(\phi) \leq 1$, and $\chi_B \in \mathcal{B}Cond^a(h)$ is a *belief condition of* a as defined in Chapter 7 (Definition 7.2.6 on page 223).

Similarly, in Chapter 7, each agent has a *guess* about the semantics used by other agents, but in general, an agent may not precisely know the semantics used by other agents. The *belief semantics table* introduced in Chapter 7 (Definition 7.2.4) says that an agent a's belief semantics table consists of a set of pairs of the form

$$\langle h, \mathcal{B}Sem_h^a \rangle$$

where $h \in A$, $\mathcal{B}Sem_h^a$ is a belief semantics over $\mathcal{BL}_i^h$ and $i \in \mathbb{N}$ is fixed. When agent a is not sure about the semantics used by an agent h, we may replace the above table by a *probabilistic belief semantics table* as follows.

DEFINITION 9.6.2 (PROBABILISTIC BELIEF SEMANTICS TABLE $\mathbf{PBelSemT}^a$ OF AGENT a) Every agent a has an associated *belief semantics table* $\mathbf{PBelSemT}^a$ which is a set of triples

$$\langle h, \{\mathcal{B}Sem_{h,1}^a, \ldots, \mathcal{B}Sem_{h,k}^a\}, \text{BSProb} \rangle$$

where $h \in A$, $\mathcal{B}Sem_{h,j}^a$ is a belief semantics over $\mathcal{BL}_i^h$ for some fixed i, and BSProb is a probability distribution over $\{\mathcal{B}Sem_{h,1}^a, \ldots, \mathcal{B}Sem_{h,k}^a\}$ such that

$$\sum_{j=1}^{k} \text{BSProb}(\mathcal{B}Sem_{h,j}^a) \leq 1.$$

For each agent h there is exactly one row in this table with h as its first entry. (There is no loss of generality in this—if no row exists for an agent h, the semantics can be membership $X \models \phi$ if and only if $\phi \in X$.)

Given a formula ϕ, the probability that a believes agent h to hold belief ϕ may now be computed as follows.

1. Find all rows in **PBT**^{a} whose first entry is h.
2. Let $\Phi_1, \ldots, \Phi_r$ be the second entry of all such rows.
3. Let X be any *hitting set* of the sets $\Phi_1, \ldots, \Phi_r$. Intuitively, we know that each Φ_i is a set of formulas, at least one of which is believes by a to be true in agent h's state.
4. Let HitSet be the set of all such hitting sets of $\Phi_1, \ldots, \Phi_r$.
5. Likewise, find the row in **PBelSemT**^{a} whose first entry is h.
6. Let $\models_1, \ldots, \models_w$ be the second entry of the only such row. Let BSProb be the third entry of this row.
7. Suppose the different entries in agent a's belief table are independent. Let $X = \{(H, \models_i) \mid H \in \text{HitSet and } H \models_i \phi\}$. Then the probability that agent a believes agent h to have ϕ true in its state is given by:

$$\sum_{(H, \models_i) \in X} \mathbf{Prob}_{\Phi_i}(h_i) \times \text{BSProb}(\models_i)$$

where h_i is the set of all elements in H that are in Φ_i and $\mathbf{Prob}_{\Phi_i}(E) = \sum_{e \in E} \mathbf{Prob}_{\Phi_i}(e)$.

9.7 Related Work

There has been an incredible amount of work on uncertainty in knowledge based and database systems (Shafer and Peal 1990). However, almost all this work assumes that we are reasoning with logic or with Bayesian nets (Koller 1998) and most work proceeds under strong assumptions about the relationships between events (e.g., most Bayesian approaches assume conditional independence between events while other approaches such as (Fagin, Halpern, and Megiddo 1990; Ng and Subrahmanian 1993b) assume that we have no knowledge of the dependencies between events). The stark reality in today's world is that most data is neither represented logically nor in Bayesian nets. Techniques to implement uncertain reasoning in packages that manipulate diverse data structures are completely lacking today. In this chapter, we have made a first step towards this goal.

This chapter introduces techniques to allow an agent developer to encode different assumptions about the relationships between events when writing probabilistic agent programs. The idea of conjunction and disjunction strategies to facilitate this was first introduced in the ProbView system (Lakshmanan, Leone, Ross, and Subrahmanian 1997) in an attempt to allow users querying probabilistic relational databases to express in their query, their knowledge of the dependencies between events. Later, Dekhtyar and Subrahmaniam (1997) extended the use of conjunction and disjunction strategies to the case of logic programs. In this chapter, the idea of conjunction and disjunction strategies are applied in the context of deontic-logic based agent programs. We are not aware of any extant work on allowing flexible dependency assumptions in the context of logics and actions.

Research on epistemic logic (e.g., (Morgenstern 1988; Moore 1985a; Kraus and Lehmann 1988)) enables reasoning about what is known and is not known at a given time. However, epistemic logics have not been used as a representation in decision making and in automated planning systems, perhaps, because the richness of these languages makes efficient reasoning very difficult. In contrast, our framework has polynomial data complexity.

Halpern and Tuttle (1992) study the semantics of reasoning about distributed systems when uncertainty is present. They develop a logic where a process has knowledge about the probability of events which facilitates decision-making by the process. We, on the other hand, consider probabilistic states, and as argued in Chapter 7, this also allows us to reason about probabilistic beliefs, i.e., probabilities are assigned to the agents' beliefs about events, rather than to the events themselves. That is, in Halpern's work (Halpern and Tuttle 1992), the beliefs of the agent are CERTAIN, but in our framework, the beliefs of the agent may themselves be uncertain (with the phenomenon when they are certain being a special case of our framework).

Poole (1997) presented a framework that allows a natural specification of multi-agent decision problems. It extends logic with a new way to handle and think about non-determinism and uncertainty in terms of independent choices made by various agents, including nature and a logic program that gives the consequence of choices. It has general independence assumption. This work is more expressive than ours, but its generality leads to complexity problems and to difficulties in using the framework.

Haddawy (1991) developed a logic that allows to write sentences that describe uncertainty in the state of the world, uncertainty of action effects, combine possibility and chance, distinguish between truth and chance and express information about probability distributions. He uses model theoretic semantics and demonstrates how his logic can be used to specification various reasoning and planning problems. The main purpose of the specification is to prove correctness, and not for programming of agents.

There are many approached for solving problems of planning under uncertainty. Kushmerick, Hanks, and Weld (1995) model uncertainty about the true state of the world with a probability distribution over the state space. Actions have uncertain effects, and each of these effects is also modeled with a probability distribution. They seek plans whose probability of success exceeds the threshold. They describe BURDIN, an implemented algorithm for probabilistic planning. We do not discuss the way the uncertainty in the state of the agents is implemented. We are only concern with the interface between the agent's state and its decision making module. The modeling of the state can be done using any technique, including this of Kushmerick et al. We focus on agent programming and not on agent planning. Other researchers extended Kushmerick et al.'s model to increase the efficiency of the planning (Haddawy, Doan, and Goodwin 1996) or to more realistic domains (Doan 1996). Thiébaux, Hertzberg, Shoaff, and Schneider (1995) developed a framework for anytime generation of plans under incomplete and ambiguous knowledge and actions with alternative and context dependent effects.

Kaelbling, Littman, and Cassandra (1998) propose to use *partially observable Markov decision processes* (POMDPs) for planning under uncertainty. Similar to BURIDAN they use a probability distributions over states to express uncertainty about the situation of the agent. They also consider the problem of non-deterministic actions and getting feedback from the environment which we mentioned only briefly.

10 Secure Agent Programs

As more and more agent applications are built and deployed, and as access to data and services is increasingly provided by such agents, the need to develop techniques to enforce security become greater and greater. For example, in the STORE example, the credit agent provides access to sensitive credit data and credit rating services which should only be accessible to users or agents authorized to make such accesses. Likewise, in the CFIT example, the current location of a Stealth autoPilot agent during a mission is a piece of classified information that should not be disclosed to arbitrary agents. In addition, as agents operate in an environment involving a variety of host systems and other agents, tools should be available that allow the agent developer to configure his agent in a way that ensures that it will not crash host computers and/or maliciously attack other agents. In general, there is a wide range of security problems that arise in an agent environment such as (but not restricted to) the following:

- Agents often communicate through messages; it may be necessary to *encrypt* such messages to prevent unauthorized agents from reading them.
- Some agents may be willing to provide certain services only to specifically authorized agents; this implies that reliable *authentication mechanisms* are needed (to check that the "client" agent is not pretending to be somebody else).
- Mobile agent *hosts* should be protected from being misused—or even crashed—by malicious and/or misfunctioning agents.
- Symmetrically, mobile agents' integrity should be protected from malicious and/or misfunctioning hosts, which—for example—might attempt to read agents' private data, and modify their code.

As research into authentication mechanisms and prevention of network "sniffers" is extensive and can be directly incorporated within agents, in this chapter we focus only on how agents can support the following two major principles of security:

Data security principle For each data-object in an agent's state, there may be restrictions on which other agents may read, write, or otherwise manipulate that data.

Action security principle For each action in an agent's repertoire, there may be restrictions on which other agents may utilize those actions.

Example 10.0.1 (CFIT) The current location of a Stealth plane agent during a mission is a piece of classified information that should not be disclosed to arbitrary agents. According to the data security principle, the plane's autoPilot agent should answer a current location request (thereby disclosing part of its data structures) only if the request comes from an authorized military agent.

To see an application of the action security principle, suppose that an autoPilot agent is asked to change the plane's altitude. Such requests should be obeyed only when they come from certified traffic control agents. Interference from other agents would turn air traffic into chaos.

The above example shows that through service requests, agents may obtain (part of) other agents' data; similarly, through service requests agents can make other agents execute actions. Therefore, in order to enforce the basic security principles described above, there must be a mechanism to ensure that while servicing incoming requests, agents will never improperly disclose any piece of sensitive or secret information, nor will they execute any undesirable actions.

To some extent, data security is analogous to database security. The oldest approaches to database security restrict query processing in such a way that no secret tuples are returned with the answer. This very simple form of filtering—called *surface security*—does not take into account the ability to infer new information from the information disclosed by the database. However, database query answers can be enriched by users through background knowledge, other data sources (e.g., databases or humans), and so on. Thus, users may be able to infer a secret indirectly from query results, even if such results contain no explicit secret. In this respect, software agents are not different: they are general computer programs, with enormous computational potentials, which may combine data obtained from different agents and derive secret information, not explicitly provided by any individual data source.

Example 10.0.2 (CFIT) Agents need not be extremely intelligent to infer secrets. Suppose the current position $\vec{p}_{now}$ of a military plane is a secret. An air traffic control agent ground_control may compute $\vec{p}_{now}$ from the current velocity $\vec{v}$ of the plane and its position $\vec{p}_t$ at the last velocity change, using the formula: $\vec{p}_{now} = \vec{p}_t + \vec{v} \cdot (now - t)$, that involves only straightforward numeric calculations.

In light of the above discussion, a stronger notion of security is needed—when an agent is responding to a request from a client agent, it must ensure that the client agent does not *derive* secrets that it wants to keep hidden from the client agent.

As agents do not know much about the inferential abilities and knowledge sources of other agents, how can they determine what information can be safely disclosed? For example, modeling human agents is a hopeless task. Humans are frequently unable to explain even their own inferences. Software agents are somewhat easier to model. For instance, if agents a and b are produced by the same company, then the developers of a may be able to encode a precise model of b inside agent a because they have access to b's code, which determines both the possible knowledge sources and the possible inferences of b. Nonetheless, even in this fortunate case, a might not know what knowledge has been gathered by b at arbitrary points in time, because this depends on which agents have been contacted by b, which in turn depends on the state of the network, and other factors that are difficult to model precisely. Thus, agents have to preserve data security using incomplete and imprecise knowledge about other agents.

In this chapter, we make the following contributions:

- First, in Section 10.1, we introduce a *completely logical agent model* that enables us to discuss agent security mechanisms.

- Second, in Section 10.2, we propose an abstract definition of what it means for an abstract agent to preserve data and action security. This apparently straightforward task turns out to be extremely complex, and involves several subtleties. It turns out that preserving the *exact* abstract notion of security described here is basically impossible, because it requires the agent in question to have a vast body of knowledge that it usually will not have.

- We attack this problem head on in Section 10.3 where we introduce a methodology for designing safe data security checks using incomplete and imprecise knowledge about other agents—these checks will be called *approximate security checks*. The methodology is developed using the abstract agent model. This has the advantage that attention is focused on the logical aspects of maintaining security in the absence of implementation choices made in *IMPACT*. We introduce two types of security checks—*static* security checks which, if checked at compile-time, guarantee that the agent will always be secure, and dynamic security checks that allow the agent to dynamically adapt to preserve security. Approximate security checks are compatible both with static security verification and with dynamic (run-time) security verification.

- In Section 10.4, we show that the problem of *exact* static security verification as well as various other related problems are undecidable. We study the different sources of complexity, and provide the good news that if we are willing to live with some constraints, then security can be guaranteed.

- *IMPACT*'s architecture for implementing of secure services and security related tools is illustrated in Section 10.5. The underlying model is based on the notion of action security introduced in Section 10.2 and on the methodology for approximate data security checks of Section 10.3.

- Related work is discussed in Section 10.6.

10.1 An Abstract Logical Agent Model

In this section, we will impose a logical model of agents on top of the framework described thus far in this book. Every agent has an associated *logical* state generalizing that of Chapter 6. In addition, at any given point in time, each agent has an associated *history* of interactions with other agents which play a role in shaping agent a's beliefs about agent b's beliefs. Each agent has an associated *inference mechanism* or *logical consequence notion* that it uses to infer data from a given body of data. Of course, it is possible that some agents use a degenerate form of inference (e.g., membership in a set of facts), while others may use first order logical reasoning, or yet other logical systems. Finally, in response to a request, each agent evaluates that request via an abstract *service evaluation function* which specifies which other agents will be contacted, and which queries/operations will be executed by the agent. In this section, we study each of these four parameters *without* concerning ourselves about security. Section 10.2 will then explain how this abstract agent model may be modified to accommodate security needs.

10.1.1 Logical Agent States

The state of an agent may be represented as a set of ground logical facts. In other words, the state of an agent may be *represented* as the set of all ground code call atoms **in**(o, $\mathcal{S}$: $f(a_1, \ldots, a_n)$) which are true in the state, where $\mathcal{S}$ is the name of a data structure manipulated by the agent, and f is one of the functions defined on this data structure. The following examples show how this may be accomplished.

Example 10.1.1 (CFIT) Consider a ground_control agent written in C. This kind of agent is likely to store the current position of planes in data structures of the following type:

```
struct 3DPoint {
    float latitude;
    float longitude;
    float altitude; }
```

The current value of the the above three fields can be represented by the atomic code call condition:

in(X, plane : *current_loc*())

where X is an object of type 3DPoint with three fields: X.latitude, X.longitude and X.altitude. The same fact-based representation can be used for the instances of a Java class such as

```
class 3DPoint {
    float latitude;
    float longitude;
    float altitude;
    ... }
```

Example 10.1.5 will show that facts are also suitable for representing class methods.

Formally, we associate with each agent a, a language that determines the syntactic structure of facts.

DEFINITION 10.1.1 (FACT LANGUAGE $\mathcal{L}_a$) Each agent a has an associated language $\mathcal{L}_a$ (a denumerable set), such that for all states $\mathcal{O}$ of a, $\mathcal{O} \subseteq \mathcal{L}_a$.

To tie this definition to *IMPACT*, we note that an *IMPACT* agent a may have as its associated fact language, the set of all ground code call atoms expressible by it.

Remark 5 Two states that satisfy the same code call conditions are identical in the abstract framework. This is a reasonable assumption, as the behavior of *IMPACT* agents depends only on the value of code call conditions ("internal" differences which do not affect the value of code call conditions may be ignored).

10.1.2 Abstract Behavior: Histories

As mentioned earlier, there are two types of *events* that may affect agent states.

action events, denoted by the corresponding action names, (we shall use for this purpose the meta-variable α, possibly with subscripts or superscripts) represent the actions that an agent has taken, either autonomously or in response to a request made by another agent;

message events represented by triples $\langle sender, receiver, body \rangle$, where *sender* and *receiver* are agents, *sender* $\neq$ *receiver*, and *body* is either a service request ρ or an *answer*, that is, a set of ground facts $Ans = \{f_1, f_2, \ldots\}$.

Formally, we need no assumptions on the syntactic structure of service requests—our results do not depend on it. However, for the purpose of writing some examples, we shall adopt service requests of the form $sn(i_1, \ldots, i_k, mi_1, \ldots, mi_m)$, where sn is a service name, $i_1, \ldots, i_k$ are its inputs, and $mi_1, \ldots, mi_m$ are its mandatory inputs, while answers will be sets of facts of the form $sn(i_1, \ldots, i_k, mi_1, \ldots, mi_m, o_1, \ldots, o_n)$, where $o_1, \ldots, o_n$ are the service outputs (see Definition 4.6.1).

We are now ready to define the basic notion of a history, as a sequence of events.

DEFINITION 10.1.2 (HISTORIES) A *history* is a possibly infinite sequence of events, such as $\langle e_1, e_2, \ldots \rangle$. We say that a history h is a *history for* a if each action in h can be executed by a, and for all messages $\langle s, r, m \rangle$ in h, either $s = a$ or $r = a$.

The *concatenation* of two histories h_1 and h_2 will be denoted by $h_1 \cdot h_2$. With a slight abuse of notation, we shall sometimes write $h \cdot e$, where e is an event, as an abbreviation for the concatenation $h \cdot \langle e \rangle$.

The notion of a history for a keeps track of a set of messages that a has interchanged with other agents, and a set of actions that a has performed. It is important to note that a history need not be complete—an agent may or may not choose to explicitly keep all information about events in its history.

Example 10.1.2 (CFIT) A history for an autoPilot agent may have the form $\langle \ldots e_1, e_2, e_3, e_4 \ldots \rangle$, where:

$e_1 = \langle \text{ground\_control}, \text{autoPilot}, \text{set:altitude}(\textit{new\_alt}) \rangle$,

$e_2 = \textit{climb}(15\textit{sec})$,

$e_3 = \langle \text{ground\_control}, \text{autoPilot}, \text{location}() \rangle$,

$e_4 = \langle \text{autoPilot}, \text{ground\_control}, \{\text{location}((50, 20, 40))\} \rangle$.

Here e_1, e_3 are request messages, e_2 is an action event, and e_4 is an answer message. Intuitively, the ground control asks the autoPilot to change the plane's altitude, then asks for the new position. Events e_2 and e_4 model the autoPilot's reactions to those requests.

As mentioned at the beginning of this section, the events in an agent's history determine the agent's current state. Accordingly, we adopt the following notation.

DEFINITION 10.1.3 (AGENT STATE AT h: $\mathcal{O}_a(h)$) For all agents a and all histories h for a, we denote by $\mathcal{O}_a(h)$, the state of a immediately after the sequence of events h. The initial state of a (i.e. the state of a when it was initially deployed) is denoted by $\mathcal{O}_a(\langle \rangle)$.

The following example illustrates the above definition.

Example 10.1.3 If h has the form $\langle \ldots e_4 \rangle$, where e_4 is the event described in Example 10.1.2, and F is the fact **in**$((50, 20, 40), \text{autoPilot}:\text{location}())$, then $\mathcal{O}_{\text{autoPilot}}(h)$ may contain the facts F and

in$(F, \mathbf{BT}^a : \text{proj-select}(\text{agent}, =, \text{ground\_control}))$, (10.1)

(recall that (10.1) means that autoPilot believes that ground_control believes that autoPilot's current position is (50, 20, 40)).

The notion of history for a captures histories that are *syntactically* correct. However, not every history for a describes a possible behavior of a. For instance, some histories are impossible because a's code will never lead to that sequence of events. Some others are impossible because they contain messages coming from agents that will never want to talk to a. The definition below models the set of histories that might actually happen.

DEFINITION 10.1.4 (POSSIBLE HISTORIES) The set of *possible histories* for a is denoted by $pos\mathcal{H}_a$. It is a subset of the set of all histories for a.

10.1.3 Agent Consequence Relation

In principle, "intelligent" agents can derive new facts from the information explicitly stored in their state. Different agents have different reasoning capabilities. Some agents may perform no reasoning on the data they store, some may derive new information using numeric calculations (as in Example 10.0.2); others may have sophisticated inference procedures.

Example 10.1.4 Given any agent a, we may regard the **in**(.,.) predicate and $=, >, <, \geq, \leq$ as standard predicates of first order logic. Then a's state can be viewed as a set of first-order formulas (the code call conditions which are true in the state), from which a may be able to infer (some) logical consequences, using the standard inferences of first-order logic.

The notion of agent consequence introduced below will model the process by which agents draw inferences based upon their state. The result of those inferences will be modeled by sets of facts.

Example 10.1.5 (CFIT) Let us reconsider Example 10.1.1. If the ground_control agent were written in Java, then it would probably represent planes with a Java class Plane, one of whose methods would be current_loc(). In this case, the private variables of the class Plane need not explicitly represent the plane's current location. For instance, by analogy with Example 10.0.2, such variables may encode the plane's position and velocity at the last time t when its velocity changed, and the method current_loc may compute the current position with the formula $\vec{p}_{now} = \vec{p}_t + \vec{v} \cdot (now - t)$. The method location can be represented by the code call

in(X, plane : *current_loc*()).

Remark 6 The same code call can be used to model a structured variable (see Example 10.1.1); the fact language constitutes a uniform way of expressing an agent's information, independently of whether it is represented explicitly or implicitly in the agent's state.

DEFINITION 10.1.5 (AGENT CONSEQUENCE RELATION) We assume that each agent a has an associated consequence relation Cn_a, that takes as input, a set of ground facts belonging to $\mathcal{L}_a$ and returns as output, a set of ground facts belonging to $\mathcal{L}_a$. $\text{Cn}_a(F)$ returns as output, all facts implied by the input set F, according to the notion of consequence adopted by a. Cn_a is required to satisfy the following general axioms:

1. $\text{Cn}_a(X) \supseteq X$;
2. $\text{Cn}_a(\text{Cn}_a(X)) = \text{Cn}_a(X)$.

We say that Cn_a is a *strong* consequence relation if it further satisfies the condition that $\text{Cn}_a^{\text{fol}}(X) \supseteq \text{Cn}_a(X)$ for all X, where $\text{Cn}_a^{\text{fol}}(F)$ denotes the set of all consequences of F using the standard consequence notion of first order logic.

Our definition of agent consequence builds upon the classical notion of an abstract consequence relation, originally proposed by Tarski (1981). Almost all standard provability relations, $\vdash$, for different proof systems ranging from classical logic to modal logics to multivalued logics, induce a function $\text{Cn}^\vdash$ as follows:

$\text{Cn}^\vdash(X) =_{def} \{\psi \mid X \vdash \psi\}$.

Conversely, each abstract consequence relation Cn_b induces a provability relation

$S \vdash_b \psi$ *if, by definition,* $\quad \forall X : S \subseteq X \subseteq \mathcal{L}_b, \ \psi \in \text{Cn}_b(X)$.

Note a subtle difference between $\vdash_b$ and Cn_b: in $S \vdash_b \phi$, S is treated as a *partial* description of a state, while the argument X of Cn_b is taken as a *complete* description of b's state.

The notion of strong consequence requires agents to be "rational" in the sense that they do not make inferences that are unsound with respect to classical logic. This is not the only possible form of rationality; some agents may make decisions on the basis of conditions that *normally* or *plausibly* hold; the consequence relation of such agents is not strong. Drawing conclusions requires resources; some agents may want to infer all valid conclusions from their state, while others may only draw inferences obtainable through a bounded number of inferences. This explains why consequence relations need not satisfy $\text{Cn}_a^{\text{fol}}(X) \subseteq \text{Cn}_a(X)$.

10.1.4 Abstract Service Request Handling

The abstract model of histories described thus far is completely general. It can model agents that respond to many requests simultaneously, by interleaving the corresponding actions; it can also model agents that respond to service requests with arbitrarily complex plans. However, for the purposes of this chapter, we shall make a few simplifying assumptions about service request handling in order to improve readability:

Assumption 1 Each agent serves one request at a time, and does not interleave its autonomous plans with the evaluation of any service requests. This assumption makes it easier

Section 10.1   An Abstract Logical Agent Model   337

to relate events to the request that triggered them, because the request itself and the sequence of triggered events are contiguous. Each event e is triggered by the last incoming request before e. This assumption can be easily eliminated by assigning an "id" to each event, and then ensuring that a response made by agent a to agent b contains information about the id of the request being responded to.

Assumption 2 Each request service follows a precise pattern of activities. First, if necessary, the server agent a contacts other agents (e.g. to get some missing information, to make a reservation, etc.); second, their answers are waited for; then, the requested actions "internal" to a (i.e., not involving communications) are executed, and finally, an answer is returned to the client (if the request specifies some output variables). This pattern makes it easier to identify the different parts of the request service relevant to security enforcement, such as the sequence of actions triggered by a request and the answer to a data request.

The above assumptions correspond to the following formal definition.

DEFINITION 10.1.6 (SERVICE REQUEST EVALUATION FUNCTIONS)   Suppose a is an agent, and h ranges over those histories for a whose last event is a request message $\langle b_h, a, \rho_h \rangle$, where ρ_h is a service request.

- A *contact evaluation function used by agent* a is a mapping cnt_a that takes h as input and returns a sequence of outgoing messages $\mathsf{cnt}_a(h) = \langle \langle a, c_1, \rho_1 \rangle, \ldots, \langle a, c_n, \rho_n \rangle \rangle, (c_i \neq B)$.
- An *action evaluation function* is a mapping act_a that takes h and a sequence of incoming messages $Resp(\mathsf{cnt}_a(h)) = \langle \langle c_1, A, Ans_1 \rangle, \ldots, \langle c_n, A, Ans_n \rangle \rangle$ (corresponding to the response received from other agents to the outgoing requests in $\mathsf{cnt}_a(h)$) as input, and returns a sequence of actions executable by a.
- A *data evaluation function* is a mapping ans_a that takes h and $Resp(\mathsf{cnt}_a(h))$ as described above as inputs, and returns an answer $\{f_1, \ldots, f_m\}$.

Finally, the *(global) service evaluation function* is

$$\zeta_a(h) = h \cdot \mathsf{cnt}_a(h) \cdot Resp(\mathsf{cnt}_a(h)) \cdot \mathsf{act}_a(h, Resp(\mathsf{cnt}_a(h))) \cdot \langle a, b_h, \mathsf{ans}_a(h, Resp(\mathsf{cnt}(h))) \rangle.$$

The triple $\langle \mathsf{cnt}_a, \mathsf{act}_a, \mathsf{ans}_a \rangle$ will be referred to as a *service request evaluation policy*. With a slight abuse of notation, the service request evaluation policy will be sometimes be identified with the global service evaluation function ζ_a.

Figure 10.1 shows a diagrammatic view of how an agent evaluates a service request. Intuitively, $\zeta_a(h)$ extends h with the events triggered by the most recent request $\langle b_h, a, \rho_h \rangle$ (which may be found at the end of h); the action part and the data part are determined on

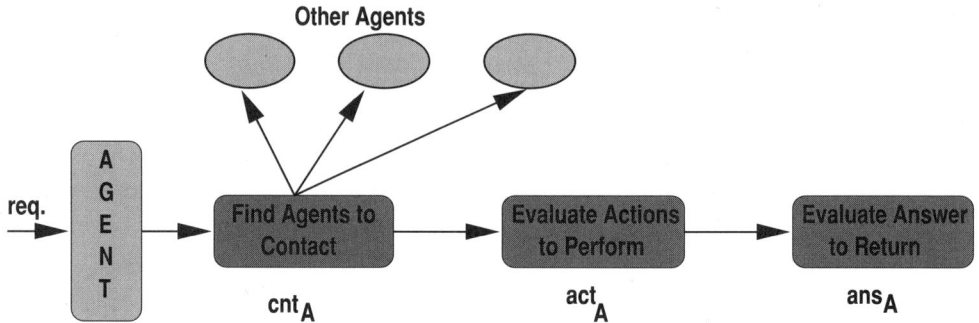

Figure 10.1
Agent Service Evaluation Procedure.

the basis of the inputs modeled by $Resp(cnt_a(h))$. The answer $ans_a(h, Resp(cnt_a(h)))$ is the data returned by a.

In *IMPACT* agents, cnt_a and act_a would be defined through *agent programs* (see Chapter 6), while ans_a would be implemented as a set of *service rules* (Definition 4.6.1).

10.2 Abstract Secure Request Handling

In the preceding section, we have introduced an abstract agent model. Here, we use that abstract model to state formally what it means for a service request evaluation policy to be *secure*.

- First, in Section 10.2.1 we will describe, for each agent a, what data and actions it wishes to protect from another agent b. When handling a service request, agent a must ensure that such data is not disclosed to agent b, and such actions are not executed on behalf of agent b.

- Second, in Section 10.2.2, we introduce the notion of a *service distortion*. Informally speaking, each agent has an associated service request evaluation function ζ_a (see Definition 10.1.6), which describes how incoming requests would be evaluated in the absence of security restrictions. A distortion function distorts ζ_a in some way, so as to protect a's own data, and to prevent a from executing undesirable actions. Incoming requests are then served using the distortion function, instead of ζ_a.

- In Section 10.2.3, we will define what it means for a distortion to preserve security, with respect to the security specifications introduced in Section 10.2.1. This task involves some subtleties that will lead to non-trivial definitions.

- Finally, in Section 10.2.4, *maximally cooperative distortions* will be introduced. The underlying idea is that, in many cases, we want security-preserving distortions to be as close as possible to the original evaluation function ζ_a, i.e., ζ_a should be distorted as little as possible when attempting to maintain security.

10.2.1 Security Specifications

In this section, we define what kinds of *data* an agent would like to protect from another agent, and also what kinds of *actions* an agent would like to avoid executing for other agents.

DEFINITION 10.2.1 (AGENT SECRETS FUNCTION Sec_a) Suppose a is an agent. Sec_a is a function which associates with any other agent $b \neq a$, a set of ground facts from $\mathcal{L}_b$, which a would like to keep secret from b.

Intuitively, a would like to prevent b from *inferring* the ground facts contained in $Sec_a(b)$.

Example 10.2.1 (CFIT) In the scenario of Example 10.0.1, the *Stealth* plane's autoPilot agent should have an associated secrets function $Sec_{\text{autoPilot}}$ such that if ground_control is a civilian agent, then (at least) all the facts **in**(x, autoPilot:*location*())) should be contained in $Sec_{\text{autoPilot}}(\text{ground\_control})$.

The concept of an agent action security function describes what actions an agent may or may not perform for another agent.

DEFINITION 10.2.2 (AGENT ACTION SECURITY FUNCTION $ASec_a$) An agent action security function associated with agent a is a function $ASec_a$ that associates with any other agent $b \neq a$, a set consisting of (i) outgoing request messages of the form $\langle a, c, \rho \rangle$ ($c \neq b$), and (ii) sequences of ground action names.

Roughly speaking, $ASec_a(b)$ contains a set of forbidden action sequences that a does not want to execute upon b's requests. It also includes requests that a is not willing to issue on behalf of b.

Example 10.2.2 (CFIT) As mentioned in Example 10.0.1, autoPilot agents should only obey the commands issued by certified air traffic control agents. For all other agents b, $ASec_{\text{autoPilot}}(b)$ should contain (among other sequences) all the simple sequences $\langle climb(x) \rangle$.

In some cases, the set $ASec_a(b)$ may be closed under action equivalence. For example, suppose there exist two actions printf(s) and fprintf(stdout,s) that execute the C functions associated with these names. These two actions are equivalent, and hence if $\alpha_1, \ldots, \alpha_9$ is a forbidden action sequence and $\alpha_2 = $ printf(s), then the action sequence α_1, fprintf(stdout, s), $\alpha_3, \ldots, \alpha_9$ should also be forbidden.

One may therefore wonder whether we should insist that if an action sequence is in $ASec_a(b)$, then every action sequence equivalent to it should also be in $ASec_a(b)$. Using the real world operation of computer systems as a guide, the answer seems to be no. To see why, consider simple email. A user may write on another user's mailbox file only through certified e-mail programs. No sequence of individual `open`, `close`, `read` and `write` operations is admitted on another user's mailbox, although some of these sequences update the mailbox exactly as the e-mail program would. Accordingly, $ASec_a(b)$ need not necessarily be closed under action equivalence.

10.2.2 Service Distortions

As we anticipated at the beginning of this section, in order to maintain security an agent may replace an unrestricted service evaluation policy (that would be applied in the absence of security specifications) with a distorted policy, that should protect the agent's data, and avoid forbidden action sequences. Distorted policies and their components will be marked with a tilde in order to distinguish them from their unrestricted counterparts.

DEFINITION 10.2.3 (SERVICE DISTORTION FUNCTIONS $\widetilde{cnt}_a, \widetilde{act}_a, \widetilde{ans}_a$) The *contact distortion function, action distortion function* and *data distortion function used by* a, denoted by $\widetilde{cnt}_a, \widetilde{act}_a$ and $\widetilde{ans}_a$, are mappings with the same input and output types as their corresponding service request functions. The *(global) service distortion function* is

$$\tilde{\zeta}_a(h) = h \cdot \widetilde{cnt}_a(h) \cdot Resp(\widetilde{cnt}_a(h)) \cdot \widetilde{act}_a(h, Resp(\widetilde{cnt}_a(h))) \cdot \langle a, b_h, \widetilde{ans}_a(h, Resp(\widetilde{cnt}_a(h))) \rangle.$$

Recall that b_h above refers to the agent making the last request message to agent a in history h.

The triple $\langle \widetilde{cnt}_a, \widetilde{act}_a, \widetilde{ans}_a \rangle$ will be referred to as *distortion policy*. With a slight abuse of notation, the distortion policy will be sometimes be identified with the global distortion function $\tilde{\zeta}_a$.

The underlying intuition is that, in order to protect security, agent a reacts to incoming requests as specified by the distortion functions $\widetilde{cnt}_a, \widetilde{act}_a$ and $\widetilde{ans}_a$. Note that the above definition does not specify what it means for a distortion to be secure. Some distortions will be secure, others may not be secure. Secure distortions will be introduced in the next section.

Example 10.2.3 (CFIT) A distortion policy for the military autoPilot agent may refuse to answer questions about the plane's current location. Then, the data distortion function $\widetilde{ans}_{autoPilot}(h, Resp)$ will return the empty set whenever the last event of h is a current location request from some unauthorized agent.

Section 10.2   Abstract Secure Request Handling   341

As the distortion function $\tilde{\zeta}_a$ determines a's reaction to incoming requests, and hence the form of a's histories, the set of possible histories for a should be *compatible* with the behavior specified by $\tilde{\zeta}_a$. Accordingly, in the following we shall assume that:

for all the possible histories $h \in \text{pos}\mathcal{H}_a$ whose last event is a request to a, the history $\tilde{\zeta}_a(h)$ is in $\text{pos}\mathcal{H}_a$ (where $\tilde{\zeta}_a$ is the distortion adopted by a).

10.2.3 Secure Service Distortions

What does it mean for a distortion to preserve security? A full answer to this question must deal both with the protection of agents' *data*, and with restrictions on the *actions* that agents may execute in response to incoming requests, as specified by the functions Sec_a and $ASec_a$ introduced in Section 10.2.1.

Let us consider data protection first. Standard approaches require systems (be they agents, databases or other packages) to include no secrets in their answers. This is definitely a reasonable security requirement, that we call *surface security*.

Recall that $\text{pos}\mathcal{H}_a$ denotes the set of *all possible histories* for an agent a.

DEFINITION 10.2.4 (SURFACE SECURITY)   A distortion policy $\tilde{\zeta}_a$ with data distortion $\widetilde{ans}_a$ and contact distortion $\widetilde{cnt}_a$ is *surface secure w.r.t.* b if for all histories $h \in \text{pos}\mathcal{H}_a$ whose last event is a service request message from b, and for all responses $Resp(\widetilde{cnt}_a(h))$,

$$\widetilde{ans}_a(h, Resp(\widetilde{cnt}_a(h))) \cap Sec_a(b) = \emptyset.$$

In other words, the answer of a (modeled by the term on the left of the intersection) should contain no secret information.

Although this somewhat minimal form of security can be satisfactory for simple client agents, it doesn't guarantee data protection from smart agents. Recall that agents can derive new information through their consequence relation.

Example 10.2.4   With reference to Example 10.1.5, an agent b which knows that the plane has been traveling at a constant velocity $\vec{v}$ for the last 30 minutes can derive the current position of the plane from its location at time $t = \text{now} - 30$. In this example, the plane's position 30 minutes ago—although not a secret in itself—suffices to let b violate a secret (the current position of the plane).

A naive approach to this problem consists of stating that *a distortion policy $\tilde{\zeta}_a$ is data secure if a's client agents can never deduce any secret*. However, this definition does not take into account the fact that security breaches might be caused by some other agent $c \neq a$. The problem is that b might come to know some secret s because it was told this by c. Clearly, agent a has in no way caused security to be violated in this situation. Under the naive definition, a's distortion policy would not be data-secure simply because c disclosed s. This would happen even in the limit case where a's distortion never answers incoming requests and maintains perfect silence!

This paradoxical situation can be avoided by adopting a more realistic notion of security. The underlying intuition is that agents are responsible only for their own answers. Roughly speaking, a distortion policy can be said to be secure if it never *increases* the set of secrets known by other agents. With respect to the previous example, a's distortion policy should be regarded as data secure as long as b cannot derive new secrets using a's answers. To state this formally, we need a couple of intermediate definitions.

DEFINITION 10.2.5 (COMPATIBLE HISTORIES $h_1 \xleftrightarrow{ab} h_2$)   Let a and b be agents. We say that two histories h_1 and h_2 are ab-*compatible*, denoted $h_1 \xleftrightarrow{ab} h_2$, if the subsequences of h_1 and h_2 obtained by removing all events but the messages of the form $\langle a, b, \ldots \rangle$ and $\langle b, a, \ldots \rangle$ coincide. Furthermore, if $h_1 \xleftrightarrow{ab} h_2$ and the last events of h_1 and h_2 coincide, then we write $h_1 \xLeftrightarrow{ab} h_2$, and say that h_1, h_2 are *strongly* ab-compatible.

Intuitively, histories h_1 and h_2 are ab-compatible iff the two histories are identical as far as messages between the agents a, b are concerned. Therefore, h_1 and h_2 might be a's and b's view (respectively) of the same global sequence of events. Note that h_1 and h_2 may differ on interactions involving agents other than a, b, but they are considered to be a, b compatible if they coincide on events involving a, b.

Example 10.2.5   Consider the two histories h_1, h_2 given below.

$h_1 = \langle b, a, \rho_1 \rangle, \langle a, c, \rho_2 \rangle, \langle c, b, \rho_3 \rangle, \langle a, b, \text{ans}_1 \rangle.$
$h_2 = \langle b, a, \rho_1 \rangle, \langle a, c, \rho_4 \rangle, \langle c, b, \rho_3 \rangle, \langle a, b, \text{ans}_1 \rangle.$

It is easy to see that histories h_1, h_2 are ab-compatible and bc-compatible, but they are not ac-compatible. Furthermore, h_1 and h_2 are strongly ab-compatible and strongly bc-compatible, as the last events of these two histories are identical.

In addition to the notion of compatible histories, we need a concise notation for the set of secrets of a that can be violated (i.e., inferred) by b at some point in time, corresponding to history h_b. Recall that we use $\mathcal{O}_b(h_b)$ to denote b's state at h_b, and that $\text{Cn}_b(\mathcal{O}_b(h_b))$ is the set of facts that can be derived by b from that state.

DEFINITION 10.2.6 (VIOLATED SECRETS) $\text{Violated}_b^a(h_b) = \text{Cn}_b(\mathcal{O}_b(h_b)) \cap Sec_a(b).$

Section 10.2   Abstract Secure Request Handling   343

We are now ready to formalize the important concept of data security, which says that for an agent's distortion policy to be data secure, it must guarantee that it will never increase the set of secrets violated by another agent.

DEFINITION 10.2.7 (DATA SECURITY)   Let $h_a \in \text{pos}\mathcal{H}_a$ be such that the last event of h_a is a request message from b. A distortion policy $\tilde{\zeta}_a$ is *data secure at* h_a if for all histories $h_b \cdot e \in \text{pos}\mathcal{H}_b$ such that $h_b \cdot e \stackrel{ab}{\Longleftrightarrow} \tilde{\zeta}_a(h_a)$,

$\text{Violated}_b^a(h_b) \supseteq \text{Violated}_b^a(h_b \cdot e)$.

If $\tilde{\zeta}_a$ is secure for all h_a satisfying the above assumptions, then we say that $\tilde{\zeta}_a$ is *data secure*.

To understand this definition, recall that $\tilde{\zeta}_a(h_a)$ is a's history immediately after it answers b's request. Thus, the condition $h_b \cdot e \in \text{pos}\mathcal{H}_b$ and $h_b \cdot e \stackrel{ab}{\Longleftrightarrow} \tilde{\zeta}_a(h_a)$, requires that $h_b \cdot e$ is a possible history for b when a's answer reaches b. Next, note that from $h_b \cdot e \stackrel{ab}{\Longleftrightarrow} \tilde{\zeta}_a(h_a)$ and the definition of $\tilde{\zeta}_a(h_a)$, it follows that e must be a message of the form $\langle a, b, \widetilde{\text{ans}}_a(h_a, Resp(\widetilde{\text{cnt}}_a(h_a)))\rangle$, that is, e is a's answer to b. Then the inclusion in Definition 10.2.7 means that the set of violated secrets (of b) does not increase after receiving a's answer. By quantifying over all possible histories $h_b \cdot e$ with the aforementioned properties, we require data to be protected no matter what actions b may take before getting the answer, possibly including sending requests to other agents and getting their answers.

Interestingly enough, the above definition encompasses the case (corresponding to strict inclusion) in which a convinces b that some previously violated secret does not hold—although in practice this may be just as hard to do as it is desirable.

Surface security can be regarded as a special case of (full) data security. Indeed, when the client agent b stores only the current answer, without drawing any conclusion from it, surface security and data security may coincide. The following is a formal statement of this fact.

THEOREM 10.2.1 (DATA SECURITY IS MORE GENERAL THAN SURFACE SECURITY)   There exist multiagent systems where surface security coincides with data security.

Proof   Consider a simple multiagent system consisting of two agents a and b. Let a's and b's possible histories have the form

$h_n = \langle q_1, a_1, \ldots, q_n, a_n \rangle$,

where each q_i is a request message from b to a, and each a_i is a's answer to q_i. Let $\mathcal{O}_b(\langle\rangle) =_{def} \emptyset$, and

$\mathcal{O}_b(h_n) =_{def} \bigcup_{i=1}^{n} a_i$.

Finally, let Cn_b be the identity function over b's states. Then $\text{Violated}_b^a(\langle\rangle) = \emptyset$, and

$\tilde{\zeta}_a$ is data secure *iff* $\text{Violated}_b^a(\langle\rangle) \supseteq \text{Violated}_b^a(h_1) \supseteq \text{Violated}_b^a(h_2) \supseteq \cdots$

$\qquad\qquad\qquad\quad$ *iff* $\forall n > 0,\ \text{Violated}_b^a(h_n) = \emptyset.$

Moreover, $\text{Violated}_b^a(h_n) = \bigcup_{i=1}^{n} a_i \cap Sec_a(b)$; therefore

$\tilde{\zeta}_a$ is data secure *iff* $\forall n > 0,\ a_i \cap Sec_a(b) = \emptyset.$

But this is equivalent to say that $\tilde{\zeta}_a$ is surface secure. ■

However, *data security does not always entail surface security*. For example, if a sends b secrets only when b already knows them (a game well-known by double-crossers), then data security is enforced, while surface security is violated.

Example 10.2.6 Consider a military autoPilot agent that knows that it has been successfully tracked by an enemy radar agent. In this case, security of the airplane's location has already been violated, and hence, the autoPilot agent can send a message to its ground_control agent without violating data security. (Had the enemy radar agent not already tracked it, executing such a send-message action might allow the plane's location to be identified if the enemy intercepts the message).

Analogous to the notion of data secure distortions is a notion of action secure distortion policies, where a requested action is replaced by a distorted version or a modified version of that action.

DEFINITION 10.2.8 (ACTION SECURE DISTORTION POLICY) Let h_a be finite history for a, whose last event is a request message $\langle b, a, \rho \rangle$. A distortion policy $\tilde{\zeta}_a$ is *action secure at* h_a iff for all sequences of incoming messages $Resp(\widetilde{cnt}_a(h))$ of the appropriate type, no message in $\widetilde{cnt}_a(h_a)$ occurs in $ASec_a(b)$, and no segment of $\widetilde{act}_a(h_a, Resp(\widetilde{cnt}_a(h)))$ is contained in $ASec_a(b)$.

If $\tilde{\zeta}_a$ is action secure at h_a for all h_a, then we simply say that $\tilde{\zeta}_a$ is *action secure*.

The intuition underlying action secure distortions is very similar to the intuition underlying data secure distortions. The two notions of security are combined in the next definition.

DEFINITION 10.2.9 (SECURE DISTORTIONS) We say $\tilde{\zeta}_a$ is *secure* at h_a iff $\tilde{\zeta}_a$ is both data secure at h_a and action secure at h_a.

10.2.4 Maximally Cooperative Secure Service Distortions

There are many different ways in which an agent can distort services. One of these ways is to provide no information or to take no action at all, which is a very uncooperative mode of behavior. At the opposite extreme, an agent may provide information or take actions that are *as close as possible* to the information/actions being requested, without compromising security. The right balance between security and cooperation depends on a number of application dependent factors, such as the *quality* of a given service and the importance of response time (searching for the most cooperative distortions may be computationally expensive).

Independently of tradeoff considerations, the above discussion assumes the existence of some notion of *nearness* or *degree of distortion* of an answer/action. If we have a set of answers (including distorted answers) that may be possibly given in response to a request, then one way of determining nearness is by having some kind of metric on the space of such possible answers. Alternatively, one may induce a partial ordering on the answers. For example, in the CFIT* scenario, suppose an agent wishes to know the current location of an helicopter agent. Suppose Loc_i denotes the location of the helicopter i minutes in the past. Thus, Loc_{30} specifies where the helicopter was 30 minutes back, Loc_{60} specifies where the helicopter was an hour back, and so on. Suppose it is acceptable to provide location information that is 30 minutes old to an agent a. Clearly, while both Loc_{30} and Loc_{60} are secure distortions of the true answer (Loc_0), the former is less distorted than the latter.

Alternatively, consider an FBI agent who looks for people who make over 150K and suppose the answer to this query according to the oracle agent is a set of names of 10 people. An answer which contains 9 of these names may be considered "nearer" to the actual answer than a list of 5 names.

Consider again the CFIT* scenario, when a tank agent asks a terrain agent for a map of a specific area. A map which includes as many details as possible, without violating security of the area in question will be the desired answer.

In a similar vein, when an agent requests an action that cannot be executed because of security reasons, we would like the responding agent to take an action that is maximally cooperative in terms of satisfying the request, but which avoids the security violation. Reserving a Jeep for an agent may be the most cooperative action when reserving a Sedan is not allowed. Analogously, suppose an agent receives a request for transportation for a specific trip. The normal course of action would be to make a flight reservation, and arrange for transportation to the airport. If for some reason, the agent cannot execute this action because of a security restriction disallowing (perhaps temporarily) such actions, then a cooperative response might be to find out about possible trains, make transportation arrangements to the train station, and reserve a train seat. In the CFIT* scenario, suppose the heli1 agent maintains information about the locations of other vehicles and a request to update the locations of vehicle1 and vehicle2 is sent to the heli1 agent by the vehicle3 agent. Suppose now that $ASec_{heli1}(vehicle3)$ which is the set of all action sequences that the heli1 agent may not perform for the vehicle3 agent, forbids execution of the update to agent vehicle2's location. That is, the heli1 agent does not honor vehicle3's request to update vehicle2's location. In this case, the heli1 agent could choose not to honor either of the two requested updates, or it could choose to updating the location of vehicle1—the latter option is clearly more cooperative than the former.

In general, suppose Ans_a is the set of answers which can be given to other agents by a. We assume that there is a partial order $\leq_a^{ans}$ on Ans_a. Similarly, suppose Act_a denotes the set of ground actions of agent a and $\leq_a^{act}$ is a partial order on the sequence of actions in Act_a.

For example, in the helicopter agent scenario, Ans_{heli1} consists of the set of all possible locations of the helicopter and these answers can be ordered according to their actual distance from one another. Another possibility is that the answers pertaining to the helicopter's location consist of pairs of the form (t_i, loc_i) indicating that the location of the helicopter at time t_i is loc_i. In this case, we may choose a partial order $\leq_{heli1}^{ans}$ such that $(t_1, loc_1) \leq_{heli1}^{ans} (t_2, loc_2)$, iff $t_1 < t_2$.

In the FBI scenario described above, the order used by the oracle agent may simply be set inclusion ($\subseteq$).

Similarly, when considering update actions for the helicopter agent, the ordering $\leq_{heli1}^{act}$ may be set inclusion over sets of updates. In this case, $\emptyset \leq_{heli1}^{act} U_1 \leq_{heli1}^{act} U_2$, where

$U_1 = \{update\text{-}loc(location, \text{vehicle1}, time\_10, 55, 60)\}$,

$U_2 = U_1 \cup \{update\text{-}loc(location, \text{vehicle2}, time\_10, 40, 30)\}$.

The next definition states formally how the orderings $\leq_a^{ans}$ and $\leq_a^{act}$ determine the relative degree of cooperation provided by different distortions.

DEFINITION 10.2.10 (DEGREES OF COOPERATION) A distortion policy $\tilde{\zeta}_a = \langle \widetilde{cnt}, \widetilde{act}, \widetilde{ans} \rangle$ is *more data (resp. action) cooperative* than a distortion policy $\tilde{\zeta}_a' = \langle \widetilde{cnt}', \widetilde{act}', \widetilde{ans}' \rangle$ if for all histories h for a, and for all responses $Resp(\widetilde{cnt}(h))$ and $Resp(\widetilde{cnt}'(h))$,

$\widetilde{ans}'(h, (\widetilde{cnt}'(h))) \leq_a^{ans} \widetilde{ans}(h, Resp(\widetilde{cnt}(h)))$

(resp. $\widetilde{ans}'(h, (\widetilde{cnt}'(h))) \leq_a^{act} \widetilde{ans}(h, Resp(\widetilde{cnt}(h)))$). Then we write $\tilde{\zeta}_a' \leq_a^{ans} \tilde{\zeta}_a$ (resp. $\tilde{\zeta}_a' \leq_a^{act} \tilde{\zeta}_a$).

Note that distortions should not be *too* cooperative. For example, $\tilde{\zeta}_a$ should not return more information than the unrestricted policy ζ_a. Similarly, $\tilde{\zeta}_a$ should not do for b more than ζ_a is willing to do. This intuition is formalized by the following definition.

DEFINITION 10.2.11 (CORRECT DISTORTIONS) Distortion $\tilde{\zeta}_a$ is *data correct* (w.r.t. ζ_a) if $\tilde{\zeta}_a \leq_a^{ans} \zeta_a$. It is *action correct* (w.r.t. ζ_a) if $\tilde{\zeta}_a \leq_a^{act} \zeta_a$. If $\tilde{\zeta}_a$ is both data correct and action correct, then we simply say that $\tilde{\zeta}_a$ is *correct*.

Now we can formalize the notion of *maximal cooperation*. The above discussion shows clearly that there must be two limits to cooperation: security preservation and correctness. A distortion is maximally cooperative if it satisfies both.

DEFINITION 10.2.12 (MAXIMALLY COOPERATIVE DISTORTIONS) Distortion $\tilde{\zeta}_a$ is *maximally data (resp. action) cooperative* (w.r.t. ζ_a), if it is correct w.r.t. ζ_a and for all distortions $\tilde{\zeta}'_a$ correct w.r.t. ζ_a,

$$\tilde{\zeta}'_a \leq^{\text{ans}}_a \tilde{\zeta}_a$$

(resp. $\tilde{\zeta}'_a \leq^{\text{act}}_a \tilde{\zeta}_a$). When $\tilde{\zeta}_a$ is both maximally data cooperative and maximally action cooperative, then we say that $\tilde{\zeta}_a$ is *maximally cooperative*.

In the following sections, we will see that the degree of cooperation may be influenced by the quality of a's incomplete/imprecise knowledge about other agents.

10.3 Safely Approximate Data Security

The notion of data secure distortion introduced in the preceding section (Definition 10.2.7) depends on several aspects of the agents b that submit service requests to a. These include:

- b's possible behaviors, formalized by the set of possible histories $\text{pos}\mathcal{H}_b$;
- b's states at arbitrary points in time, formalized by the state function $\mathcal{O}_b(.)$;
- b's consequence relation, $\text{Cn}_b(.)$.

In the real world, however, a (and its developers) can hardly be expected to successfully guess the above parameters for an arbitrary agent b that might send a request to agent a. For instance, agent b may only be willing to disclose a small part of its state, so that $\mathcal{O}_b(.)$ is not precisely known by a; similarly, b's code (and hence $\text{pos}\mathcal{H}_b$ and $\text{Cn}_b(.)$) may be unknown to agent a and its developers. Things are even more complicated when b is a human agent; even b may be unable to precisely explain its inference mechanism. This means that Definition 10.2.7 cannot be immediately used to obtain a secure distortion policy for a.

In practice, only an *approximate* idea of b's behavior and capabilities will be available to agent a. The best a can do is to use such approximations. In this section, we will specify what the approximations look like, and describe the conditions under which the approximations used by a are rich enough to guarantee security. In particular, in this section, we do the following.

- First, we define what it means for agent a to approximate agent b's history.
- Then, we describe how agent a approximates agent b's language (after all, if agent a knows nothing about agent b's language, then it cannot say much about agent b's beliefs).

- Then, we show how these two notions allow us to define how agent a approximates agent b's state, given its approximation of agent b's history and language.
- We, then, introduce a notion of how agent a can approximate agent b's inference mechanism/consequence relation so that it can infer an approximation of agent b's beliefs.
- Based on these parameters, we show that to preserve security, agent a must *overestimate* what (it thinks) agent b will know after it responds to a given request, and it must *underestimate* what (it thinks) agent b knew before giving the answer.
- Though some of these approximations are space-consuming, we show that all approximations can be *compacted*, but such compactions diminish the level of cooperation agent a gives to agent b.

Note that according to our definition of security, we wish to ensure that the set of secrets violated by agent b must not increase after agent a responds to agent b. By underestimating what agent b knows before the answer is given, we are effectively assuming that agent b knew as few secrets upfront as possible. By overestimating what agent b knows after the answer is given, we are assuming that agent b is capable of drawing a large set of inferences (perhaps larger than it really can). If we can show that our security mechanism guarantees that this overestimate of what b knows after we answer the request only violates at most as many secrets as b knew before the answer was provided, then we can rest assured that security will be preserved.

10.3.1 The Basic Idea

The intuition underlying approximate security checks is relatively simple: take the worst possible case and decide what to do on the basis of that worst-case scenario.

Example 10.3.1 (Approximate Security Check) Suppose that agent ground_control asks agent autoPilot what its location was 30 minute back. Agent autoPilot must decide how to respond on the basis of whatever information it may have about ground_control. In particular,

1. autoPilot does not know whether ground_control can derive autoPilot's current position P—which may be a secret—from a 30 minute old position;
2. autoPilot does not know whether ground_control already knows P.

In the worst possible case (according to autoPilot's incomplete knowledge), ground_control does not know P, but it knows how to derive P from a 30 minutes old position. In this scenario, if autoPilot returned its old position to ground_control, then ground_control would be able to derive P, thereby violating a new secret. Therefore, in order to be sure that data security is not violated, autoPilot should not return its old position to ground_control.

Two more scenarios are compatible with autoPilot's incomplete knowledge about ground_control:

1. It may be the case that ground_control cannot derive P from a 30 minute old position. In this case, it would be safe to tell ground_control the old location. Agent autoPilot doesn't do so, however, because it has *overestimated* what ground_control is capable of deriving, so as to correctly handle with the worst-case scenario.

2. It may be the case that ground_control already knows P. Then it would be safe to tell ground_control the old location, because this would not increase ground_control's knowledge. However, autoPilot doesn't do so because it has *underestimated* what can be derived by ground_control *before* the answer, in order to deal correctly with the worst case. Of course, no (additional) harm is done in this case by autoPilot.

This overestimation/underestimation mechanism works well for secrets that really depend on the answer, but it should *not* be applied to other secrets. This is illustrated by the following example.

Example 10.3.2 (Approximate Security Check, continued) Suppose autoPilot protects another secret, namely, its passenger list L. Agent autoPilot is asked for its current position P by ground_control. P is totally unrelated to L, therefore ground_control's knowledge about L cannot be changed by whatever answer autoPilot gives concerning P. Thus there are two possible scenarios: (i) ground_control doesn't know L, either before or after the answer; (ii) ground_control knows L both before and after the answer. Now, if we applied the overestimation-after-answer plus underestimation-before-answer mechanism to L, we would improperly detect a security violation. Indeed, according to the two possible scenarios, it is unknown whether ground_control knows L, both before and after autoPilot's answer. Then the overestimation/underestimation mechanism would say that L might be unknown before the answer and known after it. In other words, it would seem that ground_control has magically obtained the name list using autoPilot's answer about its current position.

This explains why the overestimation/underestimation mechanism should be applied only to the secrets that may be influenced by the current answer.

Summarizing, suppose a wishes to protect its data from b. Then, in order to perform approximate security checks, a needs the following items:

- an estimate of b's possible states;
- an upper bound on the set of secrets that can be derived by b *using* a*'s answer*;
- a lower bound on the set of secrets that can be derived by b (from the old state).

In turn, to approximate b's states, a needs some approximation of b's fact language (i.e., of its data structures) and of its history (which influences the actual contents of b's state). All of these approximate notions are formalized in the following sections.

10.3.2 Approximating Possible Histories

DEFINITION 10.3.1 (POSSIBLE HISTORIES APPROXIMATION) The *approximation of the possible histories for* b *used by* a is a set of histories $\text{pos}\mathcal{H}_b^a$.

In this definition, $\text{pos}\mathcal{H}_b^a$ is deliberately not restricted to histories for b, because a may have only a vague idea of b's behavior. For example, some $h \in \text{pos}\mathcal{H}_b^a$ may contain an action α that cannot be executed by b (therefore h is not an history for b), because a (mistakenly) believes that b can execute α.

Furthermore, a will typically be unable to see the messages exchanged between b and other agents. Thus, a will be forced to use incomplete descriptions of b's histories.

Example 10.3.3 Agent a may use its own history h_a as a partial description of b's history h_b. In fact, the messages between a and b should be the same in h_a and h_b. Therefore, if

$$h_a = \langle \langle b, a, \rho_1 \rangle, \langle c, a, \rho_2 \rangle, \langle a, b, Ans_1 \rangle \rangle, \tag{10.2}$$

then h_b can be any possible history of the form

$$h_1 \cdot \langle b, a, \rho_1 \rangle \cdot h_2 \cdot \langle a, b, Ans_1 \rangle \cdot h_3, \tag{10.3}$$

where h_1, h_2 and h_3 contain no message from/to a—that is, h_b can be *any possible history which is* ab-*compatible with* h_a (see Definition 10.2.5).

Example 10.3.4 In some applications, agent a may be unable to store h_a entirely because of space limitations. In this case, a may decide to keep only the last n events of the history. Consider again the previous example; if $n = 3$ and the truncated history is (10.2), then the corresponding history h_b can be any possible history of the form (10.3) where only h_2 and h_3 are required to contain no messages from/to a (i.e., only a final segment of h_b is required to be compatible with h_a). Compatibility is not required for h_1 because some old message m between a and b may have been deleted from a's truncated history (but m is still part of the global history of b).

The above example shows that the correspondence between approximate and actual histories is application-dependent and, in general, non-trivial. This correspondence is formalized as follows.

DEFINITION 10.3.2 (HISTORY CORRESPONDENCE RELATION $\stackrel{ab}{\rightsquigarrow}_h$) For all agents a and b there is an associated *correspondence relation* $\stackrel{ab}{\rightsquigarrow}_h \subseteq \text{pos}\mathcal{H}_b^a \times \text{pos}\mathcal{H}_b$.

The subscript h will often be omitted to improve readability. Intuitively, if some history $h_b \in \text{pos}\mathcal{H}_b$ matches an approximate description $h \in \text{pos}\mathcal{H}_b^a$, then we write $h \stackrel{ab}{\rightsquigarrow} h_b$. In Example 10.3.3, $\text{pos}\mathcal{H}_b^a$ coincides with $\text{pos}\mathcal{H}_a$ (the set of all possible histories for a), and $\stackrel{ab}{\rightsquigarrow}$ coincides with the compatibility relation $\stackrel{ab}{\longleftrightarrow}$. Moreover, agent a maintains an approximation of b's current history. This notion is formalized below.

DEFINITION 10.3.3 (APPROXIMATE CURRENT HISTORY H_b^a, CORRECTNESS) Let $h \in \text{pos}\mathcal{H}_a$ be the current history of a. The approximation of b's current history at h, is an approximate history $H_b^a(h) \in \text{pos}\mathcal{H}_b^a$.

We say that H_b^a is *correct* if for all $h \in \text{pos}\mathcal{H}_a$, and for all $h_b \in \text{pos}\mathcal{H}_b$ such that $h \stackrel{ab}{\longleftrightarrow} h_b$ it is the case that $H_b^a(h) \stackrel{ab}{\rightsquigarrow} h_b$.

Intuitively, the approximate current history is correct if it matches (at least) all possible histories for b compatible with a's history. In Example 10.3.3, H_b^a is the identity function, as a uses its own history as an approximation of b's current history. Clearly, in that example H_b^a is correct, as the matching relation $\stackrel{ab}{\rightsquigarrow}$ coincides with the compatibility relation $\stackrel{ab}{\longleftrightarrow}$.

10.3.3 Approximating Facts and Conditions

The first difficulty in approximating b's state is that a may have imprecise knowledge of b's fact language (i.e., of the nature of b's data structures).

Example 10.3.5 (CFIT) Agent a may have only a vague idea of how b represents locations. For example, b's representation may be the C structure illustrated in Example 10.1.1, namely:

```
struct 3DPoint {
    float latitude;
    float longitude;
    float altitude; }
```

while a may think that b uses a code call **in**(X, $autoPilot:location$()). where X has three double precision fields called lat, lon and alt.

The above example covers *syntactic variants* in the two languages (such as field names), as well as *granularity differences* (due to the different precision of the numbers involved).

Furthermore, in general, a will only have incomplete knowledge of the *contents* of b's data structures. The language adopted by a for describing approximate states should be flexible enough to model a's partial view of b's knowledge.

Example 10.3.6 Suppose agent a estimates that b's state contains at least one of the following code call conditions:

in((10, 10, 20), autoPilot : *location*())

in((10, 20, 30), autoPilot : *location*()).

In this case, a might approximate b's state using—say—a logical language with disjunction ($\vee$). Then the approximation of b's state would contain the formula

in((10, 10, 20), autoPilot : *location*()) $\vee$ **in**((10, 20, 30), autoPilot : *location*()).

Example 10.3.7 If a estimates that b's state can be any state which contains **in**(o, p : f(a)) but does not contain **in**(o, p : g(b)), then b's state could be approximated by the set of literals

{**in**(o, p : f(a)), ¬**in**(o, p : g(b))}.

No commitment to any specific language is made here. We simply assume that the abstract approximate language introduced below takes care of aspects such as those occurring in the above examples.

DEFINITION 10.3.4 (APPROXIMATE FACT LANGUAGE $\mathcal{L}_b^a$) The approximate fact language of b used by a is a denumerable set $\mathcal{L}_b^a$.

In the preceding two examples, $\mathcal{L}_b^a$ might be a standard first-order language (based on atomic code call conditions), or a propositional language (based on ground atomic code call conditions), or something even simpler, such as a set of clauses or literals (based on the same kind of atoms).

The intended meaning of the approximate language $\mathcal{L}_b^a$ is formalized by a *fact correspondence relation* that relates approximate facts to the actual data structures of b that match the approximate description.

DEFINITION 10.3.5 (FACT CORRESPONDENCE RELATION $\stackrel{ab}{\leadsto}_f$) For all agents a and b there is an associated *correspondence relation* $\stackrel{ab}{\leadsto}_f \subseteq \mathcal{L}_b^a \times \mathcal{L}_b$.

When the context allows us to distinguish $\stackrel{ab}{\leadsto}_h$ from $\stackrel{ab}{\leadsto}_f$ we will omit the subscript f so as to improve readability.

Intuitively, we write $f \stackrel{ab}{\leadsto} f_b$ if f_b is one of the possible instantiated data structures for b that match the approximate description f used by a. In Example 10.3.5, f stands for the code call atom **in**(X, autoPilot : *location*()), while f_b may stand for a C variable of type 3DPoint, whose three fields are obtained by rounding off the corresponding fields of X.

Some approximate facts f may have no counterpart in $\mathcal{L}_b$ (e.g., a may think that b can use a code call p : $g()$ when in fact this is not the case). In such cases, we write:

$f \stackrel{ab}{\not\leadsto}$ if, by definition, $\nexists f'. f \stackrel{ab}{\leadsto} f'$.

Analogously, some facts of $\mathcal{L}_b$ may have no approximate counterpart (e.g., when a does not know that b may use some code call p : $h()$). In this case we write:

$f \stackrel{ab}{\not\leadsto}$ if, by definition, $\nexists f'. f' \stackrel{ab}{\leadsto} f$.

Ground conditions (which are conjunctions of ground facts) are approximated by sets of approximate facts. Approximate conditions are matched against sets of facts from $\mathcal{L}_b$ by means of a correspondence relation derived from the correspondence relation for individual facts, $\stackrel{ab}{\leadsto}_f$.

DEFINITION 10.3.6 (APPROXIMATE CONDITIONS)   An approximate condition is a set $C \subseteq \mathcal{L}_b^a$.

DEFINITION 10.3.7 (CONDITION CORRESPONDENCE RELATION)   We say that an approximate condition $C \subseteq \mathcal{L}_b^a$ corresponds to a set of facts $C_b \subseteq \mathcal{L}_b$, denoted $C \stackrel{ab}{\leadsto}_c C_b$, if both the following conditions hold:

1. if $f \in C$ then either $f \stackrel{ab}{\not\leadsto}$ or $\exists f_b \in C_b. f \stackrel{ab}{\leadsto} f_b$.
2. if $f_b \in C_b$ then either $\stackrel{ab}{\not\leadsto} f_b$ or $\exists f \in C. f \stackrel{ab}{\leadsto} f_b$.

The first requirement above says that all elements, f, of the approximate condition must correspond to some fact f_b in the actual state unless f has no counterpart in the language $\mathcal{L}_b$ (in which case, f is ignored). Similarly, the second requirement says that each member of C_b must have a counterpart in C, with the exception of those facts f_b that are not expressible in the approximate language $\mathcal{L}_b^a$.

10.3.4 Approximating States

The approximation of a state $\mathcal{O}_b$ should tell us the following things:

- which facts are *surely true* in $\mathcal{O}_b$; this is needed to underestimate the inferences of b (inferences can be part of a correct underestimation only if they follow from conditions that are guaranteed to be true in $\mathcal{O}_b$);

- which facts *may possibly be true* in $\mathcal{O}_b$; this is needed to overestimate the inferences of b (inferences that depend on facts that *might* be in $\mathcal{O}_b$ should be considered by the overestimation);

- which facts are *new*; this is needed to identify the inferences that really depend on the last answer (see the problem discussed in Example 10.3.2); intuitively, a new secret is violated only when it is derived from some new fact.

Accordingly, approximate states are described using three sets of approximate conditions.

DEFINITION 10.3.8 (APPROXIMATE STATES $\widehat{\mathcal{O}} = \langle Nec, Poss, New \rangle$) An approximate state of b used by a is a triple $\widehat{\mathcal{O}} = \langle Nec, Poss, New \rangle$, whose elements are sets of approximate conditions (i.e., $\widehat{\mathcal{O}} \in \wp(\mathcal{L}_b^a) \times \wp(\mathcal{L}_b^a) \times \wp(\mathcal{L}_b^a)$). The three elements of an approximate state $\widehat{\mathcal{O}}$ will be denoted by $\widehat{\mathcal{O}}.Nec$, $\widehat{\mathcal{O}}.Poss$, and $\widehat{\mathcal{O}}.New$, respectively. $\widehat{\mathcal{O}}$ is required to satisfy the following inclusions:

1. $\widehat{\mathcal{O}}.Nec \subseteq \widehat{\mathcal{O}}.Poss$;
2. $\widehat{\mathcal{O}}.New \subseteq \widehat{\mathcal{O}}.Poss$.

The first inclusion says that a condition C cannot be necessarily true if it is not possibly true. The second inclusion says that all new facts must be possible.

Agent a maintains an approximation of b's current state. This is formalized in the definition below.

DEFINITION 10.3.9 (APPROXIMATE STATE FUNCTION $\mathcal{O}_b^a$, CORRECTNESS) The approximate state function $\mathcal{O}_b^a$ is a mapping which maps approximate histories from $\text{pos}\mathcal{H}_b^a$ onto approximate states of b used by a. We say that $\mathcal{O}_b^a$ is *correct* if for all approximate histories $h \in \text{pos}\mathcal{H}_b^a$, the following conditions hold:

1. if $C \in \mathcal{O}_b^a(h).Nec$, then for all h_b such that $h \overset{ab}{\leadsto} h_b$ there exists $C_b \subseteq \mathcal{O}_b(h_b)$ such that $C \overset{ab}{\leadsto} C_b$;

2. for all $C_b \subseteq \mathcal{O}_b(h_b)$ such that $h \overset{ab}{\leadsto} h_b$, if $C \overset{ab}{\leadsto} C_b$ then $C \in \mathcal{O}_b^a(h).Poss$;

3. for all possible non-empty histories $h_b \cdot e \in \text{pos}\mathcal{H}_b$ such that $h \overset{ab}{\leadsto} h_b \cdot e$, and for all $C_b \subseteq \mathcal{O}_b(h_b \cdot e)$ such that $C_b \not\subseteq \mathcal{O}_b(h_b)$, if $C \overset{ab}{\leadsto} C_b$ then $C \in \mathcal{O}_b^a(h).New$.

Intuitively, the above conditions say that an approximate state function is correct if: (i) each condition C in *Nec* corresponds to some condition C_b which is actually true in the current state of b, *whatever it may be* (note the universal quantification over h_b); thus, in case of doubt, in order to achieve correctness it is better to underestimate *Nec*; (ii) the approximations C of each set of facts C_b that might be part of b's current state should be included in *Poss* (in case of doubt, it is better to overestimate *Poss* to achieve correctness);

Section 10.3 Safely Approximate Data Security

(iii) if a set of facts is new in b's current state (because $C_b \subseteq \mathcal{O}_b(h_b \cdot e)$ and $C_b \not\subseteq \mathcal{O}_b(h_b)$), then its counterparts C should be included in *New* (that should be overestimated in case of doubt).

Example 10.3.8 Consider the scenario depicted in examples 10.3.1 and 10.3.2. Suppose the approximate language $\mathcal{L}_{\text{ground\_control}}^{\text{autoPilot}}$ contains only the facts **in**(P, autoPilot : *location*()) (where P is autoPilot's current position) or **in**(L, autoPilot : *passengers*()) (where L is autoPilot's passenger list). Recall that autoPilot doesn't know whether ground_control knows anything about P and L. Therefore, if h is autoPilot's current history, one should set:

$\mathcal{O}_{\text{ground\_control}}^{\text{autoPilot}}(h).Nec = \emptyset$,

$\mathcal{O}_{\text{ground\_control}}^{\text{autoPilot}}(h).Poss = \{\{\textbf{in}(\text{P}, \text{autoPilot} : location())\},$

$\{\textbf{in}(\text{L}, \text{autoPilot} : passengers())\},$

$\{\textbf{in}(\text{P}, \text{autoPilot} : location()),$

$\textbf{in}(\text{L}, \text{autoPilot} : passengers())\}\}$.

In other words, nothing is necessary, everything is possible. If autoPilot sent ground_control an answer message $e = \langle autoPilot, ground\_control, \{\textbf{in}(\text{P}, \text{autoPilot} : location())\}\rangle$ with its current position, then one might set:

$\mathcal{O}_{\text{ground\_control}}^{\text{autoPilot}}(h \cdot e).Nec = \{\{\textbf{in}(\text{P}, \text{autoPilot} : location())\}\}$,

$\mathcal{O}_{\text{ground\_control}}^{\text{autoPilot}}(h \cdot e).Poss = \{\{\textbf{in}(\text{P}, \text{autoPilot} : location())\},$

$\{\textbf{in}(\text{L}, \text{autoPilot} : passengers())\},$

$\{\textbf{in}(\text{P}, \text{autoPilot} : location()),$

$\textbf{in}(\text{L}, \text{autoPilot} : passengers())\}\}$,

$\mathcal{O}_{\text{ground\_control}}^{\text{autoPilot}}(h \cdot e).New = \{\{\textbf{in}(\text{P}, \text{autoPilot} : location())\},$

$\{\textbf{in}(\text{P}, \text{autoPilot} : location()),$

$\textbf{in}(\text{L}, \text{autoPilot} : passengers())\}\}$.

Note that in this example **in**(P, autoPilot : *location*()) becomes necessarily true (in some other cases, ground_control might disbelieve autoPilot, and $\mathcal{O}_{\text{ground\_control}}^{\text{autoPilot}}(h \cdot e).Nec$ would remain empty). The set of possible new conditions that become true owing to e is set to all the sets of facts that contain the answer **in**(P, autoPilot : *location*()).

Remark 7 It is important to note that an implementation does not explicitly need to store all the members of $\widehat{\mathcal{O}}.Nec$, $\widehat{\mathcal{O}}.Poss$ and $\widehat{\mathcal{O}}.New$. This would be infeasible in practice. Techniques to efficiently implement approximate states are described in Section 10.5.

10.3.5 Approximate Secrets

When agent a describes the set of secrets $Sec_a(b)$ it wishes to prevent b from inferring, the members of $Sec_a(b)$ are drawn from $\mathcal{L}_b$—as this language itself may only be partially known to agent a, a must use some approximation of its secrets function.

DEFINITION 10.3.10 (APPROXIMATE SECRETS $AppSec_a(b)$) The set of *approximate secrets* of agent a w.r.t. agent b, denoted by $AppSec_a(b)$, is some subset of $\mathcal{L}_b^a$.

Clearly, the fact correspondence relation $\overset{ab}{\leadsto}_f$ applies to approximate secrets. If $f \in AppSec_a(b)$ approximates $f' \in Sec_a(b)$, then we write $f \overset{ab}{\leadsto} f'$.

Approximate secrets should adequately represent all real secrets, as specified by the following definition.

DEFINITION 10.3.11 (APPROXIMATE SECRETS, CORRECTNESS) The set $AppSec_a(b)$ is correct w.r.t. $Sec_a(b)$ if it satisfies the following conditions:

1. for all $f_b \in Sec_a(b)$ there exists $f \in AppSec_a(b)$ such that $f \overset{ab}{\leadsto} f_b$;
2. if $f \overset{ab}{\leadsto} f_b$ and $f_b \in Sec_a(b)$, then $f \in AppSec_a(b)$.

Condition 1 says that each secret should be expressible in the approximate language $\mathcal{L}_b^a$ (otherwise, some violation might go unnoticed). Condition (2) above states the conservative principle that if a fact f may correspond to a secret, then it should be treated like a secret.

10.3.6 Approximate Consequences

Recall that b's consequence relation Cn_b is a mapping over sets of facts. Its approximate counterpart is a mapping of the same kind, based on the approximate language $\mathcal{L}_b^a$.

DEFINITION 10.3.12 (APPROXIMATE CONSEQUENCE RELATION) An approximate consequence relation of b used by a is a mapping $Cn_b^a : \wp(\mathcal{L}_b^a) \to \wp(\mathcal{L}_b^a)$.

Recall that a should maintain both an overestimate and an underestimate of b's consequence relation Cn_b. These will be denoted by OCN_b^a and UCN_b^a, respectively.

Example 10.3.9 Suppose ground_control can derive autoPilot's current position P from some previous position and velocity, P_t and V_t, provided that they are no more than 10 minutes old. Let $C_t = \{\mathbf{in}(P_t, \text{autoPilot}: location\_at(t)), \mathbf{in}(V_t, \text{autoPilot}: velocity\_at(t))\}$. Then, for all $t \geq \text{now} - 10$, a correct overestimate OCN_b^a should be such that $\mathbf{in}(P_t, \text{autoPilot}: location\_at(t)) \in OCN_b^a(C_t)$. Actually, the overestimate would still be correct if the above inclusion held for some $t < \text{now} - 10$—the important thing is that *at least* all the inferences of ground_control should be captured. However, this requirement would be too strong: we are not interested in inferences whose conclusions are neither secrets, nor can be used to derive a secret.

Symmetrically, **in**(P_t, autoPilot : *location_at(t)*) $\in UCN_b^a(C_t)$ should hold only if $t \geq$ now $- 10$. It may hold only for *some* of such t (in a limit case, $UCN_b^a(C_t)$ may be empty), but it should not hold for any $t <$ now $- 10$.

The above intuitions are formalized by the following definitions. Recall that each consequence relation Cn_b corresponds to a provability relation $\vdash_b$ over partial state descriptions and facts.

DEFINITION 10.3.13 (CORRECT UNDERESTIMATION (SOUNDNESS)) An approximate consequence relation UCN_b^a is a correct underestimation of Cn_b if whenever $C \overset{ab}{\leadsto} C_b$ and $f \overset{ab}{\leadsto} f_b$, $f \in UCN_b^a(C)$ implies $C_b \vdash_b f_b$.

In other words, UCN_b^a is a correct underestimation of Cn_b if what can be inferred using UCN_b^a is also derivable—*mutatis mutandis*—using $\vdash_b$ (and hence Cn_b).

Before proceeding to the definition of correct overestimates, we need a definition that intuitively captures the *causal dependencies* between a set C_b of facts and the facts f_b that can be derived from C_b. This is needed to focus on the secrets that are violated *because* of a's answer (see Example 10.3.2). The mapping Cn_b is not completely adequate for this purpose, because in general, when $f_b \in \text{Cn}_b(C_b)$, C_b may contain facts that are not relevant to the proof of f_b. Rather, we should say that f_b is caused by the presence of C_b when $f_b \in \text{Cn}_b(C_b)$ *and* C_b is *minimal*, i.e., if we dropped even one fact from C_b, then f_b would not be derivable anymore.

DEFINITION 10.3.14 (CAUSAL DEPENDENCIES) We say that C_b causes f_b, denoted **Causes**(C_b, f_b), if $C_b \vdash_b f_b$ and for all $C \subset C_b$, $C \nvdash_b f_b$.

We are now ready to give a formal definition of correct overestimations. Intuitively, the definition below says that $OCN_b^a(C)$ should contain all the secrets that can be derived because of C.

DEFINITION 10.3.15 (CORRECT OVERESTIMATIONS) An approximate consequence relation OCN_b^a is a correct overestimation of Cn_b if for all C_b and f_b such that C_b causes f_b and $f_b \in Sec_a(b)$, there exist C, f such that $C \overset{ab}{\leadsto} C_b$ and $f \overset{ab}{\leadsto} f_b$ such that $f \in OCN_b^a(C)$.

Remark 8 The overestimation OCN_b^a is only required to capture the *secrets* f_b that can be derived because of C_b. In other words, agent a need not model all the knowledge and inferences of b, but only those that are related to possible security violations. This feature holds promise that we will be able to design efficient security verification procedures.

10.3.7 Approximate Data Security Check

Summarizing, agent $\mathfrak{a}$ approximates $\mathfrak{b}$'s behavior by means of the functions $H_\mathfrak{b}^\mathfrak{a}$, $\mathcal{O}_\mathfrak{b}^\mathfrak{a}$, $OCN_\mathfrak{b}^\mathfrak{a}$ and $UCN_\mathfrak{b}^\mathfrak{a}$. The secrets in $Sec_\mathfrak{a}(\mathfrak{b})$ are approximated by $AppSec_\mathfrak{a}(\mathfrak{b})$. Together, these functions constitute $\mathfrak{a}$'s approximate view of $\mathfrak{b}$.

DEFINITION 10.3.16 (AGENT APPROXIMATION, CORRECTNESS) The approximation of $\mathfrak{b}$ used by $\mathfrak{a}$ (based on the approximate languages $\text{pos}\mathcal{H}_\mathfrak{b}^\mathfrak{a}$ and $\mathcal{L}_\mathfrak{b}^\mathfrak{a}$, and on the correspondence functions $\stackrel{\mathfrak{ab}}{\leadsto}_h$ and $\stackrel{\mathfrak{ab}}{\leadsto}_f$) is a quintuple

$$\mathbf{App}_\mathfrak{a}(\mathfrak{b}) = \langle H_\mathfrak{b}^\mathfrak{a}, \mathcal{O}_\mathfrak{b}^\mathfrak{a}, AppSec_\mathfrak{a}(\mathfrak{b}), OCN_\mathfrak{b}^\mathfrak{a}, UCN_\mathfrak{b}^\mathfrak{a} \rangle,$$

whose members are, respectively, a current history approximation, a current state approximation, a set of approximate secrets and two approximate consequence relations.

We say that $\mathbf{App}_\mathfrak{a}(\mathfrak{b})$ is *correct* if $H_\mathfrak{b}^\mathfrak{a}$, $\mathcal{O}_\mathfrak{b}^\mathfrak{a}$ and $AppSec_\mathfrak{a}(\mathfrak{b})$ are correct, $OCN_\mathfrak{b}^\mathfrak{a}$ is a correct overestimation of $\text{Cn}_\mathfrak{b}$, and $UCN_\mathfrak{b}^\mathfrak{a}$ is a correct underestimation of $\text{Cn}_\mathfrak{b}$.

This definition builds upon definitions of what it means for the individual components of $\mathbf{App}_\mathfrak{a}(\mathfrak{b})$ to be correct—something we have defined in preceding sections of this chapter.

Using these concepts, we wish to specify what it means for a distortion function to be approximately data secure. If we can compute an overestimate of the set of secrets violated by agent $\mathfrak{b}$ *after* agent $\mathfrak{a}$ provides an answer to its request, and we compute an underestimate of the set of secrets violated by agent $\mathfrak{b}$ *before* agent $\mathfrak{a}$ provides an answer, and if we can show that the latter is a superset of the former, then we would be able to safely guarantee data security. We first define these over/under estimates below, and then use those definitions to define what it means for a distortion function to be approximately data secure.

DEFINITION 10.3.17 (OVERESTIMATION OF VIOLATED SECRETS) For all approximate histories $h \in \text{pos}\mathcal{H}_\mathfrak{b}^\mathfrak{a}$ let

$$\mathsf{OViol}_\mathfrak{b}^\mathfrak{a}(h) =_{def} \bigcup \{OCN_\mathfrak{b}^\mathfrak{a}(C) \mid C \in \mathcal{O}_\mathfrak{b}^\mathfrak{a}(h).\text{New}\} \cap AppSec_\mathfrak{a}(\mathfrak{b}).$$

Informally, $\mathsf{OViol}_\mathfrak{b}^\mathfrak{a}(h)$ is the overestimated set of secrets that can be derived because of some new facts (the reason why only the consequences of new facts are considered is illustrated earlier via Example 10.3.2).

DEFINITION 10.3.18 (UNDERESTIMATION OF VIOLATED SECRETS) For all approximate histories $h \in \text{pos}\mathcal{H}_\mathfrak{b}^\mathfrak{a}$, let

$$\mathsf{UViol}_\mathfrak{b}^\mathfrak{a}(h) =_{def} \bigcup \{UCN_\mathfrak{b}^\mathfrak{a}(C) \mid C \in \mathcal{O}_\mathfrak{b}^\mathfrak{a}(h).\text{Nec}\} \cap AppSec_\mathfrak{a}(\mathfrak{b}).$$

In other words, $\mathsf{UViol}_\mathfrak{b}^\mathfrak{a}(h)$ is the underestimated set of secrets that can be derived from facts which are estimated to be necessarily true. The approximate counterpart of data security can now be defined.

Section 10.3   Safely Approximate Data Security   359

DEFINITION 10.3.19 (APPROXIMATE DATA SECURITY)   Let $h \in \text{pos}\mathcal{H}_a$ be a possible history for a whose last event is a request message from b, and suppose that a's response $\tilde{\zeta}_a(h)$ to this request (where $\tilde{\zeta}_a$ is a's distortion function) has the form $h' \cdot e$. We say that $\tilde{\zeta}_a$ is *approximately data secure at h* (w.r.t. $\textbf{App}_a(b)$) if

$$\text{UViol}_b^a(H_b^a(h')) \supseteq \text{OViol}_b^a(H_b^a(h' \cdot e)).$$

We reiterate that we are comparing an overestimation of the secrets violated by b because of a's answer e (right-hand side of the above inclusion), with an underestimation of the secrets violated by b before the answer (left-hand side of the inclusion). The following example illustrates this definition.

Example 10.3.10   Consider again the scenario of Example 10.3.1. Nothing is known about the ground_control agent before autoPilot's answer, so, in symbols,

$$\mathcal{O}_{\text{ground\_control}}^{\text{autoPilot}}(H_b^a(h')).Nec = \emptyset, \quad \text{and hence}$$

$$\text{UViol}_{\text{ground\_control}}^{\text{autoPilot}}(h') = \emptyset.$$

If autoPilot's answer in message e is empty, then we may assume that

$$\mathcal{O}_{\text{ground\_control}}^{\text{autoPilot}}(H_b^a(h' \cdot e)).New = \emptyset, \quad \text{and hence}$$

$$\text{UViol}_{\text{ground\_control}}^{\text{autoPilot}}(h' \cdot e) = \emptyset.$$

In this case, $\text{UViol}_b^a(H_b^a(h')) = \text{OViol}_b^a(H_b^a(h' \cdot e))$ and hence this distortion is approximately data secure at h. Alternatively, assume that the answer in e contains the secret $s = \textbf{in}(\text{P}, \text{autoPilot} : location())$. Suppose also that ground_control believes this answer, which is included in ground_control's new state. We don't know whether s was in the previous state, so s *might* be a new fact. Then,

$$\{s\} \in \mathcal{O}_{\text{ground\_control}}^{\text{autoPilot}}(H_b^a(h' \cdot e)).New, \quad \text{and hence}$$

$$s \in \text{UViol}_{\text{ground\_control}}^{\text{autoPilot}}(h' \cdot e).$$

Here $\text{UViol}_b^a(H_b^a(h')) \subset \text{OViol}_b^a(H_b^a(h' \cdot e))$. This distortion is not approximately data secure at h.

The approximate data security check works well if the approximation $\textbf{App}_a(b)$ is *correct*. The theorem below shows that, under this assumption, the approximate security check suffices to enforce the exact notion of security.

THEOREM 10.3.1 (CORRECT APPROXIMATE DATA SECURITY IMPLIES DATA SECURITY) If $\tilde{\zeta}_a$ is approximately data secure at h w.r.t $\mathbf{App}_a(b)$ and $\mathbf{App}_a(b)$ is correct, then $\tilde{\zeta}_a$ is data secure at h.

Proof We prove the contrapositive, which is equivalent. Suppose $\tilde{\zeta}_a$ is *not* data secure. Then, for some histories $h_a \in \text{pos}\mathcal{H}_a$ and $h_b \cdot e \in \text{pos}\mathcal{H}_b$, it holds that $h_b \cdot e \overset{ab}{\Longleftrightarrow} \tilde{\zeta}_a(h_a)$ and

$\text{Violated}_b^a(h_b) \not\supseteq \text{Violated}_b^a(h_b \cdot e)$.

Consequently, there exists $f_0 \in Sec_a(b)$ such that

(a) $f_0 \in \text{Violated}_b^a(h_b \cdot e)$ and
(b) $f_0 \notin \text{Violated}_b^a(h_b)$.

Now suppose $\tilde{\zeta}_a(h_a)$ has the form $h' \cdot e$ (so $h_b \overset{ab}{\leadsto} h'$).

Claim1: there exists f_1 such that $f_1 \overset{ab}{\leadsto} f_0$ and $f_1 \in \text{OViol}_b^a(H_b^a(h' \cdot e))$.

This claim can be proved with the following steps:

(c) $f_0 \in Cn_b(\mathcal{O}_b(h_b \cdot e))$ (by (a) and the def. of OViol_b^a);
(d) $\exists C_0$ such that $C_0 \subseteq \mathcal{O}_b(h_b \cdot e)$ and $\text{Causes}(C_0, f_0)$;
(e) $\exists f_1, C_1$ such that $f_1 \overset{ab}{\leadsto} f_0$, $C_1 \overset{ab}{\leadsto} C_0$ and $f_1 \in OCN_b^a(C_1)$ (by (d) and correctness of OCN_b^a);
(f) $C_0 \not\subseteq \mathcal{O}_b(h_b)$ (otherwise $f_0 \in \text{Violated}_b^a(h_b)$, contradicting (b));
(g) $C_1 \in \mathcal{O}_b^a(H_b^a(h' \cdot e)).New$ (by (d), (e), (f) and the correctness of $\mathcal{O}_b^a$ and H_b^a);
(h) $f_1 \in AppSec_a(b)$ ($f_1 \overset{ab}{\leadsto} f_0$+ correctness of $AppSec_a(b)$);
(i) $f_1 \in \text{OViol}_b^a(H_b^a(h' \cdot e))$.

Claim 1 immediately follows.

Claim2: $f_1 \notin \text{UViol}_b^a(H_b^a(h'))$.

Suppose $f_1 \in \text{UViol}_b^a(H_b^a(h'))$. We derive the following steps:

(j) $\exists C_2 \in \mathcal{O}_b^a(H_b^a(h')).Nec$ such that $f_1 \in UCN_b^a(C_2)$ (by def. of UViol_b^a);
(k) $\forall f_b$ such that $f_1 \overset{ab}{\leadsto} f_b$, $f_b \in Cn_b(\mathcal{O}_b(h_b))$ (by (j) and correctness of UCN_b^a and $\mathcal{O}_b^a$);
(l) $f_0 \in Cn_b(\mathcal{O}_b(h_b))$ (from (k), since $f_1 \overset{ab}{\leadsto} f_0$);
(m) $f_0 \in \text{Violated}_b^a(h_b)$ (from (l), since f_0 is a secret).

Section 10.3   Safely Approximate Data Security   361

But (m) contradicts (b), so Claim 2 holds. From the above claims it follows immediately that $\tilde{\zeta}_a$ is not approximately data secure. This completes the proof.   ∎

10.3.8 Compact Approximations

In many applications (especially those where security checks are performed at runtime), the overhead caused by maintaining two approximate states for each client agent and computing two approximations of its consequence relation would be unacceptable. For this reason, we introduce a *compact* version of the approximate security check, where only the state after the answer and the overestimation of b's consequences need to be computed.

DEFINITION 10.3.20 (COMPACT APPROXIMATION)   An approximation $\mathbf{App}_a(b) = \langle H_b^a, \mathcal{O}_b^a, AppSec_a(b), OCN_b^a, UCN_b^a \rangle$ based on the languages $\mathrm{pos}\mathcal{H}_b^a$ and $\mathcal{L}_b^a$ is *compact* if the following two conditions hold:

1. for all approximate histories $h \in \mathrm{pos}\mathcal{H}_b^a$, $\mathcal{O}_b^a(h).Nec = \emptyset$;
2. for all $C \subseteq \mathcal{L}_b^a$, $UCN_b^a(C) = \emptyset$.

Note that in compact approximations, the part related to the estimation of violated secrets before a's answer is in fact missing (empty). The inclusion of Definition 10.3.19 then becomes equivalent to:

$$\mathsf{OViol}_b^a\big(H_b^a(h' \cdot e)\big) = \emptyset,$$

where $h' \cdot e = \tilde{\zeta}_a(h)$. As expected, the above security condition depends only on one approximation of b's inferences, and only on the approximation of b's state *after* a's answer e.

The above equation immediately allows us to infer that the use of compact representations strengthens the notion of data security by requiring that no secret be derivable using a's answer. At first glance, this approach may appear similar to the naive security definition that requires b to derive no secret, no matter where it comes from (see Section 10.2.3). However, the paradoxical situation in which a's distortion is labeled non-secure because some other agent c has distributed a secret is avoided by compact approximations. In fact, since OViol_b^a approximates only the inferences that are *caused* by a's answer, the secrets revealed by another agent, e.g., c, would not be included in OViol_b^a. The definition of correct overestimation (based on **Causes**) and the use of the field *New* in the definition of OViol_b^a play a fundamental role in preserving this important property.

Example 10.3.11 Suppose $\widetilde{ans}_a$ returns always the empty set. Then b cannot obtain any information from a's answers, and hence its states can be correctly modeled by an approximate state function such that $\mathcal{O}_b^a(h).New$ is always empty. It follows that $\mathsf{OViol}_b^a(H_b^a(h))$ is always empty, and hence a's distortion is approximately data secure.

A nice property of compact approximations is that *every* correct approximation can be turned into a compact approximation which is correct! This is done via the following conversion operation.

DEFINITION 10.3.21 (COMPACT VERSION) The compact version of $\mathbf{App}_a(b) = \langle H_b^a, \mathcal{O}_b^a, AppSec_a(b), OCN_b^a, UCN_b^a \rangle$ is a compact approximation

$$\mathbf{Compact}(\mathbf{App}_a(b)) = \langle \mathbf{H}_b^a, \widehat{\mathcal{O}_b^a}, AppSec_a(b), OCN_b^a, (\lambda X.\emptyset) \rangle$$

where $\lambda X.\emptyset$ is the constant function that always returns $\emptyset$, and for all $h \in \text{pos}\mathcal{H}_b^a$,

$$\widehat{\mathcal{O}_b^a}(h) =_{def} \langle \emptyset, \mathcal{O}_b^a(h).Poss, \mathcal{O}_b^a(h).New \rangle.$$

The following result verifies that the compaction operator **Compact** preserves correctness.

THEOREM 10.3.2 (CORRECTNESS PRESERVATION) If $\mathbf{App}_a(b)$ is correct, then **Compact** $(\mathbf{App}_a(b))$ is correct.

Proof By definition, $\mathbf{Compact}(\mathbf{App}_a(b))$ is correct if each of its components are correct. The correctness of $H_b^a, AppSec_a(b)$ and OCN_b^a follows from the assumption that $\mathbf{App}_a(b)$ is correct. The function $\lambda X.\emptyset$ satisfies trivially the correctness condition for underestimated consequence relations. Finally, the correctness of $\tilde{\mathcal{O}}_b^a$ depends on conditions 1-3 of Definition 10.3.9. Clearly, condition 1 is satisfied because $\tilde{\mathcal{O}}_b^a(h).Nec = \emptyset$ (by definition of **Compact**). Conditions 2 and 3 are satisfied because $\mathbf{App}_a(b)$ is correct. This completes the proof. ∎

By replacing $\mathbf{App}_a(b)$ with $\mathbf{Compact}(\mathbf{App}_a(b))$, performance may be significantly improved. The price to be paid for this is a potential loss of cooperation. The following theorem says that whenever a distortion is approximately data secure w.r.t. a compact approximation of an agent, then it is also approximately data secure w.r.t. the (perhaps uncompact) approximation of the agent.

THEOREM 10.3.3 (COMPACT APPROX. SECURITY IMPLIES APPROX. SECURITY) If $\tilde{\zeta}_a$ is approximately data secure at h w.r.t. $\mathbf{Compact}(\mathbf{App}_a(b))$, then $\tilde{\zeta}_a$ is approximately data secure at h w.r.t. $\mathbf{App}_a(b)$.

Proof Suppose $\tilde{\zeta}_a$ is approximately data secure at h w.r.t. $\mathbf{Compact}(\mathbf{App}_a(b))$ and suppose $\tilde{\zeta}_a(h)$ has the form $h' \cdot e$. Then

$$\text{OViol}_b^a\bigl(H_b^a(h' \cdot e)\bigr) = \emptyset,$$

Section 10.3   Safely Approximate Data Security   363

where OViol_b^a is defined w.r.t. **Compact**($\mathbf{App}_a(b)$). Note that $\mathbf{App}_a(b)$ yields the same overestimation OViol_b^a as **Compact**($\mathbf{App}_a(b)$); it follows that also under $\mathbf{App}_a(b)$

$$\mathsf{UViol}_b^a\big(H_b^a(h')\big) \supseteq \mathsf{OViol}_b^a\big(H_b^a(h' \cdot e)\big) = \emptyset,$$

which implies that $\tilde{\zeta}_a$ is approximately data secure at h w.r.t. $\mathbf{App}_a(b)$. ∎

As a consequence of this theorem, we know that to check whether a distortion $\tilde{\zeta}_a$ is approximately data secure w.r.t. $\mathbf{App}_a(b)$, it is sufficient to check whether $\tilde{\zeta}_a$ is approximately data secure w.r.t. **Compact**($\mathbf{App}_a(b)$).

COROLLARY 9   For each distortion $\tilde{\zeta}_a$ which is approximately data secure w.r.t. **Compact** ($\mathbf{App}_a(b)$), there exists a distortion $\tilde{\zeta}_a'$ which is approximately data secure w.r.t. $\mathbf{App}_a(b)$ and at least as cooperative as $\tilde{\zeta}_a$.

The converse of Theorem 10.3.3 (and Corollary 9) does not hold, in general, and therefore choosing to use **Compact**($\mathbf{App}_a(b)$) in place of $\mathbf{App}_a(b)$ may lead to a decrease in cooperation. This is demonstrated in the following example.

Example 10.3.12   Suppose ground_control already knows autoPilot's current position, and this is recorded into $\mathbf{App}_{\mathsf{autoPilot}}(\mathsf{ground\_control})$. That is,

in(P, autoPilot:*location*()) $\in UCN_{\mathsf{ground\_control}}^{\mathsf{autoPilot}}$.

In this case, autoPilot may tell ground_control its old position P_t at time $t = $ now $- 5$. According to autoPilot's overestimation, ground_control may be able to derive autoPilot's current position from P_t, but this doesn't matter, as this secret has already been violated. However, if we adopted **Compact**($\mathbf{App}_{\mathsf{autoPilot}}(\mathsf{ground\_control})$), the secrets which are already known by ground_control would not be considered, and the answer message containing P_t would trigger a security violation.

10.3.9 Static Approximations

As answers get larger and agent approximations more sophisticated, the overhead caused by runtime checks may become unacceptable, even if compact approximations are adopted. For such applications, as well as for time-critical applications, *static* security checks are more appropriate. Such checks should guarantee *a priori* that a given distortion function is always data secure for each possible history h. The problem is that for many agents (including most *IMPACT* agents) it is simply impossible to predict upfront what the possible histories h will look like, because agents can be as powerful as arbitrary Turing machines (this aspect will be studied formally in Section 10.4). For this reason, it is necessary to *approximate the behavior of the server agent* a. When designing agent a, this may be accomplished by overestimating the set of a's possible histories, in order to cover *at least* all the possible interactions between a and b. If each such history in the overestimated set of possible histories is guaranteed to be secure at the time the agent is deployed, then security of the distortion function used by agent a is guaranteed upfront.

DEFINITION 10.3.22 (STATIC AGENT APPROXIMATION, RESTRICTION, CORRECTNESS) A static approximation **StaticApp**$_a$(b) is an approximation of b used by a such that the domain of H_b^a is extended to a set, $\text{pos}\mathcal{H}_a'$, of histories for a such that $\text{pos}\mathcal{H}_a' \supseteq \text{pos}\mathcal{H}_a$. The set $\text{pos}\mathcal{H}_a'$ will be referred to as the *approximation of a's possible histories*.

The *dynamic restriction* of **StaticApp**$_a$(b) is the agent approximation **App**$_a$(b) obtained from **StaticApp**$_a$(b) by restricting the domain of H_b^a to $\text{pos}\mathcal{H}_a$.

We say that **StaticApp**$_a$(b) is *correct* if all its components are correct. The correctness of H_b^a is obtained by extending the correctness condition of Definition 10.3.3 to all $h \in \text{pos}\mathcal{H}_a'$. The definition of correctness for the other components is unchanged.

The approximate behaviors described by $\text{pos}\mathcal{H}_a'$ may be *nondeterministic* because a's responses to incoming requests cannot be precisely known in advance. Technically, this means that $\text{pos}\mathcal{H}_a'$ is allowed to simultaneously contain two histories of the form $h \cdot e \cdot h'$ and $h \cdot e \cdot h''$, where e is a service request to a. In this framework, the data security check can be reformulated as follows.

DEFINITION 10.3.23 (STATIC DATA SECURITY) We say that the approximation $\text{pos}\mathcal{H}_a'$ of a's behavior is *statically data secure* (w.r.t. **StaticApp**$_a$(b)) if for all $h \cdot e \in \text{pos}\mathcal{H}_a'$ such that e is an answer message to b,

$$\mathsf{UViol}_b^a\big(H_b^a(h)\big) \supseteq \mathsf{OViol}_b^a\big(H_b^a(h \cdot e)\big).$$

Informally speaking, the following theorem guarantees that any agent known to be statically data secure is also data secure.

THEOREM 10.3.4 (STATIC SECURITY PRESERVATION) Let $\tilde{\zeta}_a$ be the distortion adopted by a, and let **StaticApp**$_a$(b) be a correct static approximation of b used by a. If $\text{pos}\mathcal{H}_a'$ is statically data secure, then $\tilde{\zeta}_a$ is data secure.

Proof First note that since **StaticApp**$_a$(b) is correct, then also its dynamic restriction **App**$_a$(b) is correct (straightforward from the definition). Now we prove the contrapositive of the theorem, which is equivalent. Suppose $\tilde{\zeta}_a$ is *not* data secure. Then, by Theorem 10.3.1, it is not approximately data secure w.r.t. **App**$_a$(b). Consequently, for some history $h_0 \cdot e \in \text{pos}\mathcal{H}_a$,

$$\mathsf{UViol}_b^a\big(H_b^a(h_0)\big) \not\supseteq \mathsf{OViol}_b^a\big(H_b^a(h_0 \cdot e)\big). \qquad (*)$$

Section 10.3   Safely Approximate Data Security   365

By definition of static approximation, $\text{pos}\mathcal{H}'_a \supseteq \text{pos}\mathcal{H}_a$, so $h_0 \cdot e \in \text{pos}\mathcal{H}'_a$. It follows (by definition and (*)) that $\text{pos}\mathcal{H}'_a$ is not statically data secure w.r.t. **StaticApp**$_a(\text{b})$. ∎

A related result states that a dynamic use of the same approximation may lead to more cooperative service evaluation. More precisely, the next theorem says (i) that static security is always at least as strong as dynamic security, and (ii) that a distortion may be data secure, even if the static check detects a potential violation.

THEOREM 10.3.5 (STATIC VS. DYNAMIC VERIFICATION)

1. Under the hypotheses of the above theorem, if $\text{pos}\mathcal{H}'_a$ is statically data secure, then $\tilde{\zeta}_a$ is approximately data secure w.r.t. **StaticApp**$_a(\text{b})$'s dynamic restriction.

2. There exists an agent a with distortion $\tilde{\zeta}_a$, and a correct static approximation **StaticApp**$_a(\text{b})$ based on a's history approximation $\text{pos}\mathcal{H}'_a$, such that $\tilde{\zeta}_a$ is data secure w.r.t. **StaticApp**$_a(\text{b})$'s dynamic restriction, but $\text{pos}\mathcal{H}'_a$ is not statically data secure w.r.t. **StaticApp**$_a(\text{b})$.

Proof   The proof of part 1 is contained in the proof of Theorem 10.3.4 (there we proved that if $\tilde{\zeta}_a$ is not approximately data secure w.r.t. the dynamic approximation **App**$_a(\text{b})$ then $\text{pos}\mathcal{H}'_a$ is not statically data secure w.r.t. **StaticApp**$_a(\text{b})$).

To prove part 2, suppose b is the agent defined in the proof of Theorem 10.2.1, and let **App**$_a(\text{b})$ be any correct approximation of b with $AppSec_a(\text{b}) \neq \emptyset$. Let $\tilde{\zeta}_a$ be any distortion approximately data secure w.r.t. **App**$_a(\text{b})$. Let f be any secret in $Sec_a(\text{b})$. Define $\text{pos}\mathcal{H}'_a = \text{pos}\mathcal{H}_a \cup \{\langle a, b, \{f\}\rangle\}$. Note that **App**$_a(\text{b})$ is the dynamic restriction of **StaticApp**$_a(\text{b})$. Clearly, $\text{pos}\mathcal{H}'_a$ is not statically data secure w.r.t. **StaticApp**$_a(\text{b})$ (b believes the secret f and stores it in its state). This completes the proof. ∎

10.3.10   Summary

We have introduced a methodology for building approximate security checks, based on incomplete and imprecise knowledge about client agents. The methodology is based on four items:

- an approximation $H^a_b(.)$ of b's current history;
- an approximation $\mathcal{O}^a_b(.)$ of b's current state;
- an overestimation $OCN^a_b(.)$ of the secrets that can be derived by b;
- an underestimation $UCN^a_b(.)$ of the facts that can be derived by b.

We have given criteria for correctly defining each of the above items. Some, like $H^a_b(.)$, $\mathcal{O}^a_b(.).Poss$, $\mathcal{O}^a_b(.).New$, and $OCN^a_b(.)$ should be overestimated, in case of doubt, while others like $\mathcal{O}_b^a(.).Nec$ and $UCN_b^a(.)$ should be underestimated. We have proved formally that if the above criteria are followed, then approximate security checks suffice to enforce the exact notion of data security.

This methodology has been formulated in terms of the abstract agent model of Section 10.1, and therefore it can be applied to a wide variety of agents, including agents programmed directly in procedural and object-oriented languages such as C and Java. Moreover, the approximations are based on abstract representation languages for facts and histories, which can be tailored rather freely to specific applications. The only subtle point is in the representation of secrets; we have specified which granularity problems should be avoided in order to preserve security (see Definition 10.3.11).

10.4 Undecidability Results

The techniques introduced in the preceding sections are compatible with a wide variety of security checks including, but not limited to:

Static security verification: Before deploying a given agent a, decide whether its distortion policy, $\tilde{\zeta}_a$, will be secure at all possible histories h_a for a;

Dynamic security verification: Decide at runtime whether the agent's distortion policy is secure at the current history h_a.

Clearly, if would be nice if all security checks could be implemented statically, thereby avoiding the overhead of runtime checks. Unfortunately, *IMPACT* agents can be as powerful as arbitrary Turing machines, and hence their behavior cannot be predicted, in general, as stated by the following results. The first result below states that even the relatively simple notion of surface security is undecidable.

THEOREM 10.4.1 (UNDECIDABILITY OF SURFACE SECURITY) The problem of deciding statically whether an arbitrary *IMPACT* agent is surface secure is undecidable.

Proof We prove this theorem by uniformly reducing the halting problem for arbitrary deterministic Turing machines M to a surface security verification problem. For this purpose, we simulate M with a suitable agent a that outputs a secret f when a final state of M is reached.

We start by encoding M's states $\{s_1, \ldots, s_m\}$ into the belief table $\mathbf{BT}^a$ of a. Agent a is built in such a way that $\mathbf{BT}^a$ contains always one entry of the form $\text{Enc}_{\text{state}}(s_i) =_{def}$ $\langle \text{state}, \mathcal{B}_{s_i}(s_i, \mathbf{true}) \rangle$, where s_i is the current state of M.

Secondly, we show how to encode M's tape with belief atoms. For this purpose, the first step is encoding finite string of symbols taken from M's alphabet:

Section 10.4   Undecidability Results   367

- the empty sequence is encoded by the atom **true**; formally, $\text{Enc}'_x(\langle\rangle) =_{def} \textbf{true}$;
- a nonempty sequence $\sigma = v_1 \ldots v_n$ is encoded by $\text{Enc}'_x(\sigma) =_{def} \mathcal{B}_x(v_1, \text{Enc}_x(v2 \ldots v_n))$.

(Here x can be curr, left or right; the reason of this is explained below). Now suppose the finite used portion of the tape is

$$\sigma = v_1 \ldots v_l v_0 v'_1 \ldots v'_r$$

and that M's head points to v_0. This configuration is encoded with three entries of $\mathbf{BT}^\mathfrak{a}$:

- $\text{Enc}_{\text{curr}}(\sigma) = \langle \text{curr}, \text{Enc}'_{\text{curr}}(v_0) \rangle$;
- $\text{Enc}_{\text{left}}(\sigma) = \langle \text{left}, \text{Enc}'_{\text{left}}(v_l \ldots v_1) \rangle$;
- $\text{Enc}_{\text{right}}(\sigma) = \langle \text{right}, \text{Enc}'_{\text{right}}(v'_1 \ldots v'_r) \rangle$.

This completes the encoding of M's configuration. Now we have to model M's finite control; it will be encoded through an agent program based on the following update action:

upd(*state*′, *left*′, *curr*′, *right*′)

which replaces the four entries of $\mathbf{BT}^\mathfrak{a}$ encoding state and tape with the new encoded configuration, specified by the four arguments.

Now recall that M's finite control can be regarded as a set of 5-tuples of the form

$\langle s, v, v', s', m \rangle$

where s is the current state, v is the symbol under M's head, v' is the symbol to be overwritten on v, s' is the next state and $m = \{\text{left}, \text{right}\}$ specifies the head's movement. Each such 5-tuple is encoded by an agent program rule R. If $m = \text{right}$ then R is:

$\mathbf{O}upd(\text{Enc}_{\text{state}}(S'), \langle \text{left}, \mathcal{B}_{\text{left}}(v', L)\rangle, \text{Enc}_{\text{curr}}(V_1), \langle \text{right}, R\rangle) \leftarrow$
  $\mathbf{in}(\text{Enc}_{\text{state}}(s), \mathbf{BT}^\mathfrak{a} : proj\_select(\text{agent}, =, \text{state}))\ \&$
  $\mathbf{in}(\langle \text{left}, L\rangle, \mathbf{BT}^\mathfrak{a} : proj\_select(\text{agent}, =, \text{left}))\ \&$
  $\mathbf{in}(\text{Enc}_{\text{curr}}(v), \mathbf{BT}^\mathfrak{a} : proj\_select(\text{agent}, =, \text{curr}))\ \&$
  $\mathbf{in}(\langle \text{right}, \mathcal{B}_{\text{right}}(V_1, R)\rangle, \mathbf{BT}^\mathfrak{a} : proj\_select(\text{agent}, =, \text{right}))$.

Intuitively, this rule causes replacement of the current configuration of M with the new one specified by v', s' and $m = \text{right}$. Afterward, the head points to V_1. The agent program rules for $m = \text{left}$ are symmetrical.

Finally, for each final state s of M, $\mathfrak{a}$'s agent program contains a rule

$\mathbf{O}\,send(\mathsf{b}, f) \leftarrow \mathbf{in}(\text{Enc}_{\text{state}}(s), \mathbf{BT}^\mathfrak{a} : proj\_select(\text{agent}, =, \text{state}))$

where f is a secret and $send(\mathsf{b}, f)$ is an action that sends the answer $\{f\}$ to b.

Clearly, by construction, a outputs a secret (thereby violating surface security) if and only if M terminates. This completes the proof. ∎

As a consequence, verifying data security is also undecidable.

COROLLARY 10 The problems of deciding statically whether an arbitrary *IMPACT* agent is data secure or approximately data secure, are undecidable.

Proof Immediate from theorems 10.2.1 and 10.4.1. ∎

Theorem 10.4.1 is proved by simulating an arbitrary Turing machine M with an *IMPACT* agent a. The agent's decision component implements the finite control of M; M's tape is stored by means of a's meta-level component. There are many other possible ways of encoding M's tape in a's data structures, for example through the *history component* introduced in the next section, or through some relational database package, just to mention a few. In general, if we had to restrict *IMPACT* agents to make their behavior predictable, we would have to ban every package which uses unbounded memory. Note, however, that this by itself would not automatically allow static security verification, because the number of possible agent states might still be prohibitively large.

Using similar techniques, one can show that action security cannot be decided statically.

THEOREM 10.4.2 (UNDECIDABILITY OF ACTION SECURITY) The problem of deciding statically whether an arbitrary *IMPACT* agent is action secure is not decidable.

Proof Similar to the proof of Theorem 10.4.1. An arbitrary Turing machine M can be encoded into an *IMPACT* agent as shown in the proof of Theorem 10.4.1. However, the rules that output a secret when a final state of M is reached are replaced by rules that do a forbidden action. Then the halting problem is reduced to action security verification. ∎

Clearly, the above results concern *exact* security checks. Fortunately, there exist some decidable static checks that suffice to preserve security (see Section 10.3.9). Such checks provide decidable *sufficient* conditions which, if satisfied by an *IMPACT* agent, guarantee that the problems of data security and approximate data security are decidable. The next section describes how the *IMPACT* agent architecture supports static security verification.

10.5 IMPACT Security Implementation Architecture

At this point in time, we have not implemented the security features described in this chapter in the *IMPACT* system. However, we have developed a strategy to implement the theory of this chapter within *IMPACT*, and hence, in this section, we describe this implementation architecture.

The security architecture supports both static and dynamic security verification. Static security checks may reduce or even eliminate the overhead due to run-time (dynamic) security verification. On the other hand, static security verification is in general more restrictive than dynamic security verification (Theorem 10.3.5). In addition, the architecture supports a combination of the static and dynamic approaches. In this architecture, the agent developer can articulate his security needs via three components:

History component Hist_a. This component is used to record and maintain a's history, h_a. We have shown in Section 10.3 that h_a plays an important role in approximating the histories of other agents (see Section 10.3.2), which in turn is needed to determine which secrets can be violated by b. In particular, for all client agents b, h_a is the input to the function H_b^a that approximates b's history; h_a is also involved in the correctness of H_b^a (see Definition 10.3.3). Example 10.3.3 shows how the approximate history $H_b^a(h_a)$ of b may be obtained directly from h_a.

Agent approximation program AAP_b^a. This is a set of rules that encode a's approximation of b, denoted by $\text{App}_a(b)$ in the abstract approximation framework (see Definition 10.3.16). The *IMPACT* security architecture supports *compact approximations* (Section 10.3.8), which, as the reader will recall, enhances the efficiency of computation. Recall that a compact approximation consists of the following items:

- the history approximation function H_b^a;
- the state approximation function $\mathcal{O}_b^a$;
- a set $AppSec_a(b)$ of secrets that should not be derivable by (the approximate model of) b;
- an overestimation OCN_b^a of b's inferences, used to estimate the secrets that might be violated by b using a's answers.

Moreover, a set of rules R_{slf} define an approximation $\text{pos}\mathcal{H}_a'$ of a's behavior, which is required for static security verification (see Section 10.3.9). By writing AAP_b^a, agent developers define their own approximations, as required by the application at hand.

SecP_a. This package is used to maintain, compile and execute the programs that perform static, dynamic and combined security checks.

The rest of this section is organized as follows: First, the history component is introduced. Then the agent approximation program AAP_b^a will be illustrated extensively, and the functions for static and dynamic security checks will be introduced. A final section will be devoted to action security.

10.5.1 History Component Hist_a

As pointed out in Section 10.3.2 (Example 10.3.4), agents may be unable to store their complete history because of memory limitations and/or computation time requirements.

Thus, in general, the historical archive associated with an *IMPACT* agent a consists of *some* set of events involving a. For instance, these could include requests that have been made to a and the results of those requests. Agents differ based on how they answer the following questions:

- *Which events should be stored in the historical archive?* In general, an agent a may choose to store only certain types of events. This may increase the efficiency of history manipulation, but may decrease the quality of the *approximations* of other agents' histories, which are based on a's own history (see the examples in Section 10.3.2).

- *Which attributes of these events should be stored?* Possible attributes of an answer message which an agent developer might wish to store are the requested service, the receiver, the answer, the time at which the answer was sent.

The *IMPACT* architecture's history component has been designed so as to be compatible with the generic abstract model of histories introduced in Section 10.1. The following interface functions are associated with the history component Hist_a of an *IMPACT* agent a:

- `retrieve_reqs(Sender,Receiver,Request,When)`: Retrieve all stored request messages sent by Sender to Receiver at time When, and matching Request. Parameter When has the form Op <time>, where Op is one of $<, \leq, =, \neq, \geq, >$. The above parameters may be left unspecified, in part or entirely, using the wildcard '_'. For example, the invocation `retrieve_reqs(b,_,_,> 20:jan:95:1900)` retrieves all stored request messages sent by b after the specified time.

- `retrieve_answ(Sender,Receiver,Fact,When)`: Retrieve all stored answer messages sent by Sender to Receiver at time When, and such that the answer contains a fact f which matches Fact. The variables of Fact are instantiated with f. When can be specified as explained above; wildcards may be used.

- `retrieve_actn(Act,When)`: Retrieve all stored actions that match Act, and executed at the time specified by When. The action name and/or its arguments may be left unspecified using the wildcard '_'.

Note that the history component of an IMPACT agent may be viewed as just another data structure together with the above set of associated functions. Hence, the concepts of code call and code call conditions apply directly to the history component.

DEFINITION 10.5.1 (HISTORY CONDITIONS) Suppose *RF* is one of the above three retrieval functions, and args is a list of arguments for *RF* of the appropriate type. We may inductively define history conditions as follows.

- **in**(X, Hist_a : *RF*(args)) is a history condition.

- If Op is any of $<, \leq, =, \neq, \geq, >$, and T_1, T_2 are variables or objects, then T_1 Op T_2 is a history condition.
- If χ_1, χ_2 are history conditions then $(\chi_1 \ \& \ \chi_2)$ is a history condition.

The syntactic restrictions obeyed by history conditions will be needed in Section 10.5.2. In general, Hist$_a$'s functions may occur side by side with arbitrary conditions.

Example 10.5.1 Suppose one of the possible answers to a service request is: "Request rejected: attempted security violation." In order to discourage agents from repeatedly making such attempts, agent a may refuse to provide any service for 10 days after an attempted violation. This policy can be expressed by means of *action rules* (see Section 4.6) that call the history package before serving the request. In the following, sn is an action name (and we assume there is a service with the same name), $i_1, \ldots, i_k$ are its inputs, $mi_1, \ldots, mi_m$ are its mandatory inputs, and $o_1, \ldots, o_n$ are the outputs (see Definition 4.6.1).

Do $sn(i_1, \ldots, i_k, mi_1, \ldots, mi_m, o_1, \ldots, o_n) \leftarrow$
    $T = \text{now} - 10 \text{ days},$
    not_in(X, Hist$_a$: retrieve_answ($a, \_$, attempted_violation, $>$ T)).

The history package is completed by the *history update actions* described below.

- insert_reqs(Sender,Receiver,Req), insert_answ(Sender,Receiver,Ans), insert_actn(Act): These actions append a new event to a's history.
- delete(Event): Deletes Event from the history.

Example 10.5.2 An agent may only save responses sent to police officers. In addition, the answers to police officers with security level not higher than secret are saved only for two years. This policy can be specified via the following action rules:

O insert_answ(a, Receiver, Ans) $\leftarrow$
    O *sendMessage*(a, Receiver, Ans) &
    in(Receiver, oracle : project(police, name)).

O delete(Event) $\leftarrow$
    $T = \text{now} - 2\text{years} \ \&$
    in(Event, Hist$_a$: retrieve_answ($\_, \_, \_, <$ T)) &
    in(Event.receiver, oracle : *project*(police, name)).
    Event.sender.level $\sqsubseteq$ secret.

Concurrent history update actions have the same STRIPS-like semantics as any other concurrent actions: deletions are applied first. The resulting behavior is equivalent to first applying all delete(X) actions, and then all the actions of the form insert_yyyy(X).

10.5.2 Implementing Agent Approximation

IMPACT's agent approximation framework is based on the notions introduced in Section 10.3. Recall that the approximation of agent b used by a is based on two abstract languages $\text{pos}\mathcal{H}_b^a$ and $\mathcal{L}_b^a$, for describing approximate possible histories and approximate facts, respectively. An agent developer building an *IMPACT* agent should go through the following steps:

1. He first writes a set of rules called *history approximation rules* through which he specifies how his agent approximates the history of another agent;

2. Then, he writes a set of *state approximation rules* which specifies how his agent approximates the state of another agent;

3. Then, he writes a set of *consequence approximation rules* through which he specifies how his agent captures the approximate consequence relation of another agent;

4. Finally, he writes a set of *secrets approximation rules* specifying the set of approximate secrets.

These rules have the form Property ← Condition; their intended meaning is that agent b *may* satisfy Property if Condition holds. So, for example, Property can say "b's history may contain a message from c," or something like: "b's state can possibly contain fact f," or: "b might be able to perform such and such an inference." *It is intended that two properties can be simultaneously satisfied by b only if their corresponding conditions can be simultaneously true.*

The above steps work both for *IMPACT* agents and non-*IMPACT* agents. In the case of the latter, the agent developer also needs to choose an appropriate fact language suitable for his application. The language hierarchy $\mathcal{BL}_\infty^a$ ($i \geq 0$) is one of the possible options; see Section 10.3.3 for alternative examples. We introduce another example below.

Example 10.5.3 (Agent Approximation in IMPACT: Fact Language) This is the first of a series of examples that will illustrate how agent approximations can be built in *IMPACT* when little or nothing is known about the client agent b. The reference scenario is similar to the CFIT-like scenario depicted in Example 10.1.5: Agent b may be interested in agent autoPilot's position and velocity at time t, denoted by P_t and V_t, respectively. The current location P_{now}, however, is a secret.

Here we introduce the approximate fact language $\mathcal{L}_b^{\text{autoPilot}}$. It consists of two kinds of facts:

location_at(t, P_t),
velocity_at(t, V_t).

We make no assumption on the set of coordinates (they may be cartesian, radial or whatever), nor on their precision, in accordance with the spirit of this example (almost nothing is known about b). Consequently, the variables P_t and V_t are just place-holders, they will never be instantiated in our example.

The history approximation language, on the contrary, is fixed. It consists of sets of *constraints* that describe the events in b's history and their mutual relationships.

Implementing History Approximation We now discuss how history approximations may be expressed by an agent developer in *IMPACT*.

DEFINITION 10.5.2 (HISTORY CONSTRAINT LANGUAGE)   A *history constraint* is an expression of the following type:

- requested(Sender,Receiver,Request,Time)
- told(Sender,Receiver,Answer,Time)
- done(Agent,ActionName,Time)
- T_1 Op T_2, where Op is a *comparison operator* ($<, \leq, =, \neq, \geq, >$) and T_1, T_2 may be path variables or objects.

Constraints of the form requested(...), told(...) and done(...) will be called *pure history constraints*; those of the form T_1 Op T_2 will be called *comparison constraints*.

Pure history constraints correspond to the three possible event types, that is, request messages, answer messages and action events. The argument Time is a number which denotes the time at which the event happened.

Example 10.5.4 A history h_b for b of the form $\langle \ldots \langle b, a, location() \rangle \ldots \langle a, b, \{location(pos)\} \rangle \ldots \rangle$ (containing a service request and the corresponding answer) satisfies the history constraints:

requested(b, a, $location()$, T1), told(a, b, Y, T2), T1 $\leq$ T2.

More precisely, the link between the *IMPACT* security architecture and the abstract framework is the following: *IMPACT*'s history approximations are sets $H = \{HC_1, HC_2, \ldots, HC_i, \ldots\}$, where each HC_i is a set of history constraints; a history for b, $h_b = \langle e_1, e_2, \ldots, e_i, \ldots \rangle$, corresponds to H (in symbols, $H \overset{ab}{\leadsto} h_b$) if h_b *satisfies* some $HC_i \in H$, which means that for some ground instance $HC_i\theta$ of HC_i, the following conditions hold:

- each comparison constraint in $HC_i\theta$ is true;
- each pure history constraint $c \in HC_i\theta$ *matches* some event e in h_b of the corresponding

type, in the sense that the fields Sender, Receiver, Request and Answer of c coincide with the corresponding elements of e;

• the parameters Time correctly reflect the ordering of the events; formally, for all pure history constraints c' and c'' in $HC_i\theta$, whose last paramenters are Time' and Time'', respectively, and such that c' and c'' correspond to events e_j and e_k of h_b, (respectively), it holds that Time' $\leq$ Time'' $\Leftrightarrow j \leq k$.

In the previous example, one can verify that b's history satisfies the given history constraints by applying any substitution θ such that T1$\theta \leq$ T2θ and Y$\theta = location(pos)$.

The current history approximation *function*, H_b^a, is described by a set R_{his} of *history approximation rules*

$PHC \leftarrow \chi_{\text{hist}}$,

where PHC is a pure history constraint and χ_{hist} is a history code call condition. Essentially, the above rule says that b's history *may* satisfy the history constraint PHC, provided that χ_{hist} evaluates to **true**.

Example 10.5.5 (Implementing Agent Approximation: Possible Histories) Let us reconsider the scenario introduced in Example 10.5.3. In the same spirit, little or nothing is known about the possible histories for b. The set of agents that may be contacted by b is not known. Some of them might know agent autoPilot's position and velocity P_t and V_t at different times t (for instance, such information might have been acquired with radars, or from autoPilot itself). Therefore, it cannot be excluded a priori that b is told some P_t or V_t by other agents. This is expressed via the following history approximation rules. They say that for all X $\neq$ autoPilot and T $\leq$ T1, b's history may happen to contain messages from X to b, containing P_t or V_t, or both.

(r1) told(X, b, *location_at*(T, Pt), T1) $\leftarrow$ X $\neq$ autoPilot & T $\leq$ T1.

(r2) told(X, b, *velocity_at*(T, Vt), T2) $\leftarrow$ X $\neq$ autoPilot & T $\leq$ T2.

The only assumption we make here is that the agents involved in this scenario do not talk about the future. Only old or current positions and velocities are communicated. This is expressed by T $\leq$ T1 and T $\leq$ T2.

We assume that in some cases, autoPilot itself may tell b some of its old positions. Agent autoPilot keeps all its answers in Hist$_{\text{autoPilot}}$ for one hour, then deletes them. Then, a recent answer can be in b's history only if a corresponding message is stored in Hist$_{\text{autoPilot}}$, while older messages may be in b's history regardless of Hist$_{\text{autoPilot}}$'s contents (Example 10.3.4). This can be expressed via the following rules.

(r3) told(autoPilot, b, *location_at*(T, Pt), T3) ←
    in(Ev, Hist$_{\text{autoPilot}}$: *retrieve_answ*(autoPilot, b, *location_at*(T, Pt), _)) &
    T3 ≥ Ev.time.

(r4) told(autoPilot, b, *location_at*(T, Pt), T4) ←
    T ≤ T4 &
    T4 ≤ now − 60.

Rule (**r3**) states that an answer message from autoPilot may be in b's history if there is a corresponding message Ev in autoPilot's history (second line). Message delivery might not be instantaneous; there may be a delay before the answer is received by b (third line).

Rule (**r4**) is needed because events older than 60 minutes are deleted from Hist$_{\text{autoPilot}}$. Therefore, if T4 ≤ now − 60, then an answer message from autoPilot may be in b's history while the corresponding event has been deleted from Hist$_{\text{autoPilot}}$. Condition T ≤ T4 says that P_t refers to a time point earlier than the answer delivery time. This condition is useless in (**r3**), because autoPilot cannot return any future velocity, and hence, T ≤ Ev.time ≤ T3.

To formalize the semantics of the above rules we need a notion of *derivation*, borrowed from the theory of logic programming. In the following, the word *atom* denotes an atomic code call condition or a history constraint. By *rule*, we mean any expression $H \leftarrow B$, where H is an atom (called the *head* of the rule), and B is a conjunction of atoms (the *body* of the rule).

DEFINITION 10.5.3 (RESOLVENT, DERIVATION) Let G be a conjunction of atoms A_1 & ... & A_n, and let $r = (H \leftarrow B)$ be a rule whose head can be unified with some A_i ($1 \leq i \leq n$), with a substitution θ. The *resolvent* of G and r w.r.t. θ (with *selected literal* A_i) is $(A_1 \& \ldots \& A_{i-1} \& B \& A_{i+1} \& \ldots \& A_n)\theta$.

A *standardized apart member* of a set of rules R is a variant of a rule $r \in R$, obtained by uniformly renaming R's variables with fresh variables, never used before.

A *derivation* from a set of rules R with substitutions $\theta_1 \ldots \theta_m$ is a sequence $G_0, \ldots, G_m$ such that for all $i = 1 \ldots n$, G_i is a resolvent of G_{i-1} and some standardized apart member r_i of R, w.r.t. θ_i. If $G_0, \ldots, G_m$ is a derivation from R with substitutions $\theta_1 \ldots \theta_m$, and θ is the composition of $\theta_1 \ldots \theta_m$, then we write

$$G_0 \longrightarrow_R^\theta G_m.$$

If the θ_is are all most general unifiers, then we write $G_0 \xrightarrow{\text{mg}}_R^\theta G_m$.

It is well known that if $G_0 \longrightarrow_R^\theta G_m$, then R entails $G_m \Rightarrow G_0\theta$ in classical logic (the rules in R are regarded as universally closed formulas). Similarly, suppose that HC is a set of history constraints such that $HC \longrightarrow_{R_{\text{his}}}^\theta \chi_{\text{hist}}$; intuitively, this means that if χ_{hist} is true then b's history may satisfy $HC\theta$. Now it is easy to formalize the link between *IMPACT*'s history approximation rules and the abstract function H_b^a:

$$H_b^a(h_a) =_{def} \{HC\theta\sigma \mid HC \xrightarrow{\theta}_{R_{his}} \chi_{hist} \text{ and } \sigma \in \text{Sol}(\chi_{hist})\} \qquad (10.4)$$

(here h_a denotes a's current history). In other words, once the agent developer describes a set of history approximation rules, this uniquely determines the abstract history approximation H_b^a.

Example 10.5.6 (Agent Approximation in IMPACT: Derivation from R_{his}) If R_{his} consists of the rules **(r1)**–**(r4)** defined in the previous example, and

$HC = \text{told}(X, b, \textit{velocity\_at}(T, Vt), T') \, \& \, \text{told}(Y, b, \textit{location\_at}(T, Pt), T'')$,

then there exist three derivations $HC \xrightarrow{\theta_i}_{R_{his}} \chi_{hist}^i$ ($i = 1, 2, 3$). The first one applies **(r1)** and **(r2)**, and yields:

$\chi_{hist}^1 = X \neq \text{autoPilot} \, \& \, T \leq T' \, \& \, Y \neq \text{autoPilot} \, \& \, T \leq T''$,

$HC\theta_1 = HC$.

This means that (it is estimated that) b's history may contain two events matching HC, provided that χ_{hist}^1 holds. The other derivations use **(r2)** and one of **(r3)** and **(r4)**, yielding:

$\chi_{hist}^2 = \textbf{in}(Ev_1, \text{Hist}_{\text{autoPilot}} : \textit{retrieve\_answ}(\text{autoPilot}, b, \textit{location\_at}(T, Pt), \_)) \, \&$
$\qquad\quad T' \geq Ev_1.\text{time} \, \&$
$\qquad\quad Y \neq \text{autoPilot} \, \& \, T < T''$,

$HC\theta_2 = \text{told}(\text{autoPilot}, b, \textit{velocity\_at}(T, Vt), T') \, \& \, \text{told}(Y, b, \textit{location\_at}(T, Vt), T'')$;

$\chi_{hist}^3 = T \leq T' \, \& \, T' \leq \text{now} - 60 \, \& \, Y \neq \text{autoPilot} \, \& \, T < T''$,

$HC\theta_3 = HC\theta_2$.

Again, this means that b's history may contain two events that match $HC\theta_i$ if the corresponding condition χ_{hist}^i is satisfied. For $i = 2$, checking such condition involves inspecting autoPilot's history $\text{Hist}_{\text{autoPilot}}$. This can be done either dynamically (at run time) or statically, by estimating how the history condition will be evaluated in the future (this can be done with a suitable set of rules, R_{slf}, that will be introduced below).

Implementing State Approximation Recall that an approximate state of b has three fields, *Nec*, *Poss* and *New*, that capture (respectively) the conditions which are deemed to be necessarily true, possibly true, possibly true *and* caused by the last event in b's history.

The *IMPACT* security architecture supports compact approximations, so *Nec* is not modeled (it is always empty, see Section 10.3.8). The set *New* is derived automatically from *Poss* and will be defined later. Thus, *IMPACT*'s state approximation model only needs to

Section 10.5   IMPACT Security Implementation Architecture   377

use the set *Poss*. This is done by means of a set R_{sta} of *state approximation rules*

$$\mathcal{B}_\mathfrak{a}(\mathsf{b}, f) \leftarrow HC,$$

where f is a fact from the chosen approximate fact language $\mathcal{L}_\mathsf{b}^\mathfrak{a}$ and *HC* is a set of history constraints. Intuitively, the above rule says that if b's history satisfies *HC*, then $\mathcal{B}_\mathfrak{a}(\mathsf{b}, f)$ *might* be in b's state. By writing a set of rules R_{sta}, the agent developer specifies how agent $\mathfrak{a}$ approximates the *Poss* part of agent b's state.

Example 10.5.7 (Implementing Agent Approximation: States)   As very little is known about b, the following possibilities must be taken into account:

• b may store in its state any data obtained from other agents (this doesn't mean that b actually stores all such data);

• b may keep data in its state for unbounded amounts of time (i.e., it cannot be said a priori whether a particular piece of data will be removed or replaced at some point).

This means that b's state may possibly contain any fact received from other agents. This can be expressed via the following rule:

(r5) $\mathcal{B}_{\mathsf{autoPilot}}(\mathsf{b}, \mathsf{F}) \leftarrow \mathtt{told}(\mathsf{X}, \mathsf{b}, \mathsf{F}, \mathsf{T}).$

Clearly, if more information about b were available, the body of the above rule might be enriched with further constraints. For example, by adding $\mathsf{T} \geq \mathtt{now} - 30$ one could say that b does not keep facts for more than 30 minutes. By adding $\mathsf{X} \neq \mathsf{c}$ one could say that c's messages are not stored by b.

Accordingly, the underlying link to the abstract approximation framework can be formalized as follows, where B ranges over sets of belief atoms and H is an approximate history for b:

$$\mathcal{O}_\mathsf{b}^\mathfrak{a}(H).Poss =_{def} \left\{ B\theta\sigma \mid B \xrightarrow{\theta}_{R_{\mathsf{sta}}} HC \text{ and } HC\sigma \in H \right\}. \tag{10.5}$$

In other words, once the agent developer has written a set R_{sta} of state approximation rules, he has implicitly and clearly stated what the state approximation, $\mathcal{O}_\mathsf{b}^\mathfrak{a}$ is that agent $\mathfrak{a}$ uses to reason about agent b.

Now the facts that may possibly belong to b's current state can be obtained simply by using the union $R_{\mathsf{sta}} \cup R_{\mathsf{his}}$, as shown by the next proposition.

PROPOSITION 10.5.1 $\mathcal{O}_\mathsf{b}^\mathfrak{a}(H_\mathsf{b}^\mathfrak{a}(h_\mathfrak{a})).Poss = \{B\theta\sigma \mid B \xrightarrow{\theta}_{R_{\mathsf{sta}} \cup R_{\mathsf{his}}} \chi_{\mathsf{hist}} \text{ and } \sigma \in \mathsf{Sol}(\chi_{\mathsf{hist}})\},$ where χ_{hist} ranges over history code call conditions.

Proof   First we prove the left-to-right inclusion. Assume that $B_0 \in \mathcal{O}_\mathsf{b}^\mathfrak{a}(H_\mathsf{b}^\mathfrak{a}(h_\mathfrak{a})).Poss$. By (10.5), this means that B_0 has the form $B\theta\sigma$ and for some history constraints *HC*, there is a derivation $B \xrightarrow{\theta}_{R_{\mathsf{sta}}} HC$ where $HC\sigma \in H_\mathsf{b}^\mathfrak{a}(h_\mathfrak{a})$.

This membership, by (10.4), implies that $HC\sigma$ has the form $HC'\theta'\sigma'$ and there is a derivation $HC' \xrightarrow[R_{his}]{\theta'} \chi_{hist}$ for some set of history constraints χ_{hist} with $\sigma' \in \text{Sol}(\chi_{hist})$.

By combining the ground instances of the two derivations we obtain a derivation $B_0 \xrightarrow[R_{sta}]{\theta_1} HC\sigma \xrightarrow[R_{his}]{\theta_2} \chi_{hist}\sigma'$, and hence, by setting $\theta'' = \theta_1 \circ \theta_2$, $\chi''_{hist} = \chi_{hist}\sigma'$ and $\sigma'' = \varepsilon$, where ε denotes the empty substitution, we obtain:

$$B_0 \xrightarrow[R_{sta} \cup R_{his}]{\theta''} \chi''_{hist},$$

where $\sigma'' \in \text{Sol}(\chi''_{hist})$. As a consequence,

$$B_0 \in \left\{ B\theta\sigma \mid B \xrightarrow[R_{sta} \cup R_{his}]{\theta} \chi_{hist} \text{ and } \sigma \in \text{Sol}(\chi_{hist}) \right\}.$$

Since B_0 is an arbitrary member of $\mathcal{O}_b^a(H_b^a(h_a)).Poss$, this proves that

$$\mathcal{O}_b^a(H_b^a(h_a)).Poss \subseteq \left\{ B\theta\sigma \mid B \xrightarrow[R_{sta} \cup R_{his}]{\theta} \chi_{hist} \text{ and } \sigma \in \text{Sol}(\chi_{hist}) \right\}.$$

We are left to show the opposite inclusion. For this purpose, suppose B_0 belongs to the right-hand-side of the above inclusion, that is, B_0 has the form $B\theta\sigma$, $B \xrightarrow[R_{sta} \cup R_{his}]{\theta} \chi_{hist}$ and $\sigma \in \text{Sol}(\chi_{hist})$.

This derivation can be reordered by postponing the application of R_{his}'s rules, and can be split into two segments, for some HC, θ_1 and θ_2, as follows:

$$B \xrightarrow[R_{sta}]{\theta_1} HC \xrightarrow[R_{his}]{\theta_2} \chi_{hist},$$

where $\theta = \theta_1 \circ \theta_2$. This is possible for two reasons:

1. By a well-known result in logic programming theory, called *independence from the selection rule*, we can invert the application of two rules in a derivation, provided that none of the two rules rewrites an atom introduced by the other rule.

2. The atoms in the body of R_{his}'s rules, by definition, never match the head of any rule in R_{sta}. So R_{his}'s rules can be delayed until all the necessary rules of R_{sta} have been applied.

Now the reader can easily verify (with (10.4) and (10.5)) that $HC\theta_2\sigma$ belongs to $H_b^a(h_a)$, and hence $B\theta\sigma$ (that equals B_0) belongs to $\mathcal{O}_b^a(H_b^a(h_a)).Poss$. This completes the proof. ∎

Example 10.5.8 (Implementing Agent Approximation: States (continued)) If R_{his} consists of rules (**r1**)–(**r4**), and R_{sta} contains only (**r5**), then the condition

$$B = \mathcal{B}_{autoPilot}(\text{b}, location\_at(\text{T}, \text{Pt})) \;\&\; \mathcal{B}_{autoPilot}(\text{b}, velocity\_at(\text{T}, \text{Vt}))$$

has three derivations $B \xrightarrow[R_{sta} \cup R_{his}]{\theta_i} \chi^i_{hist}$ ($i = 1, 2, 3$), where χ^i_{hist} and θ_i are as in Example 10.5.6 (the first two steps of these derivations apply (**r5**) twice, and transform B into the constraints *HC* of Example 10.5.6; the rest of the derivations coincide with those of Example 10.5.6).

The intuitive meaning of these derivations is: two facts approximated by *location_at*(T, Pt) and *velocity_at*(T, Vt) may be simultaneously stored in b's current state when any of the conditions χ_{hist}^i is satisfied. For instance, χ_{hist}^1 is satisfied whenever there exist X, Y, T′, T″, such that

$$X \neq autoPilot \,\&\, T \leq T' \,\&\, Y \neq autoPilot \,\&\, T \leq T''.$$

This is always possible, whenever there exists some agent different from autoPilot; under this assumption, our rules say that the facts (corresponding to) *location_at*(T,Pt) and *velocity_at*(T,Vt) may be part of b's current state.

However, $\mathcal{O}_b^a(H_b^a(h_a)).Poss$ is not exactly what is needed to overestimate the set of secrets violated by b. Recall that $\text{OViol}_b^a(h)$ depends on $\mathcal{O}_b^a(H_b^a(h_a)).New$. As expected, the field *New* is obtained automatically from *Poss*. Intuitively, a set of approximate facts $C = \{f_1, \ldots, f_n\}$ is *new* if it has been made true by a's *current answer*. In *IMPACT* terms, this means that the belief atoms $\mathcal{B}_a(b, f_1), \ldots, \mathcal{B}_a(b, f_n)$ should be derivable from a history condition χ_{hist} that refers to a's current answer.

Example 10.5.9 (Implementing Agent Approximations: New Facts) Consider again the derivations of Example 10.5.8. The first derivation leads to a condition χ_{hist}^1 that does not mention $\text{Hist}_{autoPilot}$. The intuitive reason is that in this derivation, the facts of *B* come from messages received from some X, Y different from autoPilot (because rules (**r1**) and (**r2**) are used). Therefore, as far as this derivation is concerned, *B* does not contain any new facts originated by autoPilot's current answer.

The second derivation leads to a condition χ_{hist}^2 that contains

in(Ev_1, $\text{Hist}_{autoPilot}$: *retrieve_answ*(autoPilot, b, *location_at*(T, Pt), _)).

If the last event Ev in $\text{Hist}_{autoPilot}$ matches the above condition, then (some of) the facts in *B* may have been created using autoPilot's current answer Ev (in this example, *location_at*(T, Pt) comes from Ev). Therefore, *B* might have just become true.

The third derivation leads to a condition χ_{hist}^3 that does not mention $\text{Hist}_{autoPilot}$, although *location_at*(T, Pt) actually comes from autoPilot. This happens because rule (**r4**) is used in that derivation; intuitively, this means that the answer of autoPilot's that originated *location_at*(T, Pt) is at least 60 minutes old, and hence it has been removed from $\text{Hist}_{autoPilot}$. Therefore, this fact cannot be new.

The above arguments concerning the second and third derivation would not be sound if the current answer were not stored in $\text{Hist}_{autoPilot}$. Some new facts might be missed.

More generally, this kind of arguments is correct if Hist_a is guaranteed to contain the current answer. We shall see later that the security check function enforces this condition by temporarily inserting the current answer into Hist_a (independently, after the security check, a may decide whether the answer should be stored in Hist_a or not).

Summarizing, if there is a solution $\sigma \in \mathsf{Sol}(\chi^2_{\mathsf{hist}})$ that binds Ev_1 to the last event of $\mathsf{Hist}_{\mathsf{autoPilot}}$, then $B\theta_2\sigma$ may be new, that is, $B\theta_2\sigma \in \mathcal{O}^a_b(H^a_b(h_a)).\mathit{New}$.

The above discussion leads us to adopt the following definition.

$$\mathcal{O}^a_b\big(H^a_b(h_a)\big).\mathit{New} =_{\mathit{def}} \big\{B\theta\sigma \mid B \xrightarrow{\theta}_{R_{\mathsf{sta}} \cup R_{\mathsf{his}}} \chi_{\mathsf{hist}},\ \sigma \in \mathsf{Sol}(\chi_{\mathsf{hist}}),\ \text{some}$$
$$\mathbf{in}(E, (\mathsf{Hist}_a : \mathit{retrieve\_answ}(a, b, \ldots))) \text{ belongs to } \chi_{\mathsf{hist}}\sigma$$
$$\text{and } E \text{ is the last event of } \mathsf{Hist}_a\big\}. \qquad (10.6)$$

Note that conditions $B \xrightarrow{\theta}_{R_{\mathsf{sta}} \cup R_{\mathsf{his}}} \chi_{\mathsf{hist}}$ and $\sigma \in \mathsf{Sol}(\chi_{\mathsf{hist}})$ state that $B\theta\sigma$ is in Poss (by Proposition 10.5.1); the other conditions say that χ_{hist} explicitly refers to the current answer of a to b (represented by E).

Implementing Consequence Approximation When the agent developer wishes to specify agent a's overestimation of b's consequence relation, OCN^a_b, he does so by writing a set R_{con} of *consequence overestimation rules*

$$\mathcal{B}_a(b, f) \leftarrow B_1 \,\&\, \ldots \,\&\, B_n,$$

where each B_i is either a belief atom of the form $\mathcal{B}_a(b, \ldots)$ or a comparison constraint $T_1 \text{ Op } T_2$.

The following is a simple example of R_{con}, extending the $\mathsf{autoPilot}$ example we have been using thus far.

Example 10.5.10 (Agent Approximation in IMPACT: Consequence Overest. I) Let us now introduce some stronger assumptions about b. Suppose it cannot be excluded that b may derive the current position, P_{now}, of $\mathsf{autoPilot}$, from some previous position P_t and velocity V_t (Example 10.1.5). Suppose, however, that $\mathsf{autoPilot}$'s trajectory changes very frequently, and hence if $t < \mathsf{now} - 10$, then we can safely assume that b cannot derive P_{now} from P_t and V_t. Then R_{con} consists of the following rule:

(**r6**) $\mathcal{B}_{\mathsf{autoPilot}}(\mathsf{b}, \mathit{location\_at}(\mathsf{now}, \mathsf{Pnow})) \leftarrow$
   $\mathcal{B}_{\mathsf{autoPilot}}(\mathsf{b}, \mathit{location\_at}(\mathsf{T}, \mathsf{Pt})) \,\&\,$
   $\mathcal{B}_{\mathsf{autoPilot}}(\mathsf{b}, \mathit{velocity\_at}(\mathsf{T}, \mathsf{Vt})) \,\&\,$
   $\mathsf{T} \geq \mathsf{now} - 10.$

Clearly, the correspondence between R_{con} and its abstract counterpart OCN_b^a can be formalized as follows. Let C and C' range over sets of approximate facts; then

$$OCN_b^a(C) =_{def} \{ \text{facts}(B\theta\sigma) \mid B \xrightarrow{\theta}_{R_{con}} C',\ \sigma \in \text{Sol}(\text{comc}C') \text{ and facts}(C')\sigma \subseteq C \}. \quad (10.7)$$

where $\text{comc}(C')$ is the set of comparison constraints in C' and $\text{facts}(C')$ is the set of facts occurring within the belief atoms of C'.

Example 10.5.11 (Implementing Agent Approximation: Consequence Overest. II) Let $C' = \mathcal{B}_{\text{autoPilot}}(b, location\_at(T, Pt))\ \&\ \mathcal{B}_{\text{autoPilot}}(b, velocity\_at(T, Vt))\ \&\ T \geq now - 10$ and $R_{con} = \{\mathbf{r6}\}$. Intuitively, C' means that autoPilot believes that its location and velocity at time $T \geq now - 10$ may be stored in b's state at some point. Under this assumption, it is estimated that b may derive $location\_at(now, Pnow)$, (i.e., autoPilot's current location), because of the following points:

- $\mathcal{B}_{\text{autoPilot}}(b, location\_at(now, Pnow)) \xrightarrow{\varepsilon}_{R_{con}} C'$, where ε is the empty substitution (the derivation consists of one application of (**r6**));
- $\text{comc}(C') = \{T \geq now - 10\}$;
- let t_0 be any number such that $t_0 \geq now - 10$; let $\sigma =_{def} [t_0/T]$; note that $\sigma \in \text{Sol}(\text{comc}(C'))$;
- $\text{facts}(\mathcal{B}_{\text{autoPilot}}(b, location\_at(now, Pnow))) = location\_at(now, Pnow)$, and
- $\text{facts}(C') = \{location\_at(T, Pt), velocity\_at(T, Vt)\}$;

and hence: $location\_at(now, Pnow) \in OCN_b^{\text{autoPilot}}(\{location\_at(t_0, Pt), velocity\_at(t_0, Vt)\})$.

Implementing Approximate Secrets The set of approximate secrets $AppSec_a(b)$ is represented in the *IMPACT* architecture by means of a set R_{sec} of *secret approximation rules*

$$\text{secret}_a(b, f) \leftarrow \chi_{cmp},$$

where f is an approximate fact from $\mathcal{L}_b^a$, and χ_{cmp} is a set of comparison constraints $T_1\ Op\ T_2$. Intuitively, the above rule means that f should be kept secret from b if χ_{cmp} is true. The link with the abstract framework is the following:

$$AppSec_a(b) =_{def} \{f\sigma \mid (\text{secret}_a(b, f) \leftarrow \chi_{cmp}) \in R_{sec} \text{ and } \sigma \in \text{Sol}(\chi_{cmp})\}. \quad (10.8)$$

Example 10.5.12 (Implementing Agent Approximation: Secrets) In our example we have one secret, declared by the following rule:

(**r7**) $\quad \text{secret}_a(b, location\_at(T, P)) \leftarrow T = now.$

Clearly, in order to show that a secret is violated, one has to derive *both* f and χ_{cmp}, simultaneously. Thus, the above rules will be used to generate conditions of the form $\mathcal{B}_a(b, f)$ & χ_{cmp}. Once implemented, the *IMPACT* security system will try to prove such conditions using the other rules and the history component.

Implementing Approximate Violations Summarizing, in *IMPACT* approximation of b used by a a set of rules of various sorts, as specified by the following definition.

DEFINITION 10.5.4 (AGENT APPROXIMATION PROGRAM, $\mathbf{AAP}_b^a$) The agent approximation program $\mathbf{AAP}_b^a$ is a set of rules with the following possible forms:

history approximation rules $PHC \leftarrow \chi_{\text{hist}}$;

state approximation rules $\mathcal{B}_a(b, f) \leftarrow HC$;

consequence approximation rules $\mathcal{B}_a(b, f) \leftarrow B_1 \& \ldots \& B_n$;

secrets approximation rules $\text{secret}_a(b, f) \leftarrow \chi_{\text{cmp}}$;

where $f \in \mathcal{L}_b^a$, *PHC* is a pure history constraint, χ_{hist} is a history code call condition, *HC* is a set of history constraints, each B_i is either a belief atom of the form $\mathcal{B}_a(b, \ldots)$ or a comparison constraint T_1 Op T_2, and χ_{cmp} is a set of comparison constraints.

The theorem below shows that the set of secrets violated by b at h_a can be obtained by computing derivations from $\mathbf{AAP}_b^a$.

THEOREM 10.5.1 (VIOLATED SECRETS AS COMPUTATIONS FROM $\mathbf{AAP}_b^a$) Let χ_{hist} range over history conditions. Then

$$\text{OViol}_b^a(h_a) = \big\{ f\theta\sigma \mid (\text{secret}_a(b, f) \leftarrow \chi_{\text{cmp}}) \in \mathbf{AAP}_b^a,$$
$$\mathcal{B}_a(b, f) \& \chi_{\text{cmp}} \xrightarrow{\theta}_{\mathbf{AAP}_b^a} \chi_{\text{hist}}, \ \sigma \in \text{Sol}(\chi_{\text{hist}}),$$
$$\text{some } \mathbf{in}(E, \text{Hist}_a : \textit{retrieve\_answ}(a, b, \ldots)) \text{ belongs to } \chi_{\text{hist}}\sigma \text{ and}$$
$$E \text{ is the last event of } \text{Hist}_a \big\}.$$

Proof Let $f_0 \in \mathcal{L}_b^a$ be an arbitrary approximate fact. By definition, $f_0 \in \text{OViol}_b^a(h_a)$ iff $f_0 \in \bigcup \{OCN_b^a(C) \mid C \in \mathcal{O}_b^a(H_b^a(h_a)).New\}$ and $f_0 \in AppSec_a(b)$.

By analogy with the proof of Proposition 10.5.1, the reader may easily verify (using equations (10.7) and (10.6)) that f_0 belongs to some of the above sets $OCN_b^a(C)$ iff f_0 has the form $f\theta\sigma$ and

1. $\mathcal{B}_a(b, f) \xrightarrow{\theta}_{R_{\text{con}} \cup R_{\text{sta}} \cup R_{\text{his}}} \chi_{\text{hist}}$ with $\sigma \in \text{Sol}(\chi_{\text{hist}})$;

2. there exists a code call condition $\mathbf{in}(E, \text{Hist}_a : \textit{retrieve\_answ}(a, b, \ldots))$ in $\chi_{\text{hist}}\sigma$ such that E is the last event of Hist_a.

Moreover, by (10.8), f_0 belongs to $AppSec_a(b)$ iff f_0 has the form $f'\sigma'$ and R_{sec} contains a rule

$$\texttt{secret}_a(b, f) \leftarrow \chi_{cmp}$$

such that $\sigma' \in \textsf{Sol}(\chi_{cmp})$. As a consequence of 1) and 2), we obtain the two points below:

a) Assume $f_0 \in \textsf{OViol}_b^a$. Then, since $\mathbf{AAP}_b^a \supseteq R_{con} \cup R_{sta} \cup R_{his}$, the derivation in 1) is also a derivation $\mathcal{B}_a(b, f) \longrightarrow_{\mathbf{AAP}_b^a}^{\theta} \chi_{hist}\sigma$. Consider a ground instance $\mathcal{B}_a(b, f_0) \longrightarrow_{\mathbf{AAP}_b^a}^{\varepsilon} \chi_{hist}\sigma$ of the above derivation. It can be immediately extended to $\mathcal{B}_a(b, f_0) \& \chi_{cmp}\sigma' \longrightarrow_{\mathbf{AAP}_b^a}^{\varepsilon} \chi_{hist}\sigma \& \chi_{cmp}\sigma'$, by appending $\& \chi_{cmp}\sigma'$ to each goal. Now, note that the empty substitution ε is in $\textsf{Sol}(\chi_{hist}\sigma \& \chi_{cmp}\sigma')$, and that $\chi_{hist}\sigma \& \chi_{cmp}\sigma'$ contains a code call condition $\mathbf{in}(E, \textsf{Hist}_a : \textit{retrieve\_answ}(a, b, \ldots))$ such that E is the last event of $\textsf{Hist}_a$.

By a standard logic programming result, this derivation can be "lifted" to a derivation $\mathcal{B}_a(b, f) \& \chi_{cmp} \longrightarrow_{\mathbf{AAP}_b^a}^{\theta'} \chi'_{hist}$. Clearly, χ'_{hist} has a solution σ'' such that $\chi'_{hist}\sigma''$ contains a code call condition $\mathbf{in}(E, \textsf{Hist}_a : \textit{retrieve\_answ}(a, b, \ldots))$ where E is the last event of $\textsf{Hist}_a$. This proves that f_0 belongs to the right-hand-side of the equation in this theorem's statement.

b) Conversely, suppose that f_0 belongs to the right-hand-side of the equation in the theorem's statement. Then we have $\mathcal{B}_a(b, f) \& \chi_{cmp} \longrightarrow_{\mathbf{AAP}_b^a}^{\theta} \chi_{hist}$, $\sigma \in \textsf{Sol}(\chi_{hist})$, and for some call $\mathbf{in}(E, \textsf{Hist}_a : \textit{retrieve\_answ}(a, b, \ldots))$ in $\chi_{hist}\sigma$, E is the last event of $\textsf{Hist}_a$. From this derivation, by dropping the part corresponding to χ_{cmp} from each goal, we obtain a derivation $\mathcal{B}_a(b, f) \longrightarrow_{\mathbf{AAP}_b^a}^{\theta} \chi'_{hist}$, where $\chi'_{hist}\sigma$ still contains the above code call condition (the part removed from χ_{hist} consists only of pure comparison constraints). The above derivation cannot use rules from R_{sec} (which match neither the initial goal nor the bodies of $\mathbf{AAP}_b^a - R_{sec}$); therefore, it is also a derivation $\mathcal{B}_a(b, f) \longrightarrow_{R_{con} \cup R_{sta} \cup R_{his}}^{\theta} \chi'_{hist}$.

It follows by 1) and 2) that $f_0 \in \bigcup \{OCN_b^a(C) \mid C \in \mathcal{O}_b^a(H_b^a(h_a)).New\}$. Moreover, note that χ_{hist} contains $\chi_{cmp}\theta$ and σ is a solution of χ_{hist}, so $\theta\sigma$ is a solution to χ_{cmp}. It follows, by (10.8), that $f\theta\sigma$—that is, f_0—is in $AppSec_a(b)$.

We may conclude that $f_0 \in \textsf{OViol}_b^a(h_a)$.

From a) and b) we immediately derive that f_0 belongs to the left-hand-side of the equation in the theorem's statement iff it belongs to the right-hand-side. This completes the proof. ∎

Example 10.5.13 (Implementing Agent Approximation: Dynamic Check) In our example, $\mathbf{AAP}_b^{autoPilot}$ consists of rules (**r1**)–(**r7**). The unique secret is specified by (**r7**), thus the security check is only concerned with derivations starting from the corresponding condition $G_0 = \mathcal{B}_{autoPilot}(b, \textit{location\_at}(\texttt{T}, \texttt{P})) \& \texttt{T} = \texttt{now}$. Only one of such derivations reaches a history condition χ_{hist} that mentions $\textsf{Hist}_{autoPilot}$. Such derivation uses rules (**r6**), (**r5**),

(r5), **(r3)**, **(r2)**, and yields a condition of the form

$\chi_{\text{hist}} = \textbf{in}(\text{Ev}_4, \text{Hist}_{\text{autoPilot}} : \textit{retrieve\_answ}(\text{autoPilot}, b, \textit{location\_at}(T_1, Pt_1), \_)) \&$

$T3_4 \geq \text{Ev}_4.\text{time} \&$

$Y_5 \neq \text{autoPilot} \& T_1 < T2_5 \&$

$T_1 \geq \text{now} - 10 \&$

$T = \text{now}.$

After evaluating the above code call to $\text{Hist}_{\text{autoPilot}}$, one can always set $T3_4 := \text{Ev}_4.\text{time}$, $Y_5 := c$, $T2_5 := T_1 + 1$, and $T := \text{now}$. Subsequently, the only constraint that might not be satisfied is the following $T_1 \geq \text{now} - 10$. Therefore, χ_{hist} has a solution if and only if the code call *retrieve_answ* finds an answer message from autoPilot to b containing a fact $\textit{location\_at}(T_1, Pt_1)$ where $T_1 \geq \text{now} - 10$.

Data security, however, is violated only if the answer message found by *retrieve_answ* is the last message of $\text{Hist}_{\text{autoPilot}}$.

Intuitively, all this means that if autoPilot tries to send b a location P_t less than 10 minutes old, then a security violation is detected. A closer look at the rules used in the derivation reveals that $\textbf{AAP}_b^{\text{autoPilot}}$ "discovers" that b might combine P_t with velocity V_t coming from another agent $Y_5 \neq \text{autoPilot}$, and derive autoPilot's current position.

The agent approximation program $\textbf{AAP}_b^a$ may be interpreted with logic programming techniques, but in general the resulting overhead may be unacceptable. Fortunately, $\textbf{AAP}_b^a$ can be *compiled* into tables that can be searched efficiently. Essentially, all the derivations are performed at compile time (perhaps using a bottom up fixpoint procedure similar to that introduced later in Chapter 12 instead of using resolution), while the evaluation of history conditions is deferred until run-time. The following function compiles $\textbf{AAP}_b^a$ into an *overestimated violation table* $\textbf{OVT}^a$, which is a set of tuples

$\langle b, f, \chi_{\text{hist}} \rangle$

where b is an agent name, f is an approximate fact from $\mathcal{L}_b^a$, and χ_{hist} is a history condition. The intended meaning of the above entry is that for all $\sigma \in \text{Sol}(\chi_{\text{hist}})$, $f\sigma$ belongs to $\text{OViol}_b^a(h_a)$.

DEFINITION 10.5.5 Function $\text{SecP}_a : \textit{CompileAAP}(\textbf{AAP}_b^a)$ sets $\textbf{OVT}^a$ to the set of all tuples $\langle b, f, \chi_{\text{hist}} \rangle$ such that:

1. $(\text{secret}_a(b, f) \leftarrow \chi_{\text{cmp}}) \in \textbf{AAP}_b^a;$

2. $(\mathcal{B}_a(b,f) \,\&\, \chi_{cmp}) \xrightarrow{mg\ \theta} _{\mathbf{AAP}_b^a} \chi_{hist}$ and χ_{hist} is a history condition;
3. the set of comparison constraints in χ_{hist} is satisfiable.

Example 10.5.14 (Implementing Agent Approximation: Violation Table) In our example $\mathbf{OVT}_{now}^a$ would contain the tuple $\langle b, location\_at(now, P), \chi_{hist} \rangle$, where χ_{hist} is the history condition illustrated in Example 10.5.13. The set of comparison constraints in χ_{hist} can be satisfied by setting: $T3_4 := \mathtt{Ev_4.time}$, $Y_5 := c$, $T2_5 := T_1 + 1$, $T := now$, and $T_1 := now - 9$.

Table $\mathbf{OVT}^a$ is searched by another function, $(SecP_a:DynOViol(b, Ans))$, that computes $\mathsf{OViol}_b^a(h_a \cdot e)$ with the algorithm illustrated below. Here, e is an event corresponding to a's current answer Ans to b.

Note that function $(SecP_a:DynOViol())$ does not modify Hist_a permanently; it checks only whether some secret would be violated if Ans were returned to b.

The following theorem states the correctness of the above functions.

THEOREM 10.5.2 (CORRECTNESS OF DYNAMIC SECURITY CHECK) Let $\mathbf{OVT}^a$ be the table constructed by $(SecP_a : CompileAAP(\mathbf{AAP}_b^a))$, and let e be an answer message from a to b with answer Ans. Then

$$\mathsf{OViol}_b^a(h_a \cdot e) = SecP_a : DynOViol(b, Ans).$$

Proof By Theorem 10.5.1 and Definition 10.5.5, an approximate fact f_0 is in $\mathsf{OViol}_b^a(h_a)$ iff there exist a triple $\langle b, f, \chi_{hist} \rangle$ in $\mathbf{OVT}^a$ and a substitution $\sigma \in \mathsf{Sol}(\chi_{hist})$ such that

1. $f\sigma = f_0$;
2. $\chi_{hist}\sigma$ contains some code call condition $\mathbf{in}(E, \mathsf{Hist}_a : retrieve\_answ(a, b, \ldots))$ where E is the last event of Hist_a.

Now, Algorithm 10.5.1 clearly returns all and only the $f\sigma$ satisfying the above properties. The theorem follows immediately. ■

Remark 9 Programmers may fill in $\mathbf{OVT}_{now}^a$ as they prefer (at their own risk), thereby tailoring dynamic security checks to the given application. The compilation mechanism provided by the *IMPACT* architecture has the advantage that it is directly linked to a methodology that formally guarantees data security preservation.

Implementing Static and Combined Security Verification The history conditions χ_{hist} in $\mathbf{OVT}^a$ cannot be evaluated before running a. Moreover, the results of Section 10.4 show that it is impossible to predict in advance the possible histories of a. Nonetheless, static security checks can be based on an estimate of a's future behavior, which in the

> **Algorithm 10.5.1 (Dynamic Security Check)**
> $\text{SecP}_a : \text{DynOViol}(b : \text{AgentName}, \text{Ans} : \text{Answer})$
>
> (⋆ output: an overestimation $\text{OVT}^a_{\text{now}}$ of the set of secrets ⋆)
> (⋆ that would be violated if Ans were returned to b   ⋆)
>
> $\text{OVT}^a_{\text{now}} := \emptyset;$
>   (⋆ Hist_a is temporarily extended with answer message e ⋆)
> $e := \textbf{new}(\textit{AnswerMessage});$
> $e.\text{sender} := a;$
> $e.\text{receiver} := b;$
> $e.\text{answer} := \text{Ans};$
> $e.\text{SendTime} := \text{now};$
>   **execute** *insert_answ(e)*;
>   (⋆ OVT^a's tuples are evaluated against the extended history ⋆)
>   **for all** tuples $\langle b, f, \chi_{\text{hist}} \rangle$ in OVT^a **do**
>   **for all** σ in $\text{Sol}(\chi_{\text{hist}})$ **do**
>   **for all** in$(V, \text{Hist}_a : \textit{retrieve\_answ}(\ldots))$ in $\chi_{\text{hist}}\sigma$ **do**
>   **if** $V = e$ **then** $\text{OVT}^a_{\text{now}} := \text{OVT}^a_{\text{now}} \cup \{f\sigma\};$
>   (⋆ Hist_a is restored ⋆)
>   **execute** *delete(e)*;
>   **return**($\text{OVT}^a_{\text{now}}$);
> **end.**

abstract framework is captured by a set of histories $\text{pos}\mathcal{H}'_a$ (Section 10.3.9). In the *IMPACT* architecture, a's possible future histories can be estimated by means of a set, R_{slf}, of *self-approximation rules* having the form

in$(e, \text{Hist}_a : \textit{fun}(\text{args})) \leftarrow \chi_{\text{cmp}},$

where *fun* is one of the functions of package Hist_a, *args* is a suitable list of arguments, and χ_{cmp} is a comparison constraint. These rules should describe the conditions χ_{cmp} under which the head may become true.

Example 10.5.15 (Self-approximation Rules) Suppose our agent autoPilot implements the service returning its old locations with the following service rule:

(**r_loc**)   *location_at*(T, Pt) ← T ≤ now − 11 & $\chi_{\textit{location\_at}}$,

where $\chi_{\textit{location\_at}}$ is the code call that actually computes Pt. Clearly, with this implementation, all answers of the form *location_at*(T, Pt) satisfy T ≤ now − 11. In general, the comparison constraints occurring in the service rules can be used to restrict, a priori, the possible future answers for a. In our example we can write

(**r8**)   in(E, $\text{Hist}_{\text{autoPilot}}$: *retrieve_answ*(autoPilot, b, *location_at*(T, P), W))
      ← T ≤ now − 11.

The problem of deciding whether some answer event e can be the last event of Hist_a at some future point is solved with a technical device. Let χ_{hist} be the final step of a derivation from $\mathbf{AAP}_b^a$. For each code call $\mathbf{in}(e, \text{Hist}_a : \mathit{fun}(\ldots, w))$ in χ_{hist}, the following constraints are added to χ_{hist}:

- $e.\texttt{time} \leq \texttt{now}$;
- if w has the form $\texttt{Op}\ t$, then $e.\texttt{time}\ \texttt{Op}\ t$ is added to χ_{hist}.

Clearly, the above constraints will always be true at run-time. During static verification they enforce the intended meaning of $\texttt{now}$ and of the time specification parameter w with conditions that can be evaluated statically. Moreover, for the selected code condition $\chi_0 = \mathbf{in}(e, \text{Hist}_a : \mathit{retrieve\_answ}(\texttt{args}))$ in χ_{hist} (if any), the constraint

- $e.\texttt{time} = \texttt{now}$

is added to χ_{hist}. This constraint will be true at run-time only if e is the last event of Hist_a. The resulting, extended set of constraints is denoted by:

$\text{ext}_{\text{now}}(\chi_{\text{hist}}, \chi_0)$.

Intuitively, if for all derivations $\text{ext}_{\text{now}}(\chi_{\text{hist}}, \chi_0) \xrightarrow{\theta}_{R_{\text{slf}}} \chi_{\text{cmp}}$ the comparison constraints χ_{cmp} are unsatisfiable, then e cannot be the last event of a's history, at any point. If some χ_{cmp} is satisfiable, then e *might* be bound to the last event of Hist_a, sooner or later.

Example 10.5.16 (Static Security Check) Consider the derivation $G_0 \xrightarrow{\theta}_{\mathbf{AAP}_b^{\text{autoPilot}}} \chi_{\text{hist}}$, illustrated in Example 10.5.13. In this case, χ_{hist} contains one call to $\text{Hist}_{\text{autoPilot}}$, namely,

$\chi_0 =_{\mathit{def}} \mathbf{in}(\text{Ev}_4, \text{Hist}_{\text{autoPilot}} : \mathit{retrieve\_answ}(\text{autoPilot}, b, \mathit{location\_at}(\text{T}_1, \text{Pt}_1), \_))$.

Thus, the extended condition in this example is:

$\text{ext}_{\text{now}}(\chi_{\text{hist}}, \chi_0) = \chi_{\text{hist}}\ \&\ \text{Ev}_4.\texttt{time} \leq \texttt{now}\ \&\ \text{Ev}_4.\texttt{time} = \texttt{now}$.

If the last parameter of *retrieve_answ* were—say—"$> \text{T}_9$", then $\text{ext}_{\text{now}}(\chi_{\text{hist}}, \chi_0)$ would contain also a constraint $\text{Ev}_4.\texttt{time} > \text{T}_9$.

Now, the extended condition $\text{ext}_{\text{now}}(\chi_{\text{hist}}, \chi_0)$ can be evaluated using (**r8**), which yields the set of comparison constraints

$\chi_{\text{cmp}} = \text{T}_1 \leq \texttt{now} - 11\ \&$
$\quad\quad\ \text{T3}_4 \geq \text{Ev}_4.\texttt{time}\ \&$
$\quad\quad\ \text{Y}_5 \neq \text{autoPilot}\ \&\ \text{T}_1 < \text{T2}_5\ \&$
$\quad\quad\ \text{T}_1 \geq \texttt{now} - 10\ \&$
$\quad\quad\ \text{T} = \texttt{now}\ \&$

        Ev$_4$.time $\leq$ now &

        Ev$_4$.time $=$ now.

The first row comes from (**r8**), while the others were already in ext$_{\text{now}}$(χ_{hist}, χ_0). This set of constraints is not satisfiable, because it contains the mutually incompatible constraints T$_1$ $\leq$ now $-$ 11 and T$_1$ $\geq$ now $-$ 10. Thus, our static security check proves that this service (*location_at*) is secure as far as b is concerned. We recall the main assumptions (encoded in the approximation rules) that support this result:

- agent b may get all sorts of information from agents different from autoPilot;
- b's state may contain any subset (possibly all) of the data obtained from other agents;
- b may derive autoPilot's current position from previous position and velocity not older than 10 minutes.

The security check certifies that under the above conditions, b will never violate autoPilot's current position *because of* autoPilot*'s answers*. The approximation of autoPilot itself (R_{slf}) introduces no further assumptions, because it has been derived from autoPilot's service rules, which are known.

Note that χ_{hist} has one extension ext$_{\text{now}}$(χ_{hist}, χ_0) for each condition χ_0 = **in**(e, Hist$_a$: *retrieve_answ*(args)) in χ_{hist}; the set of all such ext$_{\text{now}}$(χ_{hist}, χ_0) will be denoted by EXT$_{\text{now}}$(χ_{hist}).

We are now in a position to define the function for static security verification. Conceptually, this function extends the derivations from **AAP**$_b^a$ with derivations from R_{slf}, until a set of comparison constraints χ_{cmp} is obtained. If χ_{cmp} is satisfiable, then a security violation may occur. In practice, the function below exploits the compiled derivations stored in **OVT**^{a}, and computes only the derivations from R_{slf}. It returns a modified violation table **OVT**$_{\text{opt}}^a$ corresponding to possible security violations.

Intuitively, if $\langle$b, f, $\chi_{\text{hist}}\rangle$ $\in$ **OVT**$_{\text{opt}}^a$, then χ_{hist} might become true at some future point in time (according to R_{slf}), and in that case, b might violate f. In other words, the static security check coincides with

SecP$_a$: *StaticOViol*(b) = $\emptyset$.

Example 10.5.17 (Static Security Check, continued) We have seen in Example 10.5.16 that the only derivation involving Hist$_{\text{autoPilot}}$ leads (with (**r8**)) to an unsatisfiable conjunction of comparison constraints χ_{cmp}. In this case, Sol(χ_{cmp}) = $\emptyset$ and hence no tuple is added to **OVT**$_{\text{opt}}^a$ (see the above algorithm). The other derivations never mention Hist$_{\text{autoPilot}}$; this implies that EXT$_{\text{now}}$(χ_{hist}) = $\emptyset$; therefore, no tuples of **OVT**$_{\text{opt}}^a$ are obtained from such

Section 10.5   IMPACT Security Implementation Architecture   389

Algorithm 10.5.2 (Static Security Check)
$\text{SecP}_a: \textit{StaticOViol}(\text{b:AgentName})$

($\star$ output: a modified table $\textbf{OVT}^a_{\text{opt}}$ $\star$)

$\quad \textbf{OVT}^a_{\text{opt}} := \emptyset;$
$\quad$($\star$ $\textbf{OVT}^a$'s tuples are evaluated using R_{slf} $\star$)
$\quad$**for all** tuples $\langle b, f, \chi_{\text{hist}} \rangle$ **in** $\textbf{OVT}^a$ **do**
$\quad\quad$**for all** $\chi'_{\text{hist}} \in \text{EXT}_{\text{now}}(\chi_{\text{hist}})$ **do**
$\quad\quad\quad$**for all** deriv. $\chi'_{\text{hist}} \xrightarrow[R_{\text{slf}}]{\text{mg } \theta} \chi_{\text{cmp}}$ such that χ_{cmp} is a comparison constraint
$\quad\quad\quad\quad$**do if** $\text{Sol}(\chi_{\text{cmp}}) \neq \emptyset$ **then** $\textbf{OVT}^a_{\text{opt}} := \textbf{OVT}^a_{\text{opt}} \cup \{\langle b, f, \chi_{\text{hist}} \rangle\};$
$\quad$**return**($\textbf{OVT}^a_{\text{opt}}$);
end.

---

derivations. It follows that

$\text{SecP}_{\text{autoPilot}}: \textit{StaticOViol}(\text{b}) = \emptyset,$

and hence, autoPilot is statically secure.

Example 10.5.18 (Static Security Check, continued) If agent autoPilot had also another service rule

$(\mathbf{r\_loc'}) \quad \textit{location\_at}(\text{T}, \text{Pt}) \leftarrow \text{T} \leq \text{now} - 7 \ \& \ \chi',$

(where χ' computes Pt) then R_{slf} should be extended with a corresponding rule

$(\mathbf{r8'}) \quad \textbf{in}(\text{E}, \text{Hist}_{\text{autoPilot}}: \textit{retrieve\_answ}(\text{autoPilot}, \text{b}, \textit{location\_at}(\text{T}, \text{P}), \text{W})$
$\quad\quad \leftarrow \text{T} \leq \text{now} - 7.$

Now there would be another derivation $\chi_{\text{hist}} \xrightarrow[R_{\text{slf}}]{\theta} \chi'_{\text{cmp}}$ (where χ_{hist} is defined as in Example 10.5.13), such that

$\chi'_{\text{cmp}} = \text{T}_1 \leq \text{now} - 7 \ \&$
$\quad\quad \text{T3}_4 \geq \text{Ev}_4.\text{time} \ \&$
$\quad\quad \text{Y}_5 \neq \text{autoPilot} \ \& \ \text{T}_1 < \text{T2}_5 \ \&$
$\quad\quad \text{T}_1 \geq \text{now} - 10 \ \&$
$\quad\quad \text{T} = \text{now} \ \&$
$\quad\quad \text{Ev}_4.\text{time} \leq \text{now} \ \&$
$\quad\quad \text{Ev}_4.\text{time} = \text{now}.$

These comparison constraints are satisfiable with any T_1 such that $\text{now} - 10 \leq T_1 \leq \text{now} - 7$, and hence

$\text{SecP}_{\text{autoPilot}} : \textit{StaticOViol}(b) = \{\langle b, \textit{location\_at}(\text{now}, P), \chi_{\text{hist}}\rangle\}.$

This means that autoPilot may indirectly disclose the secret: $\textit{location\_at}(\text{now}, P)$, if condition χ_{hist} becomes true at some point (i.e., if autoPilot returns to b a position P_t "younger" than 10 minutes).

Another way of describing $\text{SecP}_a : \textit{StaticOViol}(b)$ is: this function *optimizes* $\mathbf{OVT}^a$ by removing all entries whose history conditions will never be satisfied (according to the self-approximation rules R_{slf}). Thus, under the assumption that R_{slf} is correct, *static and dynamic security verification can be combined* simply by substituting $\mathbf{OVT}^a_{\text{opt}}$ for $\mathbf{OVT}^a$ in $\text{SecP}_a : \textit{DynOViol}()$, with the following obvious advantages:

- dynamic security verification becomes more efficient, because less entries have to be considered;

- the resulting distortion policy is in general more cooperative than a statically secure distortion, because those services which are not guaranteed to be secure at compile time (given the necessarily imprecise predictions about a's future histories) are given another choice at run-time, instead of being restricted a priori.

In the scenario of Example 10.5.17, the combined check would return an empty table $\mathbf{OVT}^a_{\text{opt}}$; this would automatically turn off run-time verification. The scenario of Example 10.5.18 is less fortunate: there, $\mathbf{OVT}^a_{\text{opt}}$ coincides with $\mathbf{OVT}^a$, and no advantage is obtained at run-time. The reader may easily find intermediate cases where $\emptyset \subset \mathbf{OVT}^a_{\text{opt}} \subset \mathbf{OVT}^a$.

10.5.3 Explanations

When static security verification returns a non-empty table $\mathbf{OVT}^a_{\text{opt}}$, a's programmers have several options.

- They may restrict a's services, in order to obtain a statically secure distortion. For instance, in Example 10.5.18, an inspection of rule (**r8'**) used in the derivation shows that security might be violated because the service rule (**r_loc'**) may return a location which is not older than 10 minutes. The obvious solution is to replace the first condition in the body of (**r_loc'**) by $T < \text{now} - 10$.

- Programmers may refine b's approximation and self-approximation rules, to obtain sharper estimates of a's and b's behavior, hoping that a's service will turn out to be statically secure w.r.t. the refined approximations. For instance, as a first approximation, R_{slf} might be set to

(**r8″**)   **in**(E, $\text{Hist}_{\text{autoPilot}}$: *retrieve_answ*(autoPilot, b, *location_at*(T, P), W)) ← **true**.

With this rule, a potential security violation would be detected statically. A closer look at the rules used in the derivation might reveal that variable T in (**r8″**) can be restricted, and (**r8″**) would be replaced by (**r8**).

• Programmers may adopt the combined approach illustrated in a previous section, and postpone the verification of the entries of $\textbf{OVT}^{\alpha}_{\text{opt}}$ to run-time.

In order to choose between the above alternatives, programmers need some details about *how* potential violations have been derived. This is called an *explanation*, and consists of the sequence $r_1\theta_1, \ldots, r_m\theta_m$ of rules that have been applied in the derivation. Each entry of $\textbf{OVT}^{\alpha}$ and $\textbf{OVT}^{\alpha}_{\text{opt}}$ is labeled with the corresponding explanation; moreover, rules may be labeled with a description of their role (in English, HTML or other formats). When finished, *IMPACT* will provide interactive tools for browsing explanations and related information. It should be noted that explanation mechanisms may play an important role in the design of secure services and agent approximations.

10.5.4 Action Security

In the *IMPACT* security architecture, the set $ASec_a(b)$ of forbidden action sequences can be described by a list of *action security directives* of the form:

forbid <regular expr> **repair** $\{\alpha_1, \ldots, \alpha_n\}$ **where** χ,

where <regular expr> is a regular expression (see below) that describes the forbidden sequence. The rest of the directive (which is optional) says that the last action of the forbidden sequence should be replaced by the set of all actions $\alpha_i \sigma$ such that $\sigma \in \text{Sol}(\chi)$ ($1 \leq i \leq n$). For instance, these actions may provide an alternative service to b (in the spirit of *maximally cooperative distortions*, see Section 10.2.4), or "repair" the effects of the forbidden sequence. As an example of an alternative service, a forbidden *Unix* command ls, that would let b see all the contents of the current directory, may be replaced by a restricted action ls <filename 1>···<filename n>, that would show only allowed files. A repair action might be some form of *undo* or *rollback* operation (when possible).

Regular expressions consist of action names, composed with the operators ';' (sequence), '*' (closure) and '|' (alternative), that can be nested arbitrarily (';' and '|' are binary and infix, while '*' is unary and postfix). The arguments of an action may be left unspecified, using the wildcard '_'. For example, the expression

open(_,rw); read(_)*; (send(b,_)|write(_))

denotes all the sequences where a file is open in read/write mode, then a (possibly empty) number of read operations is performed, and finally either a message is sent back to b, or a write operation is performed.

Example 10.5.19 Suppose agent a is willing to manipulate files upon requests from b, with the limitation that not more than one file may be simultaneously open. In case of violations, a may be cooperative and close the first file before opening the second. This may be obtained with a directive like

forbid open(_, _); (read(_, _) | write(_, _) | seek(_, _))*; open(_, _)
    repair {close(OldFile), open(NewFile, Mode)}
    where in(OldFile, a : OpenFileTable(b)) & **O** open(NewFile, Mode).

Action security directives can be expressed also with an alternative syntax:

forbid α' **when** χ' **repair** $\{\alpha_1, \ldots, \alpha_n\}$ **where** χ.

Here the forbidden sequence is any sequence $\alpha'_1, \ldots, \alpha'_k, \alpha'$ such that $\alpha'_1, \ldots, \alpha'_k$ leave agent a in a state that makes χ' true.

Example 10.5.20 An autoPilot agent should obey a request to change the plane's trajectory only if the request does not put the plane in a dangerous situation. For example, suppose the minimal safe altitude is minAlt. If the plane is already at that altitude, a request to move to a lower altitude should be ignored. Then, the set $ASec_{\text{autoPilot}}(ground\_control)$ should contain a directive such as

forbid setAltitude(Delta)
    when in(Alt, a : *getAltitude*()) & Alt + Delta < minAlt,

(note that no repair action is specified here, so the forbidden action is simply ignored).

An equivalence relation over actions may be specified by an agent developer in *IMPACT* by means of *equivalence directives* (to be implemented) of the form

$\alpha_1 = \alpha_2$.

The equivalence relation may be pre-processed by replacing action names with compound regular expressions in forbidden sequences. For instance, the equivalence directive ls X = dir X would cause each occurrence of 'ls .' to be replaced by (ls . | dir .). The equivalence directive fput(stdin,X) = put(X) would cause each occurrence of put(_) to be replaced by (fput(stdin,_)|put(_)).

Section 10.5 IMPACT Security Implementation Architecture

The given set of action security directives can be compiled into a finite state automaton plus a set of action rules. The automaton recognizes forbidden sequences, while action rules replace the last action in the forbidden sequence with the corresponding repair action. More precisely, package $SecP_a$ provides the following functions:

$SecP_a : CompileActDir$(`<directives file>`). This function constructs a finite state automaton (a C program) which takes a stream of actions as input, and returns an integer i whenever it recognizes an instance of the i-th directive's forbidden sequence. This value can be read with the function *Forbidden* specified below. For each directive

$r_i =$ **forbid** `<regular expr>` **repair** $\{\alpha_1, \ldots, \alpha_n\}$ **where** χ,

CompileActDir produces also the rules

$\mathbf{W}X \leftarrow \mathbf{O}X \mathbin{\&} \mathbf{in}(i, SecP_a : Forbidden(X))$,
$\mathbf{O}\alpha_j \leftarrow \mathbf{O}X \mathbin{\&} \mathbf{in}(i, SecP_a : Forbidden(X)) \mathbin{\&} \chi \quad (j = 1 \ldots n).$

Intuitively, the first rule blocks (waives) the last action X of the forbidden sequence, while the other rules trigger the repair actions α_i, whose parameters may have been instantiated by evaluating χ. Note that the two rules are triggered only when action X completes an instance of `<regular expr>`, as checked by $\mathbf{in}(i, SecP_a : Forbidden(X))$. This check is performed only on the actions X that are obligatory—because $\mathbf{O}X$ holds—, and hence about to be executed. Similarly, for each directive

$r_i =$ **forbid** α' **when** χ' **repair** $\{\alpha_1, \ldots, \alpha_n\}$ **where** χ,

CompileActDir produces the rules

$\mathbf{W}X \leftarrow \mathbf{O}X \mathbin{\&} \mathbf{in}(i, SecP_a : Forbidden(X)) \mathbin{\&} \chi'$,
$\mathbf{O}\alpha_j \leftarrow \mathbf{O}X \mathbin{\&} \mathbf{in}(i, SecP_a : Forbidden(X)) \mathbin{\&} \chi' \mathbin{\&} \chi.$

$SecP_a : Forbidden(\texttt{Act})$. This function feeds action `Act` to the automaton, which returns i if the last actions executed, followed by `Act`, constitute an instance of the regular expression specified in the i-th directive. If the sequence matches two or more directives, then the least index i is returned. If no directive is matched an ok value is returned. The automaton's state is then restored to the previous value (i.e., the effects of `Act` are undone).

The action security package's specification is completed by an action *Done*(`Act`). This action tells the automaton that `Act` has actually been executed. It is called implicitly when `Act` is applied. Unlike the previous function, *Done* changes the state of the automaton.

Remark 10 The finite state automaton can be constructed using a straightforward adaptation of wellknown lexical analyzer generators such as `lex` and `flex`. The only modification concerns the tentative nature of Forbidden: it must be possible to try Act and then go back to the previous state of the automaton, in order to verify other possible actions Act. For this purpose, it suffices to store the index of the previous state, and provide a command that replaces the current state index with the previous one.

10.6 Related Work

Most research on agent security deals with issues related to the usage of agents on the Web. Attempts have been made to answer questions such as, "Is it safe to click on a given hyperlink?" or "If I send this program out into the Web to find some bargain CD's, will it get cheated?" (e.g., (Chess 1996; Chess 1998)). Others try to develop methods for finding intruders who are executing programs not normally executed by "honest" users or agents (Crosbie and Spafford 1995). In contrast, in this chapter, we focus on data security and action security in multiagent environments.

A significant body of work has also gone into ensuring that agents neither crash their host nor abuse its resources. Mostmobile-agent systems protect the hosts by (Gray, Kotz, Cybenko, and Rus 1998): (1) cryptographically verifying the identity of the agent's owner, (2) assigning access restrictions to the agent based on the owner's identity, and (3) allowing the agent to execute in a secure execution environment that can enforce these restrictions (Vigna 1998b). Java agent security relies mainly on the idea of that an applet's actions are restricted to its "sandbox," an area of the web browser dedicated to that applet (Fritzinger and Mueller 1996). Java developers claim that their Java 2 platform provides both system security and information security (Hughes 1998).

An interesting approach for safe execution of untrusted code is the Proof-Carrying Code (PCC) technique (Necula and Lee 1997). In a typical instance of PCC, a code receiver establishes a set of safety rules that guarantee safe behavior of programs, and the code producer creates a formal safety proof that proves, for the untrusted code, adherence to the safety rules. Then, the receiver is able to use a simple and fast proof validator to check, with certainty, that the proof is valid and hence the untrusted code is safe to execute. An important advantage of this technique is that although there might be a large amount of effort in establishing and formally proving the safety of the untrusted code, almost the entire burden of doing this is on the code producer. The code consumer, on the other hand, has only to perform a fast, simple, and easy-to-trust proof-checking process.

Campbell and Qian (Campbell and Qian 1998) address security issues in a mobile computing environment using a mobile agent based security architecture. This security architecture is capable of supporting dynamic application specific security customization and adaptation. In essence the idea is to embed security functions in mobile agents to enable runtime composition of mobile security systems. The implementation is based on OMG's *CORBA* distributed object orientation technology and Java-based distributed programming environment. Gray Campbell and Qian (Campbell and Qian 1998) address security issues in a mobile computing environment using a mobile agent based security architecture. This security architecture is capable of supporting dynamic application specific security customization and adaptation. In essence the idea is to embed security functions in mobile agents to enable runtime composition of mobile security systems. The implementation is based on OMG's *CORBA* distributed object orientation technology and Java-based distributed programming environment. Gray et al. consider a problem of protecting a group of machines which do not belong to the same administrative control. They propose a market-based approach in which agents pay for their resources.

Less attention has been devoted to the opposite problem, that is, protecting mobile agents from their hosts (Sander and Tschudin 1998). An example of how to protect Java mobile agents is given in (Nishigaya 1997). Hohl (Hohl 1997) proposed to protecting mobile agents from attackers by not giving the attacker enough time to manipulate the data and code of the agent. He proposed that this can be achieved by a combination of a *code mess up* and *limited lifetime of code and data* which he describes. Farmer et al. (Farmer, Guttag, and Swarup 1996) use a *state appraisal* mechanism which checks if some invariants of the agent's state hold (e.g., relationships among variables) when an agent reaches a new execution environment. Vigna (Vigna 1998a) presents a mechanism to detect possible illegal modification of a mobile agent which is based on post-mortem analysis of data—called *traces*—that are collected during agent execution. The traces are used for checking the agent program against a supposed history of execution.

At the same level of abstraction, it is necessary to deal with issues of identity verification and message exchange protection (Thirunavukkarasu, Finin, and Mayfield 1995). The techniques and methodologies illustrated in this chapter rely on the assumption that the above problems and other network security problems (Schumacher and Ghosh 1997) are dealt with correctly by the underlying implementation.

Zapf, Mueller, and Geihs (1998) consider security threats to both hosts and agents in electronic markets. They describe the preliminary security facilities implemented in their agent system AMETAS. They do not provide a formal model or an experimental results to evaluate their system.

Agent data security has many analogies with security in databases. This field has been studied intensively, e.g., (Bertino, Bettini, Ferrari, and Samarati 1996; Bertino, Samarati, and Jajodia 1993; Bonatti, Kraus, and Subrahmanian 1995; Castano, Fugini, Martella, and Samarati 1995; Jajodia and Sandhu 1991; Millen and Lunt 1992; Winslett, Smith, and Qian 1994). While this work is significant, none of it has focused on agents. We attempt to build on top of existing approaches. However, data security in autonomous agents environments raises new problems. In particular, no central authority can maintain security, but rather participants in the environment should be responsible for maintaining it.

Problems of authentication and authorization arise when databases operate in an open environment (Bina, McCool, Jones, and Winslett 1994). Bina et al. propose a framework for solving these problems using WWW information servers and a modified version of the NCSA Mosaic. Berkovits et al. (Berkovits, Guttman, and Swarup 1998) consider this problem in mobile agent systems by modeling the trust relation between the principals of the mobile agents.

We do not consider the authentication problem in our work, but rather assume that methods such as developed in (Bina, McCool, Jones, and Winslett 1994) are available. Usually these methods used cryptography and electronic signatures techniques. A tutorial text on such techniques can be found in (Stallings 1995).

Formal models for verifying security of protocols for authentication, key distribution, or information sharing may have some similarities with our formal model. Heintze and Tygar (Heintze and Tygar 1996) preent a simple model which includes the notions of traces (similar to out histories), agent states and beliefs. Our notions are more general than theirs. For example, the internal state of each agent in their model consists of three components: (1) the set of messages and keys known to the agent; (2) the set of messages and keys believed by the agent to be secret (and with whom the secrets are shared); and (3) the set of nonces recently generated by the agent. We do not make any restrictions on the agents' states and we assume that an agent can infer new information from its beliefs. We also define the notion of distortion functions that specify to the agent how to behave in order to maintain security. Their system is used to verify the security of cryptographic protocols. They present an interesting result concerning a composition of two secure protocols. They state sufficient conditions on two secure protocols A and B such that they may be combined to form a new secure protocol C. We leave for future work the problem of combining two secure service distortions.

In some systems agents are used to maintain security. For example, in the architecture presented in (Bergadano, Puliafito, Riccobene, and Ruffo 1999) of Java-based agents for information retrieval, there are two security agents: Message Security Agent (MSA) and Controller Security Agents (CSA). The MSA deals with services relating to the exchange of messages. The CSA provides services to check adequate use of resources by detecting anomalies. We do not consider the basic security problems provided by the security agents of (Bergadano, Puliafito, Riccobene, and Ruffo 1999). We proposed that the higher-level security issues considered in this chapter will be dealt with by the *IMPACT* agents themselves, and not delegated to separate servers.

Security agents are also used in Distributed Object Kernel (DOK) project (Tari 1997) for enforcing security policies in distributed and heterogeneous environments. There are three levels of agents. Top level agents are aware of all the activities that are happening in the system (or have already happened). Based on this information the agents of the top layer delegate functions to the appropriate agents. In the environments that we consider, agents cannot have information on all the activities that are happening and each agent should maintain its data and action security.

He, Sycara, and Finin (1998) proposed to implement the authorities of authentication verification service systems as autonomous software agents, called security agents, instead of building a static monolithic hierarchy as in the traditional Public Key Infrastructure (PKI) implementations. One of the open questions they present is: "How to define a suitable language for users to describe their security policy and security protocols so that the agent delegates of a user can safely transact electronic business on his behalf?" We believe that the language and framework presented in this chapter can be used for such purpose, in addition to the original purpose of programming individual agents to maintain their data and action security.

Foner (1996) discusses security problems in a multi-agent matchmaker system named Yenta. The matchmaking done by the *IMPACT* Server is much more limited. *IMPACT* servers do not have access to the agents' data as Yenta's agents have. Thus, the impact Server's security tasks are simpler. Each agent is responsible for its own data security. We believe that this approach will lead to more secure multiagent systems.

Soueina, Far, Katsube, and Koono (1998) presents a language for programming agents acting in multiagent environments. It is possible to give an agent commands such as "lie(action())" indicating that lying may be needed when the action is performed, "zone(action*)" that can be used to classify some agents as being hostile etc. Their work is based on first order logic and on concepts from game theory, but no formal semantics is given.

Other distributed object oriented systems provide some security services. *CORBA* (OMG 1998b), an object request broker framework, provides security services, such as identification and authentication of human users and objects, and security of communication between objects. These services are not currently provided by *IMPACT*, and their implementation is left for future work. *CORBA* provides some simple authorization and access control. Our model allows the application of more sophisticated security policies using the idea of service distortions.

Zeng and Wang (Zeng and Wang 1998) proposed an Internet conceptual security model using Telos. They try to detect attacks based on monitoring and analyzing of audit information. In their framework a designer can construct ontology of Internet security and then develops a set of rules for security maintenance. Their examples consider identifying security problems by analyzing network transactions. It is not clear from the papers how their rules will be used to preserve security and they do not consider data security problems.

Concordia is a framework for development and management of network-efficient mobile agent applications for accessing information anytime, anywhere and on any device supporting Java. Agent protection in *Concordia* (Koblick 1999) refers to the process of protecting agent's contents during transmission over the net. Prior to transmission an agent's bytecodes, member data and state information are encrypted through a combination of symmetric and public cryptography. In order to provide reliability, *Concordia* employs a persistent store to periodically checkpoint an agent. But, this on-disk representation may impose security risks, hence *Concordia* also encrypts this on-disk representation of an agent.

Concordia agents are mobile, they can execute anywhere on the network where they are authorized. These host servers need to be protected. Server resource protection involves two concepts: agent identification and resource permission. An agent's user identity uniquely identifies the user who launched the agent. User identity consists of either an individual user name, or a group name, plus the password which is always stored in a secure format. An agent roaming the network carries it identity. Resource permissions, which are built on top of standard Java security classes, are used to allow of deny access to machine resources.

IBM *Aglets* (Tai and Kosaka 1999) provide a framework for development and management of mobile agents. An aglet is a Java object having mobility and persistence and its own thread of execution. Security services in *Aglets* (Lande and Osjima 1998) includes authentication of the user, the host, the code and the agent, ensuring the integrity of the agent, protecting the confidential information an agent may carry, auditing and non-repudiation, i.e., an agent or server cannot deny a communication exchange if it already took place. *Aglets* provide an auditing service which records all security related activities of an agent. An aglet has credentials to indicate the implementer and also the person who launched it. A server can control and limit the behavior of aglets it receives through these credentials. The security model of *Aglets* (Lande and Osjima 1998) supports the definition of security policies and describes how these policies are enforced. The model includes principles which are entities whose identity can be authenticated. The principles include the aglet, the aglet owner (the person who launched the aglet), the aglet manufacturer (the person who implemented the aglet), the context, the domain, and domain authority. Contexts and servers are in charge of keeping the host operating system safe. A server defines a security policy to protect local machine resources. Contexts host visiting aglets and provide access to local resources. Domains identify a group of servers. Finally, a network domain authority keeps its network secure so that visiting aglets execute their tasks safely.

The security model of *Aglets* (Lande and Osjima 1998) also includes permissions, which define the capabilities of executing aglets by setting access restrictions on resource usage. Lande and Osjima (1998) define permissions as a resource, such as a file, together with appropriate actions such as reading and writing. Permissions include file permissions (to control access the local file system), network permissions (to control access to the network), window system (to open a window), context permissions (to use services of the context), and aglet permissions (to control the methods provided by an aglet).

11 Complexity Results

In the previous chapters, we have described our approach to a *software agent system*, which involves a number of different components to make an agent work in practice. As we have seen, a large number of different tasks must be or should be handled by an agent, including *location of external services*, *decision making*, *meta-reasoning* as well as *uncertain* and *temporal reasoning*. All these capabilities require proper conceptualization and formalization, which we have given in this book.

However, to put the *IMPACT* system to work, we need algorithms for solving the particular computational problems which emerge from these various tasks. And, of course, these algorithms should be decent ones, in the sense that the problems are solved in an efficient way. This calls us for the development of such algorithms.

But before we start off developing such algorithms, we have to commit to a clear understanding what "efficient" really means. Commonly, *computable in polynomial time* is understood as a synonym of "efficiently computable." Not all problems are solvable in polynomial time, and for many of them, this is provably the case. However, there is a vast body of important problems in computer science, for which it is not formally proven yet that no polynomial time algorithms do exist for solving them, even though there is strong evidence that no such algorithms do exist. An example of such problems are the NP-complete problems, which are solvable by (deterministic) algorithms in exponential time. The issue of whether any such problem can be solved by a polynomial time algorithm amounts to the famous open P = NP question.

Extending the work on NP-complete problems, the field of structural complexity theory has developed a number of techniques and tools to assess the "difficulty" of a computation problem, such that we may find how difficult solving a particular problem is. Moreover, these techniques may help us in judging whether a particular algorithm is to be considered reasonable or, under an appropriate notion, even optimal given the intrinsic problem complexity. Rather than simply classifying a problem as either "solvable in polynomial time" or by some evidence "not solvable in polynomial time, and thus intractable," a closer look on the computational cost of solving a problem should be given, as this might reveal interesting information. Such information may be, for example, which type of algorithm is appropriate for solving a problem, or which related problems do exist to which a problem at hand can be efficiently reduced to.

In this chapter, we turn to this question and address the computational cost of tasks which have to be performed by *IMPACT* agents. An exhaustive study which covers all these tasks would be an ambitious program, however, and would fill yet another book. For this reason, we focus here on a central task of the *IMPACT* architecture, namely, on agent decision making. In fact, this task is at the heart of the *IMPACT* agent system—without the agent decision layer, *IMPACT* agents are deemed to idly wait and not providing any services. Agent programs, which we have described in Chapter 6, along with different notions status sets provide a formal semantics for an agent's behavior. For an implementation of decision making, we need appropriate algorithms to compute these semantics, which suggests to perform a study of the computational complexity of the semantics.

Our plan for this chapter is as follows. As we will encounter some complexity classes which the casual reader is usually not familiar with, we recall some basic concepts of the theory of NP-completeness and beyond in the first section. We then precisely formulate in Section 11.2 the problems whose complexity is investigated, and which underlying assumptions are made in our analysis—this is indispensable for a complexity assessment. After that, we present in Section 11.3 a summary of the results and the bottom line of the conclusions that can be drawn. The reader who is merely interested in such a summary and a general discussion, may safely skip the rest of this chapter, in which the technical results are established. However, she might browse Sections 11.4 and 11.5 if she is interested in algorithms by which various kinds of status sets are computed, since such algorithms are developed in the course of the complexity analysis.

11.1 Complexity Classes

We assume at this point that the reader has some basic knowledge about computational complexity; the texts (Garey and Johnson 1979; Johnson 1990; Papadimitriou 1994) are good sources, which the reader who has little experience on complexity may consult for further background.

11.1.1 Decision Problems

The attempt to distinguish easy from hard problems has led to the widely accepted notion of *tractability* as the property that a problem can be *solved in polynomial time*, measured in the size of the problem input. The mathematical study of problem solving has for a long time centered around the simplest type of problems, namely *decision problems*.

DEFINITION 11.1.1 (DECISION PROBLEMS)   Formally, a decision problem Π consists of a pair (D, Y) of a set D of *problem instances*, which are strings from a language over a finite

Section 11.1   Complexity Classes

alphabet, and a subset Y of D which are called *"Yes"-instances*. The strings in $D \setminus Y$ are called *"No"-instances*.[1]

An algorithm correctly solves a decision problem $\Pi = (D, Y)$, if it outputs, given an instance I from D, "Yes" if $I \in Y$ holds, and outputs "No" otherwise.

The *complexity* of a decision problem, in terms of a resource such as computation time or work space, is understood as the cost of an optimal algorithm (assuming some computation model) for solving this problem. Abstracting from this optimal cost, different complexity classes have been defined which allow to roughly characterize the difficulty of a problem in the large.

DEFINITION 11.1.2 (DETERMINISTIC COMPLEXITY CLASSES)   The class P contains all decision problems Π that are solvable in polynomial time on a deterministic Turing machine (DTM), i.e., there exists a DTM M which solves Π and such that the running time of M is bounded by a polynomial in the length $|I|$ of the input I. Similarly, the class PSPACE contains all decision problems which are solvable by some DTM in polynomial work space, i.e., the number of tape cells visited by the workhead of M is bounded by a polynomial in the length of the input I.

Further complexity classes, such as EXPTIME and EXPSPACE, are defined by using other bounds on time and space, respectively.

For example, the problem ACYCLIC $= (D, Y)$ where D consists of the encodings of directed graphs (according to some standard encoding) and Y contains the (encodings of) acyclic graphs in D, can be solved in polynomial time. Informally, we say that the problem, given a graph, deciding whether the graph is acyclic, is possible in polynomial time, and thus the problem is in P.

A decision problem $\Pi = (D, Y)$ is solved by a nondeterministic Turing machine (NTM), if for every instance I of Π there is a run of M such that M outputs "Yes" if and only if I is a yes-instance. Note that no symmetric behavior is required for no-instances—M need even not halt on such instances.

DEFINITION 11.1.3 (NONDETERMINISTIC TURING MACHINES)   A decision problem Π is solvable in nondeterministic polynomial time, if Π is solved by some NTM M such that a polynomial exists which bounds for each "Yes"-instance the time of the shortest run of M

---

[1] Note that decision problems are often defined as formal languages L over a finite alphabet, such that the strings in L are the "Yes"-instances and all other strings correspond to the "No"-instances and the strings not encoding any problem instance. Under the usual assumption that the proper encodings of problem instances are easily recognized, the two formal definitions of problems are for our purposes equivalent.

which outputs "Yes." The class NP contains all decision problems which are solvable in nondeterministic polynomial time.

For example, the well-known satisfiability problem SAT $= (D, Y)$, whose problem instances D are propositional formulas $\phi = \bigwedge_{i=1}^{m} C_i$ in conjunctive normal form (CNF), and whose "Yes"-instances are the satisfiable formulas in D, is a in NP. Indeed, an assignment σ of truth values to the propositional variables $x_1, \ldots, x_n$ occurring in ϕ such that it satisfies ϕ, can be nondeterministically generated by the Turing machine (i.e., "guessed") in n steps, and the verification of the guess (i.e., checking whether σ satisfies ϕ), can be done efficiently.

Clearly, all problems in P are in NP, and as can be seen, all problems in NP are in PSPACE. It is to date unknown, however, whether any of the reverse containments holds, even though it is widely believed that none of them actually is true. Problems that are candidates for lying in the difference between NP and P are the NP-complete problems, which we introduce next.

The notion of completeness of a problem has been introduced in order to characterize the "hardest" problems in a complexity class. This notion involves the concept of *problem reduction*, which is as follows.

DEFINITION 11.1.4 (PROBLEM REDUCTION, HARDNESS, AND COMPLETENESS) A decision problem Π is polynomial-time reducible to a decision problem Π', if there is a function f which is computable in polynomial time, such that for every instance I of Π, $f(I)$ is an instance of Π' and $f(I)$ is a "Yes"-instance of Π' just if I is a "Yes"-instance of Π.

A problem Π is said to be *hard* for a class of problems C (i.e., *C-hard*), if every problem in C is polynomial-time reducible to Π. Furthermore, a problem Π is *complete* for C, if Π is hard for C and Π belongs to C.

For example, SAT is a well-known NP-complete problem. Many restrictions of SAT have been shown to be NP-complete as well. One of them is monotone 3SAT (M3SAT), which contains those instances $\phi = \bigwedge_{i=1}^{m} C_i$ of SAT such that each clause $C_i = L_{i,1} \vee L_{i,2} \vee L_{i,3}$ is a disjunction of three literals $L_{i,j}$, and either all literals in C_i are positive atoms or all are negated atoms. The complement of SAT (i.e., deciding unsatisfiability of a propositional CNF ϕ) is a well-known co-NP-complete problem, as is deciding whether a propositional formula $\phi = \bigvee_{i=1}^{m} D_i$ in disjunctive normal form (DNF) is a tautology. Similarly to SAT, this remains true if each disjunct $D_i = L_{i,1} \wedge L_{i,2} \wedge L_{i,3}$ is a conjunction of three literals $L_{i,j}$, and either all $L_{i,j}$ in D_i are atoms or all are negated atoms. We shall refer to such ϕ as *monotone 3DNF* (M3DNF) formulas.

Knowing that a problem is NP-complete or co-NP-complete is quite useful, because this tells us that one should not spend much time for developing a polynomial time algorithm

Section 11.1   Complexity Classes

(unless she wants to solve the P = NP problem, and become a famous computer scientist!), and rather look for restrictions on the problem under which a polynomial algorithm is feasible, or for a suitable heuristics which works well in practice.

It appeared that a number of problems reside between NP and PSPACE, and that there are proper, natural models of computation which express that computational nature of these problems. The most important such problems are the ones which reside in the polynomial hierarchy, which has been built upon the classes P and NP ($= \Sigma_1^P$), by allowing the use of an oracle (i.e., a subprogram) for deciding problems instantaneously.

DEFINITION 11.1.5 (ORACLE TURING MACHINE) An oracle Turing machine (OTM) is a Turing machine equipped with a query tape, on which queries to a fixed problem can be posed. Any such query is answered upon entering a designated query state in one step.

For a complexity class C, we denote by P^C (resp., NP^C) the class of all decision problems which can be solved by a deterministic (resp., nondeterministic) OTM with the help of an oracle in C.

In particular, P^{NP} (resp., NP^{NP}) is the class of problems solvable in polynomial time on a deterministic (resp., nondeterministic) Turing machine, if an oracle for a problem in NP may be used.

For the oracle classes C which we will encounter, we may also say that an oracle for solving any problem in C (a C-oracle, for short) is available, rather than only a fixed one. The reason is that all instances of problems in C can be efficiently transformed into instances of a single (fixed) C-complete problem.

The classes of the polynomial hierarchy, which is embedded in PSPACE, are shown in the left part of Figure 11.1 on the next page. In this figure, an edge directed from class C_1 to class C_2 indicates that all problems in C_1 can be efficiently transformed into some problem in C_2, and that it is strongly believed that a reduction in the other direction is not possible, i.e., any hardest problem in C_2 is more difficult than each single problem in C_1. For the decisional classes, the arcs in Figure 11.1 on the following page actually denote inclusions, i.e., the transformation of problems in C_1 to problems in C_2 is by means of the identity.

All classes of the polynomial hierarchy have complete problems, including canonical complete problems in terms of evaluating quantified Boolean formulas. A *quantified Boolean formula* (QBF) is a generalized propositional formula, in which each propositional variable x_i ranges over {*true, false*} and is governed either by an existential ($\exists$) or a universal ($\forall$) quantifier. The truth value of such a formula is obtained by eliminating all quantifiers in the obvious way and evaluating the resulting variable-free formula. For example, $\forall y_1, y_2 \exists x_1, x_2 (x_1 \wedge (\neg y_1 \vee y_2 \vee x_2) \wedge y_1)$ is a QBF. It evaluates to *false*, since on assigning e.g., *false* to both y_1 and y_2, the remaining formula is unsatisfiable.

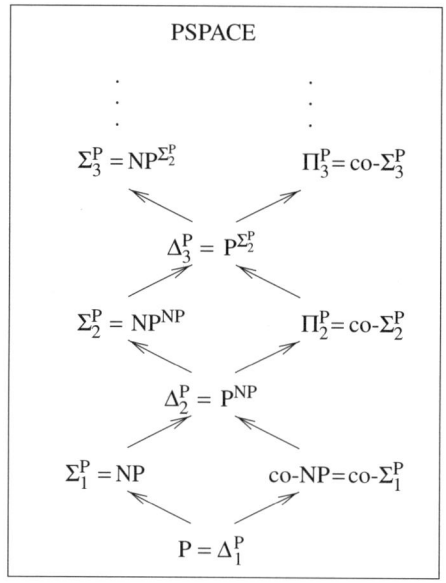
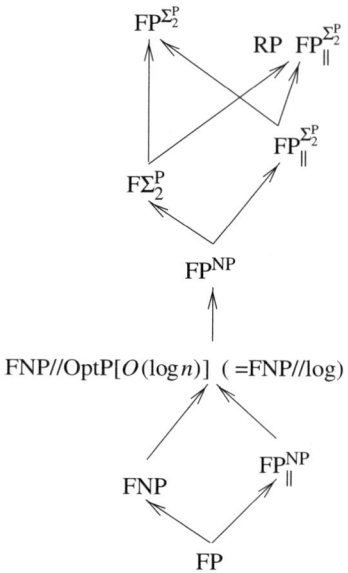

Figure 11.1
Decision (left) and Search (right) Problem Complexity Classes.

Evaluating a given QBF Φ is a classical PSPACE-complete problem. Syntactic restrictions on Φ provide problems complete for the Σ_k^P and Π_k^P classes of the polynomial hierarchy. In particular, deciding whether a QBF of the form $\exists Y^1 \forall Y^2 \cdots Q_k Y^k \phi$, where the Y^i are sets of variables and the quantifiers Q_i in front of them alternate, evaluates to *true* is a well-known Σ_k^P-complete problem. Dually, deciding whether a QBF of form $\forall Y^1 \exists Y^2 \cdots Q_k Y^k \phi$ evaluates to true is Π_k^P-complete.

11.1.2 Search Problems

In our analysis, we will also encounter problems which are not decision problems, but return a value as the solution to a problem instance, rather then reporting "Yes" or "No."

DEFINITION 11.1.6 (SEARCH PROBLEM) A *search problem* $\Pi = (D, S)$ is a generalization of a decision problem, in which for every instance $I \in D$ of the problem a (possibly empty) finite set $S(I)$ of solutions exists. To solve such a problem, an algorithm must (possibly nondeterministically) compute the solutions $S(I)$ in its computation branches, if $S(I)$ is not empty. Classes of search problems, which are also referred to as *function classes*, are defined in analogy to classes of decision problems.

Thus, while the decision problem SAT asks whether an instance I, given by a set of propositional clauses, is satisfiable, the set $S(I)$ of solutions for the corresponding search problem FSAT consists of all satisfying valuations for I.

Decision problems can be viewed as particular search problems, in which the solution set $S(I)$ is either empty or the singleton set {"Yes"}. More formally, search problems in the classes from Figure 11.1 are solved by transducers, i.e., Turing machines equipped with an output tape. If the machine halts in an accepting state, then the contents of the output tape is the result of the computation. Observe that a nondeterministic machine computes a (partial) multi-valued function. Thus, not all arcs in Figure 11.1 mean inclusion, i.e., trivial reducibility by the identity. However, if we are only interested in *some arbitrary* solution from a set of possible solutions, as e.g., in some arbitrary satisfying assignment in case of problem FSAT, then we may give up the implicit uniformity condition of having *each* solution as a possible outcome of a (nondeterministic) computation, and simple require that at *least one* of the possible solutions is returned over all branches—this is the (natural) view that we will adopt when classifying problems on agent programs. This view, adopted also, e.g., by Chen and Toda (1995) for solving optimization problems, is coherent with the notion of reduction below, and turns the arcs in Figure 11.1 into inclusions. For example, FSAT and finding some arbitrary feasible status set are problems in FP^{NP} under this view.

The concept of reduction among search problems Π_1 and Π_2 is also obtained by a proper generalization of the respective concept for decision problems, cf. (Papadimitriou 1994; Chen and Toda 1993).

DEFINITION 11.1.7 (SEARCH PROBLEM TRANSFORMATION) A search problem Π_1 is polynomial-time transformable to Π_2, if (*i*) from every instance I of Π_1, an instance $f(I)$ of Π_2 is constructible in polynomial time, such that $f(I)$ has some solution precisely if I has, and (*ii*) from every solution S of $f(I)$, a solution of I can be constructed in time polynomial in the size of S and I.

DEFINITION 11.1.8 (HARDNESS AND COMPLETENESS) As in the case of decisions problems, a search problem Π is hard for a class of search problems C, if every problem in C is polynomial-time transformable into Π. A search problem Π is complete for C, if Π is hard for C and belongs to C.

We now describe some the search problem classes that will shall encounter in this chapter. The search problem counterparts of the classes C in the polynomial hierarchy are often denoted by a prefixed "F"; some of them appear in Figure 11.1.

The Classes FP, FP^{NP}, and $FP^{\Sigma_2^P}$: These are the classes of functions computable by a deterministic Turing machine in polynomial time with no oracle, NP-oracle, and Σ_2^P-oracle, respectively. Notice that each such machine computes a single-valued function. The classes $FP_{\|}^{NP}$ and $FP_{\|}^{\Sigma_2^P}$ are refinements of the classes FP^{NP} and $F\Sigma_2^P$, respectively, and are the search problem counterparts of the classes $P_{\|}^{NP}$ and $P_{\|}^{\Sigma_2^P}$, respectively, which are not shown in the figure. These classes contain functions which are computable in polynomial time on a deterministic Turing machine which has access to an oracle in NP (resp., Σ_2^P), but where all queries to the oracle must be prepared before issuing the first oracle call. Thus, the oracle calls are non-adaptive and must essentially take place in parallel; it is commonly believed that this restricts computational power.

The Classes FNP and $F\Sigma_2^P$: FNP (resp., $F\Sigma_2^P$) contains the multi-valued functions whose solutions can be computed by a nondeterministic transducer in polynomial time (resp., in polynomial time with an NP-oracle), such that a given solution candidate can be checked in polynomial time (resp., the check is in co-NP). The class is contained in the class NPMV (resp., NPMV^{NP}), which contains all multi-valued functions computable in nondeterministic polynomial time (resp., in nondeterministic polynomial time with a NP oracle) (Fenner et al. 1997).

The Class FNP//log: FNP//log is short for the class FNP//OptP[$O(\log n)$] (Chen and Toda 1995). Intuitively, it is the class of problems such that a solution for an instance I can be nondeterministically computed by a transducer in polynomial time, if the optimal value $\text{opt}(I)$ of an NP optimization problem on I is known, where $\text{opt}(I)$ (an integer, represented in binary) must have $O(\log |I|)$ bits. NP *optimization problem* means here that the maximal (resp., minimal) value of a solution for a problem Π is computed such that, given I and an integer k, deciding whether $\text{opt}(I) \geq k$ (resp., $\text{opt}(I) \leq k$) is in NP and recognizing solutions is polynomial.

E.g., computing the largest set S of pairwise connected nodes in a given graph G (i.e., a maximum clique) is a problem in FNP//log (observe that different maximum cliques may exist). Indeed, computing the *size* of a maximum clique is an NP-optimization problem with $O(\log |I|)$ output bits, since testing whether a set S is a clique is easy (just check whether G has an edge between each pair of nodes in S), and deciding whether $\text{opt}(G) \geq k$ is in NP (guess a clique of size $\geq k$). Furthermore, if $s = \text{opt}(G)$ is known, then the transducer can nondeterministically generate and verify a clique of size s in polynomial time.

The class FNP//log reduces to FP^{NP} and roughly amounts to a randomized version of $FP_{\|}^{NP}$. Because of its nondeterministic nature, it contains problems which are not known to be solvable in $FP_{\|}^{NP}$. The most prominent of these problems is the computation of an arbitrary model of a propositional formula (Jenner and Toran 1997), which is the prototypical problem complete for the class FNP. Few natural FNP//log-complete problems are known to date and almost none arise in practical applications; our analysis shows that certain problems arising naturally in agent systems (e.g., computing a weak rational status set) are in FNP//log, and that some of them are even complete for this class.

The Class $\text{RP} \cdot \text{FP}_{\parallel}^{\Sigma_2^P}$: The class $\text{RP} \cdot \text{FP}_{\parallel}^{\Sigma_2^P}$ (Chen and Toda 1995) contains informally those problems for which a solution on input I can be found by a random polynomial time algorithm with very high probability, by using a problem in $\text{FP}_{\parallel}^{\Sigma_2^P}$ as single-call subroutine. This class is above $\text{FP}_{\parallel}^{\Sigma_2^P}$. Chen and Toda (1995) have shown that many optimization problems belong to this class whose solutions are the maximal (resp., minimal) solutions of an associated decision problem for which recognizing a solution is in co-NP. We shall use this relationship for classifying some problem into $\text{RP} \cdot \text{FP}_{\parallel}^{\Sigma_2^P}$, and refer the interested reader to (Chen and Toda 1995) for the technical details about this class. As we shall see, computing an F-preferred rational status set or a weak rational status set amount to such optimization problems, and thus the problems belong to $\text{RP} \cdot \text{FP}_{\parallel}^{\Sigma_2^P}$.

Evaluating QBFs as described on page 403 also provides complete problems for the search class counterparts of Σ_k^P. To formally describe them, we introduce the following notation.

Notation: $\phi[Y = \chi]$. Let ϕ be a propositional formula, and χ a truth value assignment to a set of propositional variables Y. Then $\phi[Y = \chi]$ is the formula obtained by substituting in ϕ for every $y_j \in Y$ its truth value according to χ. Furthermore, $\phi[Y = \emptyset]$ (resp., $\phi[Y \neq \emptyset]$) stands for $\phi[Y = \chi]$ where χ assigns **false** to every $y \in Y$ (resp., assigns **true** to at least one $y \in Y$).

For example, consider $\phi = x_1 \wedge (\neg y_1 \vee y_2 \vee x_2) \wedge y_1$. Then, for the assignment χ to $Y = \{y_1, y_2\}$ such that $\chi(y_1) = $ **true**, $\chi(y_2) = $ **false**, the formula $\phi[Y = \chi]$ is $x_1 \wedge (\neg \textbf{true} \vee \textbf{false} \vee x_2) \wedge \textbf{true}$.

Computing a truth value assignment χ such that the QBF $\forall Y^2 \exists Y^3 \cdots Q_k Y^k \phi[Y^1 = \chi]$ is true is complete for $\text{F}\Sigma_k^P$, for $k \geq 1$.

For the class FNP//log, the following problem X-maximal model is complete (Chen and Toda 1993; Chen and Toda 1995):[2] Given a SAT instance ϕ and a subset X of its variables, compute the X-part of a model M of ϕ such that $M \cap X$ is maximal, i.e., no model M' of ϕ exists such that $M' \cap X \supset M \cap X$, where a model M is identified with the set of atoms true in it.

11.2 Decision Making Problems

In this section, we describe the particular problems whose complexity is investigated, and we state our assumptions on the problem instances for which the analysis is being carried out.

---

[2] In (Chen and Toda 1995) a form of reduction among maximization problems is used slightly different from the one in (Chen and Toda 1993). It requires that the transformed instance $f(I)$ must always have solutions, but for any maximal solution S of $f(I)$, the function $g(I, S)$ is only defined if I has solutions; our proofs of FNP//log hardness can be easily adapted for this setting.

11.2.1 Problem Statements

The semantics of an agent program has been defined in terms of (various kinds) of status sets, and thus the computational problems of main interest center around the computation of such status sets from an agent's state.

In our analysis, we study four types of complexity problems, which reflect different aspects when agent decision making happens. The problems are generic for the type of status set semantics which the agent is willing to base its decisions on. Let Sem be any kind of status sets.

Consistency: The problem is deciding whether an agent program $\mathcal{P}$ is consistent on an agent state $\mathcal{O}_S$, i.e., whether $\mathcal{P}$ possesses a Sem-status set on $\mathcal{O}_S$.

Recognition: Decide whether a given status set S is a Sem-status set of an agent program $\mathcal{P}$ on an agent state $\mathcal{O}_S$.

Computation: Compute some arbitrary Sem-status set of an agent program $\mathcal{P}$ on a given agent state $\mathcal{O}_S$.

Action Reasoning: This comprises elementary reasoning about an agent's behavior in a certain situation, and comes in two different variants. The problem is deciding, from an agent program $\mathcal{P}$ and an agent state $\mathcal{O}_S$, whether the agent takes an action α under Sem-status sets, under the

- *possibility variant*, i.e., whether α is executed according to some Sem-status set, or the
- *certainty variant*, i.e., whether α is executed according to every Sem-status set.

These problems are not completely independent. For example, the consistency problem can be solved as a byproduct by an algorithm for computing an Sem-status set, and thus is not harder than the computation problem. Nonetheless, each of the problems is of its own interest, and as we shall see, their complexities differ in subtle details. Observe that the complexity of problems analogous to the ones above have been studied in the field of knowledge representation and reasoning. In particular, problem consistency and analog of action reasoning, under both the possibility and certainty variant, have been extensively studied in the context of nonmonotonic logics and logic programming, cf. (Cadoli and Schaerf 1995; Gottlob 1992a; Dantsin et al. 1997).

11.2.2 Assumptions on the Problem Instances

The computational problems we consider have been formulated in a general setting. However, when it comes to evaluating agent programs, not all parameters that appear in the problem statements may vary, but some will most likely remain unchanged. We make this explicit by the following assumptions.

Section 11.2 Decision Making Problems   409

System Background: We assume that the environment in which agent programs are evaluated does not change. That is, we assume that there is a background which consists of a software code S, an action base $\mathcal{AB}$, a set of action constraints $\mathcal{AC}$, and a set of integrity constraints $\mathcal{IC}$, each of which is fixed and does not change over time.

Fixed Agent Program: Furthermore, we assume that the agent program $\mathcal{P}$ to be evaluated is fixed.

Thus, by the above assumptions, the varying part of the input to a problem consists of the agent state $\mathcal{O}_S$, together with a status set (problem recognition) or an action atom (action reasoning). This makes sense, though, since it models running an agent's program over changing states.

The above setting corresponds to what is commonly called the *data complexity* of a program in the database field (Vardi 1982). If we would consider varying programs where the agent state is *fixed* (resp., *varying*), we would have *expression (or program) complexity and combined complexity*, which are typically one exponential higher than data complexity. This also applies in many cases to the results that we derive below. Such results can be established, for example, by using the complexity upgrading techniques for expression complexity described in (Gottlob et al. 1995).

Assumptions about the Software Code   It is easy to see that in general, evaluating an agent program built on top of arbitrary software code is not effectively possible. If no restrictions apply to the functions provided by the software package, then the evaluation of a singe code call may turn out to be an undecidable problem, and there is no algorithm for its implementation.

However, in all available commercial software packages, calls to a function are completed in a finite amount of time (even if sometimes, the user may have the feeling that processing a certain query takes infinite time), and in many cases, even quite fast measured by the size of the data structures, which resemble the current state.

Our aim is to analyze the cost of agent decision making *per se*, and to see under which circumstances this is efficiently possible. If we use a software package $S = (\mathcal{T}_S, \mathcal{F}_S, \mathcal{C}_S)$ with high intrinsic complexity, then also the evaluation of an agent programs will be time consuming, and leaves us no chance for efficient algorithms. We therefore have to make some general assumptions about the software package used, such that polynomial time algorithms are not a priori excluded.

Domain Closure Assumption: We adopt a *generalized active domain* assumption on objects, in the spirit of domain closure. All objects considered for grounding the program rules, evaluation of the action preconditions, the conditions of the actions constraints and the integrity constraints must be from $\mathcal{O}_S$, or they must be constructible from objects therein by operations from a fixed (finite) set in a number of steps that is bounded by some constant, and such that each operation is efficiently executable (i.e., in polynomial time) and involves only a number of objects bounded by some other constant. Notice that the active domain assumption is often applied in the domain of relational databases, and similar domain closure in the context of knowledge bases. In our framework, creation and use of tuples of bounded arity from values existing in a database would be a feasible object construction process, while creation of an arbitrary relation (as an object that amounts to a set of tuples) would be not.

Under this assumption, the number of objects which may be relevant to a fixed agent program $\mathcal{P}$ on a given state $\mathcal{O}_S$ is bounded by a polynomial in the number of objects in $\mathcal{O}_S$, and each such object can be generated in polynomial time. In particular, this also means that the number of ground rules of $\mathcal{P}$ which are relevant is polynomial in the size of $\mathcal{O}_S$, measured by the number of objects that it contains.

Polynomial Code Calls: We further assume that the evaluation time of code condition calls χ over a state $\mathcal{O}_S$, for any particular legal assignment of objects, is bounded by a polynomial in the size of $\mathcal{O}_S$. Moreover, we assume that given an agent state $\mathcal{O}_S$ and a set of ground actions $\mathcal{A}$, the state $\mathcal{O}'_S$ which results under weakly-concurrent execution of $\mathcal{A}$ on $\mathcal{O}_S$ (see Definition 6.2.6 on page 148) is constructible in polynomial time.

As a consequence of these assumptions, the action and integrity constraints are evaluable on an agent state $\mathcal{O}_S$ under the generalized active domain semantics in polynomial time, and the integrity constraints on the agent state $\mathcal{O}'_S$ resulting from the execution of a set of actions A grounded in the active domain, are checkable in polynomial time in the size of $\mathcal{O}_S$.[3]

Notice that these assumptions will be met in many software packages which support the use of integrity constraints (e.g., a relational database). If evaluation of the code condition calls or constraints were not polynomial, then the evaluation of the agent program would not be either.

Note 8 Throughout this chapter, we shall in proofs only encounter code call atoms querying whether a particular tuple $t = (t_1, \ldots, t_k)$ is contained in a table R of a relational database package $\mathcal{S}$, i.e., whether the logical fact $R(t)$ is true. For simplicity, we write $R(t_1, \ldots, t_k)$ for these code call atoms (and omit using a root variable for t).

---

[3] This would remain true if the integrity constraints where arbitrary fixed first-order formulas (evaluated under active domain semantics).

11.3 Overview of Complexity Results

In this section, we provide an overview of the complexity results that we have established, and discuss their implications for agent decision making.

Basically, the results may be broken into four groups of results, which emerge from the impact of the following two orthogonal restrictions on the general problem instances:

Positive vs general programs: The action program $\mathcal{P}$ is positive, i.e., occurrence of negated action status literals in the bodies of action rules is not allowed.

No vs arbitrary integrity constraints: The set $\mathcal{IC}$ of integrity constraints is empty, as opposed to consist of an arbitrary collection of integrity constraints.

A consideration of these restrictions is meaningful, since we get insight into the cost which we have to pay by using negation in agent programs, as well as if integrity constraints must be maintained in the transition to a new agent state. As we shall see, different types of Sem-status sets show a different computational behavior on these restrictions. Apart from semantical aspects, the computational cost may serve as a basis for selecting the actual semantics under which an agent should run its program.

The results that we shall derive in Sections 11.4 and 11.5 are compactly summarized in Tables 11.2 on the following page through 11.4 on page 413. They show the results for each of the four possible combinations which result from the two restrictions from above.

In these tables, the leftmost column contains the semantics Sem which we have analyzed, each row shows the complexity results for the problems we consider under this particular semantics. The entries for decision problems in the tables stand for completeness for the respective complexity classes.

In case of P, completeness under polynomial-time transformation is not meaningful, though, since every (nontrivial) problem in P is obviously complete for P under polynomial-time transformations. Here, completeness is understood in terms of logspace-reductions, i.e., polynomial-time transformations which can be computed in logarithmic workspace. Hardness for P may implicitly be present with the functions $\mathcal{F}_\mathcal{S}$ from the software code $\mathcal{S}$, as all that we know from our assumptions is that these functions can be evaluated in polynomial time. However, we remark that for all problems except recognition of a feasible status set, hardness holds even if no new objects are introduced and the agent state consists merely of a relational database, to/from which tuples may be added and/or deleted. Proofs of these results are not difficult, using the well-known result that inference from a ground datalog program (propositional Horn logic program) is P-complete, cf. (Dantsin et al. 1997).

Table 11.2
Complexity of Agent Programs with Negation, $\mathcal{IC} = \emptyset$

				Action Reasoning	
Sem-Status Set	Consistency	Computation	Pecognition	Possible	Certain
feasible	P	FP	P	NP	co-NP
rational $\equiv$ reasonable $\equiv$ F-preferred rational $\equiv$ F-preferred reasonable	P	FP	P	P	P
weak rational $\equiv$ weak reasonable	P	FP	P	NP	co-NP

				Action Reasoning	
Sem-Status Set	Consistency	Computation	Recognition	Possible	Certain
feasible	NP	FNP	P	NP	co-NP
rational	NP	FNP//log *	co-NP	Σ_2^P	co-NP
reasonable	NP	FNP	P	NP	co-NP
F-preferred rational	NP	FNP//log	co-NP	Σ_2^P	Π_2^P
F-preferred reasonable	NP	FNP//log	co-NP	Σ_2^P	Π_2^P
weak rational	NP	FNP//log	co-NP	Σ_2^P	Π_2^P
weak reasonable	NP	FNP//log	co-NP	Σ_2^P	Π_2^P

$*\ldots$ hard for both FNP and $FP_{\|}^{NP}$

The entries for the computation problems are the classes $F\mathcal{C}$ from the literature (Papadimitriou 1994; Chen and Toda 1993; Chen and Toda 1995), which we have reviewed in Section 11.1. Unless stated otherwise, they stand for completeness under the notion of polynomial-time reduction as in Definition 11.1.7 on page 405 (Papadimitriou 1994; Chen and Toda 1993). Observe that we aim here at characterizing the complexity of agent programs in terms of existing classes from the literature, rather than introducing new classes to precisely assess the complexity of some problems.

11.3.1 Bottom Line for the Computation Problem

Of all the four problems described above, from the point of view of the *IMPACT* system (and in general, for any system that attempts to determine which actions an agent must take), the

Section 11.3   Overview of Complexity Results   413

Table 11.4
Complexity of Agent Programs with Negation, arbitrary $\mathcal{IC}$

Sem-Status Set	Consistency	Computation	Recognition	Action Reasoning Possible	Certain
feasible	NP	FNP	P	NP	co-NP
rational	P	FP	P	P	P
$\equiv$ reasonable $\equiv$ F-preferred rational $\equiv$ F-preferred reasonable					
weak rational $\equiv$ weak reasonable	NP	FNP//log *	co-NP	NP	Π_2^P

$*\ldots$ hard for both FNP and $FP_{\parallel}^{NP}$

Sem-Status Set	Consistency	Computation	Recognition	Action Reasoning Possible	Certain
feasible	NP	FNP	P	NP	co-NP
rational	Σ_2^P	$F\Sigma_2^P$	co-NP	Σ_2^P	Π_2^P
reasonable	NP	FNP	P	NP	co-NP
F-preferred rational	Σ_2^P	$FP^{\Sigma_2^P} \cap RP \cdot FP_{\parallel}^{\Sigma_2^P}$ †	Π_2^P	Σ_3^P	Π_3^P
F-preferred reasonable	NP	FNP//log	co-NP	Σ_2^P	Π_2^P
weak rational	Σ_2^P	$FP^{\Sigma_2^P} \cap RP \cdot FP_{\parallel}^{\Sigma_2^P}$ †	Π_2^P	Σ_3^P	Π_3^P
weak reasonable	NP	FNP//log	co-NP	Σ_2^P	Π_2^P

$\dagger\ldots$ hard for both $F\Sigma_2^P$ and $FP_{\parallel}^{\Sigma_2^P}$

most important problem, by far, is the problem of *Computation*—given an agent program, a current agent state, a set of integrity constraints and action constraints, determine a set of actions that the agent must take. This task forms the single most important task that an agent must take, over and over again.

When considering the different semantics for agent-programs, by examining the column "computation" in the Tables 11.1–11.4, we notice that the easiest semantics to compute are given as follows:

• When *positive agent programs with no integrity constraints* are considered, the rational, weak rational, reasonable, weak reasonable, F-preferential, and P-preferential semantics are the easiest to compute, all falling into the same complexity class. The other semantics are harder to compute. Thus, in this case, we have some flexibility in choosing that out of the rational, weak rational, reasonable, weak reasonable, F-preferential, and P-preferential, that best meets the agent's epistemic needs. Note that different agents in *IMPACT* can use different semantics.

• When *positive agent programs with integrity constraints* are considered, the best semantics, from the point of view of computational complexity, are the rational, reasonable, F-preferential, and P-preferential semantics. Note that unlike the previous case, the weak rational and weak reasonable semantics are harder to compute when integrity constraints are present.

• When *arbitrary agent programs with no integrity constraints* are considered, then the easiest semantics to compute are the feasible set semantics and the reasonable status set semantics. All other semantics are harder to compute.

• When *arbitrary agent programs with integrity constraints* are considered, the same continues to be true.

In general, when considering how to compute a kind of status set, the reasonable status set semantics is generally the easiest to compute, irrespective of whether agent programs are positive or not, and irrespective of whether integrity constraints are present or not. As we have argued earlier on in the paper, reasonable status sets have many nice properties which might make them epistemologically preferable to feasible status sets and rational status sets.

11.3.2 Sources of Complexity

The results show that the complexity of agent programs varies from polynomial up to the third level of the polynomial hierarchy. Observe that in some cases, there are considerable complexity gaps between positive agent programs and agent programs which use negation (e.g., for F-preferred rational status sets).

The reason for this gap are three sources of complexity, which lift the complexity of positive agent programs from P up to Σ_3^P and Π_3^P, respectively (in the cases of F-preferred and weak rational status sets):

1. an (in general) exponential number of candidates for a feasible (resp., weak feasible) status set;

2. a difficult recognition test, which involves groundedness; and,

3. an exponential number of preferable candidates, in terms of F-preference or maximal obedience to obligations.

These three sources of complexity act in a way orthogonally to each other, and all of them have to be eliminated to gain tractability.

For the canonical semantics of positive agent programs, the rational status set semantics, all computational problems are polynomial. This contrasts with feasible status sets, for which excepting recognition, all problems are intractable. On the other hand, under the weak status set semantics, the problems apart from action reasoning are polynomial, if no integrity constraints are present. Intractability, however, is incurred in all problems as soon as integrity constraints may be used.

It is interesting to observe that for programs with negation, rational status sets are more expensive to compute than reasonable status sets in general. This is also true if no integrity constraints are present, with the exception of consistency checking and cautious action reasoning. A similar observation applies to the F-preferred and weak variants of rational and reasonable status sets in the general case. Here, the rational variants are always more complex than the reasonable ones. However, somewhat surprisingly, if no integrity constraints are present, then the complexities of the rational and reasonable variants coincide! This is intuitively explained by the fact that in absence of integrity constraints, the expensive groundedness check for rational status sets can be surpassed in many places. This is possible by exploiting the property that in this case, every feasible status set must contain some rational status set.

Another interesting observation is that for programs with negation, the F-preferential and weak variants of rational status sets have the same complexity characteristics, and similar for reasonable status sets. This is explained by the similar optimization components which are present in the semantics, namely minimization of the **F**-part vs maximization of the set of obligations which are obeyed. These are dual optimization problems, but the underlying optimization principle is the same. A similar complexity behavior is thus not much surprising. However, we note that F-preference and weak rationality are applied to different candidate spaces, namely to all rational status sets versus all A-rational status sets, respectively. This explains that in the case of positive programs, where these candidate spaces have in general different sizes (a singleton set versus an exponential set), the complexity profiles of F-preference and weak rationality are different.

Presence of integrity constraints, even of the simplest nature which is common in practice (e.g., functional dependencies (Ullman 1989) in a database), can have a detrimental effect on (variants of) rational status sets and raises the complexity by one level in the polynomial hierarchy. However, the complexity of reasonable status sets and their variants is immune to integrity constraints except for the weak reasonable status sets on positive programs. Intuitively, this is explained by the fact that the refutation of a candidate for a reasonable status set basically reduces to the computation of the rational status set of a positive agent program, and there integrity constraints do not increase the complexity. In the case of weak reasonable status sets for positive programs, we have an increase since the weakness condition may create an exponential number of candidates if the program is inconsistent.

We finally remark that we have omitted here an analysis of the complexity of optimal status sets as proposed in Section 6.5.7, in order to avoid an abundance of complexity results. Based on the results presented above, coarse bounds are straightforward. Chen and Toda (1993), Chen and Toda (1995), Jenner and Toran (1997) and references therein provide suitable complexity classes for a more accurate assessment.

11.3.3 Algorithm Design and Approximation

The question rises how the results in Tables 11.1–11.4 can be utilized for implementation issues, and what they can tell us for dealing with action decision making in practice. Of course, the complexity results are primarily of a quantitative nature, as they characterize the worst-case complexity of the agent programming language. However, as argued recently, worst-case complexity is not unrelated to average case complexity (Li and Vitanyi 1992; Vlasie 1996). Oversimplified, average-case complexity amounts to worst case complexity, if the input instances are drawn according to a particular "universal distribution" which, roughly speaking, attaches to objects having a regular structure that is simple to produce a higher probability than to objects having a random structure. This applies well to many computational problems, and as shown in Li and Vitanyi (1992), explains the fact that algorithms such as quicksort show in practice a behavior different from the one expected from the standard average case analysis, which uses uniform distribution.

Furthermore, the complexity results have also qualitative aspects, concerning feasible algorithm schemes for implementation, or approximability. For example, any of the above problems which is in NP or in FNP can be solved by an algorithm which follows a simple backtracking strategy, such that the problem is solved when a success node is reached in the computation. However, for problems with complexity beyond NP, a simple "flat" backtracking strategy in which expansion of the current computation state is done by executing a polynomial time operation, is no longer feasible. Here, the expansion of the current computation state may require the execution of an operation whose cost is beyond P. For example, for problems in Σ_2^P, a nested backtracking strategy is feasible, in which the current computation state can be expanded by the use of an NP-oracle in polynomial time—this oracle may well be implemented by an advanced flat backtracking algorithm. In general, for problems in Σ_k^P, a k-nested backtracking strategy is feasible. If a problem is complete for Σ_k^P, then a $k-1$-nested backtracking algorithm is unlikely to exist, and we should not waste time in trying to find such an algorithm.

For further discussion on issues of algorithm design and approximation, we refer the reader to (Eiter and Gottlob 1995; Eiter et al. 1997) and references therein.

11.4 Basic Complexity Results

This section contains the first part of the derivation of the complexity results which have been presented in Section 11.3. The focus in this section is on the base case, in which we have programs without integrity constraints (though cases where results on integrity constraints follow as immediate extensions of the no-integrity-constraint case are also included). As Tables 11.1 and 11.4 show, in general the presence of integrity constraints has an effect on the complexity of some problems, while it has not for others. For the latter problems, we discuss this effect in detail in the next section. In this section, as complexity results are discussed, we also develop algorithms for various status set computations.

11.4.1 Positive Programs

The most natural question is whether a feasible status set exists for program $\mathcal{P}$ on a given state $\mathcal{O}_S$. As we have seen, this is not always the case. However, for fixed positive programs, we can always efficiently find a feasible status set (so one exists), and moreover, even a rational status set, measured in the size of the input $\mathcal{O}_S$. This is possible using the algorithm **Compute-P-RSS** below, where the program $\mathcal{P}$ and possibly integrity and action constraints are in the background.

THEOREM 11.4.1 (POLYNOMIAL TIME COMPUTABILITY OF **Compute-P-RSS**) Let $\mathcal{P}$ be a fixed positive agent program (where $\mathcal{IC}$ is arbitrary). Then, given an agent state $\mathcal{O}_S$, the unique rational status set of $\mathcal{P}$ on $\mathcal{O}_S$ (so it exists) is computed by **Compute-P-RSS** in polynomial time. Moreover, if $\mathcal{IC} = \emptyset$, then deciding whether $\mathcal{P}$ has some feasible status

---

Algorithm 11.4.1 (Rational Status Sets for Positive Programs)
Compute-P-RSS($\mathcal{O}_S$: agent state)

($\star$ input is an agent state $\mathcal{O}_S$, the agent program $\mathcal{P}$ is positive; $\star$)
($\star$ output is the unique rational status set of $\mathcal{P}$, if it exists, $\star$)
($\star$ otherwise, the output is "No." $\star$)

1. $S := lfp(\mathbf{T}_{\mathcal{P}, \mathcal{O}_S})$;
2. **if** S satisfies (S2) and (S4) of a feasible status set
3. **then output** S
4. **else output** "No";

end.

set on $\mathcal{O}_S$, as well as computing any such status set, is possible in polynomial time using **Compute-P-RSS**.

Proof By Theorem 6.5.1 on page 180 and the fact that S satisfies ($S1$) and ($S3$), algorithm correctly computes the unique rational status set of $\mathcal{P}$ on $\mathcal{O}_S$.

By the assumptions that we made at the beginning of this section, Step 1 can be done in polynomial time, since a fixed $\mathcal{P}$ amounts to a ground instance which is polynomial in the size of $\mathcal{O}_S$, and we can compute $S = lfp(\mathbf{T}_{\mathcal{P},\mathcal{O}_S})$ bottom up by evaluating the sequence $\mathbf{T}_{\mathcal{P},\mathcal{O}_S}{}^i$, $i \geq 0$, until the fixpoint is reached.

Observe that, of course, checking ($S2$) (action and deontic consistency)—or part of this criterion—in algorithm **Compute-P-RSS** can be done at any time while computing the sequence $\mathbf{T}_{\mathcal{P},\mathcal{O}_S}{}^i$, and the computation can be stopped as soon as an inconsistency is detected.

Step 2, i.e., checking whether S satisfies the conditions ($S2$) and ($S4$) of the feasible status set condition is, by our assumptions, possible in polynomial time. Therefore, for fixed $\mathcal{P}$ (and tacitly assumed fixed action and integrity constraints in the background), algorithm **Compute-Pos-Rational-SS** runs in polynomial time.

If $\mathcal{IC} = \emptyset$, then Proposition 6.5.3 on page 181 implies that $\mathcal{P}$ has a feasible status set on $\mathcal{O}_S$ *if and only if* it has a rational status set. Therefore, deciding the existence of a feasible status set (and computing one) can be done by using **Compute-P-RSS** in polynomial time. ∎

The following result is immediately derivable from the previous: Given $\mathcal{P}, \mathcal{O}_S$, and a status set S, for checking whether S is rational, we merely need to test whether (*i*) $S = lfp(\mathbf{T}_{\mathcal{P},\mathcal{O}_S})$ and (*ii*) S satisfies conditions ($S2$) and ($S4$) of a feasible status set. The proof of Theorem 11.4.1 on the page before immediately tells us that these steps are executable in polynomial time.

COROLLARY 11 Let $\mathcal{P}$ be a fixed positive agent program (where $\mathcal{IC}$ is arbitrary). Then, given an agent state $\mathcal{O}_S$ and a status set S, deciding whether S is a rational status set of $\mathcal{P}$ on $\mathcal{O}_S$ is polynomial.

As any fixed positive agent program has at most one rational status set, it follows immediately that possible and certain reasoning can be performed in the same time (i.e., polynomial) as it takes to construct such a status set.

COROLLARY 12 Let $\mathcal{P}$ be a fixed positive agent program. Then, given an agent state $\mathcal{O}_S$ and a ground action α, deciding whether α is true in some (resp. every) rational status set of $\mathcal{P}$ on $\mathcal{O}_S$ is polynomial.

Since for every positive agent program $\mathcal{P}$, the rational status set, the reasonable status set, and their preferred variants coincide, the results for rational status sets in Theorem 11.4.1 on the preceding page and Corollaries 11 and 12 extend to these kinds of status sets as well.

Section 11.4   Basic Complexity Results   419

Algorithm 11.4.2 (Weak Rational Status Sets for Pos. Programs without Constraints)
Compute-PNIC-Weak-RSS($\mathcal{O}_S$: agent state)

($\star$ the agent program $\mathcal{P}$ is positive, and $\mathcal{IC} = \emptyset$; $\star$)
($\star$ input is an agent state $\mathcal{O}_S$; $\star$)
($\star$ output is a weak rational status set of $\mathcal{P}$ if one exists, $\star$)
($\star$ otherwise, the output is "No." $\star$)

1. $A := \emptyset$;
2. $GA :=$ set of all ground actions;
3. $S := lfp(\mathbf{T}_{\mathcal{P},\mathcal{O}_S,A})$;
4. **if** S is not A-feasible **then output** "No" (halt)
5. **else**
6. $\{A := A(S); GA := GA \setminus A(S);$
7. $\}$
8. **if** $GA = \emptyset$ **then output** S (halt);
9. select some ground action $\alpha \in GA$;
10. $A' := A \cup \{\alpha\}$;
11. $S' := lfp(\mathbf{T}_{\mathcal{P},\mathcal{O}_S,A'})$;
12. **if** S' is A'-feasible **then**
13. $\{A := A(S')$;
14. $GA := GA \setminus A(S')$;
15. $S := S'$;
16. $\}$
17. **goto** 8;
end.

Weak Rational Status Sets   In this subsection, we address the problem of computing a weak rational status set for a positive program. For a fixed positive agent program $\mathcal{P}$, it is possible to compute a weak rational status set on a given agent state $\mathcal{O}_S$ in polynomial time, provided that the no integrity constraints are present.

In fact, this is possible by using the algorithm **Compute-PNIC-Weak-RSS** below.

We remark that this simple algorithm can be speeded up by exploiting some further properties. The computation of S' on line 11 can be done by least fixpoint iteration starting from S rather than from the empty set (cf. Proposition 6.5.6 on page 190). The next result—whose proof is omitted here—states that the algorithm is correct and works in polynomial time.

THEOREM 11.4.2 (COMPUTE-PNIC-WEAK-RSS IS IN P)   Given a positive program $\mathcal{P}$ and an agent state $\mathcal{O}_S$, algorithm **Compute-PNIC-Weak-RSS** correctly outputs a weak rational status set of $\mathcal{P}$ on $\mathcal{O}_S$ (so one exists) if $\mathcal{IC} = \emptyset$. Moreover, for fixed $\mathcal{P}$, **Compute-PNIC-Weak-RSS** runs in polynomial time.

This result says that we can compute an arbitrary weak rational status set in polynomial time under the asserted restrictions. However, this does not mean that we can efficiently recognize a weak rational status set. The next result shows that this is in fact possible.

THEOREM 11.4.3 (DECIDING WEAKLY RATIONALITY IS POLYNOMIAL) Let $\mathcal{P}$ be a fixed positive agent program, and suppose $\mathcal{IC} = \emptyset$. Then, given an agent state $\mathcal{O}_S$ and a status set S, deciding whether S is a weak rational status set of $\mathcal{P}$ is polynomial.

Proof By Proposition 6.5.5 on page 190, S must be $A(S)$-feasible if it is a weak rational status set. Since for any set of ground actions A, testing A-feasibility is not harder than testing feasibility, by Proposition 11.4.1 on page 422 we obtain that this condition can be tested in polynomial time.

If S is $A(S)$-feasible, then, since $\mathcal{P}$ is positive and $\mathcal{IC} = \emptyset$, by Theorem 6.5.4 S is a weak rational status set, *if and only if* for every ground action $\alpha \notin A(S)$, the status set $S' = lfp(T_{\mathcal{P}, \mathcal{O}_S, A'})$ is not A'-feasible, where $A' = A \cup \{\alpha\}$. For each such α, this condition can be checked in polynomial time, and there are only polynomially many such α, hence, the required time is polynomial. Consequently, the overall recognition test is polynomial.

We remark that algorithm **Compute-PNIC-Weak-RSS** can be modified to implement the recognition test. We omit the details, however. ■

As for action reasoning from weak rational status sets, we face for the first time intractable problems in our analysis. The intuitive reason for intractability is that an exponential number of weak rational status sets might exist, all of which must be examined for answering the problem, and there seems no way of efficiently pruning this search space.

THEOREM 11.4.4 (NP-COMPLETENESS OF DECIDING **Do**-ATOMS) Let $\mathcal{P}$ be a fixed positive agent program $\mathcal{P}$, and suppose $\mathcal{IC} = \emptyset$. Then, given an agent state $\mathcal{O}_S$ and a ground action atom α, deciding whether $\alpha \in \mathbf{Do}\,(S)$ holds for (*i*) some weak rational status set (resp., (*ii*) every weak rational status set) of $\mathcal{P}$ on $\mathcal{O}_S$ is NP-complete (resp., co-NP-complete).

Proof It is not hard to see that algorithm **Compute-PNIC-Weak-RSS** is nondeterministically complete, i.e., every weak rational status set S is produced upon proper choices on line 9 of the algorithm. Therefore, by checking $\mathbf{Do}\,(\alpha) \in S$ (resp., $\mathbf{Do}\,(\alpha) \notin S$) before termination, we obtain membership in NP (resp., co-NP).

For the hardness part, we present a reduction from the complement of M3SAT 11.1.1 on page 402 for (*ii*). A similar reduction for (*i*) is described in (Eiter and Subrahmanian 1999), which we omit here.

Let $\phi = \bigwedge_{i=1}^{m} C_i$, $C_i = L_{i,1} \vee L_{i,2} \vee L_{i,3}$, be an instance of M3SAT, over atoms $X = \{x_1, \ldots, x_n\}$. In our reduction, we store the formula ϕ in a database $\mathcal{D}$. We assume that $\mathcal{D}$ has two relations POS (V_1, V_2, V_3) and NEG (V_1, V_2, V_3), in which the positive and negative clauses of ϕ are stored, and a relation VAR (V) which contains all variables. For each positive clause C_i, there exists a tuple with the variables of C_i in POS, e.g., for $x_1 \vee x_4 \vee x_2$ the tuple (x_1, x_4, x_2), and likewise for the negative clauses a tuple with the variables in NEG, e.g., for $\neg x_3 \vee \neg x_1 \vee \neg x_2$ the tuple (x_3, x_1, x_2).

The action base $\mathcal{AB}$ contains the actions $set_0(X)$, $set_1(X)$, and α; every action has empty precondition and empty Add and Del-Set. Define now the program $\mathcal{P}$ as follows.

O$(set_0(X)) \leftarrow$ VAR(X)
O$(set_1(X)) \leftarrow$ VAR(X)
  Do $\alpha \leftarrow$ **Do** $(set_0(X_1))$, **Do** $(set_0(X_2))$, **Do** $(set_0(X_3))$, POS(X_1, X_2, X_3)
  Do $\alpha \leftarrow$ **Do** $(set_1(X_1))$, **Do** $(set_1(X_2))$, **Do** $(set_1(X_3))$, NEG(X_1, X_2, X_3)

On this program, we impose the following action constraint

AC : $\{set_0(X), set_1(X))\} \hookleftarrow$ VAR(X).

We set $\mathcal{AC} = \{AC\}$ and $\mathcal{IC} = \emptyset$. Intuitively, the weak rational status sets correspond to the truth value assignment for the variables in X; the maximality of weak rationality and the constraint AC effect that each variable $x_i \in X$ is assigned exactly one of the values 0 or 1.

Then, for the database instance D describing a formula ϕ, it is easily seen that every weak rational status set of $\mathcal{P}$ on D contains **Do** α, if and only if the corresponding M3SAT instance ϕ is a "No"-instance. Since $\mathcal{P}$ is easily constructed, the result is proved. ∎

Before closing this subsection, we remark that tractability of both problems can be asserted, if a total prioritization on the weak rational status sets is used, which technically is derived from a total ordering $\alpha_1 < \alpha_2 < \cdots < \alpha_n$ on the set of all ground actions. In this case, a positive agent program $\mathcal{P}$ has a unique weak rational status set S (if one exists). This set S can be constructed by selecting on line 9 of algorithm **Compute-PNIC-Weak-RSS** always the least action from GA with respect to $<$. Thus, in the absence of integrity constraints, the unique weak rational status set can be computed in polynomial time in this case.

11.4.2 Programs with Negation

If we allow unrestricted occurrence of negated status atoms in the rule bodies, then the complexity of evaluating agents programs increases. This is not very surprising, since this way, we can express logical disjunction of positive facts. For example, the rule

P$\alpha \leftarrow \neg$**F**α

leads to two rational status sets: $S_1 = \{\mathbf{P}\alpha\}$ and $S_2 = \{\mathbf{F}\alpha\}$. Informally, this clause expresses under rational status semantics the disjunction $\mathbf{F}\alpha \vee \mathbf{P}\alpha$. Notice that under the reasonable status semantics, the above rule has only a single reasonable status set, namely S_1. However, if we add its contrapositive

F$\alpha \leftarrow \neg$**P**α,

then the resulting program has the two reasonable status sets S_1 and S_2. Thus, in the general case, both rational and reasonable status set semantics allow for expressing disjunction, and are for this reason inherently complex.

Feasible Status Sets We note here that for feasible status sets, the recognition problem is tractable under the assumptions that we made, this can be easily seen.

PROPOSITION 11.4.1   Let $\mathcal{P}$ be a fixed agent program (where $\mathcal{IC}$ is arbitrary). Then, given a state $\mathcal{O}_S$ and a status set S, deciding whether S is a feasible status set of $\mathcal{P}$ on $\mathcal{O}_S$ is possible in polynomial time.

However, as the following result shows, the search for feasible status sets is intractable in the general case.

THEOREM 11.4.5 (NP-COMPLETENESS OF THE EXISTENCE OF A FEASIBLE SET)   Let $\mathcal{P}$ be a fixed agent program and suppose $\mathcal{IC} = \emptyset$. Then, given an agent state $\mathcal{O}_S$, deciding whether $\mathcal{P}$ has a feasible status set is NP-complete, and computing some feasible status set is complete for FNP.

Proof   By Proposition 11.4.1, we can guess and check a feasible status set of $\mathcal{P}$ on $\mathcal{O}_S$ in polynomial time. Hence, the existence problem is in NP, and the computation problem is in FNP.

To show NP-hardness, we describe a reduction from M3SAT. The reduction is similar to the one in the proof of Theorem 11.4.4. As there, we suppose that an M3SAT instance ϕ on variables $x_i \in X$ is stored in relations POS (positive clauses) and NEG (negative clauses), and that all variables x_i are stored in VAR. Moreover, we assume that $\mathcal{D}$ has a relation AUX (*Var*, *Val*), which contains in the initial database D all tuples $(x_i, 0)$, for all $x_i \in X$.

Now construct the following agent program $\mathcal{P}$:

$\mathbf{P}\beta \leftarrow$
$\mathbf{F}\beta \leftarrow \mathbf{F}\alpha(X_1), \mathbf{F}\alpha(X_2), \mathbf{F}\alpha(X_3), \text{POS}(X_1, X_2, X_3)$
$\mathbf{F}\beta \leftarrow \mathbf{P}\alpha(X_1), \mathbf{P}\alpha(X_2), \mathbf{P}\alpha(X_3), \text{NEG}(X_1, X_2, X_3)$
$\mathbf{P}\alpha(X_1) \leftarrow \neg \mathbf{F}\alpha(X_1), \text{VAR}(X_1)$

The action base $\mathcal{AB}$ contains two actions α and β, which have both empty preconditions and empty add and delete sets. Thus, these actions do not have any effect on the state of the database. We set $\mathcal{AC} = \emptyset$ and $\mathcal{IC} = \emptyset$.

Then, it is easy to see that $\mathcal{P}$ has a feasible status set over $\mathcal{O}_S$, if and only if ϕ is satisfiable; the satisfying truth value assignments of ϕ correspond naturally (but not 1-1) to the feasible status sets of $\mathcal{P}$ on $\mathcal{O}_S$. (Observe that every feasible status set must either contain $\mathbf{P}\alpha(x_i)$ or contain $\mathbf{F}\alpha(x_i)$, for every x_i, but not both. Intuitively, $\mathbf{P}\alpha(x_i)$ represents that x_i is true, while $\mathbf{F}\alpha(x_i)$ represents that x_i is false.) Since for a given formula ϕ the database instance D of $\mathcal{D}$ is clearly constructible in polynomial time, it follows that the decision problem is NP-hard. Moreover, by the correspondence between feasible sets status of $\mathcal{P}$ and the satisfying assignments of ϕ, it follows immediately that computing a feasible status set is hard for FNP.

Observe that we can replace in $\mathcal{P}$ the positive atoms $\mathbf{F}\alpha(\mathtt{X_i})$ in rule bodies by $\neg\mathbf{P}\alpha(\mathtt{X_i})$, without changing the feasible status sets. Moreover, the last rule could then also be removed, and still a feasible status exists if and only if ϕ is satisfiable. ∎

This negative result raises the issue of how we can achieve tractability of programs. There are different possibilities.

One possibility is that we identify syntactic constraints under which programs are guaranteed to be tractable. However, as the form of the program in the proof of the previous theorem indicates, rather strict conditions on negation must be imposed, in order to exclude possible inconsistencies. Still, a number of different feasible and rational status sets may exist, owing to the inherent logical disjunction. In particular, the reduction in the proof of Theorem 11.4.5 works for rational status sets as well.

Another possibility is that we use an alternative semantics which is more amenable to cutting disjunctive cases. In particular, under *reasonable* status set semantics, the program in the proof of Theorem 11.4.5 either has no reasonable status set, or a unique such status set, which can be efficiently determined in polynomial time, notice that $\mathbf{F}\alpha(x_i)$ is not contained in any reasonable status set, since there is no possibility for deriving $\mathbf{F}\alpha(x_i)$ by means of the head of a program rule or by deontic closure. However, if we add the rule

$$\mathbf{F}\alpha(\mathtt{X_1}) \leftarrow \neg\mathbf{P}\alpha(\mathtt{X_1})$$

to the program, then the reasonable status sets of the resulting program $\mathcal{P}'$ coincide with the rational status sets of $\mathcal{P}$. Hence, also the computation of a reasonable status set is intractable in general. We will deal with reasonable status set in detail in Subsection 11.4.2.

From Theorem 11.4.5, the following result on action reasoning on the feasible status sets is easily derived.

THEOREM 11.4.6 (NP-COMPLETENESS FOR DECIDING **Do**-ATOMS)   Let $\mathcal{P}$ be a fixed agent program. Then, given an agent state $\mathcal{O}_S$ and a ground action α, deciding whether $\alpha \in \mathbf{Do}\,(S)$ for (*i*) every (resp., (*ii*) some) feasible status set S of $\mathcal{P}$ on $\mathcal{O}_S$, is co-NP-complete (resp., NP-complete).

Proof   A guess for a feasible status set S such that $\alpha \notin \mathbf{Do}\,(S)$ (resp., $\alpha \in \mathbf{Do}\,(S)$) can be verified in polynomial time (Proposition 11.4.1).

For the hardness part of (i), observe that the atom **Do** (β) belongs to every feasible status set of the program $\mathcal{P}$ in the proof of Theorem 11.4.5, if and only if $\mathcal{P}$ has no feasible status set. For (ii), we add the rule **Do** $\beta \leftarrow$. Then, **Do** (β) occurs in some feasible status set of the resulting program if and only if $\mathcal{P}$ has some feasible status set. This proves the result. ∎

Rational Status Sets For the existence problem, we obtain from Proposition 6.5.3 and Theorem 11.4.5 immediately the following result.

THEOREM 11.4.7 (EXISTENCE OF RATIONAL SETS IS NP-COMPLETE) Let $\mathcal{P}$ be a fixed agent program, and suppose $\mathcal{IC} = \emptyset$. Then, given an agent state $\mathcal{O}_S$, deciding whether $\mathcal{P}$ has a rational status set on $\mathcal{O}_S$ is NP-complete.

The condition that a feasible status set is grounded requires a minimality check. It turns out that this minimality check is, in general, an expensive operation. In fact, the following holds.

THEOREM 11.4.8 (DECIDING GROUNDEDNESS IS co-NP-COMPLETE) Let $\mathcal{P}$ be a fixed agent program, and suppose $\mathcal{IC} = \emptyset$. Then, given an agent state $\mathcal{O}_S$ and a feasible status set S for $\mathcal{P}$ on $\mathcal{O}_S$, deciding whether S is grounded is co-NP-complete.

Proof For refuting that S is grounded, we can guess a status set S' such that $S' \subset S$ and verify in polynomial time that S' satisfies the conditions $(S1)$–$(S3)$ of a feasible status set.

To show that the problem is co-NP-hard, we use a variant of the construction in the proof of Theorem 11.4.5. For the CNF formula ϕ there, we set up the following program $\mathcal{P}$:

$\mathbf{P}\beta \leftarrow$
$\mathbf{F}\beta \leftarrow \neg \mathbf{P}\gamma, \neg \mathbf{P}\alpha(X_1), \neg \mathbf{P}\alpha(X_2), \neg \mathbf{P}\alpha(X_3), \text{POS}(X_1, X_2, X_3)$
$\mathbf{F}\beta \leftarrow \neg \mathbf{P}\gamma, \mathbf{P}\alpha(X_1), \mathbf{P}\alpha(X_2), \mathbf{P}\alpha(X_3), \text{NEG}(X_1, X_2, X_3)$
$\mathbf{P}\alpha(X_1) \leftarrow \mathbf{P}\gamma, \text{VAR}(X_1)$

Here, γ is a new action of the same type as α and β.

It is easily seen that $S = \{\mathbf{P}\beta, \mathbf{P}\gamma\} \cup \{\mathbf{P}\alpha(x_i) \mid i = 1, \ldots, n\}$ is a feasible status set of $\mathcal{P}$. Observe that any feasible status set $S' \neq S$ such that $S' \subseteq S$ must satisfy $\mathbf{P}\gamma \notin S'$. It holds that S is grounded, if and only if formula ϕ is not satisfiable. This proves co-NP-hardness.

The reduction even allows to derive another result. In fact, observe that any rational status set of $\mathcal{P}$ is contained in S: if $\mathbf{P}\gamma \in S'$ for a status set S' which satisfies $(S1)$–$(S3)$, then clearly $S' \supseteq S$ holds, otherwise, if $\mathbf{P}\gamma \notin S'$, then $S' \subset S$ must hold. Assume w.l.o.g. that either ϕ is unsatisfiable, or all its satisfying assignments, viewed as Boolean vectors, are incomparable. Then, S is the unique rational set of $\mathcal{P}$, if and only if ϕ is unsatisfiable. As a consequence, deciding whether a nonpositive agent program has a unique rational status set is co-NP-hard as well. ∎

The complexity of the recognition problem is an immediate consequence of the previous theorem and Proposition 11.4.1.

COROLLARY 13 Let $\mathcal{P}$ be a fixed agent program, and suppose $\mathcal{IC} = \emptyset$. Then, given an agent state $\mathcal{O}_S$ and a status set S, deciding whether S is a rational status set for $\mathcal{P}$ on $\mathcal{O}_S$ is co-NP-complete.

In the absence of integrity constraints, the rational status sets coincide with the minimal feasible status sets. Using an NP oracle, we can compute a rational status set as done by **Compute-NIC-Rational-SS** below.

This algorithm correctly outputs a rational status set (so one exists) in polynomial time modulo checking the condition on line 5, which can be accomplished by calling an NP-oracle and negating the result. Hence, the problem is in FP^{NP}. This upper bound can be improved to FNP//log, since we can nondeterministically compute a rational status set as follows.

1. Compute the smallest size s of a feasible status set S,

2. nondeterministically generate, i.e., guess and check a feasible status set S such that $|S| = s$, and output it.

Step 1 amounts to an NP optimization problem whose output has $O(\log |I|)$ bits: an instance I is given by (fixed) $\mathcal{P}$ and $\mathcal{O}_S$, and the solutions are the feasible status sets (which are recognizable in polynomial time). The cost of any solution S is its cardinality $|S|$, and deciding whether $s = \text{opt}(I) \geq k$ is in NP. Furthermore, s has in binary notation $O(\log |I|)$ many bits. Step 2 is polynomial by Proposition 11.4.1. Hence, the overall algorithm proves that computing a rational status set is in FNP//log, if $IC = \emptyset$. We obtain the following result.

Algorithm 11.4.3 (Rational Status Sets for Arbitrary Programs, $\mathcal{IC} = \emptyset$)
Compute-NIC-Rational-SS($\mathcal{O}_S$: agent state)

($\star$ agent program $\mathcal{P}$ is arbitrary, but $\mathcal{IC} = \emptyset$, $\star$)
($\star$ input is an agent state $\mathcal{O}_S$; $\star$)
($\star$ output is a rational status set of $\mathcal{P}$ if one exists, $\star$)
($\star$ otherwise, the output is "No." $\star$)

1. $S := \emptyset$; $GA :=$ set of all ground action status atoms;
2. **if** S is a feasible status set **then output** S (halt);
3. **if** $GA = \emptyset$ **then output** "No" (halt);
4. select some atom $A \in GA$;
5. **if** $\not\exists$ feasible status set $S' : S \subseteq S' \subseteq S \cup (GA \setminus \{A\})$ **then** $S := S \cup \{A\}$;
6. $GA := GA \setminus \{A\}$;
7. **goto** 2.

end.

THEOREM 11.4.9 (COMPUTING RATIONAL STATUS SETS IS IN FNP//log) Let $\mathcal{P}$ be a fixed agent program, and suppose $\mathcal{IC} = \emptyset$. Given an agent state $\mathcal{O}_S$, computing any rational status set of $\mathcal{P}$ on $\mathcal{O}_S$ is in FNP//log and hard for both FNP and $\mathrm{FP}_{\parallel}^{\mathrm{NP}}$.

Proof By the previous discussion, it follows that the problem is in FNP//log. Hardness for FNP follows from the proof of Theorem 11.4.5.

Thus, it remains to show hardness for $\mathrm{FP}_{\parallel}^{\mathrm{NP}}$. We establish this by a reduction of computing a minimal model of a propositional CNF formula ϕ, i.e., find a model M (satisfying truth value assignment to the variables), such that no model M' exists with $M' \subset M$, where a model is identified with the set of variables which are true in it. $\mathrm{FP}_{\parallel}^{\mathrm{NP}}$-hardness of this problem, even if all clauses in ϕ have at most three literals, follows easily from the results in (Chen and Toda 1995) (Lemma 4.7).

The reduction is an extension of the one in the proof of Theorem 11.4.8 (note the observations on rational status sets of the program $\mathcal{P}$ there, and that a rational status set always exists).

We use six further 3-ary relations $C_1, \ldots, C_6$ for storing the clauses which are neither positive nor negative, and add respective rules deriving $\mathbf{F}\beta$. More precisely, if we set $C_0 =$ NEG and $C_7 = $ POS, then the relation C_i stores the clauses $C = L_1 \vee L_2 \vee L_3$ such that the string $p(L_1)p(L_2)p(L_3)$ of the polarities of the literals yields i in binary, where $p(L) = 1$ if L is positive, and $p(L) = 0$, if L is negative. Thus, e.g., the clause $x_1 \vee x_5 \vee \neg x_3$ is stored as tuple (x_1, x_5, x_3) in the relation C_6, since $p(x_1)p(x_5)p(\neg x_3) = 110$.

Then, the rational status set of the resulting program $\mathcal{P}'$ on the database for ϕ correspond 1-1 to the minimal models of ϕ, if ϕ is satisfiable, and the set S from there is the unique rational status set if and only if ϕ is unsatisfiable. Moreover, from any rational status set, the corresponding minimal model $M = \{x_i \mid \mathbf{P}(x_i) \in S\}$ is easily computed. Hence, computing a minimal model reduces to computing a rational status set. This implies $\mathrm{FP}_{\parallel}^{\mathrm{NP}}$-hardness, and the theorem is proved. ∎

An improvement of these bounds, in particular completeness for FNP//log, seems to be difficult to achieve. In fact, it can be shown that in the case $\mathcal{IC} = \emptyset$, computing a rational status set is polynomial time equivalent to computing a minimal model of a CNF formula, which is not known to be complete for FNP//log, cf. (Chen and Toda 1995).

Action reasoning becomes harder in the brave variant if we use rational status sets instead of feasible status sets. The reason is that we have to check groundedness of a status set, which is a source of complexity and adds another level in the polynomial hierarchy. However, for the cautious variant, there is no complexity increase.

THEOREM 11.4.10 (CO-NP-COMPLETENESS FOR DECIDING **Do**-ATOMS) Let $\mathcal{P}$ be a fixed agent program $\mathcal{P}$, and suppose $\mathcal{IC} = \emptyset$. Given an agent state $\mathcal{O}_S$ and a ground action

Section 11.4 Basic Complexity Results 427

atom α, deciding whether $\alpha \in \mathbf{Do}\,(S)$ holds for (i) every (resp., (ii) some) rational status set of $\mathcal{P}$ on $\mathcal{O}_S$ is co-NP-complete (resp., Σ_2^P-complete).

Proof For (i), observe that to disprove $\alpha \in \mathbf{Do}\,(S)$ for every rational status set S, we can guess a feasible status set S such that $\alpha \notin S$ and verify the guess in polynomial time by Proposition 11.4.1. Hence, the problem is in co-NP. Hardness follows from the reduction in the proof of Theorem 11.4.5, there, $\mathbf{Do}\,(\beta)$ belongs to every rational status set of the constructed program $\mathcal{P}$, if and only if $\mathcal{P}$ has no feasible status set.

The membership part of (ii) is easy: A guess for a rational status set S such that $\alpha \in \mathbf{Do}\,(S)$ can be verified by Proposition 11.4.1 and Theorem 11.4.8 in polynomial time with the help of an NP oracle.

The hardness part is shown by a reduction from evaluating a quantified Boolean formula (QBF) of the form $\forall X \exists Y \phi$, where ϕ is in M3SAT form; deciding this problem is well-known Π_2^P-complete (Garey and Johnson 1979). The reduction combines the reductions in the proofs of Theorems 11.4.5 and 11.4.8 in a suitable way.

We extend the database $\mathcal{D}$ from the proofs of Theorems 11.4.5 and 11.4.8, by adding two further relations XVAR and YVAR for storing the variables of X and Y, respectively. Construct a program $\mathcal{P}$, using the actions α, β, and γ from the proof of Theorem 11.4.8 as follows.

$\mathbf{P}\beta \leftarrow$
$\mathbf{F}\beta \leftarrow \neg \mathbf{P}\gamma, \neg \mathbf{P}\alpha(X_1), \neg \mathbf{P}\alpha(X_2), \neg \mathbf{P}\alpha(X_3), \text{POS}(X_1, X_2, X_3)$
$\mathbf{F}\beta \leftarrow \neg \mathbf{P}\gamma, \mathbf{P}\alpha(X_1), \mathbf{P}\alpha(X_2), \mathbf{P}\alpha(X_3), \text{NEG}(X_1, X_2, X_3)$
$\mathbf{P}\alpha(X_1) \leftarrow \neg \mathbf{F}\alpha(X_1), \text{XVAR}(X_1)$
$\mathbf{P}\alpha(X_1) \leftarrow \mathbf{P}\gamma, \text{YVAR}(X_1)$
$\mathbf{Do}\,\gamma \leftarrow \mathbf{P}\gamma$

Clearly, every feasible status set S must contain either $\mathbf{P}\alpha(x_i)$ or $\mathbf{F}\alpha(x_i)$ (but not both), for every $x_i \in X$. Moreover, if $\mathbf{P}\gamma \in S$, then $\mathbf{Do}\,\gamma \in S$ and for all $y_j \in Y$, we have $\mathbf{P}\alpha(y_j) \in S$.

Let χ be a choice among the atoms $\mathbf{P}\alpha(x_i)$ and $\mathbf{F}\alpha(x_i)$, for all $x_i \in X$. Then, χ naturally represents a truth value assignment to X in which x_i is true if $\mathbf{P}\alpha(x_i) \in \chi$ and x_i is false if $\mathbf{F}\alpha(x_i) \in \chi$. Define

$S_\chi = \chi \cup \{\mathbf{P}\beta, \mathbf{P}\gamma, \mathbf{Do}\,\gamma\} \cup \{\mathbf{P}\alpha(y_j) \mid y_j \in Y\}.$

It holds that S_χ is a feasible status set, for every choice χ. We claim that every rational status set S of $\mathcal{P}$ must be contained in some of the S_χ.

To see this, notice that no atoms with status $\mathbf{W}$ or $\mathbf{O}$ can be in S, since there is no possibility to derive such an atom. For the same reason, no atoms $\mathbf{Do}\,\alpha(v)$, $\mathbf{Do}\,\beta$, $\mathbf{F}\gamma$ and

$F\alpha(y)$ can be in S, for every $v \in X \cup Y$ and $y \in Y$. Hence, by the observation on $\mathbf{P}\alpha(x)$ and $\mathbf{F}\alpha(x)$ from above, S must be a subset of some S_χ.

It is easy to set that S_χ is not grounded, if and only if $\mathbf{P}\gamma$ can be removed from it, such that $S_\chi \{\mathbf{P}\gamma, \mathbf{Do}\,\gamma\}$ contains a feasible status set. This happens to be the case if the formula $\exists Y \phi[X = \chi]$ is true. Thus, it follows that some rational status set of $\mathcal{P}$ contains $\mathbf{Do}\,\gamma$, if and only if S_χ is a rational status set of $\mathcal{P}$ for some χ, if and only if for some χ the formula $\phi[X = \chi]$ is unsatisfiable, if and only if $\forall X \exists Y \phi$ is false. Since the database D for $\forall X \exists Y \phi$ is constructible in polynomial time, this proves (*ii*) and the theorem. ■

Of course, for positive agent programs, action reasoning is easier. In fact, in this case it is polynomial for both (*i*) and (*ii*) since a rational status set, if it exists, is unique and polynomially executable.

Reasonable Status Sets Our first result on reasonable status sets is positive: the recognition problem, even in the general setting where we have negation and integrity constraints, is tractable.

THEOREM 11.4.11 (DECIDING REASONABILITY IS POLYNOMIAL) Let $\mathcal{P}$ be a fixed agent program (where $\mathcal{IC}$ is not necessarily empty). Then, given an agent state $\mathcal{O}_S$ and a status set S, deciding whether S is a reasonable status set of $\mathcal{P}$ on $\mathcal{O}_S$ is possible in polynomial time.

Proof The assumption implies that the ground instance of $\mathcal{P}$ over $\mathcal{O}_S$ is constructible in polynomial time, and, moreover, the reduct $red^S(\mathcal{P}, \mathcal{O}_S)$ is computable in polynomial time. By Theorem 11.4.1, the unique rational status set S' of $red^S(\mathcal{P}, \mathcal{O}_S)$ is computable in polynomial time, and it remains by Theorem 6.5.1 and the definition of a reasonable status set to check whether $S = S'$ (so S' exists). Overall, this yields a polynomial-time algorithm. ■

Computing a reasonable status set, however, is clearly intractable in the general case, even in the absence of integrity constraints.

THEOREM 11.4.12 (NP-COMPLETENESS OF EXISTENCE OF A REASONABLE SET) Let $\mathcal{P}$ be a fixed agent program (where $\mathcal{IC}$ is arbitrary). Then, given an agent state $\mathcal{O}_S$, deciding whether $\mathcal{P}$ has a reasonable status set on $\mathcal{O}_S$ is NP-complete, and computing some reasonable status set S of $\mathcal{P}$ on $\mathcal{O}_S$ is complete for FNP. Hardness holds even if $\mathcal{IC} = \emptyset$.

Proof The membership part follows from Theorem 11.4.11, since a guess for S can be verified in polynomial time.

The hardness part is shown by a slight modification of the reduction in the proof of Theorem 11.4.5. We add the rule

$\mathbf{F}\alpha(X_1) \leftarrow \neg \mathbf{P}\alpha(X_1), \text{VAR}(X_1)$

Section 11.4   Basic Complexity Results   429

to the program $\mathcal{P}$ there. Then, the reasonable status sets of the resulting program $\mathcal{P}'$ coincide with the rational status sets of $\mathcal{P}$. This proves the result. (Observe that $\mathcal{P}$ has either no reasonable status set, or a unique such status set; note that $\mathbf{F}\alpha(x_i)$ is not contained in any reasonable status set of $\mathcal{P}$, since there is no possibility for deriving $\mathbf{F}\alpha(x_i)$ by means of the head of a program rule or by deontic closure.)   ∎

It is clear in the light of this result that for nonpositive programs without integrity constraints, action reasoning on the reasonable status sets is intractable. However, compared to the rational status sets, the complexity of the brave variant is lower. This is explained by the fact that no expensive groundedness test for reasonable status is needed.

THEOREM 11.4.13   Let $\mathcal{P}$ be a fixed agent program $\mathcal{P}$ (where $\mathcal{IC}$ is arbitrary). Then, given an agent state $\mathcal{O}_S$ and a ground action atom α, deciding whether $\alpha \in \mathbf{Do}\,(S)$ holds for (*i*) every (resp., (*ii*) some) reasonable status set of $\mathcal{P}$ on $\mathcal{O}_S$ is co-NP-complete (resp., NP-complete). Hardness holds even if $\mathcal{IC} = \emptyset$.

Proof   A guess for a reasonable status set S of $\mathcal{P}$ such that $\alpha \in \mathbf{Do}\,(S)$ (resp., $\alpha \notin \neg\mathbf{Do}\,(\alpha)$) can be verified in polynomial time (Proposition 11.4.11). This proves membership.

Hardness for (*i*) and (*ii*) can be easily shown by modifying the reduction in the proof of Theorem 11.4.5 by adding the rule $\mathbf{F}(\alpha(X_1)) \leftarrow \neg\mathbf{P}(\alpha(X_1))$, VAR($X_1$) and query about β for (*i*); for (*ii*), add a further rule $\mathbf{Do}\,(\beta) \leftarrow$.   ∎

Weak Status Sets   In Subsection 11.4.1, we have already considered the computation of weak rational (resp., reasonable) status sets for positive programs. In the presence of negation, the concepts of weak rational status sets and weak reasonable status set do no longer coincide. Also, the complexities of the different concepts of status sets are different.

Compared to rational (resp., reasonable) status sets, we have here to deal with relativized action closure ACl_A, which results in A-feasibility, A-rationality etc. The relativization to A does not affect the complexity.

PROPOSITION 11.4.2   Let $\mathcal{P}$ be any program (where $\mathcal{IC}$ is arbitrary). Then, given an agent state $\mathcal{O}_S$, S and A, testing A-feasibility of S (resp., A-rationality, A-reasonability), has the same complexity as testing feasibility (resp., rationality, reasonability) of S.

Since under our assumptions, a weak rational (resp., weak reasonable) status set exists if and only if an A-rational (resp., A-reasonable) status set exists for some A, we easily obtain from the proofs of Theorems 11.4.5 and 11.4.12 the following result.

THEOREM 11.4.14   Let $\mathcal{P}$ be a fixed agent program, and suppose $\mathcal{IC} = \emptyset$. Then, given an agent state $\mathcal{O}_S$, deciding whether $\mathcal{P}$ has a weak rational (resp., reasonable) status set on $\mathcal{O}_S$ is NP-complete.

> **Algorithm 11.4.4 (Weak Rational Sets for arbitrary Programs, $\mathcal{IC} = \emptyset$)**
> **Compute-NIC-WRational-SS($\mathcal{O}_S$: agent state)**
>
> ($\star$ agent program $\mathcal{P}$ is arbitrary, but $\mathcal{IC} = \emptyset$; $\star$)
> ($\star$ input is an agent state $\mathcal{O}_S$; $\star$)
> ($\star$ output is a weak rational status set of $\mathcal{P}$ if one exists, $\star$)
> ($\star$ otherwise, the output is "No." $\star$)
>
> 1. $s := \max\{|A| \mid \mathcal{P} \text{ has an } A\text{-feasible status set on } \mathcal{O}_S\}$;
> 2. Compute a set A such that $|A| = s$ and some A-feasible status set exists;
> 3. $s' := \min\{|S| \mid S \text{ is an } A\text{-feasible status set on } \mathcal{O}_S\}$;
> 4. $S :=$ any A-feasible status set such that $|S| = s'$;
> 5. **output** S;
> **end**.

The computation of any weak rational status set can be accomplished using the algorithm **Compute-NIC-WRational-SS** described below.

The steps 1.–4. can be done in polynomial time with the help of an NP oracle. Therefore, computing a weak rational status set is in FP^{NP} in the absence of integrity constraints. Notice by Proposition 6.5.5, Steps 1 and 2 can be combined by computing a status set S which is $A(S)$-feasible and such that $|A(S)|$ is maximal.

For weak reasonable status sets, we can apply an adapted version of **Compute-NIC-WRational-SS**, in which "A-feasible" is replaced by "A-reasonable." Notice that existence problem for A-feasible and A-reasonable status sets has the same complexity.

Thus, for both kinds of status sets, the computation problem is polynomial if an NP oracle may be consulted. We can improve on this upper bound and give an exact characterization of the problem in terms of the complexity class FNP//log, which comprises computation problems with an adjunct NP optimization problem (see Section 11.1 and (Chen and Toda 1995)).

In our case, this NP optimization problem consists in the computation of the numbers s and s', respectively. It is possible to combine these two steps into a single NP optimization problem, such that we can generate, given its solution, nondeterministically in polynomial time a weak rational (resp., reasonable) status set.

THEOREM 11.4.15 (COMPUTING WEAK RATIONAL SETS IS FNP//log-COMPLETE) Let $\mathcal{P}$ be a fixed agent program and suppose that $\mathcal{IC} = \emptyset$. Then, computing any weak rational (resp., weak reasonable) status set of $\mathcal{P}$ on a given agent state $\mathcal{O}_S$ is complete for FNP//log.

Proof Let GA be the set of all ground action atoms. Associate with every status set S the tuple $t_S = \langle |A(S)|, |GA| - |S| \rangle$, if S is $A(S)$-rational, and $t_s = \langle -1, 0 \rangle$ otherwise, and

Section 11.4   Basic Complexity Results   431

impose on the tuples t_S the usual lexicographic order. Then, the following holds: Any status set S such that t_S is maximal is a weak rational status set, if and only if $t_S \neq \langle -1, 0\rangle$.

Given a maximal tuple $t_S \neq \langle -1, 0\rangle$, it is clearly possible to generate a weak rational status set S nondeterministically in polynomial time, so one exists. Moreover, the tuples t_S can be easily encoded by polynomial size numbers $z(t_S)$, such that $z(t_S) > z(t_{S'})$ if and only if $t_S > t_{S'}$, e.g., define $z(\langle i, j\rangle) = (|GA| + 1)i + j$. Computing the maximum $z(t_S)$ is an NP optimization problem, and from any $z(t_S)$, the tuple t_S is easily computed. Hence, it follows that computing a weak rational status set is in FNP//log.

It remains to show hardness for this class. For this purpose, we reduce the computation of an X-maximal model (see Section 11.1) to this problem. Without loss of generality, we assume that ϕ is an M3SAT instance. Indeed, we may split larger clauses by introducing new variables, and exchange positive (resp., negative) literals in clauses by using for each variable x a new variable $\hat{x}$ which is made equivalent to $\neg x$. (All new variables do not belong to the set X.)

The reduction is similar to the one in the proof of Theorem 11.4.4. We use the action base and database from there, and introduce a further relation XVAR for storing the variables in X. Consider the following program $\mathcal{P}$:

O(set_1(X)) $\leftarrow$ XVAR(X)
Do (set_0(X)) $\leftarrow$ ¬**Do** (set_1(X)), VAR(X)
    Pα $\leftarrow$
    Fα $\leftarrow$ **Do** (set_0(X$_1$)), **Do** (set_0(X$_2$)), **Do** (set_0(X$_3$)), POS(X$_1$, X$_2$, X$_3$)
    Fα $\leftarrow$ **Do** (set_1(X$_1$)), **Do** (set_1(X$_2$)), **Do** (set_1(X$_3$)), NEG(X$_1$, X$_2$, X$_3$)

and impose on it the action constraint AC:

AC: $\{set_0$(X), set_1(X)$\}$ $\leftrightarrow$ VAR(X).

The first rule states that every variable in X should be set to true, and the second rule together with AC effects that x_i is either set to **true** or to **false**, but not both.

It is easily seen that the weak rational status sets S of $\mathcal{P}$ on the input database D for an M3SAT instance ϕ correspond 1-1 to the X-maximal models of ϕ. From every such S, the X-part of the corresponding X-maximal model is easily obtained.

Since D is efficiently constructed from ϕ in polynomial time, it follows that computing a weak rational status set is hard for FNP//log.

The proof of hardness for computing a weak reasonable status set is similar; we use an additional clause **Do** (set_1(X)) $\leftarrow$ ¬**Do** (set_0(X)), VAR(X) . This proves the result. ∎

Like in the case of positive programs, recognition of a weak rational status set S is no harder than computation, even if programs are nonpositive. The recognition problem is solved by the following algorithm.

Algorithm 11.4.5 (Recognition of Weak Rational Status Sets)
Rec-NIC-WRational($\mathcal{O}_S$: agent state; S: status set)

(⋆ agent program $\mathcal{P}$ is arbitrary, but $\mathcal{IC} = \emptyset$;   ⋆)
(⋆ input is an agent state $\mathcal{O}_S$, and a status set S;   ⋆)
(⋆ output is "Yes," if S is a weak rational status set of $\mathcal{P}$,   ⋆)
(⋆ otherwise, the output is "No."   ⋆)

    1. **if** S is not $A(S)$-feasible **or**
    2. $\exists S' \subset S$: S is $A(S)$-feasible **or**
    3. $\exists S'$: S' is $A(S')$-feasible and $A(S) \subset A(S')$
    4. **then output** "No"
    5. **else output** "Yes";
end.

The correctness of this algorithm follows from Proposition 6.5.5. However, it is not clear how to implement it such that it runs in polynomial time. The next theorem establishes that such an implementation is unlikely to exist, nor that any polynomial time algorithm for this problem is known.

THEOREM 11.4.16   Let $\mathcal{P}$ be a fixed agent program and suppose that $\mathcal{IC} = \emptyset$. Then, given an agent state $\mathcal{O}_S$ and a status set S, deciding whether S is a weak rational status set of $\mathcal{P}$ on $\mathcal{P}$ is co-NP-complete.

Proof Algorithm **Rec-NIC-WRational** can be easily rewritten as a nondeterministic polynomial time algorithm for refuting that S is a weak rational status set. Hardness is immediate from the proof of Theorem 11.4.8. ∎

A weak reasonable status set can be recognized in a similar way, as done by algorithm **Rec-WReasonable** below.

Algorithm 11.4.6 (Recognition of Weakly Reasonable Status Sets)
Rec-WReasonable($\mathcal{O}_S$: agent state; S: status set)

(⋆ agent program $\mathcal{P}$ and $\mathcal{IC}$ are arbitrary;   ⋆)
(⋆ input is an agent state $\mathcal{O}_S$, and a status set S;   ⋆)
(⋆ output is "Yes," if S is a weak reasonable status set of $\mathcal{P}$ ⋆)
(⋆ otherwise, the output is "No."   ⋆)

    1. **if** S is not $A(S)$-reasonable **or**
    2. $\exists S'$: S' is $A(S')$-reasonable and $A(S) \subset A(S')$
    3. **then output** "No"
    4. **else output** "Yes"
end.

The correctness of this algorithm follows from Proposition 6.5.5. We obtain the following result.

THEOREM 11.4.17   Let $\mathcal{P}$ be a fixed agent program (where $\mathcal{IC}$ is arbitrary). Then, given an agent state $\mathcal{O}_S$ and a status set S, deciding whether S is a weak reasonable status set is co-NP-complete. Hardness holds even if $\mathcal{IC} = \emptyset$.

Proof   Clearly, algorithm **Rec-WReasonable** can be turned into a NP-algorithm for showing that S is not a weak rational status set.

The hardness part follows by an easy modification to the proof of Theorem 11.4.5. Add as in the proof of Theorem 11.4.12 the rule

$\mathbf{F}\alpha(X_1) \leftarrow \neg \mathbf{P}\alpha(X_1), \text{VAR}(X_1),$

and add $\mathbf{O}\beta \leftarrow$. Furthermore, add the atom $\mathbf{Do}\,\beta$ in the bodies of all rules with head $\mathbf{F}\beta$.

Assume without loss of generality that the truth value assignment to X in which every variable x_i is *false* does not satisfy ϕ. Then, $S = \{\mathbf{F}(x_i) \mid x_i \in X\} \cup \{\mathbf{P}\beta, \mathbf{O}\beta\}$ is $A(S)$-reasonable. It is easily seen that S is a weak reasonable status set, if and only if ϕ is not satisfied by any assignment in which some variable x_i is true. ∎

When we switch from rational (resp., reasonable) status sets to weak versions, the complexity of action reasoning is partially affected in the absence of integrity constraints.

It is easy to see that for the brave variant, the complexity for the weak and the ordinary version of rational status sets is the same. In both cases, the straightforward guess-and-check algorithm yields the same upper bound, and the result for brave rational action reasoning has been derived without involving obligations.

For the cautious variant, we find a complexity increase, even if the complexity of the recognition problem has not changed. The reason is that the beneficial monotonicity property of finding just some feasible status set which does not contain the action α in question as a proof that α does not occur in all rational status sets, can (in a suitable adaptation) no longer be exploited.

THEOREM 11.4.18   Let $\mathcal{P}$ be a fixed agent program $\mathcal{P}$, and suppose $\mathcal{IC} = \emptyset$. Then, given an agent state $\mathcal{O}_S$ and a ground action α, deciding whether $\alpha \in \mathbf{Do}\,(S)$ holds for (*i*) every (resp., (*ii*) some) weak rational status set of $\mathcal{P}$ on $\mathcal{O}_S$ is Π_2^P-complete (resp., Σ_2^P-complete).

Proof   The proof for (*ii*) is in the discussion above. For (*i*), observe that a weak rational status set S such that $\alpha \notin \mathbf{Do}\,(S)$ can be guessed and checked with an NP oracle in polynomial time (Theorem 11.4.17).

For the hardness part of (*i*), we adapt the construction in the proof of Theorem 11.4.15 for a reduction from QBF formulas $\forall X \exists Y \phi$, where ϕ is in M3SAT form.

We use the action base $\mathcal{AB}$ from there and extend it with another action β of the same type as α. Moreover, we use the relations POS and NEG for storing the clauses of ϕ (cf. proof of Theorem 11.4.4), and replace VAR by the relations XVAR and YVAR for storing the variables in X and Y, respectively.

Then, we set up the following program:

$\mathbf{O}(set_0(X_1)) \leftarrow \text{XVAR}(X_1)$
$\mathbf{O}(set_1(X_1)) \leftarrow \text{XVAR}(X_1)$
$\mathbf{Do}\,(set_0(Y_1)) \leftarrow \neg\mathbf{Do}\,(set_1(Y_1)), \text{YVAR}(Y_1)$
$\quad\quad \mathbf{F}\beta \leftarrow \mathbf{Do}\,(set_0(X_1)), \mathbf{Do}\,(set_0(X_2)), \mathbf{Do}\,(set_0(X_3)), \text{POS}(X_1, X_2, X_3)$
$\quad\quad \mathbf{F}\beta \leftarrow \mathbf{Do}\,(set_1(X_1)), \mathbf{Do}\,(set_1(X_2)), \mathbf{Do}\,(set_1(X_3)), \text{NEG}(X_1, X_2, X_3)$
$\quad\quad \mathbf{O}(\alpha) \leftarrow$
$\quad\quad \mathbf{P}(\beta) \leftarrow \mathbf{Do}\,(\alpha)$

Furthermore, we introduce an action constraint:

$AC: \quad \{set_0(X_1), set_1(X_1)\} \hookleftarrow \text{XVAR}(X_1).$

In the above program, the agent is informally obliged by the first two clauses to set every variable $x \in X$ to both true and false, which is prohibited by AC. By the maximality of weak rational status set, the agent can safely follow one of the two obligations and assign each variable x_i in X a truth value, which creates an exponential number of possibilities. The subsequent clause, together with the minimality property of an A-rational set, forces she to assign each variable in Y a truth value. The next two clauses check whether the formula ϕ is violated. If so, then $\mathbf{F}\beta$ is derived. In this case, the agent cannot take action α as obliged from the rule $\mathbf{O}(\alpha) \leftarrow$; hence, she must violate this obligation in that case. Thus, if for a choice χ from $\mathbf{O}(set_0(x_i))$, $\mathbf{O}(set_1(x_i))$ for all $x_i \in X$ (representing a truth assignment to X), the formula $\phi[X = \chi]$ is unsatisfiable (i.e., $\forall X \exists Y \phi$ is false), then there exists a weak rational status set S such that $\alpha \notin \mathbf{Do}\,(S)$. Conversely, if $\alpha \notin \mathbf{Do}\,(S)$ for such a status set S, then a truth assignment χ to X (given by S) exists such that $\forall Y. \neg\phi[X = \chi]$ is true, i.e., $\forall X \exists Y \phi$ is false.

Consequently, $\alpha \in \mathbf{Do}\,(S)$ holds for every weak rational status set of $\mathcal{P}$ on the database D for $\forall X \exists Y \phi$ *if and only if* $\forall X \exists Y \phi$ is true. This proves Π_2^P-hardness of (i) and the result. ∎

For action reasoning with weak reasonable status sets, we obtain similar complexity results.

THEOREM 11.4.19 Let $\mathcal{P}$ be a fixed agent program. Then, given an agent state $\mathcal{O}_S$ and a ground action atom α, deciding whether $\alpha \in \mathbf{Do}\,(S)$ holds for (i) every (resp., (ii) some) weak reasonable status set of $\mathcal{P}$ on $\mathcal{O}_S$ is Π_2^P-complete (resp., Σ_2^P-complete). Hardness holds even if $\mathcal{IC} = \emptyset$.

Proof   A weak reasonable status set S such that $\alpha \notin \mathbf{Do}\,(S)$ (resp., $\alpha \in \mathbf{Do}\,(S)$) can be guessed and checked in polynomial time with an NP oracle by Theorem 11.4.17.

Hardness follows for both problems by a slight extension of the construction in the proof of Theorem 11.4.18. Add to the program $\mathcal{P}$ there the clause

$\mathbf{Do}\,(set_1(\mathrm{X})) \leftarrow \neg\mathbf{Do}\,(set_0(\mathrm{X})), \mathrm{YVAR}(\mathrm{X})$

Then, the weak reasonable status sets of the resulting program $\mathcal{P}'$ coincide with the weak rational status sets of $\mathcal{P}'$, which coincide with the weak rational status sets of $\mathcal{P}$. This proves the result for (*i*). For (*ii*), add the rule $\mathbf{Do}\,\gamma \leftarrow \neg\mathbf{Do}\,\alpha$ and query about γ.   ∎

11.4.3 Preferred Status Sets

Intuitively, adding a preference on rational or reasonable status sets does increase the complexity of the semantics. Even if we have checked that a status set S is rational (resp., reasonable), then we still have to verify that there is no other rational (resp., reasonable) status set S' which is preferred over S. This check appears to be expensive, since we have to explore an exponential candidate space of preferred rational (resp., reasonable) status sets S', and the test whether S' is in fact rational is expensive as well.

However, as it turns out, for rational status sets, preference does not lead to an increase in the complexity of action reasoning if integrity constraints are absent. On the other hand, preference does increase the complexity of action reasoning for reasonable status set. This is explained by the fact that for rational status sets, an increase in complexity is avoided since for deciding preference, it is sufficient to consider feasible status sets for ruling out a candidate S for a preferred rational set, and feasible status sets have lower complexity. For reasonable status sets, a similar property does not apply, and we enface the situation of being obliged to use reasonable status sets for eliminating a candidate.

In the rest of this chapter, we focus on F-preferred status sets. Similar results can be derived for the dual P-preferred status sets.

As for the consistency problem, it is clear that under our assumptions a F-preferred rational (resp., reasonable) status set exists just if some rational (resp., reasonable) status exists. Thus, we obtain from Theorems 11.4.7 and 11.4.12 the following corollary.

COROLLARY 14   Let $\mathcal{P}$ be a fixed agent program and suppose $\mathcal{IC} = \emptyset$. Then, given an agent state $\mathcal{O}_S$, deciding whether $\mathcal{P}$ has some F-preferred rational (resp., reasonable) status set on $\mathcal{O}_S$ is NP-complete.

For the recognition problem, one might expect a complexity increase if F-preference is applied to rational status sets. However, this is not the case. The reason is that F-preference and groundedness of a rational status set are not orthogonal sources of complexity in the absence of integrity constraints.

THEOREM 11.4.20   Let $\mathcal{P}$ be a fixed agent program, and suppose $\mathcal{IC} = \emptyset$. Then, given an agent state $\mathcal{O}_S$ and a status set S, deciding whether S is a F-preferred rational status sets of $\mathcal{P}$ on $\mathcal{O}_S$ is co-NP-complete.

Proof   By Proposition 11.4.1, one can decide in polynomial time whether S is a feasible status set. Now we exploit the following property: A feasible status set S of $\mathcal{P}$ is not a F-preferred rational status set of $\mathcal{P}$, *if and only if* there exists a feasible status set S' of $\mathcal{P}$ such that $\mathbf{F}(S') \subset \mathbf{F}(S)$ holds.

Therefore, we can refute that S is a F-preferred rational status set by guessing a status set S' and checking in polynomial time whether either S is not a feasible set, or whether S' is feasible and satisfies $\mathbf{F}(S') \subset \mathbf{F}(S)$. Hence, the problem is in co-NP.

Hardness is an immediate consequence of the proof of Theorem 11.4.8, as the candidate set S defined there satisfies $\mathbf{F}(S) = \emptyset$, and is thus F-preferred, if and only if it is grounded. ∎

The computation of an F-preferred rational status set is possible using a variant of the algorithm **Compute-NIC-Rational-SS** in Section 11.4.2 as follows. After Step 2, compute in a binary search the size s of the smallest possible $\mathbf{F}$-part over all feasible status sets of $\mathcal{P}$ on $\mathcal{O}_S$. Then, in the remaining steps of the algorithm, constrain the oracle query to existence of a feasible status set S' such that

$$S \subseteq S' \subseteq S \cup (GA \setminus \{A\}) \quad \text{and} \quad |\mathbf{F}(S')| = s.$$

This is a polynomial algorithm using an NP oracle, and hence the problem is in FP^{NP}.

A refined analysis unveils that the complexity of this problem is, like the one of computing a weak rational status set, captured by the class FNP//log.

THEOREM 11.4.21   Let $\mathcal{P}$ be a fixed agent program, and suppose $\mathcal{IC} = \emptyset$. Then, given an agent state $\mathcal{O}_S$, computing an arbitrary F-preferred rational status set of $\mathcal{P}$ on $\mathcal{O}_S$ is complete for FNP//log.

Proof   The proof of membership is similar to the FNP//log-membership proof for computing a weak rational status set. Indeed, the F-preferred status sets are the status sets S for which the tuple $t'_S = \langle |\mathbf{F}(S)|, |S| \rangle$ is minimal under lexicographic ordering, where infeasible status sets S have associated the tuple $t'_S = \langle |GA| + 1, |GA| \rangle$ and GA is the set of all ground action status atoms. From a minimal t'_S, a F-preferred rational status

Section 11.4   Basic Complexity Results   437

set can be nondeterministically constructed in polynomial time. Hence, the problem is in FNP//log.

The proof of hardness is by a reduction from the problem X-maximal model in the proof of Theorem 11.4.15, which is w.l.o.g. in M3SAT form.

We modify the program in the proof of Theorem 11.4.5 to the following program $\mathcal{P}'$:

$\mathbf{P}\beta \leftarrow$
$\mathbf{F}\beta \leftarrow \neg\mathbf{P}\alpha(X_1), \neg\mathbf{P}\alpha(X_2), \neg\mathbf{P}\alpha(X_3), \text{POS}(X_1, X_2, X_3)$
$\mathbf{F}\beta \leftarrow \mathbf{P}\alpha(X_1), \mathbf{P}\alpha(X_2), \mathbf{P}\alpha(X_3), \text{NEG}(X_1, X_2, X_3)$
$\mathbf{F}\alpha(X_1) \leftarrow \neg\mathbf{P}\alpha(X_1), \text{XVAR}(X_1)$

Here, XVAR stores the variables in X. The rational status sets of $\mathcal{P}'$ on the database D for ϕ correspond 1-1 to the models M of ϕ such that for the X-part fixed to $X \cap M$, the part of the remaining variables is minimal, i.e., to the models M such that no M' exists such that $M' \cap X = M \cap X$ and $M' \subset M$.

It is not hard to see that for every F-preferred rational status set S of $\mathcal{P}$ on D, the corresponding model M of ϕ is X-maximal. (Observe also that for every X-maximal model ϕ, there exists some F-preferred rational status set of $\mathcal{P}$ such that the corresponding model M' of ϕ satisfies $M' \cap X = M \cap X$.) Moreover, M is easily constructed from S. It follows that computing an arbitrary F-preferred rational status set is hard for FNP//log. ∎

For F-preferred reasonable status sets, we obtain similar results. However, we may allow the presence of integrity constraints without a change in the complexity.

THEOREM 11.4.22   Let $\mathcal{P}$ be a fixed agent program (where $\mathcal{IC}$ is arbitrary). Then, given an agent state $\mathcal{O}_S$ and a status set S, deciding whether S is a F-preferred reasonable status set of $\mathcal{P}$ on $\mathcal{O}_S$ is co-NP-complete. Hardness holds even if $\mathcal{IC} = \emptyset$.

Proof   By Proposition 11.4.11, we can decide in polynomial time whether S is a reasonable status set, and check that there is no reasonable status set S' such that $\mathbf{F}(S') \subset \mathbf{F}(S)$ with the help of an NP oracle.

Hardness is shown by a proper modification of the program $\mathcal{P}$ in the proof of Theorem 11.4.8. Replace the clause $\mathbf{P}\alpha(X_1) \leftarrow \mathbf{P}\gamma, \text{VAR}(X_1)$ with the clause $\mathbf{F}\alpha(X_1) \leftarrow \mathbf{F}\gamma, \text{VAR}(X_1)$, replace $\neg\mathbf{P}\gamma$ with $\neg\mathbf{F}\gamma$ in the other clauses, and add the following clauses:

$\mathbf{P}\alpha(X_1) \leftarrow \neg\mathbf{F}\alpha(X_1), \text{VAR}(X_1)$
$\mathbf{F}\alpha(X_1) \leftarrow \neg\mathbf{P}\alpha(X_1), \text{VAR}(X_1)$
$\quad \mathbf{F}\gamma \leftarrow \neg\mathbf{P}\gamma$
$\quad \mathbf{P}\gamma \leftarrow \neg\mathbf{F}\gamma$

Then, the set $S = \{\mathbf{F}\alpha(x_i) \mid x_i \in X\} \cup \{\mathbf{F}\gamma\} \cup \{\mathbf{P}\beta\}$ is a reasonable status set of the new program $\mathcal{P}'$ on the database D. It is the (unique) F-preferred reasonable status set, if and only if the formula ϕ is not satisfiable. Hence, deciding whether S is a F-preferred reasonable status set is co-NP-hard. ∎

An F-preferred reasonable status set can be computed applying an algorithm analogous to the one used for computing a F-preferred rational status set. First, compute the minimum size s of the $\mathbf{F}$-part $\mathbf{F}(S)$ over all reasonable status sets S, and then construct a reasonable status set S such that $|\mathbf{F}(S)| = s$. This matches the solution scheme for problems in FNP//log. Observe that the same algorithm can also be applied in the presence of integrity constraints.

We thus obtain the following result.

THEOREM 11.4.23 Let $\mathcal{P}$ be a fixed agent program (where $\mathcal{IC}$ is arbitray). Then, given an agent state $\mathcal{O}_S$, computing any F-preferred reasonable status set of $\mathcal{P}$ on $\mathcal{O}_S$ is complete for FNP//log. Hardness holds even if $\mathcal{IC} = \emptyset$.

Proof The membership part is in the discussion above. The hardness part can be shown by a modification of the reduction in the proof of Theorem 11.4.21. Add to the program from there the following rules:

$\mathbf{P}\alpha(X_1) \leftarrow \neg \mathbf{F}\alpha(X_1), \text{XVAR}(X_1)$
$\mathbf{P}\alpha(X_1) \leftarrow \neg \mathbf{P}\gamma(X_1), \text{YVAR}(X_1)$
$\mathbf{P}\gamma(X_1) \leftarrow \neg \mathbf{P}\alpha(X_1), \text{YVAR}(X_1)$

Here, YVAR is a relation that stores the variables that are not in X, and γ is a new action of the same type as α.

It holds that the reasonable status sets of the new program $\mathcal{P}'$ on the database D for ϕ correspond 1-1 to the models of ϕ; moreover, the F-preferred reasonable status sets S correspond 1-1 to the X-maximal models M of ϕ. Since M is easily computed from S, it follows that computing an arbitrary F-preferred reasonable status set is FNP//log-hard. ∎

For action reasoning under F-preferred rational status sets, we obtain similar results as for action reasoning under weak rational status sets. The next result shows that the certainty variant of action reasoning based on F-preferred rational status sets is Π_2^P-complete, while the corresponding possibility variant is (as expected) Σ_2^P-complete.

THEOREM 11.4.24 Let $\mathcal{P}$ be a fixed program, and suppose that $\mathcal{IC} = \emptyset$. Then, given an agent status $\mathcal{O}_S$ and a ground action α, deciding whether $\alpha \in \mathbf{Do}(S)$ holds for (*i*) every (resp., (*ii*) some) F-preferred rational status set S of $\mathcal{P}$ on $\mathcal{O}_S$ is Π_2^P-complete (resp., Σ_2^P-complete).

Proof For the membership part, observe that a guess for a F-preferred rational status set S such that $\alpha \notin \mathbf{Do}\,(S)$ (resp., $\alpha \in \mathbf{Do}\,(S)$), can be verified by checking that F is feasible, F is grounded, and that no feasible status set S' exists such that $\mathbf{F}(S') \subset \mathbf{F}(S)$. By Proposition 11.4.1, and Theorem 11.4.8, it follows that these tests can be done in polynomial time with an NP oracle. Hence, the problem is in Π_2^P (resp., Σ_2^P).

To show hardness, we employ a slight modification of the construction in the proof of case *(ii)* of Theorem 11.4.10. Add to the program $\mathcal{P}$ from there the clauses

$\mathbf{P}\alpha^*(X_1) \leftarrow \mathbf{F}\alpha(X_1), \text{XVAR}(X_1)$

$\mathbf{F}\alpha^*(X_1) \leftarrow \mathbf{P}\alpha(X_1), \text{XVAR}(X_1)$

where α^* is a new action of the same type as α. The effect of these clauses is to include $\mathbf{P}\alpha^*(x_i)$ in a rational status set, if $\mathbf{F}\alpha(x_i)$ belongs to it, and symmetrically to include $\mathbf{F}\alpha^*(x_i)$, if $\mathbf{P}\alpha(x_i)$ occurs in it. This way, the choice χ from $\mathbf{F}\alpha(x_i), \mathbf{P}\alpha(x_i)$ is mirrored in a complementary fashion on $\mathbf{F}\alpha^*(x_i), \mathbf{P}\alpha^*(x_i)$ such that the extended candidate set

$$S_\chi^* = S_\chi \cup \{\mathbf{F}\alpha^*(x_i) \mid \mathbf{P}\alpha(x_i) \in S_\chi, x_i \in X\} \cup \{\mathbf{P}\alpha^*(x_i) \mid \mathbf{F}\alpha(x_i) \in S_\chi, x_i \in X\}$$

is *not* a F-preferred rational status set, if and only if the formula $\exists Y \phi[X = \chi]$ is true.

Since any rational status set S' which is F-preferred over S_χ^* must not contain $\mathbf{P}\gamma$ and thus not $\mathbf{Do}\,\gamma$, it follows that $\mathbf{Do}\,\gamma$ is contained in some F-preferred rational status set, if and only if the formula $\forall X \exists Y \phi$ is false. This proves Σ_2^P-hardness of *(ii)*.

For the hardness part of *(i)*, add the clauses $\mathbf{Do}\,\delta \leftarrow \neg \mathbf{P}\gamma$ and $\mathbf{F}\delta \leftarrow \mathbf{P}\gamma$ to the above program, where δ is another action of the type of α. Then, the set $S_\chi^* \cup \{\mathbf{F}\delta\}$ is a rational status set of the new program, and it contains $\mathbf{Do}\,\gamma$ but not $\mathbf{Do}\,\delta$. Every rational status set S' which is F-preferred to $S_\chi^* \cup \{\mathbf{F}\delta\}$ contains $\mathbf{Do}\,\delta$ and corresponds to some truth assignment to Y which satisfies $\phi[X = \chi]$. It holds that $\mathbf{Do}\,\delta$ occurs in all F-preferred rational status sets of $\mathcal{P}$ if and only if $\forall X \exists Y \phi$ is true. This proves Π_2^P-hardness. ∎

As discussed above, for reasonable status sets F-preference leads to a complexity increase, and raises it to the level of rational status sets. However, as with the other problems on reasonable status sets, this increase is independent of whether integrity constraints are present or not. For rational status sets, this is not the case, and the complexity there is higher in the general case, as we shall see in Section 11.5.5.

THEOREM 11.4.25 Let $\mathcal{P}$ be a fixed program (where $\mathcal{IC}$ is arbitrary). Then, given an agent state $\mathcal{O}_S$ and a ground action α, deciding whether $\alpha \in \mathbf{Do}\,(S)$ holds for *(i)* every (resp., *(ii)* some) F-preferred reasonable status set S of $\mathcal{P}$ on $\mathcal{O}_S$ is Π_2^P-complete (resp., Σ_2^P-complete). Hardness holds even if $\mathcal{IC} = \emptyset$.

Proof A F-preferred reasonable status set S such that $\alpha \notin \mathbf{Do}(S)$ (resp., $\alpha \in \mathbf{Do}(S)$) can be guessed and checked in polynomial time with the help of an NP oracle (Proposition 11.4.11 on page 428, Theorem 11.4.22 on page 437).

For the hardness part, we employ a reduction the QBF problem described in the proof of Theorem 11.4.10: Decide whether a formula $\Phi = \forall X \exists Y. \phi$ where ϕ is a M3SAT instance is true. Without loss of generality, we may assume that $\phi[Y = \emptyset]$ is unsatisfiable.

We extend the reduction in the proof of Theorem 11.4.5 similar as the one in the proof of Theorem 11.4.10 for the proof of Theorem 11.4.24. We construct the following program $\mathcal{P}$, where γ is a fresh action of the same type as β:

$\mathbf{P}\beta \leftarrow$
$\mathbf{F}\beta \leftarrow \mathbf{Do}\,\gamma, \mathbf{F}\alpha(X_1), \mathbf{F}\alpha(X_2), \mathbf{F}\alpha(X_3), \text{POS}(X_1, X_2, X_3)$
$\mathbf{F}\beta \leftarrow \mathbf{Do}\,\gamma, \mathbf{P}\alpha(X_1), \mathbf{P}\alpha(X_2), \mathbf{P}\alpha(X_3), \text{NEG}(X_1, X_2, X_3)$
$\mathbf{P}\alpha(X_1) \leftarrow \neg \mathbf{F}\alpha(X_1)$
$\mathbf{F}\alpha(X_1) \leftarrow \neg \mathbf{P}\alpha(X_1)$
$\mathbf{P}\alpha^*(X_1) \leftarrow \mathbf{F}\alpha(X_1), \text{XVAR}(X_1)$
$\mathbf{F}\alpha^*(X_1) \leftarrow \mathbf{P}\alpha(X_1), \text{XVAR}(X_1)$
$\mathbf{Do}\,(\gamma) \leftarrow \neg \mathbf{F}\alpha(Y_1), \text{YVAR}(Y_1)$

For every choice χ from $\mathbf{F}\alpha(x_i), \mathbf{P}\alpha(x_i)$ for all $x_i \in X$ (representing a truth assignment to X), the program $\mathcal{P}$ has a reasonable status set S_χ^+ which contains $\mathbf{F}\alpha(y_j)$, for all $y_j \in Y$, but does not contain $\mathbf{Do}\,\gamma$.

Every reasonable status set S' which is F-preferred to S_χ^+ must contain the same atoms $\mathbf{F}\alpha(x_i)$ as S_χ^+ and encode by a choice from $\mathbf{P}\alpha(y_j), \mathbf{F}\alpha(y_j)$ for all $y_j \in Y$ a truth value assignment χ' to Y such that not all y_j are false and $\phi[X = \chi]$ is satisfied by it. Furthermore, by the last clause such a S' must contain $\mathbf{Do}\,\gamma$. Conversely, if for χ some assignment to Y exists which does not set all y_j to false and satisfies $\phi[X = \chi]$, then a reasonable status set S' exists which is F-preferred to S and contains $\mathbf{Do}\,\gamma$. It follows that $\mathbf{Do}\,\gamma$ is contained in every F-preferred reasonable status set of $\mathcal{P}$, if and only if $\forall X (\exists Y \neq \emptyset)\phi$ is true. This proves Π_2^P-hardness of (i).

For (ii), add a further rule $\mathbf{Do}\,(\delta) \leftarrow \neg \mathbf{Do}\,(\gamma)$ where δ is a fresh action of the type of β. Then, $\mathbf{Do}\,(\delta)$ belongs to some F-preferred reasonable status set of $\mathcal{P}$, if and only if $\forall X (\exists Y \neq \emptyset)\phi$ is false. This proves the theorem. ∎

11.5 Effect of Integrity Constraints

So far, we have focused in our complexity analysis mainly on agent programs where in the background no integrity constraints were present. We say mainly, since for positive

Section 11.5   Effect of Integrity Constraints   441

programs and reasonable status sets, most results that have been derived in Section 11.4 do allow for integrity constraints, and fortunately establish tractability for a number of important computation problems.

However, in the presence of negation, we have excluded integrity constraints. The reason is that in some cases, the presence or absence of integrity constraints makes a difference to the intrinsic complexity of a problem, while in other cases, there is no difference. We thus analyze in this section the effects of integrity constraints on the complexity of agent programs. As an overview and discussion of the results is given in Section 11.3, we focus here on deriving these results. Throughout this section, the following setting is used in proofs of the hardness results:

- Like in the previous section, $\mathcal{S} = (\mathcal{T_S}, \mathcal{F_S}, \mathcal{C_S})$ is a simple relational database $\mathcal{D}$ in which tuples may be inserted or deleted from tables. The integrity constraints $\mathcal{IC}$ on $\mathcal{D}$ are *functional dependencies* (FDs for short) on the tables. Notice that FDs are one of the most basic and important type of dependencies in databases (Ullman 1989).[4]

- The polynomial concurrent action execution policy is *weakly-concurrent execution* as described in Chapter 6.

11.5.1   Feasible Status Sets

As shown in the previous section, finding a rational or feasible status set of a positive agent program is polynomial, if no integrity constraints are present. While adding integrity constraints preserves polynomial time computability of rational status sets, it leads to intractability for feasible status sets.

THEOREM 11.5.1   Let $\mathcal{P}$ be a fixed agent program (where $\mathcal{IC}$ is arbitrary). Then, deciding whether $\mathcal{P}$ has a feasible status set on a given agent state $\mathcal{O_S}$ is NP-complete, and computing an arbitrary feasible status set is FNP-complete. Hardness holds even if $\mathcal{P}$ is positive.

Proof   The problem is in NP, since a feasible status set S can be guessed and checked in polynomial time, according to our assumptions (cf. Proposition 11.4.1).

We show the hardness part for the particular restriction by a reduction from the set splitting problem (Garey and Johnson 1979). Given a collection $\mathcal{S} = \{S_1, \ldots, S_m\}$ of nonempty sets over a finite set U, decide whether there exists a partitioning (or *coloring*) (C_1, C_2) of U such that every $S_i \in \mathcal{S}, i = 1, \ldots, m$, meets both C_1 and C_2 in at least one element.

---

[4] A functional dependency is a constraint $C : X \to A$ on a relation r, where A is a column of r and $X = \{X_1, \ldots, X_n\}$ is a subset of columns of r; it holds, if any two tuples in r which agree on the columns in X agree also on A. In our framework, C can be expressed as an integrity constraint e.g., as follows:
in(T1, db : *select*(r))&**in**(T2, db : *select*(r))&$(T_1.X_1 = T_2.X_1)$& $\cdots$ &$(T_1.X_n = T_2.X_n) \Rightarrow T1.A = T2.A$.

We construct from $\mathcal{S}$ an instance of the feasible status set test as follows. The database $\mathcal{D}$ has four relations:

- COLL(*Set*, *El*),
- SPLIT(*El*, *Color*),
- A1(*Set*, *El*, *Tag*), and
- A2(*Set*, *El*, *Tag*).

Intuitively, the collection $\mathcal{S}$ is stored in COLL by tuples (i, e) for every $e \in S_i$ and $S_i \in \mathcal{S}$. The table SPLIT is used for placing each element $e \in U$ either in C_1 or C_2 (i.e., coloring it), which is indicated by tuples $(e, 1)$ and $(e_2, 2)$. The tables A1 and A2 hold the occurrences of elements in sets, where each set has some label.

The action base $\mathcal{AB}$ contains *assign*(S, X, Y) and *trigger*(X, Y) described as follows:

assign: $Pre(assign(\text{S, X, Y})) = \text{COLL(S, X)}$,
$Add(assign(\text{S, X, Y})) = \{\text{SPLIT(X, Y)}\}$,
$Del(assign(\text{S, X, Y})) = \{\text{A1(S, Z, Y), A2(S, Z, Y)}\}$;

trigger: $Pre(trigger(\text{X, Y})) = \textbf{true}$,
$Add(trigger(\text{X, Y})) = \{\text{A1(X, Y, 0), A2(X, Y, 0)}\}$,
$Del(trigger(\text{X, Y})) = \emptyset$.

The program $\mathcal{P}$ has the single rule

Do (*trigger*(X, Y)) ← COLL(X, Y)

Let D be the database instance such that COLL contains the collection $\mathcal{S}$, SPLIT is empty, and A1 (resp. A2) holds for each tuple (s, e) in COLL a tuple $(s, e, 1)$ (resp. $(s, e, 2)$). Moreover, suppose that $\mathcal{IC}$ contains the FD $El \rightarrow Color$ on ASSIGN and the FD $Set \rightarrow Tag$ on A1 and A2.

Intuitively, the program forces the agent to add for every occurrence of an element in a set $S_i \in \mathcal{S}$, represented by a tuple (i, e) in COLL, a tuple $(i, e, 0)$ to both A1 and A2. This triggers a violation of the FD $Set \rightarrow Tag$ on A1 and A2. The violation must be cured by executing $assign(i, e_1, 1)$ and $assign(i, e_2, 2)$ actions for some e_1, e_2 which occur in the set S_i; by the FD $El \rightarrow Color$ on SPLIT, e_1 must be different from e_2. (Notice that, under weakly-current execution, actions $assign(i, e, 0)$ are useless, since deletions are performed before additions, and this would not cure any violation.)

Hence, it is easy to see that $\mathcal{P}$ has a feasible status set on D, if and only if $\mathcal{S}$ is colorable by some coloring (C_1, C_2). Since a coloring (C_1, C_2) is easily constructed from any feasible status set S, the result follows. ∎

The previous theorem shows that we benefit from using rational status sets instead of feasible status sets on positive programs in different respects. First, on the semantical side, we have a unique rational status set (if one exists) compared to a possible exponential number of feasible status sets, and second, on the computational side, we can compute the unique rational status set on an agent state in polynomial time, compared to the intractability of computing any feasible status set. The intractability is explained by the fact that a simple program like the one in the proof of Theorem 11.5.1 is underconstrained, and forces to explore different possibilities for the actions which are not mentioned in the program.

Unfortunately, in the presence of negation, like on the semantical side, also on the computational side the appealing properties of rational status sets vanish.

11.5.2 Rational Status Sets

The complexity of recognizing a rational status set is not affected by the presence of integrity constraints, since they can be evaluated in polynomial time. The result of Corollary 13 thus easily generalizes to this case.

THEOREM 11.5.2 Let $\mathcal{P}$ be a fixed agent program (where $\mathcal{IC}$ is arbitrary). Then, given an agent state $\mathcal{O}_S$ and a status set S, deciding whether S is a rational status set of $\mathcal{P}$ on $\mathcal{O}_S$, is co-NP-complete. Hardness holds even if $\mathcal{IC} = \emptyset$.

However, computing a rational status set becomes harder if integrity constraints are present. Because of the integrity constraints, an arbitrary feasible status set S may *no longer necessarily contain* a rational status set, and thus picking a feasible status set having smallest size does not necessarily give us a rational status set. In fact, our next result shows that deciding containment of a rational status set is intractable.

THEOREM 11.5.3 Let $\mathcal{P}$ be a fixed agent program (where $\mathcal{IC}$ is arbitrary). Then, given an agent state $\mathcal{O}_S$ and a feasible status set S for $\mathcal{P}$ on $\mathcal{O}_S$, deciding whether S contains some rational status set (resp., S is rational) is co-NP-hard.

Proof We prove this by a reduction from deciding whether a M3DNF formula $\phi = \bigvee_{i=1}^{m} D_i$ on propositional variables $X = \{x_1, \ldots, x_n\}$ is a tautology.

The database $\mathcal{D}$ contains three relations: POS(V_1, V_2, V_3) and NEG(V_1, V_2, V_3) for storing the positive and the negative disjuncts of ϕ, respectively, and a relation VAR(*Var, Value, Tag*), which contains for each pair of variable a $x \in X$ and a value $v \in \{0, 1\}$ precisely one tuple.

The initial database D contains the following tuples. For each positive disjunct $D_i = x_{i_1} \wedge x_{i_2} \wedge x_{i_3}$ from ϕ, the tuple $(x_{i_1}, x_{i_2}, x_{i_3})$ is in POS, and for each negative disjunct $D_i = \neg x_{i_1} \wedge \neg x_{i_2} \wedge \neg x_{i_3}$ the tuple $(x_{i_1}, x_{i_2}, x_{i_3})$ is in NEG. Moreover, for each propositional variables $x_i \in X$, the tuples $(x_i, 0, 0)$ and $(x_i, 1, 0)$ are in VAR.

The action base contains the three actions *all*, *set*(X, Y) and *add_var*(X, Y, Z), which have empty preconditions and the following add and delete sets:

$$all: Add(all) = Del(all) = \emptyset;$$

$$set(X, Y): Add(set(X, Y)) = \emptyset,$$
$$Del(set(X, Y)) = \{VAR(X, Y, 0)\};$$

$$add\_var(X, Y, Z): Add(add\_var(X, Y, Z)) = \{VAR(X, Y, Z)\},$$
$$Del(add\_var(X, Y, Z)) = \emptyset.$$

The program $\mathcal{P}$ is as follows:

Do $(set(X_1, Y_1)) \leftarrow$ **Do** (all), VAR(X_1, Y_1, Z_1).
  Do $(all) \leftarrow$ **Do** $(set(X_1, 0))$, **Do** $(set(X_1, 1))$, VAR(X_1, Y_1, Z_1).
  Do $(all) \leftarrow \neg$**Do** $(set(X_1, 0))$, $\neg$**Do** $(set(X_1, 1))$, VAR(X_1, Y_1, Z_1).
  Do $(all) \leftarrow$ **Do** $(set(X, 0))$, **Do** $(set(Y, 0))$, **Do** $(set(Z, 0))$, POS(X, Y, Z).
  Do $(all) \leftarrow$ **Do** $(set(X, 1))$, **Do** $(set(Y, 1))$, **Do** $(set(Z, 1))$, NEG(X, Y, Z).
Do $(add\_var(X_1, Y_1, 1)) \leftarrow$ VAR(X_1, Y_1, Z_1).

Suppose that $\mathcal{IC}$ holds the single FD *Var, Value* $\to$ *Tag* on VAR. Let S be the smallest status set S closed under **A-Cl**$(\cdot)$ and **D-Cl**$(\cdot)$ such that

Do $(S) = \{all\} \cup \{set(x_i, v), add\_var(x_i, v, 1) \mid x_i \in X, v \in \{0, 1\}\}$.

As easily checked, S is a feasible status set of $\mathcal{P}$ on the initial database D.

We note that any feasible status set $S' \subset S$ such that conditions $(S1)$–$(S3)$ of a feasible status set hold must not contain **Do** (all), while it must contain exactly one of **Do** $(set(x_i, 0))$ and **Do** $(set(x_i, 1))$, for every $x_i \in X$. However, no such S' satisfies the FD *Var, Value* $\to$ *Tag* on VAR: either the tuples $(x_i, 1, 0)$ and $(x_i, 1, 1)$ are in VAR, or the tuples $(x_i, 0, 0)$ and $(x_i, 0, 1)$; this means that the FD *Var, Value* $\to$ *Tag* is violated on VAR.

It holds that S contains some rational status set (resp., that S is rational), if and only if formula ϕ is a tautology. The result follows. ∎

The complexity of computing a rational status set, stated in the next result, is at the second level of the polynomial hierarchy.

THEOREM 11.5.4 Let $\mathcal{P}$ be a fixed agent program (where $\mathcal{IC}$ is arbitrary). Then, given an agent state $\mathcal{O}_S$, deciding whether $\mathcal{P}$ has a rational status set on $\mathcal{O}_S$ is Σ_2^P-complete, and computing any rational status set is FΣ_2^P-complete.

Proof The problems are in Σ_2^P and FΣ_2^P, respectively, since a rational status set S can be guessed and verified in polynomial time with the help of an NP oracle (cf. Theorem 11.5.2).

Section 11.5   Effect of Integrity Constraints   445

To show that the problems are hard for Σ_2^P and $F\Sigma_2^P$, respectively, we extend the construction in the proof of Theorem 11.5.3, such that we encode the problem of computing, given a QBF $\exists Y \forall X \phi$, where ϕ is M3DNF, an assignment χ to the Y-variables such that $\forall X \phi[Y = \chi]$ is true.

We use an additional relation YVAR for storing the Y-variables, and add the rule

Do $(set(\text{Y}, 1)) \leftarrow \neg \textbf{Do}\,(set(\text{Y}, 0))$

This rule enforces a choice between **Do** $(sety_j, 0)$ and **Do** $(sety_j, 1)$, for all $y_j \in Y$ (representing a truth assignment to Y). Extended by the set S from the proof of Theorem 11.5.3, each such choice χ generates a candidate S_χ for a rational status set.

It holds that every rational status set of $\mathcal{P}$ on D must be of the form S_χ, for some choice χ. Moreover, the rational status sets of $\mathcal{P}$ on D correspond to the sets S_χ such that the formula $\forall X \phi[Y = \chi]$ is true. Therefore, deciding whether $\mathcal{P}$ has a rational status set on D is Σ_2^P-hard, and computing any rational status set is hard for $F\Sigma_2^P$. ∎

For action reasoning, we obtain from the preceding theorem easily the following result.

THEOREM 11.5.5   Let $\mathcal{P}$ be a fixed agent program (where $\mathcal{IC}$ is arbitrary). Then, given an agent state $\mathcal{O}_S$ and a ground action α, deciding whether $\alpha \in \textbf{Do}\,(S)$ holds for (i) every (resp., (ii) some) rational status set of $\mathcal{P}$ on $\mathcal{O}_S$ is (i) Π_2^P-complete (resp., (ii) Σ_2^P-complete).

Proof   Membership is immediate from Theorem 11.5.2: A guess for a rational status set S such that $\alpha \notin \textbf{Do}\,(S)$ (resp., $\alpha \in \textbf{Do}\,(S)$) can be verified with an NP oracle.

For the hardness parts, observe that $all \in \textbf{Do}\,(S)$ for every rational status set of the program $\mathcal{P}$ in the proof of Theorem 11.5.4; thus, by querying about all, hardness for (i) holds. The hardness part of (ii) follows from Theorem 11.4.10. ∎

11.5.3   Reasonable Status Sets

For reasonable status sets, we find in all cases better computational properties than for rational status sets. This is explained by the fact that the criterion for a reasonable status set is much stronger than the one for a rational status set, such that the presence of integrity constraints has no effect on the tractability vs intractability issue of recognizing a reasonable status set. In both cases, a reasonable status set can be recognized in polynomial time (Proposition 11.4.11). Therefore, the same complexity results hold for programs with and without integrity constraints (see Section 11.4.2).

11.5.4   Weak Status Sets

Positive Programs   The recognition problem is no longer known to be polynomial if no integrity constraints are present in general. This is a consequence of the proof of the previous theorem.

THEOREM 11.5.6 Let $\mathcal{P}$ be a fixed positive agent program (where $\mathcal{IC}$ is arbitrary). Then, given an agent state $\mathcal{O}_\mathcal{S}$ and a status set S on $\mathcal{O}_\mathcal{S}$, deciding whether S is a weak rational status set of $\mathcal{P}$ is co-NP-complete.

Proof To show that S is not a weak rational status set, we can proceed as follows. Check whether S is not $A(S)$-rational; if this is not the case (i.e., S is $A(S)$-rational), then guess some status set S' such that S' is $A(S')$-rational and $A(S') \supset A(S)$. Since checking A-rationality is polynomial if $\mathcal{P}$ is positive (we need to check whether $S = \mathit{lfp}(\mathbf{T}_{\mathcal{P},\mathcal{O}_S,A})$ and S is A-feasible, which is polynomial by Propositions 11.4.2 and 11.4.1), the problem is in co-NP.

The hardness part is shown by a reduction from the complement of problem M3SAT, for which we adapt the reduction in the proof of Theorem 11.4.4. As there, the database has relations POS, NEG, and VAR for storing an M3SAT instance ϕ on variables X. We introduce a further relation AUX(*Var*, *Val*), on which we impose the FD *Var* $\to$ *Val*.

The initial database D stores ϕ in POS, NEG, and VAR as usual, and AUX contains all tuples $(x_i, 0)$ for $x_i \in X$. Clearly, D satisfies the FD *Var* $\to$ *Val* on AUX.

The action base $\mathcal{AB}$ is modified by setting

$Add(set_v(X)) = \{\text{AUX}(Y, 1)\}$ and $Del(set_v(X)) = \{\text{AUX}(X, 0)\}$, $v \in \{0, 1\}$.

The program $\mathcal{P}$ is modified as follows.

$\mathbf{O}(set_0(X)) \leftarrow \text{VAR}(X)$
$\mathbf{O}(set_1(X)) \leftarrow \text{VAR}(X)$
   $\mathbf{F}\alpha \leftarrow \mathbf{Do}\,(set_0(X_1)), \mathbf{Do}\,(set_0(X_2)), \mathbf{Do}\,(set_0(X_3)), \text{POS}(X_1, X_2, X_3)$
   $\mathbf{F}\alpha \leftarrow \mathbf{Do}\,(set_1(X_1)), \mathbf{Do}\,(set_1(X_2)), \mathbf{Do}\,(set_1(X_3)), \text{NEG}(X_1, X_2, X_3)$
   $\mathbf{P}\alpha \leftarrow$

In addition, we have the action constraint

AC: $\{set_0(X), set_1(X)\} \nleftrightarrow \text{VAR}(X)$.

Then, on the initial database D, the status set

$S = \{\mathbf{O}(set_0(x_i)), \mathbf{O}(set_1(x_i)), \mathbf{P}(set_0(x_i)), \mathbf{P}(set_1(x_i)) \mid x_i \in X\} \cup \{\mathbf{P}\alpha\}$

is a $\{\alpha\}$-rational status set, and hence $A(S)$-rational by Proposition 6.5.5. Moreover, it holds that S is a weak rational status set, if and only if there exists no status set S' such that S' is $A(S')$-feasible and $A(S') \supset A(S)$. Observe that any such S' must contain either $\mathbf{Do}\,(set_0(x_i))$ or $\mathbf{Do}\,(set_1(x_i))$, for every $x_i \in X$, and thus corresponds to a truth value assignment. Indeed, taking $set_0(x_i)$ or $set_1(x_i)$ for any x_i adds the tuples $(x_j, 1)$ to AUX, for all variables x_j. For preservation of the FD *Var* $\to$ *Val* on AUX, the tuple $(x_j, 0)$ must

Section 11.5   Effect of Integrity Constraints   447

then be removed from AUX, which requests taking either $set_0(x_j)$ or $set_1(x_j)$. On the other hand, for any truth value assignment χ to X which satisfies ϕ, a status S' can be obtained such that S' is $A(S')$-rational and $A(S') \supset A(S)$.

Therefore, it holds that S is a weak rational status set if and only if ϕ is unsatisfiable, i.e., a "No"-instance of M3SAT. Since D is easily constructed from ϕ, this proves co-NP-hardness and the theorem.   ∎

As we have seen in Section 11.4.1, a weak rational (resp., reasonable) status set of a fixed positive agent program without integrity constraints can be computed in polynomial time using the algorithm **Compute-PNIC-Weak-RSS**. A similar polynomial algorithm in the presence of integrity constraints is unlikely to exist.

THEOREM 11.5.7   Let $\mathcal{P}$ be a fixed positive agent program (where $\mathcal{IC}$ is arbitrary). Given an agent state $\mathcal{O}_S$, deciding whether $\mathcal{P}$ has a weak rational status set on $\mathcal{O}_S$ is NP-complete.

Proof   Under the assumption, a weak rational status set exists if and only if some A-rational status set exists. By Theorem 6.5.2 we can nondeterministically decide the existence of an A-rational status set in polynomial time by guessing a set A of ground actions, computing $S = lfp(\mathbf{T}_{\mathcal{P},\mathcal{O}_S,A})$ and then checking whether S is A-feasible. Consequently, by Propositions 11.4.2 and 11.4.1 the problem is in NP.

NP-hardness can be shown by a slight extension to the reduction in the proof of Theorem 11.5.6. Without loss of generality, the M3SAT formula ϕ from the reduction there is only satisfiable if a designated variable x_1 is set to **true**. Thus, if we add the rule **Do** $set_1(x_1) \leftarrow$ to the program $\mathcal{P}$, then the resulting program $\mathcal{P}'$ has a weak rational status set if and only if ϕ is satisfiable.   ∎

For the computation problem, we have the algorithm **Compute-P-WRational-SS** below, which makes use of an NP oracle.

This algorithm computes a weak rational status set in polynomial time modulo evaluating the condition on line 2, which can be done by a call to the NP oracle. It computes the last element A_k in a maximal chain $A_0 = \emptyset \subset A_1 \subset \cdots \subset A_k$ of A_i-rational status set, which is a weak rational status set. Its correctness follows from the characterization of weak rational status sets in Section 6.5.5. Therefore, the problem is in FP^{NP}. Observe that in case $\mathcal{IC} = \emptyset$, the NP-oracle can be replaced by a polynomial time algorithm, such that we obtain an overall polynomial algorithm similar to **Compute-PNIC-Weak-RSS**.

Like in other cases, the FP^{NP} upper bound for the computation problem can also be lowered to FNP//log in this case.

THEOREM 11.5.8   Let $\mathcal{P}$ be a fixed positive agent program (where $\mathcal{IC}$ is arbitrary). Then, computing a weak rational status set is in FNP//log and hard for both FNP and $FP^{NP}_{\parallel}$.

> **Algorithm 11.5.1 (Computation of Weakly Rational Status Sets for Positive Programs)**
> Compute-P-WRational-SS($\mathcal{O}_S$: agent state)
>
> ($\star$ agent program $\mathcal{P}$ is positive, and $\mathcal{IC}$ is arbitrary; $\star$)
> ($\star$ input is an agent state $\mathcal{O}_S$; $\star$)
> ($\star$ output is a weak reasonable status, if one exists, $\star$)
> ($\star$ otherwise, the output is "No." $\star$)
>
> 1. $A_{new} := \emptyset$, $GA :=$ set of all ground actions;
> 2. $exists\_larger := \exists A \supseteq A_{new} \exists S'((S' = lfp(\mathbf{T}_{\mathcal{P},\mathcal{O}_S,A})) \land (S'$ is $A(S')$-feasible));
> 3.   **if** $exists\_larger$ **then**
> 4.   { $S := lfp(\mathbf{T}_{\mathcal{P},\mathcal{O}_S,A_{new}})$;
> 5. $A_{old} := A(S)$;
> 6. $GA := GA \setminus A_{old}$;
> 7.   }
> 8.   **else if** $A_{new} = \emptyset$ **then output** "No (halt);
> 9.   **if** $GA = \emptyset$ **then output** S (halt)
> 10. **else**
> 11. { choose some $\alpha \in GA$;
> 12. $A_{new} := A_{old} \cup \{\alpha\}$;
> 13. $GA := GA \setminus \{\alpha\}$;
> 14.   **goto** 2.
> 15. }
> **end**.

Proof A weak rational status set can be computed as follows. Compute first the maximum size $s = |A(S)|$ over all status sets S such that S is $A(S)$-rational. Then, generate nondeterministically a status set S which is $A(S)$-rational and such that $|A(S)| = s$, and output this set (so one exists).

The correctness of this algorithm follows from Proposition 6.5.5. Moreover, checking whether S is $A(S)$-rational is polynomial if $\mathcal{P}$ is positive, as follows from Propositions 11.4.2 and 11. Consequently, step 1 of the algorithm amounts to an NP-optimization problem whose output has $O(\log |I|)$ bits, which implies that computing a weak rational status set is in FNP//log.

FNP-hardness follows from the proof of Theorem 11.5.7: The weak rational status sets of the program from the proof of this theorem correspond to the satisfying assignments of an M3SAT instance, whose computation is easily seen to be FNP-complete.

For the proof of $FP_{\parallel}^{NP}$-hardness, we use the fact that given instances $I_1, \ldots, I_n$ of any arbitrary fixed co-NP-complete problem Π, computing the binary string $B = b_1 \cdots b_n$ where $b_i = 1$ if I_i is a "Yes"-instance of Π and $b_i = 0$ otherwise, is $FP_{\parallel}^{NP}$-hard (this is easily seen; cf. also Lemma 4.7 of (Chen and Toda 1995).

We choose for this problem the recognition of a weak rational status set S of a fixed positive agent program $\mathcal{P}$, which is co-NP-complete by Theorem 11.5.6. We assume that

Section 11.5 Effect of Integrity Constraints   449

$\mathcal{P}$ is the program from the proof of this result, and S the status set constructed over the database D for a formula ϕ. We observe that $\mathcal{P}$ has weak rational status set on $\mathcal{P}$, and that S is the unique weak rational status set, if and only if the formula ϕ is unsatisfiable. Thus, from any arbitrary weak rational status set S' of $\mathcal{P}$ over D, it is immediate whether S is weak rational or not. Consequently, computing weak rational status sets $S_1, \ldots, S_n$ of $\mathcal{P}$ over given databases $D_1, \ldots, D_n$ is $\text{FP}_{\parallel}^{\text{NP}}$-hard.

It remains to show that the computation of $S_1, \ldots, S_n$ can be reduced to the computation of a single weak rational status set S of a fixed program $\mathcal{P}'$ over a database D'. For this purpose, we merge the databases D_i into a single database. This is accomplished by tagging each tuple in D_i with i, i.e., add a new attribute A in each relation, and each tuple obtains value i on it, A is added on the left hand side of each functional dependency. Moreover, an additional argument T for the tag is introduced in each action, and all literals in a rule have the same fresh variable T in the tag position.

Then, the resulting program $\mathcal{P}'$ has some weak rational status set S on the union D' of the tagged D_i's, and from any such S weak rational status sets $S_1, \ldots, S_n$ of $\mathcal{P}$ on each D_i are easily obtained in polynomial time. Since D' is polynomial-time constructible from $D_1, \ldots, D_n$, this proves $\text{FP}_{\parallel}^{\text{NP}}$-hardness. ∎

We finally address the problem of action reasoning.

THEOREM 11.5.9 Let $\mathcal{P}$ be a fixed positive agent program (where $\mathcal{IC}$ is arbitrary). Then, given an agent state $\mathcal{O}_S$ and a ground action atom α, deciding whether $\alpha \in \mathbf{Do}(S)$ holds for (*i*) every (resp., (*ii*) some) weak rational status set of $\mathcal{P}$ on $\mathcal{O}_S$ is Π_2^P-complete (resp., NP-complete).

Proof The membership part of (*i*) is easy from Theorem 11.5.6. A guess for a weak rational status set S such that $A \notin \mathbf{Do}(S)$ can be verified with an NP oracle in polynomial time. For the membership part of (*ii*), suppose S is an A rational status set. Then, since $\mathcal{P}$ is positive, any A'-rational status set S' such that $A' \supseteq A$ satisfies $S' \supseteq S$. Therefore, it suffices to guess a status set S such that S is $A(S)$-rational and $A \in \mathbf{Do}(S)$. Since the guess can be verified in polynomial time, membership in NP follows.

Hardness for (*ii*) follows from Theorem 11.4.4. The hardness part for (*i*) can be shown by a suitable extension of the construction in the proof of Theorem 11.5.6, such that validity of a quantified Boolean formula $\forall Y \exists X \phi$, can be decided, where ϕ is in M3SAT form.

Without loss of generality, we assume that no clause of ϕ has all its variables from Y, and that ϕ can only be satisfied if a particular variable $x_1 \in X$ is set to **true**. We introduce besides POS, NEG, VAR (which stores $X \cup Y$), and AUX(which must satisfy the FD *Var* → *Val*) new relations XVAR and YVAR for (redundantly) storing the variables in X and Y, respectively.

The actions $set_0(X)$, $set_1(X)$, and α are modified such that they have empty preconditions and empty Add- and Del-sets. Furthermore, we introduce two new actions $upd(X, X')$ and $add(Y)$ as follows:

upd: $Pre(upd(X, X')) = $ **true**, $\qquad$ add: $Pre(add(Y)) = $ **true**,
$\qquad Add(upd(X, X')) = \{\text{AUX}(X', 1)\}$, $\qquad\quad Add(add(Y)) = \{\text{AUX}(Y, 1)\}$,
$\qquad Del(upd(X, X')) = \{\text{AUX}(X, 0)\}$; $\qquad\quad\; Del(add(Y)) = \emptyset$.

Finally, we add to the program $\mathcal{P}$ in the proof of Theorem 11.5.6 the following rules (let $v \in \{0, 1\}$):

$\quad$ **Do** $(add(Y_1)) \leftarrow \text{YVAR}(Y_1)$
$\quad$ **Do** $(upd(Y_1, Y_1)) \leftarrow $ **Do** $(set_v(Y_1))$, $\text{YVAR}(Y_1)$
$\quad$ **Do** $(upd(X_1, X_2)) \leftarrow $ **Do** $(set_v(X_1))$, $\text{XVAR}(X_1)$, $\text{XVAR}(X_2)$

The modifications have the following effect. The first rule adds for each $y_j \in Y$ the tuple $(y_j, 1)$ to AUX and thus causes a violation of the FD $Var \rightarrow Val$. This must be cured by executing $upd(y_j, y_j)$, which requests that y_j is assigned a value (i.e., either $set_0(y_j)$ or $set_1(y_j)$ is taken). Assigning a truth value to some variable $x_i \in X$ (i.e., executing $set_0(x_i)$ or $set_1(x_i)$) adds a tuple $(x_j, 1)$ to AUX for each $x_j \in X$, which causes a violation of the FD $Var \rightarrow Tag$ for $x_j \neq x_i$ (observe that $(x_i, 0)$ is removed). Each such violation must be cured by assigning x_j a truth value.

Thus, every weak rational status set of the constructed program on D contains either **Do** $(set_0(y_j))$ or **Do** $(set_1(y_j))$, for each $y_j \in Y$ (but not both), i.e., embodies a choice χ.

On the other hand, for each such choice χ (representing a truth assignment to Y), by the assumption on ϕ a weak rational status set exists: if all obligations $set_0(x_i)$, $set_1(x_i)$, $x_i \in X$ are violated, then we obtain a respective A-feasible status set S_χ, and therefore, since the program is positive, a weak rational status set $S' \supseteq S_\chi$ exists. It holds that S_χ is weak rational, if and only if $\exists X\phi[Y = \chi]$ is unsatisfiable. Observe that, by our assumption on x_1, every weak rational S' such that $S' \supset S_\chi$ contains **Do** $(set_1(x_1))$.

It follows that $set_1(x_1) \in $ **Do** (S) holds for every weak rational status set S of the program on D if and only if ϕ is true. This proves the hardness part for (i) and the result. ∎

Programs with Negation We obtained that for positive programs, presence of integrity constraints increases the complexity of weak rational (resp., weak reasonable) status sets in general. We thus ask whether integrity constraints have a similar effect for programs with negation.

As for weak reasonable status sets, we find that integrity constraints do not increase the complexity. This has already been established for the recognition problem and action

Section 11.5   Effect of Integrity Constraints   451

reasoning in Theorems 11.4.17 and 11.4.19, respectively. It remains to consider the problems of consistency and computation.

THEOREM 11.5.10   Let $\mathcal{P}$ be a fixed agent program (where $\mathcal{IC}$ is arbitrary). Then, given agent state $\mathcal{O}_S$, deciding whether $\mathcal{P}$ has a weak reasonable status set on $\mathcal{P}_S$ is NP-complete, and computing any weak reasonable status set of $\mathcal{P}$ on $\mathcal{O}_S$ is complete for FNP//log.

Proof   By Theorems 11.4.14 and 11.4.15, it remains to prove the membership part. Under the assumptions, a weak reasonable status exists if and only if some A-reasonable status set S exists. Propositions 11.4.2 and 11.4.1 imply that deciding $A(S)$-reasonability of S is polynomial. Therefore, a guess for S can be verified in polynomial time. Hence, the consistency problem is in NP.

We can obtain a weak reasonable status set by first computing the maximum s over all $|A(S)|$ such that S is $A(S)$-reasonable, and then generating nondeterministically an $A(S)$-reasonable status set S such that $|A(S)| = s$. Computing s amounts to an NP optimization problem with $O(\log |I|)$ bits; hence, the problem is in FNP//log.   ∎

For weak rational status sets, the existence problem is equivalent to the existence of some A-rational status set. From Proposition 11.4.2 on page 429 and the proof of Theorem 11.5.4 on page 444 (whose hardness part does not involve obligation) we thus obtain the following result.

THEOREM 11.5.11   Let $\mathcal{P}$ be a fixed agent program (where $\mathcal{IC}$ is arbitrary). Then, given an agent state $\mathcal{O}_S$, deciding whether $\mathcal{P}$ has a weak rational status set on $\mathcal{P}$ is Σ_2^P-complete.

For the computation of a weak rational status set, we can use a modified version of the algorithm **Compute-NIC-WRational-SS**, by replacing A-feasible sets with A-rational sets. This increases the complexity, as we have to replace the NP oracle by a Σ_2^P oracle. Thus, the problem belongs to $FP^{\Sigma_2^P}$. This can be complemented by a probabilistic upper bound.

THEOREM 11.5.12   Let $\mathcal{P}$ be a fixed agent program (where $\mathcal{IC}$ is arbitrary). Then, computing any weak rational status set of $\mathcal{P}$ on a given agent state $\mathcal{O}_S$ is in $FP^{\Sigma_2^P} \cap RP \cdot FP_\|^{\Sigma_2^P}$ and hard for both $F\Sigma_2^P$ and $FP_\|^{\Sigma_2^P}$.

Proof   Membership in $FP^{\Sigma_2^P}$ was discussed above. Membership in $RP \cdot FP_\|^{\Sigma_2^P}$ can be established using results from (Chen and Toda 1995). In fact, the computation of a weak rational status set in the most general setting can be easily expressed as a maximization problem (MAXP) as defined in (Chen and Toda 1995), such that the instance-solution relation is co-NP-decidable; for such problems, $RP \cdot FP_\|^{\Sigma_2^P}$ is an upper bound.

Hardness for $F\Sigma_2^P$ is immediate from the proof of Theorem 11.5.4 on page 444 (existence of a rational status set), since **O** does not occur in the program constructed. Hardness for $FP_{\|}^{\Sigma_2^P}$ can be established as follows. Let Π be any Σ_2^P-complete problem. Then, computing, given instances $I_1, \ldots, I_n$ of Π, the binary string $B = b_1 \cdots b_n$ where $b_i = 1$ if I_i is a "Yes"-instance and $b_i = 0$ otherwise, is easily seen to be hard for $FP_{\|}^{\Sigma_2^P}$.

From the proof of Theorem 11.5.4 on page 444, we know that deciding whether a fixed agent program $\mathcal{P}$, in which **O** does not occur, has a rational status set on a given database D is Σ_2^P complete. Thus, for given databases $D_1, \ldots, D_n$, computing the string B is $FP_{\|}^{\Sigma_2^P}$-hard.

The different instances can be combined into a single instance of a new fixed program as follows. Take a fresh action α, which does not occur in $\mathcal{P}$ such that $Pre(\alpha) = \textbf{true}$ and $Add(\alpha) = Del(\alpha) = \emptyset$. Add the atom $\textbf{Do}\,\alpha$ in the body of each rule in $\mathcal{P}$, and add the rule $\textbf{O}\alpha \leftarrow$. Then the resulting program $\mathcal{P}_0$ has some weak rational status set S on each D_i, and for any such S it holds $\alpha \in \textbf{Do}\,(S)$ if and only if $\mathcal{P}_0$ has a rational status set on D_i.

The databases D_i can be merged into a single database D' for a new fixed program $\mathcal{P}'$, in the same way as described in the proof of Theorem 11.5.8 on page 447, by tagging the databases D_i with i and taking their union. This program $\mathcal{P}'$ has some weak rational status set S on D', moreover, for every such S, it holds that $\alpha(i) \in \textbf{Do}\,(S)$ if and only if $\mathcal{P}$ has a rational status set on D_i, thus, from an S the binary string B is easily computed.

Since the database D' is polynomial-time constructible from $D_1, \ldots, D_n$, it follows that computing a weak rational status set is hard for $FP_{\|}^{\Sigma_2^P}$. ∎

Next we consider the recognition problem. Here, the complexity increases if integrity constraints are allowed.

THEOREM 11.5.13 Let $\mathcal{P}$ be a fixed agent program (where $\mathcal{IC}$ is arbitrary). Then, given an agent state $\mathcal{O}_S$ and a status set S, deciding whether S is a weak rational status set of $\mathcal{P}$ on $\mathcal{O}_S$ is Π_2^P-complete.

Proof For the membership part, consider the following algorithm for the complement problem. First, check whether S is not an $A(S)$-rational status set. If S is found $A(S)$-rational, then guess $A' \supset A(S)$ and S' and check whether S' is A'-rational. Since checking A-rationality of S is in co-NP (apply Proposition 11.4.2 on page 429 and Theorem 11.5.2 on page 443), this is an Σ_2^P algorithm. Thus, the original problem is in Π_2^P.

For the hardness part, we adapt the construction in the proof of Theorem 11.5.3 for QBF formulas $\exists Y \forall X \phi$, by adding the $\exists Y$ quantifier block.

We use the database $\mathcal{D}$, the actions base $\mathcal{AB}$, and the integrity constraints as there, but add to $\mathcal{D}$ another relation YVAR for storing the Y-variables (the X-variables are in VAR) and introduce another action αd with empty precondition and add and delete sets.

We add the following clauses in the program:

$$\mathbf{O}(\alpha) \leftarrow$$
$$\mathbf{O}(set(Y, 0)) \leftarrow \text{YVAR}(Y)$$
$$\mathbf{O}(set(Y, 1)) \leftarrow \text{YVAR}(Y)$$
$$\mathbf{Do}\,(set(Y, 0)) \leftarrow \mathbf{Do}\,(\alpha), \neg\mathbf{Do}\,(set(Y, 1)), \text{YVAR}(Y)$$
$$\mathbf{Do}\,(\alpha) \leftarrow \mathbf{Do}\,(set(Y, 0)), \text{YVAR}(Y)$$
$$\mathbf{Do}\,(\alpha) \leftarrow \mathbf{Do}\,(set(Y, 1)), \text{YVAR}(Y).$$

Let $\mathcal{P}'$ be the resulting program, and set up the action constraint

AC: $\{set(Y, 0), set(Y, 1)\} \looparrowleft \text{YVAR}(Y).$

The additional rules state that the agent is obliged to execute α and to set every variable $y_j \in Y$ to true and false, which is prohibited by AC. Moreover, each y_j must have assigned a value if α is executed, and if some variable receives a value, then α is executed. Consequently, if α is executed, then every y_j gets precisely one value, and if α is not executed, then no y_j gets a value.

Let S_0 be the status sets defined by

$$S_0 = S \cup \{\mathbf{O}\alpha, \mathbf{P}\alpha\} \cup \{\mathbf{O}(set(y_j, v)), \mathbf{P}(set(y_j, v)) \mid y_j \in Y, v \in \{0, 1\}\},$$

where S is the status set from the proof of Theorem 11.5.3 on page 443. Then, S_0 is an $A(S)$-rational status set, in which all the obligations from the new rules are violated.

We claim that S_0 is the (unique) weak rational status set of $\mathcal{P}'$ if and only if $\forall Y \exists X \neg \phi$ is true.

($\Rightarrow$) Suppose S_0 is weak rational, and let χ be an arbitrary choice χ from $set(y_j, 0)$, $set(y_j, 1)$, for all $y_j \in Y$ (representing a truth assignment to Y). Then, it is impossible to find an A-rational status set where the obligation followed in A correspond to χ.

In particular, the status set

$$S_\chi = S_0 \cup \chi \cup \{\mathbf{Do}\,\alpha\}$$

is not weak rational. As easily checked, S_χ is $A(S_\chi)$-feasible. Hence, some $S' \subset S$ must exist which satisfies the conditions $(S1)$–$(S3)$ of $A(S_\chi)$-feasibility. Consequently, $\forall X\,\phi[Y = \chi]$ is false. It follows that $\forall Y \exists X\,\neg\phi$ is true.

($\Leftarrow$) Suppose $\forall Y \exists X \neg\phi$ is true. Consider any weak rational status set S of $\mathcal{P}'$. Then, either (i) $\alpha \in S$ and $A(S)$ defines a choice χ from $\mathbf{Do}\,set(y_j, 0)$, $\mathbf{Do}\,set(y_j, 1)$, for all $y_j \in Y$ (representing a truth assignment); or (ii) $A(S) = A(S_0)$ holds.

Assume (*i*) holds and consider the following two cases:

(1) **Do** (*all*) $\notin S$. Then, exactly on of the actions $set(x_i, 0)$, $set(x_i, 1)$ must be in **Do** (*S*), for every $x_i \in X$. But then, executing **Do** (*S*) violates the integrity constraints $\mathcal{IC}$, which contradicts that *S* is a weak rational status set.

(2) **Do** (*all*) $\in S$. Since by assumption $\forall X \phi[Y = \chi]$ is false, there exists some $S' \subset S$ which satisfies the conditions (*S*1)–(*S*3) of *A*(*S*)-feasibility. Again, this means that *S* is not *A*(*S*)-rational and thus contradicts weak rationality of *S*.

Hence, case (*i*) is impossible, which means that case (*ii*) must apply to *S*. Consequently, S_0 is a weak rational status set. It can be seen that $S = S_0$ must hold. This proves the result. ■

The last result that we turn to in this subsection is action reasoning under weak rational status sets. Here we face the full complexity of all conditions that we have imposed on a status set.

THEOREM 11.5.14   Let $\mathcal{P}$ be a fixed agent program. Let $\mathcal{O}_S$ be a given agent state and let α be a given ground action. Then, deciding whether $\alpha \in$ **Do** (*S*) holds for (*i*) every (resp., (*ii*)) some) weak rational status set of $\mathcal{P}$ on $\mathcal{O}_S$ is Π_3^P-complete (resp., Σ_3^P-complete).

Proof   The membership part is routine: a guess for a weak rational status set *S* such that $\alpha \notin$ **Do** (*S*) (resp., $\alpha \in$ **Do** (*S*)) can be verified with an Σ_2^P oracle in polynomial time (Theorem 11.5.13 on page 452).

For the hardness part, we extend the construction in the proof of Theorem 11.5.13 on page 452 to QBFs of form $\forall Z \exists Y \forall X \phi$, by adding another quantifier block. We introduce a new relation ZVAR for storing the variables in *Z*, and add the following clauses to the program:

O(*set*(Z, 0)) ← ZVAR(Z),
O(*set*(Z, 1)) ← ZVAR(Z),
Do (*set*(Y, 0)), ← ¬**Do** (*set*(Y, 1)), ZVAR(X).

Denote the resulting program by $\mathcal{P}''$. Moreover, we impose a further action constraint

AC':   {*set*(Z, 0), *set*(Z, 1)} ↩ ZVAR(Z).

This forces the agent to make in every weak rational status set a choice χ from **Do** (*set*(z_i, 0)) and **Do** (*set*(z_i, 1)), for all $z_i \in Z$. Upon such a choice (which represents a truth assignment), $\mathcal{P}''$ behaves like $\mathcal{P}'$. Thus, for any such choice χ, a weak rational status set *S* including χ contains **Do** α if and only if $\exists Y \forall X \phi[Z = \chi]$ is true.

It follows that **Do** α belongs to every weak rational status set of $\mathcal{P}''$ if and only if $\forall Z \exists Y \forall X \phi$ is true. This proves Π_3^P-hardness of (*i*). For (*ii*), we add the rule **Do** (β) ← ¬**Do** (α) in the program, where β is a fresh action of the type of α. Let $\mathcal{P}^*$ be the resulting program.

It holds that $\mathcal{P}^*$ has some weak rational status set containing $\mathbf{Do}\,\beta$ if and only if $\mathcal{P}''$ has some weak rational status set not containing $\mathbf{Do}\,\alpha$. This implies Σ_3^P-hardness of (ii). ∎

11.5.5 Preferred Status Sets

Imposing integrity constraint on the agent state acts differently on rational versus reasonable status sets. It appears that for rational status sets, we have a complexity increase, while for reasonable status sets, the complexity remains unchanged (see Section 11.4.3).

As for the consistency problem, under the assumptions a F-preferred rational (resp., reasonable) status set exists if and only if a rational (resp., reasonable) status set exists. Thus, from Theorems 11.5.4 and 11.4.12 on page 428, we obtain the following corollary.

COROLLARY 15 Let $\mathcal{P}$ be a fixed agent program (where $\mathcal{IC}$ is arbitrary). Then, given an agent state $\mathcal{O}_S$, deciding whether $\mathcal{P}$ has some F-preferred rational (resp., reasonable) status set on $\mathcal{P}$ is Σ_2^P-complete (resp., NP-complete).

In the presence of integrity constraints, the recognition problem for F-preferred rational status sets migrates to the next level of the polynomial hierarchy. For the proof of this result, we use the following convenient lemma.

LEMMA 11.5.1 Let $\Phi' = \forall Z \exists Y' \forall X' \phi'$ be a QBF such that ϕ' is in DNF, where Z may be void. Then, a formula $\Phi = \forall Z \exists Y \forall X \phi$, where ϕ is in M3DNF, is constructible in polynomial time, such that

(1) the formula $\forall Z X\, \phi[Y = \emptyset]$ is true;

(2) Φ' is equivalent to $\forall Z (\exists Y \neq \emptyset) \forall X\, \phi$.

Proof Without loss of generality, Φ' is already monotone. Suppose $Y' = \{y_1, y_2, \ldots, y_n\}$ and let $Y = Y' \cup \{y_0\}$. Consider the formula

$$\forall Z (\exists Y \neq \emptyset) \forall X' ((\neg y_0 \wedge \cdots \wedge \neg y_n) \vee \phi'). \tag{11.1}$$

This formula is clearly equivalent to Φ'. Construct next the formula

$$\forall Z (\exists Y' \neq \emptyset) \forall X' [(\forall W \psi) \vee \phi'], \tag{11.2}$$

where $W = \{w_1, \ldots, w_n\}$ and $\psi = (\neg y_0 \wedge w_1) \vee (\neg w_1 \wedge \neg y_1 \wedge w_2) \vee (\neg w_2 \wedge \neg y_2 \wedge w_3) \vee \cdots \vee (\neg w_{n-1} \wedge \neg y_{n-1} \wedge w_n) \vee (\neg w_n \wedge \neg y_n)$. The formula (11.2) is equivalent to (11.1). Indeed, observe that $\forall W \psi$ is equivalent to $\neg y_0 \wedge \cdots \wedge \neg y_n$. To see this, suppose first $\forall W \psi$ is true. Then, for every $i = 0, \ldots, n$ consider a truth value assignment χ_i to W such that $w_j = 0$, for every $j \leq i$, and $w_j = 1$, for all $j > i$. Then, $\psi[W = \chi_i] \leftrightarrow \neg y_j$. Hence, $\neg y_0 \wedge \cdots \wedge \neg y_n$ is true. Conversely, suppose $\neg y_0 \wedge \cdots \wedge \neg y_n$ is true. Toward a contradiction, suppose $\psi[W = \chi]$ is false for some truth value assignment χ to W. Hence, by the first disjunct in ψ, w_1 is false in χ, which means by the second disjunct that w_2 is false in $\chi, \ldots$, that w_n is false in χ. However, the last disjunct in ψ is $\neg w_n \wedge \neg y_n$. Thus, this disjunct and hence $\psi[W = \chi]$ is true, which is a contradiction.

By elementary quantifier pulling (no variable from $Z \cup X'$ occurs in ψ), formula (11.2) is equivalent to

$$\forall Z(\exists Y \neq \emptyset) \forall X'W(\psi \vee \phi'), \tag{11.3}$$

and $\forall Z X'W(\psi \vee \phi)[Y = \emptyset]$ is true. By using further universally quantified variables $W' = \{w'_1, \ldots, w'_n\}$, we fleet ψ into M3DNF form and obtain

$$\forall Z(\exists Y \neq \emptyset) \forall W W' \left[\bigvee_{w_i \in W} (w_i \wedge w'_i) \vee \bigvee_{w_i \in W} (\neg w_i \wedge \neg w'_i) \vee \psi[W/\neg W'] \vee \phi' \right] \tag{11.4}$$

where $\phi[W/\neg W']$ means the obvious substitution of W'-literals for W-literals such that the formula is monotone. Clearly, (11.4) is equivalent to (11.3). By replicating literals in disjuncts, the lemma is proven. ∎

THEOREM 11.5.15 Let $\mathcal{P}$ be a fixed agent program (where $\mathcal{IC}$ is arbitrary). Then, given an agent state $\mathcal{O}_S$ and a status set S, deciding whether S is a F-preferred rational status set of $\mathcal{P}$ on $\mathcal{O}_S$ is Π_2^P-complete.

Proof Checking whether S is a rational status set can be done with a call to an NP oracle (Theorem 11.5.2 on page 443), and a rational status set S' such that $\mathbf{F}(S') \subset \mathbf{F}(S)$ can be guessed and checked in polynomial time with an NP oracle. Hence, showing that S is not a F-preferred rational status set is in Σ_2^P.

The proof of hardness is an extension to the proof of Theorem 11.5.3. We encode the $\exists Y \forall X \phi$ QBF problem, where ϕ is in M3DNF form, by adding a further block of quantifiers $\exists Y$ in the construction. For convenience, we may start from the formula $\exists Y \forall X \phi$ as in Lemma 11.5.1 on the preceding page, and encode the failure of condition (2) of it; this is a Π_2^P-hard problem.

We use the database relations POS and NEG from the proof of Theorem 11.5.3 on page 443 for storing the positive and negative disjuncts of ϕ, respectively. The relation VAR however, is extended by an additional tag column to the format VAR(*Var, Value, Tag, Tag1*). The additional tag *Tag1* indicates whether a variable is from X (value 0) or from Y (value 1).

We impose two FDs on VAR: *Var, Value* $\rightarrow$ *Tag* and *Var* $\rightarrow$ *Tag1*.

The action base $\mathcal{AB}$ is the same, with the only difference that *add_var* has a fourth parameter W and that each occurrence of VAR(X, Y, Z) is replaced by VAR(X, Y, Z, W).

We modify and extend the program $\mathcal{P}$ to a program $\mathcal{P}'$ as follows. First, each occurrence of an atom VAR(X, Y, Z) is replaced by VAR(X, Y, Z, 0), and *add_var*(X, Y, 1) is replaced

Section 11.5   Effect of Integrity Constraints

by $add\_var(X, Y, 1, 0)$. We then add the rules

(1) $\mathbf{F}(set(X, 1)) \leftarrow \mathbf{Do}\,(set(X, 0)), \text{VAR}(X, Y, Z, 1)$
(2) $\mathbf{Do}\,(set(X, 1)) \leftarrow \neg\mathbf{Do}\,(set(X, 0)), \text{VAR}(X, Y, Z, 1)$

For every choice χ from $\mathbf{Do}\,(set(y_j, 0))$, $\mathbf{Do}\,(set(y_j, 1))$, for all $y_j \in Y$ (representing a truth value assignment to Y), we obtain a candidate S_χ for a F-preferred rational status set which is a feasible status set of $\mathcal{P}'$. This candidate is the deontic and action closure of the set

$$S \cup \chi \cup \{\mathbf{F}(set(y_j, 1)) \mid set(y_j, 0) \in \mathbf{Do}\,(\chi)\},$$

where S is the feasible status set from the proof of Theorem 11.5.3 on page 443 (adapted for add_var).

For the choice $\chi = \chi_0$ which sets all y_j to **false**, S_χ has a maximal **F**-part over all χ; this is also the maximal **F**-part possible for any rational status set of $\mathcal{P}'$. Moreover, by Lemma 11.5.1 on page 455 and the construction of $\mathcal{P}'$, this S_{χ_0} is a rational status set.

We claim that S_{χ_0} is F-preferred if and only if $\exists Y \neq \emptyset \forall X\, \phi$ is false. The result follows from this claim.

($\Rightarrow$) Suppose S_{χ_0} is F-preferred. Then, no rational status set S' exists such that $\mathbf{F}(S') \subset \mathbf{F}(S)$. In particular, for every $\chi \neq \chi_0$ the set S_χ is not a rational status set. As in the proof of Theorem 11.5.3, we conclude that the formula $\forall X\, \phi[Y = \chi]$ must be false. Hence, $\exists Y \neq \emptyset \forall X\, \phi$ is false.

($\Leftarrow$) Suppose S_{χ_0} is not F-preferred. Then, there exists a rational set S' such that $\mathbf{F}(S') \subset \mathbf{F}(S)$. By clause (1) and deontic consistency of S', at most one of $set(y_j, 0)$ and $set(y_j, 1)$ is in $\mathbf{Do}\,(S')$, for every $y_j \in Y$; moreover, by the clause (2), precisely one of them is in S'. Thus, S' includes a choice χ representing a truth value assignment to Y. For this choice, the program $\mathcal{P}'$ essentially reduces under rational status set semantics to the program $\mathcal{P}$ for $\phi[Y = \chi]$ from the proof of Theorem 11.5.3 on page 443. (Observe that only clauses (1) and (2) allow to derive status information for any action $set(y_j, 1)$.) It is not hard to see that the set S there is the unique rational status set of $\mathcal{P}$, if a rational status set exists. It follows that for the choice χ, the formula $\forall \phi[Y = \chi]$ is true. Since $S' \neq S_{\chi_0}$, we have $\chi \neq \chi_0$. Consequently, $(\exists Y \neq \emptyset)\forall X\, \phi$ is true. ∎

Since the recognition of F-preferred rational status sets is gets more complex in the presence of integrity constraints, also the complexity of computing such a status set increases. The increase is one level in the polynomial hierarchy.

THEOREM 11.5.16   Let $\mathcal{P}$ be a fixed agent program (where $\mathcal{IC}$ is arbitrary). Then, given an agent state $\mathcal{O}_S$, computing any F-preferred rational status set of $\mathcal{P}$ on $\mathcal{O}_S$ (so one exists), is in $\text{FP}^{\Sigma_2^P} \cap \text{RP} \cdot \text{FP}_{\|}^{\Sigma_2^P}$ and hard for both $\text{F}\Sigma_2^P$ and $\text{FP}_{\|}^{\Sigma_2^P}$.

Proof Modify the algorithm **Compute-NIC-Rational-SS** in Section 11.4.2 as follows. After Step 2, compute the smallest size s of the **F**-part over all rational status sets of $\mathcal{P}$ on $\mathcal{O}_S$. Then, in the remaining steps, constrain the oracle queries to existence of a rational status set S' such that $S \subseteq S' \subseteq (GA \setminus \{A\})$ and $|\mathbf{F}(S')| = S$. Since the oracle queries are in Σ_2^P (cf. Theorem 11.5.4), the problem is in $\mathrm{FP}^{\Sigma_2^P}$. Membership in $\mathrm{RP} \cdot \mathrm{FP}_{\|}^{\Sigma_2^P}$ follows from the fact that computing a F-preferred rational status set can be easily expressed as a maximization problem (MAXP) as defined in (Chen and Toda 1995), whose instance-solution relation is co-NP-decidable; $\mathrm{RP} \cdot \mathrm{FP}_{\|}^{\Sigma_2^P}$ is an upper bound for such problems (Chen and Toda 1995).

Hardness for $F\Sigma_2^P$ is immediate from the proof of Theorem 11.5.4 on page 444 (compute a rational status set), since each rational status set of the program $\mathcal{P}$ constructed there is F-preferred. The lower bound of hardness for $\mathrm{FP}_{\|}^{\Sigma_2^P}$ can be shown following the argument in the proof of Theorem 11.5.12 on page 451, where we reduce the computation of the binary string B for instances $I_1, \ldots, I_n$ of the Σ_2^P-complete complement of the recognition problem for F-preferred rational status sets.

We may suppose that the program is $\mathcal{P}'$ from the proof of Theorem 11.5.15 on page 456, and that the set S to check over database D is the set S_{χ_0}, which is rational and has the maximal **F**-part over all rational status sets. Similar as in the proof of Theorem 11.5.12 on page 451, we tag databases D_i by introducing a new column T in each table which is added on the left hand side of each FD, and we add for the tag a variable T to each action scheme. Then, the F-preferred rational status sets of the obtained program $\mathcal{P}''$ over the union $\widehat{D}$ of all tagged databases D_i, are given by the unions of the F-preferred rational status sets S_i of $\mathcal{P}''$ over each tagged database D_i. Hence, from any F-preferred status set S of $\mathcal{P}''$, the desired string B can be efficiently computed. Moreover, $\widehat{D}$ is constructible in polynomial time from $I_1, \ldots, I_n$. It follows that computing a F-preferred rational status set is $\mathrm{FP}_{\|}^{\Sigma_2^P}$-hard. ∎

The last result of this subsection and the chapter concerns action reasoning for F-preferred rational status sets. We find that this problem has the same complexity as for weak rational status sets, and is thus at the third level of the polynomial hierarchy.

THEOREM 11.5.17 Let $\mathcal{P}$ be a fixed agent program (where $\mathcal{IC}$ is arbitrary). Then, given an agent state $\mathcal{O}_S$ and a ground action α, deciding whether $\alpha \in \mathbf{Do}(S)$ holds for (*i*) every (resp., (*ii*) some) F-preferred rational status set S of $\mathcal{P}$ on $\mathcal{O}_S$ is Π_3^P-complete (resp., Σ_3^P-complete).

Proof The membership part is similar as in the case $\mathcal{IC} = \emptyset$ (Theorem 11.4.24 on page 438), but we use a Σ_2^P oracle instead of a NP oracle for recognizing a F-preferred rational status set (Theorem 11.5.15 on page 456).

For the hardness part of (i), we extend the construction in the proof of Theorem 11.5.15 on page 456. We add another block of quantifiers $\forall Z$ in front of the formula Φ, and encode evaluating the formula $\forall Z(\exists Y \neq \emptyset)\forall X\phi$ as in Lemma 11.5.1 on page 455.

The action base and the database are the same, and field $Tag1$ has value 2 for identifying the Z variables. We add to the program $\mathcal{P}'$ the following clauses:

$\mathbf{F}(set(X_1, 1)) \leftarrow \mathbf{Do}\,(set(X_1, 0)), \text{VAR}(X_1, Y_1, Z_1, 2)$
$\mathbf{F}(set(X_1, 0)) \leftarrow \mathbf{Do}\,(set(X_1, 1)), \text{VAR}(X_1, Y_1, Z_1, 2)$
$\mathbf{Do}\,(set(X_1, 1)) \leftarrow \neg\mathbf{Do}\,(set(X_1, 0)), \text{VAR}(X_1, Y_1, Z_1, 2)$

The clauses effect a choice μ from $\mathbf{Do}\,(set(z_i, 0))$, $\mathbf{Do}\,(set(z_i, 1))$, for all $z_i \in Z$ (representing a truth value assignment to Z), which is passed to the rest of the program. Observe that here, different from the choice rules for Y, the $\mathbf{F}$-parts deduced from different choices μ and μ' are incomparable.

Add to the program another rule

$\mathbf{Do}\,(\alpha) \leftarrow \mathbf{Do}\,(set(X_1, 1)), \text{VAR}(X_1, Y_1, Z_1, 1),$

where α is a fresh action with empty precondition and empty Add- and Del-sets, and let $\mathcal{P}''$ be the resulting program.

It holds that $\mathbf{Do}\,(\alpha) \in S$ for every F-preferred rational status set S of $\mathcal{P}''$ if and only if $\forall Z(\exists Y \neq \emptyset)(\forall X)\phi$ is true.

To see this, notice that the previous rule is applicable in a F-preferred rational status set S if and only if $\{set(y_j, 1) \mid y_j \in Y\} \not\subseteq \mathbf{F}(S)$ holds. Moreover, each candidate S_χ from the proof of Theorem 11.5.15 on page 456, extended for the choice μ according to the new rules, contains $\mathbf{Do}\,(\alpha)$ just if $\chi \neq \chi_0$. It follows that $\mathbf{Do}\,(\alpha)$ is contained in every F-preferred rational status set of $\mathcal{P}''$ if and only if $\forall Z(\exists Y \neq \emptyset)\forall X\phi$ is true. This proves Π_3^P-hardness of (i).

For (ii), add the rule $\mathbf{Do}\,(\beta) \leftarrow \neg\mathbf{Do}\,(\alpha)$ to $\mathcal{P}''$, where β is an fresh action of the same type as α. It is easy to see that $\mathbf{Do}\,(\beta)$ belongs to some F-preferred status set of the resulting program $\mathcal{P}^*$ if and only if $\mathbf{Do}\,(\alpha)$ does not belong to every F-preferred status set of $\mathcal{P}''$, i.e., $\forall Z(\exists Y \neq \emptyset)\forall X\phi$ is false. Thus, (ii) is Σ_3^P-hard. ∎

11.6 Related Work

To our knowledge, no systematic and comprehensive studies of the computational properties of other agent frameworks which are comparable to our framework have been carried out so far. In particular, no attempts toward a sharp classification of the computational complexity of agent decision tasks have been made. As for the BDI-architecture, e.g., Rao (1995) and

Rao, Georgeff (1995, 1998) have described algorithms showing that decision problems in BDI-logics are decidable, pointing out that their complexity is not higher than the one of the underlying temporal logic component. A rich source of complexity results on modal logics—which may be used for describing agents—is (Halpern and Moses 1992), where the focus is on classical decision problems. Many more complexity results on multi-agent systems, including common knowledge, evolving knowledge, logical omniscience, are discussed in the book of Fagin, Halpern, Moses, and Vardi (1995), where further references can be found. Complexity results on nonmonotonic modal logics—modeling nonmonotonic agents—are contained, e.g., in (Marek and Truszczyński 1991; Gottlob 1992a; Eiter and Gottlob 1992; Marek and Truszczyński 1993; Schwarz and Truszczyński 1996; Donini et al. 1997).

A comparative study of the computational complexity of different agent frameworks would be an interesting subject—the result would contribute to a more detailed picture of the properties the different approaches have. However, since the layout and formal underpinnings of various agent frameworks such as those in (Shoham 1993; Cohen and Levesque 1990a; Rao and Georgeff 1991; Bratman et al. 1988; Hindriks et al. 1997) are quite different, it is not a priori clear how the complexities of these systems should be compared. Another issue, refining the complexity view, is the expressive power in terms of capability to represent decision processes of inherent complexity. The capability of agent programs in that respect may be formally assessed in the spirit of similar concepts for advanced logical database queries languages (Eiter et al. 1997). This subject is left for further investigations.

12 Implementing Agents

We have developed a software environment called the *IMPACT* Agent Development Environment (*IADE* for short). *IADE* provides a set of software tools using which an agent developer may configure his or her agent. As we have already seen in Chapter 11, the diverse semantics supported by *IMPACT* have widely varying complexities. For positive agent programs, the rational, reasonable, F-preferential rational, and F-preferential reasonable status set semantics are polynomially computable even when integrity constraints are present. However, as we have already seen via the STORE, CHAIN and CFIT examples, encoding agents naturally seems to require negation. In the presence of negation, Chapter 11 tells us that the "cheapest" semantics to compute are the feasible status set semantics and the reasonable status set semantics, as computing such status sets falls within the class FNP when integrity constraints are present. Though this is intractable, of all the other semantics, this is the "most" tractable. Furthermore, we have argued in Chapter 6 that the reasonable status set semantics has epistemically more desirable qualities than the feasible status set semantics. As a consequence, the current version of the *IMPACT* Agent Development Environment supports the computation of the reasonable status set semantics.

Notwithstanding this, as remarked above, computing reasonable status sets of arbitrary agent programs with negation falls in the class FNP. As agents need to compute reasonable status sets on a continuous basis, the *IADE* implements a class of agents for which computing reasonable status sets is polynomial in the presence of integrity constraints, and under certain conditions on the integrity constraints, action constraints, and code calls. Such agents are called *regular agents*, and their associated agent programs, integrity constraints and action constraints are called regular agent programs, regular integrity constraints, and regular action constraints, respectively.

The main aim of this chapter is to:

• First define (in Section 12.1), a class of agents called *weakly regular agents* that serve as a stepping stone to later defining regular agents.
• Derive various theoretical properties of weakly regular agents that make the design of a computation procedure to compute regular agents polynomial. This is done in Section 12.2.
• Extend the definition of weak regular agents to define regular agents—the central contribution of this chapter. This is done in Section 12.3.

- Describe two algorithms used when a regular agent is compiled, and show that these algorithms are correct. This is done in Section 12.4.
- Describe a special computation package we have built called the *Query Maintenance Package* (or *QMP* for short). This package specifies
  - Data structures used by *IADE* to ensure that status sets are succinctly (implicitly) represented in a state independent compact data structure and
  - Define functions that manipulate the above *QMP* data structures to explicitly compute a status set and/or explicitly compute a new set of actions to be done when the agent's state is changed through the receipt of messages from other agents.

These contributions are described in Section 12.5.

- Describe in detail our implementation of *IADE* and how an agent developer might use it to develop agents. This is done in Section 12.6.
- Provide experimental results that describe the behavior of our algorithms. This is done in Section 12.7.

12.1 Weakly Regular Agents

In this section, we will first identify a class of agent programs called *weakly regular agent programs* (*WRAPs* for short)—later, these are extended to *regular agent programs* (*RAPs* for short) that are guaranteed to possess polynomially computable reasonable status sets. *WRAPs* are characterized by three basic properties:

1. *Strong Safety.* In addition to the safety requirement on rules introduced in Chapter 4 (Definition 4.2.5), code call conditions are required to satisfy some additional conditions which ensure that they always return finite answers.

2. *Conflict-Freedom.* The set of rules in a *WRAP* should not lead to conflicts—for example, the rules must not force an agent to do something it is forbidden to do.

3. *Deontic Stratifiability.* This is a property in the spirit of stratification in logic programs (Apt, Blair, and Walker 1988), which prevents problems with negation in rule bodies. However, as we will see, deontic stratification is more complex than ordinary stratification due to (i) the presence of deontic modalities in rule bodies, and (ii) the fact that rules can be inconsistent due to conflicting modalities in rule heads.

12.1.1 Strong Safety

As described in Chapter 4, for a code-call to be executable at run-time, its arguments must be instantiated. Safety is a *compile-time* check that ensures that all code calls generated at *run-time* have instantiated parameters. However, executability of a code call condition does

Section 12.1   Weakly Regular Agents

not depend solely on safety. For example, consider the simple code call condition

in(X, $\mathtt{math}:geq(25))$.

This code call condition attempts to execute a function that computes all integers greater than or equal to 25. Though this code call condition is safe, it leads to an infinite set of possible answers, leading to non-termination. In fact, the problem is even more insidious. Consider, for instance, the code call condition

in(X, $\mathtt{math}:geq(25))$ & **in**(Y, $\mathtt{math}:square(X))$ & $Y \leq 2000$.

This code call condition may find all numbers that are less than 2000 and that are squares of an integer greater than or equal to 25. Clearly, over the integers there are only finitely many ground substitutions that cause this code call condition to be true. Furthermore, this code call condition is safe. However, its evaluation may never terminate. The reason for this is that safety requires that we first compute the set of all integers that are greater than 25, leading to an infinite computation. This means that in general, we must impose some restrictions on code call conditions to ensure that they are finitely evaluable.

Suppose the developer of an agent examines the code calls supported by a given data structure and specifies which of them are finite and which are not. As is well known, determining whether a function is finite or not is undecidable (cf. Rogers Jr. 1967), and hence, input from the agent developer is imperative.

DEFINITION 12.1.1 (BINDING PATTERN)   Suppose we consider a code call $\mathcal{S} : f(\mathtt{a}_1, \ldots, \mathtt{a}_n)$ where each $\mathtt{a}_i$ is of type τ_i. A *binding pattern* for $\mathcal{S} : f(\mathtt{a}_1, \ldots, \mathtt{a}_n)$ is an n-tuple $(bt_1, \ldots, bt_n)$ where each bt_i (called a *binding term*) is either:

1. A value of type τ_i, or

2. the expression ♭ denoting that this argument is bound to an unknown value.

We require that the agent developer must specify a *finiteness* predicate that may be defined via a *finiteness table* having two columns—the first column is the name of the code call, while the second column is a binding pattern for the function in question.[1] Intuitively, suppose we have a row of the form

$\langle \mathcal{S} : f(\mathtt{a}_1, \mathtt{a}_2, \mathtt{a}_3), (\flat, 5, \flat) \rangle$

---

[1] In the *IMPACT* implementation, we ask the user to represent the infinite, rather than finite code calls. This is because in most cases, we expect code calls to be finite—thus, representing relatively few infinite code calls might reduce the burden on the agent developer. In addition, the implementation allows an extra "constraint" column, and variables in binding patterns. Thus, a user can write that a code call $\mathtt{d}: f(\mathtt{X}, \mathtt{Y})$ yields an infinite answer when $X > 400$. We have chosen to keep the presentation in this chapter in the current form to make it more easily understandable.

in the finiteness table. Then this row says that the answer returned by any code call of the form $S : f(\cdot, 5, \cdot)$ is finite. In other words, as long as the second argument of this code call is 5, the answer returned is finite, irrespective of the values of the first and third arguments. Clearly, the same code call may occur many times in a finiteness table with different binding patterns.

Example 12.1.1 (Finiteness Table for AutoPilot Agent in CFIT Example) An example of a finiteness table is given below.

Code Call	Binding Pattern
autoPilot : *readGPSData*(SensorId)	(b)
autoPilot : *calculateLocation*(Location, FlightRoute, Speed)	(b, b, b)
autoPilot : *calculateNFlightRoutes*(CurrentLocation, No_go, N)	(b, b, 1)
autoPilot : *calculateNFlightRoutes*(CurrentLocation, No_go, N)	(b, b, 2)
autoPilot : *calculateNFlightRoutes*(CurrentLocation, No_go, N)	(b, b, 3)

This indicates that autoPilot : *readGPSData*() and autoPilot : *calculateLocation*() always return a finite number of answers. The code call autoPilot : *calculateNFlight-Routes*(CurrentLocation, No_go, N) returns up to N flight routes when $N \neq 0$. If $N = 0$, then an infinite number of flight routes (which start at CurrentLocation and avoid the given No_go areas) may be returned. Our finiteness table above indicates that when $1 \leq N \leq 3$, autoPilot : *calculateNFlightRoutes*() will only return a finite number of answers. Notice that this table is incomplete since it does not indicate that a finite number of answers will be returned when $N > 3$.

From the fact that any code call of the form $S : f(\cdot, 5, \cdot)$ has a finite answer, we should certainly be able to infer that the code call $S : f(20, 5, 17)$ has a finite answer. In order to make this kind of inference, we need to associate an ordering on binding patterns. We say that $b \leq val$ for all values, and take the reflexive closure. We may now extend this $\leq$ ordering to binding patterns.

DEFINITION 12.1.2 (ORDERING ON BINDING PATTERNS) We say a binding pattern $(bt_1, \ldots, bt_n)$ is *equally or less informative* than another binding pattern $(bt'_1, \ldots, bt'_n)$ if, by definition, for all $1 \leq i \leq n$, $bt_i \leq bt'_i$.

We will say $(bt_1, \ldots, bt_n)$ is *less informative* than $(bt'_1, \ldots, bt'_n)$ *if and only if* it is equally or less informative than $(bt'_1, \ldots, bt'_n)$ and $(bt'_1, \ldots, bt'_n)$ is not equally or less informative than $(bt_1, \ldots, bt_n)$. If $(bt'_1, \ldots, bt'_n)$ is less informative than $(bt_1, \ldots, bt_n)$, then we will say that $(bt_1, \ldots, bt_n)$ is *more informative* than $(bt'_1, \ldots, bt'_n)$.

Section 12.1   Weakly Regular Agents   465

Suppose now that the developer of an agent specifies a finiteness table FINTAB. The following definition specifies what it means for a specific code call atom to be considered finite w.r.t. FINTAB.

DEFINITION 12.1.3 (FINITENESS)   Suppose FINTAB is a finite finiteness table, and $(bt_1, \ldots, bt_n)$ is a binding pattern associated with the code call $\mathcal{S} : f(\cdots)$. Then FINTAB is said to *entail the finiteness of* $\mathcal{S} : f(\mathtt{bt}_1, \ldots, \mathtt{bt}_n)$ *if, by definition,* there exists an entry of the form $\langle \mathcal{S} : f(\ldots), (bt'_1, \ldots, bt'_n)\rangle$ in FINTAB such that $(bt_1, \ldots, bt_n)$ is more informative than $(bt'_1, \ldots, bt'_n)$.

Below, we show how the finiteness table introduced for the autoPilot agent entails the finiteness of some simple code calls.

Example 12.1.2 (Finiteness Table)   Let FINTAB be the finiteness table given in Example 12.1.1 on the facing page. Then FINTAB entails the finiteness of autoPilot : *readGPSData* (5) and
autoPilot : *calculateNFlightRoutes*($\langle 221, 379, 433\rangle$, Ø, 2) but it does not entail the finiteness of autoPilot : *calculateNFlightRoutes*($\langle 221, 379, 433\rangle$, Ø, 0) (since this may have an infinite number of answers) or autoPilot : *calculateNFlightRoutes*($\langle 221, 379, 433\rangle$, Ø, 5) (since FINTAB is not complete).

According to the above definition, when we know that FINTAB entails the finiteness of the code call $\mathcal{S} : f(\mathtt{bt}_1, \ldots, \mathtt{bt}_n)$, then we know that every code call of the form $\mathcal{S} : f(\ldots)$ whose arguments satisfy the binding requirements are guaranteed to yield finite answers. However, defining strong safety of a code call condition is more complex. For instance, even if we know that $\mathcal{S} : f(\mathtt{t}_1, \ldots, \mathtt{t}_n)$ is finite, the code call atom **not_in**(X, $\mathcal{S} : f(\mathtt{t}_1, \ldots, \mathtt{t}_n)$) may have an infinite answer. Likewise, comparison conditions such as s > t may have finite answers in some cases and infinite answers in other cases, depending upon whether we are evaluating variables over the reals, the integers, the positive reals, the positive integers, etc. In the sequel, we make two simplifying assumptions, though both of them can be easily modified to handle other cases:

1. First, we will assume that every function f has a complement $\bar{f}$. An object o is returned by the code call $\mathcal{S} : \bar{f}(\mathtt{t}_1, \ldots, \mathtt{t}_n)$ *if, by definition,* o is not returned by $\mathcal{S} : f(\mathtt{t}_1, \ldots, \mathtt{t}_n)$. Once this occurs, all code call atoms **not_in**(X, $\mathcal{S} : f(\mathtt{t}_1, \ldots, \mathtt{t}_n)$) may be rewritten as **in**(X, $\mathcal{S} : \bar{f}(\mathtt{t}_1, \ldots, \mathtt{t}_n)$) thus eliminating the negation membership predicate. When the agent developer creates FINTAB, he must also specify the finiteness conditions (if any) associated with function calls $\bar{f}$.

2. Second, in the definition of strong safety below, we assume that all comparison operators involve variables over types having the following property.

Downward Finiteness Property. A type τ is said to have the *downward finiteness property if, by definition,* it has an associated partial ordering $\leq$ such that for all objects x of type τ, the set $\{o' \mid o'$ is an object of type τ and $o' \leq o\}$ is finite.

It is easy to see that the positive integers have this property, as do the set of all strings ordered by the standard lexicographic ordering. (Later, we will show how this property may be relaxed to accommodate the reals, the negative integers, and so on.)

We are now ready to define strong safety.

DEFINITION 12.1.4 (STRONG SAFETY) A safe code call condition $\chi = \chi_1 \& \ldots \& \chi_n$ is *strongly safe* w.r.t. a list $\vec{X}$ of root variables if there is a permutation π witnessing the safety of χ modulo $\vec{X}$ such that for each $1 \leq i \leq n$, $\chi_{\pi(i)}$ is strongly safe modulo $\vec{X}$, where strong safety of $\chi_{\pi(i)}$ is defined as follows:

1. $\chi_{\pi(i)}$ is a code call atom.
Here, let the code call of $\chi_{\pi(i)}$ be $\mathcal{S} : f(\mathtt{t_1}, \ldots, \mathtt{t_n})$ and let the binding pattern $\mathcal{S} : f(\mathtt{bt_1}, \ldots, \mathtt{bt_n})$ be defined as follows:
   (a) If t_i is a value, then $bt_i = t_i$.
   (b) Otherwise t_i must be a variable whose root occurs either in $\vec{X}$ or in $\chi_{\pi(j)}$ for some $j < i$. In this case, $bt_i = \mathtt{b}$.
Then, $\chi_{\pi(i)}$ is strongly safe if FINTAB entails the finiteness of $\mathcal{S} : f(\mathtt{bt_1}, \ldots, \mathtt{bt_n})$.

2. $\chi_{\pi(i)}$ is $\mathtt{s} \neq \mathtt{t}$.
In this case, $\chi_{\pi(i)}$ is strongly safe if each of $\mathtt{s}$ and $\mathtt{t}$ is either a constant or a variable whose root occurs either in $\vec{X}$ or in $\chi_{\pi(j)}$ for some $j < i$.

3. $\chi_{\pi(i)}$ is $\mathtt{s} < \mathtt{t}$ or $\mathtt{s} \leq \mathtt{t}$.
In this case, $\chi_{\pi(i)}$ is strongly safe if $\mathtt{t}$ is either a constant or a variable whose root occurs either in $\vec{X}$ or somewhere in $\chi_{\pi(j)}$ for some $j < i$.

4. $\chi_{\pi(i)}$ is $\mathtt{s} > \mathtt{t}$ or $\mathtt{s} \geq \mathtt{t}$.
In this case, $\chi_{\pi(i)}$ is strongly safe if $\mathtt{t} < \mathtt{s}$ or $\mathtt{t} \leq \mathtt{s}$, respectively, are strongly safe.

It is important to note that if we consider variables over types that do *not* satisfy the downward finiteness property (as in the case of the reals), then Case 1 and Case 2 above jointly define strong safety—all code calls of the forms shown in Cases 3 and 4 are not strongly safe. Thus, the definition of strong safety applies both to types satisfying the downward finiteness property and to types that do not satisfy it.

Algorithm **safe_ccc** defined in Chapter 4 may easily be modified to handle a strong safety check, by replacing the test "select all $\chi_{i_1}, \ldots, \chi_{i_m}$ from L such that χ_{i_j} is safe modulo $\vec{X}$" in step (4) of that algorithm by the test "select all $\chi_{i_1}, \ldots, \chi_{i_m}$ from L such that χ_{i_j} is *strongly*

Section 12.1   Weakly Regular Agents   467

safe modulo $\vec{X}$." As a consequence, it is not hard to see that strong safety can be checked in time proportional to the product of the time taken to check safety and the time to look up items in FINTAB. The former is quadratic (using appropriate data structures, even linear) in the length of the code call condition, and the latter is linear in the number of entries in FINTAB.

DEFINITION 12.1.5 (STRONGLY SAFE AGENT PROGRAM)   A rule r is *strongly safe* if it is safe, and $B_{cc}(r)$ is a strongly safe code call condition. An agent program is *strongly safe* if all rules in it are strongly safe.

We will require that all agent programs be strongly safe—even though this increases the development cycle time, and compilation time, these are "one time" costs that are never incurred at run time. Hence, the price is well worth paying. When we know that an agent program rule r is strongly safe, we are guaranteed that the computation of the set of instances of the head of the rule that is true involves only finite subcomputations.

12.1.2   Conflict-Freedom

In the preceding section, we have argued that for an agent program to be considered a *WRAP*, it must be strongly safe w.r.t. the finiteness table FINTAB specified by the agent developer. In this section, we specify another condition for being a *WRAP*—namely that the agent program must be guaranteed to never encounter a conflict.

The deontic consistency requirement associated with a feasible status set mandates that all feasible status sets (and hence all rational and reasonable status sets) must be *deontically consistent*. Therefore, we need some way of ensuring that agent programs are conflict-free, and this means that we first need to define what a conflict is.

DEFINITION 12.1.6 (CONFLICTING MODALITIES)   Given two action modalities Op, Op' ∈ {**P, F, O, Do, W**} we say that Op *conflicts with* Op' if there is an entry "×" in the following table at row Op and column Op':

Op\Op'	P	F	O	W	Do
P		×			
F	×		×		×
O		×		×	
W			×		
Do		×			

Observe that the conflicts-with relation is symmetric, i.e., if Op conflicts-with Op', then Op' conflicts-with Op.

We may now use the definition of conflicting modalities to specify what it means for two ground action status literals to conflict.

DEFINITION 12.1.7 (CONFLICTING ACTION STATUS LITERALS) Suppose L, L' are two action status literals. L is said to *conflict with L' if, by definition,*

- L and L' are unifiable and their modalities conflict, or
- L and L' are of the form $L = \mathsf{Op}\,(\alpha(\vec{t}))$ and $L' = \neg\mathsf{Op}\,'(\alpha(\vec{t'}))$, where $\mathsf{Op}\,(\alpha(\vec{t}))$, $\mathsf{Op}\,'(\alpha(\vec{t'}))$ are unifiable, and the entry "×" is in the following table at row Op and column $\neg\mathsf{Op}\,'$:

Op\¬Op'	¬P	¬F	¬O	¬W	¬Do
P	×				
F		×			
O	×		×		×
W				×	
Do	×				×

For example, the action status atoms $\mathbf{F}\alpha(a, b, X)$ and $\mathbf{P}\alpha(Z, b, c)$ conflict. However, $\mathbf{F}\alpha(a, b, X)$ and $\neg\mathbf{P}\alpha(Z, b, c)$ do not conflict. Furthermore, $\neg\mathbf{P}\alpha(Z, b, c)$ and $\mathbf{Do}\,\alpha(Z, b, c)$ conflict, while the literals $\mathbf{P}\alpha(Z, b, c)$ and $\neg\mathbf{Do}\,\alpha(Z, b, c)$ do not conflict. As these examples show, the conflicts-with relation is *not* symmetric when applied to (complemented) action status literals. Before defining what it means for two rules to conflict, we point out that an agent's state is constantly changing. Hence, when our definition says that an agent program does not conflict, then this must apply not just to the current state, but to all possible states the agent can be in. We will first define conflicts w.r.t. a single state, and then define a conflict free program to be one that has no conflicts in all possible states.

DEFINITION 12.1.8 (CONFLICTING RULES W.R.T. A STATE) Consider two rules r_i, r_j (whose variables are standardized apart) having the form

$r_i\colon \mathsf{Op}_i(\alpha(\vec{t})) \leftarrow B(r_i)$

$r_j\colon \mathsf{Op}_j(\beta(\vec{t'})) \leftarrow B(r_j)$.

We say that r_i and r_j *conflict* w.r.t. an agent state $\mathcal{O}_S$ if Op_i conflicts with Op_j, and there is a substitution θ such that:

- $\alpha(\vec{t}\theta) = \beta(\vec{t'}\theta)$;
- $(B_{cc}(r_i) \wedge B_{cc}(r_j))\theta\gamma$ is true in $\mathcal{O}_S$ for some substitution γ that causes $(B_{cc}(r_i) \wedge B_{cc}(r_j))\theta$ to become ground;

- if $\text{Op}_i \in \{\mathbf{P}, \mathbf{Do}, \mathbf{O}\}$ (resp., $\text{Op}_j \in \{\mathbf{P}, \mathbf{Do}, \mathbf{O}\}$) then $\alpha(\vec{t}\theta)$ (resp., $\beta(\vec{t'}\theta)$) is executable in $\mathcal{O}_S$; and

- $(B_{as}(r_i) \cup B_{as}(r_j))\theta$ contains no pair of conflicting action status literals.

Intuitively, the above definition says that for two rules to conflict in a given state, they must have a unifiable head and conflicting head-modalities, and furthermore, their bodies must be deontically consistent (under the unifying substitution) and the code call components of their bodies must have a solution. The above definition merely serves as a stepping stone to defining a conflict free agent program.

DEFINITION 12.1.9 (CONFLICT FREE PROGRAM)   An agent program, $\mathcal{P}$, is said to be *conflict free if and only if* it satisfies two conditions:

1. For every possible agent state $\mathcal{O}_S$, there is no pair r_i, r_j of conflicting rules in $\mathcal{P}$.
2. For any rule $\text{Op}_i(\alpha(\vec{t})) \leftarrow \ldots, (\neg)\text{Op}_j(\alpha(\vec{t'})), \ldots$ in $\mathcal{P}$, $\text{Op}_i(\alpha(\vec{t}))$ and $(\neg)\text{Op}_j(\alpha(\vec{t'}))$ do not conflict.

Unfortunately, as the following theorem shows, the problem of determining whether an agent program is conflict-free in the above definition is undecidable, because checking the first condition is undecidable.

THEOREM 12.1.1 (UNDECIDABILITY OF CONFLICT FREEDOM CHECKING)   The problem of deciding whether an input agent program $\mathcal{P}$ satisfies the first condition of conflict-freedom is undecidable. Hence, the problem of deciding whether an input agent program $\mathcal{P}$ is conflict free is undecidable.

Proof   The undecidability of this problem is inherited from the undecidability of the problem whether a function $f \in \mathcal{F}$ from a software code $\mathcal{S} = (\mathcal{T}, \mathcal{F})$ returns a particular value on at least one agent state $\mathcal{O}_S$. We may choose for $\mathcal{S}$ a standard relational database package, and let f be a Boolean query on the database written in SQL. Then, it is undecidable whether f evaluates to true over some (finite) database, i.e., agent state $\mathcal{O}_S$; this follows from well-known results in the area of database theory. In particular, relational calculus is undecidable, and every query in relational calculus an be expressed in SQL; see (Abiteboul, Hull, and Vianu 1995). Now, define the rules:

r_1: $\mathbf{P}(\alpha) \leftarrow$
r_2: $\mathbf{F}(\alpha) \leftarrow \mathbf{in}(\mathbf{true}, \texttt{oracle}:f())$

Then, the rules r_1 and r_2 are conflict free if and only if f does not return **true**, over any database instance. This proves the result. ∎

The ability to check whether an agent program is conflict free is very important. When an agent developer builds an agent, in general, s/he cannot possibly anticipate all the future states of the agent. Thus, the developer must build guarantees into the agent which ensure that no conflicts can possibly arise in the future. However, in general, as checking conflict freedom of agent programs is undecidable, we cannot hope for an effective algorithm to check conflict freedom. However, there are many possible ways to define *sufficient* conditions on agent programs that guarantee conflict freedom. If an agent developer encodes his agent program in a way that satisfies these sufficient conditions, then he is guaranteed that his agent is going to be conflict free. The concept of a conflict freedom implementation defined below provides such a mechanism.

DEFINITION 12.1.10 (CONFLICT-FREEDOM TEST) A *conflict-freedom test* is a function cft that takes as input any two rules r_1, r_2, and provides a boolean output such that: if cft $(r_1, r_2) = $ **true**, then the pair r_1, r_2 satisfies the first condition of conflict freedom.

Note that conflict freedom tests provide a sufficient (i.e., sound) condition for checking whether two rules r_1 and r_2 satisfy the first condition in the definition of conflict freedom. The second condition can be directly checked using the definition of what it means for two action status literals to conflict. This motivates the definition of a conflict-free agent program relative to conflict freedom test below.

DEFINITION 12.1.11 (CONFLICT-FREE AGENT PROGRAM W.R.T. cft) An agent program $\mathcal{P}$ is *conflict free w.r.t.* cft if and only if for all pairs of distinct rules $r_i, r_j \in \mathcal{P}$, cft $(r_i, r_j) = $ **true** and all rules in $\mathcal{P}$ satisfy the second condition in the definition of conflict free programs.

Intuitively, different choices of the function cft may be made, depending upon the complexity of such choices, and the accuracy of such choices (i.e., how often does a specific function cft return "**false**" on arguments (r_i, r_j) when in fact r_i, r_j do not conflict?). In *IADE*, the agent developer can choose one of several conflict-freedom tests to be used for her application (and she can add new ones to his list). Some instances of this test are given below.

Example 12.1.3 (Head-CFT, cft_h) Let r_i, r_j be two rules of the form

$r_i \colon \mathsf{Op}_i(\alpha(\vec{t})) \leftarrow B_i$
$r_j \colon \mathsf{Op}_j(\beta(\vec{t'})) \leftarrow B_j.$

Now let the head conflict-freedom test cft_h be as follows:

$$\mathsf{cft}_h(r_i, r_j) = \begin{cases} \textbf{true}, & \text{if either } \mathsf{Op}_i, \mathsf{Op}_j \text{ do not conflict, or} \\ & \alpha(\vec{t}) \text{ and } \beta(\vec{t'}) \text{ are not unifiable;} \\ \textbf{false}, & \text{otherwise.} \end{cases}$$

Section 12.1   Weakly Regular Agents   471

Example 12.1.4 (Body Code Call CFT, cft_{bcc})   Let us continue using the same notation as in Example 12.1.3 on the preceding page. Now let the body-code conflict-freedom test cft_{bcc} be as follows,

$$\text{cft}_{bcc}(r_i, r_j) = \begin{cases} \textbf{true}, & \text{if either } \textsf{Op}_i, \textsf{Op}_j \text{ do not conflict, or} \\ & \alpha(\vec{t}) \text{ and } \beta(\vec{t'}) \text{ are not unifiable, or} \\ & \textsf{Op}_i, \textsf{Op}_j \text{ conflict and } \alpha(\vec{t}), \beta(\vec{t'}) \text{ are unifiable via mgu } \theta \text{ and} \\ & \text{there is a pair of contradictory code call atoms in } B_{cc}(r_1\theta), \\ & B_{cc}(r_2\theta); \\ \textbf{false}, & \text{otherwise.} \end{cases}$$

The expression "there exist a pair of contradictory code call atoms in $B_{cc}(r_1\theta), B_{cc}(r_2\theta)$" means that there exist code call atoms of form $\textbf{in}(\textsf{X}, \textsf{cc})$ and $\textbf{not\_in}(\textsf{X}, \textsf{cc})$ which occur in $B_{cc}(r_1\theta) \cup B_{cc}(r_2\theta)$, or comparison atoms of the form $\textsf{s}_1 = \textsf{s}_2$ and $\textsf{s}_1 \neq \textsf{s}_2$; $\textsf{s}_1 < \textsf{s}_2$ and $\textsf{s}_1 \geq \textsf{s}_2$ etc.

Example 12.1.5 (Body-Modality-CFT, cft_{bm})   The body-modality conflict-freedom test is similar to the previous one, except that action status atoms are considered instead. Now let cft_{bm} be as follows:

$$\text{cft}_{bm}(r_i, r_j) = \begin{cases} \textbf{true}, & \text{if } \textsf{Op}_i, \textsf{Op}_j \text{ do not conflict or} \\ & \alpha(\vec{t}), \beta(\vec{t'}) \text{ are not unifiable or} \\ & \textsf{Op}_i, \textsf{Op}_j \text{ conflict, and } \alpha(\vec{t}), \beta(\vec{t'}) \text{ are unifiable via mgu } \theta \text{ and} \\ & \text{literals } (\neg)\textsf{Op}_i\alpha(\vec{t''}) \text{ in } B_{as}(r_i\theta) \text{ for } i = 1, 2 \text{ exist} \\ & \text{such that } (\neg)\textsf{Op}_1 \text{ and } (\neg)\textsf{Op}_2 \text{ conflict;} \\ \textbf{false}, & \text{otherwise.} \end{cases}$$

Example 12.1.6 (Precondition-CFT, cft_{pr})   Often, we might have action status atoms of the form $\textbf{P}\alpha, \textbf{Do}\,\alpha, \textbf{O}\alpha$ in a rule. For a rule r_i as shown in Example 12.1.3 on the facing page, we denote by $r_i^\star$ the new rule obtained by appending to B_i the precondition of any action status atom of the form $\textbf{P}\alpha, \textbf{Do}\,\alpha, \textbf{O}\alpha$ (appropriately standardized apart) from the head or body of r_i. Thus, suppose r is the rule

$\textbf{Do}\,\alpha(X, Y) \leftarrow \textbf{in}(X, \textsf{d}: f(Y)) \,\&\, \textbf{P}\beta \,\&\, \textbf{F}\gamma(Y).$

Suppose $pre(\alpha(X, Y)) = \textbf{in}(Y, \textsf{d}_1: f_1(X))$ and $pre(\beta) = \textbf{in}(3, \textsf{d}_2: f_2())$. Then $r^\star$ is the rule

$\textbf{Do}\,\alpha(X, Y) \leftarrow \textbf{in}(X, \textsf{d}: f(Y)) \,\&\, \textbf{in}(Y, \textsf{d}_1: f_1(X)) \,\&\, \textbf{in}(3, \textsf{d}_2: f_2()) \,\&\, \textbf{P}\beta \,\&\, \textbf{F}\gamma(Y).$

We now define cft_{pr} as follows.

$$\text{cft}_{pr}(r_i, r_j) = \begin{cases} \textbf{true} & \text{if } \text{cft}_{bcc}(r_i^\star, r_j^\star) = \textbf{true} \\ \textbf{false} & \text{otherwise.} \end{cases}$$

The following theorem tells us that whenever we have actions that have safe preconditions, then the rule $r^\star$ obtained as described above from a safe (resp., strongly safe) rule is also safe (resp., strongly safe).

THEOREM 12.1.2 Suppose r is a rule, and $\alpha(\vec{X})$ is an action such that some atom $\mathsf{Op}\,\alpha(\vec{t})$ appears in r's body where $\mathsf{Op} \in \{\mathbf{P}, \mathbf{O}, \mathbf{Do}\}$. Then:

1. If r is safe and $\alpha(\vec{X})$ has a safe precondition modulo the variables in $\vec{X}$, then $r^\star$ is safe.
2. If r is strongly safe and $\alpha(\vec{X})$ has a strongly safe precondition modulo $\vec{X}$, then $r^\star$ is strongly safe.

Proof

(1) To show that $r^\star$ is safe we need to show that the two conditions defining safety hold for $r^\star$. Suppose r is of form

$$A \leftarrow B_{cc}(r) \,\&\, \mathsf{Op}\,\alpha(\vec{t}) \,\&\, B^+_{as,rest}(r) \,\&\, B^-_{as}(r).$$

where the precondition of $\alpha(\vec{X})$ is $\chi(\vec{Y})$ (both standardized apart from r) where $\vec{Y}$ contains all variables occurring in α's precondition. Then $r^\star$ is the rule

$$A \leftarrow B_{cc}(r) \,\&\, \chi(\vec{Y}\theta) \,\&\, \mathsf{Op}\,\alpha(\vec{t}) \,\&\, B^+_{as,rest}(r) \,\&\, B^-_{as}(r)$$

where θ is the substitution $\vec{X} = \vec{t}$. Since χ is safe modulo $\vec{X}$, $\chi(\vec{Y}\theta)$ is safe modulo the list of variables in $\vec{t}$. As all variables in $\vec{t}$ occur in $B^+_{as}(r)$, $\chi(\vec{Y}\theta)$ is safe modulo the variables in $B^+_{as}(r)$. It follows immediately that $B_{cc}(r) \,\&\, \chi(\vec{Y}\theta)$ is safe modulo the variables in $B^+_{as}(r)$. Thus, $r^\star$ satisfies the first definition of safety. The second condition in the definition of safety is trivially satisfied since the only new variables in $r^\star$ are in $B_{cc}(r^\star)$.

(2) Follows immediately from the strong safety of α's precondition and part (1) above.

Note 9 Throughout the rest of this chapter, we will assume that an arbitrary, but fixed conflict-freedom test is used.

12.1.3 Deontic Stratification

In this section, we define the concept of what it means for an agent program $\mathcal{P}$ to be *deontically stratified*—this definition extends the classical notion of stratification in logic programs introduced by (Apt, Blair, and Walker 1988). The first concept we define is that of a layering function.

DEFINITION 12.1.12 (LAYERING FUNCTION) Let $\mathcal{P}$ be an agent program. A *layering function* ℓ is a map $\ell : \mathcal{P} \to \mathcal{N}$.

A layering function assigns a nonnegative integer to each rule in the program, and in doing so, it groups rules into layers as defined below.

Section 12.1   Weakly Regular Agents   473

DEFINITION 12.1.13 (LAYERS OF AN AGENT PROGRAM)   If $\mathcal{P}$ is an agent program, and ℓ is a layering function over $\mathcal{P}$, then the i-th layer of $\mathcal{P}$ w.r.t. ℓ, denoted $\mathcal{P}_i^\ell$, is defined as:

$$\mathcal{P}_i^\ell = \{r \in \mathcal{P} \mid \ell(r) = i\}.$$

When ℓ is clear from context, we will drop the superscript and write $\mathcal{P}_i$ instead of $\mathcal{P}_i^\ell$.

The following example presents some simple layering functions.

Example 12.1.7 (Layering Functions)   Consider the agent program $\mathcal{P}$ given below.

r_1: **Do** *execute_flight_plan*(Flight_route) ←
  in(automated, autoPilot : *pilotStatus*(pilot_message)),
  Do *create_flight_plan*(No_go, Flight_route, Current_location)

If the plane is on autopilot and a flight plan has been created, then execute it.

r_2: **O** *create_flight_plan*(No_go, Flight_route, Current_location) ←
  O *adjust_course*(No_go, Flight_route, Current_location)

If our agent is required to adjust the plane's course, then it is also required to create a flight plan.

r_3: **O** *maintain_course*(No_go, Flight_route, Current_location) ←
  in(automated, autoPilot : *pilotStatus*(pilot_message)),
  ¬ **O** *adjust_course*(No_go, Flight_route, Current_location)

If the plane is on autopilot and our agent is not obliged to adjust the plane's course, then our agent must ensure that the plane maintains its current course.

r_4: **O** *adjust_course*(No_go, Flight_route, Current_location) ←
  O *adjustAltitude*(Altitude)

If our agent must adjust the plane's altitude, then it is obliged to also adjust the plane's flight route as well.

Note that for simplicity, these rules use constant valued parameters for *maintain_course* and *adjust_course*. A more realistic example may involve using autoPilot : *calculateLocation*() to determine the plane's next location (i.e., the value for current_location), autoPilot : *calculateFlightRoute*() to determine a new flight route w.r.t. this value for current_location (i.e., the value for flight_route), etc.

Let the function ℓ_1 assign 0 to rule r_4, 1 to rules r_2, r_3, and 2 to rule r_1. Then ℓ_1 is a layering function which induces the program layers $\mathcal{P}_0^{\ell_1} = \{r_4\}$, $\mathcal{P}_1^{\ell_1} = \{r_2, r_3\}$, and $\mathcal{P}_2^{\ell_1} = \{r_1\}$. Likewise, the function ℓ_2 which assigns 0 to rule r_4 and 1 to the remaining rules is also a layering function. In fact, the function ℓ_3 which assigns 0 to all rules in $\mathcal{P}$ is also a layering function.

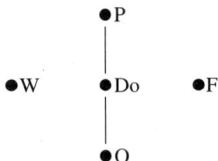

Figure 12.1
Modality ordering.

Using the concept of a layering function, we would like to define what a *deontically stratifiable* agent program is. Before doing so, we introduce a simple ordering on modalities.

DEFINITION 12.1.14 (MODALITY ORDERING) The partial ordering "$\leq$" on the set of deontic modalities $M = \{\mathbf{P}, \mathbf{O}, \mathbf{Do}, \mathbf{W}, \mathbf{F}\}$ is defined as follows (see Figure 12.1): $\mathbf{O} \leq \mathbf{Do}$, $\mathbf{O} \leq \mathbf{P}$, $\mathbf{Do} \leq \mathbf{P}$, and $\mathsf{Op} \leq \mathsf{Op}$, for each $\mathsf{Op} \in M$. Furthermore, for ground action status atoms A and B, we define that $A \leq B$ if $A = \mathsf{Op}\,\alpha$, $B = \mathsf{Op}'\alpha$, and $\mathsf{Op} \leq \mathsf{Op}'$ all hold.

Intuitively, the ordering reflects deontic consequence of one modality from another under the policy that each obligation is strictly obeyed, and that taking an action implies that the agent is permitted to execute it. We are now ready to define what it means for an agent program to be deontically stratifiable.

DEFINITION 12.1.15 (DEONTICALLY STRATIFIABLE AGENT PROGRAM) An agent program $\mathcal{P}$ is *deontically stratifiable* if there exists a layering function ℓ such that:

1. For every rule $r_i : \mathsf{Op}_i(\alpha(\vec{t})) \leftarrow \ldots, \mathsf{Op}_j(\beta(\vec{t'})), \ldots$ in $\mathcal{P}_i^{\ell}$, if $r : \mathsf{Op}\,(\beta(\vec{t''})) \leftarrow \cdots$ is a rule in $\mathcal{P}$ such that $\beta(\vec{t'})$ and $\beta(\vec{t''})$ are unifiable and $\mathsf{Op} \leq \mathsf{Op}_j$, then $\ell(r) \leq \ell(r_i)$.
2. For every rule $r_i : \mathsf{Op}_i(\alpha(\vec{t})) \leftarrow \ldots, \neg\mathsf{Op}_j(\beta(\vec{t'})), \ldots$ in $\mathcal{P}_i^{\ell}$, if $r : \mathsf{Op}\,(\beta(\vec{t''})) \leftarrow \cdots$ is a rule in $\mathcal{P}$ such that $\beta(\vec{t'})$ and $\beta(\vec{t''})$ are unifiable and $\mathsf{Op} \leq \mathsf{Op}_j$, then $\ell(r) < \ell(r_i)$.

Any such layering function ℓ is called a *witness* to the stratifiability of $\mathcal{P}$.

The following example presents a couple of agent programs, and discusses why they are (or are not) deontically stratifiable.

Example 12.1.8 (Deontic Stratifiability) Consider the agent program and layer functions given in Example 12.1.7 on the preceding page. Then the first condition of deontic stratifiability requires $\ell(r_2) \leq \ell(r_1)$ and $\ell(r_4) \leq \ell(r_2)$. Also, the second condition of deontic stratifiability requires $\ell(r_4) < \ell(r_3)$. Thus, ℓ_1 and ℓ_2 (but not ℓ_3) are witnesses to the stratifiability of $\mathcal{P}$.

Note that some agent programs are not deontically stratifiable. For instance, let $\mathcal{P}'$ contain the following rule:

r'_1: **Do** *compute_currentLocation*(report) ←
    ¬ **Do** *compute_currentLocation* (report)

Here, the author is trying to ensure that a plane's current location is always computed. The problem is that the second condition of deontic statifiability requires $\ell(r'_1) < \ell(r'_1)$ which is not possible, so $\mathcal{P}'$ is not deontically stratifiable. Note however that if we replace r'_1 with "**Do** *compute_currentLocation* (report) ← ", then $\mathcal{P}'$ would be deontically stratifiable.

It is worth noting that if $\mathcal{P}$ is deontically stratifiable, then condition (2) in the definition of a conflict free agent program (Definition 12.1.9 on page 469) is immediately true. Informally speaking, if we have a positive literal in the body of a rule, then the rule can only fire if that literal is derived—this means that heads conflict. Otherwise, if the literal is negative, then the rule must be in a lower layer than itself, which is impossible.

12.1.4 Weakly Regular Agent Programs

We are now almost ready to define a weakly regular agent program. It is important to note that weak regularity depends upon a variety of parameters including a finiteness table **FINTAB** and a conflict freedom implementation. In addition, we need a definition of what it means for an action to be strongly safe.

DEFINITION 12.1.16 (STRONGLY SAFE ACTION) An action $\alpha(\vec{X})$ is said to be *strongly safe* w.r.t. **FINTAB** if its precondition is strongly safe modulo $\vec{X}$ and each code call from the add list and delete list is strongly safe modulo $\vec{Y}$, where $\vec{Y}$ includes all root variables in $\vec{X}$ as well as in the precondition of α.

The intuition underlying strong safety is that we should be able to check whether a (ground) action is safe by evaluating its precondition. If so, we should be able to evaluate the effects of executing the action.

We now define a weakly regular agent program.

DEFINITION 12.1.17 (WEAK REGULAR AGENT PROGRAM) Let $\mathcal{P}$ be an agent program, **FINTAB** a finiteness table, and cft a conflict-freedom test. Then, $\mathcal{P}$ is called a *weakly regular agent program* (*WRAP* for short) w.r.t. **FINTAB** and cft, if the following three conditions all hold:

Strong Safety: All rules in $\mathcal{P}$ and actions α in the agent's action base are strongly safe w.r.t. **FINTAB**.

Conflict-Freedom: $\mathcal{P}$ is conflict free under cft.

Deontic Stratifiability: $\mathcal{P}$ is deontically stratifiable.

The following example presents an example of a *WRAP*, as well as an agent program that is not a *WRAP*.

Example 12.1.9 (Sample WRAP) Let $\mathcal{P}$ be the agent program given in Example 12.1.7 on page 473 and suppose that all actions in $\mathcal{P}$ are strongly safe w.r.t. a finiteness table FINTAB. Consider the conflict freedom test cft $_h$. Then $\mathcal{P}$ is a *WRAP* as it is conflict free under cft $_h$ and as it is deontically stratified according to Example 12.1.8 on page 474. Now, suppose we add the following rule to $\mathcal{P}$:

r_5: **W***create_flight_plan*(no_go, flight_route, current_location) ←
    not_in(automated, *autoPilot*:*pilotStatus*(pilot_message))

This rule indicates that our agent is not obligated to adjust the plane's course if the plane is not on autopilot. Note that as cft $_h(r_2, r_5)$ = **false**, our new version of $\mathcal{P}$ is not conflict free and so $\mathcal{P}$ would no longer be a *WRAP*.

12.1.5 Weakly Regular Agents

The framework in Chapter 6 specifies that in addition to an agent program, each agent has an associated set $\mathcal{IC}$ of integrity constraints, specifying conditions that an agent state must satisfy, and action constraints $\mathcal{AC}$, which describe conditions under which a certain collection of actions may not be concurrently executed. In order for an agent to evaluate what it must do in a given state, the ability to effectively or even polynomially evaluate the agent program is not enough—effective (respectively polynomial) evaluation of the integrity and action constraints is also required.

DEFINITION 12.1.18 (STRONGLY SAFE INTEGRITY AND ACTION CONSTRAINTS) An integrity constraint of the form $\psi \Rightarrow \chi$ is *strongly safe if, by definition,* ψ is strongly safe and χ is strongly safe modulo the root variables in ψ. An action constraint $\{\alpha_1(\vec{X}_1), \ldots, \alpha_k(\vec{X}_k)\} \hookleftarrow \chi$ is *strongly safe* if and only if χ is strongly safe.

Note 10 We will generally assume that integrity constraints and action constraints do *not* refer to the msgbox package. This will become necessary to assume in Section 12.5.1, and does not restrict our framework very much from a practical point of view.

The following example presents some action and integrity constraints, together with a specification of which ones are strongly safe.

Example 12.1.10 (Integrity and Action Constraints) Let $\mathcal{IC}$ be the following integrity constraint:

in(X_1, autoPilot : *pilotStatus*(Pilot_message)) &
in(X_2, autoPilot : *pilotStatus*(Pilot_message)) $\Rightarrow X_1 \neq X_2$

This indicates each pilot message can denote at most one pilot status. Here, $\mathcal{IC}$ is strongly safe if **FINTAB** has a row of the form $\langle$autoPilot : *pilotStatus*(a_1), (b)$\rangle$.
Let $\mathcal{AC}$ be the following action constraint:

{*adjust_course*(No_go, FlightRoute, CurrentLocation),
 maintain_course(No_go, FlightRoute, CurrentLocation)} $\hookleftarrow$

This indicates that the plane cannot adjust its course and maintain its course at the same time. Here, regardless of **FINTAB**, $\mathcal{AC}$ is strongly safe.

Last, but not least, the notion of concurrency used by the agent must conform to strong safety.

DEFINITION 12.1.19 (STRONGLY SAFE NOTION OF CONCURRENCY) A notion of concurrency, **conc**, is said to be *strongly safe* if for every set $\mathcal{A}$ of actions and every agent state $\mathcal{O}_S$, it holds that if all members of $\mathcal{A}$ are strongly safe, then so is **conc**($\mathcal{A}, \mathcal{O}_S$).

The reader may easily verify that the three notions of concurrency proposed in Chapter 6 are all strongly safe.

DEFINITION 12.1.20 (WEAKLY REGULAR AGENT) An agent a is *weakly regular* if its associated agent program is weakly regular and the action constraints, integrity constraints, and the notion of concurrency in the background are all strongly safe.

12.2 Properties of Weakly Regular Agents

In this section, we will describe some theoretical properties of regular agents which will help us compute their reasonable status sets efficiently (i.e., in polynomial time data complexity).

This section is divided up into the following parts. First, we show that every deontically stratifiable agent program (and hence every *WRAP*) has a so-called "canonical layering". Then we will show that every *WRAP* has an associated fixpoint computation method—the fixpoint computed by this method is the only possible reasonable status set the *WRAP* may have.

12.2.1 Canonical Layering

As we have seen in the preceding section, an agent program may have multiple witnesses to its deontic stratifiability, and each of these witnesses yields a *different layering*. In this section, we will define what we call a *canonical layering* of a WRAP $\mathcal{P}$.

Given an agent program $\mathcal{P}$, we denote by $\mathsf{wtn}(\mathcal{P})$ the set of all witnesses to the deontic stratifiability of $\mathcal{P}$. The *canonical layering* of $\mathcal{P}$, denoted $\mathsf{can}^\mathcal{P}$ is defined as follows.

$$\mathsf{can}^\mathcal{P}(r) = \min\{\ell_i(r) \mid \ell_i \in \mathsf{wtn}(\mathcal{P})\}.$$

The following example shows the canonical layering associated with the *WRAP* we have encountered earlier on in this chapter.

Example 12.2.1 (Canonical Layering) Consider the agent program and layer functions given in Example 12.1.7 on page 473. Recall that $\ell_1 \in \mathsf{wtn}(\mathcal{P})$, $\ell_2 \in \mathsf{wtn}(\mathcal{P})$, and $\ell_3 \notin \mathit{wtn}(\mathcal{P})$. Here, the layering ℓ_0 at $\mathcal{P}_0^{\ell_0} = \{r_4, r_1, r_2\}$ and $\mathcal{P}_1^{\ell_0} = \{r_3\}$ satisfies $\mathsf{can}^\mathcal{P} = \ell_0$.

The following proposition asserts that $\mathsf{can}^\mathcal{P}$ is always a witness to the deontic stratifiability of an agent program $\mathcal{P}$.

PROPOSITION 12.2.1 Let $\mathcal{P}$ be an agent program which is deontically stratifiable. Then $\mathsf{can}^\mathcal{P} \in \mathsf{wtn}(\mathcal{P})$, i.e., $\mathsf{can}^\mathcal{P}$ is a witness to the deontic stratifiability of $\mathcal{P}$.

Proof

1. *Item 1 of deontic stratifiability.* Suppose $r_i : \mathsf{Op}_i(\alpha(\vec{t})) \leftarrow \ldots, \mathsf{Op}_j(\beta(\vec{t'})), \ldots$ is in $\mathcal{P}_i$, and $r : \mathsf{Op}(\beta(\vec{t''})) \leftarrow \cdots$ is a rule in $\mathcal{P}$ such that $\beta(\vec{t'})$ and $\beta(\vec{t''})$ are unifiable and $\mathsf{Op} \leq \mathsf{Op}_j$. Since $\mathcal{P}$ is deontic stratifiable in every layering $\ell \in \mathsf{wtn}(\mathcal{P})$ it is the case that $\ell(r) \leq \ell(r_i)$. Taking minimal values as in the definition of $\mathsf{can}^\mathcal{P}$, it follows that $\mathsf{can}^\mathcal{P}(r) \leq i = \mathsf{can}^\mathcal{P}(r_i)$.

2. *Item 2 of deontic stratifiability.* As in the previous case, for rules r_i and r as in the second stratifiability condition, every layering $\ell \in \mathsf{wtn}(\mathcal{P})$ satisfies $\ell(r) < \ell(r_i)$. Thus, it follows that $\mathsf{can}^\mathcal{P}(r) < \mathsf{can}^\mathcal{P}(r_i)$.

Note 11 Throughout this book, whenever we discuss a *WRAP*, unless stated otherwise we will use its canonical layering.

12.2.2 Fixpoint Operators for *WRAPs*

In Chapter 6, we have shown how we may associate with any agent program $\mathcal{P}$ an operator $\mathbf{T}_{\mathcal{P},\mathcal{O}_S}$ which maps a status set S to another status set, and we have characterized the rational status of a positive agent program as the least fixpoint of this operator. We will use the powers of this operator in the characerization of the reasonable status set of a *WRAP*. We introduce the following definition.

Section 12.2   Properties of Weakly Regular Agents   479

DEFINITION 12.2.1 ($\mathbf{T}^i_{\mathcal{P},\mathcal{O}_S}(S)$ AND $\mathbf{T}^\omega_{\mathcal{P},\mathcal{O}_S}(S)$ OPERATORS)   Suppose $\mathcal{P}$ is an agent program, $\mathcal{O}_S$ an agent state, and S is a status set. Then, the operators $\mathbf{T}^i_{\mathcal{P},\mathcal{O}_S}$, $i \geq 0$, and $\mathbf{T}^\omega_{\mathcal{P},\mathcal{O}_S}$ are defined as follows:

$$\mathbf{T}^0_{\mathcal{P},\mathcal{O}_S}(S) = S,$$
$$\mathbf{T}^{(i+1)}_{\mathcal{P},\mathcal{O}_S}(S) = \mathbf{T}_{\mathcal{P},\mathcal{O}_S}\bigl(\mathbf{T}^i_{\mathcal{P},\mathcal{O}_S}(S)\bigr),$$
$$\mathbf{T}^\omega_{\mathcal{P},\mathcal{O}_S}(S) = \bigcup_{i=0}^\infty \mathbf{T}^i_{\mathcal{P},\mathcal{O}_S}(S).$$

An example of the behavior of the $\mathbf{T}_{\mathcal{P},\mathcal{O}_S}$ operators is given below.

Example 12.2.2 ($\mathbf{T}_{\mathcal{P},\mathcal{O}_S}$ *Operator*)   Let $\mathcal{P}$ contain rules r_1, r_2, r_4 from the agent program given in Example 12.1.7 on page 473, let $\mathcal{O}_S$ indicate that the plane is on autopilot, and let $S = \{\mathbf{O}adjustAltitude(5000)\}$. Then

$\mathbf{T}^0_{\mathcal{P},\mathcal{O}_S}(S) = \{\mathbf{O}\ adjustAltitude(5000)\},$

$\mathbf{T}^1_{\mathcal{P},\mathcal{O}_S}(S) = \{\mathbf{O}\ adjust\_course(no\_go,\ \text{flight\_route},\ \text{current\_location}),$
       $\mathbf{Do}\ adjustAltitude(5000), \mathbf{P}adjustAltitude(5000)\} \cup \mathbf{T}^0_{\mathcal{P},\mathcal{O}_S}(S),$

$\mathbf{T}^2_{\mathcal{P},\mathcal{O}_S}(S) = \{\mathbf{O}\ create\_flight\_plan(no\_go,\ \text{flight\_route},\ \text{current\_location}),$
       $\mathbf{Do}\ adjust\_course(no\_go,\ \text{flight\_route},\ \text{current\_location}),$
       $\mathbf{P}\ adjust\_course(no\_go,\ \text{flight\_route},\ \text{current\_location})\} \cup \mathbf{T}^1_{\mathcal{P},\mathcal{O}_S}(S),$

$\mathbf{T}^3_{\mathcal{P},\mathcal{O}_S}(S) = \{\mathbf{Do}\ create\_flight\_plan(no\_go,\ \text{flight\_route},\ \text{current\_location}),$
       $\mathbf{P}\ create\_flight\_plan(no\_go,\ \text{flight\_route},\ \text{current\_location})\} \cup \mathbf{T}^2_{\mathcal{P},\mathcal{O}_S}(S),$

$\mathbf{T}^4_{\mathcal{P},\mathcal{O}_S}(S) = \{\mathbf{Do}\ execute\_flight\_plan(\text{flight\_route})\} \cup \mathbf{T}^3_{\mathcal{P},\mathcal{O}_S}(S),$

$\mathbf{T}^5_{\mathcal{P},\mathcal{O}_S}(S) = \{\mathbf{P}\ execute\_flight\_plan(\text{flight\_route})\} \cup \mathbf{T}^4_{\mathcal{P},\mathcal{O}_S}(S),$ and

$\mathbf{T}^6_{\mathcal{P},\mathcal{O}_S}(S) = \mathbf{T}^5_{\mathcal{P},\mathcal{O}_S}(S),$ so $\mathbf{T}^\omega_{\mathcal{P},\mathcal{O}_S}(S) = \mathbf{T}^5_{\mathcal{P},\mathcal{O}_S}(S).$

Note that by removing rule r_3 from $\mathcal{P}$, we turned $\mathcal{P}$ into a positive *WRAP*. To see why this was necessary, suppose $\mathcal{P}$ included r_3. Then both $\mathbf{O}$ *maintain_course*(no_go, flight_route, current_location) and $\mathbf{O}$ *adjust_course*(no_go, flight_route, current_location) would be members of $\mathbf{T}^1_{\mathcal{P},\mathcal{O}_S}(S)$. This is not good since the plane cannot maintain and adjust its course at the same time. Later in this chapter, we shall introduce a fixpoint operator for general *WRAPs* which effectively solves this problem.

We remark that the increase of the sequence $\mathbf{T}^i_{\mathcal{P},\mathcal{O}_S}(S)$ in the previous example is not incidental. In fact, the operator $\mathbf{T}_{\mathcal{P},\mathcal{O}_S}$ is *inflationary*, i.e., $S \subseteq \mathbf{T}_{\mathcal{P},\mathcal{O}_S}(S)$ always holds. This important property will be exploited below.

Positive WRAPs Recalling from Chapter 6 that $lfp(\mathbf{T}_{\mathcal{P},\mathcal{O}_S}) = \bigcup_{i=0}^{\infty} \mathbf{T}_{\mathcal{P},\mathcal{O}_S}^i$ is the only candidate for being a rational status set of a positive agent program, using the identity $\mathbf{T}_{\mathcal{P},\mathcal{O}_S}^i(\emptyset) = \mathbf{T}_{\mathcal{P},\mathcal{O}_S}^i$ we may restate Theorem 6.5.1 as follows.

PROPOSITION 12.2.2 Let $\mathcal{P}$ be a *positive* agent program. Then, a status set S is a rational status set of $\mathcal{P}$ *if and only if* $S = \mathbf{T}_{\mathcal{P},\mathcal{O}_S}^{\omega}(\emptyset)$ and S is a feasible status set of $\mathcal{P}$.

The preceding result guarantees that *positive* agent programs always have an iteratively computable least fixpoint. This fixpoint is a rational status set, and thus a reasonable status set, if S satisfies deontic consistency as well as the action constraints and integrity constraints. If the program is weakly regular, then we obtain the following result—in the sequel, if r is a rule, $\mathcal{O}_S$ is an agent state, S is a status set, and θ is a substitution, we define a special predicate $AR(r, \theta, S)$ to be true if:

1. $r\theta$ is ground;
2. $B_{cc}(r\theta)$ is true in $\mathcal{O}_S$;
3. $B_{as}^{+}(r\theta) \subseteq S$;
4. $\neg . B_{as}^{-}(r\theta) \cap S = \emptyset$;
5. For every atom $\mathsf{Op}\,\alpha \in B_{as}^{+}(r\theta) \cup head(r\theta)$ where $\mathsf{Op} \in \{\mathbf{P}, \mathbf{Do}, \mathbf{O}\}$, the action α is executable in $\mathcal{O}_S$.

That is, $AR(r, \theta, S)$ is true just if the instance $r\theta$ of r "fires" and adds $head(r\theta)$ to $\mathbf{App}_{\mathcal{P},\mathcal{O}_S}(S)$.

PROPOSITION 12.2.3 Let $\mathcal{P}$ be a *positive* agent program, and suppose that $\mathcal{P}$ is weakly regular. Then, $\mathcal{P}$ has at most one rational status set on $\mathcal{O}_S$, and $S = \mathbf{T}_{\mathcal{P},\mathcal{O}_S}^{\omega}(\emptyset)$ is the (unique) rational status set if and only if S satisfies the action and the integrity constraints.

Proof That $\mathcal{P}$ has at most one rational status set follows from Proposition 12.2.2. Since S is deontically and action closed, it remains to verify that S is deontically consistent. Suppose this is not the case. Then, at least one of the three conditions (D1)–(D3) of deontic consistency of S is violated. For each case, we derive a contradiction, which proves the result:

(D1) $\mathbf{O}\alpha \in S$ and $\mathbf{W}\alpha \in S$, for some ground action α. This means that there are rules r and r' in $\mathcal{P}$ with heads $\mathbf{O}(\beta(\vec{t}))$ and $\mathbf{W}(\beta(\vec{t'}))$ such that, standardizing their variables apart, for some ground substitution θ it holds that $\beta(\vec{t}\theta) = \beta(\vec{t'}\theta)$; $(\exists)(B_{cc}(r) \wedge B_{cc}(r'))\theta$ is true and $\beta(\vec{t}\theta)$ is executable w.r.t. $\mathcal{O}_S$; and $B_{as}(r) \cup B_{as}(r')$ is true in S, and hence does not contain a pair of conflicting literals. However, this means that the rules r and r' conflict w.r.t. $\mathcal{O}_S$. This implies that cft $(r, r') = $ **false**, and provides a contradiction to the conflict-freedom condition of the definition of weak regularity.

(D2) $\mathbf{P}\alpha \in S$ and $\mathbf{F}\alpha \in S$. As in the previous case, we conclude that for each agent state $\mathcal{O}_S$, $\mathcal{P}$ contains rules r and r' with heads $\mathbf{F}(\beta(\vec{t}))$ and $\mathsf{Op}\,(\beta(\vec{t}'))$, respectively, where $\mathsf{Op} \in \{\mathbf{P}, \mathbf{Do}, \mathbf{O}\}$, such that r and r' are conflicting w.r.t. $\mathcal{O}_S$. Again, this contradicts the fact that $\mathcal{P}$ is weakly regular.

(D3) $\mathbf{P}\alpha \in S$ but α is not executable in $\mathcal{O}_S$. Then, there must exist a rule $r \in \mathcal{P}$ and a θ such that $\mathrm{AR}(r, \theta, S)$ is true, $head(r\theta) \in \mathbf{App}_{\mathcal{P},\mathcal{O}_S}(S)$, and $head(r\theta) = \mathsf{Op}\,\alpha$, where $\mathsf{Op} \in \{\mathbf{P}, \mathbf{Do}, \mathbf{O}\}$. The definition of $\mathbf{App}_{\mathcal{P},\mathcal{O}_S}(S)$ implies that α must be executable in $\mathcal{O}_S$. This is a contradiction.

A straightforward corollary of the above result is that when action constraints and integrity constraints are absent, then weak regular agent programs are guaranteed to have a rational status set.

Though positive agent programs may appear to be unnecessarily restrictive, they are in fact very useful to express many complex agent applications. For instance, the logistics application described in Chapter 13 is an example of a highly nontrivial positive agent program used for a real world application.

As for arbitrary agent programs, we observe that like for positive agent programs iterating the $\mathbf{T}_{\mathcal{P},\mathcal{O}_S}$ operator on $\emptyset$ will eventually lead to a fixpoint $\mathbf{T}^\omega_{\mathcal{P},\mathcal{O}_S}$ of the $\mathbf{T}_{\mathcal{P},\mathcal{O}_S}$ operator; this is true even if we start from an arbitrary set S.

PROPOSITION 12.2.4   Suppose $\mathcal{P}$ is any agent program and $\mathcal{O}_S$ is any agent state. Then, for every S, $\mathbf{T}^\omega_{\mathcal{P},\mathcal{O}_S}(S)$ is a fixpoint of $\mathbf{T}_{\mathcal{P},\mathcal{O}_S}$ and $\mathbf{T}^\omega_{\mathcal{P},\mathcal{O}_S}(S)$ is action closed.

Proof   Let $X = \mathbf{T}^\omega_{\mathcal{P},\mathcal{O}_S}(S)\,(= \bigcup_{i=0}^\infty \mathbf{T}^i_{\mathcal{P},\mathcal{O}_S}(S))$. We have to show that $\mathbf{T}_{\mathcal{P},\mathcal{O}_S}(X) = X$ holds. Since, as remarked above, $\mathbf{T}_{\mathcal{P},\mathcal{O}_S}$ is inflationary, $X \subseteq \mathbf{T}_{\mathcal{P},\mathcal{O}_S}(X)$ holds; it thus remains to show $\mathbf{T}_{\mathcal{P},\mathcal{O}_S}(X) \subseteq X$, i.e., that each atom $A \in \mathbf{T}_{\mathcal{P},\mathcal{O}_S}(X)$ is in X. The are two cases to consider.

(1) $A \in \mathbf{App}_{\mathcal{P}}(X)$. Then, a rule $r \in \mathcal{P}$ and a θ exist such that $head(r\theta) = A$ and $\mathrm{AR}(r, \theta, X)$ is true, i.e.,

(a) $r\theta$ is ground;
(b) $B_{cc}(r\theta)$ is true in $\mathcal{O}_S$;
(c) $B^+_{as}(r\theta) \subseteq X$ and
(d) $\neg.B^-_{as}(r\theta) \cap X = \emptyset$;
(e) For every atom $\mathsf{Op}\,\alpha \in B^+_{as}(r\theta) \cup H(r\theta)$ where $\mathsf{Op} \in \{\mathbf{P}, \mathbf{Do}, \mathbf{O}\}$, the action α is executable in $\mathcal{O}_S$.

Since $B^+_{as}(r\theta)$ is finite and $\mathbf{T}_{\mathcal{P},\mathcal{O}_S}$ is inflationary, the third condition implies that $B^+_{as}(r\theta) \subseteq \mathbf{T}^k_{\mathcal{P},\mathcal{O}_S}(S)$ holds for some $k \geq 0$. Furthermore, the fourth condition implies that $\neg.B^-_{as}(r\theta) \cap$

$\mathbf{T}^k_{\mathcal{P},\mathcal{O}_S}(S) = \emptyset$. This means that AR$(r, \theta, \mathbf{T}^k_{\mathcal{P},\mathcal{O}_S}(S))$ is true; hence, $A \in \mathbf{T}_{\mathcal{P},\mathcal{O}_S}(\mathbf{T}^k_{\mathcal{P},\mathcal{O}_S}(S)) \subseteq \mathbf{T}^{k+1}_{\mathcal{P},\mathcal{O}_S}(S)$, which means $A \in X$.

(2) $A \in$ **A-Cl**(X). Then, a $B \in X$ and a $k \geq 0$ exist such that $B \leq A$ and $B \in \mathbf{T}^k_{\mathcal{P},\mathcal{O}_S}(S)$. Hence, $A \in \mathbf{T}^{k+1}_{\mathcal{P},\mathcal{O}_S}(S)$ holds, and thus $A \in X$.

This proves that $\mathbf{T}^\omega_{\mathcal{P},\mathcal{O}_S}(S)$ is a fixpoint of $\mathbf{T}_{\mathcal{P},\mathcal{O}_S}$. The argument in case (2) implies that $X = \mathbf{T}^\omega_{\mathcal{P},\mathcal{O}_S}(S)$ is action-closed. ∎

General WRAPs We now extend the fixpoint operator in the preceding subsection to arbitrary *WRAPs*. We will define below an operator $\Gamma^\ell_{\mathcal{P},\mathcal{O}_S} \uparrow \omega$ that evaluates (from bottom to top) the layers of a *WRAP* generated by a layering function ℓ.

The operator $\Gamma^\ell_{\mathcal{P},\mathcal{O}_S} \uparrow i$ evaluates the layer i by computing the fixpoint $\mathbf{T}^\omega_{\mathcal{P}_i,\mathcal{O}_S}$ for the program $\mathcal{P}_i$, starting from the result that has been computed at the previous layer $i - 1$. The operator $\Gamma^\ell_{\mathcal{P},\mathcal{O}_S} \uparrow \omega$ accumulates the computation of all layers. Formally, the definition is as follows.

DEFINITION 12.2.2 ($\Gamma^\ell_{\mathcal{P},\mathcal{O}_S} \uparrow i$ AND $\Gamma^\ell_{\mathcal{P},\mathcal{O}_S} \uparrow \omega$ OPERATORS)   Suppose $\mathcal{P}$ is a deontically stratified program witnessed by layering function ℓ, and suppose the layers of $\mathcal{P}$ induced by ℓ are $\mathcal{P}_0, \ldots, \mathcal{P}_k$. The operators $\Gamma^\ell_{\mathcal{P},\mathcal{O}_S} \uparrow i(S)$ and $\Gamma^\ell_{\mathcal{P},\mathcal{O}_S} \uparrow \omega(S)$ are defined as follows.

$$\Gamma^\ell_{\mathcal{P},\mathcal{O}_S} \uparrow 0(S) = \mathbf{T}^\omega_{\mathcal{P}_0,\mathcal{O}_S}(\emptyset)$$
$$\Gamma^\ell_{\mathcal{P},\mathcal{O}_S} \uparrow (i+1)(S) = \mathbf{T}^\omega_{\mathcal{P}_{i+1},\mathcal{O}_S}\left(\Gamma^\ell_{\mathcal{P},\mathcal{O}_S} \uparrow i(S)\right)$$
$$\Gamma^\ell_{\mathcal{P},\mathcal{O}_S} \uparrow \omega(S) = \bigcup_{i=0}^{k} \Gamma^\ell_{\mathcal{P},\mathcal{O}_S} \uparrow i(S).$$

We write $\Gamma^\ell_{\mathcal{P},\mathcal{O}_S} \uparrow i$ and $\Gamma^\ell_{\mathcal{P},\mathcal{O}_S} \uparrow \omega$ for $\Gamma^\ell_{\mathcal{P},\mathcal{O}_S} \uparrow i(\emptyset)$ and $\Gamma^\ell_{\mathcal{P},\mathcal{O}_S} \uparrow \omega(\emptyset)$, respectively. The following example illustrates the computation of $\Gamma^\ell_{\mathcal{P},\mathcal{O}_S} \uparrow \omega$.

Example 12.2.3 ($\Gamma^\ell_{\mathcal{P},\mathcal{O}_S} \omega$ Operator)   Let $\mathcal{O}_S$ indicate that the plane is on autopilot and let $\mathcal{P}$ contain all rules for the agent program given in Example 12.1.7 on page 473. Additionally, let $\mathcal{P}$ contain the following rule:

r_0:   **O** *adjustAltitude*(5000) ←

Then $\mathcal{P}$ is a *WRAP* which is witnessed by layering function ℓ where $\mathcal{P}^\ell_0 = \{r_0, r_4\}$ and $\mathcal{P}^\ell_1 = \{r_1, r_2, r_3\}$. Here,

$\Gamma^\ell_{\mathcal{P},\mathcal{O}_S} \uparrow 0 = \{$**O** *adjustAltitude*(5000),

  O *adjust_course*(*no_go*, flight_route, current_location),
  Do *adjustAltitude*(5000), **P** *adjustAltitude*(5000),
  Do *adjust_course*(*no_go*, flight_route, current_location),
  P *adjust_course*(*no_go*, flight_route, current_location)$\}$,

$\Gamma^\ell_{\mathcal{P},\mathcal{O}_S} \uparrow 1 = \{$**O** *create_flight_plan*(*no_go*, flight_route, current_location),
Do *create_flight_plan*(*no_go*, flight_route, current_location),
P *create_flight_plan*(*no_go*, flight_route, current_location),
Do *execute_flight_plan*(flight_route),
P *execute_flight_plan*(flight_route)$\} \cup \Gamma^\ell_{\mathcal{P},\mathcal{O}_S} \uparrow 0$, and
$\Gamma^\ell_{\mathcal{P},\mathcal{O}_S} \uparrow 2 = \Gamma^\ell_{\mathcal{P},\mathcal{O}_S} \uparrow 1$, so $\Gamma^\ell_{\mathcal{P},\mathcal{O}_S} \uparrow \omega = \Gamma^\ell_{\mathcal{P},\mathcal{O}_S} \uparrow 1$.

Note that although r_3 was included in $\mathcal{P}$, it never had a chance to fire as it had to be assigned to the second layer. Thus, we have some insight into why this fixpoint operator solves the problem mentioned in Example 12.2.2 on page 479.

The theorem below tells us that for *all* layerings $\ell \in \mathsf{wtn}(\mathcal{P})$, $\Gamma^\ell_{\mathcal{P},\mathcal{O}_S} \uparrow \omega$ is a reasonable status set of any *WRAP* that has no associated action constraints or integrity constraints. For the proof of this result, we use the following technical lemma, which says that in the computation of $\Gamma^\ell_{\mathcal{P},\mathcal{O}_S} \uparrow \omega$, the applicability of rules is preserved.

Let us denote $S^\ell_{0,j} = \mathbf{T}^j_{\mathcal{P}_0,\mathcal{O}_S}(\emptyset)$, for all $j \geq 0$, and $S^\ell_{i+1,j} = \mathbf{T}^j_{\mathcal{P}_{i+1},\mathcal{O}_S}(\Gamma^\ell_{\mathcal{P},\mathcal{O}_S} \uparrow i)$, for all $i, j \geq 0$, i.e., $S^\ell_{i,j}$ contains the result of computing $\Gamma^\ell_{\mathcal{P},\mathcal{O}_S} \uparrow \omega$ after step j in level i. We shall drop the superscript ℓ when it is clear from the context. Note that $S_{i,j}$ monotonically increases, i.e., $S_{i,j} \subseteq S_{i',j'}$ if $(i, j) < (i', j')$ under the standard lexicographic ordering.

LEMMA 12.2.1 Suppose $\mathcal{P}$ is a *WRAP*, and let $\ell \in \mathsf{wtn}(\mathcal{P})$. If, for some rule $r \in \mathcal{P}_i$ and stage $S_{i,j}$, it is the case that $\mathrm{AR}(r, \theta, S_{i,j})$ is true, then $\mathrm{AR}(r, \theta, S_{i',j'})$ is true, for every stage $S_{i',j'}$ such that $(i, j) < (i', j')$, and $\mathrm{AR}(r, \theta, S)$ is true where $S = \Gamma^l_{\mathcal{P},\mathcal{O}_S} \uparrow \omega$.

Proof Suppose that $\mathrm{AR}(r, \theta, S_{i,j})$ is true. Thus,

1. $r\theta$ is ground,
2. $B_{cc}(r\theta)$ is true in $\mathcal{O}_S$,
3. $B^+_{as}(r\theta) \subseteq S_{i,j}$,
4. $\neg.B^-_{as}(r\theta) \cap S_{i,j} = \emptyset$, and
5. for every atom $\mathsf{Op}\,\alpha \in B^+_{as}(r\theta) \cup \{A\}$ such that $\mathsf{Op} \in \{\mathbf{P}, \mathbf{O}, \mathbf{Do}\}$, α is executable in $\mathcal{O}_S$.

As $S_{i,j} \subseteq S_{i',j'} \subseteq S$ holds for all i', j' as in the statement of the lemma, proving $\neg.B^-_{as}(r\theta) \cap S = \emptyset$ will establish the lemma. Assume this is not true, i.e., an atom $A \in \neg.B^-_{as}(r\theta) \cap S$ exists. This implies that there exists a rule $r' \in \mathcal{P}$ such that for some θ' and i^*, j^*, $\mathrm{AR}(r', \theta', S_{i^*,j^*})$ is true and $head(r'\theta') \leq A$. Condition (2) of deontic stratifiability implies $\ell(r') < \ell(r)$, and thus $i^* < i$ can be assumed. As the stages in the construction of S monotonically increase, it follows that $head(r'\theta')$ and A are contained in $S_{i,j}$; thus, $\neg.B_{as}^-(r\theta) \cap S_{i,j} \neq \emptyset$. This means that $\text{AR}(r, \theta, S_{i,j})$ is not true, which is a contradiction. Thus, $\neg.B_{as}^-(r\theta) \cap S = \emptyset$. ∎

THEOREM 12.2.1   Suppose $\mathcal{P}$ is a *WRAP*. Let $\ell \in \text{wtn}(\mathcal{P})$ be any witness to the regularity of $\mathcal{P}$. If $\mathcal{IC}$ and $\mathcal{AC}$ are both empty, then $\Gamma_{\mathcal{P}, \mathcal{O}_S}^\ell \uparrow \omega$ is a reasonable status set of $\mathcal{P}$ w.r.t. $\mathcal{O}_S$.

Proof   Let $S = \Gamma_{\mathcal{P}, \mathcal{O}_S}^\ell \uparrow \omega$. To show that S is a reasonable status set of $\mathcal{P}$, we must show that S is a feasible status of $\mathcal{P}' = red^S(\mathcal{P}, \mathcal{O}_S)$, and no smaller $S' \subset S$ exists which satisfies conditions (S1)–(S3) of feasibility for $\mathcal{P}'$.

To show that S is a feasible status set of $\mathcal{P}'$, we must show that (S1) S is closed under program rules of $\mathcal{P}'$, that (S2) S is deontically and action consistent, that (S3) S is action closed, and that (S4) the state consistency condition is satisfied.

(S1) To see that S is closed under rules from $\mathcal{P}'$, suppose there exists a rule r in $\mathcal{P}'$ of the form $r: A \leftarrow L_1, \ldots, L_n$ such that $\text{AR}(r, \theta, S)$ is true on $\mathcal{O}_S$ for some θ. As r is in fact ground (and thus $r\theta = r$ and θ is irrelevant) and $B_{as}^-(r) = \emptyset$, this implies

(a) $B_{cc}(r)$ is true on $\mathcal{O}_S$.

(b) $B_{as}^+(r) \subseteq S$, and

(c) for every atom $\text{Op}\, \alpha \in B_{as}^+(r) \cup \{A\}$ such that $\text{Op} \in \{\mathbf{P}, \mathbf{O}, \mathbf{Do}\}$, α is executable in $\mathcal{O}_S$.

We have to show that $A \in S$. As $B_{as}^+(r)$ is finite, item (b) implies that $B_{as}^+(r) \subseteq \Gamma_{\mathcal{P}, \mathcal{O}_S}^\ell \uparrow k$ for some integer k. Let k^* be the least such integer. For each atom $A \in B_{as}^+(r)$, there is rule $r' \in \mathcal{P}$ and a ground substitution θ' such that $r'\theta'$ is applied in the construction of $\Gamma_{\mathcal{P}, \mathcal{O}_S}^\ell \uparrow \omega$ and $head(r'\theta') \leq A$ (i.e., A is either included directly by applying $r'\theta'$, or indirectly by applying $r'\theta'$ and action closure rules). The rule r stems from the ground instance $r''\theta''$ of a rule $r'' \in \mathcal{P}$. Item (1) of deontic stratifiability implies that $\ell(r') \leq k^* \leq \ell(r'')$ holds. As $\Gamma_{\mathcal{P}, \mathcal{O}_S}^\ell \uparrow k^* \subseteq S$ and $\neg.B_{as}^-(r''\theta'') \cap S = \emptyset$, it follows that the rule $r''\theta''$ is applied in the construction of $\Gamma_{\mathcal{P}, \mathcal{O}_S}^\ell \uparrow \omega$, and thus $head(r''\theta'') = A$ is included in S.

(S2) Since $\mathcal{AC} = \emptyset$, S is trivially action consistent. To see that S is deontically consistent, assume it is not. Thus, it must violate some deontic consistency rule (D1)–(D3). As in the proof of Proposition 12.2.3 on page 480, it can be shown using Lemma 12.2.1 on the preceding page that each such violation raises a contradiction.

(S3) Clearly, $\mathbf{A}\text{-}\mathbf{Cl}(S) = \bigcup_{i=0}^\infty \mathbf{A}\text{-}\mathbf{Cl}(\Gamma_{\mathcal{P}, \mathcal{O}_S}^\ell \uparrow i)$ holds by definition of S and the fact that $\mathbf{A}\text{-}\mathbf{Cl}(X) = \bigcup_{X' \in \mathcal{C}} \mathbf{A}\text{-}\mathbf{Cl}(X')$ holds for every collection $\mathcal{C}$ of subsets of an arbitrary status set X such that $\bigcup_{X' \in \mathcal{C}} X' = X$. Applying Proposition 12.2.4 on page 481, it follows $\mathbf{A}\text{-}\mathbf{Cl}(S) = S$.

(S4) This is trivial as $\mathcal{IC} = \emptyset$ is assumed.

At this stage, we have shown that S is a feasible status set of $\mathcal{P}'$. To establish that S is rational, suppose $S' \subset S$ is a status set satisfying conditions (S1)–(S3) for $\mathcal{P}'$. Let $S_{i,j}$ be

Section 12.2   Properties of Weakly Regular Agents   485

the first stage in the construction of S such that $S_{i,j} \setminus S' \neq \emptyset$. Let $A \in S_{i,j} \setminus S'$ be any atom. It follows that there exist a rule $r \in \mathcal{P}_i$ and a θ such that $A = head(r\theta)$ and $AR(r, \theta, S_{i,j-1})$ is true. By Lemma 12.2.1 on page 483, also $AR(r, \theta, S)$ is true; item (4) of the definition of $AR(r, \theta, S)$ implies that the rule r' obtained from $r\theta$ by removing $B^-_{as}(r\theta)$ belongs to $\mathcal{P}'$. Furthermore, the minimality of $S_{i,j}$ implies that $B^+_{as}(r')$ $(= B^+_{as}(r\theta))$ is contained in S'. Thus, $AR(r', \theta, S')$ is true. This implies $A \in S'$, which is a contradiction. Thus, a feasible status set $S' \subset S$ of $\mathcal{P}$ does not exist. This proves the result. ∎

From this result, we can conclude that the outcome of the stepwise $\Gamma^\ell_{\mathcal{P},\mathcal{O}_S} \uparrow \omega$ construction is a fixpoint of the global $\mathbf{T}_{\mathcal{P},\mathcal{O}_S}$ operator.

COROLLARY 16   Let $\mathcal{P}$ be a *WRAP* and let $\ell \in \mathsf{wtn}(\mathcal{P})$. Then, $S = \Gamma^\ell_{\mathcal{P},\mathcal{O}_S} \uparrow \omega$ is a fixpoint of $\mathbf{T}_{\mathcal{P},\mathcal{O}_S}$.

Proof   Theorem 12.2.1 on the preceding page and Lemma 6.5.1 imply that S is a pre-fixpoint of $\mathbf{T}_{\mathcal{P},\mathcal{O}_S}$, i.e., $\mathbf{T}_{\mathcal{P},\mathcal{O}_S}(S) \subseteq S$ holds. Since, as pointed out above, $\mathbf{T}_{\mathcal{P},\mathcal{O}_S}$ is inflationary, i.e., $S \subseteq \mathbf{T}_{\mathcal{P},\mathcal{O}_S}(S)$ holds, the result follows. ∎

The above theorem shows that when a *WRAP* $\mathcal{P}$ has no associated integrity constraints and action constraints, then $\Gamma^\ell_{\mathcal{P},\mathcal{O}_S} \uparrow \omega$ is guaranteed to be a reasonable status set of $\mathcal{P}$. The following result shows that any reasonable status set of $\mathcal{P}$ must be of this form, and in fact coincides with $\Gamma^\ell_{\mathcal{P},\mathcal{O}_S} \uparrow \omega$.

THEOREM 12.2.2   Suppose $\mathcal{P}$ is a *WRAP*, $\ell \in \mathsf{wtn}(\mathcal{P})$ and S is any reasonable status set of $\mathcal{P}$. Then, $S = \Gamma^\ell_{\mathcal{P},\mathcal{O}_S} \uparrow \omega$.

Proof   To prove this result, it is sufficient to show by induction on $i \geq 0$ that for every rule $r \in \mathcal{P}_i$ and ground substitution θ it is the case that

$$AR(r, \theta, S) \longleftrightarrow \exists j. AR(r, \theta, S_{i,j}).$$

Without loss of generality, we assume that $\mathcal{P}_0 = \emptyset$.

Then, the base case $i = 0$ is trivial, as $\mathcal{P}_0$ contains no rules. For the inductive case, assume the statement holds for all $j \leq i$ and consider the case $i + 1 > 0$. We have to show that

$$\forall r \in \mathcal{P}_{i+1} \forall \theta. AR(r, \theta, S) \longleftrightarrow \exists j. AR(r, \theta, S_{i+1,j})$$

holds. We consider the two directions of this equivalence.

($\Longleftarrow$) Suppose that $AR(r, \theta, S_{i+1,j})$ is true for a particular j. We have to show that $AR(r, \theta, S)$ is true. By the definition of predicate AR, it remains to show that (i) $B^+_{as}(r\theta) \subseteq S$ and (ii) $\neg. B^-_{as}(r\theta) \cap S = \emptyset$. We prove this by induction on $j \geq 0$.

For the base case $j = 0$, we obtain from item 1 of deontic stratifiability that for each atom $A \in B^+_{as}(r\theta)$, there exists a rule $r' \in \mathcal{P}_{i'}$ where $i' \leq i$ and a substitution θ' such that $head(r'\theta') \leq A$ and $AR(r', \theta', S_{i',j'})$ is true for some $j' \geq 0$. Then, by the outer induction hypothesis on i, it follows that AR(r', θ', S) is true, which implies $A \in S$. Thus, (i) holds. For (ii), truth of AR$(r, \theta, S_{i+1,j})$ implies that no atom $A \in \neg.B_{as}^-(r\theta)$ is contained in $S_{i+1,j}$. Item 2 of deontic stratifiability of $\mathcal{P}$ implies that every rule r' such that $head(r'\theta') \leq A$ for some θ' is contained in $\mathcal{P}_{i'}$ for some $i' \leq i$. Furthermore, $S_{i',j'} \subseteq S_{i+1,j}$ implies that AR$(r', \theta', S_{i',j'})$ is false, for every $j' \geq 0$. Hence, by the outer induction hypothesis on i, AR(r', θ', S) is false. This implies $A \notin S$, and hence $\neg.B_{as}^-(r\theta) \cap S = \emptyset$ is true. This concludes the proof of the inner base case $j = 0$.

For the inner induction step, suppose the statement holds for all $j' \leq j$ and consider $j + 1 > 0$. The proof of (i) is similar to the case $j = 0$, but takes into account that r' and θ' for A may also be such that $r' \in \mathcal{P}_{i+1}$ and AR$(r', \theta', S_{i+1,j'})$ holds where $j' \leq j$. In this case, the inner induction hypothesis on j implies that AR(r', θ', S) is true. The proof of (ii) is analogous to the case $j = 0$.

($\Rightarrow$) We have to show that AR(r, θ, S), where $r \in \mathcal{P}_{i+1}$, implies that $\exists j.$AR$(r, \theta, S_{i+1,j})$ is true. We prove the following equivalent claim. Let $\mathcal{P}' = red^S(\mathcal{P}, \mathcal{O}_S)$. Then, for every atom $A \in \mathbf{T}_{\mathcal{P}',\mathcal{O}_S}^\omega(\emptyset)$ for which $r \in \mathcal{P}_{i+1}$ and θ exist such that $A = head(r\theta)$ and AR(r, θ, S) is true, $\exists j.$AR$(r, \theta, S_{i+1,j})$ is true. The proof is by induction on the stages $\mathbf{T}_{\mathcal{P}',\mathcal{O}_S}^k(\emptyset)$, $k \geq 0$, of the fixpoint iteration for $\mathcal{P}'$.

The base case $k = 0$ is trivial, since $\mathbf{T}_{\mathcal{P}',\mathcal{O}_S}^0(\emptyset) = \emptyset$. For the induction step, suppose the statement holds for all $k' \leq k$, and consider $k + 1 > 0$. Let $A \in \mathbf{T}_{\mathcal{P}',\mathcal{O}_S}^{k+1}(\emptyset) \setminus \mathbf{T}_{\mathcal{P}',\mathcal{O}_S}^k(\emptyset)$ and r, θ as in the premise of the statement. From item (1) of deontic stratifiability of $\mathcal{P}$, the outer induction hypothesis on i, and the inner induction hypothesis on k, it follows that each $A \in B_{as}^+(r\theta)$ is contained in S_{i+1,j_A} for some $j_A \geq 0$. Since $B_{as}^+(r\theta)$ is finite, $B_{as}^+(r\theta) \subseteq S_{i+1,j}$ holds where $j = \max\{j_A \mid A \in B_{as}^+(r\theta)\}$. To show that AR$(r, \theta, S_{i+1,j})$ holds for this j, it remains to show that $\neg.B_{as}^-(r\theta) \cap S_{i+1,j} = \emptyset$ holds. Item (2) of deontic stratifiability and the outer induction hypothesis imply that no atom $A \in \neg.B_{as}^-(r'\theta')$ is contained in $S_{i+1,j}$; thus, $\neg.B_{as}^-(r'\theta') \cap S_{i+1,j} = \emptyset$, where $j \geq 0$ is arbitrary. This proves that AR$(r, \theta, S_{i+1,j})$ holds, and thus $\exists j.$AR$(r', \theta', S_{i+1,j})$ is true. This concludes the proof of the inner induction step on $k + 1$, and also the proof of the outer inductive step $i + 1$. ∎

The following are immediate corollaries of the above result.

COROLLARY 17   Suppose $\mathcal{P}$ is a *WRAP*, and suppose ℓ_1, ℓ_2 are in wtn$(\mathcal{P})$. Then $\Gamma_{\mathcal{P},\mathcal{O}_S}^{\ell_1} \uparrow \omega = \Gamma_{\mathcal{P},\mathcal{O}_S}^{\ell_2} \uparrow \omega$.

COROLLARY 18   Suppose $\mathcal{P}$ is a *WRAP* and let $\ell \in$ wtn$(\mathcal{P})$ be arbitrary. If $\Gamma_{\mathcal{P},\mathcal{O}_S}^{\ell_1} \uparrow \omega$ satisfies the action and integrity constraints $\mathcal{AC}$ and $\mathcal{IC}$, respectively, then $\Gamma_{\mathcal{P},\mathcal{O}_S}^{\ell_1} \uparrow \omega$ is the (unique) reasonable status of $\mathcal{P}$ on $\mathcal{O}_S$. Otherwise, $\mathcal{P}$ has no reasonable status set on $\mathcal{O}_S$.

Section 12.3   Regular Agent Programs   487

This last result will play a *fundamental role* in the design of algorithms to compute the reasonable status set of a *WRAP* (if one exists). All that is required is to iteratively compute $\Gamma^{\ell_1}_{\mathcal{P},\mathcal{O}_S} \uparrow \omega$, and then to check if $\Gamma^{\ell_1}_{\mathcal{P},\mathcal{O}_S} \uparrow \omega$ satisfies the integrity and action constraints associated with the current state of the agent.

12.3 Regular Agent Programs

In this section, we define what it means for a *WRAP* to be *bounded*. A regular agent program then is a program which is weakly regular and bounded. Intuitively, boundedness means that by repeatedly unfolding the positive parts of the rules in the program, we will eventually get rid of all positive action status atoms. Thus, in this section, we will associate with any agent program $\mathcal{P}$ an operator Unfold$_\mathcal{P}$ which is used for this purpose. Before doing so, we need some additional syntax. Let us call any positive action status atom Op α occurring in the body of a rule r, a *prerequisite* of r.

DEFINITION 12.3.1 (PREREQUISITE-FREE (PF) CONSTRAINT)   A prerequisite-free (pf) constraint is defined as follows:

• **true** and **false** are distinguished pf-constraints (with obvious meaning).

• the body of each rule r such that $B^+_{as}(r) = \emptyset$ (i.e., r contains no prerequisites) is a pf-constraint.

• If γ_1, γ_2 are pf-constraints, then so are γ_1 & γ_2 and $\gamma_1 \vee \gamma_2$.

DEFINITION 12.3.2 (PREREQUISITE-FREE CONSTRAINT RULE)   A prerequisite-free constraint rule is of the form

$A \leftarrow$ pfc

where A is an action status atom and pfc is a pf-constraint.

An agent program $\mathcal{P}$ may certainly contain rules r which have prerequisites Op α. Each such prerequisite might be replaced by the body of a rule r' which derives Op α. This way, the prerequisites can be eliminated from r, replacing them by rule bodies. This step may introduce new prerequisites from the body of some rule r', though; such prerequisites may be eliminated by repeating the process.

The operator Unfold$_\mathcal{P}$ is used to describe this process. Informally, it maps a set R of pf-constraint rules, which compactly represent already unfolded rules from $\mathcal{P}$, to another set Unfold$_\mathcal{P}(R)$ of pf-constraint rules, implementing the unfolding step described above, but using pf-constraint rules from R rather than rules r' from $\mathcal{P}$. The operator Coll$_\mathcal{P}$ introduced next is an intermediate operator for defining Unfold$_\mathcal{P}$.

DEFINITION 12.3.3 (OPERATOR COLL$_\mathcal{P}$) Let $\mathcal{P}$ be an agent program and R be a set of pf-constraint rules which are standardized apart. Suppose $\mathsf{Op} \in \{\mathbf{P}, \mathbf{O}, \mathbf{Do}, \mathbf{W}, \mathbf{F}\}$ and let α be any action name. Then the *collect set*, $\mathrm{Coll}_\mathcal{P}(R, \mathsf{Op}, \alpha)$, is defined as the following set of pf-constraints:

$$\mathrm{Coll}_\mathcal{P}(R, \mathsf{Op}, \alpha) = \Big\{ \gamma \mid \mathsf{Op}\,\alpha(\vec{X}) \leftarrow \gamma_0 \in R,$$
$$\text{there exists a rule } r \in \mathcal{P} \text{ such that } head(r) = \mathsf{Op}'\alpha(\vec{t}), \mathsf{Op}' \leq \mathsf{Op},$$
$$B_{as}^+(r) = \{\mathsf{Op}_1\alpha_1(\vec{t}_1), \ldots, \mathsf{Op}_k\alpha_k(\vec{t}_k)\},$$
$$\mathsf{Op}_i\alpha_i(\vec{X}_i) \leftarrow \gamma_i \in R, i = 1, \ldots, k,$$
$$\text{and } \gamma = \gamma_0 \vee \Big[(\vec{X} = \vec{t}) \& B_{cc}(r) \& \bigwedge_{i=1}^k ((\vec{X}_i = \vec{t}_i) \& \gamma_i) \& B_{as}^-(r)\Big] \Big\}$$

Here, an equality formula $(\vec{X} = \vec{t})$ stands for the conjunction of all equality atoms $X = t$, where X and t are from the same position of $\vec{X}$ and $\vec{t}$, respectively.

What this operator does is the following. It takes a pf-constraint rule from R which defines $\mathsf{Op}\,\alpha(\vec{X})$ through its body γ_0, and weakens this constraint γ_0 (i.e., increases the set of solutions) by taking the disjunction with an unfolded rule r whose head either defines an instance of the action status atom $\mathsf{Op}\,\alpha(\vec{X})$, or of an action status atom $\mathsf{Op}'\alpha(\vec{X})$ which, by deontic and action closure rules, defines an instance of $\mathsf{Op}\,\alpha(\vec{X})$. The unfolding of rule r is obtained by replacing each positive action status atom $\mathsf{Op}_i\alpha_i(\vec{t}_i)$ in r's body with the body γ_i of a pf-constraint rule pfc_i from R which defines $\mathsf{Op}_i\alpha(\vec{X}_i)$.

Informally, one may think of the rules in R as being known for sure. For instance, if $\mathsf{Op}\,\alpha(\vec{X}) \leftarrow \gamma_0$ is in R, then one may think of this as saying that all instances θ of $\alpha(\vec{X})$ such that the existential closure of $\gamma_0\theta$ is true in the current agent state are true. The $\mathrm{Coll}_\mathcal{P}$ operator takes such an R as input, and uses the rules in $\mathcal{P}$ to identify ways of weakening the constraint γ_0, thus extending the set of ground instances of $\alpha(\vec{X})$ satisfying the above condition.

Note 12 We will assume that when no pf-constraint rule in R has $\mathsf{Op}\,\alpha(\vec{X})$ in the head, then that R is augmented via the insertion of the pf-constraint rule $\mathsf{Op}\,\alpha(\vec{X}) \leftarrow$ **false**. The rest of our treatment is based on this assumption.

We remark that in the above definition, the constraint γ may be simplified by obvious operations such as pushing through equalities, or eliminating **true/false** subparts of a constraint; we do not pursue the issue of simplifications further here.

The following simple example illustrates the use of the Coll operator.

Example 12.3.1 (Coll$_\mathcal{P}$ Operator) Let $\mathcal{P}$ be the agent program in Example 12.1.7 on page 473 and let

$R = \{\mathbf{O}adjustAltitude(5000) \leftarrow \mathbf{in}(\mathtt{Alt}, \mathtt{autoPilot}\!:\!getAltitude()) \,\&\, (\mathtt{Alt} < 4000)\}.$

Section 12.3   Regular Agent Programs   489

Then

$\text{Coll}_\mathcal{P}(R, \mathbf{O}, \textit{adjust\_course}(\texttt{X}, \texttt{Y}, \texttt{Z})) = \{(\texttt{X} = \textit{no\_go}) \ \& \ (\texttt{Y} = \textit{flight\_route}) \ \&$
$\hspace{4cm} (\texttt{Z} = \textit{current\_location}) \ \& \ (\texttt{Altitude} = 5000) \ \&$
$\hspace{4cm} \textbf{in}(\texttt{Alt}, \texttt{autoPilot} : \textit{getAltitude}()) \ \&$
$\hspace{4cm} (\texttt{Alt} < 4000)\}.$

Note that this expression can be simplified by removing the unused (Altitude = 5000) conjunct.

The operator Unfold$_\mathcal{P}$ defined below uses Coll$_\mathcal{P}$ to compute a single constraint for each Op and each action name α.

DEFINITION 12.3.4 (OPERATOR UNFOLD$_\mathcal{P}$)

$\text{Unfold}_\mathcal{P}(\text{Op}, \alpha, R) = \text{Op}\,\alpha(\vec{X}) \leftarrow \bigvee_{\gamma \in \text{coll}_\mathcal{P}(R, \text{Op}, \alpha)} \gamma, \quad \text{and}$

$\text{Unfold}_\mathcal{P}(R) = \bigcup_{\text{op}, \alpha} \text{Unfold}_\mathcal{P}(\text{Op}, \alpha, R).$

Note. When Coll$_\mathcal{P}(R, \text{Op}, \alpha)$ is empty in the above definition, the right hand side of the above implication is set to false.

The operator Unfold$_{\mathcal{P}, Op, \alpha}$ may be iterated; its powers are (as usual) denoted by Unfold$_\mathcal{P}^0$(Op, α, R) = R, Unfold$_\mathcal{P}^{i+1}$(Op, α, R) = Unfold$_\mathcal{P}$(Op, α, Unfold$_\mathcal{P}^i$(Op, α, R)), $i \geq 0$, and similar with Unfold$_\mathcal{P}$. The following simple example illustrates the use of the Unfold operator.

Example 12.3.2 (Unfold$_\mathcal{P}$ Operator) Let $\mathcal{P}$ be the agent program in Example 12.2.3 on page 482 and let $R = \emptyset$. Then, applying simplifications in place,

$\text{Unfold}_\mathcal{P}^0(R) = \emptyset,$

$\text{Unfold}_\mathcal{P}^1(R) = \{\mathbf{O}/\mathbf{Do}/\mathbf{P} \ \textit{maintain\_course}(\textit{no\_go}, \textit{flight\_route}, \textit{current\_location}) \leftarrow$
$\hspace{2cm} \textbf{in}(\text{automated}, \texttt{autoPilot} : \textit{pilotStatus}(\texttt{pilot\_message})) \ \&$
$\hspace{2cm} \neg \ \mathbf{O} \ \textit{adjust\_course}(\textit{no\_go}, \textit{flight\_route}, \textit{current\_location}),$
$\hspace{2cm} \mathbf{O}/\mathbf{Do}/\mathbf{P} \ \textit{adjustAltitude}(5000) \leftarrow \ \},$

$\text{Unfold}_\mathcal{P}^2(R) = \{\mathbf{O}/\mathbf{Do}/\mathbf{P} \ \textit{adjust\_course}(\textit{no\_go}, \textit{flight\_route}, \textit{current\_location}) \leftarrow$
$\hspace{2cm} (\texttt{Altitude} = 5000)\} \cup \text{Unfold}_\mathcal{P}^1(R),$

$\text{Unfold}_\mathcal{P}^3(R) = \{\mathbf{O}/\mathbf{Do}/\mathbf{P} \ \textit{create\_flight\_plan}(\textit{no\_go}, \textit{flight\_route},$
$\hspace{2cm} \textit{current\_location}) \leftarrow$
$\hspace{2cm} (\texttt{No\_go} = \textit{no\_go}) \ \& \ (\texttt{Flight\_route} = \textit{flight\_route}) \ \&$
$\hspace{2cm} (\texttt{Current\_location} = \textit{current\_location}) \ \&$
$\hspace{2cm} (\texttt{Altitude} = 5000)\} \cup \text{Unfold}_\mathcal{P}^2(R),$

$\text{Unfold}_{\mathcal{P}}^4(R) = \{\textbf{Do/P } \textit{execute\_flight\_plan}(\textit{flight\_route}) \leftarrow$
$\qquad\qquad\text{in}(\text{automated}, \texttt{autoPilot}:\textit{pilotStatus}(\texttt{pilot\_message}))$ &
$\qquad\qquad(\texttt{No\_go} = \textit{no\_go})$ & $(\texttt{Flight\_route} = \textit{flight\_route})$ &
$\qquad\qquad(\texttt{Current\_location} = \textit{current\_location})$ &
$\qquad\qquad(\texttt{Altitude} = 5000)\} \cup \text{Unfold}_{\mathcal{P}}^3(R),$

and $\text{Unfold}_{\mathcal{P}}^5(R) = \text{Unfold}_{\mathcal{P}}^4(R)$.

Note that in this example, $\textbf{O/Do/P}\,\alpha(\vec{X}) \in \text{Unfold}_{\mathcal{P}}^i(R)$ (or $\textbf{Do/P}\,\alpha(\vec{X}) \in \text{Unfold}_{\mathcal{P}}^i(R)$) indicates that $\{\textbf{O}\,\alpha(\vec{X}), \textbf{Do}\,\alpha(\vec{X}), \textbf{P}\,\alpha(\vec{X})\} \subseteq \text{Unfold}_{\mathcal{P}}^i(R)$ ($\{\textbf{Do}\,\alpha(\vec{X}), \textbf{P}\,\alpha(\vec{X})\} \subseteq \text{Unfold}_{\mathcal{P}}^i(R)$).

When we iteratively compute $\text{Unfold}_{\mathcal{P}}^i$, it is important to note that we may often *redundantly* fire the same rule in $\text{Coll}_{\mathcal{P}}$ many times without deriving anything new. Constraint equivalence tests may be used to terminate this.

This raises the question what it means for two pf-constraints to be equivalent. We provide a simple model theoretic answer to this question below, and then explain what a constraint equivalence test is.

DEFINITION 12.3.5 (BISTRUCTURE)   A *bistructure* for an agent program $\mathcal{P}$ is a pair $(\mathcal{O}_S, S)$ where $\mathcal{O}_S$ is a possible state of the agent in question, and S is a status set.

We now define what it means for a bistructure to satisfy a pf-constraint.

DEFINITION 12.3.6 (SATISFACTION OF A GROUND PF-CONSTRAINT BY A BISTRUCTURE)   A bistructure $(\mathcal{O}_S, S)$ *satisfies*

1. a ground code call condition χ if χ is true in $\mathcal{O}_S$;
2. a ground action status atom $\neg\text{Op}\,\alpha$ if $\text{Op}\,\alpha \notin S$;
3. a conjunction pfc_1 & pfc_2 if it satisfies pfc_1 and pfc_2;
4. a disjunction $\text{pfc}_1 \vee \text{pfc}_2$ if it satisfies either pfc_1 or pfc_2.

DEFINITION 12.3.7 (SOLUTIONS OF A PF-CONSTRAINT W.R.T. A BISTRUCTURE)   Suppose pfc is a pf-constraint involving free variables $\vec{X}$. The *solutions* of pfc w.r.t. a bistructure $(\mathcal{O}_S, S)$ is the set of all ground substitutions θ such that $(\mathcal{O}_S, S)$ satisfies pfcθ.

We are now ready to define what it means for two constraints to be equivalent in the presence of an arbitrary but fixed underlying agent program $\mathcal{P}$.

DEFINITION 12.3.8 (a-EQUIVALENT PF-CONSTRAINTS)   Suppose a is an agent, and pfc_1, pfc_2 are pf-constraints involving variables $\vec{X}$, $\vec{Y}$ respectively. Let $\vec{X}'$, $\vec{Y}'$ be subvectors of $\vec{X}$, $\vec{Y}$ respectively of the same length. Then pfc_1, pfc_2 are said to be $(a, \vec{X}', \vec{Y}')$-*equivalent*, denoted $\text{pfc}_1 \sim_{a,\vec{x}',\vec{y}'} \text{pfc}_2$ if for every bistructure $(\mathcal{O}_S, S)$ such that S is a reasonable

Section 12.3   Regular Agent Programs   491

status set of a's agent program w.r.t. state $\mathcal{O}_S$, it is the case that $\pi_{\vec{X}'}(\mathsf{Sol}(\mathsf{pfc}_1)) = \pi_{\vec{Y}'}(\mathsf{Sol}(\mathsf{pfc}_2))$ where $\mathsf{Sol}(\mathsf{pfc}_i)$ denotes the set of all solutions of pfc_i and $\pi_{\vec{Z}}(\mathsf{Sol}(\mathsf{pfc}_i))$ denotes the set of projections of solutions of pfc_i on the variables in $\vec{Z}$.

The intuition behind the above definition is that two PFCs may appear in the body of two different pf-constraint rules. Each of these rules may "output" some variables in the body to the head. The condition involving the check that $\pi_{\vec{X}'}(\mathsf{Sol}(\mathsf{pfc}_1)) = \pi_{\vec{Y}'}(\mathsf{Sol}(\mathsf{pfc}_2))$ above ensures that the outputs of the constraints involved are identical, when we restrict it to the variables specified.

In general, the problem of checking equivalence of two PFCs is easily seen to be undecidable, and as a consequence, we introduce the notion of a pf-constraint equivalence test below which provides a sufficient condition for two pfc's to be equivalent.

DEFINITION 12.3.9 (PF-CONSTRAINT EQUIVALENCE TEST) A *pf-constraint equivalence check test* $\mathsf{eqi}_{a,\vec{X}',\vec{Y}'}$ is a function that takes as input two pf-constraints $\mathsf{pfc}_1, \mathsf{pfc}_2$, such that if $\mathsf{eqi}_{a,\vec{X}',\vec{Y}'}(\mathsf{pfc}_1, \mathsf{pfc}_2) = \mathbf{true}$ then $\mathsf{pfc}_1, \mathsf{pfc}_2$ are equivalent w.r.t. $\mathcal{P}$.

We will often write eqi instead of $\mathsf{eqi}_{a,\vec{X}',\vec{Y}'}$ when the parameters $a, \vec{X}', \vec{Y}'$ are clear from context. Note that just as in the case of conflict freedom tests, a pf-constraint equivalence test merely implements a *sufficient* condition to guarantee equivalence of two pf-constraint rules. It may well be the case that $\mathsf{pfc}_1, \mathsf{pfc}_2$ are in fact equivalent on all agent states, but $\mathsf{eqi}(\mathsf{pfc}_1, \mathsf{pfc}_2) = \mathsf{false}$.

Some examples of constraint equivalence tests are given below.

Example 12.3.3 (Renaming Permutation Equivalence) The function eqi^{rp} returns **true** on two pf-constraints $\mathsf{pfc}_1, \mathsf{pfc}_2$ whose variables are standardized apart if and only if there is a renaming substitution θ such that $\{C\theta \mid C \in \mathsf{pfc}_1^*\} = \{C'\theta \mid C' \in \mathsf{pfc}_2^*\}$ where pfc_i^* is a conjunctive normal form representation of pfc_i.

Example 12.3.4 (Rewrite-Based Equivalence) Another way to check equivalence of two pf-constraints is to expect the agent developer to write a set, RW, of rewrite rules of the form

condition $\rightarrow \mathsf{pfc}_1 = \mathsf{pfc}_2$

where *condition* is a code call condition not involving the $\mathbf{in}(\cdot, \cdot)$ predicate, i.e., it only involves comparison operations $=, <, \leq, >, \geq$. RW encodes domain knowledge about what equivalences hold in the data structures and actions involved. It may be viewed as an equational theory (Plaisted 1993). Let $\Upsilon^k(\mathsf{pfc})$ denote the set of all PFC's that pfc can be rewritten to by applying at most k rules in RW.

We say that $\mathsf{pfc}_1, \mathsf{pfc}_2$ are k-equivalent w.r.t. RW if and only if $\Upsilon^k(\mathsf{pfc}_1) \cap \Upsilon^k(\mathsf{pfc}_2) \neq \emptyset$.

It is easy to see that as long as each rule in the equational theory RW is sound (i.e., it accurate w.r.t. the data structures and actions in question), this is a valid pf-constraint equivalence test.

Based on the notion of equivalent pf-constraints, we may define a notion of equivalence for sets of pf-constraint rules as follows.

DEFINITION 12.3.10 (EQUIVALENCE OF TWO SETS OF PF-CONSTRAINT RULES) Two sets R_1, R_2 of pf-constraint rules are equivalent w.r.t. a pf-constraint equivalence test eqi, denoted $R_1 \equiv_{\text{eqi}} R_2$, if there is a bijection $\psi : R_1 \to R_2$ such that for all $r_1 \in R_1$, eqi($r_1, \psi(r_1)$) = **true** and r_1, r_2 both have heads of the form $\text{Op}\,\alpha(\cdot)$, i.e., their heads involve the same action name and the same deontic modality.

We now define the notion of a bounded agent program. Informally, an agent program $\mathcal{P}$ is bounded, if after unfolding rules in $\mathcal{P}$ a certain number of times, we end up with a set of pf-constraints which does not change semantically if we do further unfolding steps.

DEFINITION 12.3.11 (b-BOUNDED AGENT PROGRAM) An *agent program* $\mathcal{P}$ is *bounded* w.r.t. an equivalence check test eqi if there is an integer b such that eqi(Unfold$_\mathcal{P}^b(R)$, Unfold$_\mathcal{P}^{b+1}(R)$) = **true**, for any set of pf-constraints R. In this case, $\mathcal{P}$ is (eqi, b)-bounded.

Observe that when $\mathcal{P}$ is a program which does not contain a truly recursive collection of rules, then $\mathcal{P}$ is (eqi, b)-bounded where eqi is an arbitrary pf-constraint equivalence test such that eqi(pfc, pfc) = **true** for every pfc and b is the number of rules in $\mathcal{P}$. Thus, only truly recursive rules—which seem to play a minor rule in many agent programs in practical applications—may prevent boundedness. If, moreover, $\mathcal{P}$ is deontically stratified and has a layering $\mathcal{P}_0, \ldots, \mathcal{P}_k$ then $\mathcal{P}$ is even (eqi, $k+1$)-bounded.

Rather than unfolding a *WRAP* $\mathcal{P}$ in bulk, we can unfold it along a layering $\ell \in \text{wtn}(\mathcal{P})$ using a pf-constraint equivalence test eqi$^{(i)}$ which is suitable for each layer $\mathcal{P}_i$. Such an eqi$^{(i)}$ may be selected automatically by the implementation *IMPACT* Agent Development Environment (*IADE*), or the agent designer may be prompted to select one from a catalogue or provide his/her own equivalence test implementation. In particular, if $\mathcal{P}_i$ contains no set of truly recursive rules, then a test eqi$^{(i)}$ which always returns true is suitable, which can be automatically selected.

Let us define sets of pf-constraint rules R_i^l, $i \geq 0$, as follows:

$R_0^\ell = \emptyset$,
$R_{i+1}^\ell = \text{Unfold}_{\mathcal{P}_i}^b\left(R_i^\ell\right)$, for all $i \geq 0$,

where $\mathcal{P}_i$ (the i'th layer of $\mathcal{P}$) is (b, eqi$^{(i)}$)-bounded. The *unfolding of $\mathcal{P}$ along ℓ* is given by the set R_{k+1}^ℓ, where k is the highest nonempty layer of $\mathcal{P}$.

DEFINITION 12.3.12 (b-REGULAR AGENT PROGRAM) Suppose a layering ℓ and equivalence tests eqi$^{(i)}$ ($i \geq 0$) have been fixed for an agent program $\mathcal{P}$. Then, $\mathcal{P}$ is said to be a *b-regular agent program* w.r.t. ℓ and the eqi$^{(i)}$, if $\mathcal{P}$ is a *WRAP*, $\ell \in \text{wtn}(\mathcal{P})$, and each layer $\mathcal{P}_i$ of $\mathcal{P}$ is (eqi$^{(i)}$, b)-bounded.

DEFINITION 12.3.13 (REGULAR AGENT)   An agent is said to be *regular* w.r.t. a layering ℓ and a selection of pf-constraint equivalence tests $\text{eqi}^{(i)}$, if it is weakly regular and its associated agent program is b-regular w.r.t. ℓ and the $\text{eqi}^{(i)}$, for some $b \geq 0$.

In the above definition, an agent's regularity depends on several parameters ℓ, $\text{eqi}^{(i)}$, and b. The implementation may use them as follow: it generates a layering of an agent program $\mathcal{P}$, and equivalence tests $\text{eqi}^{(i)}$ are fixed for each layer $\mathcal{P}_i$ with the help of the agent developer. It then sets b to a default value, and iteratively constructs the sequence $R_0^\ell, R_1^\ell, \ldots, R_{k+1}^\ell$; if in some step, the equivalence test

$$\text{eqi}^{(i)}\left(\text{Unfold}_\mathcal{P}^b(R), \text{Unfold}_\mathcal{P}^{b+1}(R)\right)$$

returns false, then an error is flagged at compile time. The b parameter can be reset by the agent developer. However, for most agents, a sufficiently large b (e.g., $b = 500$) may be adequate.

12.4 Compile-Time Algorithms

In this section, we develop algorithms used in the compilation phase—that is, when the agent developer has built the agent and is either testing it, or is about to deploy it. This phase has two major components—checking if an agent is weakly regular, and computing an "initial" reasonable status set of the agent.

12.4.1 Checking Weak Regularity

In this section, we present an algorithm, **Check_WRAP**, for checking whether a given agent program $\mathcal{P}$ is weakly regular. As we have already discussed methods for checking safety and strong safety of code call conditions earlier on in this book, we will focus our discussion on checks for the conflict-freedom and deontic stratifiability conditions. Note that these two conditions are *closely interlinked*. It is easy to use the strong safety check algorithm to check whether an agent is safe because this algorithm can be directly used to verify whether an action is strongly safe, an action constraint is strongly safe, and an integrity constraint is strongly safe.

The conflict-freedom conditions can be readily checked, as they do not depend on a layering ℓ. The function cft (r_i, r_j) is used to check the first conflict freedom condition, while adapted efficient unification algorithms, e.g., (Paterson and Wegman 1978), may be used to check the second condition. However, the check for deontic stratification conditions is more complex. Different methods can be applied, and we outline here a method which is based on computing the (maximal) strongly connected components of a graph $G = (V, E)$. This method extends similar methods for finding stratifications of logic programs, cf. (Ullman 1989).

A *strongly connected component* (*SCC*) of a directed graph $G = (V, E)$ is a maximal set $C \subseteq V$ of vertices (maximal w.r.t. set inclusion) such that between every pair of vertices $v, v' \in C$, there exists a path from v to v' in G involving only vertices from C. For any graph G, we can define its *supergraph* $S(G) = (V^*, E^*)$ as the graph whose vertices are the strongly connected components of G, and such that there is an edge $C \to C'$ in E^*, if there is an edge from some vertex $v \in C$ to some vertex $v' \in C'$ in the graph G. Note that the supergraph $S(G)$ is acyclic. Using Tarjan's algorithm, see e.g. (Moret and Shapiro 1991), the SCCs of G, and thus the supergraph $S(G)$, is computable in time $O(|V| + |E|)$, i.e., in linear time from G.

The method for checking the stratification conditions is now to build a graph G whose vertices are the rules in $\mathcal{P}$. There is an edge from rule r to rule r' if $\ell(r') \leq \ell(r)$ follows from one of the two deontic stratification conditions. From the SCCs of G, we may easily check whether $\mathcal{P}$ is deontically stratified, and from $S(G)$, a layering $\ell \in \text{wtn}(\mathcal{P})$ witnessing this fact can be obtained by a variant of topological sorting. The following example discusses the graph and supergraph associated with an example agent program, and illustrates the intuition underlying this algorithm.

Example 12.4.1 (Layering Through Graphs) Let $\mathcal{P}$ be the agent program given in Example 12.2.3 on page 482. Then the first condition of deontic statifiability requires $\ell(r_0) \leq \ell(r_4) \leq \ell(r_2) \leq \ell(r_1)$. Also, the second condition of deontic statifiability requires $\ell(r_4) < \ell(r_3)$. Thus, we obtain the following graph G:

$$r_1 \longrightarrow r_2 \longrightarrow r_4 \longrightarrow r_0$$
$$\uparrow$$
$$r_3$$

In other words, $E = \{(r_1, r_2), (r_2, r_4), (r_4, r_0), (r_3, r_4)\}$ and $V = \{r_0, r_1, r_2, r_3, r_4\}$. Since there are no cycles in G, supergraph $S(G) = (V^*, E^*)$ where $V^* = \{\{r_i\} \mid r_i \in V\}$ and $E^* = \{(\{r_i\}, \{r_j\}) \mid (r_i, r_j) \in E\}$. Here, since each vertex has its own SCC, $\mathcal{P}$ is deontically stratified. Furthermore, our variant of "reverse" topological sort reveals that $\ell(r_0) = 0$, $\ell(r_4) = 1$, $\ell(r_2) = \ell(r_3) = 2$, and $\ell(r_1) = 3$.

The algorithm, **Check_WRAP**, used to check whether an agent program $\mathcal{P}$ is weakly regular is shown below.

The following example shows how the above algorithm works on an example agent program.

Example 12.4.2 (Algorithm Check_WRAP) Let $\mathcal{P}$ be the agent program given in Example 12.2.3 on page 482. Then **Check_WRAP**($\mathcal{P}$) begins by ensuring that every rule and action in $\mathcal{P}$ is strongly safe w.r.t. our FINTAB. It also ensures that there are no conflicts

Section 12.4   Compile-Time Algorithms   495

Algorithm 12.4.1
Check_WRAP($\mathcal{P}$)

(⋆ input is an agent program $\mathcal{P}$, a conflict-freedom test cft , and a finiteness table FINTAB ⋆)
(⋆ output is a layering $\ell \in \text{wtn}(\mathcal{P})$, if $\mathcal{P}$ is regular and "no" otherwise   ⋆)

1. **If** some action α or rule r in $\mathcal{P}$ is not strongly safe **then return** "no" and **halt**.
2. **If** some rules $r: \text{Op}(\alpha(\vec{X}))$ and $r': \text{Op}'(\alpha(\vec{Y}))$ in $\mathcal{P}$ exist such that cft $(r, r') = \textit{false}$, **then return** "no" and **halt**.
3. **If** a rule $r: \text{Op}_i(\alpha(\vec{X})) \leftarrow \ldots, (\neg)\text{Op}_j(\alpha(\vec{Y})), \ldots$ is in $\mathcal{P}$ such that $\text{Op}_i(\alpha(\vec{X}))$ and $\text{Op}_j(\alpha(\vec{Y}))$ conflict, **then return** "no" and **halt**.
4. Build the graph $G = (V, E)$, where $V = \mathcal{P}$ and an edge $r_i \to r$ is in E for each pair of rules r_i and r as in the two stratifiability conditions.
5. Compute, using Tarjan's algorithm, the supergraph $S(G) = (V^*, E^*)$ of G.
6. **If** some rules r_i, r as in the second stratifiability condition exists such that $r_i, r \in C$ for some $C \in V^*$, **then return** "no" and **halt else** set $i := 0$.
7. For each $C \in V^*$ having out-degree 0 (i.e., no outgoing edge) in $S(G)$, and each rule $r \in C$, define $\ell(r) := i$.
8. Remove each of the above C's from $S(G)$, and remove all incoming edges associated with such nodes in $S(G)$ and set $i := i + 1$;
9. **If** $S(G)$ is empty, i.e., $V^* = \emptyset$, **then return** ℓ and **halt else** continue at 7.

---

between or within $\mathcal{P}$'s rules. If everything is ok, it builds the graph G and supergraph $S(G)$ given in Example 12.4.1 on the facing page and ensures that $\mathcal{P}$ is deontically stratifiable. If it is not, then $\mathcal{P}$ cannot be a *WRAP* so an error message is returned and the algorithm halts. Otherwise, since v_0^* has no outgoing edges, ℓ assigns r_0 to layer $i = 0$, v_0^* and (v_4^*, v_0^*) are removed from $S(G)$, and i is incremented. Since $V^* \neq \emptyset$, we continue the loop by assigning $\ell(r_4)$ to layer $i = 1$, removing v_4^*, (v_2^*, v_4^*), (v_3^*, v_4^*) from $S(G)$, and incrementing i. V^* is still nonempty so ℓ assigns r_2 and r_3 to layer $i = 2$ (since v_2^* and v_3^* now have no outgoing edges), v_2^*, (v_1^*, v_2^*), v_3^* are removed from $S(G)$, and i is incremented. Finally, ℓ assigns r_1 to layer $i = 3$, v_1^* is removed from $S(G)$, i is incremented, and layering ℓ is returned since V^* is now empty.

The following theorem states that Algorithm **Check_WRAP** is correct.

THEOREM 12.4.1   For any agent program $\mathcal{P}$, **Check_WRAP**($\mathcal{P}$) returns w.r.t. a conflict-freedom test cft and a finiteness table FINTAB, a layering $\ell \in \text{wtn}(\mathcal{P})$ if $\mathcal{P}$ is a *WRAP*, and returns "no" if $\mathcal{P}$ is not regular.

Proof   It is straightforward to show that if **Check_WRAP** returns a layering ℓ, then $\mathcal{P}$ is weakly regular and $\ell \in \text{wtn}(\mathcal{P})$ holds. On the other hand, suppose the algorithm returns "no". If it halts in step 2 or 3, then the first (resp. second) condition of conflict freedom is violated for any layering ℓ, and thus $\mathcal{P}$ is not weakly regular. If it halts in step 6, then, by definition of G, a sequence of rules $r_0, r_1, \ldots, r_n$, $n \geq 1$, exists such that any layering ℓ satisfying the stratifiability conditions must, without loss of generality, satisfy $\ell(r_0) \leq \ell(r_1) \leq \cdots \leq \ell(r_n)$ and $\ell(r_n) < \ell(r_0)$. However, this means $\ell(r_0) < \ell(r_0)$, which implies that such an ℓ is impossible. Thus, the algorithm correctly returns that $\mathcal{P}$ is not weakly regular. ∎

Complexity of Algorithm Check_WRAP. We start by observing that steps 5 through 9 can be implemented to run in time linear in the size of G by using appropriate data structures, that is, in $O(|\mathcal{P}|^2)$ time (note that $S(G)$ is not larger than G).

In Step 1, checking whether an action α or a rule r is strongly safe can be done in time linear in the size of the description of α or the size of r, respectively, times the size of FINTAB. If we suppose that the action base $\mathcal{AB}$ in the background and the FINTAB are fixed, this means that Step 1 is feasible in $O(\|\mathcal{P}\|)$ time, where $\|\mathcal{P}\|$ is the size of the representation of $\mathcal{P}$, i.e., in linear time. The time for Step 2 depends on the time required by cft (r, r')—if $t_{cft}(\mathcal{P})$ is an upper bound for the time spent on a call of cft (r, r'), then Step 2 needs $O(|\mathcal{P}|^2 \cdot t_{cft}(\mathcal{P}))$ time. Step 3 can be done in $O(\|\mathcal{P}\| t_u(\mathcal{P}))$ time, where $t_u(\mathcal{P})$ is the maximal time spent on unifying two atoms in $\mathcal{P}$. Finally, Step 4 can be done in $O(|\mathcal{P}|^2 t_u(\mathcal{P}))$ time.

Thus, extending the assumption for Step 1 by further assuming that atoms and rule bodies have size bounded by a constant—an assumption that is certainly plausible, since the number of literals in a rule body is not expected to exceed 20, say, and each literal will, as a string, hardly occupy more than 1024 characters—we obtain that **Check_WRAP**($\mathcal{P}$) can be executed in $O(|\mathcal{P}|^2 t_{cft}(\mathcal{P}))$ time. This bound further decreases to $O(|\mathcal{P}| t_{cft}(\mathcal{P}))$ time if for each action α and modality Op, only a few rules (bounded by a constant) with head Op $\alpha(\cdot)$ exist in $\mathcal{P}$. These assumptions on the "shape" of the rules and the program seem to be reasonable with respect to agent programs in practice. Thus, we may expect that **Check_WRAP** runs in $O(|\mathcal{P}| \cdot t_{cft}(\mathcal{P}))$ time. In particular, for an efficient implementation of a cft as in Examples 12.1.3 on page 470– 12.1.5 on page 471, it runs in $O(|\mathcal{P}|)$ time, i.e., in linear time in the number of rules.

We conclude this subsection with the remark that **Check_WRAP** can be modified to compute the canonical layering can$^\mathcal{P}$ as follows. For each node $C \in V^*$, use two counters $out(C)$ and $block(C)$, and initialize them in step 5 to the number of outgoing edges from C in E^*. Steps 7 and 8 of **Check_WRAP** are replaced by the following steps:

7'. Set $U := \emptyset$;
    while some $C \in V^*$ exists such that $block(C) = 0$ **do**
    $U := U \cup \{C\}$;
    Set $out(C') := out(C') - 1$ for each $C' \in V^*$ such that $C' \rightarrow C$;

Set $block(C') := block(C') - 1$ for each $C' \in V^*$ such that $C' \to C$ due to the first stratification condition but not the second stratification condition.

for each rule r in $\bigcup U$ **do** $\ell(r) := i$;

8'. Set $i := i + 1$;

Remove each node $C \in U$ from $S(G)$, and set $block(C) := out(C)$ for each retained node C.

When properly implemented, steps 7' and 8' can be executed in linear time in the size of $S(G)$, and thus of G. Thus, the upper bounds on the time complexity of **Check_Regular** discussed above also apply to the variant which computes the canonical layering.

Thus, at this stage we have provided a complete definition of a weakly regular agent program, together with an efficient compile-time algorithm for determining whether an agent program is weakly regular or not.

12.4.2 Computing Reasonable Status Sets

As we have already remarked previously in this chapter, computing the unique reasonable status set (if one exists) of a regular agent program can be done by first computing the status set $\Gamma_{\mathcal{P},\mathcal{O}_S}^{\ell_1} \uparrow \omega$ and then checking if this status set satisfies the integrity and action constraints.

Even though Algorithm **Reasonable_SS** can be executed on weakly regular agent programs, rather than *RAPs*, there is no guarantee of termination in that case. The following theorem states the result that for a regular agent, its reasonable status set on an agent state is effectively computable.

Algorithm 12.4.2
Reasonable-SS($\mathcal{P}, \ell, \mathcal{IC}, \mathcal{AC}, \mathcal{O}_S$)

($\star$ input is a regular agent consisting of a RAP $\mathcal{P}$, a layering $\ell \in \text{wtn}(\mathcal{P})$, $\star$)
($\star$ a strongly safe set $\mathcal{IC}$ of integrity constraints, $\star$)
($\star$ a strongly safe set $\mathcal{AC}$ of action constraints, and an agent state $\mathcal{O}_S$, $\star$)
($\star$ output is a reasonable status set S of $\mathcal{P}$ on $\mathcal{O}_S$, if one exists, and "no" otherwise. $\star$)

1. $S := \Gamma_{\mathcal{P},\mathcal{O}_S}^{l} \uparrow \omega$;
2. $\mathbf{Do}(S) := \{\alpha \mid \mathbf{Do}(\alpha) \in S\}$;
3. **while** $\mathcal{AC} \neq \emptyset$ **do**
   select and remove some $ac \in \mathcal{AC}$;
   if ac is not satisfied w.r.t. $\mathbf{Do}(S)$ **then return** "no" and **halt**;
4. $\mathcal{O}_S' :=$ apply $\mathbf{conc}(\mathbf{Do}(S), \mathcal{O}_S)$; ($\star$ resulting successor state $\star$)
5. **while** $\mathcal{IC} \neq \emptyset$ **do**
   select and remove some $ic \in \mathcal{IC}$;
   if $\mathcal{O}_S' \not\models ic$ **then return** "no" and **halt**.
6. **return** S and **halt**.

THEOREM 12.4.2   If $\mathfrak{a}$ is a regular agent, then algorithm **Reasonable_SS** computes a reasonable status set (if one exists) in finite time.

Proof   We have to show that each of the steps 1–5 of the algorithm can be done in finite time. As for step 1, the boundedness of the agent program $\mathcal{P}$ associated with $\mathfrak{a}$ ensures that the set $\Gamma^l_{\mathcal{P},\mathcal{O}_S} \uparrow \omega$ is computable within a bounded number of steps: For computing $\Gamma^l_{\mathcal{P},\mathcal{O}_S} \uparrow i$, we must compute the operator $\mathbf{T}^\omega_{\mathcal{P}_i,\mathcal{O}_S}$ from (Def. 12.2.1 on page 479) associated with the layer $\mathcal{P}_i$, which needs to apply the operator $\mathbf{T}_{\mathcal{P}_i\mathcal{O}_S}$ only a bounded number of times. Furthermore, the number of nonempty layers $\mathcal{P}_i$ is bounded as well. An inductive argument shows that in each step $S_0, S_1, S_2, \ldots S_m = \Gamma^l_{\mathcal{P},\mathcal{O}_S} \uparrow \omega$ of the fixpoint computation, any rule r from the layer $\mathcal{P}_i$ currently considered instantiates due to strong safety only to a finite number of ground rules r' which fire. These r' can be effectively computed from the status set S_k derived so far (where $S_0 = \emptyset$), proceeding as follows. Let Θ be the set of ground substitutions such that $B^+_{as}(r)$ is true w.r.t. S_k. Since, by induction hypothesis, S_k is finite, Θ can be computed in finite time. Next, for each $\theta \in \Theta$, the set of all ground substitutions γ that satisfy $B_{cc}(r\theta)$ is finite and is effectively computable. For each such γ, it is effectively checkable whether for the ground instance $r' = r\theta\gamma$ of r, the part $B^-_{as}(r')$ is true w.r.t. S_k (i.e., $\neg.B^-_{as}(r') \cap S_k = \emptyset$), and whether for each atom $\text{Op}\alpha$ from $B^+_{as}(r') \cup \{head(r')\}$ such that $\text{Op} \in \{\mathbf{O}, \mathbf{Do}, \mathbf{P}\}$ it holds that α is executable in $\mathcal{O}_S$. The instances of r which fire are precisely all rules of this form. Since this yields only finitely many new action status atoms, also S_{k+1} is finite and effective computable. It follows that $\Gamma^l_{\mathcal{P},\mathcal{O}_S} \uparrow \omega$ is computed within finite time.

Step 2 is simple. Step 3 can be effectively accomplished: Strong safety of each action constraint $ac: \{\alpha_1(\vec{X}_1), \ldots, \alpha_k(\vec{X}_k)\} \hookleftarrow \chi$ ensures that χ has only finitely many solutions θ, which can be effectively computed; furthermore, matching the head $\alpha_1(\vec{X}_1), \ldots, \alpha_k(\vec{X}_k)$ to atoms $\alpha_1(\vec{t}_1), \ldots, \alpha_k(\vec{t}_k)$ in $\mathbf{Do}(S)$ such that $\alpha_i(\vec{X}_i\theta') = \alpha_i(\vec{t}_i)$, $i = 1, \ldots, k$, where θ' extends θ, can be done in polynomial time in the size of $\mathbf{Do}(S)$.

The new agent state $\mathcal{O}'_S$ in Step 4 is, by specification, effectively computable. Finally, also Step 5 can be done in finite time, since strong safety implies that for each integrity constraint $ic: \psi \Rightarrow \chi$ in $\mathcal{IC}$, the body ψ has only a finite number of ground instances $\psi\theta$ which are true in the agent state, and they are effectively computable; since χ is strongly safe checking whether $\chi\theta$ is true is possible in finite time. ∎

This leaves us with the question *in what time* the reasonable status set can be computed. We cannot be sure, a priori, hat this is possible in polynomial time, as strong safety of rules just ensures a finite but arbitrarily large of solutions to a code call; likewise, comparison atoms $\mathtt{X} < \mathtt{t}$, where $\mathtt{t}$ is e.g. an integer, may instantiate to an exponential number of solutions (measured in the number of bits needed to store $\mathtt{t}$). Thus, we need some further assertions to guarantee polynomial-time evaluability.

Section 12.4   Compile-Time Algorithms

For convenience, call an occurrence of a variable X in a strongly safe code call condition χ *loose* w.r.t. a set $\vec{X}$ of variables, if X is not from $\vec{X}$ and does not occur as the result of a code call **in**(X, ·) or **not_in**(X, ·) in χ. Intuitively, a loose occurrence of a variable X may be instantiated without accessing the agent state, with some value drawn from X's domain. Based on this, loose occurrence of a variable X in a strongly safe action, rule, integrity and action constraint is defined in the obvious way.

THEOREM 12.4.3   Suppose a is a fixed regular agent. Assume that the following holds:

(1) Every ground code call $S : f(d_1, \ldots, d_n)$ has a polynomial set of solutions, which is computed in polynomial time; and

(2) no occurrence of a variable in a's description loose.

Furthermore, assume that assembling and executing **conc**(**Do**(S), $\mathcal{O}_S$) is possible in polynomial time in the size of **Do**(S) and $\mathcal{O}_S$. Then, algorithm **Reasonable_SS** computes a reasonable status set (if one exists) on a given agent state $\mathcal{O}_S$ in polynomial time (in the size of $\mathcal{O}_S$).

Proof   We have to argue that each of the steps 1–5 can be done in polynomial time, rather than in arbitrary finite time. This can be accomplished by refining the analysis in the proof of Theorem 12.4.2 on the facing page.

As for Step 1, the cardinality of the set Θ of substitutions such that $B_{as}^+(r)$ is true w.r.t. the already derived status set S_k is polynomial in the the size of S_k. Under the assumptions, this set is computable in polynomial time. Next, for each $\theta \in \Theta$, the assumptions imply that the set Γ_θ contains only polynomially many assignments γ, each of which is computable in polynomial time. The check whether $B_{as}^-(r')$ where $r' = (r\theta\gamma)$ is true w.r.t. S_k is easy, and the test whether r' is actually fired is feasible in time polynomial in the size of $\mathcal{O}_S$. Overall, the number of instances r' of r which eventually fire is polynomial in the size S_k and the agent state.

This means the number $N_k = |S_k|$ of atoms Op α that are derived after k steps of firing rules (where $N_0 = 0$), is bounded by $p(N_{k-1}, |\mathcal{O}_S|)$, where p is some polynomial and $|\mathcal{O}_S|$ is the size of the agent state, and S_k is computable in polynomial time. Since $\mathcal{P}$ is associated with a regular agent, the number of steps in computing $S := \Gamma^l_{\mathcal{P}, \mathcal{O}_S} \uparrow \omega$ is bounded by some (a priori known) constant b. Thus, it follows that the number of atoms in S is polynomial, and that S is computable in polynomial time. This shows that Step 1 is computable in polynomial time.

Step 3 can be done in polynomial time, since the assumptions imply that each body χ of an action constraint *ac* has only a polynomial number of solutions, which are computable in polynomial time, and matching the head of *ac* against S is polynomial. Step 4 can be done in polynomial time, since assembling and executing **conc**(**Do**(S), $\mathcal{O}_S$) is polynomial and **Do**(S) is polynomial in the size of $\mathcal{O}_S$, which means that the size of the resulting state $\mathcal{O}'_S$ is polynomial in the size of $\mathcal{O}_S$.

Finally, Step 5 is polynomial, since the body ψ of each integrity constraint $ic: \psi \Rightarrow \chi$ has a polynomial number of solutions θ, which are computable in polynomial time, and checking whether $\chi\theta$ is true in state $\mathcal{O}'_S$ is polynomial in the size of $\mathcal{O}'_S$ (and thus of $\mathcal{O}_S$).
∎

Forbidding loose occurrences of a variable X in an atom such as X < t is not overly restrictive in general; using a special domain function $types:dom(\tau)$, which returns the elements of type τ, we can eliminate the loose occurrence by joining the code call atom **in**(X, $types:dom(\tau)$), where τ is the domain of X. Or, we might use a special domain comparison function $types:less\_than(\tau, X)$, which returns all values of τ which are less than X, and replace X < t by **in**(X, $types:less\_than(\tau, t)$). Due to the assumed downward finiteness property, the latter has a guaranteed finite set of solutions, which is not true for **in**(X, $types:dom(\tau)$) if τ is infinite.

12.5 The Query Maintenance Package

In this section, we will describe how RAPs are implemented within the *IMPACT* architecture via a specialized package called the *Query Maintenance Package*. The basic idea behind this package is simple. Agents need to *continuously* recompute their reasonable status sets, based on the latest set of state changes that have occurred (which in turn are triggered by messages received). We would like to reduce this run-time computation load on the agent as much as possible. We do this by ensuring that when the agent is deployed, a certain data structure called the **QMPtab** defined in Section 12.5 is initialized. The **QMPtab** contains a succinct, non ground description of the agent's reasonable status set at *any given point in time*, i.e., it is state independent. With every operator Op ∈ {**O**, **P**, **Do**, **F**, **W**}, and every action $\alpha(\vec{X})$ with all nonground parameters, it associates a single query, which when evaluated against the current agent state specifies which instances of Op $\alpha(\vec{X})$ are true in the current reasonable status set of the agent. Then, in Section 12.5.1, we describe a set of functions that may be used, both at run-time and compile time, to perform computations based on the **QMPtab**. These operators perform the basic computations needed by any agent.

The QMPtab Data Structure The **QMPtab** is a table having the schema (Opr, Action, PFC) where:

1. Op is one of the five operators **F, P, O, Do, W**;
2. Action is of the form $\alpha(X_1, \ldots, X_n)$ where α is an action name having schema $(\tau_1, \ldots, \tau_n)$ and each $X_i \in Var(\tau_i)$ (i.e., each X_i is a variable over objects of type τ_i);
3. PFC is a pf-constraint.

For each Op $\in$ {**F, P, O, Do, W**} and each action name α, **QMPtab** contains *exactly one* row having Opr = Op and Action = $\alpha(\ldots)$.

Example 12.5.1 A small example **QMPtab** is shown below.

Op	Action	PFC
O	$\alpha(X)$	**in**(X, d : f(a, b)) & $X < 5$.
Do	$\alpha(X)$	**in**(X, d : f(a, b)) & $X < 2$.
F	$\alpha(X)$	**in**(X, d : f(a, b)) & $X > 10$.
P	$\alpha(X)$	**in**(X, d : f(a, b)) & $X < 8$.
W	$\alpha(X)$	false

Intuitively, the first row of this table says that to determine the set of all action status atoms of the form $\mathbf{O}\alpha(t)$ that are true in this agent's unique reasonable status set, all we need to do is to evaluate the code call condition **in**(X, d : f(a, b)) & $X < 5$ w.r.t. the current state of the agent. The other rows in this table may be similarly interpreted. Note that the **QMPtab** therefore does not depend on the state, though the evaluation of the entries in the PFC column certainly does.

In general, given any **QMPtab**, we may associate with it a unique status set **SS(QMPtab)** as follows:

SS(QMPtab) = {Op $\alpha(\vec{X}\theta)$ | there is a row $r \in$ **QMPtab** such that r.Op = Op, r.Action = $\alpha(\vec{X})$, $\alpha(\vec{X}\theta)$ is ground and r.PFCθ is true}.

Here, truth of the pf-constraint r.PFC is with respect to the current agent state. As we can see, QMP may be used to succinctly represent status sets. What we would *like* is to ensure that at any given point in time **SS(QMPtab)** is in fact the unique reasonable status set of the underlying RAP with w.r.t. the agent's state at that point in time.

The basic idea is to first compute such a **QMPtab** when the agent is deployed. As changes occur, we would like to use the **QMPtab** to rapidly compute the set of all **Do**-actions that the agent must perform, given the occurrence of the changes. This will be done via the qmp:update function described in Section 12.5.1.

12.5.1 QMP Function Calls

The QMP package supports a set of function calls. The input/output signatures of these function calls, together with the intended use of these function calls is listed here—succeeding sections discuss their implementation.

- qmp:init(action base $\mathcal{AB}$; software code $\mathcal{S}$)

This function initializes the **QMPtab** so that **SS(QMPtab)** coincides with the unique reasonable status set of the agent program. This is done by first directly computing $\text{Unfold}_\mathcal{P}^b$. If $\text{Op}\,\alpha \leftarrow \chi$ is in $\text{Unfold}_\mathcal{P}^b$, then the triple $(\text{Op}, \alpha, \chi)$ is placed in **QMPtab**. The implementation of qmp:init is described in Section 12.5.1.

- qmp:eval(action status atom $\text{Op}\,\alpha(\vec{t})$; agent state $\mathcal{O}_\mathcal{S}$; software code $\mathcal{S}$)

Given an action status atom $\text{Op}\,\alpha(\vec{t})$, may associate with it a pfc-constraint γ by finding the pfc-constraint γ' associated with $\text{Op}\,\alpha(\vec{X})$ in **QMPtab** and setting $\gamma = \gamma'\,\&\,\vec{X} = \vec{t}$. We then need to evaluate γ over the current agent state and output the set of all solutions to γ on $\mathcal{O}_\mathcal{S}$. The qmp:eval function does this, building on top of the existing implementation of the HERMES Heterogeneous Reasoning and Mediator System developed at the University of Maryland (Adali et al. 1996; Brink et al. 1995; Lu et al. 1996).

- qmp:update(software code $\mathcal{S}$)

At any given point t in time, the agent has a reasonable status set. When the state of the agent changes through the receipt of one or more messages, the agent must determine what new actions must be performed, i.e., it must compute the set of all actions of the form $\text{Do}\,\alpha(\vec{t})$ that are true in the new reasonable status set of the agent (w.r.t. the state of the agent after receipt of the messages). The qmp:update algorithm tries to avoid a brute-force computation of this set.

We will now describe the three functions from above in more detail.

The qmp:init Function Note that for any Op and any action $\alpha(\vec{X})$, $\text{Unfold}_\mathcal{P}^i$ contains exactly one rule of the form

$$\text{Op}\,\alpha(\vec{X}) \leftarrow \text{pfc}_i.$$

This pf-constraint can be represented in a straightforward way as an AND/OR tree. The leaves of the tree are either code call conditions, or negated action status atoms, while the interior nodes are labeled with either the connective $\vee$ or $\&$. For example, consider the following pf-constraint rule.

$$\mathbf{P}\beta(X, Y) \leftarrow Y = a\,\&\,\mathbf{in}(X, \mathcal{S} : f(a, a)) \vee$$
$$Y = a\,\&\,\mathbf{in}(X, \mathcal{S} : f(a, b))\,\&\,\neg\mathbf{Do}\gamma(X).$$

Section 12.5 The Query Maintenance Package

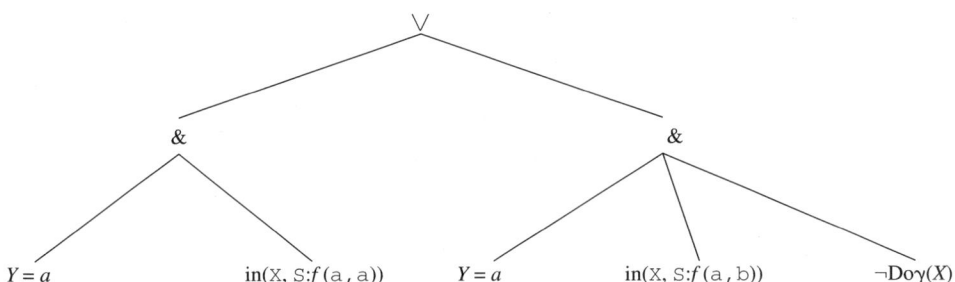

Figure 12.2
An example AND/OR tree associated with a pf-constraint.

Figure 12.2 shows the AND/OR tree associated with the body of this pf-constraint rule. Note that this AND/OR tree is nothing more than a parse tree associated with a pf-constraint. When unfolding is performed, and pfc_i is updated to a new AND/OR parse tree pfc_{i+1} the AND/OR parse tree associated with pfc_i can be straightforwardly extended to one associated with pfc_{i+1}.

It is important to note that the AND/OR tree associated with a pf-constraint may often contain repeated code calls and/or code calls whose answers are subsets of other code calls. In such cases, there are alternative representations (e.g., a directed acyclic graph) and various ways to optimize such trees by modifying standard query optimization methods in databases (Ullman 1989). We will not go into this issue in greater detail.

The qmp:eval Function Consider any pair $(\mathsf{Op}, \alpha(\vec{X}))$. After unfolding the RAP out completely using the qmp:init function, this pair has an associated pf-constraint in **QMPtab** which is represented as an AND/OR tree. The qmp:eval function evaluates these pf-constraints bottom up (i.e., starting from leaf nodes). It associates a SOL field with each non-leaf node in the AND/OR tree. This field is intended to find the set of all solutions of the pf-constraint rooted at that node, and is initially set to be empty. The following algorithm specifies how to associate a SOL field with a non-leaf node and compute the final answer.

1. **Associating SOL Fields with Interior Nodes.**

(a) *The node is an "&" node.* In this case, the children of the node fall into three categories. Either they are code call atoms, or they are negated action status atoms, or they are the root of a tree representing a sub-pf-constraint. In this case, we may proceed as follows. Recursively evaluate the conjunction of the code call part and the sub-pf-constraint part—these must be evaluable as they are each strongly safe. Let Θ be the set of all solutions of this evaluation.

Now observe that every variable occurring in a negative action status literal part (e.g., $\neg\mathsf{Op}'\beta(\vec{Y})$) must occur in the evaluated part, and hence, each solution $\theta \in \Theta$ instantiates each such variable. For each $\theta \in \Theta$ check if $\neg\mathsf{Op}'\beta(\vec{Y}\theta)$ is true for *each* negated literal that is a child of the "&" node referenced above. Set *SOL* to $\{\theta \mid \theta \in \Theta$ and $\neg\mathsf{Op}'\beta(\vec{Y}\theta)$ is true for all negated action status atoms that are children of $\Theta\}$.

(b) *The node is an "$\vee$" Node.* Recursively evaluate all its children. If $C_1, \ldots, C_n$ are its children, and these children have $SOL_1, \ldots, SOL_n$ as their solutions, respectively, let $SOL = \bigcup_{i=1}^{n} SOL_i$.

2. **Returning the Answer.** Return the set $\{\pi_{\vec{x}}(\theta) \mid \theta \in SOL(ROOT)\}$ where *ROOT* is the root of the tree associated with $(\mathsf{Op}, \alpha(\vec{X}))$.

Notice that for the above procedure to work, for each ground negated action status atom $\neg\mathsf{Op}'\beta(\vec{Y}\theta)$, we must already know the set of solutions of $\mathsf{Op}'\beta(\vec{Y})$. This means that we must always invoke the qmp:eval function bottom up starting with action status atoms defined in the bottom most layer of the RAP, and work our way up.

Let us illustrate this procedure on the example AND/OR tree shown in Figure 12.2 on the preceding page. We assume of course, that $\neg\mathbf{Do}\gamma(X)$ has been evaluated prior to the evaluation of this parse tree. The evaluation of the left "&" node is straightforward. Let us suppose this returns two substitutions, $\theta_1 = \{X/c, Y/a\}$ and $\theta_2 = \{X/b, Y/a\}$. Now evaluate the right "&" expression. This is done by first executing the code call condition $Y = a \,\&\, \mathsf{in}(X, \mathcal{S} : f(a, b))$. Let us assume this returns two substitutions, $\sigma_1 = \{X/a, Y/a\}$ and $\sigma_2 = \{X/b, Y/a\}$. For each of these two substitutions, we invoke $\mathbf{Do}\gamma(X)$. Suppose $\mathbf{Do}\gamma(a)$ fails, but $\mathbf{Do}\gamma(b)$ succeeds. Then SOL of the right "&" node consists just of σ_1. SOL of the root is now $\{\sigma_1, \theta_1, \theta_2\}$. The algorithm restricts them to the variables (x, y), so it just returns $\{\sigma_1, \theta_1, \theta_2\}$.

The qmp:update Function All changes to the state of the agent occur in one of two ways—(i) either the agent computes a reasonable status set which causes it to perform some state-changing actions, or (ii) the agent receives some messages from other agents that cause it to compute a new reasonable status set and take the actions prescribed in that new reasonable status set.

The first case above is clearly one that is triggered by the agent itself after computing a valid reasonable status set, so no new reasonable status set needs to be computed.

One the other hand, case (ii) above forces the agent to find a new reasonable status set based on the messages received. When an agent is regular, it can have at most one reasonable status set, viz. **SS(QMPtab)**. If **SS(QMPtab)**, when evaluated agains the state of the agent *after* the messages are received, satisfies the integrity and action constraints, then we know that it is reasonable.

In order to determine what actions to execute concurrently, the agent only needs to perform the steps listed below. In what follows, when we refer to "evaluation" of a status atom, $\mathsf{Op}\,\alpha(\vec{X})$, we mean finding the set of all ground instances of that status atom such that the pf-constraint associated with $\mathsf{Op}\,\alpha(\vec{X})$ is true.

(1) Create a graph whose vertices are action status atoms as follows:

 – For each row r in **QMPtab** such that $r.\mathsf{Opr} = \mathbf{Do}$ and $r.\mathsf{Action} = \alpha(\vec{X})$ create the node $\mathbf{Do}\alpha(\vec{X})$.
 – If $\mathsf{Op}\,\beta(\vec{X})$ is a node in the graph, corresponding to the row r in **QMPtab** with $r.\mathsf{Opr} = \mathsf{Op}$ and $r.\mathsf{Action} = \beta(\vec{X})$, and a negated action status atom $\neg\mathsf{Op}'\beta'(\vec{t})$ appears in r. PFC, then $\mathsf{Op}'\beta'(\vec{Y})$ is a node in the graph, where $\mathsf{Op}'\beta'(\vec{Y})$ is in **QMPtab**, and there is an edge in the graph from $\mathsf{Op}'\beta'(\vec{Y})$ to $\mathsf{Op}\,\beta(\vec{X})$.

As $\mathcal{P}$ is a RAP, it is easy to see that this graph is acyclic. Given an action status atom A in this graph, $pred(A)$ is the set of all action status atoms A' such that there is a direct edge from A' to A in the graph. Initially, all nodes are unmarked.

(2) **while** there is an unmarked node left **do**

 – Select an action status atom $\mathsf{Op}\,\beta(\vec{X})$ such that all $B \in pred(\mathsf{Op}\,\beta(\vec{X}))$ are marked.
 – Evaluate $\mathsf{Op}\,\beta(\vec{X})$. The code call part of the associated pfc can be evaluated using any incremental view maintenance algorithm in the literature. (By selecting only action status atoms using the previous condition, we know that the negative action status atoms associated with $\mathsf{Op}\,\beta(\vec{X})$'s associated pf-constraint have been fully evaluated).
 – Mark the node labeled $\mathsf{Op}\,\beta(\vec{X})$.

(3) Let

$$DoSet = \bigcup_{DoNodes} \{\mathbf{Do}\alpha(\vec{X}\sigma) \mid \mathbf{Do}\alpha(\vec{X}\sigma) \text{ is evaluated to be true}\},$$

where *DoNodes* is the set of all nodes in this graph labeled with an action status atom of the form $\mathbf{Do}(\cdot)$.

(4) The P-, F- part etc. can be computed similarly, reusing already computed nodes. The actions in DoSet are merged by calling **conc**(Do(DoSet), $\mathcal{O}_S$), and it is checked whether executing the resulting action satisfies the action and integrity constraints.

12.6 The *IMPACT* Agent Development Environment (*IADE*)

Our implementation of the regular agent program paradigm consists of two major parts. The first part is the *IMPACT* Agent Development Environment (*IADE* for short), which is used by the developer to build and compile agents. The second part is the run-time part that

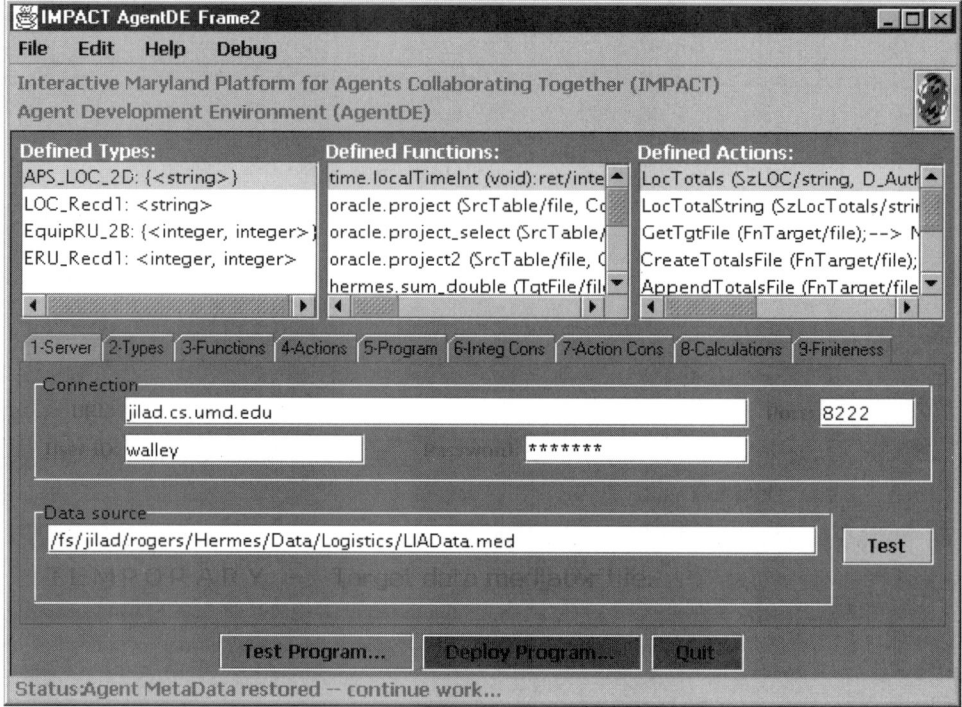

Figure 12.3
Main *IADE* Screen.

allows the agent to autonomously update its reasonable status set and execute actions as its state changes. Below, we describe each of these two parts. *IADE* supports their tasks as follows.

• First, it provides an easy to use, network accessible graphical user interface through which an agent developer can specify the data types, functions, actions, integrity constraints, action constraints, notion of concurrency and agent program associated with his/her agent.

• Second, it provides support for compilation and testing. In particular, *IADE* allows the agent developer to specify various parameters (e.g., conflict freedom test, finiteness table) he wants to use for compilation. It implements the `qmp:init` algorithm and also accesses the `qmp:eval` algorithm. It allows the agent developer to view the reasonable status set associated with his agent program w.r.t the current state of the agent.

Section 12.6 The *IMPACT* Agent Development Environment (*IADE*)   507

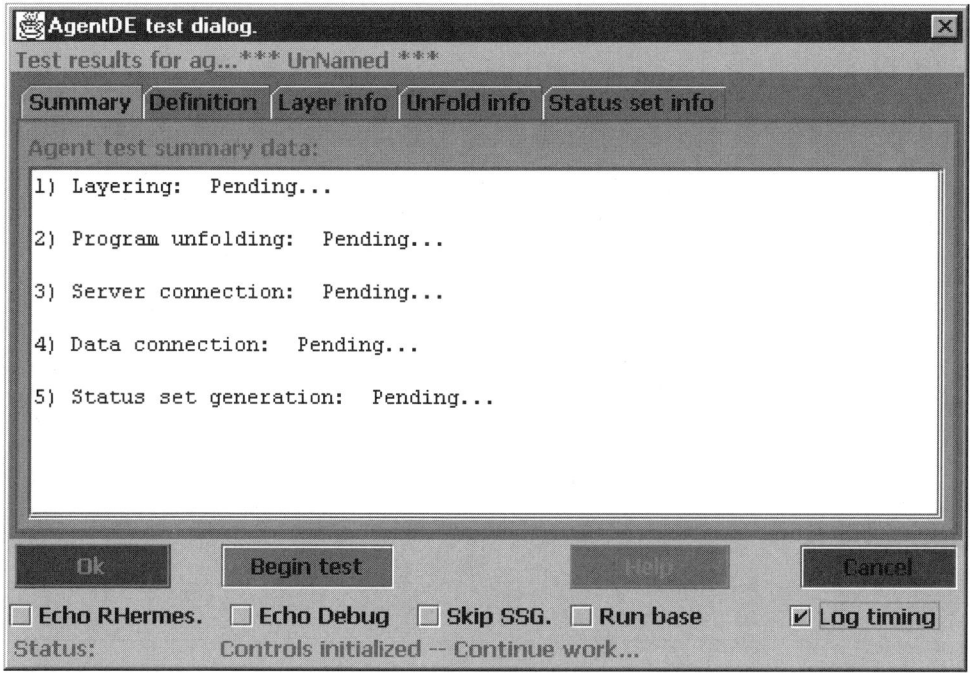

Figure 12.4
IADE Test Dialog Screen Prior to Program Testing.

The *IADE* includes the safety, strong safety, conflict freedom algorithms, and the **Check_WRAP** algorithms (the last is slightly modified). The unfold algorithm currently works on positive agent programs—this is being extended to the full fledged case.

Figure 12.3 on the preceding page shows a screendump of *IADE*'s top-level screen. When the agent developer brings up this screen, he may use the "URL" and "PORT" entries in this screen to specify connect information for his agent. He can specify where the data objects associated with this agent are located in the "Data source" entry. The three windows labeled "Defined Types", "Defined Functions" and "Defined Actions" at the top allow the user to browse types, functions and actions defined to date, using the scrollbars shown. The nine tabs below allow the agent developer to specify new types, functions, etc. The tab marked "calculations" allows the user to specify the conflict freedom test he wants to use, and the notion of concurrency he wants to use, while the tab marked "finiteness" allows the user to specify the finiteness table.

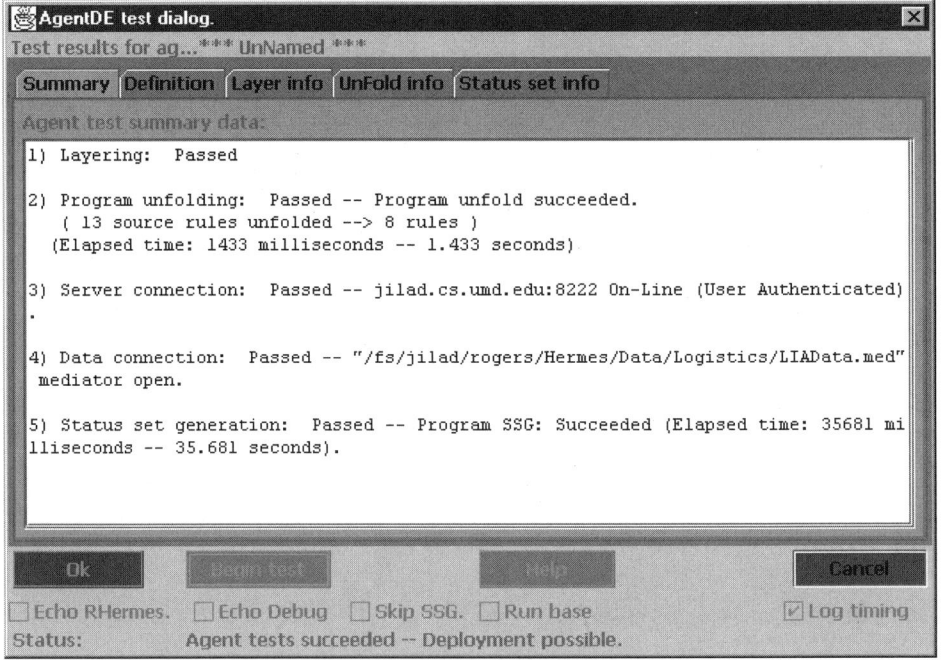

Figure 12.5
IADE Test Execution Screen.

Figure 12.4 on the preceding page specifies what happens when the agent developer presses the "Test Program" button in the Figure 12.3 on page 506 screen. The new dialog that comes up is a debug window that shows that no layering has been done (yet), no unfolding has been done yet, etc.

When the user presses the "Begin Test" button in the screen of Figure 12.4 on the preceding page, the window shown in the screen of Figure 12.5 is brought up. It shows the time taken for program unfolding, the fact that the server connection has been tested and established to work, etc. In the specific example screen shown in Figure 12.5, the agent program being considered is one used for a live logistics demonstration on a large amount of US Army War Reserves data. This application will be described in further detail in Chapter 13.

Once the status sets have been generated after the test execution phase is completed, the user can press the "Unfold Info" tab (to see the unfolded program) or the "Layer Info" tab (to see the layers of the agent program) or the "Status Set Info" tab (to see status information). Figure 12.6 on the next page shows the results of viewing the unfold information.

Section 12.6   The *IMPACT* Agent Development Environment (*IADE*)

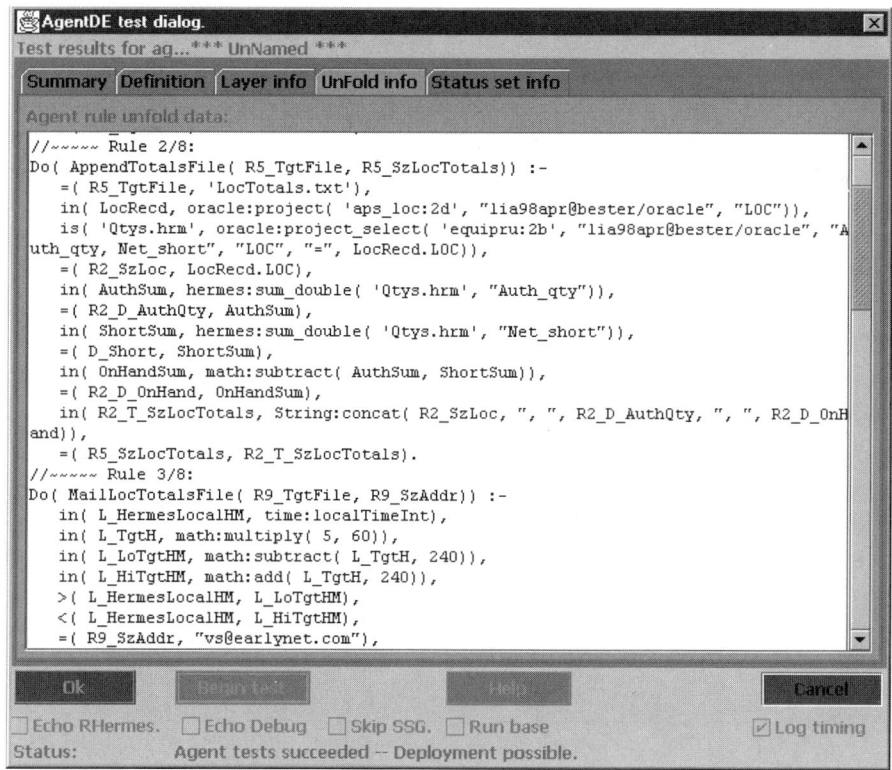

Figure 12.6
IADE Unfold Information Screen.

When the user selects the "Status set Info" tab, he sees the screen shown in Figure 12.7 on the following page. Note that this screen has tabs on the right, corresponding to the various deontic modalities. By selecting a modality, the agent developer can see what action status atoms associated with that modality are true in the status set. Figure 12.7 on the next page shows what happens when the user wishes to see all action status atoms of the form **Do**(·) in the status set.

Figure 12.8 on page 511 shows the interface used to specify the "finiteness" table. As mentioned earlier on in this chapter, in the *IMPACT* implementation, we actually represent code calls that are infinite in this table, using some extra syntax. Specifically, the first row of the table shown in Figure 12.8 on page 511 says that when $Q > 3$ and $R < 4$, all code calls of the form $\mathrm{domain}_1 : \mathit{function}_1(Q, R)$ are infinite.

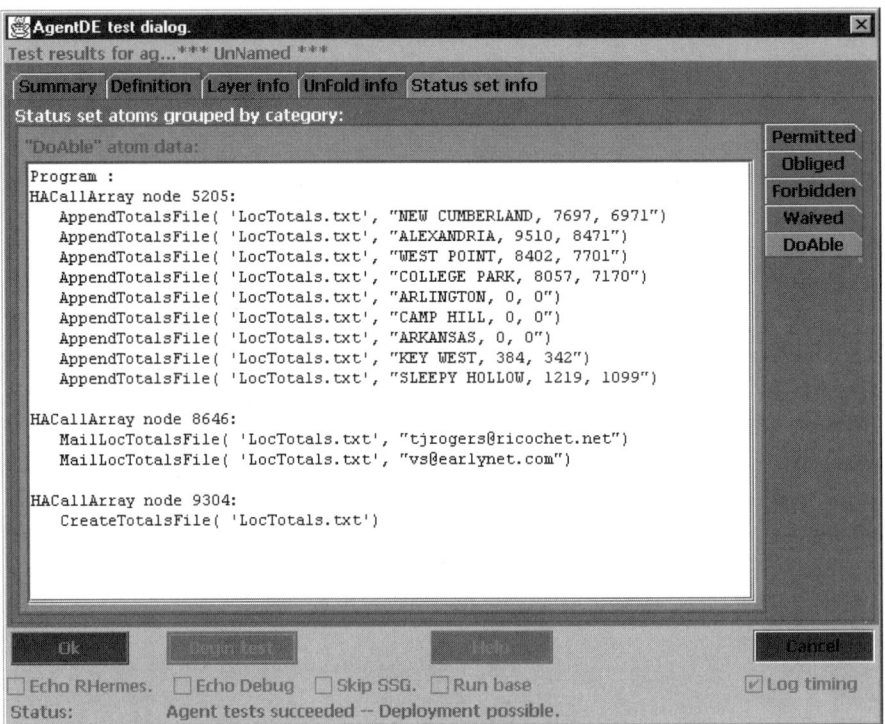

Figure 12.7
IADE Status Set Screen.

Figure 12.9 on page 512 shows the interface used by the agent developer to specify what notion of concurrency he wishes to use, what conflict freedom implementation he wishes to use and what semantics he wishes to use. Each of the items in the figure have associated drop-down menus (not visible in the picture). The last item titled "Calculation Method" enables us (as developers of *IMPACT*) to test different computation algorithms. It will be removed from the final *IMPACT* release.

It is important to note that the above interfaces are only intended for use by the agent developer, and the status set computations shown in Figure 12.7 are for the agent developer's testing needs. The run-time execution module runs as a background applet and performs the following steps: (i) Monitoring of the agent's message box, (ii) execution of the **Update_Reasonable_SS** algorithm, and (iii) concurrent execution of the actions α such that $\mathbf{Do}(\alpha)$ is in the updated reasonable status set.

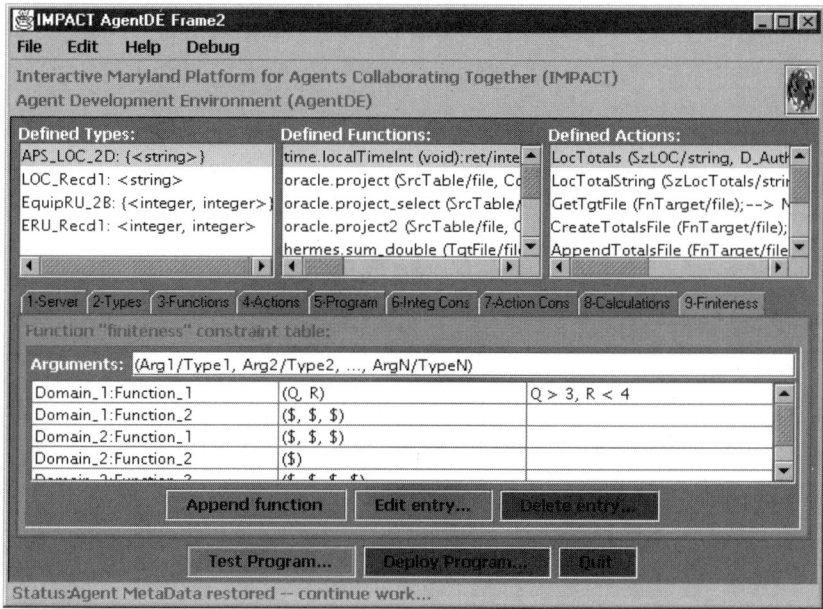

Figure 12.8
IADE (In-)Finiteness Table Screen.

12.7 Experimental Results

In this section, we overview experiments with different aspects of the *IMPACT* Agent Development Environment.

12.7.1 Performance of Safety Algorithm

Figure 12.10 on the following page shows the performance of our implemented safety check algorithm. In this experiment, we varied the number of conjuncts in a code call condition from 1 to 20 in steps of 1. This is shown on the x-axis of Figure 12.10 on the next page. For each $1 \leq i \leq 20$, we executed the **safe_ccc** algorithm 1000 times, varying the number of arguments of each code call from 1 to 10 in steps of 1, and the number of root variables occurring in the code call conditions from 1 to twice the number of conjuncts (i.e., 1 to $2i$). The actual conjuncts were generated randomly once the number of conjuncts, number of arguments, and number of root variables was fixed. For each fixed number $1 \leq i \leq 20$ of conjuncts, the execution time shown on the y-axis represents the average over 1000

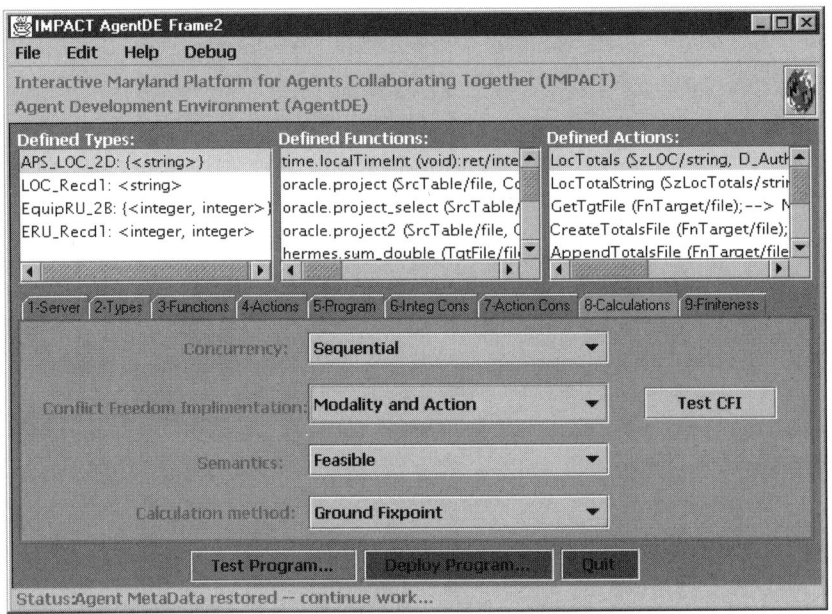

Figure 12.9
IADE Option Selection Screen.

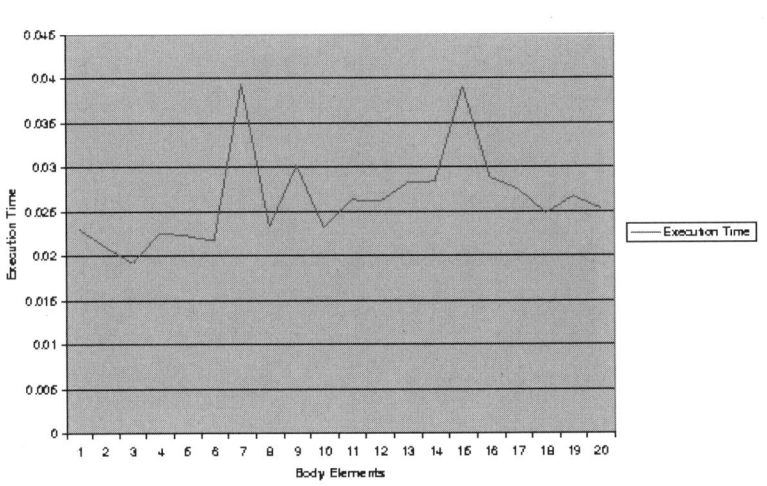

Figure 12.10
Safety Experiment Graph.

Section 12.7 Experimental Results

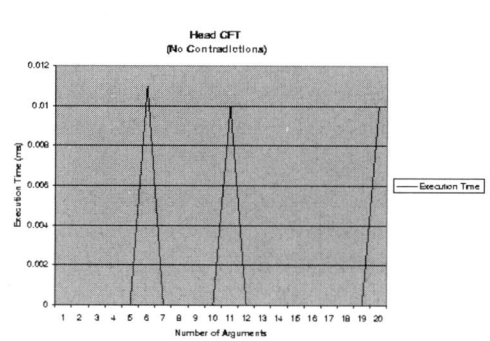

(a) HeadCFT returning "**true**"

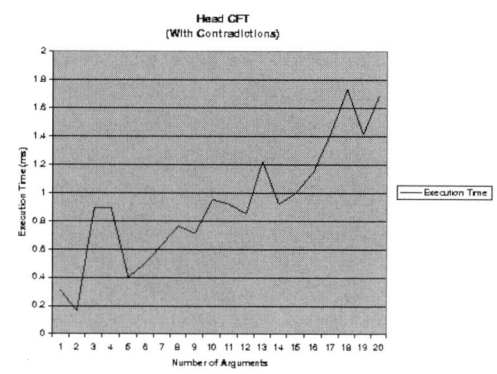

(b) HeadCFT returning "**false**"

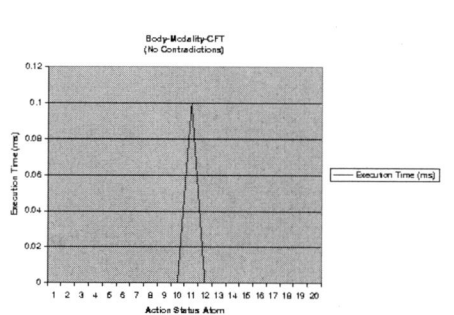

(c) BodyModalityCFT returning "**true**"

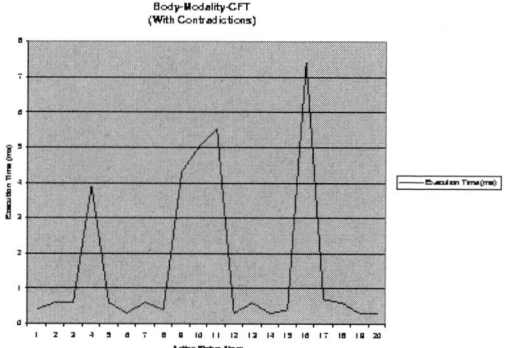

(d) BodyModalityCFT returning "**false**"

Figure 12.11
Performance of Conflict Freedom Tests.

runs with varying values for number of arguments and number of variables. Times are given in milliseconds. The reader can easily see that algorithm **safe_ccc** is extremely fast, taking between 0.02 milliseconds and 0.04 milliseconds. Thus, checking safety for an agent program with a 1000 rules can probably be done in 20–40 milliseconds.

Notice that the bounds used in our experiments are a good reflection of reality—we do not expect to see many agent programs with more than 20 conjuncts in the code call part of a single rule body. This is both difficult for a human being to write, and is difficult to read.

12.7.2 Performance of Selected Conflict Freedom Tests

In *IADE*, we have implemented the Head-CFT and Body-Modality-CFT—several other CFTs are being implemented to form a library of CFTs that may be used by agent developers. Figure 12.11 on the preceding page shows the time taken to execute the Head-CFT and Body-Modality-CFTs. Note that Head-CFT is clearly much faster than Body-Modality-CFT when returning "false"—however, this is so because Head-CFT returns "false" on many cases when Body-Modality-CFT does not do so. However, on returns of "**true**," both mechanisms are very fast, usually taking time on the order of $\frac{1}{100}$ to $\frac{1}{10}$ of a millisecond, with some exceptions. These very small times also explain the "zigzag" nature of the graphs—even small discrepancies (on the order of $\frac{1}{100}$ of a second) appear as large fluctuations in the graph. Even if an agent program contains a 1000 rules (which we expect to be an exceptional case), one would expect the Body-Modality-CFT to only take a matter of seconds to conduct the one-time, compile-time test—a factor that is well worth paying for in our opinion.

12.7.3 Performance of Deontic Stratification Algorithm

We conducted experiments with the **Check_WRAP** algorithm. Our experiments did not include timings on the first two steps of this algorithm as they pertain to safety and conflict freedom tests rather than to deontic stratification, and experimental results on those two tests have already been provided above. Furthermore, our experiments generated graphs randomly (as described below) and the programs associated with those graphs can be reconstructed from the graphs.

In our experiments, we randomly varied the number of rules from 0 to 200 in steps of 20, and ensured the there were between n and $2n$ edges in the resulting graph, where n is the number of rules (vertices). The precise number was randomly generated. For each such selection, we performed twenty runs of the algorithm. The time taken to generate the graphs was included in these experimental timings. Figures 12.12 (a) and (b) show the results of our experiments.

Figure 12.12(a) shows the time taken to execute all but the safety and conflict freedom tests of the **Check_WRAP** algorithm. The reader will note that the algorithm is very fast, taking only about 260 milliseconds on an agent program with 200 rules. Figure 12.12(b) shows the relationship between the number of SCCs in a graph, and the time taken to compute whether the agent program in question is deontically stratified. In this case, we note that as the number of SCCs increases to 200, the time taken goes to about 320 milliseconds. Again, the deontic stratifiability requirement seems to be very efficiently computable.

Section 12.8   Related Work   515

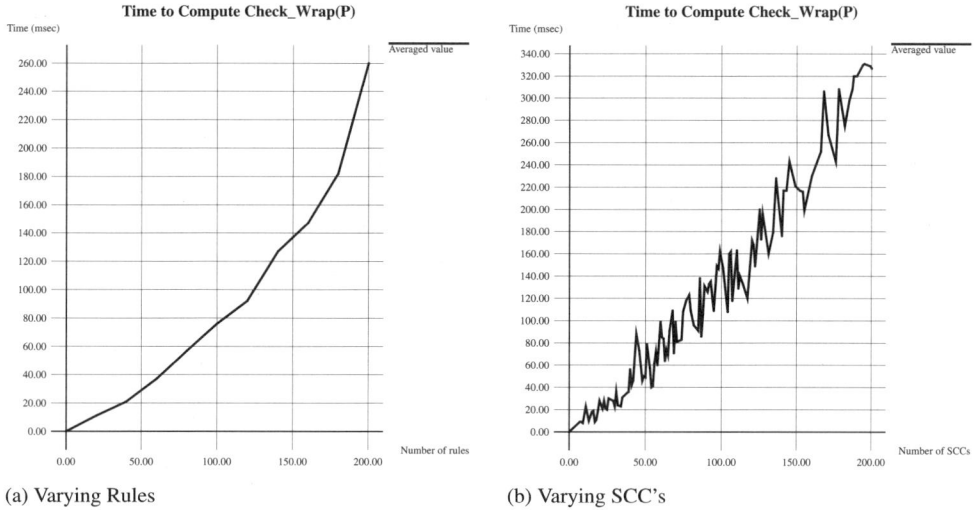

(a) Varying Rules   (b) Varying SCC's

Figure 12.12
Performance of Deontic Stratification.

12.7.4 Performance of Unfolding Algorithm

We were unable to conduct detailed experiments on the time taken for unfolding and the time taken to compute status sets as there are no good benchmark agent programs to test against, and no easy way to vary the very large number of parameters associated with an agent. In a sample application shown in Figures 12.6 on page 509 and 12.7 on page 510, we noticed that it took about 7 seconds to unfold a program containing about 10 rules, and to evaluate the status set took about 32 seconds. However, in this application, massive amounts of Army War reserves data resident in Oracle as well as in a multi-record, nested, unindexed flat file were accessed, and the times reported include times taken for Oracle and the flat file to do their work, plus network times. We did not yet implement any optimizations, like caching etc.

12.8 Related Work

There has been relatively little work in defining a formal semantics for agent programming languages: exceptions include the various pieces of work described in Chapter 6. In this chapter, we have attempted to define a polynomially implementable class of agent programs and described how we implemented this class of programs.

As defined in this chapter, a regular agent program satisfies four conditions—strong safety, conflict freedom, deontic stratifiability, and a boundedness condition. Each of these parameters has been studied in the literature, at least to some extent, and we have built upon those works.

- The concept of safety is related to the notion of *mode realizability* in logic programs (Rouzaud and Nguyen-Phoung 1992; Boye and Maluszynski 1995). In order to evaluate the truth or falsity of some atoms in a logic program, certain arguments of that atom may need to be instantiated. This is similar, but not identical to the notion of safety where we have similar conditions on code call conditions. Strong safety requires the important finiteness property in addition to this.

- The concept of conflict freedom has been studied in logic programming when negations are allowed in both the head and the body of a rule. Such logic programs were introduced by (Gelfond and Lifschitz 1991) and contradiction removal in such programs was studied extensively by Pereira's group (Alferes and Pereira 1996). Our work differs from these in the sense that we are looking for syntactic conditions on agent programs (rather than logic programs) that guarantee that under all possible states of the agent, conflicts will not occur. Such a test can be encoded at compile time.

- The notion of deontic stratifiability of an agent program, builds directly on top of the concept of a stratified logic program introduced by Apt and Blair (1988). We extend the concept of stratified logic programs to the case of a deontic stratified agent program modulo a conflict freedom test. Checking deontic stratifiability is somewhat more complex than checking ordinary stratifiability, and hence, our algorithms to do this are new.

- The notion of boundedness of an agent program builds upon the well known idea of unfolding (or partial evaluation) in logic programs. This area has been recently studied formally for semantics of (disjunctive) logic programs (wellfounded as well as stable) in (Brass and Dix 1997; Brass and Dix 1998; Brass and Dix 1999). The use of Tarjan's algorithm for computing the well-founded semantics in almost linear time has been explicitly addressed e.g., in (Berman, Schlipf, and Franco 1995; Dix, Furbach, and Niemela 1999).

To date, we are not aware of any existing work on the semantics of agent programs that is polynomial and that has been implemented. In this chapter, we have described a wide variety of parameters (e.g., conflict freedom tests, finiteness tables, etc.) that go into the design and development of an agent, and we have provided experimental data showing that these algorithms work effectively. To our knowledge, this is one of the first attempts to do this for a *generic, application independent* agent programming paradigm.

13 An Example Application

Based on the theory of agent programs defined in this book, we have developed a significant, highly non-trivial logistics application for the US Army Logistics Integration Agency's War Reserves planning. In this chapter, we will:

- Describe the *War Reserves data set problem* faced by the US Army;
- Describe the architecture used to address this problem;
- Describe our solution to the above problem, using *IMPACT*.

13.1 The Army War Reserves (*AWR*) Logistics Problem

At any given point of time, the US Army has a set of ships deployed worldwide containing "prepositioned stocks." Whenever a conflict arises anywhere in the world, one or more of these ships can set sail to that location, and the prepositioned stocks on board those ships can be immediately used to set up a base of operations.

However, this strategy would not be very useful if the stocks on the ship are either (i) insufficient, or (ii) sufficient, but not in proper working order. Readiness of these ships refers to the answer to the question: Does the ship have most of the items it should have on board the ship in proper working order?

As the *AWR* data describing the contents and readiness of the ships in question has evolved over the years, there has been considerable variance in the formats and structures in which data has been stored. Specifically, two data sources are used:

- A body of data is stored in a system called *LOGTAADS* (Logistics—The Army Authorization Document System), which consists of a single-file, multitable structure. In other words, this file consists of a set of distinct (actually four) tables. The *WM_MOC* file contains 68,146 records, no functions were available to access this data—hence, we had to implement our own functions to do so (Schafer, Rogers, and Marin 1998).

- A body of Oracle data. This data contains an *EquipRU* and a *Apr_loc* file comprising of 4,721 and 155 records, respectively.

Logisticians responsible for the readiness of the Army War Reserves need the following types of services in order to successfully accomplish the goal of maintaining high levels of readiness.

1. **Query Services:** They need to be able to execute a variety of queries such as:

(a) *Find me the "overall status" of all AWR ships?*
This query may access information on all ships from the logtaads and oracle data sources, and merge them together, using a crude measure of readiness to define the overall status of a ship. In our implementation, this "crude measure" of readiness merely finds the ratio (termed percentage fill) of the actual number of parts on the ship, to the number of parts that should be on the ship.

(b) *Find me a breakdown of the fill of the ship Alexandria[1] for each supply item class?*
Supply items on ships are classified into "P" items, "A" items, "B/C" items, "BN TF" items, "BDE CS/CSS" items and "EAD CS/CSS" items. For example, if the logistician finds that the percentage fill mentioned above is too crude an estimate for his requirements, he may pose this more sophisticated query in order to obtain a clearer picture of the state of the different ships.

(c) *Find me unit level information on the "BN TF" supply items in the Alexandria?*
This query may be posed when the logistician is still not satisfied with the level of detail—here he wants to know exactly how many of each "BN TF" item are actually on the ship.

2. **Alert Services:** In addition, logisticians need to be able to obtain automatic "alerts" when certain conditions arise. For example, a logistician tracking the Alexandria may wish to obtain an alert by e-mail everytime the percentage fill on the Alexandria drops below 80%. Alternatively, another logistician may want to receive an e-mail whenever the percentage fill of "BN TF" items drops below 85%. In such a case, he may want the unit level data as well for the Alexandria to be mailed to him.

3. **Update Services:** Third, multiple logisticians may be working with and manipulating the *AWR* data over time. Whenever an update occurs to the *AWR* data set (either made by the logistician or elsewhere), the effect of these updates need to be incorporated and actions such as the alert services described above might need to be taken.

4. **Analytic Services:** The alert services may be closely coupled to analytic services. For example, when the percentage fill on the Alexandria drops below 70%, the logistician may want an Excel chart to be created, showing a graphical rendering of supply items (x-axis) and percentage fill for that supply item alone (on the y-axis). Instead of mailing the raw data to the appropriate recipients, he may want this chart to be mailed. Creating such a chart requires the ability to interoperate with an Excel "agent".

---

[1] Owing to the sensitive nature of this application, names of US Army ships have been replaced with fictitious names, and the data shown below is not "real" data.

Section 13.3 *AWR* Agent Implementation   519

In our current implementation, we have implemented Query services and Alert services, but still have not completed the implementation of update services and analytic services—something we plan to do shortly.

13.2 *AWR* Agent Architecture

Figure 13.1 shows the *AWR* architecture we are planning to build for this application. The items shown in light are ones we have implemented, while those shown in dark are ones still to be implemented.

Both the *LOGTAADS* and Oracle data sets are accessible via agents built by us that support accessing those data sets. In addition, there is a $awrMediator$ agent that provides an integrated view across these two data sources.

• The $locTotals$ agent provides one and only one service. When requested to provide high level percentage fill data on US Army ships, it returns a table having four attributes—a ship's name, its authorized quantity, its on-hand quantity, and its percentage fill (which is the ration of the on-hand quantity to the authorized quantity).

• The $locERCTotals$ agent also provides only one service. Given any ship, it is capable of creating a composite file containing the breakdown by category ("P," "A," "B/C," "BN TF,"

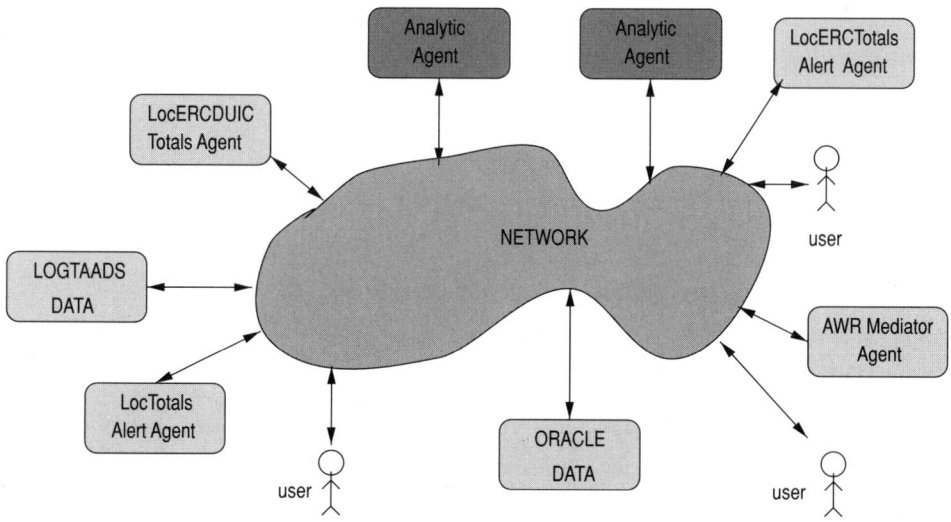

Figure 13.1
Architecture of the multiagent *AWR* system.

"BDE CS/CSS," and "EAD CS/CSS") for the ship in question. As different users express interests in different ships, it then e-mails them the ship's ERC totals at a specific time each day.

• The locERCDUICTotals agent can provide much more detailed information. Instead of providing aggregate information about a set of items (e.g., all "A" items or all "BN TF" items), it provides on hand quantity, and authorized quantity information for all authorized supply items.

At this stage, we have not implemented the analytic agents shown in Figure 13.1 on the preceding page. We are currently working on this.

13.3 *AWR* Agent Implementation

In this section, we briefly describe the way we implemented two of the agents described above.

13.3.1 The locTotals Agent

We describe below, the various components associated with the locTotals agent. The main aim of this agent is to notify a set of subscribers about the status of all *AWR* ships. Each subscriber specifies a time at which they want to be notified (e.g., at 8 am daily, every Monday at 8 am, etc.), and where (i.e., at what e-mail address) they wish to be notified at those times.

Types This particular agent manipulates four data types:

• LOC_Recd1
which has the schema: (LOC/string).

• APS_LOC_2D
which is a set of LOC_Recd1 records.

• ERU_Recd1
which has the schema: (R_Auth_Qty/Integer, R_Net_short/Integer).

• EquipRU_2B
which is a set of ERU_Recd1 records.

Functions The following ten functions are supported by the locTotals agent. Notice that the locTotals agent spans five packages—Oracle, a *HERMES* package, a math package, a time package, and a string manipulation package.

• $time : localTimeInt() \rightarrow$ Integer.
This code call returns the current local time.

Section 13.3   *AWR* Agent Implementation   521

- oracle : *project*(SrcTable, ConInfo, ProjectFlds) → APS_LOC_2D.
This indicates that one of the functions supported by the locTotals agent is a call to Oracle, on the data types listed. The calls returns an object of type *APS_LOC_2D*, i.e., it returns a set of records containing a single string field.
- oracle : *project_select*(SrcTable, ConInfo, ProjectFlds, ConsField, ConsOp, Constr) → EquipRU_2B.
This function returns as output, a set of pairs $\langle R\_Auth\_Qty/\text{Integer}, R\_Net\_short/\text{Integer} \rangle$.
- oracle : *project2*(SrcTable, ConInfo, ProjectFlds) → polymorphic.
This function takes as input an Oracle table located at a specified location and a set of fields, and projects out the appropriate fields. Note the polymorphic nature of this function—the output type depends on the specified fields. The *IADE* can automatically infer the output type.
- In addition, some "workhorse" functions supported are:
  - hermes : *sum_double*(TgtFile, SzTgtField) → Integer.
  - math : *subtract*(Val_1, Val_2) → Integer.
  - math : *add*(Val_1, Val_2) → Integer.
  - math : *multiply*(Val_1, Val_2) → Integer.
  - math : *divide*(Val_1, Val_2) → Integer.
  - string : *concat*(Val_1, Val_2, Val_3, Val_4, Val_5) → String.

Note that the above math operations represent integer, rather than real-valued arithmetic.

Actions   The following nine actions are supported by the locTotals agent. In *IMPACT*, there is no need to specify preconditions, add and delete lists for generic file manipulation actions and message management actions as these are handled automatically. The preconditions, add and delete lists for the other actions are empty.

- *LocTotals*(SzLOC, D_AuthQty, D_OnHand).
This action takes a shipname (SzLOC) as input and computes its authorized quantity and its OnHand quantity from the *LOGTAADS* and Oracle data.
- *LocTotalString*(SzLocTotals).
This action is used to convert the answer returned by the *LocTotals* action above into a string.
- *GetTgtFile*(FnTarget).
This action gets a file.
- *CreateTotalsFile*(FnTarget).
This action creates a file.

- *AppendTotalsFile*(FnTarget, SzLocTotals).

This action takes a target file and a string denoting the totals for a ship, and concatenates the latter to the existing file. The idea is that this action is called once for each ship.

- *LogLocTotals*(FnTarget).

This action executes the *CreateTotalsFile* action followed by the *AppendTotalsFile* action.

- *ValidateTimeInterval*(L_Hour, L_MinuteSpan).

This action validates the given time interval.

- *GetEmailAddr*().

This action gets an e-mail address. For now, this action is hardcoded to just get one e-mail address.

- *MailLocTotalsFile*(R9_TgtFile, R9_SzAddr).

This action mails the specified file to the specified e-mail address.

Agent Program We list below the 13 rules in this agent program.

r1: **Do** *LocTotals*(SzLOC, D_AuthQty, D_OnHand) ←

   in(LocRecd, oracle : *project*('aps_loc : 2d', "lia98apr@bester/oracle", "LOC")),

   is('Qtys.hrm', oracle : *project* ('equipru : 2b', "lia98apr@bester/oracle",
                             "Auth_qty, Net_short", "LOC", "=", LocRecd.LOC)),

   =(SzLOC, LocRecd.LOC),

   in(AuthSum, hermes : *sum_double*('Qtys.hrm', "Auth_qty")),

   =(D_AuthQty, AuthSum),

   in(ShortSum, hermes : *sum_double*('Qtys.hrm', "Net_short")),

   in(OnHandSum, math : *subtract*(AuthSum, ShortSum)),

   =(D_OnHand, OnHandSum).

This rule executes an action called *LocTotals* that accesses an Oracle relation at a location denoted by *lia98apr@bester* and computes the totals for all ships, together with the percentage fills. It is important to note that the *LocTotals* action has no effects—so in fact, this rule only serves to say that a set of ground status atoms of the form *LocTotals*(SzLOC, D_AuthQty, D_OnHand) is in any status set of the agent. The following rule takes the set of these ground status atoms and merges them into a massive string.

r2: **Do** *LocTotalString*(R2_SzLocTotals) ←

   Do *LocTotals*(R2_SzLoc, R2_D_AuthQty, R2_D_OnHand),

   in(R2_T_SzLocTotals, string : *concat*(R2_SzLoc, ",", R2_D_AuthQty, ",",
   R2_D_OnHand)),

   =(R2_SzLocTotals, R2_T_SzLocTotals).

Section 13.3   *AWR* Agent Implementation

r3: **Do** *GetTgtFile*(R3_F_Name) ←
=(R3_F_Name, 'LocTotals.txt').

This rule gets a file called *'LocTotals.txt'*.

r4: **Do** *CreateTotalsFile*(R4_TgtFile) ←
Do *GetTgtFile*(R4_TgtFile).

Likewise, this rule creates a file. The meaning of the following rules is more or less self-explanatory.

r5: **Do** *AppendTotalsFile*(R5_TgtFile, R5_SzLocTotals) ←
Do *GetTgtFile*(R5_TgtFile), **Do** *LocTotalString*(R5_SzLocTotals).

r6: **Do** *LogLocTotals*(R6_TgtFile) ←
Do *CreateTotalsFile*(R6_TgtFile), **Do** *AppendTotalsFile*(R6_TgtFile, R6_SzLocTotals).

r7: **Do** *ValidateTimeInterval*(L_TgtHour, L_TgtMinuteSpan) ←
in(L_HermesLocalHM, time : *localTimeInt*()),
in(L_TgtH, math : *multiply*(L_TgtHour, 60)),
in(L_LoTgtHM, math : *subtract*(L_TgtH, L_TgtMinuteSpan)),
in(L_HiTgtHM, math : *add*(L_TgtH, L_TgtMinuteSpan)),
>(L_HermesLocalHM, L_LoTgtHM),
<(L_HermesLocalHM, L_HiTgtHM).

The following rules execute the mail actions to a small group of two subscribers—vs and rogers. Depending upon the time of day, the notifications are sent to different e-mail addresses. For example, rule 8 sends e-mail to vs at *vs@earlynet.com* during one time interval, while rule 9 and 10 send him notifications to other addresses at other time intervals. The three rules after that do likewise for rogers.

r8: **Do** *GetEmailAddr*(SzAddr) ←
Do *ValidateTimeInterval*(5, 240), =(SzAddr, "vs@earlynet.com").

r9: **Do** *GetEmailAddr*(SzAddr) ←
Do *ValidateTimeInterval*(6, 240), =(SzAddr, "vs@cs.umd.edu").

r10: **Do** *GetEmailAddr*(SzAddr) ←
Do *ValidateTimeInterval*(15, 240), =(SzAddr, "vs@latenite.com").

r11: **Do** *GetEmailAddr*(SzAddr) ←
Do *ValidateTimeInterval*(5, 240), =(SzAddr, "tjrogers@ricochet.net").

r12: **Do** *GetEmailAddr*(SzAddr) ←
Do *ValidateTimeInterval*(6, 240), =(SzAddr, "rogers@cs.umd.edu").

r13: **Do** *GetEmailAddr*(SzAddr) ←
Do *ValidateTimeInterval*(15, 240), =(SzAddr, "rogers@interserv.com").

As the reader will see from Figure 12.5 on page 508, the time taken for unfolding the locTotals agent is relatively small—1.433 seconds. *IADE* contains an optimization—for actions that have no effects, there is no need to evaluate the associated pf-constraint. This causes several rules in the unfolded program to be thrown away which explains why a set of 13 source rules is replaced by 8 rules after the unfolding process is complete. The total time taken to evaluate these rules over the distributed data sources described in Chapter 12 is 25.681 seconds.

13.3.2 The locERCTotals Agent

The locERCTotals agent is similar to the locTotals agent. For each ship, instead of producing aggregate level information, it provides information for the various categories of supply items. We now describe the design of this agent.

Types The locERCTotals agent uses the same four types used by the locTotals agent. This is not a surprise, as the data accessed by this agent is identical to the data accessed by the locTotals agent.

Functions The locERCTotals agent uses the same functions used by the locTotals agent except for the oracle:*project2*() and math:*divide*() functions.

Actions The nine actions implemented in the locERCTotals agent are listed below. Unless mentioned otherwise, all actions have empty preconditions, add lists and delete lists.

- *Loc_Names*(SzLoc).

This action computes the name of all ships used to store the Army War Reserves.

- *Cd2ERC*(SzCD, SzERC).

This action generates something called a "pacing" code from the data character passed into it.

- *LocERC_Totals*(SzLoc, SzERC, L_AuthQty, L_OnHand).

This action is similar to the *LocTotals* action in the locTotals agent—the main difference is that given any ship (SzLoc) and any supply category (SzERC), it finds the totals for that category.

- *LocERC_TotalString*(SzLoc, SzERC, SzLocERCTotals).

This action is similar to the *LocTotalString* action described for the locTotals agent. Given any ship (SzLoc) and any supply category (SzERC), it converts the totals for that ship and supply category into a string.

Section 13.3   *AWR* Agent Implementation   525

- *ValidateTimeInterval*(L_Hour, L_MinuteSpan).

This action is identical to the one used by the locTotals agent.

- The following actions are self explanatory:

- *GetTargets*(F_Name, SzLoc, SzAddr).

- *CreateLocERCTotalsFile*(F_TgtFile).

This action executes a body of code which creates such a file.

- *AppendTotalsFile*(F_TgtFile, SzLoc, SzERC, SzLocERCTotals).

This function also executes a body of code that performs the desired append action.

- *LogLocERCTotals*(F_TgtFile, SzLoc, SzERC).

- *MailLocERCTotals*(F_TgtFile, SzLoc, SzAddr).

Agent Program   The agent program associated with the locERCTotals agent contains a total of 17 rules and is shown below.

r1: **Do** *Loc_Names*(SzLoc) ←
　　　in(LocRecd, oracle : *project*('aps_loc : 2d', "lia98apr@bester/oracle", "LOC")) ,
　　　=(SzLoc, LocRecd.LOC).

r2: **Do** *Cd2ERC*(SzCode, SzERC) ←
　　　=(SzCode, "A"), =(SzERC, "Ship 0 CD code").

r3: **Do** *Cd2ERC*(SzCode, SzERC) ←
　　　=(SzCode, "B"), =(SzERC, "P").

r4: **Do** *Cd2ERC*(SzCode, SzERC) ←
　　　=(SzCode, "C"), =(SzERC, "A").

r5: **Do** *Cd2ERC*(SzCode, SzERC) ←
　　　=(SzCode, "D"), =(SzERC, "B/C").

r6: **Do** *LocERC_Totals*(SzLoc, SzERC, L_AuthQty, L_OnHand) ←
　　　Do *Loc_Names*(SzLoc),
　　　Do *Cd2ERC*(SzCd, SzERC),
　　　is('Qtys.hrm', oracle : *project_selectN* ('equipru : 2b', "lia98apr@borg/oracle",
　　　　　　　　　　　"Auth_qty, Net_short", 2, "LOC", "=", SzLOC,
　　　　　　　　　　　"Erc", "=", SzCd
　　　in(L_AuthQty, hermes : *sum_double*('Qtys.hrm', "Auth_qty")),
　　　in(L_Short, hermes : *sum_double*('Qtys.hrm', "Net_short")),
　　　in(LOnHand, hermes : *subtract*(L_AuthQty, L_Short)).

r7: **Do** *LocERC_TotalString*(SzLoc, SzERC, SzLocERCTotals) ←
　　　Do *LocERC_Totals*(SzLoc, SzERC, L_AuthQty, L_OnHand),

in(SzLocERCTotals, string : *concat*(SzLoc, ",", SzERC,",", L_AuthQty, ",", L_OnHand,",")).

r8: **Do** *ValidateTimeInterval*(L_TgtHour, L_TgtMinuteSpan) ←
  in(L_HermesLocalHM, time : *localTimeInt*()),
  in(L_TgtH, math : *multiply*(L_TgtHour, 60)),
  in(L_LoTgtHM, math : *subtract*(L_TgtHour, L_TgtMinuteSpan)),
  in(L_HiTgtHM, math : *add*(L_TgtH, L_TgtMinuteSpan)),
  >(L_HermesLocalHM, $L_LoTgtHM$),
  <(L_HermesLocalHM, $L_HiTgtHM$).

r9: **Do** *GetTargets*(F_Name, SzLoc, SzAddr) ←
  Do *ValidateTimeInterval*(8, 240),
  =(SzLoc, "COLLEGE PARK"),
  =(F_Name, '*CP_LocERCTotals.txt*'),
  =(SzAddr, "*vs@cs.umd.edu*").

r10: **Do** *GetTargets*(F_Name, SzLoc, SzAddr) ←
  Do *ValidateTimeInterval*(8, 240),
  =(SzLoc, "WEST POINT"),
  =(F_Name, '*WP_LocERCTotals.txt*'),
  =(SzAddr, "*dj4149@exmail.usma.army.mil*").

r11: **Do** *GetTargets*(F_Name, SzLoc, SzAddr) ←
  Do *ValidateTimeInterval*(2, 240),
  =(SzLoc, "WEST POINT"),
  =(F_Name, '*WP_LocERCTotals.txt*'),
  =(SzAddr, "*jschafer@earlybird.com*").

r12: **Do** *GetTargets*(F_Name, SzLoc, SzAddr) ←
  Do *ValidateTimeInterval*(15, 240),
  =(SzLoc, "WEST POINT"),
  =(F_Name, '*WP_LocERCTotals.txt*'),
  =(SzAddr, "*jschafer@latenite.com*").

r13: **Do** *GetTargets*(F_Name, SzLoc, SzAddr) ←
  Do *ValidateTimeInterval*(8, 240),
  =(SzLoc, "ALEXANDRIA"),
  =(F_Name, '*AX_LocERCTotals.txt*'),
  =(SzAddr, "*rogers@cs.umd.edu*").

r14: **Do** *GetTargets*(F_Name, SzLoc, SzAddr) ←
  Do *ValidateTimeInterval*(15, 240),
  =(SzLoc, "ALEXANDRIA"),

=(F_Name, *'AX_LocERCTotals.txt'*),
=(SzAddr, "*rogers@latenite.com*").

r15: **Do** *CreateLocERCTotalsFile*(F_TgtFile) ←
Do *GetTargets*(F_TgtFile, SzLoc, szAddr).

r16: **Do** *AppendTotalsFile*(F_TgtFile, SzLoc, SzERC, SzLocERCTotals) ←
Do *GetTargets*(F_TgtFile, SzLoc, szAddr).
Do *LocERC_TotalString*(SzLoc, SzERC, SzLocERCTotals).

r17: **Do** *MailLocERCTotals*(F_TgtFile, SzLoc, SzAddr) ←
Do *GetTargets*(F_TgtFile, SzLoc, szAddr).

The *IMPACT* Agent Development environment takes 150 milliseconds to unfold this agent program, rendering the 17 rules listed above as a set of 30 agent program rules. Computing the status set (which involves computing these 30 pf-constraints associated with the unfolded agent program) takes a total of 35.386 seconds, including all network costs.

14 Conclusions

Chapter 1 of this book lays out a set of basic goals and desiderata that we believe any program called an "agent" must satisfy, and that we believe an infrastructure supporting interactions between multiple agents must satisfy. Subsequently, in Chapters 2 onward, we have described a wide variety of contributions, including the *IMPACT* architecture, how *IMPACT* servers support a wide variety of generic interoperability needs, how *IMPACT* agents may be built, how these agents can make intelligent decisions, reason about commitments both now and in the future, reason about uncertainty, and so on. The important, and as yet unanswered questions at this stage are:

1. *Do the contributions in Chapters 2–13 successfully address the needs and desiderata described in Chapter 1?*

2. *In addition, do these desiderata support the kinds of agent behavior required by other researchers, e.g., Hayes (1999); Lesser (1999)?*

3. Finally, what are the answers to the three important questions, **(Q1)**, **(Q2)**, **(Q3)** raised in Section 1.5. To refresh the reader's mind, these questions are recapitulated below.

(Q1) *What is an agent?*

(Q2) *If program P is not considered to be an agent according to some specified definition of agenthood, is there a suite of tools that can help in "agentizing" P?*

(Q3) *Once a specific definition of agenthood is chosen, what kind of software infrastructure is required to support interactions between such agents, and what core set of services must be provided by such an infrastructure?*

In this chapter, we attempt to answer these questions.

14.1 Progress Towards the Ten Desiderata

Section 1.5 provides ten desiderata which, to our mind, any notion of "agenthood" must satisfy. In this section, we review how our framework supports these ten desiderata, and also assess where it falls short and what research is needed to make up the shortfall.

14.1.1 Desiderata (D1) and (D2)

Desideratum **(D1)** says that "anybody who has a software program P, either custom designed to be an agent, or an existing legacy program, must be able to *agentize* their program and *plug* it into the provided solution." Similarly, Desideratum (**D2**) says that a theory of agents must take into account that data is stored in a wide variety of data structures and is manipulated by an existing corpus of algorithms.

IMPACT supports this very strongly, both in its theory and in its implementation. In fact, Chapter 4 is devoted to describing the following concepts: *code call conditions* provide a syntax using which, queries and requests to arbitrary legacy and/or specialized data structures may be executed. It also describes the *state* of the agent as a set of objects of any set of data types whatsoever, as long as the set of data types used by the agent is specified when the agent is built. It supports the concept of an *integrity constraint* over such diverse data structures. Likewise, in Chapter 6 onward, we notice that agent programs, action constraints, temporal agent programs, probabilistic agent programs, etc., are all built on top of arbitrary data structures accessible via the code call mechanism.

The implementation of *IMPACT* uses a pre-existing software package developed at the University of Maryland called *WebHermes* (Adali, S., et al. 1997) which supports execution of code call conditions over a wide variety of data structures and software packages. These currently include (or have included in the past), relational database management systems (Oracle, Ingres, Dbase, Paradox), an object oriented system (ObjectStore), a multimedia system called MACS (Brink, Marcus, and Subrahmanian 1995), a video information system called AVIS (Adali, Candan, Chen, Erol, and Subrahmanian 1996), a geographic data structure called a PR-quadtree, arbitrary flat files (as long as their schemas are specified), a US Army route planner over free terrain (Benton and Subrahmanian 1994), a variety of US Army logistics data including specialized Oracle and nested multirecord TAADS data (Schafer, Rogers, and Marin 1998), a variety of US Army simulation data from a massive program called JANUS deployed by the Simulation, Training and Instrumentation Command, a face recognition program, and so on.

14.1.2 Desideratum (D3)

Desideratum (**D3**) says that "a theory of agents must *not* depend upon the set of actions that the agent performs. Rather, the set of actions that the agent performs must be a *parameter* that is taken into account in the semantics."

This is certainly the case in *IMPACT*. When an agent developer builds an agent, s/he can specify, through the *IMPACT* Agent Development Environment, a set of actions that his or her agent can perform. For each of these actions, he specifies a codebase, and a set of preconditions, add and delete lists. This feature is not only present in the implementation—it is also an essential component of the theory underlying agent programs. As we can see in Chapter 6, an agent's associated semantics (feasible status set, rational status set, reasonable status set, etc.) depend fundamentally upon the agent's associated agent program, as well as upon the agent's actions' effects, which determine if a new state (reached by executing these actions) satisfies the integrity constraints or not.

14.1.3 Desideratum (D4)

Desideratum **(D4)** says that "every agent should execute actions based on some *clearly articulated* decision policy."

The entire goal of Chapters 6, 7, 8 and 9 is to allow the agent developer to define decision policies based on his application needs. An agent program, defined in Chapter 6 specifies the operating principles/decision policy of the agent. It provides a number of alternative semantics that an agent developer may "choose" for his agent to use.

Thus, from a *theoretical* point of view, we have successfully provided a language for articulating decision policies based on just a set of data structures if needed, but also based on sophisticated forms of temporal reasoning, meta-reasoning and prediction, and reasoning with uncertainty. From the point of view of *implementation* methods, however, our current *IMPACT* system handles agent programs (actually *regular* agents as described in Chapter 12).

14.1.4 Desideratum (D5)

This desideratum says that any agent construction framework must allow agents to perform "reasoning about beliefs."

Chapter 7 extends the concept of an agent program proposed in Chapter 6 to the case where agents reason about the beliefs of other agents, about what other agents believe about other agents, about what other agents are permitted or obligated to do, and so on. It proposes the concept of a *meta-agent program* and shows that the semantics of meta-agent programs cleanly extends that of agent programs. Furthermore, it shows that meta-agent programs can be directly implemented on top of an implementation of ordinary agent programs. The effect of this startling result is that the *IADE* can be used to implement meta-agent programs if its interface is extended to allow the user to articulate his "meta-reasoning" conditions and his belief atoms (see Chapter 7), his belief tables, his belief semantics tables, and so on. We anticipate extending the *IADE* to accomplish this in the near future.

14.1.5 Desideratum (D6)

Desideratum **(D6)** of our agent framework says that "any infrastructure to support multiagent interactions *must* provide two important types of security—security on the agent side, to ensure that an agent (if it wishes) can protect some of its information and services, and security on the infrastructural side so that one agent cannot masquerade as another."

As the reader can see from Chapter 10, we have shown that agent security can be split into two components—*data security* and *action security*. We have shown that maintaining security is undecidable in general. However, we have proposed the notions of *approximate security* and shown that *IMPACT* agents can maintain security by trading off some cooperativeness. In addition, our notions of security may build on top of existing, well understood authentication mechanisms. For instance, checking authentication using a specific authentication program is an *action* that an agent may take!

On the implementation side, however, the *IADE* currently forces the agent developer to explicitly specify actions to handle his agent's security needs. In addition, no mechanisms exist in the current *IADE* implementation to specify the various "approximation" components specified in Chapter 10. Successfully addressing this problem is a major priority of our ongoing effort.

Chapter 8 involves another extension to the case where agents may reason about its past, present and future states, as well as reason about actions it is permitted to do, obliged to do, forbidden from doing, both now, in the past, and in the future. Chapter 9 extends agent programs to allow users to articulate decision policies in uncertain environments.

14.1.6 Desideratum (D7) and (D8)

Desideratum (D7) says, in effect, that agents must be efficient, relative to an oracle to handle API calls to the underlying code base on top of which the agent is built. Desideratum (D8) says that implementing polynomial fragments of agent programming languages is critical.

We have carefully studied, in Chapter 11, the complexity of computing appropriate status sets of agent programs. Chapter 11's theoretical complexity results show that for positive agent programs with integrity constraints, the reasonable and feasible status sets can be efficiently (i.e., polynomially) computed. In Chapter 12, we provide concrete implementation mechanisms. In particular, we show via our implementation that if we are willing to pay a price at the time an agent is deployed (a one time cost), then we may end up with huge savings at run time as far as status set computation is concerned.

One extension that we are currently working on is to extend *regular* agent programs to the case of meta-agent programs, temporal agent programs, and probabilistic agent programs, so that polynomial versions of those agent programs are also available.

14.1.7 Desideratum (D9)

Desideratum (D9) deals with *reliability*—can we ensure that if the "agent infrastructure" crashes, then all agents' activities will not come to a grinding halt?

In *IMPACT*, the *IMPACT* Servers are the ones that provide the so called "agent infrastructure." Agents need to use the server only when either (i) they do not understand what another agent's terminology or defined types refer to, or (ii) when they need to find an agent that provides a specific service they want. We have provided for reliability of *IMPACT* servers via replication of these servers at distributed nodes, as described in Chapter 2, and by minimizing the dependency of individual agents on *IMPACT* servers. Even if all replicas of the *IMPACT* servers go down, agents in *IMPACT* can still function and interact with one another, as long as the underlying communications medium (wired or wireless network) is up.

14.1.8 Desideratum (D10)

Last, but not least, desideratum (D10) says that "the only way of testing the applicability of any theory is to build a software system based on the theory, to deploy a set of applications based on the theory, and to report on experiments based on those applications. Thus, an implementation *must be validated* by a set of deployed applications."

As reported in Chapter 13, we have validated our theory and implementation via two applications: one for the US Army Logistics Integration Agency's Army War Reserves agent, while the other is an agent application for the US Army Simulation, Training and Instrumentation Command (STRICOM).

14.2 Agent Desiderata Provided by Other Researchers

Our research supports various requirements about agents specified by other researchers. Prior to this work, most definitions of agents were *behavioral* in the sense that whether a program was considered an agent or not depended upon how the program behaved. In contrast, in this book, we have proposed a *structural* definition of agents in which we specify what software components must be contained within an agent. Shoham (1999) provides a list of parameters that have typically been used to characterize a software agent. This list of parameters is a set of behavioral requirements articulated by various researchers. We outline Shoham's requirements (as well as a few more) below, together with an assessment of how *IMPACT* supports these requirements, and where it falls short.

- *Ongoing execution.* This criterion says that software agents function continuously over time. In fact, as described by the Agent Decision Cycle in Chapter 6, the reader can see that all *IMPACT* agents are continuously functioning.
- *Autonomy.* Autonomy means that agents do not require human supervision. Autonomous agents can easily be built in *IMPACT*. We have shown, in Chapter 6, how clock driven agents can be built, which automatically take certain actions based on occurrence of clock events. Likewise, the credit agent in Chapter 8 may automatically notify a customer whose

credit has an overdue payment every 10 days. In general, an autonomous agent is one that takes actions without explicit intervention by the user on behalf of whom the action is being taken. *IMPACT* agent programs contain rules that can trigger actions whenever a state change occurs, and as our notion of a state change is powerful enough to include clock ticks, database updates, random event occurrence, etc., our framework is rich enough to trigger actions based on such events.

• *Adaptiveness.* This parameter is also a behavioral parameter which says that agents should be able to adapt over time to the needs of specific users. It is important to note that adapting is an action. In *IMPACT*, an agent can log all transactions performed by a user into its state (thus maintaining a history of the sort shown in Chapter 10), and then determine what actions to take on a user's behalf, and how to perform these actions, based on the log.

• *Intelligence.* This is an extremely vague requirement that agents be able to perform different types of reasoning such as probabilistic reasoning, planning, etc. In *IMPACT*, as shown in Chapter 9, agents can certainly reason in the presence of uncertainty. Furthermore, in *IMPACT*, agents can plan, by specifically triggering planning actions in the agent decision cycle. The coupling of action to state in *IMPACT* is very generic. Actions in *IMPACT* can include invoking route planners and flight planners (as in the CFIT example), performing statistical data mining style analyses (as in the credit agent), and so on.

• *Agent Awarenenss.* This parameter requires that agents be able to model other agents, reason about them, and so on. As we have shown in Chapter 7, using the map paradigm, *IMPACT* agents may reason about the state, as well as the actions of other agents. Furthermore, agents can participate in auctions and engage in strategic negotiations with other agents (Chapter 8).

• *Mobility.* *IMPACT* agents can be mobile, because mobility is an action that any agent can execute. So is cloning. In addition, as shown in Chapter 6, Java applets may themselves be viewed as *IMPACT* agents.

• *Anthropomorphism.* This parameter says that agents should have the ability to deal with beliefs, obligations, and other such modalities, and also convey "emotions" through graphical or voice actions. Of course, this is straightforward to encode in an *IMPACT* agent. By its very design, an agent program allows an agent to explicitly describe what it may or may not do, what its obligations are, and so forth. In the same vein, if the state of the agent satisfies certain conditions executing an action that displays a "happy face" or a "grumpy face" can be directly encoded as an agent program rule.

• *Reactivity.* Reactive agents are those that can automatically react to events. It is apparent from the preceding paragraph that *IMPACT* agents can react to events, because events are state changes as far as the agent is concerned.

- *Evaluating Courses of Action.* Several researchers such as Bratman, Israel, and Pollack (1988) and Schoppers and Shapiro (1997), require agents to have the ability to evaluate alternative courses of actions, and adopt one that is optimal w.r.t. some objective function of interest to the agent. In chapter 6, we have defined an "optimal status set" semantics for agent programs that accomplishes this. First, an agent developer can select a semantics for his agent (feasible, rational, reasonable, etc.). Each status set according to the selected semantics is considered to be a possible course of action. The one that is optimal w.r.t. some cost function specified by the agent developer is then selected by the agent, and the actions in it are concurrently executed.

- *Communication.* Another well accepted requirement of agents is the ability to communicate with other agents and to comprehend the content of these communications. In *IMPACT*, agents communicate with other agents via the msgbox package. Sending messages, reading messages, flushing the message box, are all actions that the agent might take. Agents can *comprehend* what messages other agents are sending via the *IMPACT* servers that maintain thesaurus and type information.

- *Planning.* As agents are required to act intelligently on behalf of one or more individuals, agents must be able to plan in order to accomplish these objectives. Here, *IMPACT*'s way of accomplishing planning by agents is quite different from methods traditionally adopted in artificial intelligence and in agent research in particular, (Schoppers and Shapiro 1997), Bratman, Israel, and Pollack (1988). In *IMPACT*, *planning* is an action. An agent can plan for a contingency by explicitly invoke a planning code base, specific to the agent. This makes sense to us. Database retrieval agents, for instance, should not be forced to do AI planning. In the CHAIN example, the truck agent may plan its route using a road map, while in the CFIT agent, planning may be done using 3-d models of the world. Both require invocation of different planners. Thus, in our framework, we have provided the ability to "plug in" different planners into *IMPACT* agents.

- *Negotiation.* There has been extensive work on negotiation in multiagent systems, based on the initial idea of contract nets, due to Smith and Davis (1983). In chapter 8, we have provided a detailed example of how strategic models of negotiation can be encoded into *IMPACT* agents.

Appendix A

Code Calls and Actions in the Examples

A.1 Agents in the CFIT Example

A.1.1 AutoPilot Agents

The autoPilot agent ensures that the plane stays on its allocated flight path. The task of the autoPilot agent is to ensure that the plane stays on-course, and make appropriate adjustments when the physical dynamics of the plane cause it to veer off course.

Code Calls

1. Determine the current location of the plane.
   autoPilot: *location*() → `3DPoint`

2. Determine the pilot status of the plane, i.e., whether it is *automated, semi-automated, semi-manual* or *manual*.
   autoPilot: *pilotStatus*(`Pilot_message`) → `PilotStatusString`

3. Get the current flight route of the plane
   autoPilot: *getFlightRoute*() → `Path`

4. Get the next `SensorId`. Each time this code call is called the next sensor from the queue is returned. All the sensors are maintained in a circular queue.
   autoPilot: *getSensorId*() → `String`

5. Read the GPS Data from the sensor with `SensorId`
   autoPilot: *readGPSData*(`SensorId`) → `GPSDataReport`

6. Given the `CurrentLocation`, `CurrentFlightRoute` and a set of `No_go` regions, adjust the flight route of the plane
   autoPilot: *adjustFlightRoute*(`CurrentFlightRoute, CurrentLocation, No_go`) → `Path`

7. Given the `CurrentLocation` of the plane and a set of `No_go` areas, calculate a flight path for the plane
   autoPilot: *calculateFlightRoute*(`CurrentLocation, No_go`) → `Path`

8. Given the `CurrentLocation` of the plane and a set of `No_go` areas, calculate N alternative flight paths for the plane
   autoPilot: *calculateNFlightRoutes*(`CurrentLocation, No_go, N`) → `ListofPaths`

9. Get the current `Altitude` of the plan
   autoPilot: *getAltitude*() → `Altitude`

10. Set the altitude of the plane to `Altitude`
    autoPilot: *setAltitude*(`Altitude`) → `Boolean`

11. Given the current `Altitude` of the plane calculate the new altitude of the plane
    autoPilot: *calculateNewAltitude*(`Altitude`) → `Altitude`

12. Get the current `Velocity` of the plane
    autoPilot: *velocity*() → `Velocity`

13. Given the current location, flight route and speed of the plane calculate the next location of the plane
    autoPilot: *calculateLocation*(`Location, FlightRoute, Velocity`) → `3DPoint`

14. Return the list of passengers on the plane
    autoPilot: *passengers*() → `ListOfPassengers`

Actions

1. Collect GPS Data from the sensor with SensorId.

Name: *collectGPSData*(SensorId)
Pre: **in**(SensorId, autoPilot: *getSensorId*())
Del: {}
Add: **in**(SensorId, autoPilot: *getSensorId*())&
     in(GPSData, autoPilot: *readGPSData*(SensorId))

2. Adjust course of the plane

Name: *adjust_course*(No_go, FlightRoute, CurrentLocation)
Pre: **in**(No_go, msgbox: *getVar*(Msg.Id, "No_go"))
Del: **in**(CurrentFlightRoute, autoPilot: *getFlightRoute*())
Add: **in**(CurrentLocation, autoPilot: *location*())&
     in(CurrentFlightRoute, autoPilot: *getFlightRoute*())&
     in(FlightRoute, code call)
where code call is
autoPilot: *adjustFlightRoute*(CurrentFlightRoute, CurrentLocation, No_go)

3. Maintain the flight route of the plane

Name: *maintain_course*(No_go, Flight_route, Current_location)
Pre: **in**(No_go, msgbox: *getVar*(Msg.Id, "No_go"))&
     in(CurrentLocation, autoPilot: *location*())&
     in(CurrentRoute, autoPilot: *getFlightRoute*())&
     = (*CurrentRoute, allocatedFlightPath*)
Del: {}
Add: {}

4. Return the control of the plane to the pilot

Name: *return_control*()
Pre: **in**(automated, autoPilot: *pilotStatus*(pilot_message))
Del: **in**(automated, autoPilot: *pilotStatus*(pilot_message))
Add: **in**(manual, autoPilot: *pilotStatus*(pilot_message))

5. Create a flight plan for the plane

Name: *create_flight_plan*(No_go, Flight_route, Current_location)
Pre: **in**(No_go, msgbox: *getVar*(Msg.Id, "No_go"))&
     in(CurrentLocation, autoPilot: *location*())
Del: **in**(CurrentRoute, autoPilot: *getFlightRoute*())
Add: **in**(No_go, msgbox: *getVar*(Msg.Id, "No_go"))&
     in(CurrentLocation, autoPilot: *location*())&
     in(FlightRoute, autoPilot: *calculateFlightRoute*(CurrentLocation, No_go))

6. Execute the flight plan of the plane

Name: *execute_flight_plan*(Flight_route)
Pre: **in**(No_go, msgbox: *getVar*(Msg.Id, "No_go"))&
     in(CurrentLocation, autoPilot: *location*())
Del: {}
Add: **in**(No_go, msgbox: *getVar*(Msg.Id, "No_go"))&
     in(CurrentLocation, autoPilot: *location*())&
     in(FlightRoute, autoPilot: *calculateFlightRoute*(CurrentLocation, No_go))

7. Adjust the altitude of the plane

Name: *adjustAltitude*(Altitude)
Pre: **in**(CurrentAltitude, autoPilot: *getAltitude*())
Del: **in**(CurrentAltitude, autoPilot: *getAltitude*())

Section A.1   Agents in the CFIT Example   539

Add: **in**(CurrentAltitude, autoPilot: *getAltitude*())&
    in(Altitude, autoPilot: *calculateNewAltitude*(CurrentAltitude))

8. Compute the current location of the plane

Name: *compute_currentLocation*(Report)
Pre: **in**(Report, msgbox: *getVar*(Msg.Id, "Report"))
Del: **in**(OldLocation, autoPilot: *location*())
Add: **in**(OldLocation, autoPilot: *location*())&
    in(FlightRoute, autoPilot: *getFlightRoute*())&
    in(Velocity, autoPilot: *velocity*())&
    in(NewLocation, code call)

where code call is
autoPilot: *calculateLocation*(OldLocation, FlightRoute, Velocity)

A.1.2 Satellite Agents

These agents monitor the position of several planes simultaneously. Every Δt units of time, each satellite agent broadcasts a report. Each satellite agent specifies where it believes the plane is at that point in time.

Code Calls

1. Broadcast GPS data
satellite: *broadcastGPSData*() $\rightarrow$ SatelliteReport

Actions

1. Broadcast satellite report

Name: *broadcast*(Report)
Pre: {}
Del: {}
Add: **in**(Report, satellite: *broadcastGPSData*())

A.1.3 GPS Agents

This agent takes reports from multiple satellite agents and merges them together. The gps agent then feeds the GPS-based location of the plane to the autoPilot agent, which consults the terrain agent below before taking corrective action.

Code Calls

1. Merge the two satellite reports into a single satellite report
gps: *mergeGPSData*(Report1, Report2) $\rightarrow$ SatelliteReport

2. Return the satellite id of the next satellite in the queue. All available satellites are maintained in a circular queue, each time this code call is invoked the next satellite in the queue is returned
gps: *getNextSatellite*() $\rightarrow$ String

3. Receive the GPS data sent from the Satellite and store it as a satellite report
gps: *receiveFrom*(Satellite) $\rightarrow$ SatelliteReport

Actions

1. Collect GPS data from Satellite

Name: *collect_data*(Satellite)
Pre: **in**(Satellite, gps: *getNextSatellite*())
Del: {}

Add: **in**(Satellite, gps: *getNextSatellite*())&
    in(Report, gps: *recieveFrom*(Satellite))

2. Merge satellites reports of Satellite1 and Satellite2

Name: *merge_data*(Satellite1, Satellite2)
Pre: **in**(Satellite1, gps: *getNextSatellite*())&
    in(Satellite2, gps: *getNextSatellite*())
Del: {}
Add: **in**(Satellite1, gps: *getNextSatellite*())&
    in(Satellite2, gps: *getNextSatellite*())&
    in(Report1, gps: *recieveFrom*(Satellite1))&
    in(Report2, gps: *recieveFrom*(Satellite2))&
    in(Report, gps: *mergeGPSData*(Report1, Report2))

A.1.4 Terrain Agents

The terrain agent takes a coordinate in the globe, and generates a terrain map for the region. In this example, a special kind of terrain map is retrieved called a *Digital Terrain Elevation Data* (DTED) map. The terrain agent provides to the autoPilot agent a set of "no-go" areas. Using this set, the autoPilot agent can take corrective action, if necessary.

Code Calls

1. Given a 2D Point generate the terrain map for that point
terrain: *generateTerrainMap*(Point) → TerrainMap

2. Determine the No_go areas of a plane given its FlightRoute
terrain: *determineNogo*(FlightRoute) → TerrainMap

Actions

1. Given the FlightRoute of a plan determine the set of No_go areas on that flight route

Name: *determineNogo*(FlightRoute)
Pre: **in**(FlightRoute, msgbox: *getVar*(Msg.Id, "FlightRoute"))
Del: {}
Add: **in**(FlightRoute, msgbox: *getVar*(Msg.Id, "FlightRoute"))&
    in(No_go, terrain: *determineNogo*(FlightRoute))

A.1.5 Action Constraints

{*compute_currentLocation*(Report),
adjust_course(No_go, FlightRoute, CurrentLocation)} ↩

This action constraint states that the actions compute_currentLocation and adjust_course may never be executed concurrently. This is because the adjust_course action requires the current location of the plane as input, and the compute_currentLocation action computes the required input.

{*collect_data*(Satellite), *merge_data*(Satellite1, Satellite2)} ↩
$$\text{Satellite} = \text{Satellite1}.$$
{*collect_data*(Satellite), *merge_data*(Satellite1, Satellite2)} ↩
$$\text{Satellite} = \text{Satellite2}.$$

These two action constraints state that the gps agent cannot concurrently execute the action merge_data and collect_data, if the satellite it is collecting data from is one of the satellites whose data it is merging.

A.2 Agents in the STORE Example

A.2.1 Credit Agents

This agent does nothing more sophisticated than providing access to a credit database. In the USA, many department stores issue their own credit cards, and as a consequence, they automatically have access to (at least some) credit data for many customers. The credit agent may in fact access a variety of databases, not just one.

Code Calls

1. Provide the credit information of the customer with social security number Ssn with the Type of detail
credit: *provideCreditInfo*(Ssn, Type) → FinanceRecord

2. Check the credit records of the customer with name Name and social security number Ssn
credit: *checkCredit*(Ssn, Name) → Real

3. Determine the list of customers to notify about their pending credit debts
credit: *customer_to_be_notified*() → < String, String, Time >

4. Return the financial records of the customer with social security number Ssn
credit: *getFinanceRec*(Ssn) → FinanceRecord

5. Send a notice to the customer Name with social security number Ssn
credit: *sendNotice*(Ssn, Name) → Boolean

Actions

1. Terminate the credit of the customer with social security number Ssn

Name: *terminateCredit*(Ssn)
Pre: in(Ssn, msgbox: *getVar*(Msg.Id, "Ssn"))
Del: in(FinanceRec, credit: *getFinanceRec*(Ssn))
Add: {}

2. Notify the customer with name Name and social security number Ssn

Name: *notifyCustomer*(Ssn, Name)
Pre: in(Ssn, msgbox: *getVar*(Msg.Id, "Ssn"))&
in(Name, msgbox: *getVar*(Msg.Id, "Name"))
Del: in(Ssn, msgbox: *getVar*(Msg.Id, "Ssn"))&
in(Name, msgbox: *getVar*(Msg.Id, "Name"))
Add: in(Status, credit: *sendNotice*(Ssn, Name))

3. Provide credit report of the customer with name Name and social security number Ssn. Credit reports are prepared in high detail

Name: *provideCreditReport*(Ssn, Name)
Pre: in(Ssn, msgbox: *getVar*(Msg.Id, "Ssn"))&
in(Name, msgbox: *getVar*(Msg.Id, "Name"))
Del: in(Ssn, msgbox: *getVar*(Msg.Id, "Ssn"))&
in(Name, msgbox: *getVar*(Msg.Id, "Name"))
Add: in(CreditReport, credit: *provideCreditInfo*(Ssn, high))

4. Check the credit record of customer with social security number Ssn to see if he has an overdue payment

Name: *checkCredit*(Ssn)
Pre: in(Ssn, msgbox: *getVar*(Msg.Id, "Ssn"))&
in(Name, msgbox: *getVar*(Msg.Id, "Name"))
Del: in(Ssn, msgbox: *getVar*(Msg.Id, "Ssn"))&
in(Name, msgbox: *getVar*(Msg.Id, "Name"))
Add: in(Overdue, credit: *checkCredit*(Ssn, Name))

A.2.2 Profiling Agents

This agent takes as input the identity of a user. It then asks the credit agent for information on this user's credit history, and analyses the credit data. Credit information typically contains detailed information about an individual's spending habits. The profiling agent may then classify the user as a "high" spender, an "average" spender, or a "low" spender.

Code Calls

1. Classify users as high, medium or low spenders
profiling: *classifyUser*(Ssn) → UserProfile

2. Select all records of relation Relation
profiling: *all*(Relation) → SetsOfRecords

3. List the social security numbers of a given Category of users
profiling: *listUsers*(Category) → ListOfStrings

Actions

1. Update the profiles of customers who are classified as high spenders

Name: *update_highProfile*(Ssn, Name, Profile)
Pre: in(spender(high), profiling: *classifyUser*(Ssn))
Del: {}
Add: in(⟨Ssn, Name, Profile⟩, profiling: *all*('highProfile'))

2. Update the profiles of customers who are medium spenders

Name: *update_mediumProfile*(Ssn, Name, Profile)
Pre: in(spender(medium), profiling: *classifyUser*(Ssn))
Del: {}
Add: in(⟨Ssn, Name, Profile⟩, profiling: *all*('mediumProfile'))

3. Update the profiles of customers who are low spenders

Name: *update_lowProfile*(Ssn, Name, Profile)
Pre: in(spender(low), profiling: *classifyUser*(Ssn))
Del: {}
Add: in(⟨Ssn, Name, Profile⟩, profiling: *all*('lowProfile'))

4. Classify the user with name Name and social security number Ssn as a high, medium or low spender

Name: *classify_user*(Ssn, Name)
Pre: in(Ssn, msgbox: *getVar*(Msg.Id, "Ssn"))&
   in(Name, msgbox: *getVar*(Msg.Id, "Name"))
Del: in(Ssn, msgbox: *getVar*(Msg.Id, "Ssn"))&
   in(Name, msgbox: *getVar*(Msg.Id, "Name"))
Add: in(UserProfile, profiling: *classifyUser*(Ssn))

5. Inform the saleNotification agent

Name: *inform_sale_notifier*(Ssn, Name, Profile)
Pre: in(Ssn, msgbox: *getVar*(Msg.Id, "Ssn"))&
   in(Name, msgbox: *getVar*(Msg.Id, "Name"))&
   in(Profile, msgbox: *getVar*(Msg.Id, "Profile"))&
   = (Profile, riskProfile)
Del: {}
Add: in(Status, code call)
where code call is
msgbox: *sendMessage*(profiling, saleNotification, "Ssn, Name, riskprofile")

A.2.3 ProductDB Agents

This agent provides access to one or more product databases reflecting the merchandise that the department store sells. Given a desired product description, this agent may be used to retrieve tuples associated with this product description.

Code Calls

1. Return product description
productDB: *provideDescription*(ProductId) → ProductDescription

A.2.4 Content-Determination Agents

This agent tries to determine what to show the user. It takes as input, the user's request, and the classification of the agent as determined by the profiling agent. It executes a query to the productDB agent, which provides it a set of tuples. It then uses the user classification provided by the profiling agent to filter these tuples. In addition, the contentDetermin agent may decide that when it presents the items selected to the user, it will run advertisements on the bottom of the screen, showing other items that "fit" this user's high-spending profile.

Code Calls

1. Prepare a presentation for a product
contentDetermin: *preparePresentation*(ProductId, UserRequest, UserProfile) Presentation

A.2.5 Interface Agents

This agent takes the objects identified by the contentDetermin agent and weaves together a multimedia presentation.

A.2.6 Sale-Notification Agents

This agent identifies a user's profile, determines which of the items going on sale "fits" the user's profile, and takes an appropriate action, such as mailing the user a list of enclosed items determined above.

Code Calls

1. Identify a user profile
saleNotification: *identifyProfile*(Ssn, Name) → ⟨UserProfile, UserAddress⟩

2. Determine the items on sale that fit a user's profile
saleNotification: *determineItems*(ListOfItemsOnSale, Profile) → ListOfItems

Actions

1. Mail brochures to the customer address CustomerAddress, containing the list of items ListOfItems

Name: *mailBrochure*(CustomerAddress, ListOfItems)
Pre: **in**(⟨Profile, CustomerAddress⟩, saleNotification: *identifyProfile*(Ssn, Name))
     & **in**(ListOfItems, code call)
where code call is
saleNotification: *determineItems*(ListOfItems, Profile)
Del: {}
Add: {}

A.2.7 Action Constraints

$\{update\_highProfile(\texttt{Ssn1}, \texttt{Name1}, \texttt{Profile}), update\_lowProfile(\texttt{Ssn2}, \texttt{Name2}, \texttt{Profile})\} \hookleftarrow$
$\qquad \textbf{in}(\texttt{spender(high)}, \texttt{profiling}: classifyUser(\texttt{Ssn1})) \ \&$
$\qquad\qquad\qquad\qquad\qquad\qquad\qquad \texttt{Ssn1} = \texttt{Ssn2} \ \& \ \texttt{Name1} = \texttt{Name2}$

$\{update\_userProfile(\texttt{Ssn1}, \texttt{Name1}, \texttt{Profile}), classify\_user(\texttt{Ssn2}, \texttt{Name2})\} \hookleftarrow$
$\qquad\qquad\qquad\qquad\qquad\qquad \texttt{Ssn1} = \texttt{Ssn2} \ \& \ \texttt{Name1} = \texttt{Name2}$

The first action states that if the user is classified as a high spender, then the profiling agent cannot execute *update_highProfile* and *update_lowProfile* concurrently. In contrast, the second action constraint states that the profiling agent cannot classify a user profile if it is currently updating the profile of that user.

A.3 Agents in the CHAIN Example

A.3.1 Plant Agents

This agent monitors available inventory, and makes sure that inventories does not fall below some determined threshold values. Moreover, the plant agent determines the amount of stock needed, finds out the supplier, and places orders. Once the plant agent places orders with the suppliers, it must ensure that the transportation vendors can deliver the items to the company's location. For this, it consults a shipping agent, which in turn may consult a truck agent or an airplane agent. It also monitors the performance of suppliers.

Code Calls

1. Return the amount available of part Part_id in the inventory
plant: *monitorInventory*(Part_id) → Integer

2. Update inventory to set the amount of Part_id to Amount
plant: *updateInventory*(Part_id, Amount) → Boolean

3. Choose a supplier of Part_id
plant: *chooseSupplier*(Part_id) → String

4. Determine the amount of Part_id to order
plant: *determineAmount*(Part_id) → Integer

Actions

1. Order Amount of Part_id from Supplier when the amount in the inventory falls below the threshold lowInInventory

Name: *orderPart*(Part_id, Amount, Supplier)
Pre: **in**(AmountAvailable, plant: *monitorInventory*(Part_id)) &
$\qquad$ AmountAvailable $\leq$ lowInInventory
Del: {}
Add: **in**(Amount, plant: *determineAmount*(Part_id)) &
$\qquad$ **in**(Supplier, plant: *chooseSupplier*(Part_id))

A.3.2 Supplier Agents

This agents basically monitors two databases, one for the committed stock the supplier has, and the other for the uncommitted stock the supplier has. When the plant agent requests a particular amount of some part, it consults these databases, serves the plant agent if it has the available stock, and updates its databases.

Section A.3   Agents in the CHAIN Example   545

Code Calls

1. Monitor the stock of Part_id, and return either amount_available if there is Amount of Part_id, or amount_not_available if there is not Amount of Part_id available
supplier: *monitorStock*(Amount, Part_id) → StatusString

2. Ship the Amount of Part_id from Src to Dest by using Method
supplier: *shipFreight*(Amount, Part_id, Method, Src, Dest) → Boolean

3. Return the constant too_low_threshold
supplier: *too_low_threshold*(Part_id) → Integer

4. Return the constant low_threshold
supplier: *low_threshold*(Part_id) → Integer

5. Return the product status of part Part_id
supplier: *productStatus*(Part_id) → ProductStatusString

6. Determine the amount of part Part_id to order
supplier: *determineAmount*(Part_id) → Integer

7. Place an order for part Part_id
supplier: *placeOrder*(Part_id) → Boolean

8. Place an order for part Part_id by fax
supplier: *placeOrderByFax*(Part_id) → Boolean

9. Handle Amount of shipment of part Part_id to company Company
supplier: *handleShipment*(Company, Part_id, Amount) → Boolean

Actions

1. Respond to part requests of other agents

Name: *respond_request*(Part_id, Amount, Company)
Pre: **in**(Part_id, msgbox: *getVar*(Msg.Id, "Part_id"))&
    in(Amount, msgbox: *getVar*(Msg.Id, "Amount"))&
    in(Company, msgbox: *getVar*(Msg.Id, "Company"))
Del: **in**(Part_id, msgbox: *getVar*(Msg.Id, "Part_id"))&
    in(Amount, msgbox: *getVar*(Msg.Id, "Amount"))&
    in(Company, msgbox: *getVar*(Msg.Id, "Company"))
Add: **in**(varstatus, supplier: *productStatus*(Part_id))

2. Update the stock database

Name: *update_stockDB*(Part_id, Amount, Company)
Pre: **in**(Part_id, msgbox: *getVar*(Msg.Id, "Part_id"))&
    in(Amount, msgbox: *getVar*(Msg.Id, "Amount"))&
    in(Company, msgbox: *getVar*(Msg.Id, "Company"))&
    in(X, supplier: *select*('uncommitted', id, =, Part_id))&
    X.amount > Amount
Del: **in**(X, supplier: *select*('uncommitted', id, =, Part_id))&
    in(Y, supplier: *select*('committed', id, =, Part_id))
Add: **in**(⟨part_id, X.amount − Amount⟩, supplier: *select*('uncommitted', id, =, Part_id))&
    in(⟨part_id, Y.amount + Amount⟩, supplier: *select*('committed', id, =, Part_id))

3. Order Amount_to_order units of part Part_id

Name: *order_part*(Part_id, Amount_to_order)
Pre: **in**(Part_id, msgbox: *getVar*(Msg.Id, "Part_id"))&
    in(supplies_low, supplier: *low_threshold*(Part_id))&
    in(amount_not_available, supplier: *monitorStock*(supplies_low, Part_id))

Del: {}
Add: **in**(Amount_to_order, supplier: *determineAmount*(Part_id))&
  in(Status, supplier: *placeOrder*(Part_id))

4. Order Amount_to_order units of part Part_id by fax

Name: *fax_order*(Company, Part_id, Amount_to_order)
Pre: **in**(Part_id, msgbox: *getVar*(Msg.Id, "Part_id"))&
  in(supplies_low, supplier: *low_threshold*(Part_id))&
  in(amount_not_available, supplier: *monitorStock*(supplies_low, Part_id))
Del: {}
Add: **in**(Amount_to_order, supplier: *determineAmount*(Part_id))&
  in(Status, supplier: *placeOrderByFax*(Part_id))

5. Ship Amount units of part Part_id to Company

Name: *shipped*(Company, Part_id, Amount)
Pre: **in**(Part_id, msgbox: *getVar*(Msg.Id, "Part_id"))&
  in(Amount, msgbox: *getVar*(Msg.Id, "Amount"))&
  in(Company, msgbox: *getVar*(Msg.Id, "Company"))
Del: **in**(Part_id, msgbox: *getVar*(Msg.Id, "Part_id"))&
  in(Amount, msgbox: *getVar*(Msg.Id, "Amount"))&
  in(Company, msgbox: *getVar*(Msg.Id, "Company"))
Add: **in**(Status, supplier: *handleShipment*(Company, Part_id, Amount))

A.3.3 Shipping Agents

This agents coordinates the shipping of parts by consulting to truck and airplane agents.

Code Calls

1. Prepare shipping schedule
shipping: *prepareSchedule*(Part_id, Amount, Src, Dest) → Schedule

2. Determine a truck to ship Amount of Part_id from Src to Dest
shipping: *determineTruck*(Part_id, Amount, Src, Dest) → String

3. Determine an airplane to ship Amount of Part_id from Src to Dest
shipping: *determineAirplane*(Part_id, Amount, Src, Dest) → String

Action

1. Find a truck to ship Amount of Part_id from Src to Dest

Name: *findTruck*(Part_id, Amount, Src, Dest)
Pre: **in**(Part_id, msgbox: *getVar*(Msg.Id, "Part_id"))&
  in(Amount, msgbox: *getVar*(Msg.Id, "Amount"))&
  in(Src, msgbox: *getVar*(Msg.Id, "Src"))&
  in(Dest, msgbox: *getVar*(Msg.Id, "Dest"))
Del: {}
Add: **in**(TruckId, shipping: *determineTruck*(Part_id, Amount, Src, Dest))

2. Find an airplane to ship Amount of Part_id from Src to Dest

Name: *findAirplane*(Part_id, Amount, Src, Dest)
Pre: **in**(Part_id, msgbox: *getVar*(Msg.Id, "Part_id"))&
  in(Amount, msgbox: *getVar*(Msg.Id, "Amount"))&
  in(Src, msgbox: *getVar*(Msg.Id, "Src"))&
  in(Dest, msgbox: *getVar*(Msg.Id, "Dest"))
Del: {}
Add: **in**(PlaneId, shipping: *determineAirplane*(Part_id, Amount, Src, Dest))

Section A.3   Agents in the CHAIN Example   547

A.3.4 Truck Agents

This agent provides and manages truck schedules using routing algorithms.

Code Calls

1. Return the current location of the truck
$\text{truck}: location() \rightarrow \texttt{2DPoint}$

2. Given a `highway` and the current location of the truck calculate the destination of the truck
$\text{truck}: calculateDestination(\texttt{From}, \texttt{Highway})\ \texttt{2DPoint}$

Actions

1. Drive from location `From` to location `To` on highway `Highway`

Name: *drive*(From, To, Highway)
Pre: **in**(From, truck: *location*())
Del: **in**(From, truck: *location*())
Add: **in**(From, truck: *location*())&
   in(To, truck: *calculateDestination*(From, Highway))

A.3.5 Airplane Agents

This agent provides and manages airplane freight cargo.

Code Calls

1. Return the current location of the plane
$\text{airplane}: location() \rightarrow \texttt{3DPoint}$

2. Return the current angle of the plane
$\text{airplane}: angle() \rightarrow \texttt{Angle}$

3. Return the current speed of the plane
$\text{airplane}: speed() \rightarrow \texttt{Speed}$

4. Given the current speed, current location and angle of the plane calculate the next position of the plane
$\text{airplane}: calculateNextLocation(\texttt{Location}, \texttt{Speed}, \texttt{Angle}) \rightarrow \texttt{3DPoint}$

Actions

1. Fly from location `From` to location `To`

Name: *fly*(From, To)
Pre: **in**(From, airplane: *location*())
Del: **in**(From, airplane: *location*())
Add: **in**(From, airplane: *location*())&
   in(Speed, airplane: *speed*())&
   in(Angle, airplane: *angle*())&
   in(To, airplane: *calculateNextLocation*(From, Speed, Angle))

A.3.6 Action Constraints

$\{update\_stockDB(\texttt{Part\_id1}, \texttt{Amount1}, \texttt{Company1}),$
   $update\_stockDB(\texttt{Part\_id2}, \texttt{Amount2}, \texttt{Company2})\} \hookleftarrow$
      $\texttt{Part\_id1} = \texttt{Part\_id2}\ \&$
      $\textbf{in}(\texttt{X}, \text{supplier}: select('uncommitted', \text{id}, =, \texttt{Part\_id1}))\ \&$
      $\texttt{X.amount} < \texttt{Amount1} + \texttt{Amount2}\ \&$
      $\texttt{Company1} \neq \texttt{Company2}.$

{*respond_request*(Part_id1, Amount1, Company1),
 respond_request(Part_id2, Amount2, Company2)} $\hookleftarrow$ Part_id1 = Part_id2 &
 Company1 $\neq$ Company2.

The first constraint states that if the two update_stockDB actions update the same Part_id and the total amount available is less than the sum of the requested amounts, then these actions cannot be concurrently executable. The second constraint states that if two companies request the same Part_id, then the supplier agent does not respond to them concurrently. That is, the supplier agent processes requests one at a time.

A.4 Agents in the CFIT* Example

A.4.1 Tank Agents
Code Calls

1. Drive forward at speed Speed (0 to Max speed)
tank: *goForward*(Speed) $\rightarrow$ Boolean

2. Drive backward at speed Speed (0 to Max speed)
tank: *goBackward*(Speed)

3. Turn left by Degrees degrees (0 to 360)
tank: *turnLeft*(Degrees)

4. Turn right by Degrees degrees (0 to 360)
tank: *turnRight*(Degrees)

5. Determine current position in 2D
tank: *getPosition*() $\rightarrow$ 2DPoint

6. Get current heading
tank: *getHeading*() $\rightarrow$ Heading

7. Aim the gun at 3D point Point
tank: *aim*(Point) $\rightarrow$ Boolean

8. Fire the gun using the current aim
tank: *fire*() $\rightarrow$ Boolean

9. Compute the distance between two 2D points
tank: *computeDistance*(X, Y) $\rightarrow$ Distance

10. Retrieve the maximum range for the gun
tank: *getMaxGunRange*() $\rightarrow$ Distance

11. Calculate the next position of the tank when driving with Speed from CurrentLocation
tank : *calculate-NextPosition*(CurrentLocation, Speed) $\rightarrow$ 2DPoint

12. Find all vehicles within Distance units of traffic circle given by (XCoord,YCoord,VarRadius)
tank: *FindVehiclesInRange*(Distance, XCoord, YCoord, VarRadius) $\rightarrow$ ListOfVehicles

Actions

1. Drive from 2D point From to 2D point To at speed Speed

Name: *drive*(From, To, Speed)
Pre: in(From, tank: *getPosition*())
Del: in(From, tank: *getPosition*())
Add: in(CurrentLocation, tank: *getPosition*())&
 in(To, tank: *calculateNextPosition*(CurrentLocation, Speed))

Section A.4 Agents in the CFIT* Example   549

2. Drive route Route given as a sequence of 2D points at speed Speed

Name: *driveRoute*(Route, Speed)
Pre: in(Route(0).Position, tank: *getPosition*())
Del: in(Route(0).Position, tank: *getPosition*())
Add: in(Route(Route.Count).Position, code call)
where code call is
tank: *calculateNextPosition*(Route(Route.Count − 1).Position, Speed).

3. Attack vehicle at position Position from position MyPosition

Name: *attack*(MyPosition, Position)
Pre: in(MyPosition, tank: *getPosition*())&
    in(Distance, tank: *computeDistance*(MyPosition, Position))&
    in(maxRange, tank: *getMaxGunRange*())&Distance < maxRange
Del: {}
Add: {}

A.4.2 Terrain Route Planning Agent

Code Calls

1. Sets current map to Map
route: *useMap*(Map) → Boolean

2. Compute a route plan on the current map for a vehicle of type VehicleType from SourcePoint to DestinationPoint given in 2D. Returns a route plan as a sequence of points in plane.
route: *getPlan*(SourcePoint, DestinationPoint, VehicleType)
→ SequenceOf2DPoints

3. Given SourcePoint and DestinationPoint on the current map, determine the likely routes of a vehicle of type VehicleType whose initial route segment is Route, given as a sequence of points in the plane. It returns a sequence of route-probability pairs.
route: *groundPlan*(SourcePoint, DestinationPoint, VehicleType, Route)
→ (Route, Probability)

4. Compute a flight plan on the current map from SourcePoint to DestinationPoint given in 3D. Returns a flight plan as a sequence of points in space
route: *flightPlan*(SourcePoint, DestinationPoint) → SequenceOf3DPoints

5. Determines whether two points are visible from each other on the given map. For example if a hill lies between the two points, they are not visible from each other. This is useful to determine whether an agent can see another agent or whether an agent can fire upon another agent.
route: *visible*(Map, Point1, Point2) → Boolean

Actions

1. Compute a route plan on map Map for a vehicle of type VehicleType from SourcePoint to Destination-Point given in 2D.

Name: *planRoute*(Map, SourcePoint, DestinationPoint, VehicleType)
Pre: SourcePoint ≠ DestinationPoint
Del: {}
Add: in(true, route: *useMap*(Map))&
    in(Plan, route: *getPlan*(SourcePoint, DestinationPoint, VehicleType))

2. Given SourcePoint and DestinationPoint on map Map determine the likely routes of a vehicle of type VehicleType whose initial route segment is Route, given as a sequence of points in the plane

Name: *evaluateGroundPlan*(Map, SourcePoint, DestinationPoint, VehicleType, Route)
Pre: SourcePoint ≠ DestinationPoint

Del: {}
Add: **in**(true, route: *useMap*(Map))&
　　　　in(RP, route: *groundPlan*(SourcePoint, DestinationPoint, VehicleType, Route))

3. Compute a flight plan on map Map from SourcePoint to DestinationPoint given in 3D.

Name: *planFlight*(Map, SourcePoint, DestinationPoint)
Pre: SourcePoint $\neq$ DestinationPoint
Del: {}
Add: **in**(true, route: *useMap*(Map))&
　　　　in(Plan, route: *flightPlan*(SourcePoint, DestinationPoint))

A.4.3 Tracking Agent

This agent continuously scans the area for enemy vehicles. It maintains a list of enemy vehicles, assigning each an agent id. It tries to determine the vehicle type for each enemy vehicle. When it detects a new vehicle, it adds it to its list, together with its position. Since the tracking agent only keeps track of enemy vehicles which are on the ground, the position is in the plane. This could be for example an *AWACS* plane.

Code Calls

1. Get position for agent with id AgentId
tracking: *getPosition*(AgentId) $\to$ 2DPoint

2. Get the type of agent for agent with id AgentId. It returns the most likely vehicle type together with the probability
tracking: *getTypeOfAgent*(AgentId) $\to$ (VehicleType, Probability)

3. Return the list of all agents being tracked
tracking: *getListOfAgents*() $\to$ ListOfAgentIds

4. Find the list of agents in the given Image
tracking: *findobjects*(Image) $\to$ ListOfAgentIds

5. Return the list of neutralized agents
tracking: *getListOfNeutralizedAgents*() $\to$ ListOfAgentIds

6. Return the marking information in the given Image
tracking: *marking*(Image) $\to$ MarkingInformation

7. Return the turrent information in the given Image
tracking: *turrent*(Image) $\to$ TurrentInformation

A.4.4 Coordination Agent

Code Calls

1. Determine whether a vehicle of type VehicleType1 at position Position1 can attack a vehicle of type VehicleType2 at position Position2. For example a tank is not able to attack a fighter plane unless it is on the ground.
coord: *canBeAttackedNow*(VehicleType1, Position1, VehicleType2, Position2)
$\to$ Boolean

2. Given an agent id for an enemy vehicle, determine the best position, time and route for an attack to be successful. Also return the estimated probability of success
coord: *findAttackTimeAndPosition*(AgentId) $\to$ (Position, Time, Route, Probability)

3. Given a set of ids for friendly agents, compute a plan for a coordinated attack against the enemy agent with id EnemyId. The friendly agents participating in the coordinated attack are taken from the set SetOfAgentIds
coord: *coordinatedAttack*(SetOfAgentIds, EnemyId) $\to$ AttackPlan

Section A.4   Agents in the CFIT* Example   551

Actions

1. Given a set of ids for friendly agents, compute a plan for a coordinated attack against the enemy agent with id `EnemyId`. The friendly agents participating in the coordinated attack are taken from the set `SetOfAgentIds`.

Name: *attack*(SetOfAgentIds, EnemyId)
Pre: SetOfAgentIds $\neq \emptyset$
Del: {}
Add: **in**(AP, coord: *coordinatedAttack*(SetOfAgentIds, EnemyId))

A.4.5   Helicopter Agents

Code Calls

1. Change flying altitude to `Altitude` (0 to `Maximum` altitude)
heli: *setAltitude*(Altitude) $\rightarrow$ Boolean

2. Get current altitude
heli: *getAltitude*() $\rightarrow$ Altitude

3. Change flying speed to `Speed` (0 to `Maximum` speed)
heli: *setSpeed*(Speed) $\rightarrow$ Boolean

4. Get current speed
heli: *getSpeed*() $\rightarrow$ Speed

5. Change flying heading to `Heading` (0 to 360)
heli: *setHeading*(Heading) $\rightarrow$ Boolean

6. Get current heading
heli: *getHeading*() $\rightarrow$ Heading

7. Aim the gun at the 3D point given by `Position`
heli: *aim*(Position) $\rightarrow$ Boolean

8. Fire the gun using the current aim
heli: *fire*() $\rightarrow$ Boolean

9. Determine the current position in space
heli: *getPosition*() $\rightarrow$ 3DPoint

10. Compute heading to fly from 2D point `Src` to 2D point `Dst`
heli: *computeHeading*(Src, Dst) $\rightarrow$ Heading

11. Compute the distance between two 3D points
heli: *computeDistance*(X, Y) $\rightarrow$ Distance

12. Retrieve the maximum range for the gun
heli: *getMaxGunRange*() $\rightarrow$ Distance

13. Calculate the next position of the helicopter given its `CurrentPosition`, its `Speed` and
heli: *calculateNextPosition*(CurrentPosition, Speed) $\rightarrow$ 3DPoint

Actions

1. *Fly*() from 3D point `From` to 3D point `To` at altitude `Altitude` and with speed `Speed`

Name: *fly*(From, To, Altitude, Speed)
Pre: **in**(From, heli: *getPosition*())
Del: **in**(From, heli: *getPosition*())
Add: **in**(CurrentPosition, heli: *getPosition*())&
   in(To, heli: *calculateNextPosition*(CurrentPosition, Speed))

2. *FlyRoute*(Path) where `Path` is a sequence of quadruples consisting of: a 3D point, altitude, speed and angle

Name: *flyRoute*(Path)

Pre: **in**(Path(0).Position, heli: *getPosition*())
Del: **in**(Path(0).Position, heli: *getPosition*())
Add: **in**(Path(Path.Count).Position, code call), where code call is
heli: *calculateNextPosition*(Path(Path.Count − 1).Position, Speed)

3. Attack vehicle at position Position in space from position MyPosition

Name: *attack*(MyPosition, Position)
Pre: **in**(MyPosition, heli: *getPosition*())&
  in(Distance, heli: *computeDistance*(MyPosition, Position))&
  in(maxRange, heli: *getMaxGunRange*())& Distance < maxRange
Del: {}
Add: {}

A.4.6 AutoPilot Agents
Code Calls

1. Return the current location of the plane.
autoPilot: *location*() → 3DPoint

2. Return the current status of the plane.
autoPilot: *planeStatus*() → PlaneStatus

3. Return the current flight route of the plane
autoPilot: *getFlightRoute*() → Path

4. Return the current Velocity of the plane
autoPilot: *velocity*() → Velocity

5. Given the current location, flight route and speed of the plane calculate the next location of the plane
autoPilot: *calculateLocation*(Location, FlightRoute, Velocity) → 3DPoint

6. Return the current Altitude of the plan
autoPilot: *getAltitude*() → Altitude

7. Set the altitude of the plane to Altitude
autoPilot: *setAltitude*(Altitude) → Boolean

8. Detect the possible dangerous situations to warn the pilot
autoPilot: *detectWarning*() → WarningType

9. Determine the specific cause and specific information of the warning type
autoPilot: *determineSpecifics*(WarningType) → SpecificInformation

10. Send a warning signal to the pilot
autoPilot: *warnPilot*(WarningType, WarningSpecificInfo) → SignalType

11. Send a warning signal to the base station
autoPilot: *sendSignalToBase*(WarningType, WarningSpecificInfo) → SignalType

Actions

1. Compute the current location of the plane

Name: *compute_currentLocation*(Report)
Pre: **in**(Report, msgbox: *getVar*(Msg.Id, "Report"))
Del: **in**(OldLocation, autoPilot: *location*())
Add: **in**(OldLocation, autoPilot: *location*())&
  in(FlightRoute, autoPilot: *getFlightRoute*())&
  in(Velocity, autoPilot: *velocity*())&
  in(NewLocation, code call)

where code call is
autoPilot: *calculateLocation*(OldLocation, FlightRoute, Velocity)

2. Warn the pilot with WarningType and with specific information WarningSpecificInfo

Name: *warn_pilot*(WarningType, WarningSpecificInfo)
Pre: **in**(WarningType, autoPilot: *detectWarning*())&
    in(WarningSpecificInfo, autoPilot: *determineSpecifics*(WarningType))
Del: {}
Add: **in**(Status, autoPilot: *warnPilot*(WarningType, WarningSpecificInfo))

3. Send a signal to the base station to give a warning of WarningType with specific information WarningSpecificInfo

Name: *signal_base*(WarningType, WarningSpecificInfo)
Pre: **in**(WarningType, autoPilot: *detectWarning*())&
    in(WarningSpecificInfo, autoPilot: *determineSpecifics*(WarningType))
Del: {}
Add: **in**(Status, autoPilot: *sendSignalToBase*(WarningType, WarningSpecificInfo))

4. Decrease the altitude of the plane

Name: *decrease_altitude*(newaltitude)
Pre: {}
Del: **in**(OldAltitude, autoPilot: *getAltitude*())
Add: **in**(status, autoPilot: *setAltitude*(newaltitude))

Action Constraints

in(S, heli: *getSpeed*()) $\hookleftarrow$ $S <$ maxSpeed
in(A, heli: *getAltitude*()) $\hookleftarrow$ $A <$ maxAltitude

Action Constraints

{*attack*(MyPos, P)} $\hookleftarrow$ **in**(P, heli1: *getPosition*()) & **in**(MyPos, heli: *getPosition*())
{*attack*(MyPos, P)} $\hookleftarrow$ **in**(P, heli2: *getPosition*()) & **in**(MyPos, heli: *getPosition*())
{*attack*(MyPos, P)} $\hookleftarrow$ **in**(P, heli3: *getPosition*()) & **in**(MyPos, heli: *getPosition*())
{*attack*(MyPos, P)} $\hookleftarrow$ **in**(P, heli4: *getPosition*()) & **in**(MyPos, heli: *getPosition*())

where heli1, ..., heli4 are the friendly agents of the agent in question.

References

Abbadi, A. E., D. Skeen, and F. Cristian (1985). An Efficient, Fault-tolerant Protocol for Replicated Data Management. In *Proceedings of the 1985 SIGACT-SIGMOD Symposium on Principles of Data Base Systems*, Portland, Oregon, pp. 215–229.

Abiteboul, S., R. Hull, and V. Vianu (1995). *Foundations of Databases*. Addison Wesley.

Adali, S., K. S. Candan, S.-S. Chen, K. Erol, and V. S. Subrahmanian (1996). Advanced Video Information Systems: Data Structures and Query Processing. *Multimedia Systems 4*(4), 172–186.

Adali, S., K. S. Candan, Y. Papakonstantinou, and V. S. Subrahmanian (1996, June). Query Caching and Optimization in Distributed Mediator Systems. In *Proceedings of ACM SIGMOD Conference on Management of Data*, Montreal, Canada.

Adali, S., et al. (1997). Web hermes user manual. http://www.cs.umd.edu/projects/hermes/UserManual/index.html.

Ahmed, R., et al. (1991, December). The Pegasus Heterogeneous Multidatabase System. *IEEE Computer 24*(12), 19–27.

Alferes, J. J. and L. M. Pereira (1996). Reasoning with Logic Programming. In *Springer-Verlag Lecture Notes in Artificial Intelligence*, Volume 1111.

Allen, J. (1984). Towards a General Theory of Action and Time. *Artificial Intelligence 23*(2), 123–144.

Allen, J. F. and G. Ferguson (1994). Actions and Events in Interval Temporal Logic. *Journal of Logic and Computation 4*(5), 531–579.

Alur, R. and T. A. Henzinger (1992, June). Logics and Models of Real Time: A Survey. In J. W. de Bakker, C. Huizing, W. P. de Roever, and G. Rozenberg (Eds.), *Proceedings of Real-Time: Theory in Practice*, Volume 600 of *Lecture Notes in Computer Science*, pp. 74–106. Berlin, Germany: Springer-Verlag.

Apt, K. (1990). Logic Programming. In J. van Leeuwen (Ed.), *Handbook of Theoretical Computer Science*, Volume B, Chapter 10, pp. 493–574. Elsevier Science Publishers B.V. (North-Holland).

Apt, K. and H. Blair (1988). Arithmetic Classification of Perfect Models of Stratified Programs. In R. Kowalski and K. Bouwen (Eds.), *Proceedings of the Fifth Joint International Conference and Symposium on Logic Programming (JICSLP-88)*, pp. 766–779. MIT Press.

Apt, K., H. Blair, and A. Walker (1988). Towards a Theory of Declarative Knowledge. In J. Minker (Ed.), *Foundations of Deductive Databases and Logic Programming*, pp. 89–148. Washington DC: Morgan Kaufmann.

Åquist, L. (1984). Deontic Logic. In D. Gabbay and F. Guenthner (Eds.), *Handbook of Philosophical Logic, Volume II*, Chapter II.11, pp. 605–714. D. Reidel Publishing Company.

Arens, Y., C. Y. Chee, C.-N. Hsu, and C. Knoblock (1993). Retrieving and Integrating Data From Multiple Information Sources. *International Journal of Intelligent Cooperative Information Systems 2*(2), 127–158.

Artale, A. and E. Franconi (1998). A Temporal Description Logic for Reasoning about Actions and Plans. *Journal of Artificial Intelligence Research 9*, 463–506.

Baker, A. B. and Y. Shoham (1995). Nonmonotonic Temporal reasoning. In D. Gabbay, C. Hogger, and J. Robinson (Eds.), *Handbook of Logic in Artificial Intelligence and Logic Programming*. Oxford University Press.

Baldoni, M., L. Giordano, A. Martelli, and V. Patti (1998b). A Modal Programming Language for Representing Complex Actions. manuscript.

Baldoni, M., L. Giordano, A. Martelli, and V. Patti (1998a). An Abductive Proof Procedure for Reasoning about Actions in Modal Logic Programming. In *Workshop on Non Monotonic Extensions of Logic Programming at ICLP '96*, Volume 1216 of *Lecture Notes in AI*, pp. 132–150. Springer-Verlag.

Baldwin, J. F. (1987). Evidential Support Logic Programming. *Journal of Fuzzy Sets and Systems 24*, 1–26.

Baral, C. and M. Gelfond (1993). Representing Concurrent Actions in Extended Logic Programming. In R. Bajcsy (Ed.), *Proceedings of the 13th International Joint Conference on Artificial Intelligence*, Chambery, France, pp. 866–871. Morgan Kaufman.

Baral, C. and M. Gelfond (1994). Logic Programming and Knowledge Representation. *The Journal of Logic Programming 19/20*, 73–148.

Baral, C., M. Gelfond, and A. Provetti (1995). Representing Actions I: Laws, Observations, and Hypothesis. In *AAAI '95 Spring Symposium on Extending Theories of Action*.

Baral, C. and J. Lobo (1996). Formal Characterization of Active Databases. In D. Pedreschi and C. Zaniolo (Eds.), *Workshop of Logic on Databases (LID '96)*, Volume 1154 of *Lecture Notes in Computer Science*, San Miniato, Italy, pp. 175–195.

Bateman, J. A. (1990). Upper Modeling: organizing knowledge for natural language processing. In *5th International Workshop on Natural Language Generation, 3–6 June 1990*, Pittsburgh, PA. Organized by Kathleen R. McKeown (Columbia University), Johanna D. Moore (University of Pittsburgh) and Sergei Nirenburg (Carnegie Mellon University).

Bayardo, R., et al. (1997). Infosleuth: Agent-based Semantic Integration of Information in Open and Dynamic Environments. In J. Peckham (Ed.), *Proceedings of ACM SIGMOD Conference on Management of Data*, Tucson, Arizona, pp. 195–206.

Bell, C., A. Nerode, R. Ng, and V. S. Subrahmanian (1994, November). Mixed Integer Programming Methods for Computing Non-Monotonic Deductive Databases. *Journal of the ACM 41*(6), 1178–1215.

Bell, C., A. Nerode, R. Ng, and V. S. Subrahmanian (1996). Implementing Deductive Databases by Mixed Integer Programming. *ACM Transactions on Database Systems 21*(2), 238–269.

Ben-Eliyahu, R. and R. Dechter (1994). Propositional Semantics for Disjunctive Logic Programs. *Annals of Mathematics and Artificial Intelligence 12*, 53–87.

Benthem, J. v. (1991). *The logic of time*. Kluwer Academic Publishers.

Benthem, J. v. (1995). Temporal logic. In D. Gabbay, C. Hogger, and J. Robinson (Eds.), *Handbook of Logic in Artificial Intelligence and Logic Programming*, pp. 241–350. Oxford University Press.

Benton, J. and V. S. Subrahmanian (1994). Using Hybrid Knowledge Bases for Missile Siting Problems. In I. C. Society (Ed.), *Proceedings of the Conference on Artificial Intelligence Applications*, pp. 141–148.

Bergadano, F., A. Puliafito, S. Riccobene, and G. Ruffo (1999, January). Java-based and secure learning agents for information retrieval in distributed systems. *INFORMATION SCIENCES 113*(1–2), 55–84.

Berkovits, S., J. Guttman, and V. Swarup (1998). Authentication for Mobile Agents. In G. Vigna (Ed.), *Mobile agents and security*, Volume 1419 of *Lecture Notes in Computer Science*, pp. 114–136. New York, NY: Springer-Verlag.

Berman, K. A., J. S. Schlipf, and J. V. Franco (1995, June). Computing the Well-Founded Semantics Faster. In A. Nerode, W. Marek, and M. Truszczynski (Eds.), *Logic Programming and Non-Monotonic Reasoning, Proceedings of the Third International Conference*, Volume 928 of *Lecture Notes in Computer Science*, Berlin, Germany, pp. 113–126. Springer-Verlag.

Bertino, E., C. Bettini, E. Ferrari, and P. Samarati (1996). A Temporal Access Control Mechanism for Database Systems. *IEEE Transactions on Knowledge and Data Engineering 8*(1), 67–80.

Bertino, E., P. Samarati, and S. Jajodia (1993, November). Authorizations in relational database management systems. In *Proceedings of the 1st ACM Conference on Computer and Communication Security*, Fairfax, VA.

Bina, E. J., R. M. McCool, V. E. Jones, and M. Winslett (1994). Secure Access to Data over the Internet. In *Proceedings of the Third International Conference on Parallel and Distributed Information Systems (PDIS 94)*, Austin, Texas, pp. 99–102. IEEE-CS Press.

Birmingham, W. P., E. H. Durfee, T. Mullen, and M. P. Wellman (1995). The Distributed Agent Architecture of the University of Michigan Digital Library (UMDL). In *AAAI Spring Symposium Series on Software Agent*.

Blakeley, J. (1996, June). Data Access for Masses through OLE DB. In H. V. Jagadish and I. S. Mumick (Eds.), *Proceedings of ACM SIGMOD Conference on Management of Data*, Montreal, Canada, pp. 161–172.

Blakeley, J. and M. Pizzo (1998, June). Microsoft Universal Data Access Platform. In L. M. Haas and A. Tiwary (Eds.), *Proceedings of ACM SIGMOD Conference on Management of Data*, Seattle, Washington, pp. 502–503.

Bonatti, P., S. Kraus, and V. S. Subrahmanian (1995, June). Foundations of Secure Deductive Databases. *IEEE Transactions on Knowledge and Data Engineering 7*(3), 406–422.

Bond, A. H. and L. Gasser (1988). An Analysis of Problems and Research in DAI. In A. H. Bond and L. Gasser (Eds.), *Readings in Distributed Artificial Intelligence*, pp. 3–35. San Mateo, California: Morgan Kaufmann.

Boole, G. (1854). *The Laws of Thought*. Macmillan, London.

Bowersox, D. J., D. J. Closs, and O. K. Helferich (1986). *Logistical Management: A Systems Integration of Physical Distribution, Manufacturing Support, and Materials Procurement*. New York: Macmillan.

Box, D. (1998, January). *Essential COM (The Addison Wesley Object Technology Series)*. Addison Wesley.

Boye, J. and J. Maluszynski (1995). Two Aspects of Directional Types. In *Proceedings of the 12th International Conference on Logic Programming*, Tokyo, Japan, pp. 747–761. MIT Press.

Brass, S. and J. Dix (1997). Characterizations of the Disjunctive Stable Semantics by Partial Evaluation. *The Journal of Logic Programming 32*(3), 207–228. (Extended abstract appeared in: Characterizations of the Stable Semantics by Partial Evaluation *LPNMR, Proceedings of the Third International Conference, Kentucky*, pages 85–98, 1995. LNCS 928, Springer-Verlag).

Brass, S. and J. Dix (1998). Characterizations of the Disjunctive Well-founded Semantics: Confluent Calculi and Iterated GCWA. *Journal of Automated Reasoning 20*(1), 143–165. (Extended abstract appeared in: Characterizing D-WFS: Confluence and Iterated GCWA. *Logics in Artificial Intelligence, JELIA '96*, pages 268–283, 1996. Springer-Verlag, LNCS 1126.).

Brass, S. and J. Dix (1999). Semantics of (Disjunctive) Logic Programs Based on Partial Evaluation. *The Journal of Logic Programming 38*(3), 167–213. (Extended abstract appeared in: Disjunctive Semantics Based upon Partial and Bottom-Up Evaluation, *Proceedings of the 12th International Logic Programming Conference, Tokyo*, pages 199–213, 1995. MIT Press.).

Bratman, M., D. Israel, and M. Pollack (1988). Plans and Resource-Bounded Practical Reasoning. *Computational Intelligence 4*(4), 349–355.

Breibart, Y. and H. Korth (1997, May). Replication and Consistency: Being Lazy Helps Sometimes. In *Proceedings of the 16th ACM SIGACT-SIGMOD-SIGART Symposium on Principles of Database Systems*, Tucson, Arizona, pp. 173–184.

Brewka, G. and J. Dix (1999). Knowledge Representation with Extended Logic Programs. In D. Gabbay and F. Guenthner (Eds.), *Handbook of Philosophical Logic, 2nd Edition, Volume 6, Methodologies*, Chapter 6. Reidel Publishing Company. Shortened version also appeared in Dix, Pereira, Przymusinski (Eds.), *Logic Programming and Knowledge Representation*, Springer-Verlag, LNAI 1471, pages 1–55, 1998.

Brewka, G., J. Dix, and K. Konolige (1997). *Nonmonotonic Reasoning—An Overview*. Number 73 in CSLI Lecture Notes. CSLI Publications, Stanford University.

Brink, A., S. Marcus, and V. Subrahmanian (1995). Heterogeneous Multimedia Reasoning. *IEEE Computer 28*(9), 33–39.

Brooks, R. A. (1986). A robust layered control system for mobile robot. *IEEE Journal of Robotics and Automation 2*(1), 14–23.

Buneman, P., J. Ullman, L. Raschid, S. Abiteboul, A. Levy, D. Maier, X. Qian, R. Ramakrishnan, V. S. Subrahmanian, V. Tannen, and S. Zdonik (1996). Mediator Languages—A Proposal for a Standard. Technical report, DARPA's I3/POB working group.

Cadoli, M. and M. Schaerf (1995). Tractable Reasoning via Approximation. *Artificial Intelligence 74*(2), 249–310.

Campbell, A. E. and S. C. Shapiro (1998, January). Algorithms for Ontological Mediation. Technical Report 98-02, Department of Computer Science, SUNY Buffalo. ftp://ftp.cs.buffalo.edu/pub/tech-reports/98-02.ps.Z.

Campbell, R. and T. Qian (1998, December). Dynamic Agent-based Security Architecture for Mobile Computers. In *The Second International Conference on Parallel and Distributed Computing and Networks (PDCN'98)*, Australia.

Candan, K. S., B. Prabhakaran, and V. S. Subrahmanian (1996, November). CHIMP: A Framework for Supporting Multimedia Document Authoring and Presentation. In Proceedings of *ACM Multimedia Conference*, Boston, MA.

Carey, M. J., et al. (1995, March). Towards Heterogeneous Multimedia Information Systems: The Garlic Approach. In *Fifth International Workshop on Research Issues in Data Engineering—Distributed Object Management*, Taipei, Taiwan, pp. 203–214.

Castano, S., M. G. Fugini, G. Martella, and P. Samarati (1995). *Database Security*. Addison Wesley.

Cattell, R. G. G., et al. (Ed.) (1997). *The Object Database Standard: ODMG-93*. Morgan Kaufmann.

Chawathe, S., et al. (1994, October). The TSIMMIS Project: Integration of Heterogeneous Information Sources. In *Proceedings of the 10th Meeting of the Information Processing Society of Japan*, Tokyo, Japan. Also available via anonymous FTP from host db.stanford.edu, file/pub/chawathe/1994/tsimmis-overview.ps.

Chellas, B. (1980). *Modal Logic*. Cambridge University Press.

Chen, Z.-Z. and S. Toda (1993). The Complexity of Selecting Maximal Solutions. In *Proceedings of the 8th IEEE Structure in Complexity Theory Conference*, San Diego, CA, pp. 313–325. IEEE Computer Society Press.

Chen, Z.-Z. and S. Toda (1995). The Complexity of Selecting Maximal Solutions. *Information and Computation 119*, 231–239.

Chess, D. M. (1996). Security in Agents Systems. http://www.av.ibm.com/InsideTheLab/Bookshelf/ScientificPapers/.

Chess, D. M. (1998). Security Issues in Mobile Code Systems. In G. Vigna (Ed.), *Mobile agents and security*, Volume 1419 of *Lecture Notes in Computer Science*, pp. 1–14. New York, NY: Springer-Verlag.

Chittaro, L. and A. Montanari (1998). Editorial: Temporal representation and reasoning. *Annals of Mathematics and Artificial Intelligence 22*, 1–4.

Cohen, P. and H. Levesque (1990a). Intention is Choice with Commitment. *Artificial Intelligence 42*, 263–310.

Cohen, P. R. and H. Levesque (1990b). Rational Interaction as the Basis for Communication. In P. R. Cohen, J. L. Morgan, and M. E. Pollack (Eds.), *Intentions in Communication*, pp. 221–256. Cambridge, MA: MIT Press.

Coradeschi, S. and L. Karlsson (1997). A Behavior-based Decision Mechanism for Agents Coordinating using Roles. In *International Workshop on Agent Theories, Architectures, and Languages*, Providence, RI, pp. 100–105.

Cormen, T. H., C. E. Leiserson, and R. L. Rivest (1989). *Introduction to Algorithms*. McGraw-Hill.

Creamer, J., M. O. Stegman, and R. P. Signore (1995, February). *The ODBC Solution: Open Database Connectivity in Distributed Environments/Book and Disk*. McGraw-Hill.

Crosbie, M. and E. Spafford (1995, November). Applying genetic programming to intrusion detection. In *Proceedings of the AAAI 1995 Fall Symposium series*.

Dagan, I. (1998). Contextual Word Similarity. In R. Dale, H. Moisl, and H. Somers (Eds.), *A Handbook of Natural Language Processing*. New York: Marcel Dekker. to appear.

Damasio, C. V., W. Nejdl, and L. M. Pereira (1994). An Extended Logic Programming System for Revising Knowledge Bases. In *Proceedings of the 4th International Conference on Principles of Knowledge Representation and Reasoning (KR'94)*, Bonn, Germany, pp. 607–618. Morgan Kaufmann.

Dantsin, E., T. Eiter, G. Gottlob, and A. Voronkov (1997, June). Complexity and Expressive Power of Logic Programming. In *Proceedings of the Twelfth IEEE International Conference on Computational Complexity (CCC '97)*, Ulm, Germany, pp. 82–101. IEEE Computer Society Press.

Date, C. J. (1995). *An Introduction to Database Systems* (sixth ed.). Addison Wesley.

Dayal, U. (1983). Processing Queries Over Generalization Hierarchies in a Multidatabase System. In M. Schkolnick and C. Thanos (Eds.), *Proceedings of the 9th International Conference on Very Large Data Bases*, Florence, Italy, pp. 342–353. VLDB Endowment/Morgan Kaufmann.

Dayal, U. and H.-Y. Hwang (1984). View Definition and Generalization for Database Integration in a Multidatabase System. *IEEE Transactions on Software Engineering 10*(6), 628–645.

Dean, T. and D. McDermott (1987). Temporal data base management. *Artificial Intelligence 32*(1), 1–55.

Dechter, R., I. Meiri, and J. Pearl (1991). Temporal Constraint Networks. *Artificial Intelligence 49*, 61–95.

Decker, K., K. Sycara, and M. Williamson (1997). Middle Agents for the Internet. In *Proceedings of the International Joint Conference on Artificial Intelligence*, Nagoya, Japan, pp. 578–583.

Dekhtyar, A. and V. S. Subrahmanian (1997). Hybrid Probabilistic Logic Programs. In L. Naish (Ed.), *Proceedings of the 14th International Conference on Logic Programming*, Leuven, Belgium, pp. 391–405. MIT Press. Extended version accepted for publication in Journal of Logic Programming, http://www.cs.umd.edu/TRs/authors/Alex_Dekhtyar.html.

Dignum, F. and R. Conte (1997). Intentional Agents and Goal Formation. In *International Workshop on Agent Theories, Architectures, and Languages*, Providence, RI, pp. 219–231.

Dignum, F. and R. Kuiper (1997). Combining Deontic Logic and Temporal logic for Specification of Deadlines. In *Proceedings of Hawaii International Conference on System Sciences, HICSS-97*, Maui, Hawaii.

Dignum, F., H. Weigand, and E. Verharen (1996). Meeting the deadline: on the formal specification of temporal Deontic constraints. *Lecture Notes in Computer Science 1079*, 243–.

d'Inverno, M., D. Kinny, M. Luck, and M. Wooldridge (1997). A Formal Specification of dMARS. In *International Workshop on Agent Theories, Architectures, and Languages*, Providence, RI, pp. 146–166.

Dix, J. (1995). Semantics of Logic Programs: Their Intuitions and Formal Properties. An Overview. In A. Fuhrmann and H. Rott (Eds.), *Logic, Action and Information. Proc. of the Konstanz Colloquium in Logic and Information (LogIn'92)*, pp. 241–329. DeGruyter.

Dix, J., U. Furbach, and I. Niemela (1999). Nonmonotonic Reasoning: Towards Efficient Calculi and Implementations. In A. Voronkov and A. Robinson (Eds.), *Handbook of Automated Reasoning*. Elsevier Science Publishers. to appear.

Doan, A. (1996). Modeling Probabilistic Actions for Practical Decision-Theoretic Planning. In *Proceedings of the Third International Conference on Artificial-Intelligence Planning Systems*, Edinburgh, Scotland, UK.

Dogac, A., et al. (1996a, February). A Multidatabase System Implementation on CORBA. In *Proceedings of the 6th International Workshop on Research Issues in Data Engineering—Interoperability of Nontraditional Database Systems (RIDE-NDS '96)*, New Orleans, Louisiana, pp. 2–11.

Dogac, A., et al. (1996b, June). METU Interoperable Database System. In H. V. Jagadish and I. S. Mumick (Eds.), *Proceedings of ACM SIGMOD Conference on Management of Data*, Montreal, Canada, pp. 552.

Donini, F. M., D. Nardi, and R. Rosati (1997). Ground Nonmonotonic Modal Logics. *Journal of Logic and Computation 7*(4), 523–548.

Dubois, D., J. Land, and H. Prade (1991, June). Towards Possibilistic Logic Programming. In *Proceedings of the Eighth International Conference on Logic Programming*, Paris, France, pp. 581–595. MIT Press.

Dubois, D., J. Lang, and H. Prade (1994). Automated Reasoning Using Possibilistic Logic: Semantics, Belief Revision, and Variable Certainty Weights. *IEEE Transactions on Knowledge and Data Engineering 6*(1), 64–71.

Dubois, D. and H. Prade (1988). Certainty and Uncertainty of Vague Knowledge and Generalized Dependencies in Fuzzy Databases. In *Proceedings of International Fuzzy Engineering Symposium*, Yokohama, Japan, pp. 239–249.

Dubois, D. and H. Prade (1989). Processing Fuzzy Temporal Knowledge. *IEEE Transactions on Systems, Man and Cybernetics 19*(4), 729–744.

Dubois, D. and H. Prade (1991). Epistemic Entrenchment and Possibilistic Logic. *Artificial Intelligence 50*(2), 223–239.

Dubois, D. and H. Prade (1995, August). Possibility Theory as a Basis for Qualitative Decision Theory. In *Proceedings of the Fourteenth International Joint Conference on Artificial Intelligence, IJCAI 95*, Montreal, Quebec, Canada, pp. 1924–1932. Morgan Kaufmann.

Durfee, E. H. (1988). *Coordination of Distributed Problem Solvers*. Boston: Kluwer Academic Publishers.

Eiter, T. and G. Gottlob (1992). Reasoning with Parsimonious and Moderately Grounded Expansions. *Fundamenta Informaticae 17*(1, 2), 31–53.

Eiter, T. and G. Gottlob (1995, January). The Complexity of Logic-Based Abduction. *Journal of the ACM 42*(1), 3–42.

Eiter, T., G. Gottlob, and N. Leone (1997, December). On the Indiscernibility of Individuals in Logic Programming. *Journal of Logic and Computation 7*(6), 805–824.

Eiter, T., G. Gottlob, and H. Mannila (1997, September). Disjunctive Datalog. *ACM Transactions on Database Systems 22*(3), 364–417.

Eiter, T., V. Subrahmanian, and T. Rogers (1999, May). Heterogeneous Active Agents, III: Polynomially Implementable Agents. Technical Report INFSYS RR-1843-99-07, Institut für Informationssysteme, Technische Universität Wien, A-1040 Vienna, Austria.

Eiter, T. and V. S. Subrahmanian (1999). Heterogeneous Active Agents, II: Algorithms and Complexity. *Artificial Intelligence 108*(1–2), 257–307.

Emden, M. v. (1986). Quantitative Deduction and its Fixpoint Theory. *Journal of Logic Programming 4*(1), 37–53.

Etzioni, O., N. Lesh, and R. Segal (1994). Building softbots for UNIX. In O. Etzioni (Ed.), *Software Agents—papers from the 1994 Spring Symposium*, pp. 9–16.

Etzioni, O. and D. S. Weld (1995, August). Intelligent Agents on the Internet: Fact, Fiction, and Forecast. *IEEE Expert 10*(4), 44–49.

Fagin, R. and J. Halpern (1989, August). Uncertainty, Belief and Probability. In *Proceedings of the 11th International Joint Conference on Artificial Intelligence, IJCAI 89*, Detroit, MI, pp. 1161–1167. Morgan Kaufmann.

Fagin, R., J. Halpern, Y. Moses, and M. Vardi (1995). *Reasoning about Knowledge*. Cambridge, Massachusetts: MIT Press. 2nd printing.

Fagin, R., J. Y. Halpern, and N. Megiddo (1990, July/August). A logic for reasoning about probabilities. *Information and Computation 87*(1/2), 78–128.

Fagin, R. and M. Vardi (1986). Knowledge and Implicit Knowledge in a Distributed Environment. In *Proceedings of 1986 Conference on Theoretical Aspects of Reasoning about Knowledge*, pp. 187–206. Morgan Kaufmann.

Fankhauser, P., B. Finance, and W. Klas (1996). IRO-DB: Making Relational and Object-Oriented Database Systems Interoperable. In P. M. G. Apers, M. Bouzeghoub, and G. Gardarin (Eds.), *Proceedings of the 5th International Conference on Extending Database Technology*, Volume 1057 of *Lecture Notes in Computer Science*, Avignon, France, pp. 485–489. Springer-Verlag.

Farmer, W. M., J. D. Guttag, and V. Swarup (1996, September). Security for Mobile Agents: Authentification and State Appraisal. In E. Bertino, H. Kurth, G. Martella, and E. Montolivo (Eds.), *Proceedings of the Fourth ESORICS*, Volume 1146 of *Lecture Notes in Computer Science*, pp. 118–130. Rome, Italy: Springer-Verlag.

Fenner, S., S. Homer, M. Ogihara, and A. Selman (1997). Oracles That Compute Values. *SIAM Journal on Computing 26*(4), 1043–1065.

Ferguson, I. A. (1992). Towards an Architecture for adaptive, rational, mobile agents. In E. Werner and Y. Demazeau (Eds.), *Decentralized Artificial Intelligence, Volume 3*, pp. 249–262. Germany: Elsevier Science Publishers.

Fiadeiro, J. and T. Maibaum (1991). Temporal Reasoning over Deontic Specifications. *Journal of Logic and Computation 1*(3), 357–395.

Finin, T., R. Fritzon, D. McKay, and R. McEntire (1994, July). KQML—A Language and protocol for Knowledge and Information Exchange. In *Proceedings of the 13th International Workshop on Distributed Artificial Intelligence*, Seattle, WA, pp. 126–136.

Finin, T., et al. (1993). Specification of the KQML Agent-Communication Language (Draft Version). The DARPA Knowledge Sharing Initiative External Interfaces Working Group.

Foltz, P. W. and S. T. Dumais (1992). Personalized information delivery: An analysis of filtering methods. In *Proceedings of ACM CHI Conference on Human Factors in Computing Systems—Posters and Short Talks*, Posters: Designing for Use. Monterey, CA.

Foner, L. N. (1993). What's an agent anyway? A Sociological Case Study. Technical Report Agents Memo 93-01, MIT, Media Laboratory.

References

Foner, L. N. (1996). A Security Architecture for Multi-Agent Matchmaking. In *Second International Conference on Multi-Agent Systems (ICMAS96)*, Japan.

Foner, L. N. (1997, February). Yenta: A Multi-Agent, Referral-Based Matchmaking System. In W. L. Johnson and B. Hayes-Roth (Eds.), *Proceedings of the 1st International Conference on Autonomous Agents*, New York, NY, pp. 301–307. ACM Press.

Frakes, W. B. and R. Baeza-Yates (Eds.) (1992). *Information Retrieval Data Structures and Algorithms*. Prentice-Hall.

Franklin, S. and A. Graesser (1997). Is it an Agent, or just a Program?: A Taxonomy for Autonomous Agents. In J. P. Muller, M. J. Wooldridge, and N. R. Jennings (Eds.), *Intelligent agents III: Proceedings of the Third International Workshop on Agent Theories, Architectures, and Languages*. Springer-Verlag.

Fritzinger, S. and M. Mueller (1996). Java Security. `http://java.sun.com/docs/white/index.html`.

Garcia-Molina, H., et al. (1997). The TSIMMIS Approach to Mediation: Data Models and Languages. *Journal of Intelligent Information Systems 8*(2), 117–132.

Garey, M. and D. S. Johnson (1979). *Computers and Intractability—A Guide to the Theory of NP-Completeness*. New York: W. H. Freeman.

Gasser, L. and T. Ishida (1991). A Dynamic Organizational Architecture For Adaptive Problem Solving. In *Proceedings of the 9th Conference on Artificial Intelligence*, Anaheim, CA, pp. 185–190. AAAI Press/MIT Press.

Gelfond, M. and V. Lifschitz (1988). The Stable Model Semantics for Logic Programming. In *Logic Programming: Proceedings Fifth International Conference and Symposium*, Cambridge, Massachusetts, pp. 1070–1080. MIT Press.

Gelfond, M. and V. Lifschitz (1991). Classical Negation in Logic Programs and Disjunctive Databases. *New Generation Computing 9*, 365–385.

Gelfond, M. and V. Lifschitz (1993). Representing Actions and Change by Logic Programs. *The Journal of Logic Programming 17*(2), 301–323.

Genesereth, M. R. and R. E. Fikes (1992, June). Knowledge Interchange Format, Version 3.0 Reference Manual. Technical Report Logic-92-1, Computer Science Department, Stanford University. http://www-ksl.stanford.edu/knowledge-sharing/papers/kif.ps.

Genesereth, M. R. and S. P. Ketchpel (1994). Software Agents. *Communications of the ACM 37*(7), 49–53.

Genesereth, M. R. and N. J. Nilsson (1987). *Logical Foundations of Artificial Intelligence*. Morgan Kaufmann.

Georgeff, M. and A. Lansky (1987). Reactive Reasoning and Planning. In *Proceedings of the Conference of the American Association of Artificial Intelligence*, Seattle, WA, pp. 677–682.

Giacomo, G. D., Y. Lesperance, and H. Levesque (1997). Reasoning about Concurrent Execution, Prioritized Interrupts, and Exogenous Actions in the Situation Calculus. In *Proceedings of the International Joint Conference on Artificial Intelligence*, Nagoya, Japan.

Ginsberg, M. L. and D. E. Smith (1987). Reasoning About Action I: A Possible Worlds Approach. In F. Brown (Ed.), *Proceedings of the Workshop "The Frame Problem in Artificial Intelligence"*, pp. 233–258. Morgan Kaufmann. also in Artificial Intelligence, 35(165–195), 1988.

Glicoe, L., R. Staats, and M. Huhns (1995). A Multi-Agent Environment for Department of Defense Distribution. In *IJCAI 95 Workshop on Intelligent Systems*.

Gmytrasiewicz, P. and E. Durfee (1992). A Logic of Knowledge and Belief for Recursive Modeling. In *Proceedings of the 10th National Conference on Artificial Intelligence*, San Jose, CA, pp. 628–634. AAAI Press/MIT Press.

Gmytrasiewicz, P., E. Durfee, and D. Wehe. (1991). A Decision-Theoretic Approach to Coordinating Multiagent Interactions. In *Proceedings of the 12th International Joint Conference On Artificial Intelligence*, Sydney, Australia, pp. 62–68. Morgan Kaufmann.

Goldberg, D., D. Nichols, B. Oki, and D. Terry (1992, December). Using collaborative filtering to weave an information tapestry. *Communications of the ACM 35*(12), 61–70.

Gottlob, G. (1992a, June). Complexity Results for Nonmonotonic Logics. *Journal of Logic and Computation 2*(3), 397–425.

Gottlob, G. (1992b, March). On the Power of Pure Beliefs or Embedding Default Logic into Standard Autoepistemic Logic. Technical Report CD-TR 92/34, Christian Doppler Laboratory for Expert Systems, TU Vienna. Extended Abstract in Proceedings IJCAI-93, Chambery, France, pp. 570–575.

Gottlob, G. (1995a). The Complexity of Propositional Default Reasoning Under the Stationary Fixed Point Semantics. *Information and Computation 121*(1), 81–92.

Gottlob, G. (1995b). Translating Default Logic into Standard Autoepistemic Logic. *Journal of the ACM 42*(4), 711–740.

Gottlob, G., N. Leone, and H. Veith (1995). Second-Order Logic and the Weak Exponential Hierarchies. In J. Wiedermann and P. Hajek (Eds.), *Proceedings of the 20th Conference on Mathematical Foundations of Computer Science (MFCS '95)*, Volume 969 of *Lecture Notes in Computer Science*, Prague, pp. 66–81. Full paper available as CD/TR 95/80, Christian Doppler Lab for Expert Systems, Information Systems Department, TU Wien.

Gray, J., P. Helland, P. O'Neil, and D. Shasha (1996). The dangers of replication and a solution. In *Proceedings of ACM SIGMOD Conference on Management of Data*, Montreal, Quebec, pp. 173–182.

Gray, R., D. Kotz, G. Cybenko, and D. Rus (1998). D'Agents: Security in Multiple-language, Mobile-Agent System. In G. Vigna (Ed.), *Mobile agents and security*, Volume 1419 of *Lecture Notes in Computer Science*, pp. 154–187. New York, NY: Springer-Verlag.

Gruber, T. R. and G. R. Olsen (1994). An ontology for engineering mathematics. In J. Doyle, P. Torasso, and E. Sandewall (Eds.), *Fourth International Conference on Principles of Knowledge Representation and Reasoning*, Bonn, Germany. Morgan Kaufmann.

Guha, R. V. and D. B. Lenat (1994, July). Enabling Agents to Work Together. *Communications of the ACM, Special Issue on Intelligent Agents 37*(7), 126–142.

Guntzer, U., W. Kiessling, and H. Thone (1991, May). New Directions for Uncertainty Reasoning in Deductive Databases. In J. Clifford and R. King (Eds.), *Proceedings of ACM SIGMOD Conference on Management of Data*, Denver, Colorado, pp. 178–187.

Gupta, P. and E. T. Lin (1994, September). DataJoiner: A Practical Approach to Multi-Database Access. In *Proceedings of the Third International Conference on Parallel and Distributed Information Systems*, Austin, Texas. IEEE-CS Press.

Haddadi, A. (1995). Towards a Pragmatic Theory of Interactions. In *International Conference on Multi-Agent Systems*, pp. 133–139.

Haddawy, P. (1991). *Representing Plans under Uncertainty: A Logic of Time, Chance and Action*. Ph. D. thesis, University of Illinois. Technical Report UIUCDCS-R-91-1719.

Haddawy, P., A. Doan, and R. Goodwin (1996). Efficient Decision-Theoretic Planning: Techniques and Empirical Analysis. In *Proceedings of the Third International Conference on Artificial-Intelligence Planning Systems*, Edinburgh, Scotland, UK.

Halpern, J. and Y. Moses (1992). A Guide to the Completeness and Complexity for Modal Logics of Knowledge and Belief. *Artificial Intelligence 54*, 319–380.

Halpern, J. and Y. Shoham (1991). A propositional modal interval logic. *Journal of the ACM 38*(4), 935–962.

Halpern, J. Y. and M. Tuttle (1992). Knowledge, Probability and Adversaries. Technical report, IBM. IBM Research Report.

Hansson, S. (1994). Review of Deontic Logic in Computer Science: Normative System Specification. *Bulletin of the Interest Group on Pure and Applied Logic (IGPL) 2*(2), 249–250.

Hayes-Roth, B. (1995). An Architecture for Adaptive intelligent systems. *Artificial Intelligence 72*(1-2), 329–365.

He, Q., K. P. Sycara, and T. W. Finin (1998, May). Personal Security Agent: KQML-Based PKI. In K. P. Sycara and M. Wooldridge (Eds.), *Proceedings of the 2nd International Conference on Autonomous Agents (AGENTS-98)*, New York, pp. 377–384. ACM Press.

Heintze, N. and J. Tygar (1996, January). A model for secure protocols and their compositions. *IEEE Transactions on Software Engineering 22*(1), 16–30.

Hendler, J. and D. McDermott (1995). Planning: What it could be, An introduction to the special issue on Planning and Scheduling. *Artificial Intelligence 76*(1–2), 1–16.

Hendler, J., A. Tate, and M. Drummond (1990). Systems and techniques: AI planning. *AI Magazine 11*(2), 61–77.

Findriks, K. V., F. S. de Boer, W. van der Hoek, and J. J. C. Meyer (1997). Formal Semantics for an Abstract Agent Programming Language. In *International Workshop on Agent Theories, Architectures, and Languages*, Providence, RI, pp. 204–218.

Hohl, F. (1997). An Approach to Solve the Problem of Malicious Hosts in Mobile Agent Systems. http://inf.informatik.uni-stuttgart.de:80/ipvr/vs/mitarbeiter/hohlfz.en%gl.html.

Holler, E. (1981). *Distributed Systems-Architecture and Implementation: An Advanced Course*, Chapter Multiple Copy Update. Lecture Notes in Computer Science. Berlin, Germany: Springer-Verlag.

Horstmann, C. S. and G. Cornell (1997). *Core Java 1.1: Fundamentals (Sunsoft Press Java Series)*. Palo Alto, CA: Prentice-Hall.

Horty, J. F. (1996). Agency and obligation. *Synthese 108*, 269–307.

Hughes, M. (1998). Application and enterprise security with the JAVA^{TM} 2 platform. http://java.sun.com/events/jbe/98/features/security.html.

Ishizaki, S. (1997). Multiagent Model of Dynamic Design: Visualization as an Emergent Behavior of Active Design Agents. In M. Huhns and M. Singh (Eds.), *Readings in Agents*, pp. 172–179. Morgan Kaufmann.

Jajodia, S. and R. Sandhu (1991, May). Toward a Multilevel Relational Data Model. In *Proceedings of ACM SIGMOD Conference on Management of Data*, Denver, Colorado.

Jenner, B. and J. Toran (1997, January). The Complexity of Obtaining Solutions for Problems in NP and NL. In L. Hemaspaandra and A. Selman (Eds.), *Complexity Theory Retrospective II*, pp. 155–178. Springer-Verlag.

Johnson, D. S. (1990). A Catalog of Complexity Classes. In J. van Leeuwen (Ed.), *Handbook of Theoretical Computer Science*, Volume A, Chapter 2, pp. 67–161. Elsevier Science Publishers

Kaelbling, L. P., M. L. Littman, and A. R. Cassandra (1998). Planning and Acting in Partially Observable Stochastic Domains. *Artificial Intelligence 101*, 99–134.

Kanger, S. (1972). Law and Logic. *Theoria 38*(3), 105–132.

Kiessling, W., H. Thone, and U. Guntzer (1992, March). Database Support for Problematic Knowledge. In *Proceedings of the 3rd International Conference on Extending Database Technology, EDBT'92*, Volume 580 of *Lecture Notes in Computer Science*, Vienna, Austria, pp. 421–436.

Kifer, M. and V. S. Subrahmanian (1992). Theory of Generalized Annotated Logic Programming and its Applications. *Journal of Logic Programming 12*(4), 335–368.

Koblick, R. (1999, March). Concordia. *Communications of the ACM 42*(3), 96–97.

Koehler, J. and R. Treinen (1995). Constraint Deduction in an Interval-based Temporal Logic. In M. Fisher and R. Owens (Eds.), *Executable Modal and Temporal Logics*, Volume 897 of *Lecture Notes in Artificial Intelligence*, pp. 103–117. Springer-Verlag.

Koller, D. (1998). Structured Probabilistic Models: Bayesian Networks and Beyond. In *Proceedings of the Fifteenth National Conference on Artificial Intelligence, AAAI '98*, Madison, Wisconsin. AAAI Press/MIT Press. http://robotics.Stanford.EDU/~koller/Invited98.

Koubarakis, M. (1994). Complexity Results for First Order Theories of Temporal Constraints. In *Proceedings 4th International Conference on Principles of Knowledge Representation and Reasoning (KR-94)*, Bonn, Germany, pp. 379–390.

Kowalski, R. (1995). Using metalogic to reconcile reactive with rational agents. In *Meta-Logics and Logic Programming*. MIT Press.

Kowalski, R. and F. Sadri (1998). Towards a unified agent architecture that combines rationality with reactivity. draft manuscript.

Kraus, S. and D. Lehmann (1988). Knowledge, Belief and Time. *Theoretical Computer Science 58*, 155–174.

Kraus, S., K. Sycara, and A. Evenchik (1998). Reaching agreements through argumentation: a logical model and implementation. *Artificial Intelligence 104*(1–2), 1–69.

Kraus, S., J. Wilkenfeld, and G. Zlotkin (1995). Multiagent Negotiation Under Time Constraints. *Artificial Intelligence 75*(2), 297–345.

Krogh, C. (1995). Obligations in Multi-Agent Systems. In Aamodt, Agnar, and Komorowski (Eds.), *Proceedings of the Fifth Scandinavian Conference on Artificial Intelligence (SCAI '95)*, Trondheim, Norway, pp. 19–30. ISO Press.

Kuokka, D. and L. Harada (1996). Integrating Information via Matchmaking. *Journal of Intelligent Informations Systems 6*(3), 261–279.

Kushmerick, N., S. Hanks, and D. Weld (1995). An Algorithm for probabilistic planning. *Artificial Intelligence 76*(1–2), 239–286.

Labrou, Y. and T. Finin (1997a, February). A Proposal for a new KQML Specification. Technical Report TR CS-97-03, Computer Science and Electrical Engineering Department, University of Maryland Baltimore County, Baltimore, MD 21250. http://www.cs.umbc.edu/~jklabrou/publications/tr9703.ps.

Labrou, Y. and T. Finin (1997b). Semantics for an Agent Communication Language. In *International Workshop on Agent Theories, Architectures, and Languages*, Providence, RI, pp. 199–203.

Ladkin, P. (1986). Primitives and units for time specification. In *Proceedings of the Fifth National Conference on Artificial Intelligence (AAAI-86)*, Volume 1, Philadelphia, PA, pp. 354–359. Morgan Kaufmann.

Ladkin, P. (1987). The Completeness of a Natural System for Reasoning with Time Intervals. In J. McDermott (Ed.), *Proceedings of the 10th International Joint Conference on Artificial Intelligence*, Milan, Italy, pp. 462–465. Morgan Kaufmann.

Lakshmanan, V. S., N. Leone, R. Ross, and V. S. Subrahmanian (1997, September). ProbView: A Flexible Probabilistic Database System. *ACM Transactions on Database Systems 22*(3), 419–469.

Lakshmanan, V. S. and F. Sadri (1994a, September). Modeling Uncertainty in Deductive Databases. In *Proceedings of the 5th International Conference on Database Expert Systems and Applications, (DEXA'94)*, Volume 856 of *Lecture Notes in Computer Science*, Athens, Greece, pp. 724–733.

Lakshmanan, V. S. and F. Sadri (1994b, November). Probabilistic Deductive Databases. In *Proceedings of the International Logic Programming Symposium, (ILPS'94)*, Ithaca, New York, pp. 254–268. MIT Press.

Lakshmanan, V. S. and N. Shiri (1999). A Parametric Approach with Deductive Databases with Uncertainty. accepted for publication in IEEE Transactions on Knowledge and Data Engineering.

Lamport, L. (1994, May). The Temporal Logic of Actions. *ACM Transactions on Programming Languages and Systems 16*(3), 872–923.

Lande, D. B. and M. Osjima (1998). *Programming and Deploying Java Mobile Agents with Aglets*. Massachusetts: Addison Wesley.

Leban, B., D. McDonald, and D. Forster (1986). A Representation for Collections of Temporal Intervals. In *Proceedings of the 5th National Conference on Artificial Intelligence*, Volume 1, Philadelphia, PA, pp. 367–371. Morgan Kaufmann.

Lee, H., J. Tannock, and J. S. Williams (1993). Logic-based reasoning about actions and plans in artificial intelligence. *The Knowledge Engineering Review 11*(2), 91–105.

Lenat, D. (1995, November). CYC: A Large Scale Investment in Knowledge Infrastructure. *Communications of the ACM 38*(11), 32–38.

Li, M. and P. Vitanyi (1992). Average Case Complexity under the Universal Distribution Equals Worst Case Complexity. *Information Processing Letters 42*, 145–150.

Liu, L., L. Yan, and M. Ozsu (1997). Interoperability in Large-Scale Distributed Information Delivery Systems. In A. Dogac, L. Kalinichenko, M. Ozsu, and A. Sheth (Eds.), *Advances in Workflow Systems and Interoperability*. Springer-Verlag.

Lloyd, J. (1984, 1987). *Foundations of Logic Programming*. Berlin, Germany: Springer-Verlag.

Lobo, J., J. Minker, and A. Rajasekar (1992). *Foundations of Disjunctive Logic Programming*. Cambridge, MA: MIT Press.

Lobo, J. and V. S. Subrahmanian (1992). Relating Minimal Models and Pre-Requisite-Free Normal Defaults. *Information Processing Letters 44*, 129–133.

Lu, J., G. Moerkotte, J. Schue, and V. S. Subrahmanian (1995, May). Efficient Maintenance of Materialized Mediated Views. In M. Carey and D. A. Schneider (Eds.), *Proceedings of ACM SIGMOD Conference on Management of Data*, San Jose, CA, pp. 340–351.

Lu, J., A. Nerode, and V. S. Subrahmanian (1996). Hybrid Knowledge Bases. *IEEE Transactions on Knowledge and Data Engineering 8*(5), 773–785.

Luke, S., L. Spector, D. Rager, and J. Hendler (1997). Ontology-based Web Agents. In *Proceedings of First International Conference on Autonomous Agents*, Marina del Rey, CA, pp. 59–66.

Maes, P. (1989). The dynamics of action selection. In *Proceedings of the International Joint Conference on Artificial Intelligence*, Detroit, MI, pp. 991–997.

Manna, Z. and A. Pnueli (1992). *Temporal Logic of Reactive and Concurrent Systems*. Addison Wesley.

Manola, F., et al. (1992, March). Distributed Object Management. *International Journal of Intelligent and Cooperative Informations Systems 1*(1), 5–42.

Marcus, S. and V. S. Subrahmanian (1996). Foundations of Multimedia Database Systems. *Journal of the ACM 43*(3), 474–523.

Marek, W. and V. S. Subrahmanian (1992). The Relationship Between Stable, Supported, Default and Auto-Epistemic Semantics for General Logic Programs. *Theoretical Computer Science 103*, 365–386.

Marek, W. and M. Truszczyński (1991). Autoepistemic Logic. *Journal of the ACM 38*(3), 588–619.

Marek, W. and M. Truszczyński (1993). *Nonmonotonic Logics—Context-Dependent Reasoning*. Springer-Verlag.

Martelli, M., V. Mascardi, and F. Zini (1997). CaseLP: a Complex Application Specification Environment based on Logic Programming. In *Proceedings of ICLP'97 Post Conference Workshop on Logic Programming and Multi-Agents*, Leuven, Belgium, pp. 35–50.

Martelli, M., V. Mascardi, and F. Zini (1998). Towards Multi-Agent Software Prototyping. In *Proceedings of The Third International Conference and Exhibition on The Practical Application of Intelligent Agents and Multi-Agent Technology (PAAM98)*, London, UK, pp. 331–354.

Mayfield, J., Y. Labrou, and T. Finin (1996). Evaluation of KQML as an Agent Communication Language. In M. Wooldridge, J. P. Müller, and M. Tambe (Eds.), *Proceedings on the IJCAI Workshop on Intelligent Agents II: Agent Theories, Architectures, and Languages*, Volume 1037 of *LNAI*, Berlin, Germany, pp. 347–360. Springer-Verlag.

McDermott, D. (1982, December). A temporal logic for reasoning about processes and plans. *Cognitive Science 6*, 101–155.

Meyer, J.-J. C. and R. Wieringa (Eds.) (1993). *Deontic Logic in Computer Science*. Chichester: John Wiley & Sons.

Microsoft (1999). The Component Object Model: Technical Overview. Adapted from an article appearing in Dr. Dobbs Journal, December 1994, http://www.microsoft.com/com/comPapers.asp.

Millen, J. and T. Lunt (1992, May). Security for Object-Oriented Database Systems. In *Proceedings of the IEEE Symposium on Research in Security and Privacy*, Oakland, CA.

Minton, S., M. D. Johnston, A. B. Philips, and P. Laird (1992). Minimizing conflicts: a heuristic repair method for constraint satisfaction and scheduling problems. *Artificial Intelligence 58*, 161–205.

Moore, R. (1985a). A Formal theory of Knowledge and Action. In J. Hobbs and R. Moore (Eds.), *Formal Theories of the Commonsense World*. Norwood, N.J.: ABLEX publishing.

Moore, R. (1985b). Semantical Considerations on Nonmonotonic Logics. *Artificial Intelligence 25*, 75–94.

Moret, B. M. E. and H. D. Shapiro (1991). *Design and Efficiency*, Volume I of *Algorithms from* **P** *to* **NP**. Redwood City, CA: Benjamin/Cummings Publishing Company.

Morgenstern, L. (1988). *Foundations of a Logic of Knowledge, Action, and Communication*. Ph. D. thesis, New York University.

Morgenstern, L. (1990). A Formal Theory of Multiple Agent Nonmonotonic Reasoning. In *Proceedings of the 8th National Conference on Artificial Intelligence, AAAI'90*, Boston, Massachusetts, pp. 538–544. AAAI Press/ MIT Press.

Moulin, B. and B. Chaib-Draa (1996). An Overview of Distributed Artificial Intelligence. In G. M. P. O'Hare and N. R. Jennings (Eds.), *Foundations of Distributed Artificial Intelligence*, pp. 3–55. John Wiley & Sons.

Neches, R., R. Fikes, T. Finin, T. Gruber, R. Patil, T. Senator, and W. R. Swarton (1991). Enabling Technology for Knowledge Sharing. *AI Magazine 12*(3), 57–63.

Necula, G. C. and P. Lee (1997). Research on Proof-Carrying Code on Mobile-Code Security. In *Proceedings of the Workshop on Foundations of Mobile Code Security*. http://www.cs.cmu.edu/~necula/pcc.html.

Ng, R. and V. S. Subrahmanian (1993a). A Semantical Framework for Supporting Subjective and Conditional Probabilities in Deductive Databases. *Journal of Automated Reasoning 10*(2), 191–235.

Ng, R. and V. S. Subrahmanian (1993b). Probabilistic Logic Programming. *Information and Computation 101*(2), 150–201.

Ng, R. and V. S. Subrahmanian (1995). Stable Semantics for Probabilistic Deductive Databases. *Information and Computation 110*(1), 42–83.

Niezette, M. and J. Stevenne (1992). An Efficient Symbolic Representation of Periodic Time. In *Proceedings First International Conference on Information and Knowledge Management*, Baltimore, Maryland.

Nilsson, N. (1986). Probabilistic Logic. *Artificial Intelligence 28*, 71–87.

Nilsson, N. J. (1980). *Principles of Artificial Intelligence*. Morgan Kaufmann.

Nirkhe, M., S. Kraus, D. Perlis, and M. Miller (1997). How to (plan to) meet a deadline between Now and Then. *Journal of Logic and Computation 7*(1), 109–156.

Nishigaya, T. (1997). Design of Multi-Agent Programming Libraries for Java. http://www.fujitsu.co.jp/hypertext/free/kafka/paper

OMG (1997, January). A Discussion of the Object Management Architecture. Technical Report, OMG, http://www.omg.org.

OMG (1998a, January). CORBA/IIOP2.2 Specification. Technical Report 98.02.1, OMG. http://www.omg.org.

OMG (1998b, December). CORBAServices: Common Services Specification. Technical Report 98-12-09, OMG. http://www.omg.org/.

Ozsu, M. T., U. Dayal, and P. Valduriez (Eds.) (1994). *Distributed Object Management*. San Mateo, California: Morgan Kaufmann. Edited collection of papers presented at the International Workshop on Distributed Object Management, held in August 1992 at the University of Alberta, Canada.

Papadimitriou, C. H. (1994). *Computational Complexity*. Addison Wesley.

Paterson, M. and M. Wegman (1978). Linear Unification. *Journal of Computer and System Sciences 16*, 158–167.

Patil, R., R. E. Fikes, P. F. Patel-Schneider, D. McKay, T. Finin, T. Gruber, and R. Neches (1997). The DARPA Knowledge Sharing Effort. In M. Huhns and M. Singh (Eds.), *Readings in Agents*, pp. 243–254. Morgan Kaufmann.

Pearl, J. (1988). *Probabilistic Reasoning in Intelligent Systems: Networks of Plausible Inference*. Morgan Kaufmann.

Plaisted, D. (1993). Equational Reasoning and Term Rewriting Systems. In D. Gabbay, C. Hogger, and J. Robinson (Eds.), *Handbook of Logic in Artificial Intelligence and Logic Programming*, Volume 1, pp. 274–364. Oxford: Clarendon Press.

References

Poole, D. (1997). The independent choice logic for modeling multiple agents under uncertainty. *Artificial Intelligence 94*(1–2), 7–56.

Rabinovich, A. (1998). Expressive Completeness of Temporal Logic of Action. *Lecture Notes in Computer Science 1450*, 229–242.

Rao, A. S. (1995). Decision Procedures for Propositional Linear-Time Belief-Desire-Intention Logics. In M. Wooldridge, J. Müller, and M. Tambe (Eds.), *Intelligent Agents II—Proceedings of the 1995 Workshop on Agent Theories, Architectures and Languages (ATAL-95)*, Volume 890 of *LNAI*, pp. 1–39. Berlin, Germany: Springer-Verlag.

Rao, A. S. and M. Georgeff (1991). Modeling Rational Agents within a BDI-Architecture. In J. F. Allen, R. Fikes, and E. Sandewall (Eds.), *Proceedings of the International Conference on Knowledge Representation and Reasoning*, Cambridge, MA, pp. 473–484. Morgan Kaufmann.

Rao, A. S. and M. Georgeff (1995, June). Formal models and decision procedures for multi-agent systems. Technical Report 61, Australian Artificial Intelligence Institute, Melbourne.

Rao, A. S. and M. Georgeff (1998). Decision Procedures for BDI-Logics. *Journal of Logic and Computation 8*(3), 293–342.

Reiter, R. (1978). On Closed-World Databases. In H. Gallaire and J. Minker (Eds.), *Logic and Data Bases*, pp. 55–76. New York: Plenum Press.

Reiter, R. (1980). A Logic for Default Reasoning. *Artificial Intelligence 13*, 81–132.

Rogers Jr., H. (1967). *Theory of Recursive Functions and Effective Computability*. New York: McGraw-Hill.

Rosenschein, J. S. and G. Zlotkin (1994). *Rules of Encounter: Designing Conventions for Automated Negotiation Among Computers*. Boston: MIT Press.

Rosenschein, S. J. (1985). Formal Theories of Knowledge in AI and Robotics. *New Generation Computing 3*(4), 345–357.

Rosenschein, S. J. and L. P. Kaelbling (1995). A Situated View of Representation and Control. *Artificial Intelligence 73*, 149–173.

Ross, S. (1997). *A First Course in Probability*. Prentice-Hall.

Rouzaud, Y. and L. Nguyen-Phuong (1992). Integrating Modes and Subtypes into a Prolog Type Checker. In *Proceedings of the International Joint Conference/Symposium on Logic Programming*, pp. 85–97. MIT Press.

Rus, D., R. Gray, and D. Kotz (1997). Transportable Information Agents. In M. Huhns and M. Singh (Eds.), *Readings in Agents*, pp. 283–291. Morgan Kaufmann.

Russell, S. J. and P. Norvig (1995). *Artificial Intelligence: A Modern Approach*. Englewood Cliffs, NJ: Prentice-Hall.

Salton, G. and M. McGill (1983). *Introduction to Modern Information Retrieval*. McGraw-Hill.

Sander, T. and C. Tschudin (1998). Protecting Mobile Agents Against Malicious Hosts. In G. Vigna (Ed.), *Mobile agents and security*, Volume 1419 of *Lecture Notes in Computer Science*, pp. 44–60. New York, NY: Springer-Verlag.

Sandholm, T. (1993, July). An Implementation of the Contract Net Protocol Based on Marginal Cost Calculations. In *Proceedings of the 11th National Conference on Artificial Intelligence*, Washington, DC, pp. 256–262. AAAI Press/The MIT Press.

Sandholm, T. and V. Lesser (1995). Coalition Formation Amongst Bounded Rational Agents. In *Proceedings of the International Joint Conference on Artificial Intelligence*, Montreal, Canada, pp. 662–669. Morgan Kaufmann.

Schafer, J., T. J. Rogers, and J. Marin (1998, September). Networked Visualization of Heterogeneous US Army War Reserves Readiness Data. In S. Jajodia, T. Ozsu, and A. Dogac (Eds.), *Advances in Multimedia Information Systems, 4th International Workshop, MIS'98*, Volume 1508 of *Lecture Notes in Computer Science*, Istanbul, Turkey, pp. 136–147. Springer-Verlag.

Schoppers, M. and D. Shapiro (1997). Designing Embedded Agents to Optimize End-User Objectives. In *International Workshop on Agent Theories, Architectures, and Languages*, Providence, RI, pp. 2–12.

Schroeder, M., I. de Almeida Mora, and L. M. Pereira (1997). A Deliberative and Reactive Diagnosis Agent based on Logic Programming. In M. W. J. P. Muller and N. Jennings (Eds.), *Intelligent Agents III: Lecture Notes in Artificial Intelligence Vol. 1193*, pp. 293–307. Springer-Verlag.

Schumacher, H. J. and S. Ghosh (1997, July). A fundamental framework for network security. *Journal of Network and Computer Applications 20*(3), 305–322.

Schwartz, R. and S. Kraus (1997). Bidding Mechanisms for Data Allocation in Multi-Agent Environments. In *International Workshop on Agent Theories, Architectures, and Languages*, Providence, RI, pp. 56–70.

Schwarz, G. and M. Truszczynski (1996). Nonmonotonic Reasoning is Sometimes Simpler! *Journal of Logic and Computation 6*, 295–308.

Shafer, G. and J. Peal (Eds.) (1990). *Readings in uncertain reasoning*. Morgan Kaufmann.

Shehory, O. and S. Kraus (1998). Methods for Task Allocation via Agent Coalition Formation. *Artificial Intelligence 101*(1–2), 165–200.

Shehory, O., K. Sycara, and S. Jha (1997). Multi-Agent Coordination through Coalition Formation. In *International Workshop on Agent Theories, Architectures, and Languages*, Providence, RI, pp. 135–146.

Sheth, B. and P. Maes (1993, March). Evolving agents for personalized information filtering. In *Proceedings of the 9th Conference on Artificial Intelligence for Applications (CAIA'93)*, Orlando, FL, pp. 345–352. IEEE Computer Society Press.

Shoham, Y. (1993). Agent Oriented Programming. *Artificial Intelligence 60*, 51–92.

Shoham, Y. (1999, March/April). What we talk about when we talk about software agents. *IEEE Intelligent Systems 14*, 28–31.

Siegal, J. (1996). *CORBA Fundamentals and Programming*. New York: John Wiley and Sons.

Silberschatz, A., H. Korth, and S. Sudarshan (1997). *Database System Concepts*. McGraw-Hill.

Singh, M. P. (1997). A Customizable Coordination Service for Autonomous Agents. In *International Workshop on Agent Theories, Architectures, and Languages*, Providence, RI, pp. 86–99.

Singh, M. P. (1998). Toward a model theory of actions: How Agents do it in branching time. *Computational Intelligence 14*(3), 287–305.

Smith, R. G. and R. Davis (1983). Negotiation as a Metaphor for Distributed Problem Solving. *Artificial Intelligence 20*, 63–109.

Soley, R. M. and C. M. Stone (Eds.) (1995). *Object Management Architecture Guide* (third ed.). John Wiley & Sons.

Sonenberg, E., G. Tidhar, E. Werner, D. Kinny, M. Ljungberg, and A. Rao (1992). Planned Team Activity. Technical Report 26, Australian Artificial Intelligence Institute, Australia.

Soueina, S. O., B. H. Far, T. Katsube, and Z. Koono (1998). MALL: A multi-agent learning language for competitive and uncertain environments. *IEICE TRANSACTIONS ON INFORMATION AND SYSTEMS 12*, 1339–1349.

Sta, J.-D. (1993). Information filtering: A tool for communication between researchers. In *Proceedings of ACM INTERCHI'93 Conference on Human Factors in Computing Systems—Adjunct Proceedings*, Short Papers (Posters): Help and Information Retrieval, pp. 177–178.

Stallings, W. (1995). *Title Network and Internetwork Security: Principles and Practice*. Englewood Cliffs: Prentice-Hall.

Stoffel, K., M. Taylor, and J. Hendler (1997). Efficient Management of Very Large Ontologies. In *Proceedings of American Association for Artificial Intelligence Conference (AAAI-97)*, Providence, RI, pp. 442–447. AAAI Press/MIT Press.

Subrahmanian, V. S. (1987, September). On the Semantics of Quantitative Logic Programs. In *Proceedings of the 4th IEEE Symposium on Logic Programming*, pp. 173–182. Computer Society Press.

Subrahmanian, V. S. (1994). Amalgamating Knowledge Bases. *ACM Transactions on Database Systems 19*(2), 291–331.

References

Sycara, J. and D. Zeng (1996a). Coordination of multiple intelligent software agents. *International Journal of Intelligent and Cooperative Information Systems 5*, 181–211.

Sycara, K. and D. Zeng (1996b). Multi-Agent Integration of Information Gathering and Decision Support. In *European Conference on Artificial Intelligence (ECAI '96)*.

Sycara, K. P. (1987). *Resolving Adversarial Conflicts: An Approach to Integrating Case-Based and Analytic Methods*. Ph. D. thesis, School of Information and Computer Science, Georgia Institute of Technology.

Tai, H. and K. Kosaka (1999, March). The Aglets Project. *Communications of the ACM 42*(3), 100–101.

Takeda, H., K. Iwata, M. Takaai, A. Sawada, and T. Nishida (1995). An ontology-based cooperative environment for real-world agents. In V. Lesser (Ed.), *Proceedings of the First International Conference on Multi-Agent Systems*, San Francisco, CA, MIT Press.

Tambe, M., L. Johnson, and W.-M. Shen (1997). Adaptive Agent Tracking in Real-World Multiagent Domains. In M. Huhns and M. Singh (Eds.), *Readings in Agents*, pp. 504–508. Morgan Kaufmann.

Tari, Z. (1997, June). Using agents for secure access to data in the Internet. *IEEE Communications Magazine 35*(6), 136–140.

Tarski, A. (1981, January). *Logic, Semantics, Metamathematics*. Hackett Pub Co.

Thiébaux, S., J. Hertzberg, W. Shoaff, and M. Schneider (1995). A stochastic model of actions and plans for anytime planning under uncertainty. *International Journal for Intelligent Systems 10*(2).

Thirunavukkarasu, C., T. Finin, and J. Mayfield (1995, November). Secret Agents—A Security Architecture for the KQML Agent Communication Language. In *Intelligent Information Agents Workshop, held in conjunction with Fourth International Conference on Information and Knowledge Management CIKM'95*, Baltimore, MD.

Thomas, B., Y. Shoham, A. Schwartz, and S. Kraus (1991, August). Preliminary Thoughts on an Agent Description Language. *International Journal of Intelligent Systems 6*(5), 497–508.

Thomas, R. H. (1979, June). A Majority Consensus Approach to Concurrency Control for Multiple Copy Data Bases. *ACM Transactions on Database Systems 4*(2), 180–209.

Tomasic, A., L. Raschid, and P. Valduriez (1998). Scaling Access to Data Sources with DISCO. *IEEE Transactions on Knowledge and Data Engineering 10*(5), 808–823.

Tork Roth, M., et al. (1996, June). The Garlic Project. In H. V. Jagadish and I. S. Mumick (Eds.), *Proceedings of ACM SIGMOD Conference on Management of Data*, Montreal, Canada, pp. 557–558.

Twok, C. T. and D. Weld (1996). Planning to Gather Information. In *Proceedings of the 13th National Conference on Artificial Intelligence*, Portland, Oregon, pp. 32–39.

Ullman, J. D. (1989). *Principles of Database and Knowledge Base Systems*. Computer Science Press.

Ushioda, A. (1996). Hierarchical clustering of words and application to NLP tasks. In *Proceedings of the 4th workshop on very large corpora*, Copenhagen.

Vardi, M. (1982). Complexity of Relational Query Languages. In *Proceedings 14th ACM Symposium on Theory of Computing*, San Francisco, CA, pp. 137–146. ACM Press.

Vere, S. and T. Bickmore (1990). Basic Agent. *Computational Intelligence 4*, 41–60.

Verharen, E., F. Dignum, and S. Bos (1997). Implementation of a Cooperative Agent Architecture Based on the Language-Action Perspective. In *International Workshop on Agent Theories, Architectures, and Languages*, Providence, RI, pp. 26–39.

Vigna, G. (1998a). Cryptographic Traces for Mobile Agents. In G. Vigna (Ed.), *Mobile agents and security*, Volume 1419 of *Lecture Notes in Computer Science*, pp. 137–153. New York, NY: Springer-Verlag.

Vigna, G. (Ed.) (1998b). *Mobile agents and security*. New York, NY: Springer-Verlag. Lecture Notes in Computer Science, Volume 1419.

Vila, L. (1994, March). A Survey on Temporal Reasoning in Artificial Intelligence. *AI Communications 7*(1), 4–28.

Vinoski, S. (1997, February). CORBA: Integrating Diverse Applications Within Distributed Heterogeneous Environments. *IEEE Communications Magazine 35*(2), 46–55.

Vlasie, D. (1996). The Very Particular Structure of the Very Hard Instances. In *Proceedings of the Thirteenth National Conference on Artificial Intelligence, AAAI-96*, Portland, Oregon, pp. 266–270. AAAI Press/MIT Press.

Weinstein, P. and W. P. Birmingham (1997, August). Service Classification in a Proto-Organic Society of Agents. In *Proceedings of the IJCAI-97 Workshop on Artificial Intelligence in Digital Libraries*, Nagoya, Japan.

White, J. (1997, April). Mobile Agents. In J. M. Bradshaw (Ed.), *Software Agents*. Cambridge, MA: MIT Press.

Wiederhold, G. (1993). Intelligent Integration of Information. In *Proceedings of ACM SIGMOD Conference on Management of Data*, Washington, DC, pp. 434–437.

Wilder, F. (1993). *A Guide to the TCP/IP Protocol Suite*. Artech House.

Winslett, M., K. Smith, and X. Qian (1994, December). Formal Query Languages for Secure Relational Databases. *ACM Transactions on Database Systems 19*(4), 626–662.

Woelk, D., P. Cannata, M. Huhns, W. Shen, and C. Tomlinson (1993, January). Using Carnot for Enterprise Information Integration. In *Second International Conference on Parallel and Distributed Information Systems*, San Diego, CA, pp. 133–136.

Wooldridge, M. and N. Jennings (1997). Formalizing the Cooperative Problem Solving Process. In M. Huhns and M. Singh (Eds.), *Readings in Agents*, pp. 430–440. Morgan Kaufmann.

Wooldridge, M. J. and N. R. Jennings (1995). Agent Theories, Architectures and Languages: A survey. In M. J. Wooldridge and N. R. Jennings (Eds.), *Intelligent Agents*, Volume 890 of *Lecture Notes in Artificial Intelligence*, pp. 1–39. Springer-Verlag.

Zadeh, L. A. (1965). Fuzzy Sets. *Information and Control 8*(3), 338–353.

Zaniolo, C., S. Ceri, C. Faloutsos, R. T. Snodgrass, V. S. Subrahmanian, and R. Zicari (1997). *Advanced Database Systems*. Morgan Kaufmann.

Zapf, M., H. Mueller, and K. Geihs (1998). Security requirements for mobile agents in electronic markets. *Lecture Notes in Computer Science 1402*, 205–217.

Zeng, L. and H. Wang (1998, August). Towards a Multi-Agent Security System: A Conceptual Model for Internet Security. In *Proceedings of Fourth AIS (Association for Information Systems) Conference*, Baltimore, Maryland.

Index

Symbols

(θ, γ)-Executability, **146**
$B_{as}^+(r)$, 160, 175
$B_{cc}^+(r)$, 175, 234
$B_{other}^+(r)$, 234
$B_{as}^-(r)$, 184, 186
$B_{cc}^-(r)$, 234
$B_{other}^-(r)$, 234
$B_{cc}(r)$, 160
F-concurrent, **150**, 151, 154, 156
F-preference, 192
S-concurrent, 150, **150**, 151
$\Gamma^{[]}(a)$, **229**
$\Pi_b^{action}(\mathcal{BS})$, **227**
$\neg.B^-(r)$, 160
$\neg.B_{as}^-(r)$, 175
$\neg.B_{cc}^-(r)$, 175
$\models_{\mathcal{BS}em_h^a}$, **222**
d_G, **60**
$ACT(\gamma)$, **221**
$ACT(\Phi)$, **220**
$App_{\mathcal{BP},\mathcal{O}}(\mathcal{BS})$, **234**
$\mathbf{BBT^a}$, **216**
$\mathcal{BAt}_1(a, b)$, **213**
$\mathcal{BAt}_i(a, b)$, 214
$\mathcal{B}_a(b, \chi)$, **213**
$\mathcal{BCond}^a(h)$, **223**
$\mathcal{BL}_i^a$, **214**
$\mathcal{BL}_\infty^a$, **244**
$\mathcal{BL}it_i(a, b)$, **214**
$\mathcal{BL}it_\infty(a, b)$, **215**
$\mathcal{BL}it_\infty(a, A)$, **225**
$\mathbf{BSemT^a}$, **217**
$\mathcal{BS}em_h^a$, **217**, 220
$\mathcal{BS}em_{tank2}^{heli2}$, 218
$\mathcal{BS}em_{heli1}^{tank1}$, 218
$\mathbf{BT^a}$, **221**
$CCC(\gamma)$, **221**
$CCC(\Phi)$, **220**
$a : bel\_ccc\_act(\sigma)$, 243
$[\rho]$, **227**
$[]$, **227**
$\flat$, **463**
$cd(\cdot, \cdot)$, **58**
EXPSPACE, **401**
EXPTIME, **401**
NPMV^{NP}, **406**
NPMV, **406**
PSPACE, 402–404
$\otimes_{ig}$, **303**
$\otimes_{in}$, **303**
$\otimes_{nc}$, **303**
$\otimes_{pg}$, **303**

$\mathcal{AB}$, **146**
$\mathcal{AC}$, **158**
$\mathcal{AS}$, 147, 148, 150–152, 154–156, 160
$\mathcal{BS}$, **226**
$\mathcal{BP}$, **225**
$\mathcal{C}$, **76**
$\mathcal{F}$, **76**
$\mathcal{S}$, **76**
$\mathcal{T}$, **76**
conc, **147**, 156, 168
Sem$_{feas}$, 219
Sem$_{rat}$, 219
Sem$_{reas}$, 219
Σ-node, 41
$App_{\mathcal{PP},\mathcal{O}_S}(\mathcal{PS})$, **308**
$App_{\mathcal{P},\mathcal{O}_S}(S)$, 174
$A_{\mathcal{P},\mathcal{O}_S}(\hat{S})$, 190
$TPA_{\mathcal{P},\mathcal{O}_S}$, 189
$T_{\mathcal{P},\mathcal{O}_S}$, 190, 191
$T_{\mathcal{PP},\mathcal{O}_S}$, **314, 315**
red$^{\mathcal{BS}}(\mathcal{BP}, \mathcal{O}_S)$, **242**
$\wp$
  (as graph mapping), **41**
$\mathcal{S}^{ext}$, **230**, 242, 246, 247
GUI
  Java, **117**
  Tcl/Tk, **117**
ground_control, 334
IMPACT, 242
$\Pi_\sigma^{action}(\mathcal{BS})$, **227**
$\Pi_b^{state}(\mathcal{BS})$, **227**
$\Pi_\sigma^{state}(\mathcal{BS})$, **227**
Info(a), see $\Gamma^{[]}(a)$ 229
map, **225**
mar, **225**
nt, 39
no_go, **9**
Nouns, 39, **39**
$a\_part(\chi)$, **223**
$h\_part(\chi)$, **223**
$\mathcal{SH}$, 42
$\mathbf{BT^a}$: B-proj-select(r, h, ϕ) **222**
$\mathbf{BT^a}$: proj-select(agent, =, h), **221**
$v: nt$, **39**
implement_service, **99**
safe_ccc, **87**
FIPA, 3
InfoSleuth, 17
$\mathfrak{Trans}^{action}(\mathcal{BS}, b)$, **245**
$\mathfrak{Trans}^{action}(\mathcal{BS})$, **244**
$\mathfrak{Trans}$, **244**
$\mathfrak{Trans}(\mathcal{BP})$, 245, 248, 249
$\mathfrak{Trans}^{state}(\mathcal{BS}, b)$, **245**
v, 39

Verbs, 39, **39**
autoPilot, 145, 157, 163, 169, 170, 330, 334, 339, 340, 392
clock, 168, 170
credit, 141, 166, 169
gps, 145, 158, 165, 170
ground_control, 330, 332, 334, 335, 339, 344, 348, 349, 355, 356, 359, 363, 392
oracle, 345
plant, 162, 169, 195
profiling, 145, 158, 165, 169
radar, 344
saleNotification, 166, 170
salesMonitor, 168
satellite, 141
shipping, 162, 169
supplier, 144, 151, 157, 161, 162, 168, 176
terrain, 163, 169, 171, 209
truck, 141
CFIT, 145, 157, 163, 169, 170, 330, 332, 351
Info($\cdot$), **229**
CFIT*, 345
STORE, 145, 158, 165, 169
CHAIN, 144, 149, 151, 157, 161, 168, 175, 176, 178, 180, 184
3SAT, 402

A

$\mathbf{A}_{\mathcal{P}, \mathcal{O}_S}(S)$, 190
a_part(χ), **223**
$\mathcal{AB}$, **146**
$\mathcal{AC}$, **158**
ACCESS, 13, 36
ACT(γ), 221
ACT(Φ), **220**
action
 delayed, 11, 14
 strongly safe, **475**
action atom, *see* atom, action 143
action atoms
 compatible, **213**
action base, *see* base, action 146
action closure, *see* closure, action 174
action code, **143**
action consistency, *see* consistency, action 173
 for map, 231
 of $\mathcal{PS}$, **309**
action constraint, *see* constraint, action 157
action constraint satisfaction, *see* satisfaction, action constraint 158
action events, 333
action execution, **147**
action policy, 32, 34, 35
action rule, 160, *see* rule, action 160

action secure distortion policy, *see* distortion, policy, action secure 344
action status atom, *see* atom, action status 160
actions, 33
ACYCLIC, **401**
Add, **143**
adminImpact, 117–119, **122**
agent, 29
 airplane, 13
 autoPilot, 8, 10, 11, 17, 19, 20, 22, 32–34, 145, 157, 163, 169, 170, 330, 334, 339, 340, 392
 clock, **168**, 170
 content determination, 6
 coordination, **210**
 credit, 5, 8, 31, 141, 166, 169, 329
 enemy vehicle, **209**
 gps, 9, 10, 17, 32, 63, 145, 158, 165, 170
 ground_control, 330, 332, 334, 335, 339, 344, 348, 349, 355, 356, 359, 363, 392
 helicopter, **210**
 interface, 6
 inventory, 12
 location, 9, 11
 locERCTotals, 519, 524, 525
 locTotals, 519–521, 524
 oracle, **345**
 plant, 13, 14, 18, 21, 30, 36, 162, 169, 195
 product database, 5
 profiling, 5, 8, 17, 19, 31, 34, 46, 145, 158, 165, 169
 radar, **344**
 regular, **493**
 saleNotification, 6, 166, 170
 sales, 17
 salesMonitor, **168**
 satellite, 9, 32, 35, 57, 141
 shipping, 13, 162, 169
 supplier, 13, 14, 18, 22, 32, 36, 144, 151, 157, 161, 162, 168, 176
 tank, 18
 terrain, 9, 35, 40, 163, 169, 171, **209**
 tracking, **210**
 transportation, 14
 truck, 13, 19, 141
 weakly regular, 477
Agent-0, **204**
agent action security function, *see* function, agent action security 339
agent applications, 2
 data integration agents, 1
 mobile agents, 2
 monitoring interestingness, 2
 personalized visualization, 2
 software interoperability agents, 2
agent approximation, *see* approximation, agent 358

Index

agent approximation program, *see* approximation, agent, program 382
agent architecture, 19
  deliberative, 51
  hybrid, 51
  reactive, 51
agent consequence relation, *see* relation, agent consequence 335
agent decision cycle algorithm, **168**
agent decision making, *see* decision making, agent 17
agent program, 143, 161, 167, **171**, 172, 174, 177–185, 187–190, 193, 194, 197, 198, 202, 203, 205
  b-bounded, **492**
  b-regular, **492**
  deontically stratifiable, 474
  probabilistic, **304**
  regular, 186
  weak regular, **475**
agent secrets function, *see* function, agent secrets 339
agent state, 333, **334**, 368, 396
Agent-0, 19
agentize, 3, 21, 529
AgentTable, 45, 61, **122**
annihilator, 303
annotated ccc
  satisfaction of an, **307**
annotation item, *see* item, annotation 304
$\mathbf{App}_{\mathcal{P},\mathcal{O}_S}(S)$, 174
$\mathbf{App}_{\mathcal{BP},\mathcal{O}}(\mathcal{BS})$, **234**
apply, 97, 98
apply, 97
approximate
  condition, **353**
  consequence relation, **356**, 357, 358, 372
  current history, *see* history, approximate current 351
  data security, 331, *see* security, data, approximate 359
  fact language, **352**, 372, 377
  facts, 372, 384
  history, *see* history, approximate 354
  language, 353, 356, 358
  secrets, **356**, 358, 372
  secrets, correctness, **356**
  security check, 331, **348**, 349, 359, 361, 365
  state, **354**, 355
  state function, 354, **354**, 361
approximation
  agent, **358**, 363, 372, 391
    program, 369, **382**, 384
    static, **364**
  compact, **361**, 362
  current history, 358
  history, 365, 373, 374
  possible history, **350**

rule
  consequence, 372
  history, *see* history, approximation rule 372
  secrets, 372
  state, 372
$\mathcal{AS}$, 147, 148, 150–152, 154–156, 160
associativity, 303
atom
  action, 143, **143**, 160
  action status, 160, **160**, 171, 172, 174, 176, 181, 192
  code call, 160
attributes
  service description, 53
automaton
  finite state, 19

B

$\flat$, **463**
backtracking, 416
base
  action, **146**, 148, 154, 155, 159, 168, 172, 193, 195, 197, 202, 203
base language, 22
base types, **97**
$\mathbf{BBT}^a$, **216**
$\mathcal{B}Cond^a(h)$, **223**
BDI, 17, 19
BDI-agents, **204**
$\mathcal{B}_a(b, \chi)$, **213**
$\mathbf{BT}^a$
  as distinguished datatype, 226
$\mathcal{B}At_1(a, b)$, **213**
$\mathcal{B}At_i(a, b)$, 214
$\mathcal{BL}_i^a$, **214**
$\mathcal{B}Lit_i(a, b)$, **214**
$\mathcal{B}Lit_\infty(a, b)$, **215**
belief
  atom, 212, **213**, 382
  languages
    of level 0, **214**
    of level 1, **214**
  literal, **213**
    nested, **214**
    of level 1, **213**
  semantics table, 212, **217**
  table, 212, **221**
    basic, 212, **216**
    compatibility, 247
belief data structures, 209
belief formulae
  general, **215**
belief semantics table
  probabilistic, **324**

belief status set
  action closed, **233**
  deontically closed, **232**
belief table
  probabilistic, **324**
belief-semantics table, 211
beliefs, 7, 8, 10, 11, 14, 32, 35
BSemT^a
  as distinguished datatype, 226
binding pattern, **463**, 464–466
  ordering on, **464**
binding term, **463**
bistructure, 490, **490**
$\mathcal{BL}^a_\infty$, 244
bottomline, 303
$\mathcal{BP}$, **225**
  reduct of, **242**
BT^a : B-proj-select(r, h, ϕ), **222**
$\mathcal{BS}$, **226**
BSemT^a, **217**
BSemT^a : select(agent, =, h)
  as distinguished datatype, 226
BT^a : B-proj-select(r, h, ϕ)
  as distinguished datatype, 226
BT^a, **221**

C
$\mathcal{C}$, **76**
 conc, 147, 156, 168
Carnot, 105, 107
causal dependency, *see* dependency, causal 357
CCC(γ), 221
CCC(Φ), **220**
cd($\cdot$, $\cdot$), **58**
cf, 195, 196
CFT, **471**
C-hard, **402**
class, **117**
  hierClass, **117**
  tableClass, **117**
  thesClass, **117**
closure
  action, **174**, 175, 181, 200
  of $\mathcal{BS}$, **234**
  relatived, 189
  relativized, **188**
  deontic, **174**, 175, 181, 200
  of $\mathcal{BS}$, 233
CNF, **402**
coalition formation, 18
code call
  probabilistic, **297**
  software, 159

code call condition
  annotated, **304**
  compatible, **213**
  history, 374, 377, 382
code calls
  basic, 229
  extended, 209, **229**, 243
coherence
  local, *see* local coherence 236
COINS, 21, 74
COM, 115, 116
commutativity, 303
compact approximation, *see* approximation, compact 361
compact version, **362**
comparison constraint, *see* constraint, comparison 373
compatibility, 237
  with **BSemT**^{a}, 231
  with **BT**^{a}, 231
  wrt **BSemT**^{a}, **238**
  wrt **BT**^{a}, **237**
compatible history, *see* compatible, history 342
complete, **402**
completeness, **402**, **405**
complexity classes
  deterministic, **401**
component
  strongly connected, 494, **494**
ConGolog, **205**
concurrency
  notion of, **147**, 156, 168
  strongly safe, **477**
  weak, 156
concurrent execution, 142, 148
  full, **150**, 151, 156
  sequential, 150, **150**, 151
  weak, **148**, 149–151
condition
  belief, 222, *see* condition, belief 222, **223**, 231, 243
  history, *see* history, condition 370
condition correspondence relation, *see* relation, condition correspondence 353
conflict free, **469**
conflict freedom
  test, **470**
conflicting modalities, **467**
consequence approximation rule, *see* approximation, rule, consequence 372
consistency
  action, **173**, 175, 178
  for $\mathcal{BS}$, **231**
  deontic, **173**, 175, 177, 178
  for $\mathcal{BS}$, **231**
  state, 175

constraint
  action, 143, **157**, 158, 159, 168, 171, 186, 197, 200, 203
  comparison, **373**
  history, 373, 375, 377, 382
  integrity, 142, 147, 159, 168, 171, 175, 178, 179, 185, 190, 191, 202, 203
  prerequisite-free, **487**
  pure history, **373**, 374, 382
contract net, 18, 207, *see* net, contract 288
correct distortion, *see* distortion, correct 346
correct overestimations, *see* overestimations, correct 357
correct underestimation, *see* underestimation, correct 357
cost function, 195
  weak/strong monotonic, 196

D
heterogeneous, 15
data complexity, 409
data security, *see* security, data 343
Datalog, 16
dbImpact, 117–119, **122**
  db_create, 120, **128**
  db_getAgentInfo, 121, **130**, 138, 139
  db_getAgents, 121, **130**, 139
  db_getAgentTypes, 121, **130**, 139
  db_getServicesToDelete, 121, **131**
  db_getServices, 121, **131**
  db_init, 117, 120, 122, **128**, 137, 138
  db_insertAgent, 121, **131**, 139
  db_insertService, 122, **132**, 140
  db_quit, 120, 122, **128**
  db_removeAgent, 121, **132**
  db_removeAllServices, 122, **133**
  db_removeId, 122, **132**
  db_removeService, 122, **132**
  hier_create, 119, **123**
  hier_emptyId, 119, **124**, 136
  hier_firstId, 119, **124**, 136
  hier_flush, 120, **127**
  hier_getKids, 119, **125**, 134
  hier_getNames, 119, **125**, 133, 134
  hier_getNodeId, 120, **126**, 134, 140
  hier_getParent, 119, **125**, 134
  hier_getPath, 120, **126**, 135–138
  hier_getRoots, 119, **124**, **125**, 133
  hier_init, 117, 119, 122, **123**, 133, 134, 137, 140
  hier_insert, 120, **126**
  hier_lastId, 119, **124**, 136
  hier_quit, 119, 122, **124**
  hier_remove, 120, **127**
  hier_search, 119, **125**, 135, 136
  hier_setCosts, 120, **126**
  query_distance, 121, **129**
  query_findSource, 121, **130**, 137
  query_nn, 121, **129**, 137
  query_range, 121, **129**, 138
  tcp_echo, 119, **123**
  tcp_exit, 119, **123**
  thes_getCategories, 120, **127**, 135
  thes_getSynonyms, 120, **128**, 136
  thes_init, 117, 120, 122, **127**, 135, 137
  thes_quit, 120, 122, **127**
decision making
  agent, 17
decision policy, *see* policy, decision 22
decision problem, 400, **400**, 401–403, 405, 407, 460
degrees of cooperation, **346**
Del, 143
delayed action, *see* action, delayed 14
deontic closure, *see* closure, deontic 174
deontic consistency, *see* consistency, deontic 173
  for map, 231
  of $\mathcal{P}S$, 309
dependency
  causal, **357**
derivation
  resolvent, **375**
d_G, **60**
DISCO, 106
distance
  (between nodes), **42**
  function, 42, 49
distance function, 58, 61
  composite, 58, **58**, 59, 61
distortion
  action secure, 344
  contact, 341
  correct, **346**
  data, 341
  data secure, 344, 347
  degree of, 345
  function, *see* function, distortion 338
  maximally cooperative, 338, **347**, 391
  policy, 340, 341, 343, 346, 366, 390
    action secure, **344**
    secure, 347
  secure, **344**, 345
  security-preserving, 338
  service, 338, 397
  statically secure, 390
Distributed Problem Solving, 52
distribution
  probability, **297**

E

efficiently computable, 399
execution
  weakly concurrent, 410
expressiveness, 222
EXPTIME, **401**
EXPSPACE, **401**
S^{ext}, 242, 244, 246, 247
extended code calls, **229**

F

$\mathcal{F}$, **76**
fact correspondence relation, *see* relation, fact correspondence 352
fact language, **333**, 335, 351, 372
  approximate, *see* approximate, fact language 352
feasibility
  local, 247
feasible belief status set, *see* status set, belief, feasible 238
feasible execution triple, **146**, 147, 148, 150–152, 154
feasible probabilistic status set, *see* status set, probabilistic, feasible 311
feasible status set, *see* status set, feasible 175
find_nn, 60, 69, 121
  algorithm, **64**
  ANSTABLE, 61, 64
  next_nbr, 61, 64
  num_ans, 61
  relax_thesaurus, 62
  search_service_table, 61, 64
  Todo, 61, 64
finite state automaton, *see* automaton, finite state 19
finiteness, **465**
finiteness property
  downward, 466
finiteness table, 463–465, **465**, 475, 476, 495, 506, 507
fragments, 23
FSAT, 405
function
  agent action security, **339**
  agent secrets, **339**
  approximate state, *see* approximate, state function 354
  distortion, 338, 364, 396
  service distortion, **340**
  service request evaluation, **337**, 338

G

$\Gamma^{[]}(a)$, **229**
Garlic, 105, 106

graph
  weighted directly acyclic, **41**
grounded, 241
groundedness
  of a probabilistic status set, **311**
  rational status set, **178**
  wrt BS, **241**

H

h_part(χ), **223**
hard, **402**
hardness, **402**, **405**
Head-CFT, **470**
heterogeneous data, *see* data, heterogenous 15
history, 332, **334**, 335, 340–344, 347, 350, 351, 359, 363, 366, 369, 371, 373, 374
  approximate, 354, 358, 361, 369, 372, 377
  approximate current, **351**
  approximation language, 373
  approximation rule, **372**, 374, 376, 382
  code call condition, *see* code call condition, history 374
  compatible, **342**
  component, 369, **369**, 370, 382
  condition, **370**, 379, 382, 384, 385, 390
  constraint, *see* constraint, history 373
  constraint language, **373**
  correspondence relation, **351**
  package, 371
  possible, **335**
  update actions, 371

I

identity, 303
IDL, **110**
IDL*IDL*, **114**
ignorance, 303
IMPACT server, **117**
  architecture, **117**
  handle, **117**
induced status set, **227**
Info($\cdot$), **229**
Info(a), *see* $\Gamma^{[]}(a)$ 229
Info($\cdot$), 230
InfoSleuth, 105
InfoSleuth, 107
input item atom, *see* item atom, input 55
inputs
  service description, 53, 55
integrity constraint, *see* constraint, integrity 142
intentions, 17
`isagent`, 3, 29
item, **54**
  annotation, **304**

Index

item atom
  input, 55, **55**
  output, 55, **55**
item list, *see* list, item 55

J
Java agent, **146**

K
KIF, 21, 74

L
languages
  logical, 16
layering
  canonical, 477, 478, **478**, 496, 497
layering function, **472**
layers
  of an agent program, **473**
list
  item, **55**
literals
  action status
    conflicting, **468**
local
  coherence, **236**
  feasibility, **231**
logical languages, *see* languages, logical 16

M
M3SAT, 152, 154, 402, 420–422, 427, 431, 433, 437, 440, 446–449
map, **225**
MapObject, 13
mar, **225**
maximally cooperative distortions, *see* distortion, maximally cooperative 347
maximum clique, 406
MAXP, 451, 458
mechanisms
  bidding, 18
  negotiating, 18
mediators, 20
message events, 333
message manager, 31
meta agent program, 209, 212, 224, 225
meta agent rule, **225**
metaknowledge, 32, 34–36
metric, **49**, **58**
MIND, 105
modality ordering, **474**
mode realizability, 516
monotonicity, 303

Multi-Agent systems, 52
MULTIBASE, 105

N
name, **143**
  service description, 31, 39, 53
NASA hierarchy, 68, 69
net
  contract, **288**, 290
"No"-instance, **401**
no-go areas, 35, 57
noun-term, 38, **39**, 59
nounID, **46**
Nouns, **39**

O
ODBC, 16
OLE, 115
ontologies, 72
optimization problem, 405–407, 415, 425, 430, 431, 448, 451
OQL, 16
ORB, 110, 113–115
OTM, 403
output item atom, *see* item atom, output 55
outputs
  service description, 53
overestimations
  correct, **357**

P
$\wp$
  (as a graph mapping), **41**
permutation equivalence
  renaming, 491
$\Pi_b^{action}(BS)$, **227**
$\Pi_\sigma^{action}(BS)$, **227**
$\Pi_b^{state}(BS)$, **227**
$\Pi_\sigma^{state}(BS)$, **227**
plant, *see* agent, plant 14
policy
  decision, 22
polynomial hierarchy, 403–405, 414, 426, 444, 455, 457, 458
polynomial-time computable, 399, 400, 403, 406, 410, 416, 421, 423, 424, 427, 432, 436, 446, 452, 458
possible history, *see* history, possible 335
possible history approximation, *see* approximation, possible history 350
Pre, **143**
Precondition-CFT, **471**
preference, **191**
  strong, 192
  weak, **192**

prefixpoint, 314
proactive systems, *see* systems, proactive 6
probabilistic agent program, *see* agent program, probabilistic 304
probabilistic code call
 coherent, **300**
probabilistic code call atom, **301**
probabilistic code call condition, **301**
probabilistic conjunction strategy ⊗, **302**
probabilistic state consistency, *see* state consistency, probabilistic 310
probabilistic status set, *see* status set, probabilistic 306
problem reduction, **402**
program
 agent, *see* agent program 161
 meta agent, 209, 212, 224, 225
program closure
 of $\mathcal{BS}$, **235**
BT^a : proj-select(agent, =, h), **221**
PSPACE, 402–404
pure history constraint, *see* constraint, pure history 373

Q
QBF, 403, 404, 407, 427, 433, 440, 445, 452, 454–456

R
random variable, **297**, 299–301, 320, 321
range, **66**
 algorithm, **66**
 range, 66, 69, 121
 expand, 66
 RelaxList, 67
 Todo, 66
range computation, 66
range retrieval, **49**
rational probabilistic status set, *see* status set, probabilistic, rational 311
reactive systems, *see* systems, reactive 6
reasonable probabilistic status set, *see* status set, probabilistic, reasonable 312
reasonable status set, *see* status set, reasonable 184
recognition problem, 409, 411
Recognition Problem, 412, 413
recognition problem, 414, 415, 420, 422, 425, 428, 431, 433, 436, 445, 448, 450, 452, 455, 457, 458
red$^{\mathcal{BS}}(\mathcal{BP}, \mathcal{O}_S)$, **242**
regularity, 475, 480, 484, 493
relation
 agent consequence, **335**
 approximate consequence, *see* approximate, consequence relation 356

condition correspondence, **353**
fact correspondence, **352**, 356
history correspondence, *see* history, correspondence relation 351
resolvent derivation, *see* derivation, resolvent 375
RETZINA, 52
$[\rho]$, **227**
rule
 action, 160
rules
 conflicting, **468**

S
$\mathcal{S}$, **76**
safety
 strong, **466**, 467, 472, 475, 477, 498, 507
SAT, 402, 405, 407
satisfaction
 action constraint, **158**
satisfaction of an annotated ccc, *see* annotated ccc, satisfaction of an 307
schema, **143**
search problem transformation, **405**
secrets
 approximate, *see* approximate, secrets 356
 violated, 358
secrets approximation rule, *see* approximation, rule, secrets 372
secure distortion, *see* distortion, secure 344
security, 23, 33, 46, 531
 data, 330, 331, 343, **343**, 349, 358, 361, 364, 366, 368, 385, 394, 395, 397
 approximate, 331, 359, **359**, 360, 368
 static, **364**
 surface, 330, **341**, 343, 366, 368
Sem$_{feas}$, 219
Sem$_{rat}$, 219
Sem$_{reas}$, 219
semantic equivalence, 41
sequence, 221, 227, **227**, 228, 229, 231, 245, 247
server, 29, 37, 46
 registration, 37–39, 45
 synchronization module, **49**
 thesaurus, 37, 47, 62
 type, 37
 yellow pages, 37, 48, 53, 57, 63, 68
service description, 31, 53, **55**, 56
 inputs
  discretionary, 31
  mandatory, 31
 outputs, 31
service description attributes, *see* attributes, service description 53

Index 579

service description inputs, *see* inputs, service description 53
service description name, *see* name, service description 53
service description outputs, *see* outputs, service description 53
service distortion function, *see* function, service distortion 340
service name, **39**
service request evaluation function, *see* function, service request evaluation 337
service rules, 338
Service Table, 67
services, 39
  dictionary, 15
  matchmaking, 21, 38, 58, 59, 68
    nearest neighbor, **48**, **60**
    range, 49, 66
  ontological, 15
  registration, 15
  security, 15
  thesauri, 15
  yellow pages, 3, 14, 15, 21, 37
ServiceTable, 45, 61, 69, **122**
SHADE, 21, 74
σ
  as a sequence, **227**
Σ-Hierarchy, **41**, 62
Σ-node, 41
node
  Σ, 41
similar matches, 68, 74
SMART algorithm, 21, 74
software agent, 1
software infrastructure, 3
SQL, 16
state
  of an agent, **79**, 89, 92, 93
state approximation rules, *see* approximation, rule, state 372
state consistency
  probabilistic, **310**
state-independent, 196
static agent approximation, *see* approximation, agent, static 364
static data security, *see* security, data, static 364
status set, **172**, 174, 175
  belief, *see* belief status set 226, **226**
    feasible, **238**
  feasible, 171, 172, 175
  induced, *see* induced status set 227
  optimal *Sem*, 196
  probabilistic, 306, **306**, 308–317, 319, 322
    feasible, **311**

rational, **311**, 314, 315, 319
resonable, **312**
rational, 178, 182, 200, 407, 414, 415, 417–421, 423–429, 431, 433, 435–437, 439, 441, 443–446, 452, 456–458
  A-, 447, 451
  $A(S)$-, 452, 453
  F-preferred, 436–439, 455–459
  F-preferred , 437
  weak, 186, 188, 414, 419–421, 430–436, 446–455, 458
  wrt $\mathcal{BS}$, **241**
reasonable, 171, 184, 201
  weak, 188
  wrt $\mathcal{BS}$, **242**
relativized, 188
status sets
  probabilistic
    feasible, 312
strongly safe, 467, **467**, 472, 477, 493, 494, 496, 498, 503
  as an IC, **476**
surface security, *see* security, surface 341
synchronization module, **49**
systems
  proactive, 6
  reactive, 6

T
$\mathcal{T}$, **76**
$\mathbf{T}_{\mathcal{PP},\mathcal{O}_S}$, **314**, **315**
TCP/IP, **117**, 122
temporal reasoning, 32
$\mathbf{TPA}_{\mathcal{P},\mathcal{O}_S}$, 189
$\mathbf{T}_{\mathcal{P},\mathcal{O}_S}$, 190, 191
tractability, 400
$\mathfrak{Trans}^{\text{action}}(\mathcal{BS}, \text{b})$, **245**
$\mathfrak{Trans}$, 244, **244**, 245, 249
  inductive definition, 243
$\mathfrak{Trans}(\mathcal{BP})$, 245, 248, 249
$\mathfrak{Trans}^{\text{state}}(\mathcal{BS}, \text{b})$, **245**
transducer, 20, **405**
Turing machine
  deterministic, **401**, 406
  nondeterministic, **401**, 402, 403
  oracle, **403**
type hierarchy, 54, **54**
type variable, 54, **54**

U
uncertainty, 11, 13, 32
  about beliefs, 296
  about beliefs about others actions, 296

uncertainty (*contd.*)
  about effects, 295
  about state, 295
  positional, 295
underestimation
  correct, **357**
US ARMY, 209

V
verbID, **46**
Verbs, **39**

violated secrets, **342**, 343, *see* secrets, violated 358, 361
vocabulary, 41

W
Wintertree Software, *see ThesDB* 47
wrapper, 20, 29

Y
yellow pages, 48
"Yes"-instance, 154, 401, **401**, 448, 452